Introduction to Social Psychology

Introduction to Social Psychology

James T. Tedeschi
Svenn Lindskold
Paul Rosenfeld

West Publishing Company
St. Paul New York Los Angeles San Francisco

Copyeditor: Kathy Massimini
Artist: Barbara Hack Barnett
Interior Designer: Biblio Book Design
Composition: Better Graphics
Production Coordination: The Quarasan Group, Inc.
Cover: Mr. and Mrs. Isaac Phelps Stokes; John Singer Sargent (1856–1925); oil on canvas; 84¼ × 39¾ (2/4 × 101 cm.); The Metropolitan Museum of Art, bequest of Edith Minturn Phelps Stokes (Mrs. I.N.), 1938; Copyright © 1982 by The Metropolitan Museum of Art.

Photo Credits

2 Stock, Boston: Cary Wolinsky; **5** Springer/Bettman Film Archive; **8** Magnum Photos, Inc.; **12** Magnum Photos, Inc.: Paul Fusco; **16** Jeffrey Grosscup; **20** Magnum Photos, Inc.: Leonard Freed; **24** Robert Rosenthal; **27** Black Star; **34** Jeffrey Grosscup; **38** By permission of the Houghton Library, Harvard University; **39** Black Star: Jean-Claude Lejeune; **44** Jeffrey Grosscup; **46** Jeffrey Grosscup; **51** Freelance Photographer's Guild: Mendoza; **58** Black Star: Arnold Zann; **60** Jeffrey Grosscup; **64** Freelance Photographer's Guild: Jan A. Wein; **69** Black Star: Fred Ward; **72** Jeffrey Grosscup; **76** Gamma Liaison; **83** Magnum Photos, Inc.: Burt Glinn; **85** (top) Roy Baumeister (bottom) Jeffrey Grosscup; **86** Black Star: Steve Shapiro; **91** C. R. Snyder; **99** Fritz Heider; **102** Magnum Photos, Inc.: Alex Webb; **110** Black Star: Anne Dockery; **115** Freelance Photographer's Guild: Dan Esber; **117** Jeffrey Grosscup; **120** Jeffrey Grosscup; **126** National Aeronautics and Space Administration; **129** Freelance Photographer's Guild: Carole Graham; **138** Black Star: Stephen Shames; **141** Jeffrey Grosscup; **142** AP/Wide World Photos; **145** Black Star: Barry L. Schuttler; **146** Charles E. Osgood; **151** Jeffrey Grosscup; **156** Stock, Boston: Patricia Hollander Gross; **160** Magnum Photos, Inc.: Richard Kalvar; **165** Robert Meyers; **167** Icek Ajzen; **168** Jeffrey Grosscup; **178** Magnum Photos, Inc.: Alex Webb; **183** Jeffrey Grosscup; **184** Magnum Photos, Inc.: Alex Webb; **190** Photoworld; **193** AP/Wide World Photos; **198** Black Star; **204** Freelance Photographer's Guild: Mike Valeri; **209** Jeffrey Grosscup; **210** Professor Stanley Milgram; **212** Herbert Kelman; **214** Stock, Boston: Owen Franken; **220** Freelance Photographer's Guild: Colin Blackburn; **224** Freelance Photographer's Guild: Leonard Lee Rue III; **227** Black Star; **232** Black Star: John Blair; **238** Black Star; **243** Black Star: Stephen Shames; **246** (top) Richard Felson (bottom) Jeffrey Grosscup; **250** AP/Wide World Photos; **255** Jeffrey Grosscup; **262** Jeffrey Grosscup; **263** Alice M. Isen; **264** Jeffrey Grosscup; **269** Jeffrey Grosscup; **272** Magnum Photos, Inc.: Terry Evans; **274** Jeffrey Grosscup; **278** Freelance Photographer's Guild: Peter Karas; **284** Magnum Photos, Inc.: Gilles Peress; **286** Black Star: J. M. Richardson; **292** Freelance Photographer's Guild: Joseph Crachiola; **297** Magnum Photos, Inc.: Dennis Stock; **299** George Levinger; **301** Jeffrey Grosscup; **302** Stock, Boston: George Bellerose; **306** Jeffrey Grosscup; **309** Black Star; **317** Magnum Photos, Inc.: Leonard Freed; **320** Magnum Photos, Inc.: Leonard Freed; **322** Black Star: Michael Weisbrot; **323** Sandra Bem; **327** Jeffrey Grosscup; **329** Magnum Photos, Inc.: Richard Kalvar; **332** Magnum Photos, Inc.: Alex Webb; **337** Black Star: Michael Hayman; **340** Magnum Photos Inc.: Roger Malloch; **344** Black Star: Charles Zirkle; **350** Jeffrey Grosscup; **351** Marvin Shaw; **354** Photoworld; **356** Jeffrey Grosscup; **360** Jeroboam, Inc.: Peeter Vilms; **364** Photo Researchers, Inc.: Bettye Lane; **368** Elizabeth Loftus; **372** Freelance Photographer's Guild: Carolyn A. McKeone; **375** Jeffrey Grosscup; **378** Warren Meyers; **385** Freelance Photographer's Guild; **387** Freelance Photographer's Guild;

50 West Kellogg Boulevard
P.O. Box 43526
St. Paul, Minnesota 55164

Printed in the United States of America

Library of Congress Cataloging in Publication Data

Tedeschi, James T.
Social psychology.

Bibliography: p. 390
Includes index.
1. Social psychology. I. Lindskold, Svenn.
II. Rosenfeld, Paul. III. Title.
HM251.T356 1985 302 84-20981

ISBN 0-314-85306-5

Dedication with much love to
Val, Joy, Abraham, and Judes

Contents

Chapter 13 Applying social psychology 361

Preface

Oh, no, not ANOTHER social psychology textbook! While this statement is hardly music to our ears, we recognize the implicit question contained in it. Why does the world need another one? Part of the answer is reflected by Bob Dylan's lyrics, "The times they are a changing." In the two year gestation period for this book artificial hearts have been implanted in two men, women have flown in space shuttles and run for the second highest political office in the United States, and microcomputers have become as commonplace as videotape recorders. Equally rapid change has occurred in social psychology. A new textbook is needed to keep a finger on the pulse of a science that will not sit still.

Consider the enormous change that has occurred in the content of social psychology texts over the past three decades. One best selling text (Newcomb, 1950) contained chapters on socialization, culture, class, and personality, as well as social motivation, language, and mass behavior. With increased knowledge and specialization, these topics have either lost their mystery, as in the case of cultural differences, or have become separate disciplines, as with linguistics. In a sense social psychology has increased in depth but has decreased in scope.

Textbook authors must be wary of writing a book that looks too different from preceding ones. Teachers develop a pattern of teaching and have expectations about what a text should contain and the order of presentation. These expectations may serve to create cultural lag, but they also provide some historical continuity for social psychology. We have tried throughout to provide material instructors expect to find in a social psychology textbook, but it may not always be presented in the order or context of older texts. We have tried throughout to give a fair and reasonably complete treatment of the most recent developments in the field without totally neglecting "classic" theories and experiments. Thus, while we have included a great deal of fresh material in distinctive chapters on the self, self-presentation, aggression, and the sexes, the book contains the up-to-date versions of standard chapters on person perception, attitudes, social influence, prosocial behavior, and attraction. We want to make it very clear that this book is not a revised edition of the 1976 textbook. *Social Psychology* by Tedeschi and Lindskold, which was aimed for a professional audience, including graduate students and our research-oriented colleagues. This entirely new book was written for undergraduates who have never had exposure to social psychology. We have tried to write a user-friendly text that has a sense of humor, but also provides a solid foundation for understanding contemporary theories and research. The chapters have been written so that instructors can assign them out of sequence to correspond to their preferred order of presentation.

In the two years it has taken to write this book many people have helped us in one way or another. We would like to thank the following students and colleagues who have taken the time and effort to read and comment on various versions of the manuscript: David Schroeder, University of Arkansas; Dan McGrath, Northeastern University; Michael O'Malley, University of Colorado; Brian Blake, Cleveland State; Stuart Karabenick, Eastern Michigan University; Rowland Miller, Sam Houston University; Glenn Littlepage, Middle Tennessee State; Katherine Klein, North Carolina State; Elaine Hatfield, University of Hawaii; Steven Fugita, University of Akron; Richard Petty, University of Missouri; Dana Anderson, Nancy Bossert, Michael Bond, Gladys Brown, Tim Davis, Wendy Eidenmuller, Steve Galich, John Gamble, Evan Graber, Joann Horai, Jim Jaccard, John Kennedy, Linda Jackson, Frank Kardes, Steve Knouse, James Kurre, Lisa Lubomski, Valerie Melburg, Tony Menditto, Robert Meyers, Amelie and Dieter Mummendey, Brian Mullen, Nancy Norman, Barbara Quigley-Fernandez, Charles Redinius, Marc Riess, Catherine Riordan, Vaunie Struble, Kwok-Choi Wan, Barry Weller.

We made full use of micro and mainframe computers in developing and disseminating copies of the manuscript, as well as in electronic transmission between co-authors. We appreciate the expert technical advice we received from Isabel Nirenberg, Kathy Krieger, Ed Raven, and other staff members of the Computer Center at SUNY-Albany, Denny Galletta and Dennis Strouble, the microcomputer mavens at Penn State-Behrend, and all-round micro trouble-shooters Alan Rowoth and Tom Hubbard. We are also very grateful to Mary Sellen, head librarian at Penn State-Behrend, who showed us how to find many of our references through a computerized card catalog.

Many people were involved in the production of this book. Our initial editor, Barbara Brune got the project under way, and Clark Baxter with his keen editorial judgment and great sense of humor got the job done. For the last several months we had day-to-day contact with Kim Theesfeld, our outstanding production editor. We greatly appreciate her dedication to this project. Jeff Grosscup, the photo editor, and Maureen Brombach of the marketing department deserve recognition for their contributions to the production and dissemination of the book. We enjoyed working with this high quality production team.

We want to thank our families, loved ones, and friends for their understanding and support despite our tendency over the past two years to act like anti-social social psychologists. Now that the book is done, we promise to be more attentive.

January 25, 1985

James T. Tedeschi. Albany, NY

Svenn Lindskold. Athens. OH

Paul Rosenfeld. Erie, PA

Introduction to Social Psychology

The scientific approach to the world around us is exploratory, tentative, relativistic, quantitative; it constructs temporary working hypotheses and discards them; it expresses its conclusions in terms of relative probabilities, not of absolute certainties.

Eugene Rabinowitz

It is a sign of one's maturity to be able to live with an unfinished world view.

Herbert Feigl

The search for truth is more precious than its possession.

Gotthold Lessing

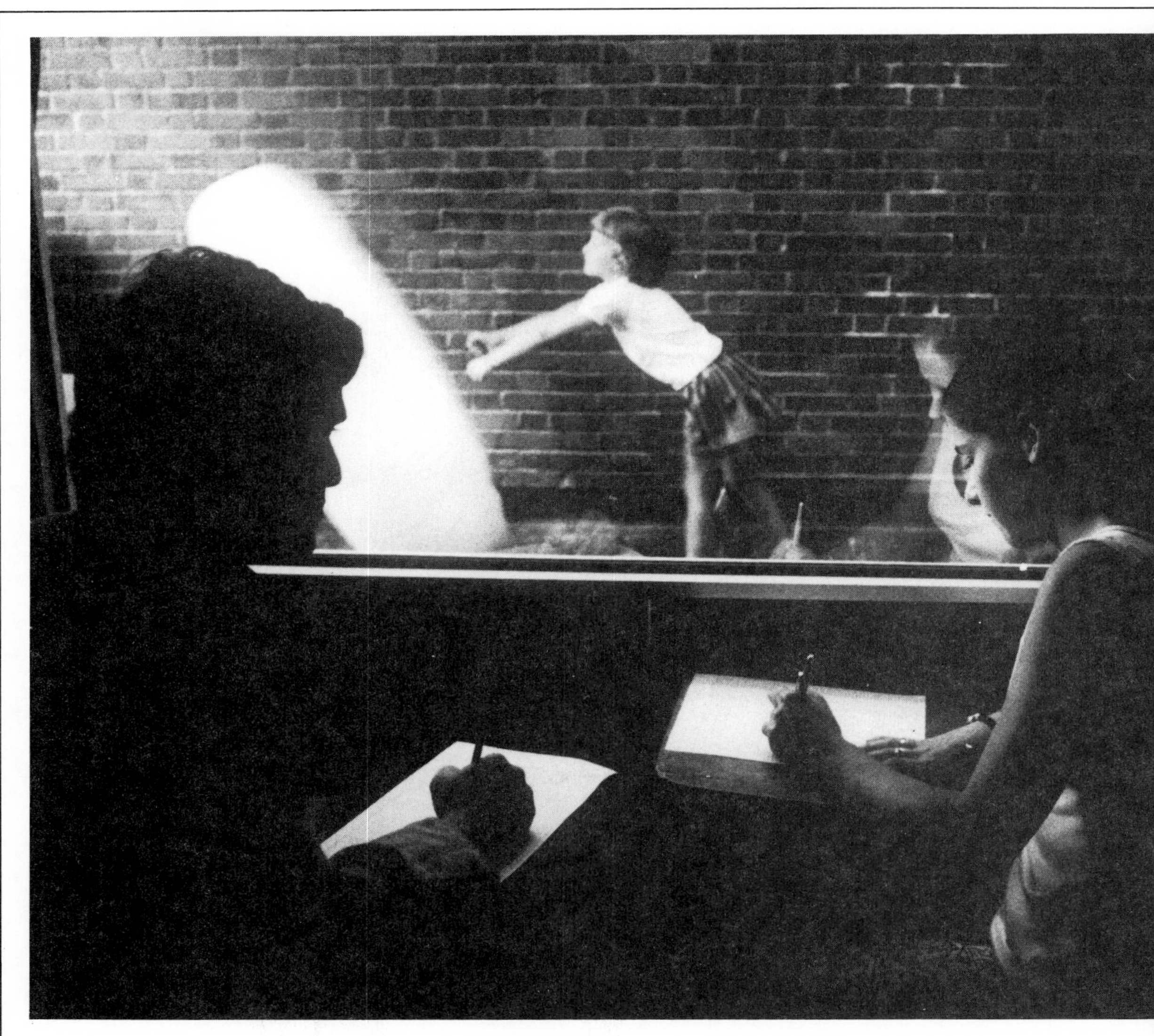

1
An orientation to social psychology and its methods

Alternative explanations of behavior

Within the city of Amsterdam in the Netherlands among the canals and tree-lined streets stands one of the most unusual art museums in the world. The paintings in the museum are representative of the impressionist school of the late nineteenth century. Their brilliant colors and swirling forms catch the eye. Brilliance not only radiates from the paintings, but it also emanates through the ceiling. The Vincent van Gogh Museum is constructed so that sunlight seeps through openings in the ceiling, honoring it's namesake's celebration of light.

This serene setting belies the tumultuous life of a troubled genius. Just before midnight in December 1888, Vincent van Gogh cut off the lower part of his left ear, gave it to a prostitute named Rachel, and requested that she "keep this object carefully" (Runyan, 1981, p. 1070). This was the first in a series of bizarre acts that continued until his suicide two years later.

Why did van Gogh cut off his ear? In a fascinating article, William Runyan (1981) reviews more than a dozen explanations offered over the years that attempt to answer this question. There are of course many ways to skin a cat, and any given action may be interpreted as having different meanings, causes, and explanations. The purpose of scientific inquiry is to narrow down and select among the alternative ways of explaining behavior.

In this book, we explore one way of explaining behavior—through social psychology. It is not the only scientific approach to understanding behavior. Political science, sociology, anthropology, history, ecomonics, and biology also are concerned with the study of human behavior. However, the problems studied and the methods of investigation employed are different for the various social and behavioral sciences. While social psychologists can borrow and learn from these other disciplines, social psychology stands as a separate and distinct field in which human behavior can be studied.

What is social psychology?

Social psychology is the scientific study of the thoughts, actions, and interactions of individuals as affected by the actual, implied, or imagined presence of others (cf. Allport, 1968). Social stimuli affect the thoughts and motivations of an individual, and these internal or **intrapsychic** factors affect that individual's subsequent interactions with other people.

The social emphasis distinguishes social psychology from psychology, and the emphasis on the individual distinguishes it from sociology. Social psychology, however, is a cousin to both of its older relatives and retains many concepts and theories borrowed from them. Nevertheless, social psychology remains a distinct and separate discipline.

Psychologists usually study the individual apart from a social context and are concerned with various internal processes, such as perception, thinking, learning, motivation, and emotions. Runyan's psychological explanation for van Gogh's strange action in cutting off his ear is that his rational thinking processes were disturbed by frightening auditory hallucinations, resulting in a psychotic breakdown. Another psychological explanation offered by Runyan is that van Gogh experienced guilt because of his homosexual attraction for the artist Paul Gaugin. This psychoanalytic interpretation views van Gogh's self-mutilation as a symbolic self-castration, which serves as punishment for unacceptable impulses.

Sociologists examine human behavior in the context of larger units, such as classes, groups, organizations, and institutions. Internal or intrapsychic processes tend to be treated as less important in the context of significant outward pressures on the behavior of individuals. These pressures usually take the form of rules or norms that govern behavior and the sanctions that are associated with them. People play roles that are structured for them in groups, and rules govern their behavior within roles (Harre and Secord, 1972). A sociological explanation for van Gogh's behavior centers on the artist's role as social outcast (a deviant role). He identified with other social outcasts, including prostitutes. His self-mutiliation and "gift" to Rachel reflected his acceptance of a role as social pariah and of the judgment of worthlessness that others attribute to persons occupying deviant roles.

Social psychologists attempt to use both individual and sociological factors in explaining behavior. They believe that intrapsychic processes have an important role in determining the behavior of the person. The social context of behavior however, provides the social stimuli, motives, and goals for an individual. Consider one of the oldest hypotheses in social psychology: frustration leads to aggression (see Chapter 8). Interfering with the goal-directed behavior of people leads to inner arousal that in turns causes them to direct aggressive responses toward target persons. The frustration typically arises from the actions of other people, which serve as the social stimuli. The inner arousal occurs as a function of the frustration and leads to the aggressive behavior.

Runyan (1981) offers several social psychological explanations for van Gogh's behavior. He bases one on the frustration-aggression hypothesis. Van Gogh may have been frustrated by two events that closely preceded his dramatic action: (1) his brother Theo, with whom he was extremely close, got engaged to be married, and hence Vincent felt his relationship with his brother to be threatened; and (2) his personal friendship with Paul Gaugin was in turmoil, and Paul had left France. Vincent may have experienced these

Self-portrait of Vincent van Gogh after he cut off his ear. Why such strange behavior? Social psychologists analyze the intrapsychic processes and external social stimuli that determine an individual's behavior. Several factors, such as psychosis and social rejection explain van Gogh's action.

social events as frustrating; his goal of expressing and receiving love from others may have caused him to be very agitated or aroused. The frustration-induced arousal led to aggression in the form of self-punitive behavior.

Another robust finding in social psychological research is that people imitate the behavior of other people (Bandura, 1977). Runyan notes that van Gogh had ample opportunity to attend and observe the bull fights in Arles, France. Of course a matador is a hero, displaying grace and courage in the face of a fighting bull. When a matador performs well, the crowd may give him permission to cut the ear off the defeated bull. By tradition, the matador displays the ear to the crowd and then gives it as a gift to his favorite woman friend. Van Gogh in his own way may have been imitating the matador by giving his own ear to a prostitute.

You ask, "But which explanation is correct?" What *really* was the reason van Gogh cut off his ear? The view of the present authors is that each of the explanations points to factors that may have contributed to van Gogh's actions. We cannot rule out any of the theories and therefor cannot reach any conclusion about the matter. The various explanations given by psychologists, sociologists, and social psychologists for the actions of Vincent van Gogh are a result of each adopting different **levels of analysis.** Table 1-1 presents the level of analysis adopted by members of each discipline within the social sciences.

Like the story of the three blind men grasping various parts of an elephant and describing them differently depending on what they had grabbed, the kind of answer given to any question of human behavior depends on the focus of the investigator. It is not contradictory to believe that because van Gogh was a social outcast, he became psychotic; he also may have repressed homosexual tendencies. A full portrait of this artist most likely would require all of these interpretations. Social psychologists offer explanations for a wide range of human experiences and actions. This book concentrates on these explanations even though matters are complicated by the fact that there are two social psychologies.

Two social psychologies

There is no psychology of groups which is not essentially and entirely a psychology of individuals.

Floyd Allport (1924)

Homonyms are words that look and sound alike but have different meanings. Although we may play pool or swim in a pool, a bathing suit is as inappropriate in the former as a cueball is to the latter. Similarly, a student usually can take a course in social psychology either in a psychology or a sociology department. Though the course titles are identical, they probably will be quite different in both content and method. The two social psychologies, like identical twins separated at birth and living in far-away countries, share a common name but speak different languages, have diverse interests, and go about their daily business according to their own idiosyncratic patterns.

Table 1-1 Levels of analysis and focus of study used by psychologists, sociologists, and social psychologists

FIELD	LEVEL OF ANALYSIS	FOCUS OF STUDY
Psychology	Perception, thinking learning, motivation	Individual
Sociology	Norms, organizations, classes, institutions	Group
Social Psychology	Attraction, aggression, influence, helping	Face-to-face interactions

The first two social psychology texts were both published in 1908-one by McDougall, a psychologist, and the other by Ross, a sociologist. According to McDougall (1908), the task of social psychology is "to show how, given the native propensities and capacities of the individual human mind, all the complex mental life of society is shaped by them" (p. 15). Ross's definition of social psychology emphasizes the social situation: "[It is the study of] the planes and currents that come into existence among men in consequence of their association" (p. 1). These differences in emphasis have persisted to the present day. The psychologically oriented social psychologist emphasizes thinking, perceiving, motivation, and learning while the sociologically oriented social psychologist emphasizes groups, organizations, social norms and roles, and social interaction.

The two social psychologies also are different with respect to their research methods. The psychologists prefer the controlled environment of the laboratory. House (1977) found that 86 percent of all studies published in the two leading psychological social psychology journals were conducted in laboratories. Sociologists typically carry out their studies of social psychology through survey and field investigations. It may in fact be easier to study factors related to individuals in the laboratory, but behavior in groups and organizations may be better observed in everyday settings.

We can observe the tendency toward intellectual isolationism in the research reports of the two kinds of social psychologists. According to Liska (1977), reports in the *Journal of Personality and Social Psychology*, the most prominent journal sponsored by psychological social psychologists, seldom reference works published in sociologically oriented journals. Social psychology textbooks, including this one, almost exclusively are written by psychologists.

In a survey of the research and professional activities of social psychologists identified with both camps, little or no overlap was found in research methods, texts, journal citations, journals read, journals published in, and academic department in which Ph.D. was earned (Wilson and Schafer, 1978). Table 1-2 summarizes the most frequent research methods used by psychological and sociological social psychologists.

Psychological social psychology: a brief history

We can trace the origins of experimental social psychology to an investigation of a phenomenon you may have experienced many times yourself. Have you ever

Table 1–2 Research techniques used by psychological and sociological social psychologists

PSYCHOLOGICAL SOCIAL PSYCHOLOGY	SOCIOLOGICAL SOCIAL PSYCHOLOGY
Lab experiments (46%)	Survey research (38%)
Survey research (13%)	Library research (19%)
Field studies (12%)	Field studies (19%)
Field experiments (12%)	Lab experiments (13%)
Natural experiments (8%)	Field experiments (5%)
Library research (6%)	Natural experiments (5%)
Archival research (2%)	Other (1%)
Other (1%)	

Source: Based on "Is social psychology interdisciplinary?" by D. W. Wilson and R. B. Schafer, 1978, *Personality and Social Psychology Bulletin, 4,* pp. 548-552.

Does the presence of others affect an individual's performance? Norman Triplett, who conducted the first social psychology experiment in 1897, observed that the presence of others enhanced the performance of bicyclists in races.

noticed a difference between activities requiring considerable physical energy when you do them by yourself and when you do them with other people? Do you put out more effort when people are watching you than when they are not? Most people would agree that the presence of others makes running easier and that they run faster and play harder when there is an audience. But can we be confident of these commonsense observations?

In 1897 Triplett published what generally is accepted as the first social psychology experiment. It was designed to answer the question: does the presence of others affect an individual's performance? Triplett noticed that winning riders in bicycle races were paced by another person. Triplet devised a laboratory procedure to put his informal observation to a more stringent test. Children were given fishing reels and were asked to reel in the line as fast as they could. Each child either carried out the task alone or when paired with another child. The children wound the reels faster when in pairs than when alone. This **social facilitation effect** is the earliest of social psychological principles, and the explanation for it is still a matter of dispute among social psychologists.

In 1924 Floyd Allport, who also conducted social facilitation research, published a textbook that has been and continues to be influential even today. We can explain social facilitation effects from the perspective of the individual or from dynamics of group processes (Hendrick, 1977). Allport clearly and powerfully presented an individual analysis, a trend that has continued and has been expanded into many other areas of research.

In the context of an individualistic approach to understanding social behavior, Thurstone developed the first attitude scale in 1927. During the 1930s and 1940s, the study of attitudes dominated social psychology. This emphasis was bolstered by the practical concerns associated with World War II. The military was interested in how to maintain morale among troops and in the factors that made propaganda more or less effective. Government agencies recruited social psychologists to help find ways to change the attitudes of people (Hendrick, 1977).

Social psychologists performed a few laboratory studies during the 1930s, but it was during the war years that the experimental method became the preferred way of testing hypotheses and theories. Kurt Lewin (1951) was one of the most influential social psychologists of that period. He stressed what he called **action research**—the study of fundamental knowledge in the context of real social problems. Psychologists then could apply the knowledge they discovered to resolving the problems; that is, their research could become a basis for both knowledge and action. According to Lewin (1951), "As far as methodoloy is concerned, one has to emphasize that laws can be established in psychology only by an experimental procedure" (p. 204).

Lewin produced a large number of distinguished student-scholars in social psychology (Marrow, 1969). From the network of personal associations and the power of the scientific method, the use of experiments has become firmly established among contemporary social psychologists with a psychological orientation. Thus, the unit of analysis is the individual and the method of choice is the laboratory experiment.

By the mid-1950s, social psychology was firmly established as a laboratory science. A major stimulus for research was Festinger's *Theory of Cognitive Disso-*

nance, which appeared in 1957 (see Chapter 6). In the early 1960s, a classic experiment performed by Schachter and Singer (1962) reoriented thinking about the nature of human emotions. Milgram's (1963) sensational study of obedience also had a lasting impact on the field. The late 1960s and the 1970s reflected the emergence of cybernetics and computers, as social psychologists focused on how people perceived one another and themselves and how they processed information about the social world (see Chapter 5). In the present decade, increasing emphasis has been given to theory and research about the self. How we think about ourselves and how we present ourselves to others has become one of the "hot" areas of research that is likely to continue into the next decade.

Acquiring knowledge in social psychology: why science?

The trouble with scientists is that they can't leave well enough alone.

Art Buchwald

Social psychology is a science because of the way it goes about evaluating explanations of human behavior. Scientific procedures must fulfill three requirements: (1) hypotheses must be evaluated on the basis of information gathered in a way to minimize the biases of the scientist; (2) data gathered to test hypotheses must be made available for public examination; and (3) the hypotheses should be falsifiable in the sense that clear tests can show them to be wrong (if they are). We examine why these three requirements are considered important criteria for the development of scientific knowledge.

In the movie *Altered States* the lead character, Eddie Jessup, combined sensory deprivation with hallucinogenic drugs in an effort to find the ultimate truth about humanity. At first he simply hallucinated about the origins of human beings. Later he began to regress physically to a primitive apelike state, a process that nearly destroyed him and his wife. Jessup's sobering conclusion after returning from his exotic "trip" is that there is no ultimate truth, that truth is something all people determine for themselves based on their own experiences.

Think of the many beliefs you have. The sun rises in the East everyday and sets in the West, the earth is round, objects fall down and not up, smoking leads to cancer, and so on. Do you have any beliefs you feel are false? If you consider something to be untrue or meaningless, you of course do not believe it; but no one is infallible. Human beings are prone to making mistakes. As the Roman poet Seneca said, "To err is human." Perfection is reserved for the gods. When we examine the source of our beliefs, our confidence in their truth may be shaken.

The orgins of beliefs

In 1877 Charles Sanders Peirce, perhaps the greastest of American philosophers, published a famous little essay entitled *The Fixation of Belief.* It examines the four most popular methods of acquiring beliefs. Peirce persuasively argued that these common methods are prone to error and bias, hence beliefs drawn from them are apt to be unreliable.

Authority

The most common way of acquiring beliefs is through the **method of authority**. We believe something is true because someone of authority tells us. This is certainly the easiest way of developing beliefs. However, authorities must obtain their information from somewhere even though they might adopt beliefs arbitrarily and without applying any method. It is for this reason that Peirce (1951) considered authorities to be unreliable sources of information. According to Peirce, there are two kinds of authorities: dogmatic and expert. The **dogmatic authority** is someone who makes statements that cannot be checked; that is, the claimed knowledge is personal and not open to public examination. For example, if someone tells us that she saw a ghost, we can believe it or not, but we cannot prove that she did or did not actually see the ghost. Similarly, if Jessup had a revelation on his exotic trip and reported it to us, we cannot check to see if he actually had this sudden, illuminating experience. Whether an individual chooses to believe a dogmatic authority depends more on trust than on the individual's independent ability to evaluate the information transmitted.

An **expert authority** is someone whose assertions can be checked independently. Parents, television newscasters, physicians, and teachers are commonly encountered expert authorities. Experts, like everyone else, are affected by their own interests and values, and the information they convey is not screened carefully for such biases. Peirce believed that the self-interests of all authorities made them unreliable as sources for the acquisition of knowledge. Although we can obtain a second opinion, agreement among authorities sharing the same self-interests, such as attorneys, physicians, and clinical psychologists, does not necessarily lead to increased reliability of information.

Personal experience

The **a priori method** is a second way people can arrive at beliefs, according to Peirce. It refers to instances when people accept beliefs because they seem plausible or because they have gained evidence through personal experience or common sense. This was Jessup's method in trying to discover the origins of the human species. It is the "seeing is believing" and "show me, I'm from Missouri" school of common sense. What we believe as a matter of common sense simply may represent a consensus of bias among people who share a common culture. A reliance on the a priori method would make knowledge acquisition a totally subjective process and hence a matter of taste.

Knowledge is not a democratic matter in the sense that if a majority believes something it is then true. History and anthropology alert us to be aware of the multitude of occasions when a great majority of people believed something that was later found to be untrue. For example, in the Dark Ages most people believed the world was flat, unmoving, and the center of the universe. Indeed, the person who did not believe these "truths" was threatened with dire punishment by a grand inquisitor. Remember that Galileo had to recant his heresy about the movement of the earth.

Common sense can be just as wrong today as in the Dark Ages. Modern social psychological research frequently has provided evidence that flies in the face of common sense. It has been shown that people in groups make riskier decisions than lone individuals make; yet we tend to think of people in groups as more conservative (see Chapter 12). Another reliable finding is: the less money people are given to tell a lie, the more they will come to believe the lie (see Chapter 5). Many people believe that the more a person can gain from a lie, the more that person believes the lie. It is examples like these that led Peirce (1951) to reject the method of direct experience as a basis for the development of knowledge.

Tenacity

The third method used by the typical person in the acquisition of beliefs is tenacity. This **method of tenacity** involves the belief that something is true because we want it to be true, then persuading ourselves over and over again that it is true. Consider the story of a patient who insisted to her psychiatrist that she was dead. The psychiatrist decided to convince her that the bizarre belief was incorrect. He asked her if dead people bleed. When she said no, he pricked her finger. The woman stared at the blood and then confessed that she was wrong: "Dead people do bleed!" Once people commit themselves to a point of view, it is difficult to help them change their minds. As Peirce (1951) said, "Men cling spasmodically to the views they already take . . . learning to turn with contempt and hatred from anything which might disturb it" (pp. 89-90).

Tenacious believers can reinterpret almost any event in terms of their preferred beliefs. An interesting example of this flexibility of interpretation occurred a number of years ago when a dam gave way in a southern area of the United States (Gergen & Gergen, 1981). The gushing water inflicted major damage upon a religious college and several deaths resulted. The surrounding areas, however, were relatively untouched. You might think that such an experience so localized to the religious college would lead many to question their faith. Instead, students at the college interpreted the catastrophic event as an act of grace from God, who "had touched them in His special way." Peirce (1951) rejected the method of tenacity because it is error prone. He advocated a method not used by the average person, the **method of science**.

Scientific method

By following a prescribed series of steps, scientists can eliminate the problems associated with the methods of authority, direct experience, and tenacity. The scientific method poses questions directly to nature as the final arbiter of truth. The goal of gaining answers that are independent of the biases and desires of scientists can be approximated if they take sufficient care in following rather rigorous standards and procedures.

Two important characteristics of the scientific method are its public and self-corrective aspects. A person, like Jessup, who reaches conclusions merely through private experiences is not a scientist. Scientists must report their methods and results publicly, so they can be scrutinized and perhaps criticized by other scientists. Doubters may be able to follow the same methods to see if the results are reliable.

Suppose we observe a blind man circumnavigating obstacles as he walks down the street. We may explain that his success is due to learning. He may have been walking the street for a long period of time, and by bumping into things, he has learned where they are. How might this hypothesis be tested? Place him in the school gymnasium where you have previously arranged some obstacles, then ask him to walk around. What you are likely to discover is that the blind man will circumnavigate the obstacles you have put in his path. What does this result say about the learning hypothesis? It is obviously wrong, so we search for a new hypothesis, undertake a new test, and continue to recycle this process until we gain evidence that does not contradict our hypothesis. This is the self-corrective aspect of the scientific method.

There is a significant weakness in the scientific method. It cannot provide us with absolute certainty about beliefs. We may say that given the available evidence it would be plausible, consistent, or reasonable to believe X, but we can never say that we are certain beyond any doubt that X is true. It is probably never the case that we can eliminate all possible alternative hypotheses so that only one hypothesis would be consistent with the available evidence. This is why we may consider truth to be an approximation, a matter of more or less, rather than of either/or. A summary of the four methods of acquiring beliefs is presented in Table 1-3.

Research methods in social psychology

A discovery is said to be an accident meeting a prepared mind.

Albert Szent-Gyorgyi

Social psychologists depend on systematic and controlled observations to learn about human behavior. Most people are curious about what is going on around them. They make observations and construct explanations for what they see. Ordinary observations are unsystematic and uncontrolled, however, and

Table 1-3 Peirce's four ways of acquiring knowledge

METHOD	ADVANTAGE	DISADVANTAGE
Authority	Easy and quick	Evidence often cannot be checked and is biased.
Personal experience	Allows for self-discovery	Consensus of the masses is often wrong.
Tenacity	Maintains stable belief system	Impedes acquisition of new knowledge.
Science	Self-corrective	Slow, tedious and is at best an approximation.

hence unreliable. Suppose you notice that males appear to be more impatient and impolite than females while both wait in the cashier's line at the grocery store. Is this a general fact or is the behavior specific to your neighborhood or to the time of day? If you stood and watched all day long, would the few incidents you observed be repeated, or was the difference in males and females confined to a few people while you were in the store? Social psychologists would make systematic observations, perhaps by visiting a number of stores in the city at different times of the week and day. If this systematic way of making observations reliably establishes that males are more aggressive than females, the investigator has discovered a fact; that is, the investigator has made a definite observation which can be reliably reported.

A hypothesis is a tentative explanation of a fact. If males were more aggressive in grocery stores, such behavior might be attributed to male hormones (testosterone), to sex-linked child-rearing practices, to more stringent time demands on men, or to any number of other possible hypotheses.

A controlled test of an hypothesis in which one or more factors are manipulated is an **experiment**. We could create a laboratory situation in which male and female subjects had to wait in line for coupons associated with a game. Suppose our hypothesis is that the behavior of males is more negative when they are waiting in line with other males than when they are positioned next to females; that is, males might react negatively when crowded by members of the same sex. To test this hypothesis, we might contrive an experiment in which students must wait for their coupons in line with members of the same sex or with members of the opposite sex. If males are more aggressive than females only when they are positioned next to other males, then the crowding hypothesis would be supported.

A complex explanation of phenomena involving a number of hypotheses is a **theory**. Scientific theories typically contain a set of basic concepts and statements about the relationships between them. A theory of crowding behavior not only should be able to explain why males are more impatient when waiting in line than females are, but it should be able to explain many other reactions to crowding by other people. A theory is much more general than any single hypothesis and has the function of organizing hypotheses and interpreting facts. Theories can be tested only through the predictions contained in specific hypotheses, however. Research typically provides tests of a variety of hypotheses associated with a theory, and researchers must judge the merit of the theory in the context of a large body of evidence. Of course no theory is perfect, and scientists are in continual search for better theories.

Research techniques can be divided into those aiming to establish facts and generate hypotheses and into those designed to test hypotheses. The goal of observational research is to establish facts and explore possible hypotheses. Experimental research is directed to hypothesis testing and theory evaluation. As we will see, each set of techniques has its place in the scientific study of human social behavior, and each also has some disadvantages.

Observational methods

One of the joys in attending an outdoor concert is to watch other people. These observations are unsystematic and unplanned. Social psychologists know what they want to observe before venturing into the field and carefully plan the procedures that they will use. The site to be visited, the measuring instruments to be used, and who will be observed are well thought out prior to the actual investigation. Among observational methods are field studies, participant observation, and unobtrusive measures.

Field studies offer social psychology investigators the advantage of "planting situations" in natural settings in order to observe behavior. Studying youth at a havitual gathering place can constitute a field study.

Box 1-1

A soft-drink identification of geographical location

Much have I learned from my teachers, more from my colleagues and most from my students.
Talmud

Shortly after moving from New York to western Pennsylvania, Paul Rosenfeld went into a grocery store to buy a soft drink. "Where do you keep the soda?" he asked. "*Soda?* Oh, you mean *pop,*" answered the clerk. "In the back near the kielbasa section."

Armed with the discovery that the term a person uses for a soft drink can be an unobtrusive measure of where he is from, Dr. Rosenfeld used it as an example in one of his classes. "People from New York drink *soda,* but in the Midwest they drink *pop.*"

"Wait a minute," said a student. "I'm from New England, and we drink tonic."

Before Dr. Rosenfeld could respond, another student in the back of the room lazily raised his hand and said in a laid-back voice, "Hey, man, I'm from California, and we drink *Coke.*"

"Well, I was referring to a general term for all soft drinks, not a specific brand."

"No, man," retorted the student. "In California when you ask someone for a *Coke,* they ask you what kind—like *orange, root beer,* or *lemon and lime.* They use it the same way you dudes from New York use *soda.*"

Thanks to our students, our unobtrusive measure has been made more sensitive: soda in New York, pop in the Midwest, tonic in New England, and Coke in California. We still are trying to determine what people in the South say.

Field studies

A **field study** is an observational method where the investigator simply observes without intervening to change behavior in any way. For example, a field study carried out at an indoor shopping mall in Seattle, Washington, recorded whether passersby looked at a one-year-old infant standing or playing next to a bench (Robinson, Lockard, and Adams, 1979). As might be expected, from knowledge of socialization practices in the United States (see Chapter 11) more females than males looked at the child.

Field studies give researchers the advantage of studying people in natural surroundings. As in "Candid Camera," people are observed behaving unselfconsciously. An example of how language is used differently in various regions of the United States is described in Box 1-1. A distinct disadvantage of a field study is the researcher's lack of control over the many factors that occur in the situation. Although facts can be established, the lack of control in field studies renders them rather unreliable as tests of hypotheses.

Participant observation

Participant observation consists of an investigator joining the people being investigated. In a classic study of this type, several social psychologists joined an end-of-the-world group (Festinger, Riecken, and Schachter, 1956). They wanted to see how the disconfirming effects of the group's prediction would alter its members' attitudes toward the group. When the world did not end, the members did not give up their faith in the group—instead, their faith was even stronger! They believed the goodness of their group had been instrumental in saving the world. We have much more to say about this study in Chapter 6.

Box 1-2

How much beer do you drink?

Unobtrusive measures are useful particularly when the behavior under investigation might be considered socially undesirable. If a researcher came to your house and asked how much beer you drank each week, what would you say? Is it anyone's business how much beer you drink: If you admit to consuming three or four six-packs, might this revelation make you look bad?

A comparison of unobtrusive measures with what respondents said to direct questions showed a lack of correspondence between their words and deeds concerning beer consumption (Webb, Campbell, Schwartz, Sehcrest, and Grove, 1981). The investigator asked people how much beer they drank each week. Only 15 percent of the people in the homes surveyed admitted to drinking any beer. The maximum amount admitted by the drinkers was eight cans per week. The investigator also examined the trash in back of the respondents' houses and discovered that the garbage from 77 percent of the homes contained cans; more than half of these had more than eight cans. The average number of disgarded beer cans in the houses with more than eight cans was fifteen. Unless beer cans can undergo mitosis, many people were having more tall cool ones than they were revealing. The moral of the story is that social psychologists have to be concerned about the reactivity of their measurements. They must build in checks to validate the responses of research participants.

The main advantage of participant observation is that it allows the investigator to get closer to the phenomenon than would be possible by other means. By becoming members of the end-of-the-world group, social psychologists were able to learn more about the way such people think. The disadvantage of participant observation, however, is that such close presence may affect the behavior under investigation. By joining this small and highly ridiculed group, the social psychologists may have added to the group's stability and encouraged good feelings about the group among its members.

Unobtrusive measures

People about to be photographed often assume unnatural poses or facial expressions. In a similar way, people who are under observation or who are subjected to various forms of psychological measurements may react to the measuring instruments. One solution investigators have for such **reactivity to measurements** is to develop less direct forms of measurement. **Unobtrusive measures** allow social psychologists to assess relevant facts without directly measuring them. Subjects are unaware of the observation. For instance, floor tile wear could be used as an indicator of the popularity of a museum exhibit. A drop in water pressure from toilet flushes has been reported in New York City following the last episode of "M*A*S*H" and the "1984 Super Bowl." Thus, water pressure may be an indirect measure of how many people are watching television. An interesting study that used unobtrusive measures is described in Box 1-2.

The major advantage of unobtrusive measures is that they allow psychologists to measure behavior without either interfering with it or creating concern about social desirability. On the other hand, we cannot always be sure that an unobtrusive measure is assessing that in which we are interested. The floor tile near a museum exhibit may be worn out because the exhibit is popular or because it is situated near the rest rooms. Ethical questions also may be raised about some forms of unobtrusive measurement. If you have some doubt about the ethics associated with invading the privacy of citizens and going through their garbage, so do the authors of this textbook.

Archival Research

Archival research makes use of information that has been collected for some other purpose. The U.S. Census, the files of the Federal Bureau of Investigation, and the *New York Times* are examples of large data bases often used in archival research. Social psychologists used archival data in one study as a basis to investigate the difference between physical assaults and homicides (Felson, 1980). An analysis of police reports indicated that personal insult by the victim was an important stimulus for homicidal assaults.

As with other research techniques, archival research has its advantages and disadvantages. On the plus side is the availability of the data and the lowered cost of obtaining it. Indeed, it might be virtually impossible for the investigator to acquire such data in any other way. What a person tells the police after assaulting someone might be quite different from what that same person would say to a psychologist several months or years later. A disadvantage in the use of archival data is the psychologists' inability to make the kinds of measurements that might be most relevant to their purposes. The police would not ask the same questions or gather the same information about a suspect as would a social psychologist who is carrying out a scientific investigation. Police records also represent the work of separate officers who may carry out their duties in very different ways. Thus, the collection of data is unsystematic and uncontrolled. An archival study is only as good as the data base.

Survey research

Surveys are a part of popular culture. Ratings of television shows are based on survey data from only a tiny fraction of the population. The results of elections frequently are predicted with great accuracy soon after the polls close. The success of a survey depends upon the method of selecting respondents. The responses

"...Very *concerned!*"

Source: Reprinted with permission from The Saturday Evening Post, Society, a division of BFL & MS, Inc. © 1984.

of those questioned serve as the basis for making general statements about the entire population that the respondents are chosen to represent.

Surveys gain their predictive power through representative sampling. Just as a doctor drawing blood from your finger assumes that it is typical of blood everywhere in your body, so the survey researcher assumes that samples drawn from a larger population are representative of the rest. A **representative sample** is a small number of people who are like the population under investigation in all relevant ways. If you are conducting a survey on voting patterns, you would not include people who were not citizens or who were under the age of twenty-one because they are not representative of the voting population. Accurate predictions of voting patterns require careful selection of respondents who are likely to vote.

The major advantage of survey research is that it allows the researcher to assess what the population as a whole feels about certain issues and how they behave. Many national surveys use samples of a few hundred respondents or even less. The effectiveness of surveys may be limited because of the questions asked and because the respondents may have to react to sensitive issues. How accurate do you think the responses would be to a question such as: "How often did you beat your husband (wife) during the last year?"

Surveys will lead to erroneous conclusions if the sample used is not truely representative of the larger population. A famous case of an unrepresentative sample occurred before the 1936 election between Roosevelt and Landon. The magazine *Literary Digest* published the results of a survey predicting that Landon, a Republican, would beat the Democatic incumbent by a landslide. Of course Roosevelt won the election in a landslide. What went wrong? A close look at the magazine's sampling techniques explains the inaccurate prediction. The sample was chosen from a list of car and telephone owners. In 1936 possession of a car and/or telephone was a sign of wealth. Because wealthy people tend to vote Republican and poor people tend to vote Democratic, the sample was biased in the direction of Republicans and was not representative of the voting population.

Correlational research

A **correlation** is a statistic measuring the degree of association between sets of data. This statistic measures the degree to which changes in the value of one variable are related to changes in another. For example, the number of hours viewers spend watching violent programs on television may be related to the amount of aggressive behavior they display.

Correlations can range from +1 to −1. A correlation of +1 indicates a perfect positive relationship. As applied to viewing television violence, it would mean that in every case the number of hours viewers spend watching violent programs would predict exactly the degree of aggressive behavior they exhibit. At the other extreme, a negative correlation tells the investigator that as variable *a* increases, variable *b* decreases, and vice versa. For example, it has been found that the more shy or socially anxious people are, the less they function well in public situations (Schlenker and Leary, 1982).

The major advantage of correlational research to social psychologists is that it is a quick and inexpensive way to determine relationships between many variables. Correlations may inform us about relationships that could not be studied in any other way. For example, researchers have established that the rate of suicides is correlated negatively with the business cycle. When times are good, there are fewer suicides, but when economic conditions deteriorate, the rate of suicides increases (Henry and Short, 1954).

The primary disadvantage of correlational research is summarized in this dictum: "Correlation does not imply causation." Because two variables are correlated does not mean one caused the other. The reason for the difficulty in interpreting cause-effect relationships from correlations has to do with the **third variable problem** (Jung, 1982). If variables x and y are corre-

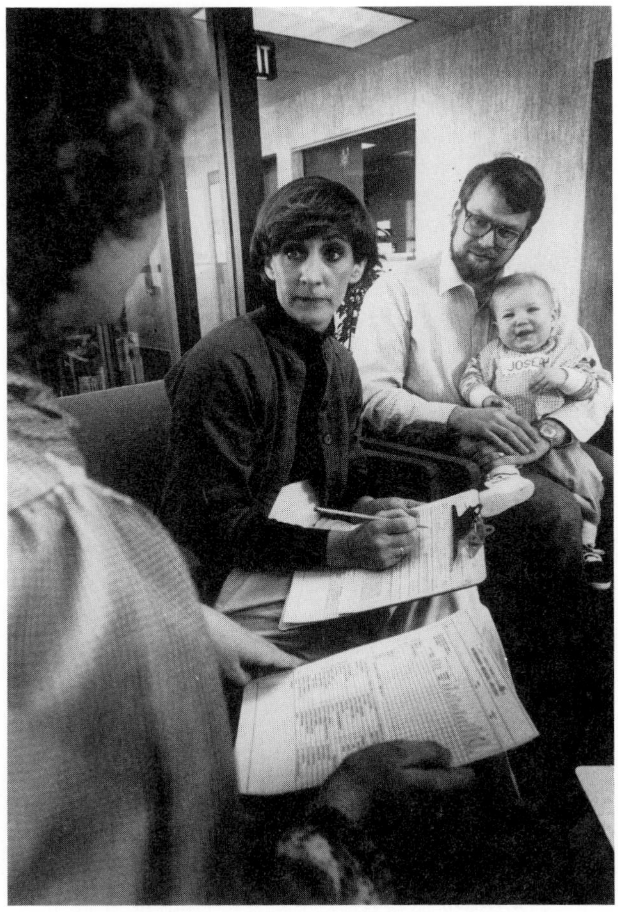

Interviewer obtains responses to questions in a survey. By studying a representative sample of these families, investigators are able to predict the behavior of a particular population, such as why parents choose to have only one child.

Box 1-3

Sometimes extraneous variables are superfluous

Research has shown that apparently trivial differences in treatment between experimental conditions can have a dramatic influence on the outcome, although not every independent or extraneous variable makes a difference. In 1928 H. B. Hovey had a group of 171 people take two different versions of an IQ test (Rosnow, 1981). They took the first version in a quiet room. The group was then given the other form of the test in another room under conditions that would remind you of trying to study in dorms during homecoming weekend. Among other things, there were seven bells, five buzzers, a bright spotlight, a phonograph (no stereos in those days), two organ pipes, three metal whistles, a large circular saw, a photographer taking pictures, and four students doing acrobatics.

The subjects did as well in the second test as in the first. We learn an important lesson from this study: although control of outside variables is a desirable goal of laboratory research, their intrusion does not automatically mean that the behavior of all subjects will be affected dramatically.

lated, it is possible that x causes y, y causes x, or a third variable causes both x and y. For example, because deterioration in economic conditions is associated with an increase in suicides does not mean that poverty causes suicides. It may be the case that decreases in income are associated with greater family conflicts, which in turn are associated with psychological depression and suicides. Thus, it may not be money but family conflict that is the cause of suicides.

Experimental methods

Social psychologists who are interested in hypothesis testing prefer to use **experimental methods**. These procedures involve an active manipulation and control over factors being studied so that a conclusion can be reached about cause-effect relationships. Among these methods are laboratory, field, and natural experiments.

Laboratoy experiments

An experiment is a test of an hypothesis requiring the planned comparison of two or more conditions. Suppose you notice how friendly your classmates become just before examinations. Its not unusual to see students bunched together anxiously waiting to get into the room to take a final examination. Do people like to have other people around when they feel anxious? This hypothesis can be tested with an experiment.

The person who performs the test is referred to as an **experimenter**. Research participants are referred to as **subjects**. The factors manipulated by the experimenter are called the **independent variables**. The impact of the independent variables on some behavior is measured, and this measure is called the **dependent variable**. Its value is assumed to depend upon the conditions and values of the independent variables. In a classic study of the "misery likes company" hypothesis, an experimenter induced anxiety in subjects by telling them that they would be receiving painful electric shocks (the independent variable). The subjects were then given an opportunity to sit alone or with other people. Their choice was the dependent variable. In general, when subjects were anxious, they had a stronger desire to be with others than when they were not anxious (Schachter, 1959).

Subjects are assigned randomly to conditions. **Random assignment** means that the condition to which a subject will be assigned is determined by chance. Each subject has an equal opportunity to be assigned to any condition of the experiment. This procedure reduces the probability that some characteristic of the subjects will be related systematically to experimental conditions. If this individual difference factor were not controlled by random assignment, something about the subjects and not about the independent variable might be the cause of differences between conditions. Uncontrolled factors that vary systematically with independent variable manipulations are called **extraneous variables**. One of the most important strengths of laboratory experiments is the ability they offer researchers to control extraneous variables. Box 1-3 provides an example showing that not all extraneous variables make a difference in experiments.

An important characteristic of an experiment is the deliberate contrivance of contrasting conditions. Subjects with high anxiety in Schachter's (1959) experiment were led to believe that they were going to receive painful shocks. The subjects in this condition are referred to as the **experimental group** because they were exposed to an independent variable inducing them to experience high anxiety. The comparison group that expected less painful shocks and experienced a low level of anxiety is called the **control group**, because this group was exposed to all aspects of the experiment except for the independent variable. The degree of anxiety is controlled to be at a low level.

What conclusion can we draw from the fact that subjects in the high-anxiety conditions had a stronger preference for waiting with other people? Because random assignment effectively equated the groups initially in terms of abilities, motivation, intelligence, and personality traits, something in the situation must have caused the difference. If all the extraneous variables were eliminated, then the cause of the affiliative behavior must have been the anxiety created by the threat of painful shock.

To the degree we are confident that it was the independent variable causing the observed difference in the dependent variable, our experiment is said to have **internal validity**. If additional research shows that this cause-effect relationship occurs in other situations that create anxiety (other than fear of shocks) and with different kinds of subjects (other than college students), our experimental findings are said to have external validity (Campbell and Stanley, 1963). **External validity** refers to researchers' ability to generalize the findings they obtain in particular experiments. Researchers strive to maximize both the internal and external validity of their experiments.

Clearly, the major advantage of laboratory experiments is that they allow the discovery of cause-effect relationships. This is a major goal of science and explains why laboratory experiments are the preferred method of social psychologists. The laboratory has the advantage of providing experimenters with a high degree of control over subject selection and assignment and control over extraneous variables.

In carrying out laboratory experiments, researchers must take care not to make the situation so artificial, atypical, or unusual that participants behave in uncharacteristic ways. The desire for tight control must be balanced by procedures designed to elicit "real behavior" from subjects. One way to confirm the external validity of laboratory research is to follow up results with experiments in real-world settings.

Field experiments

Field experiments are tests of hypotheses carried out under real-life conditions. Researchers who carry out field experiments attempt methodologically to have the best of both worlds. They combine the control exerted in laboratory experiments with the relevance of behavior occurring without the artificiality sometimes associated with the laboratory. There is no need to invent cover stories, and subjects often do not know that they are participating in an experiment. Field situations offer social psychologists opportunities to study behavior that would be difficult to examine in the laboratory.

Suppose you wanted to purchase an item in a store but did not have quite enough money. Do you think the clerk would let you have the item for less money? Would your sex or race affect the probability that the clerk would be generous? These questions were examined. Confederates entered convenience stores and attempted to buy an item that cost between $1.15 and $1.50. While paying for the item, confederates "found" that they only had a dollar. The confederates asked the

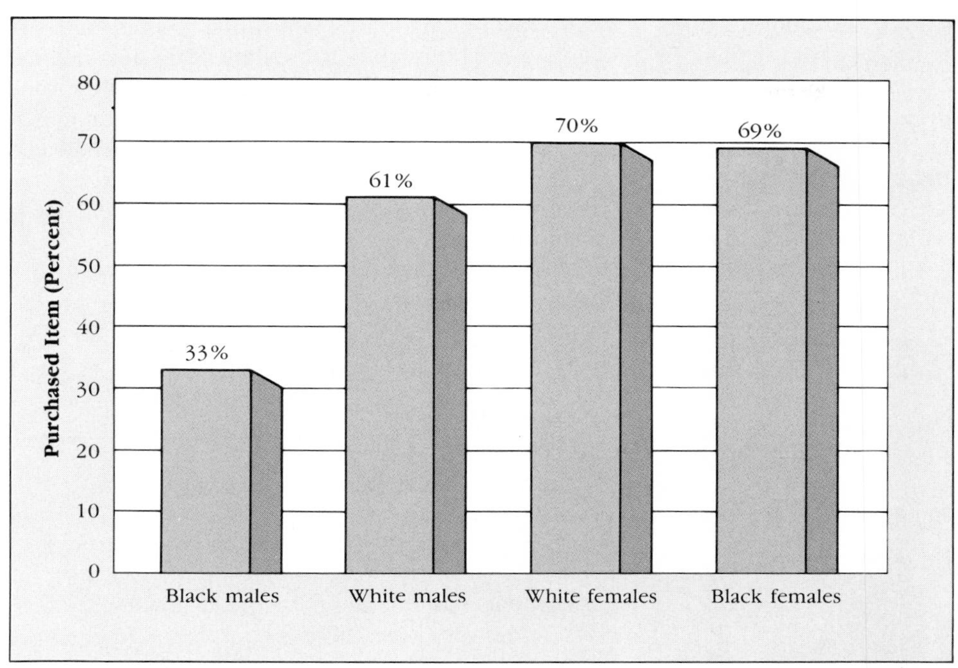

Source: Based on "Race, sex and helping in the marketplace" by J. C. Brigham and C. B. Richardson, 1979, *Journal of Personality and Social Psychology*, *9*, 314-322.

Figure 1-1 Field experiment testing how race and sex affect generosity.

clerks if it would be alright to take the item anyway. In this study, convenience store clerks were the subjects, and the independent variables were the sex (male or female) and the race (black or white) of the shoppers. The dependent variable was whether the clerks would allow the shoppers to leave the store with the product. Both independent variables affected the clerks' behavior. As can be seen in Figure 1-1, white shoppers were more often allowed to take the product than black shoppers were; females were treated more generously than males (Brigham and Richardson, 1979).

The lack of artificiality and the elimination of reactivity by subjects because they are unaware that they are in an experiment are distinct advantages of field experiments. What such studies gain in reality and relevance, however, they almost invariably lose in control over extraneous variables. Any flight from the laboratory allows numerous confounding variables, such as noise, temperature, and presence of other people to interfere with the internal validity of the experiment. The lessening of control weakens confidence in conclusions reached about cause-effect relationships.

Natural experiments

A **natural experiment** is a field experiment where Mother Nature manipulates the independent variable. Natural disasters, such as fires and earthquakes, often wreak havoc on some unfortunate people while sparing others in what appears to be a random fashion. The opportunistic researcher can take advantage of this natural manipulation by making comparisons between the affected and spared groups.

A natural experiment of this type was undertaken when a major fire broke out in southern California during a severe drought in the late 1970s. Over two hundred homes were destroyed in the Santa Barbara area. Due to variable wind conditions and the location of firefighting equipment, some houses in the same area were untouched. This natural manipulation was the occasion that brought researchers to investigate the reactions of victims and nonvictims to the disaster.

People whose homes were damaged attributed the disaster to bad luck. Nonvictims in the same neighborhoods claimed their homes escaped damage because of their protective actions (Parker, Brewer, and Spencer, 1980). As we point out in Chapter 4, this finding supports the results of numerous laboratory experiments indicating that people claim control over good outcomes but deny responsibility for bad outcomes.

Natural disasters, such as floods, produce opportunities for natural experiments. Researchers can study and compare the behavior of victims and nonvictims without creating laboratory or field situations to affect subjects.

One advantage of a natural experiment over a field experiment is the occurrence of the independent variable without the intrusion of the experimenter. There also are many events that could not be manipulated realistically or ethically. Social psychologists cannot create disasters, riots, panic, lynchings, suicides, homicides, revolutions, and many other events. If such events are to be studied, something other than laboratory experiments are required. The major disadvantage of natural experiments is that they occur rarely and their appearance usually cannot be predicted. Social psychologists attempting to make careers by performing natural experiments could well have much leisure time on their hands.

The social psychology of the experiment

Collecting data about human behavior is itself a social process.

Henry Riecken

Experiments with human participants are social situations. At the very least, there is contact and interaction between the experimenter and the subject. In social psychological research, other people are often present. These conditions introduce a number of extraneous variables that must be controlled if experiments are to be internally valid. Considerable attention has been given to the problems and the controls to be used. The focus on the effects of social factors has become an area of interest in itself and is referred to as the **social psychology of the experiment**.

In retrospect it may appear perplexing that social psychologists would ignore the social dynamics in the laboratory for the first fifty years in the history of social psychology. Social psychology is a product of a difficult and tenuous marriage of social philosophy and scientific method which is employed so successfully by the natural and biological sciences. Many people were and are skeptical that something as complex as human behavior could ever be understood by the methods of science. Psychologists may have felt the need to prove their scientific status and hence became preoccupied (some would say obsessed) with the goals of precision, standardization, and control. The laboratory was viewed as a kind of test tube, a "methodologically sterile environment for the study of behavior" (Adair, 1973, p. vii). Subjects in experiments were perceived as passively responding to psychological stimuli; there were "docile input-output machines"

(Jung, 1982, p. 203). It was assumed that the process of observing did not affect the behavior that was observed (Craig and Metze, 1979). The researcher was viewed as engaging in "immaculate perception."

Clearly humans are not inanimate or passive objects merely responding to the physical forces impinging on them. Research participants are thinking, problem-solving human beings who are cognizant of the fact that their behavior is being scrutinized intensely and that they actively influence the nature of the experimental situation (Jung, 1982; Orne, 1962). As Rosenzweig (1933) stated: "When one works with human materials one must reckon with the fact that everyone is a psychologist . . . carrying on a train of psychological activity that is rather about the experiment than a part of it" (p. 37).

Demand characteristics

Participants in experiments make use of whatever information is available to them in defining the nature of the situation. Some subjects may discover or believe they have discovered the experimenter's hypothesis. Some perhaps perceive a cue in the situation indicating what the experimenter would like them to do. Rosenzweig (1933) suggested that "a subject who acts in this way commits what we shall call the 'opinion error': he entertains opinions about the experiment—what its purpose is and what he may reveal in it—instead of simply reacting in a naive manner" (p. 343).

Orne (1962) referred to **demand characteristics** as cues that might influence the subject to respond in a particular way. The intonations of voice, body position, facial expression, or eye contact by the experimenter; the arrangement of equipment used; campus rumors about the experiment; or any other cues may function to tip off the subject to the experimenter's hypothesis, which in turn can lead to an artifactual result. An **artifact** is a finding due to extraneous and uncontrolled factors and not to the independent variable that serves as test of the hypothesis of interest.

Orne (1962) cautioned that if uncontrolled cues rather than independent variable manipulations were the main source of changes in a dependent variable, an experiment would be contaminated; that is, it would lack internal validity. In his investigations of hypnosis, Orne wanted to distinguish between what subjects do because they are in a trance and what they would do simply because they are subjects in an experiment.

Orne had difficulty in finding a task subjects would refuse to do. In one case, he gave each subject two thousand sheets of paper containing rows of random numbers and instructed them to add adjacent numbers. To complete just one sheet properly required 224 additions. Subjects had their watches taken away and were told to continue working until the experimenter returned. Five and one-half hours later, Orne gave up!

Orne made the task more difficult and even more meaningless. Subjects were instructed to do the number-adding task and, after completing each sheet, to pick up a card telling them what to do next. Every card said the same thing. They were to tear up the sheet into no less than thirty-two pieces and go on to the next sheet. Once again subjects worked for several hours until they finally stopped. Although Orne meant to construct a meaningless task in the context of an experiment, subjects believe it must have some purpose. Many in this study believed Orne was giving them a test of endurance.

Not only will subjects comply with pressures to continue working on tedious tasks, but they also will perform dangerous actions. Orne and Evans (1965) asked subjects to pick up a poisonous snake barehanded, retrieve a dissolving coin from a fuming nitric acid solution, and throw the container of acid into the face of an experimental assistant. Fifteen out of eighteen subjects complied with all three requests. They later said they thought the snake was not really poisonous and that the assistant would somehow be protected. In the context of an experiment, even the most outlandish requests are obeyed without question because participants trust the researcher.

It may seem obvious that the experimenter can check for demand characteristics by simply asking subjects how aware they were of various cues and what they thought the hypotheses of the study were. Such postexperimental interviews may not be effective because of what Orne (1969) has called a **pact of ignorance**.

> [The subject] knows that if he has "caught on" to some apparent deception and had an excess of information about the experimental procedure, he may be disqualified from participation and thus have wasted his time. The experimenter is aware that the subject who

> knows too much or has "caught on" to his deception will have to be disqualified; disqualification means running yet another subject, still further delaying completion of the study. Hence, neither party to the inquiry wants to dig very deeply. (p. 153)

The reluctance of subjects to report information that may be damaging to the experiment was shown by Quigley-Fernandez and Tedeschi (1978). Confederate entered the waiting room from the laboratory area and informed a waiting subject that he had just been given a multiple-choice test. He said it was very difficult and he did not do well, but the experimenter went over the items afterward. He then told the subject that alternative "C" was the most frequent correct choice. Taking his coat and books from a chair, the confederate beat a hasty retreat from the laboratory area. Subjects were then given a very difficult multiple-choice test containing sixteen items. The items were constructed in order for the correct answers to be divided equally among alternatives A, B, C, and D. Subjects answered, however, with C on the average of seven times. When later asked if they had heard anything that might help them on the test, the great majority of subjects indicated complete ignorance.

A demand characteristics interpretation of an experiment is only another hypothesis researchers develop after they obtain evidence. As such this interpretation should be subjected to the same kind of test as any other hypothesis. Because it seems plausible to interpret a particular study in terms of demand characteristics, the investigator cannot grant the hypothesis any special privilege. Although it is difficult to control for demand cues, careful preparation of an experiment, including preliminary pilot collection of data and critical comments derived from colleagues and students, usually will catch the more blatant cues.

Experimenter effects

People used to have visions of scientists modeled after eccentric eighteenth century English gentlemen who, being independently wealthy, could leisurely test hypotheses out of a sincere curiosity for uncovering the truth. This quaint image was replaced by the view of scientists as kinds of logic machines or robots who systematically carried through a set of experimental procedures to obtain highly objective results. These idealized images are no longer maintained among scientists themselves. Experimenters are error-prone and biased human beings who often have vested interests in the way results turn out. Bias can be introduced into a research project and directly can affect a participant's behavior, such as demand characteristics that are not controlled. Experimental bias also can contribute to inaccurate recording and analysing of data.

Rosenthal (1969) identified three basic types of experimenter effects. Included among **biosocial factors** are characteristics related to the experimenter's age, physical appearance, sex, and race. Often biosocial factors have no impact on the behavior of research participants. There are situations in which people are sensitive and react to biosocial cues, however. For example, the presence of a black experimenter decreased antiblack prejudice reported by white subjects (Summers and Hammonds, 1966). On the other hand, race had no impact on the responses of patients to interviews (Womack and Wagner, 1967).

A second type of experimenter bias is **psychosocial**, which refers to psychological characteristics of the experimenter, such as friendliness, intimidating manner, and social anxiety. What would happen, for example, if a male experimenter smiled at all the female participants but not at the male participants? If a sex difference was found in such an experiment, it would not be possible to say whether the effect was due to an actual difference between males and females or whether the uncontrolled and systematically different behavior of the experimenter produced the finding. Although this example is hypothetical, Berkowitz and Zigler (1965) reported that subjects were more responsive to an attractive than to a less liked experimenter. Careful training of experimenters and the use of a large number of them should eliminate psychosocial effects. It is unlikely that all experimenters would be alike, hence using a number of them should randomize the psychosocial factors across conditions in an experiment. If a particular biasing factor associated with one experimenter is a part of the experiment, it will be represented in all conditions of the study and is not likely to be the cause of any difference among conditions.

Experimenter expectancy effects constitute the third type of experimenter effect pointed to by Rosenthal. Experimenters carefully have planned their research projects, have hypotheses about what should happen, believe they will happen, and may act in such

Box 1-4

Pfungst pfinds a pfatal pflaw

Experimenters may not intend to emit cues regarding their purposes to participants, and the latter may not be consciously aware of them; but such cues may nevertheless affect behavior (Nisbett and Wilson, 1977). This point may be illustrated by a story of a horse, Clever Hans. By tapping his hoof in response to a query, Hans was able to perform four arithmetic functions, tell time to the minute, give the value of German coins, and indicate the exact date of any day mentioned. A skeptical German psychologist by the name of Osker Pfungst carried out a six-week study of Clever Hans. He discovered that Hans was able to answer correctly only if the questioner knew the correct answer. If Hans could not see the person asking the question, he could not give the correct response. Furthermore, he noted that most people tended to lean forward slightly after asking a question. As Hans approached the correct number of taps, they would raise their heads a tad. Pfungst reasoned that the head inclination was a cue to Hans to begin tapping, and the raising of the head was a cue to stop. A little experiment confirmed this hypothesis (Rosenthal, 1969).

a way as to artifactually confirm their expectations. This kind of **self-fulfilling prophesy** is assumed to be a nondeliberate phenomenon, (see Box 1-4).

There are rare occasions when deliberate fudging of data does occur. Psychologists recently were shocked to discover that Sir Cyril Burt, one of the foremost authorities on the nature of human intelligence, probably made up much of his data. He was so convinced that intelligence was hereditary, there was little need to gather new evidence to support the theory. This is a case of a scientist using the method of tenacity.

In carrying out social psychological research, psychologists may have a problem with unintended and subtle experimenter expectancy effects. In a demonstration of the experimenter expectancy effect, Rosenthal and Fode (1963) had student experimenters perform a study in which subjects rated photographs of people's faces on a scale where +10 meant extreme success and −10 meant extreme failure. One group of experimenters were led to believe that subjects would average +5, the other group expected an average score of −5. The results showed that the subjects in the positive expectancy group rated the photographs significantly higher than subjects in the negative expectancy group rated them.

Rosenthal's studies have been criticized by Barber and Silver (1968). The experimenter expectancy effect was demonstrated with college students but not trained professional scientists. The students simply may have presented Rosenthal with the results he so obviously expected. This is a sound criticism; however, the experimenter expectancy effect has been shown to occur outside the laboratory. Rosenthal and Jacobson (1968) found that if teachers were led to believe that some of their students had higher IQs than others, these students actually scored higher on standardized IQ tests several months later. Apparently, the teachers' belief that some students were more intelligent than their peers led to preferential treatment, which in turn produced a difference that initially did not exist. Social psychologists have taken the lesson to heart. By using many experimenters in any particular study and by keeping them "blind" or ignorant of the hypothesis, psychologists can reduce and control experimenter expectancy effects.

Subject effects

Characteristics, traits, attitudes, and motivations of participants may affect how they behave in an experiment. For example, groups with egalitarian leaders were found to have better morale and productivity than those with authoritarian or laissez-faire leaders (Lewin, Lippitt, and White). The participants were American children. When the study was carried out in India, groups with authoritarian leaders were more productive (Meade 1967). The suggestion is that cul-

Biography

Robert Rosenthal

Robert Rosenthal was born on 2 March 1933 in Giessen, Germany. He moved to the United States during World War II, and became a naturalized citizen in 1946. Dr. Rosenthal traces his eventual career choice as a psychologist to his youth. He was one of those kids whom others just naturally wanted to tell their problems to. This choice became more concrete when Rosenthal enrolled at UCLA. Still somewhat unsure of his exact major, he put down psychology because it gave him the freedom to take courses in a number of different disciplines in which he was interested. After taking his first psychology course, however, Rosenthal was "hooked", and eventually received his doctoral degree in Clinical Psychology from UCLA. He has subsequently held faculty appointments at the University of North Dakota, Ohio State University and Boston University before joining the faculty at Harvard University where he has been a Professor of Social Psychology since 1967.

Dr. Rosenthal is best known for his classic research demonstrating that an experimenter's awareness of a hypothesis can result in a self-fulfilling prophecy causing the hypothesis to be confirmed. Like many other great discoveries in the history of psychology, Dr. Rosenthal's discovery of the self-fulfilling prophecy in experimental research was *serendipitous,* i.e., accidental, and happened while he was carrying out his doctoral dissertation research on the Freudian defense mechanism of projection. His subjects were divided into groups that were to receive success, failure or neutral feedback on a bogus intelligence test. Then they were to rate the degree of success or failure of individuals portrayed in various photographs. Rosenthal hypothesized that the subjects who experienced success would rate the people in the photographs as more successful than would subjects who did not experience success.

Before the experiment began Rosenthal gave his subjects a pretest in which they rated photographs in the same manner as would be used following the experiment. When he checked the scores for the three groups on the pre-test alone, he noticed that they differed in a way that made it more likely that his experimental hypothesis would be confirmed. Thus, the groups differed before the experiment actually began, an effect Rosenthal was able to trace to his own knowledge of the hypothesis which he was subtly and unintentionally communicating to subjects. Further research showed that this phenomenon was widespread and applicable to nonlaboratory situations, such as teacher's expectations affecting the performance of their students and therapists' expectations affecting the psychological and physical health of clients.

In recent years, Dr. Rosenthal has given increasing attention to the study of nonverbal communications and their role in heterosexual interactions and attempts to deceive others. He has also maintained a strong interest in the experimental and statistical techniques used by psychologists. Within the past several years, he has helped to develop and popularize the technique of *meta-analysis,* which allows for the statistical comparison of the results of a series of related experiments.

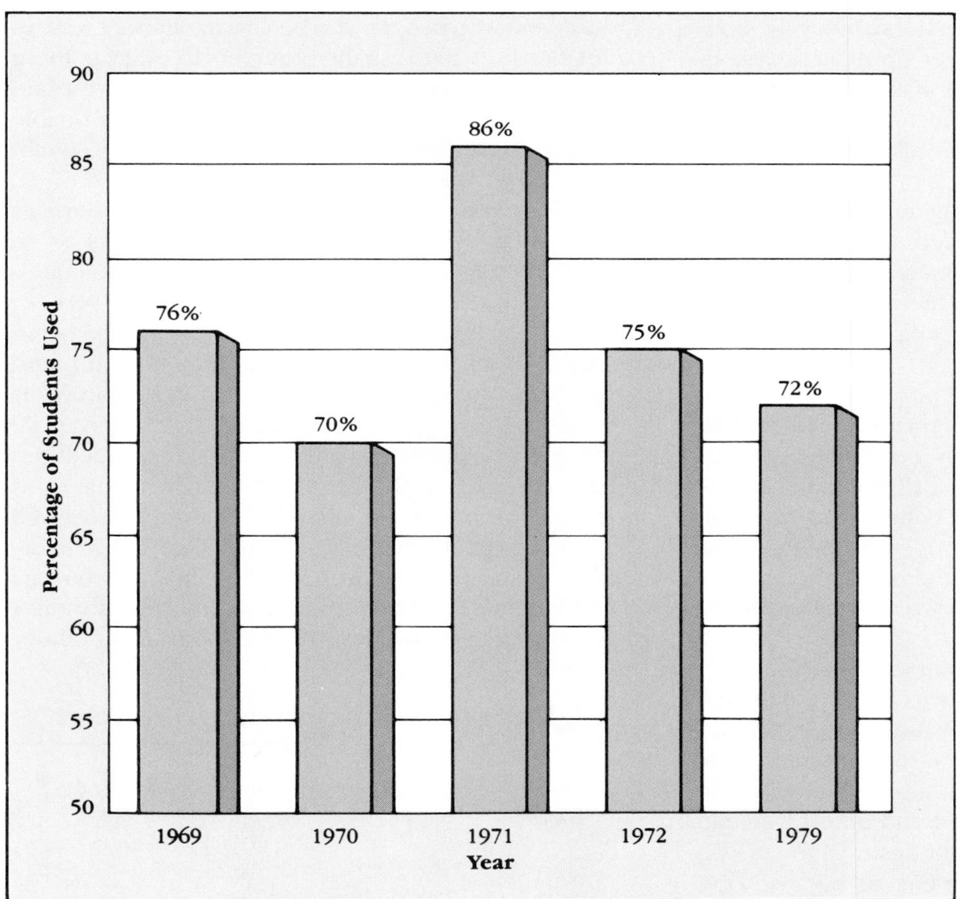

Figure 1-2 College students used in Social Psychology research.

Source: Based on data from "Social psychology research during the 1970s: Predominance of experimentation and college students" by K. C. Higbee, R. J. Millard, and J. R. Folkman, 1982, *Personality and Social Psychology Bulletin*, *8*, 180-183.

tural difference reflected in the attitudes and motivations of people can restrict the generalization of research findings.

As long ago as 1946 McNemar noted, "The existing science of human behavior is largely the science of the behavior of sophomores" (p. 333). If the albino rat is the favorite of the animal psychologist, the college sophomore is the favorite of the social psychologist. As can be seen in Figure 1-2, in a series of surveys of social psychological research covering the years of 1969 (Higbee and Wells, 1972), 1970-1972 (Higbee, Lott, and Graves, 1976), and 1979 (Higbee, Milland, and Folkman, 1982), it consistently has been found that college students were used in well over 70 percent of the studies reported in the leading journals. Because most experiments in social psychology have been carried out in American university settings, it is possible that the theories and generalizations made are applicable only to Americans or perhaps only to American college students. This state of affairs is now being addressed by a burgeoning and vigorous discipline of cross-cultural psychology.

Four different roles subjects may adopt in an experiment have been identified (Weber and Cook, 1972). The **cooperative subject** seeks to help the experimenter by trying to discover the hypothesis and then behaving in a way to confirm it. Naturally, social psychologists would like to know if their hypotheses are true, not just that subjects are friendly, cooperative, and willing to confirm the hypotheses.

Some subjects are obstreperous, obnoxious, and resentful, adopting a negativistic role. Masling (1966) has characterized the **negativistic subject** as motivated to disrupt the experimenter's plans and disconfirm a hypothesis. Such behavior has been referred to by Masling as a "screw you effect." This may be an initial attitude of the participant toward being controlled by another person, or it may be in reaction to some negative event transpiring in the experiment, such as a subject being exposed to electric shock. Negativistic subjects, like cooperative subjects, are responding to factors other than the independent variable. They do not contribute to an internally valid test of an hypothesis.

Some participants approach an experiment with a fear that the psychologist is evaluating their mental stability. These participants may be characterized as **evaluatively apprehensive** (Rosenberg, 1965, 1969). Some people wrongly believe that psychologists have an uncanny ability to uncover their deepest and most hidden motivations, therefore, the strategy they adopt in experiments is to avoid being evaluated negatively.

From an experimenter's point of view, the most desirable role adopted by participants is as **faithful subjects**. According to Fillenbaum (1966), faithful subjects do what they are told without trying to discover or confirm a hypothesis. Adoption of this role may occur because of disinterest and uninvolvement, because it is the simplest and quickest way to satisfy a research participation requirement, or because of a desire to contribute to the scientific enterprise. Faithful subjects try to react to the situation as they believe they normally would outside of the laboratory. Fortunately, most research participants appear to adopt a faithful subject role.

Situated identities

It has been argued that many results in social psychology experiments can be explained in terms of **situated identities** (Alexander and Rudd, 1981). There are cues in the situation, as well as restrictions and opportunities for behavior, implying that acting in one way rather than another will allow the actor to establish a positive identity. Whether or not behavior of subjects in an experiment is a function of a desire to present a positive identity to others can be determined by doing two things: (1) ask observers to predict what a person will do in the given situation; and (2) present observers with people who behave in different ways in this situation, then ask the observers to evaluate these people. When observers both predict a behavior and evaluate that behavior most positively, it is reasonable to suggest that subjects may behave in a way to establish a positive identity in the situation.

A look at the dynamics of a college classroom may help to clarify this concept. How do students act in class? They listen, take notes, occasionally ask a question or make a cogent point. A student who verbally challenges the professor, shouts obscenities, or attempts to write his or her own views on the board would be acting unpredictably. He or she probably would receive a negative evaluation. Suppose we move to a neighboring bar. Now the situated identities have changed. In the bar, argumentative behavior is more appropriate and taking notes would be viewed as evidence of psychological malfunctioning. Situations establish rules governing the kinds of behaviors and identities that are appropriate and that are most apt to gain a person positive evaluations from others.

Ethics of social psychological research

The rights of reseachers are limited by the rights of subjects.

Ernest Wallwork

Ethical problems sometimes arise when psychologists use human participants in laboratory experiments. Psychologists have expressed their concern about these problems in a number of recent scholarly writings (cf. Diener and Crandall, 1978; Kimmel 1981; Reynolds, 1982; Sieber, 1982). Most of the issues boil down to the same basic conflict between the rights of individuals and the possible benefits of the research to society. Each study must be evaluated to ascertain whether the possible benefits to humanity outweigh the costs to human participants, an evaluation that is referred to as a **cost-benefit analysis**.

Among the problems of concern to social psychologists are the occasions when participants will suffer pain or anxiety, the frequent use of deception, and invasion of privacy. In considering each of these problems, we also consider the proposed ethical solutions to these problems, including informed consent, careful debriefing procedures, role playing techniques, and safeguarding the anonymity and privacy of participants.

Pain and anxiety

Although medical and biological research frequently may involve physical pain and life-threatening events, social psychology seldom involves this kind of risk to participants. On occasion, participants have been asked to endure electric shocks or irritating white noise, but these stimuli, although unpleasant, do no permanent physiological harm to a person.

The ethical notion of **risk** is defined as any situation that produces unpleasant consequences to a person not likely to be experienced in the course of everyday behavior (APA, 1981), Obviously, a person is not likely to encounter electric shocks and white noise in daily activities, so these are considered situations in which the research participant is at risk.

In a study examining the effects of battle stress on performance of military trainees, sixty-six men were aboard a plane at an altitude of five thousand feet when a propeller on the plane stopped whirling and they were informed that there was an emergency (Berkun, Bialek, Kern, and Yagi, 1962). These passengers, who were army recruits in basic training, heard a pilot-to-tower conversation over their earphones indicating the plane to be in danger. The plane passed over the airfield and the trainees saw ambulances and fire trucks preparing for a crash landing. The pilot then indicated that the landing gear would not work properly and ordered the steward to prepare the passengers for a crash landing in the nearby ocean. At this point, the steward passed out questionnaires to the passengers, which served as measures of performance under stress, and blood and urine samples were taken for analysis. We can imagine the fear provoked in these recruits during this episode. What right does anyone have to place them in such circumstances?

The cost-benefit argument is that the gain in knowledge useful to national security outweighs the harm done to these sixty-six individuals. This justification probably would not be acceptable under today's more stringent ethical standards for conducting social psychological research. Although there are a number of circumstances where participants in research technically may be at risk, the degree of risk is seldom as severe as in the military study of stress. Some form of psychological discomfort, such as anxiety, embarrassment, and anger, may accompany participation in an experiment.

The widespread adoption of the **principle of informed consent** provides safeguards for participants against some of the worst forms of abuse and harm. This principle was first instituted at the Nuremberg war trials following World War II because of the abuses documented as occurring in Nazi concentration camps. People had been thrown into ice water to determine how long it would take them to die, others were infected with deadly diseases in order to have a sufficient supply of the disease on hand, and still others had dye injected into their eyes to see if Aryan blue eyes could be mass produced. These and even worse "experiments" led to an informed consent principle in biomedical and psychological research in the United States.

In its current interpretation, the principle of informed consent involves three components: (1) participation in psychology experiments is to be voluntary, (2) subjects are to be informed of any risks or dangers that might influence their decision to partici-

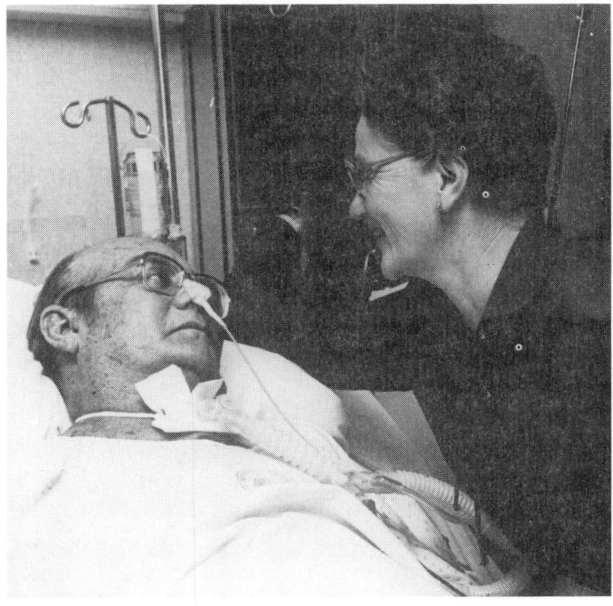

What right do researchers have to place people in real or simulated risky situations when they conduct experiments? Because of the laws that govern the principle of informed consent, Dr. Barney Clark was given a "suicide key" in order to terminate the experiment with his mechanical heart if he wished.

Box 1-5

Dr. Barney Clark and the suicide key

In December 1982 Dr. Barney Clark was the recipient of the first human artificial heart transplant. Soon after the successful operation, a number of media reports mentioned the fact that Dr. Clark was given a "suicide key" through which he could shut off the mechanism controlling his artificial heart. In an age when so many legal battles have been waged over disconnecting life-support systems from individuals in permanent comas, granting Dr. Clark a suicide key seems inconsistent with the usual medical doctrine of maintaining life for as long as possible.

The reasons for Dr. Clark's suicide key stem from an application of the principle of informed consent. Because the effects of artificial hearts in humans were unknown, Dr. Clark's transplant was considered a path-breaking but very risky experiment. Informed consent requires that a subject be able to withdraw from the experiment at any time. In Dr. Clark's case, withdrawal would mean stopping the heart and bringing about his own death. In this rather unusual set of circumstances, the principle of informed consent gave Dr. Clark the right to commit suicide! Do you think the principle of informed consent was correctly applied in this case?

pate, and (3) subjects are to be free to withdraw from an experiment at anytime without penalty.

Many courageous people have volunteered to take experimental drugs or undergo new surgical procedures so that others might benefit from the knowledge gained. Similarly, the principle of informed consent allows the informed participant in social psychological research to engage in a form of self-sacrifice to further the development of knowledge about human behavior. Informed consent may go as far as presenting a subject with the option to commit suicide, as is described in Box 1-5.

Deception

Knowing about the procedures and purposes of a social psychological experiment may invalidate the behavior under investigation. To avoid this problem and to disguise from the subjects what actually is being studied, laboratory-oriented social psychologists typically use deception. A frequently used rule of thumb by social psychologists is that deception does not violate informed consent procedures unless it concerns procedures involving risk. Experimenters cannot deceive subjects about receiving shocks, but they can deceive them about what is being studied.

Consider the case of Steve, an eighteen-year-old college student who has been participating in a study of the effects of hypnosis on problem-solving ability. The early sessions went well, helping his concentration, reducing his fatigue, and teaching him to control pain. Then Steve was given a posthypnotic suggestion that he would have trouble hearing. Shortly afterward, Steve was asked to interpret a set of slides. He became confused, angry, and terrified when he noticed other people in the room were talking to him, but he could neither hear nor understand what they were saying. What Steve did not know was that he had been told a lie about the purpose of the study. The focus was on testing a hypothesis that widespread paranoia among the aged was a result of hearing loss. Steve's earlier sessions were designed to make him a good hypnotic subject (Hunt, 1982; Zimbardo and Anderson, 1981).

If Steve had been told the hypothesis of the study, he might not have shown paranoid reactions when experiencing apparent hearing loss. Some psychologists would argue that without informed consent, this study should not have been done. Others object to any form of deception. Ethical controversy followed Milgram's studies of obedience in the 1960s. Social psychologists seriously began to debate the morality of lying in the name of seeking the truth (Rosnow, 1981). Kelman (1967), for example, argued that the credibility of psychologists would be destroyed by widespread use of deception, and the respect and trust required between researcher and participant would be undermined. Nevertheless, an increase in the use of deception occurred during the period 1959-1969 from 41 to 66 percent of the studies reported in the leading social psychology journal (Gross and Fleming, 1982). The percentage of studies using deception are shown in Figure 1-3.

Concern about demand characteristics, experimenter expectancy, and subject effects has been an important factor in the decision of psychologists to use deception. There also are occasions where honesty would cause the subject to react in artificial or non-natural ways. For example, many experiments make use of a confederate, who plays a rehearsed role, but who is represented as a peer of the subject and also is participating in the experiment. Many social psychologists would agree with an influential paper written by Aronson and Carlsmith (1968) that deception is a necessary and vital part of laboratory experiments. Furthermore, interviews revealed that a majority of students considered deception an appropriate part of experiments.

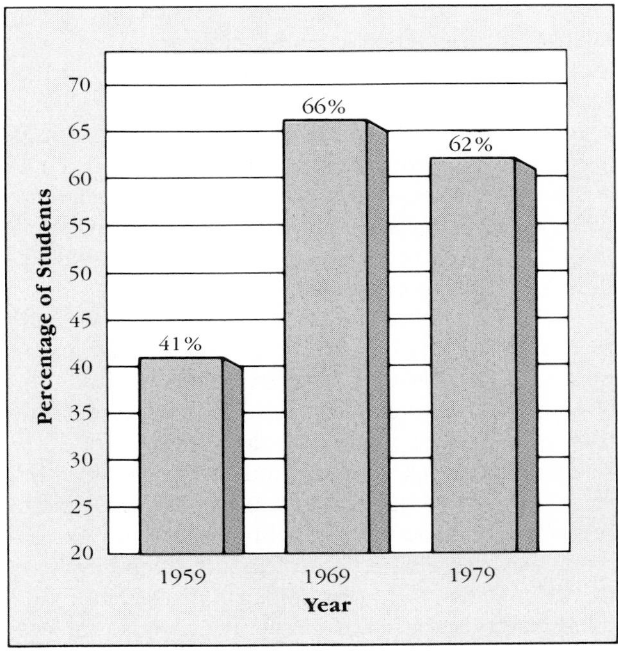

Figure 1-3 Use of deception in Social Psychology.

Source: Based on "Twenty years of deception in social psychology" by A. E. Gross and I. Fleming, 1982, *Personality and Social Psychology Bulletin*, *8*, 402-408.

Unlike business people and politicians, scientists do not use deception as a technique for exploiting people. Indeed, an ethical requirement is that all of the deceptions be revealed in a thorough debriefing as soon as the experiment is over. **Debriefing** involves honestly and patiently telling the subject the true nature of the experiment. The procedures are reviewed, the rationale for deceptions explicated, and any questions subjects may have are answered. The goal is to ensure that subjects leave the experimental situation no worse than when they entered. Subjects may benefit from the experience by gaining a sense of what it is like to be in an experiment. They can determine if they might be interested in becoming scientists and gain some knowledge of the particular hypothesis under investigation.

Ethics of field investigations

What are the ethical responsibilities of the scientist who ventures out into the public arena to carry out research? One argument is that when people go out in public they have given their consent to be observed by others, including social psychologists. As long as people are not exposed to conditions not likely to be encountered in their daily lives, and as long as they remain anonymous, the consensus is that no real ethical problem exists. Indeed, many field investigations are quite innocuous. People at a racetrack were asked before and after they placed bets, how confident they were about their selection of a horse (Knox and Inkster, 1968). These subjects were more confident after than before placing bets. This is hardly a significant invasion into people's daily lives; it represents events that occur to them without the intervention of an experimenter.

To embarrass people or to make them feel anxious or guilty is another matter. We are familiar with Alan Funt filming people in embarrassing situations and then showing these situations on national television

Table 1–4 Some ethical problems associated with social psychological research

PROBLEM	SOLUTION
Pain and Anxiety	The principle of informed consent dictates that subjects are to be informed of any risks or dangers which might influence their decision to participate.
Embarrassment	Subjects are free to withdraw from an experiment at anytime without penalty.
Coercion of subjects	Participation in psychology experiments is voluntary.
Deception of subjects	After the experiment subjects are given a thorough debriefing.
Invasion of privacy (field research)	Public behavior can be investigated if the subjects are anonymous and not exposed to conditions they would otherwise not encounter.

on "Candid Camera." Funt acquired the permission of the people involved prior to televising it, but not before surreptitiously filming their behavior. People in Western society have a right to protect their opinions, attitudes, beliefs, and behaviors from others access (Diener and Crandall, 1978). Supreme Court Justice Louis Brandeis once said that the right to be left alone was the right most valued by a civilized person.

A study of homosexual behavior in public toilets (Humphreys, 1970) may be considered invasion of privacy. The experimenter posed as a lookout who was to warn the participants if someone was coming. By serving this function, he was able to observe a large number of homosexual acts. It can be argued that the men involved, by allowing the experimenter to serve as lookout, thereby granted him permission to observe them.

It is because investigators usually can find justifications for what they do that most institutions oversee human research. Colleges and universities, have established **Institutional Review Boards** (IRBs). An IRB is composed of representative members of the institution and one or two members from the community at large. Because IRBs have greater distance and less vested interest than the invesigators, their ethical judgments tend to be less biased. The task of an IRB is to examine the goals and methods of an experiment, to judge questions of ethics, risk, and benefits, and to help investigators maintain a high standard of conduct for their scientific work. Some of the ethical problems of concern to IRBs are summarized in Table 1-4.

Summary

The dramatic example of van Gogh cutting off his ear demonstrates that there are many ways to explain human behavior. Social psychology is a way that emphasizes social stimuli and interactions with other people. Historically, two versions of social psychology evolved from psychology and sociology.

The methods of authority, common sense, and tenacity produce biases in the acquiring of knowledge. The scientific method seeks to reduce biases through a series of systematic steps we must follow in order to acquire evidence. The two features of the scientific method that distinguish it from other methods of seeking truth are its requirements for public demonstration and its self-corrective nature.

Social psychologists use a number of scientific methods in devising and testing explanations of human social behavior. Observational methods, including field studies, participant observation, unobtrusive measures, and archival, survey, and correlational research, are directed toward establishing facts and exploring hypotheses. Experimental methods, including laboratory, field, and natural experiments, are carried out to test hypotheses and evaluate theories. Many social psychologists prefer laboratory experiments because the ability to randomize subjects and control extraneous variables can establish strong internal validity for their research. The advantages and disadvantages of various research techniques are summarized in Table 1-5.

Table 1–5 A summary of the advantages and disadvantages of various research methods in social psychology

METHOD	ADVANTAGES	DISADVANTAGES
Participant observation	Allows close investigation of a phenomenon.	The behavior being studied may be influenced.
Unobtrusive measures	Obtains measures of behavior free from social desirability bias.	May not be an accurate index of behavior, and its usage may entail an unethical invasion of privacy.
Archival research	Reactivity problem is reduced since data typically collected by others; allows determination of effects over time.	The process may be time-consuming and boring; some necessary data may not be available.
Survey research	Can determine characteristics of a large population from responses of a relatively small sample.	Sensitive questions may result in socially desirable responses; biased samples can lead to inaccurate conclusions.
Correlational research	Can determine relationships between variables which for ethical or practical reasons couldn't be obtained by other methods.	Correlation doesn't imply causation.
Laboratory experiments	Can determine cause-effect relationships; great control can be exerted over variables.	Artificiality may result in behavior which is unnatural.
Field experiments	Behavior is studied in a more natural environment than the lab.	Loss of control may allow intrusion of extraneous variables.
Natural experiments	The independent variable is manipulated without the experimenter's intrusion.	Their occurrence is unpredictable and rare.

The psychology experiment is itself a social situation. Extraneous variables in the form of demand characteristics, biosocial, social, and psychological factors associated with the experimenter, including the latter's expectations, may affect the dependent variable and therefore must be controlled. Furthermore, care must be taken that situated identities are not made relevant to the experimental situation.

Stringent ethical standards must be applied to research. The problem of pain and anxiety experienced by participants is resolved by the principle of informed consent. Participation is voluntary and subjects are fully informed of any risks beforehand. Deception commonly is used in experiments because psychologists desire to disguise the true purposes of the study. It also is possible for subjects to discover the experimenter's hypothesis if deception is not used. Deceptions are temporary and nonexploitative in nature, and they are revealed to participants in a full debriefing following an experiment.

Glossary

A priori method The acceptance of beliefs in the absence of experience because they appear plausible.

Action research A strategy advocated by Kurt Lewin (1951) advising researchers to acquire basic knowledge by performing experiments in the context of real social problems.

Archival research The use of existing documents or data bases to investigate a phenomenon.

Artifact A result attributable to some factor other than the independent variable.

Biosocial and psychosocial factors Characteristics of the experimenter that may elicit unplanned and uncontrolled reactions from subjects.

Control group A group of subjects who are exposed to all aspects of the experimental procedures except for the independent variable.

Cooperative subject Participant who tries to discover the hypothesis and then behave in a way to confirm it in order to help the experimenter.

Correlation A statistic that measures the degree of relationship between two variables.

Cost-benefit analysis Evaluation of whether the benefits of research are greater than the costs to the participants.

Debriefing Explanation given to subjects following an experiment about its procedures and its true purposes.

Demand characteristics Unintentional cues in an experiment that inform the subjects about the hypothesis being tested.

Dependent variable A measure obtained to assess the effects of the independent variable.

Dogmatic authority Someone who says something is true and whose statements cannot be checked.

Ethical risk The discomfort a subject is likely to experience in an experiment not typically encountered in everyday life.

Evaluation apprehension Concern by subjects that they appear normal or average, which leads them to behave differently than they would when not under the scrutiny of an experimenter.

Experiment A test of a hypothesis carried out under controlled conditions and involving the manipulation of variables.

Experimental group A group of subjects who are exposed to some level of an independent variable.

Experimenter Researcher who makes planned and controlled observations.

Experimenter expectancy effect An unintentional action or procedure implemented by an experimenter that has the effect of leading to a predicted finding.

Expert authority Someone whose statements concerning the truth can be checked by others.

External validity of an experiment Researchers' ability to generalize the findings they obtain in particular experiments to other situations and to different subjects.

Extraneous variables Factors not of primary interest that, if left uncontrolled in an experiment, could obscure the meaning of the results because they vary with the independent variable.

Fact A definite observation made under controlled conditions reliably reported by independent observers.

Faithful subjects Participants who try to react in an experiment as they believe they would outside the laboratory.

Field experiment A test of a hypothesis carried out in a real-life (nonlaboratory) setting.

Field study An observational research method where the investigator avoids intervening in any way to change behavior.

Hypothesis A possible explanation or an educated hunch about the relationships among variables and behavior.

Independent variable A factor introduced and manipulated in an experiment to assess its effects on processes or behaviors of subjects.

Institutional Review Board (IRB) A committee established to oversee procedures of human research and to judge questions of ethics, risks, and benefits.

Internal validity of an experiment The degree to which the observed changes in the dependent variable are caused by observed changes in the independent variable.

Intrapsychic Internal, unseen processes that may affect a person's behavior.

Levels of analysis Different concepts and methods developed to explain and study particular phenomena, typically but not always unique to one of the social sciences and referring to events that can be scaled from small to large.

Method of authority We believe something to be true because someone tells us so.

Method of science A self-corrective and public procedure for approximating the truth, including observation, hypothesis formation, hypothesis testing, and hypothesis evaluation.

Method of tenacity Maintaining a belief even in the face of disconfirming evidence.

Natural experiment An experiment where the

manipulation of the independent occurs through an act of nature (e.g., natural disasters).

Negativistic subject Participant who tries to disrupt the experiment or disconfirm the experimenter's hypotheses.

Pact of ignorance Implicit agreement whereby subjects do not reveal suspicions about the procedures or hypotheses of the experimenter, who in turn does not probe too vigorously to discover what subjects believe.

Participant observation A method of study where the researcher joins the people being investigated.

Principle of informed consent An ethical standard for research requiring that subjects be fully informed of any risks, that participation must be voluntary, and that subjects should be free to discontinue at any time.

Random assignment The distribution of subjects so each has an equal opportunity to be assigned to any condition of the experiment.

Reactivity to measurement Biased responses to measuring instruments attributable to the subject's awareness of being observed.

Representative sample A sample drawn so that members have certain characteristics in the same proportion as of the population to which the survey researcher wishes to generalize.

Self-fulfilling prophesy A sequence in which experimenters' expectations lead to behaviors that cause the expected events to occur.

Situated identity Situations often dictate the kind of behavior that will allow a person to project the most positive identity.

Social facilitation effect Performance on familiar tasks is improved and performance on new tasks is hindered by the presence of others, as found by Triplett (1897) in the first social psychology experiment.

Social psychology Scientific study of how the thoughts, actions and interactions of individuals are affected by the actual, implied, or imagined presence of other people.

Social psychology of the experiment Systematic study of the experiment as a social situation involving the experimenter and the participants.

Subject A research participant.

Theory A set of consistent propositions yielding testable hypotheses offered to explain and integrate a set of facts.

Third variable problem Because correlated variables may both be caused by a third variable, causation cannot be inferred from a correlation.

Unobtrusive measures Indirect measures of behavior obtained by social psychologists after the behavior has been performed and without subjects' awareness of the observation.

Recommended Readings

Kidder, Louise. (1981). *Research methods in social relations.* New York: Holt, Rinehart, and Winston.
A classic text for advanced students interested in conducing nonlaboratory research.

Kimmel, Alan (Ed.). (1981). *Ethics of human subject research.* San Francisco, CA: Jossey-Bass.
A collection of brief but clearly written chapters on the ethics associated with carrying out research with human participants.

Reich, John. (1982). *Experimenting in society.* Glenview, IL: Scott, Foresman.
A well-written introduction to using research methods for the study of real-world phenomena; contains reprints and analyses of a number of field studies.

Rosenthal, Robert, & Rosnow, Ralph. (1984). *Essentials of behavioral research: Methods and data analysis.* New York: McGraw-Hill.
The latest work on research methods by two of the leading experts in the field.

There are three things extremely hard, Steel, a Diamond, and to know one's self.

Benjamin Franklin

2
Self-knowledge

The self as performer and critic

It is the end of summer and time once again to buy clothes for the upcoming semester. With credit cards in hand, you make a trip to the shopping mall and try unsuccessfully to squeeze your body into a pair of jeans. After a few more tries, you find a winner—a pair tight enough to accentuate physical virtues but loose enough to allow the breathing process to continue unimpaired. Even after trying them on though, you are not sure about how they look. You turn to your companion and ask for an opinion. At the same time, you look into a full-length mirror and gaze at the image. You recognize the person haughtily peering back at you. A quick glance at the face reveals a dark tan, brown eyes, a large but straight nose, a wide smile, and a strong chin. Dropping your gaze toward the new jeans, you notice a spare tire around the middle, a reminder of the many beer blasts you enjoyed during the summer vacation. Still, the jeans do look good because they fit tightly around the behind and reach just to the shoe tops. Your friend tells you the jeans look great.

Notice that the way you look at yourself is not fundamentally different from the way you look at others. You take this ability of self-evaluation for granted. It seems a mundane and unexceptional human capacity. The ability for self-reflection, however, has fascinated philosophers for thousands of years and plays an integral role in modern anthropology, sociology, psychology, and the humanities.

Think again of your image in the mirror. Imagine yourself intently studying it—praising its virtues and condemning its faults. After a while a thought may occur: "If that person in the mirror is me, who is doing the evaluating?" The ultimate realization that the evaluator is also us, that we are both subject and object, performer and critic, conscious and self-conscious is one that has captivated serious students of human behavior and led them to speculate, theorize, and empirically investigate the significance of this human capacity for understanding behavior.

The term **self** has been given to the capacity of humans to act and reflect on their actions, to be a knower and to be known simultaneously. In Chapter 2, we take a comprehensive look at the various theories that have been devised to explain the nature and functions of the self from the philosophical speculations developed at the beginning of the twentieth century to the concerns of modern laboratory-oriented social psychologists.

Sources of self-knowledge

It is impossible to conceive of a self-arising outside social experience.

George Herbert Mead

No Man is an Isle unto Himself.

John Donne

The awareness we have of ourselves as unique individuals may be a historically recent development (Brandt, 1980). From anthropological evidence, it appears that most early people were so tied to their social and family structures that the notion of individuals separate from their social institutions did not exist. Even today in oriental societies, the person achieves identity through group membership rather than through individual initiative (Bond, Leung, and Wan, 1982).

Consider what kind of person you would be had you been born in the jungles of New Guinea, in the rural areas of contemporary China, or in Africa as a pigmy. Not only would you be a different person psychologically, it is likely that you would look different. For example, if born in China (even of the same parents), you would probably be shorter and thinner than you are now. The way you hold yourself and the way you walk would be different. Your values, goals, and most importantly your idea of who you are would be drastically different than they are now. Where did you develop your ideas about yourself? What is the "self"? Let us examine the answers social psychologists have given to these two questions.

Self-recognition

When a cat sees its image in a mirror, it is apt to walk around and look behind it. A dog may bark at its image. These animals do not recognize themselves. The ability to recognize a material self is probably a necessary step in the formation of the self. It is doubtful that a newborn baby has a sense of self. The world of the newborn has been described as a "blooming, buzzing confusion" (James, 1890). Babies cannot distinguish their bodies from other parts of the environment. Parents note the delight of an infant when he or she discovers its feet and begins to play with them at two or three months of age. When a rouge mark was placed on their noses and a mirror was held up to their faces, only 25 percent of babies 9-12 months of age showed any inclination to reach for their nose; but 75 percent of children 21-25 months of age did (Lewis and Brooks, 1978). Only gradually does the individual learn to discriminate self from environment.

The ability for self-recognition is not unique among humans. The higher apes also possess a capacity for self-recognition. When full-length mirrors were placed in the cages of chimpanzees, they acted as if the images were strangers at first. In a few days, however, they began to groom themselves in front of the mirror. After ten days of experience with the mirrors, the chimps were anesthetized and an odorless, nonirritating red dye was placed on the eyebrow and back of one ear. The chimps then were placed back in their cages without the mirror. They never touched the dye spots. When the mirror was returned to their cages, the chimps were observed to touch and rub the dye spots frequently (Gallup, 1977). This capacity for self-recognition does not exist among monkeys or other species lower on the phylogenetic scale.

Self, selves, and homunculi

Is there one "true" self? There is a common tendency to think of the self as an inner person who runs the outer person like people drive automobiles. This conception of the self, sometimes referred to as the **homunculus,** leads us into conceptual problems. For example, the question can be raised: "If the inner person runs the outer person, who runs the inner person?" In other words, is there an inner, inner self? This kind of thinking leads us to an infinite regress because there always can be another person behind the one we are examining. The homunculus concept of the self is rejected by most social psychologists.

William James (1890), the first psychologist to make an enduring contribution to understanding the self, argued that there is not just one self. Rather, each person has many selves. James differentiated between three aspects of self: the material, the social, and the spiritual.

The **material self** consists of a person's body, clothes, family, home, and possessions. We view each of these as being intimately entwined with our sense of who we are. If others praise the jeans we wear or the car we drive, we feel praised. When others derogate any of our material possessions, we feel personally affronted. When a relative dies or a possession is stolen, we experience a loss of part of ourselves.

The **social self** consists of all the impressions we make on others and the recognition we receive from them. James argued that we have as many social selves as there are people who recognize and carry around an image of us. People desire to gain favorable evaluations from others and thus act in a way meant to please them. This often requires acting in quite different ways, depending on the audience. According to James (1890):

> "Many a youth who is demure enough before his parents and teachers, swears and swaggers like a pirate among his "tough" young friends. We do not show ourselves to our children as to our club-companions, to our customers as to the laborers we employ, to our own masters and employers as to our intimate friends. (pp. 46-47)

The **spiritual self** refers to our unique human capacity for self-reflection. It refers to the process of experiencing. The spiritual self is contemplative and has ideas about the meaning of life, the origins of the universe, and the mystery of human consciousness.

"Arthur, this is my wife, Sally. And this is my personal computer."

Biography

William James

The James family frequently was disturbed by the smells and explosions emanating from William's chemistry laboratory at home. In college he majored in chemistry, but changed majors and finally graduated from the Harvard Medical School. He then traveled the Amazon with Louis Agassiz, an outstanding biologist. In these travels, William fell victim to smallpox, which contributed to the vision problems and severe back pains that plagued him for many years. He also suffered from periodic episodes of severe depression, which he vividly described in some of his writings.

William was the oldest child in a wealthy New York family. He lived and studied in Europe and finally moved to Cambridge, Massachusetts. His next younger brother was Henry James, Jr., the novelist. If you have read any of his novels, you know of his reputation for involved sentences and plots. It has been said that William wrote texts like a novelist and that Henry wrote novels like a psychologist.

William taught physiology as an instructor at Harvard. Over the years, the content of the course shifted to psychology until all mention of physiology was dropped from the course title. At this time, he began work on the *Principles of Psychology,* one of the classic books in the field. *Principles of Psychology,* published in 1890, took William twelve years to write and contains thirteen hundred pages. He also wrote *The Varieties of Religious Experience,* which is required reading even today for anyone interested in the relationship of psychology and religion.

William was an excellent teacher who had a reputation for enthusiasm and energetic lectures. For his time, he also was known for his close relations with students; he was often seen walking to class in the company of students. He may have been the first professor in the United States to solicit course evaluations from his students.

As he grew older, James grew more interested in philosophy and earned international recognition for his scholarship in this field (Adelson, 1982; Fancher, 1979).

James recognized the dual nature of human experience, which he referred to as ***I*** and ***Me.*** The *I* is the knower who has a continuous stream of experience. This "stream of consciousness" contains our perceptions, current memories, thoughts, and values. As we are swept on to other experiences, our stream of consciousness changes and only some of the residues of the past remain in our mind. The *Me* is the object of experience and is represented by the material, social, and spiritual selves. The *I* is existential, momentary, and fleeting, while the *Me* is more substantial, autobiographical, and permanent.

Research tends to support the distinctions made by James. People asked to describe themselves typically begin with some aspects of the material self, such as age, height, or gender (Kuhn and McPartland, 1954). McGuire and his colleagues (McGuire and McGuire, 1982; McGuire, McGuire, Child and Fijioka, 1978; McGuire and Padawar-Singer, 1976) have discovered that people of all ages emphasize in their self-descriptions those characteristics that make them distinctive. Very tall and very short school children described themselves in terms of height more often than other children, and overweight children mentioned their weight more than children of average weight. Self-identification by reference to ethnicity also followed a distinctiveness rule. For example, black children were more likely to mention their color in response to the *Who Am I* test if they were in a class dominated by whites than if they were in a class consisting of a larger proportion of blacks. Similarly, children were more apt to mention their sex if the other sex was numerically preponderant in their households.

The social mirror

Mirror, mirror on the wall, who is the fairest of them all.

Snow White and the Seven Dwarfs

The sociologist Charles Horton Cooley (1909) proposed that we learn about ourselves from others. He used the analogy of a mirror or "looking glass." The self develops through perceptions of how it appears in the eyes of others. Our parents say we are cute, our teachers tell us we are bright (but maybe not very motivated), and the behavior of our friends implies that we are likable. The people around us act as a social mirror, reflecting back and telling us who we are and what we are like.

Each person has many selves, one of which consists of the unique human capacity for self-reflection and contemplation.

According to Cooley, the development of the self depends on three abilities that we possess: (1) to imagine our own appearance, (2) to imagine another person's evaluation of that appearance, and (3) to experience some self-feeling, such as pride or mortification. Without interaction with other people, we would have no concept of our self. It is only in groups that "human nature comes into existence. Man does not have it at birth . . . he cannot acquire it except through fellowship, and it decays in isolation" (Cooley, 1909, p. 30). The reflections of social mirrors are as real as the one in which the jeans shopper looked at the shopping mall. As Jimi Hendrix once sang, the world is a "room full of mirrors."

Social comparison processes

Leon Festinger's (1954) theory of social comparisons is an elaboration of Cooley's notion of the **looking-glass self**. According to Festinger, the self is not a part of physical reality but is constructed in the minds of people. **Physical reality** is made up of objects, colors, distances, weights, temperatures, and measurements of material substances. We acquire knowledge of physical reality through our sense organs. We validate our perceptions of physical reality through concrete means and with measuring devices, such as rulers, telescopes, and thermometers. We construct **social reality** rather than directly perceive it, and we can apprehend it only in the context of other people. Newcomers to any culture often feel confused because the way others perceive things is so different from what they have learned.

How can we tell whether our perceptions of social reality are correct? According to social comparison theory, evaluation of social reality depends on the agreement of other people, a process referred to as **consensual validation**. If you believe your social psychology exam was difficult, you cannot validate your judgment with some instrument like a ruler or a thermometer. Instead, you ask your classmates how they did, and by comparing yourself with others, you gain a sense of whether the exam was difficult or whether you just did not perform well on it. Social reality, including self-concept, is developed, maintained, and changed through social comparisons.

Festinger (1954) distinguished between **comparative appraisals**, which consist of a person's active comparisons against the standards, abilities, or attributes of other relevant people, and **reflected appraisals**, which are the inferences people make about the way others perceive them. By using comparative appraisals, students may form judgments of their own abilities as compared to their classmates. If most other students read faster, then the person forms a judgment of the self as a slow reader. If judgments of your own reading speed are based on what you believe others consider it to be, you are using reflected appraisals. We can use both comparative and reflective appraisals in forming a self-concept. An unusual case of high dependence on reflected appraisal and lack of comparisons in the formation of self-concept is described in Box 2-1.

Comparative appraisals

Are you good looking? Intelligent? Wealthy? An assessment of your physical reality may inform you that you are so many feet and inches high, but is that tall? Without making social comparisons, the question is not answerable. A person who is five feet eight inches may be tall in a pygmy tribe, but extremely short for a player on a professional basketball team. When the question, "Are you tall?" is asked, the appropriate response is, "Compared to whom?"

Festinger (1954) proposed that we choose to make social comparisons with people similar to ourselves. The weekend tennis player does not use Martina Navratalova or John McEnroe as standards to judge their own level of play. The people selected for making social comparisons are similar to us in *relevant* ways (Goethals and Darley, 1977). Age, sex, and general athletic ability may be relevant factors in making comparisons of tennis skill. The middle-aged tennis player does use younger people or those of the opposite sex as relevant comparison others.

The use of sex as a criterion for choosing others for comparison was found when students were told that members of the same sex or opposite sex performed better on a test that they were about to take (Zanna, Goethals, and Hill, 1975). After taking the test, the students were given scores but no interpretation of how they did compared to other students. When given an opportunity to obtain information about how others had performed, the students asked for information about others of the same sex, irrespective of what they had been told earlier about which of the sexes performed better on the test. Similarly, children in grade school preferred information about how children in their own grade performed as opposed to information about children in other grades (Suls, Gastorf, and Lawhon, 1978).

People who are striving to achieve at a higher level may make comparisons with others who have more ability than themselves. This tendency was found among Princeton University students. They took a subtest of the Miller Analogies Test. The test was described as one used to evaluate candidates for admission to graduate and professional schools. Each student was provided with his or her test result and then given an opportunity to find out how others had done. These students tended to be interested in the scores obtained by others who ranked a little higher than themselves. By making such comparisons, the students could ascertain how well they had done. As can be seen in Table 2-1, the students were not inter-

Box 2-1

John Stuart Mill had no comparison group

The *Autobiography of John Stuart Mill,* the nineteenth century British philosopher, reveals an interesting example of self-concept development. His concept of himself lacked social comparisons except for his father, James Mill, who was a famous philosopher and served as the sole teacher of his son. John Stuart Mill spent most of his time studying and did not play with other children. He learned Greek and Latin by the time he was three years old and mastered calculus soon afterward. He edited his father's history of India when he was twelve. Yet, as indicated in his autobiography, John had no idea that any of his accomplishments were extraordinary. He had no social standards against which to make comparisons, and his father treated his achievements as unexceptional.

ested in obtaining information about others who had done poorly on the test. There was a distinct preference for information about the performance of others of the same sex (Feldman and Ruble, 1981). The higher numbers in Table 2-1 indicate greater rated interest in learning about the scores that others obtained.

Similarity of physical attractiveness has been found to be a criterion that women use when choosing those with whom they compare themselves. (Miller, 1982). Coeds took a test that was either relevant to physical attractiveness (Opposite Sex Social Skills Text) or irrelevant (Logical Reasoning Test). Preference for information about the performance of others was strongly determined by similarity of physical attractiveness, whether or not it was relevant to the test (Miller 1982). Physical attractiveness may be an important attribute, at least for women, which people use to infer the likelihood of successful performance. It is therefore a **related ability** that may be used to infer other abilities of a person.

A specific test of the related abilities hypothesis

Table 2–1 Ratings of students' interest in the performance of others by sex and ability

SUBJECTS	ABILITY LEVEL				
	High	Upper Middle	Middle	Lower Middle	Low
Males					
Male group	3.4	3.5	3.1	0.9	1.0
Female group	2.7	2.4	2.1	0.3	0.5
Females					
Male group	2.5	1.9	1.7	0.4	0.5
Female group	2.8	3.0	2.6	1.1	1.0

Source: Based on "Social comparison strategies: Dimensions offered and options taken" by N. S. Feldman and D. N. Ruble, 1981, *Personality and Social Psychology Bulletin, 7,* p. 14. Adapted by permission of Sage Publications, Inc.

allowed subjects to choose information about how others had performed in practice sessions prior to taking a test. They were told either that practice did or did not affect performance on the test. When practice was related to test performance, subjects preferred information about others who had similar levels of practice and who were standard setters. When practice was not diagnostic of how people would perform on the test, however, these criteria for choosing others for comparison were less important (Wheeler, Koestner, and Driver, 1982).

Reflected appraisals

A mirror reflects an image to the viewer. In a similar way, the attitudes and evaluations of others provide us with impressions of what we are like. People do not always directly tell us what their impressions are, but we consider their actions to be indicative of their attitudes. There is considerable room for error in this process. It does not matter what people think of us, what matters is what we think their impressions are.

Psychoanalytic theory emphasizes the importance of childhood experiences in the development of the individual. We have prolonged and intimate contact with a few significant other people in early life. It could be expected that the reflected appraisals from these people would be especially important for the development of self-concept (Sullivan, 1953). The self-concepts of children typically are found to be very similar to the impression they believe their parents have of them (Hamachek, 1971).

There is evidence that reflected appraisals have an impact on both self-concept and subsequent behavior. For example, telling children they were tidy was much more effective in preventing littering than was a lecture about littering (Miller, Brickman, and Bolen, 1975). As can be seen in Figure 2-1, children who were lectured about tidiness continued to litter as much as children who were told nothing about tidiness. Similar findings were obtained when children were told they had good ability to do arithmetic. Exhorting children to work harder or telling them they *should* do well was not effective, but telling them they had the ability improved their performance in arithmetic (Miller et al., 1975).

When someone directly communicates evaluations, there is little room for error. Often there is a lack of correlation between the actual perceptions of others and what people believe these perceptions are (Shrauger and Schoeneman, 1979; Felson, 1981). Individuals have a tendency to *project* their self-evaluations and assume that others perceive them as they perceive themselves. The social mirror is distorted, as in a fun house, and the image reflected is what the person expects to see rather than what a true mirror would reflect.

The results of one study suggests that the perceptions of others and self-perceptions are correlated strongly when people have known each other for a long time. Married couples, who had known each other for an average of 7.6 years, filled out the Edwards Personality Preference Inventory. They rated themselves on a series of personality traits and then rated their spouses on the same traits. There was a significant correlation between self-ratings and spouse ratings (Edwards and Klockars, 1981). In another study, husbands and wives were asked to describe themselves, their spouses, and how their spouses would describe them (Moore, 1964). Self-descriptions were closer to how the subjects described themselves than to how spouses described them. On the other hand, the person's beliefs about the spouse's appraisals were not totally disparate from the actual description. We may conclude that reflected appraisals represent both the actual perceptions of others and self-serving projections.

Labeling theory

Sociological social psychologists have proposed a process very much like reflected appraisal. Becker (1963) and Scheff (1966) proposed that people refer to those who engage in deviant or unusual conduct with labels. For example, people may be labeled as "gay," "mentally ill," or "juvenile delinquent." Labeling by others leads the individual to perceive the self in a corresponding way. Once individuals apply deviant labels to themselves, their actions become consistent with the new self-definition, and they act in deviant ways. A tragic example of this process is described in Box 2-2.

Public actions, such as imprisonment, serve to validate labels for persons and change their identities (Becker, 1963; Lauer and Handel, 1977; Scheff, 1966). Differences in self-descriptions were found among institutionalized and noninstitutionalized juvenile delinquents (Dorn, 1968). Self-deprecating and self-contradictory descriptions were given by 52 percent of the

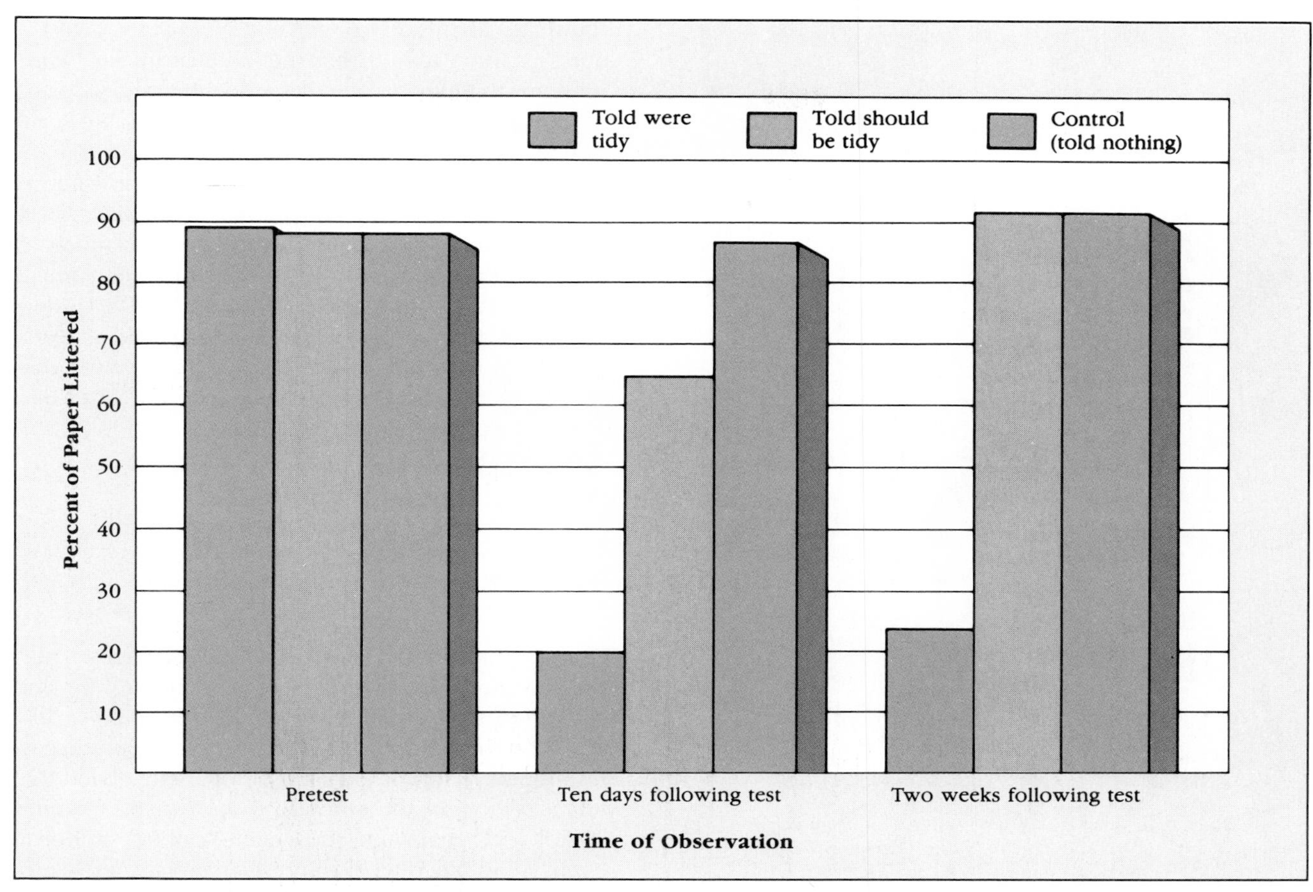

Figure 2-1 Littering behavior and self-concept.

Source: Based on "Attribution versus persuasion as a means for modifying behavior" by R. L. Miller, P. Brickman, and D. Bolen, 1975, *Journal of Personality and Social Psychology*, 31, 430–441.

institutionalized delinquents, but only 22 percent of the noninstitutionalized delinqents and 16 percent of nondelinquents gave such derogatory depictions of themselves.

To become a bum apparently involves a labeling process. Unemployed people, migrant workers, alcoholics, and others escaping from one kind of problem or another congregate on Skid Row. The more time they spend on Skid Row, the greater their acceptance of the values of this subculture. The outside society labels them as bums, so they begin to consider themselves accordingly (Spradley, 1970; Wallace, 1968). A similar action, labeling, self-definition, and reaction sequence occurs as a person evolves from novice to professional thief (Mauer, 1976).

Self-perception theory

Oh wad some power the giftee gie us
To see oursels as others see us!

Robert Burns, To a Louse

While it is clear that people learn about themselves by looking into the social mirror, they also act as observers of their own behavior. **Self-perception theory** assumes that we make inferences about our interior lives based on self-observations (Bem, 1972). We are particularly likely to engage in self-perceptions when our actions are taken without clear conscious planning. Much of our behavior is "mindless" in the sense that it is carried out automatically or out of habit without planning or conscious thinking of any sort

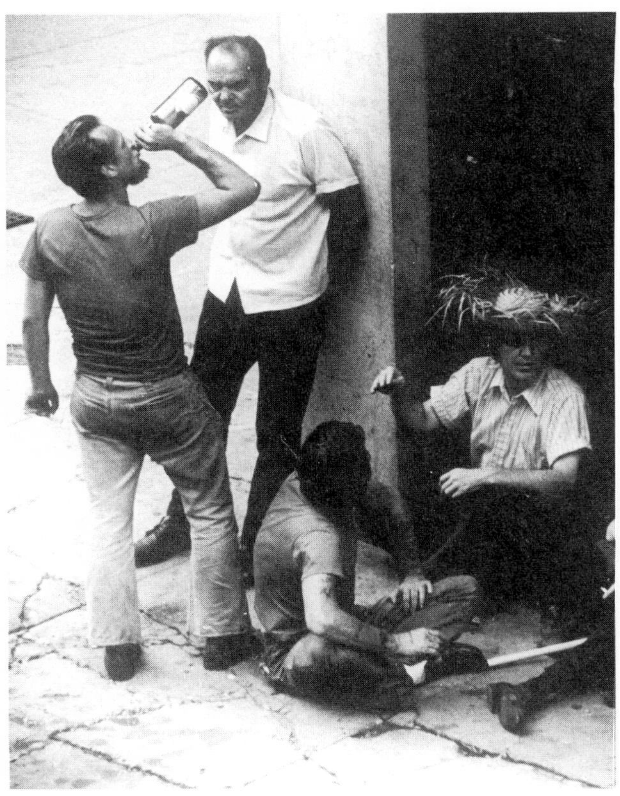

Society labels individuals who engage in deviant or unusual conduct. Acceptance of the label of "bum" characterizes those who line Skid Row. People who consider themselves as bums because they are labeled so will act accordingly.

(see Box 2-3). If we are sitting at the table eating and conversing, we usually are not preoccupied with our prior conceptions of what does and does not taste good. The topic of conversation is the focus of attention. If someone should ask if you like the wine, you remember drinking it and conclude that you must like it. Presumably you would not have drunk it if you had not liked it. Your answer does not depend upon a prior attitude toward wine, but rather on an inference based on self-perception.

Research has shown that people who are induced to smile rate cartoons as funnier than people who are not induced to smile (Laird, 1974). If they are smiling, they infer that the cartoons must have been funny. When people are induced to nod their heads up and down, they agree more often than those who shake their heads from side to side (Wells and Petty, 1980). A comedian once noted that the Chinese make better Christians than Westerners because when the Chinese read the Bible they read up and down, while Westerners read from side to side.

Self-perception theory has important implications for human motivation. When people are paid money for doing something, they do not like it as much as when they do it and are not paid, or when they initiate the action themselves (Deci and Ryan, 1980). Undertaking an action without clear external reasons leads the actor to infer that he or she must have values that led to the behavior. Developing this kind of **intrinsic motivation** is a goal of parenting.

Self-perception of emotions

If you are patient in one moment of anger, you will escape a hundred days of sorrow.

Chinese proverb

When we experience emotions, the autonomic nervous system is activated, increasing heart rate and respiration rate, causing sweating of the palms, dilation of pupils, and other reactions. Our experience of an emotion is so immediate and totally involving that we easily believe the emotion to be caused by these physiological reactions. Yet, a century of physiological research has failed to distinguish one pattern of emotions from another in terms of arousal cues or endocrinal secretions. There is no "anger juice" that is different from "love juice," nor is there a "jealousy center" in the brain that is different from an "envy center." If the arousal pattern is the same for all emotions, varying only in degree, how can we tell which emotion we are experiencing? Two interesting theories have been offered to answer this question: an evolutionary theory of facial expression and a two-factor theory of information processing that emphasizes social cues.

Facial expression and emotions

An evolutionary theory proposed by Izard (1977) states that facial expressions are inherited and the recognition of the various ways we can arrange the muscle groupings of our faces provides the basis by which we experience particular emotions. This facial expression theory may be considered a variant of self-

Box 2-2

Forty-eight years in a mental hospital by mistake

At the age of fifteen, Katerina Yasinchuk came alone from the Ukraine to the United States. She met a young man and had a baby, but both soon died. Katerina was found wandering the streets of Chicago in tears by the police; they took her to a mental hospital. The speech was incoherent, and no one could understand what she was saying. The diagnosis was that she was mentally ill, and she was institutionalized.

Hospital records showed that Katerina continued to speak for six more years. Then, in 1927 she stopped talking altogether. Labeled as a schizophrenic, she began to fulfill the expectations of hospital attendants by acting like one.

Thirty-five years later a new hospital director ordered linguists to attempt communication with the silent patient. Katerina responded when addressed in her native Ukranian language. Forty-eight years after being institutionalized and at the age of seventy-one, Katerina was released. She died at the age of eighty-six in 1983.

perception theory because it is self-observation that provides the basis for inferences about a person's internal states. Ekman and Friesen (1975) found that twenty-four muscle groups of the human face are associated with different emotions. Furthermore, the intensity of emotions is correlated with the activity of specific muscles (Ekman, Friesen, and Ancoli, 1980).

Two implications of the facial expression theory have been studied. First, if specific muscle patterns of the face are inherited and are invariably associated with specific emotions, people everywhere should express emotions in the same way. We would therefore expect people who have had little contact with Western civilization to be able to recognize the emotions of an American and vice versa. It has been found that Fore Islanders of the Far East were able to identify various emotional expressions of photographed Westerners (Ekman and Friesen, 1975). Similar results were obtained when photographs of Fore Islanders posing emotions were presented to Westerners for recognition. We should note, however, that although recognition of certain emotions, such as happiness, were unmistakable, more subtle emotions were less readily identifiable.

A second implication of the facial expression theory of emotions is that we can change our emotional experiences by putting on a different face, much as actors changed masks in the ancient Greek theater. In an attempt to affect subjects' reactions to slides of either Ku Klux Klan members or of children playing, subjects were asked to put either a frown or a smile on their faces. The type of picture had a large effect on subjects' moods; facial expressions of the subjects also had a small but significant impact. Subjects who frowned reported feeling more aggressive than subjects who smiled, whichever slide had been presented to them (Laird, 1974).

In a similar study, subjects were asked to suppress or exaggerate expressions of pain when they received a series of electric shocks (Lanzetta, Cartwright-Smith and Kleck, 1976). Subjects who disguised their reactions reported feeling less pain than those who openly expressed pain. Unfortunately, this evidence also could be interpreted in terms of demand cues, because the researchers might have biased the reporting of moods or pain by instructions regarding these emotions. When conscious inferences about what they were supposed to feel were controlled, the facial ex-

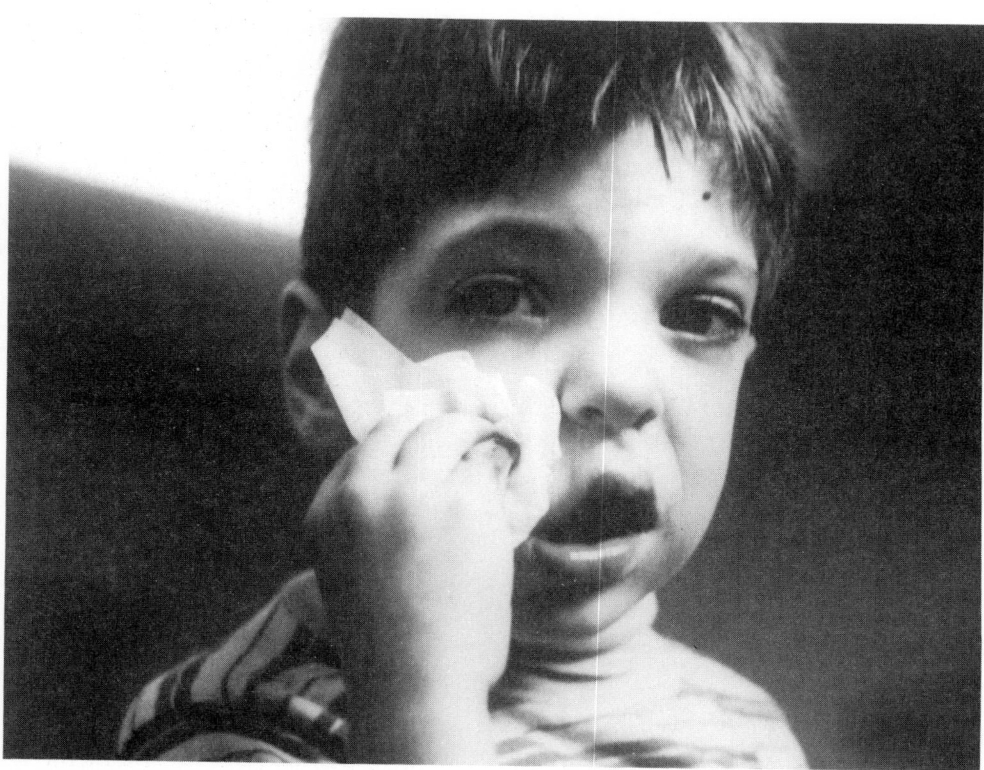

In 1977, Carroll Izard proposed that facial muscle patterns are inherited and associated with specific emotions. The unhappiness in this boy's face is recognizable to peoples of all cultures because civilizations everywhere express emotions in the same way.

pressions of subjects had no effect on their emotional experiences (Tourangeau and Ellsworth, 1978). On the other hand, studies in which facial expressions are arranged mechanically indicate that moods are affected by the specific arrangements of muscle groups. It is probably fair to conclude that self-perception of facial expressions plays some role in the experience of emotions.

Schachter's two-factor theory of emotions

Schachter (1964) has proffered an information-processing view of how people attribute emotions to themselves. When we are in a social situation and experience a state of physiological arousal, we have expectations and past learning to guide us in interpreting which emotion we must be experiencing. **Two factors** are necessary for the labeling of an emotion: physiological arousal and social cues (See Figure 2-2).

A typical emotional experience includes the definition of a social situation (perception of a stimulus) and physiological arousal. The perception of the stimulus and the experience of arousal occur simultaneously (Reisenzein, 1983). If you were walking to the zoo and were confronted by an escaped lion, your perception of the lion and your physiological arousal would occur at the same time. An interpretation of which emotion you are experiencing would then be made in the context of the situation. Past learning and expectations about the behavior of lions would lead you to label your arousal as fear. This analysis is similar to the James-Lange theory of emotions (Izard, 1977), suggesting that we do not run from lions because we are afraid, we are afraid because we run from lions. The fundamental assumption of the two-factor theory of emotions is that we must be aware of physiological

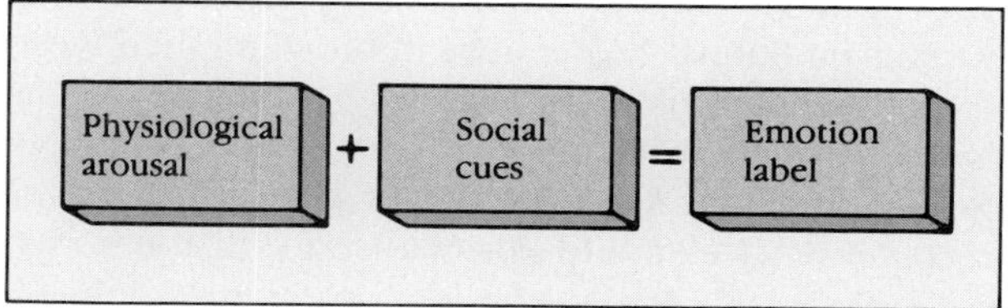

Figure 2-2 Illustration of Schachter's two-factor theory of emotions.

Box 2-3

Habitual behavior and mindlessness

William James said that habit is the flywheel of society. If we had to pay attention to everything we do, most of our time would be devoted to concentrating on the movements associated with walking, grasping, or talking. Most of us do these and many other complicated things, such as driving an automobile, almost automatically. Jokes are told about people who cannot walk and chew gum at the same time, but most people can. The development of habits allows us to think about other things while carrying on various activities.

There are times when we react mindlessly to other people, especially if they appear to give acceptable reasons for their behaviors. For example, when a person approached a xerox machine that was being used and asked to use it to copy five pages, the user denied the person access more than 50 percent of the time. However, when the requester asked to use the xerox machine "because I have to make some copies," over 90 percent of the users granted that person access (Langer, Blank, and Chanowitz, 1978). People are in such a habit of accepting reasons for different behaviors, they often do not pay attention to what actually is being said.

arousal and link it to the situation before we experience a recognizable emotion.

The initial test of two-factor theory had subjects report to an experiment described as the study of a vitamin compound, given the fictitious name "suproxin," on vision (Schachter and Singer, 1962). Some of the subjects were given injections of epinephrine, which is a stimulant and causes undifferentiated physiological arousal. Another group of subjects were given a placebo, a saline solution known to have no physiological effects. The basic idea of the study was that if subjects experienced arousal, as they would if they had been given epinephrine but had no available explanation for it, they would look to social cues in the situation to label their emotional experience. If subjects could attribute the arousal state to the drug, they would not need to make their self-attributions dependent upon available social cues.

In order to follow this logic, some subjects in the epinephrine condition were told to expect such symptoms of arousal as pounding heart, trembling of the hands, and flushing of the face (*informed condition*); some were told to expect side effects, such as itching, headache, and numbness of the feet (*misinformed condition*); and some were told nothing (*ignorant condition*).

Each subject in each condition was paired with a confederate while they both waited for "Suproxin" to take effect. In *euphoric conditions*, the behavior of the confederate included shooting paper balls at a waste basket, playing with hula hoops, verbally expressing positive feelings, and inviting the subject to join in the fun. In anger conditions the experimenter asked the subject and the confederate to complete a questionnaire containing offensive questions, such as, "With how many men (other than your father) has your mother had extramarital relations?" The confederate made increasingly angry comments about the questions and finally exclaimed that he would no longer participate; he ripped up the questionnaire and stomped out of the room.

Subjects were asked to fill out a series of mood scales, and observers measured the extent to which subjects initiated positive or negative behavior. As would be expected from the two-factor theory, subjects who ingested epinephrine and were misinformed or ignorant about the arousal side effects were more affected by the behavior of the confederate than were subjects who were informed. In euphoric conditions the former two groups reported being happier, and observers rated their behavior as more positive than subjects in the informed condition. A similar pattern of results was obtained with subjects in the anger conditions.

In the case of unexplained arousal, the person experiences arousal prior to any perception of stimuli that could have created it. The person searches for an explanation and uses social cues to define the specific emotion he or she is experiencing. Subjects who experienced arousal could not attribute it to the pill (in the misinformed condition) because they specifically were told it would create quite different side effects. They had to search for some other explanation for their arousal state, and the social situation involving the confederate provided the cues for labeling the emotion.

The Schachter and Singer study has been the target of numerous criticisms (Cotton, 1981; Leventhal, 1980). For example, the degree of euphoria or anger experienced by subjects in the misinformed and ignorant conditions should be greater than the degree of each experienced by subjects in the placebo conditions, because the latter did not experience drug-induced arousal. When there is no arousal, there should be little emotion. Yet, the drug-aroused subjects did not express moods any different from subjects in the control conditions (Plutchik and Ax, 1967). In addition, all of the behavior measures were recorded by observers who also could see the behavior of the confederate. As a consequence, the behavior of the confederate could have influenced the observers' ratings of the subjects' behavior.

It is possible that subjects actually did not experience the emotional states of euphoria or anger, but merely imitated the confederate. A study based on this hypothesis showed that subjects who read only about the euphoric and angry conditions tended to imitate the responses of subjects in the original study (Strickler, 1967).

A number of researchers have been unable to replicate the findings of Schachter and Singer (Marshall and Zimbardo, 1979; Maslach, 1979). Their studies suggest that unexplained arousal is always interpreted negatively. It is somewhat frightening for people to experince arousal without knowing why. In a review of the research testing the two-factor theory, Cotton (1981) concluded that "Schachter's theory at this juncture can be considered only tentative, with little empircal verification" (p. 373). Moreoever, Reisenzein (1983) concluded that arousal may be a rather insignificant part of emotions. The mental (cognitive) component of emotions is more important than the traditional emphasis on physiological factors has allowed (Averill, 1981). Thus, although the two-factor theory has greatly influenced the way social psychologists think about emotions, serious questions remain about its accuracy.

Misattribution of arousal

In the 1940s and 1950s, general theories of behavior were devised proposing that behavior is initiated or driven by internal physiological states of tension or arousal (Hilgard and Bower, 1975). For example, an animal deprived of food for some period of time was assumed to experience tension—a kind of hunger itch. As a consequence the animal was propelled into action related to satisfying the need—a kind of behavioral scratch. Social psychologists have extended this basic mechanism to explain aggression, passionate love, change of beliefs, phobias, other neurotic symptoms, and much else.

The two-factor theory of emotions and the Schachter and Singer study testing it suggested the possibility that a person might reattribute arousal generated by one source and identify it as related to some other experience. **Misattribution** of arousal occurs when a person mistakenly believes that the cause of arousal is something other than it actually is. Berscheid and Walster (1978) relate misattribution to passionate love. Anyone who has been passionately in love will attest to experiencing high levels of arousal. According to Berscheid and Walster, people may reattribute arousal generated from some other source and identify it as erotic love.

A former colleague of ours offered misattribution as the reason for the timing of his marriage proposal. He and his friend were watching game six of the 1977 World Series between the Los Angeles Dodgers and the New York Yankees. That was the night Reggie Jackson hit three home runs to help the Yankees win

Box 2-4

Reattribution therapy

Many theories have been developed about the process of psychotherapy since Freud expounded on psychoanalysis at the turn of the century. Stanley Strong (1982) offered one of the more recent theories. He maintained that when people view the self as ineffective or unstable, they may be motivated to seek help through counseling or psychotherapy. The therapist's task is to encourage them to reattribute the cause of their undesirable behavior.

A case study reported by Neale (cited by Valins and Nisbett, 1972) can be interpreted in terms of reattribution therapy. A twenty-five-year-old unmarried man sought therapy because he thought he was gay, and as a consequence, he experienced feelings of depression and anxiety. He thought he was a homosexual because he frequently found himself watching the crotches of other men. He believed his penis was abnormally small, and he could not enjoy sexual intercourse.

The therapist informed the client that his penis was normal in size, but that looking at objects on the same plane as one's line of vision foreshorten them. The client was encouraged to look at himself in the mirror and to read some material about male physiology. The therapist further explained "crotch watching" as normal curiosity and an attempt by the client to gain social comparison information. The client's anxiety about not quite measuring up contributed to his sexual incapacity. Concern about the small size of his penis embarrassed him in the presence of his female partner. By having the patient modify his attributions about homosexual tendencies and reattribute his sexual reactions to concern over the size of his penis, the therapist was able to relieve the client's depression and fears of homosexuality. The man's enjoyment of heterosexual intercourse was increased.

the series. Our friend, a staunch Yankee fan, got extremely excited by Reggie's performance. In the heat of arousal, he proposed to his friend who had become more irresistible with each stroke of Reggie's bat. The arousal generated by the ball game had been reattributed to the presence of the lovely lady.

Misattribution and adjustment

Clinical psychologists have not failed to notice the significance of misattribution for understanding maladjusted behavior. A frequent reason people seek psychotherapy is that distressing emotions, such as fear and anxiety, interfere with their daily functioning. They may experience new difficulties with their friends, cannot sleep, or perhaps have felt impaired in their sexual functioning. The case study of a man concerned about the size of his penis illustrates the misattribution process (see Box 2-4). Since physiological arousal is associated with these unpleasant situations, therapeutic gain might be achieved if the clients could be led to reattribute arousal to some nonemotional source (Harvey and Weary, 1981; Janis and Rodin, 1979).

Hanson and Bleechman explored the possibility of using misattribution in enhancing sexual experiences (cited in West and Wicklund, 1980). Married couples were asked to take a pill, actually a placebo, before going to bed. One group was informed that the pill was a stimulant, a second group was informed that it was a tranquilizer, while a third group was told it would have no effect. All couples were instructed to have intercourse that night and to later complete a questionnaire about their experiences. According to a misattribution hypothesis, subjects who believed they took a stimulant should attribute part of their sexually induced arousal to the pill, and as a result they should enjoy sex less. The subjects who believed they had ingested a tranquilizer and expected less arousal should attribute all of their arousal to the sexual experience and should enjoy it all the more.

The results were as predicted: intercourse was most enjoyed when arousal was overattributed to sex and least enjoyed when misattributed to a pill. These results, however, could be interpreted in other ways. For example, subjects who believed they had taken a tranquilizer may have been more relaxed after taking the pill, and relaxation would have increased the pleasure of the sexual experience.

In a controversial study, Storms and Nisbett (1970) examined misattribution with respect to another bedroom problem, insomnia. Student insomniacs were given a placebo to be taken before going to bed. Half of the subjects were led to expect the pill to arouse them, and the remainder were told it would relax them. The problem for insomniacs is that when they go to bed, they are wide awake and cannot relax. If they could attribute their arousal to some outside source, such as a pill, they should be able to relax and go to sleep. On the other hand, when they are told that a placebo, having no physiological effects, will relax them, they cannot attribute the arousal to the pill. Therefore, the arousal should be attributed to insomnia and this focus on themselves should make falling asleep a continuing problem. As expected from this reasoning, subjects in the arousing pill group were able to fall asleep sooner than those in the tranquilizer group.

The typical placebo effect in most research is that subjects are influenced by whatever they are told about a pill containing no active chemical agents. It would therefore have been expected that telling subjects a placebo would relax them actually would produce the effect and hence aid them to go to sleep. The *reverse placebo effect* obtained by Storms and Nisbett (1970) is not what would have been expected from knowledge of placebo effects. Several attempts to replicate the reverse placebo effect have not been successful. Indeed, a direct placebo effect has been found (Bootzin, Herman, and Nicassio, 1976; Kellogg and Barron, 1975).

The self-concept as a processor of information

A person shows himself in the way he opens an orange. Some tear jaggedly with fingers, some slice with a thumbnail, some spiral latitudinally, while others go at the longitude.

William Least Heat Moon, Blue Highways

The sources of information about the self, as we have seen, include self-recognition, our physical possessions, learning to interpret social cues, labeling of emotional states and social comparisons. We are not just passive absorbers of outside stimuli but actively select from available information. We have a limited capacity to process information. There is the feel of clothes against our bodies, the sounds of people talking, the floor and rug under our feet, the pictures on the wall, the telephone on the table, and so on. Because it is impossible to take in all of this information, we are very selective to what we pay attention and in what we process. The average person's attention is limited to about seven (plus or minus two) bits of information (Miller, 1956).

The **cocktail party phenomenon** has been used to illustrate the selectivity of perception. At a noisy party, you are able to maintain a conversation by tuning in a particular person's voice while tuning out the rest of the noise. Yet, if someone elsewhere in the room should mention your name, there is a good chance you would notice even though you were not attending to that person's conversation. The attention-grabbing power of information relevant to the self has been demonstrated in the laboratory (Moray, 1959). Subjects are often unaware that they have processed such self-relevant information (Bargh, 1982).

Processing through schemata

We would be unable to interpret our experiences if we could not have access to our past experiences through memory; but memory is highly selective. Sir Frederick Bartlett (1932) proposed that we do not recall events exactly as they occurred; we reconstruct events as we think they must have been. Bartlett read an unusual American Indian story to British students. During recall, the students typically distorted the story by changing the unfamiliar details to things with which they were familiar. Bartlett interpreted his data as showing that people remember by using general mental categories, which he called **schemas**, to file away incoming information. Schemas are abstract organizations of ideas, concepts, and beliefs that guide us in the coding of information in our memory.

New information is integrated into existing schemas. Specific pieces of information are linked with schemas to reconstruct the recalled event. Experience may be made to fit a category and thus be changed (or biased) during storage. In addition, the act of reconstruction may change the information that has been stored. Our memory process works in this way: abstract cognitive categories allow us to remember much while we retain only a fraction of incoming information. For example, if someone asked you to recall the color of the house you lived in as a child, you may recall only that it was a brick house; but by applying a schema about the color of bricks, you might answer that the house was reddish brown (Wingfield, 1979). This process leads to much error and distortion. As Mark Twain said: "It isn't so astonishing the number of things that I can remember, as the number of things I can remember that aren't so."

Johnson, Bransford, and Solomon (1973) provided an experimental demonstration of distortion in memory. They found that individuals who read that John pounded the nail into the wall tended to recall that a hammer was mentioned in the original version. This potential for distortion is a cost we all incur for the benefit of efficiency in the face of information overload.

Hazel Markus (1977; 1980) proposed that the self-concept consists of a series of generalizations about the self that come about through past experience and enable the efficient processing of self-related information. These generalizations, which Markus (1977) called self-schemas, "function as selective mechanisms which determine whether information is attended to, how it is structured, how much importance is attached to it, and what happens to it subsequently" (p. 64).

We are not passive absorbers of outside information but actively select what we listen to and process. If anyone at a noisy cocktail party mentions our name, we probably will hear it because self-relevant information captures our attention.

Markus assumed that people constantly are trying to understand themselves; they do this most efficiently by organizing social experiences into various abstract categories. A young lady noticing the stares of male admirers and the whistles of construction workers may organize these experiences by classifying herself as "sexy." The skinny man whose bumbling attempts at conversation lead to social ineptness may, like many of the characters portrayed by Woody Allen, think of himself as a "schnook."

Most self-schemas can be labeled with traitlike terms, such as talkative, generous, and creative, all of which imply some action and can be inferred on the basis of past actions. Once formed, these self-categorizations guide the processing of future incoming information. The sexy lady befriends those who praise her beauty, ignores people who call her shallow, directs conversations to emphasize physical attributes, and avoids intellectual discussions. In order to make sense out of available information, we selectively process that which past experience indicates is important for us.

Markus reasoned that if individuals are provided with information for which they have an available self-schema, they should be able to process the information faster than when they have no such self-schema available. To test this hypothesis, Markus (1977) formed three groups of subjects in terms of self-ratings on a measure of independence: a group of independents, a group of dependents, and a group that had no pronounced self-schema on this dimension (aschematic). All subjects were asked to press a button when presented with an adjective that was self-descriptive. Aschematic subjects reacted to fewer adjectives. When they did indicate adjectives as self-descriptive, they were slower than the other two groups in pressing the button. As might be expected, independent and dependent persons reacted more often and more quickly to adjectives that were congruent with their self-schemas.

Self-schemas act as filters. Congruent information is processed easily, but information contradicting self-schemas is resisted. This filtering effect of self-schemas was shown among socially sensitive subjects who refused to accept an experimenter's statement that they had obtained low scores on a social sensitivity test (Sweeney and Moreland, 1980).

Another implication of the self-schema notion is that we can learn faster and recall more easily information that is associated with categories regarding the self. The "medical student syndrome" illustrates this principle. Medical students often experience symptoms of the various diseases they study. This reaction may represent organization of information in terms of self-schemas and may help students remember the symptoms for examinations. In a study supporting this interpretation, subjects were given a list of adjectives to memorize (Rogers, Kuiper, and Kirker, 1977). Various groups were given commonly used strategies for facilitating such memorization. When reading through the list, one group was told to decide whether the particular adjective was descriptive of themselves. This self-reference group remembered the adjectives better than the group in a control condition. Self-reference activates schemas that enrich new material with previously existing knowledge, thereby facilitating later recall of the information.

The ease of processing information consistent with self-schemas was demonstrated among introductory psychology students, who had been identified as masculine, feminine, or androgynous on the basis of self-ratings of traits (Markus, Crane, Bernstein, and Siladi, 1982). Eight weeks after the initial self-ratings, the students were provided with a list of twenty words, eight masculine, eight feminine, and four neutral. They were asked to describe past incidents from their own behavior as evidence that they possessed the traits implied by these words. The results are shown in Figure 2-3. As can be seen, students who possessed masculine schemas were able to provide more examples of incidents when given a masculine word, those who possessed feminine schemas cited more incidents when given a feminine word. Androgynous students provided just as many incidents to masculine or feminine words. Apparently, we remember more about our past behavior if the incidents are congruent with our self-schemas.

The fact that information is organized in the context of self-schemas provides us with a better memory about our own experiences than about the actions of other people (Kuiper and Rogers, 1979; Lord, 1978). One consequence of this information-storage bias is that actors tend to take more credit for accomplishments on the job than they attribute to their co-workers (Ross and Sicoly, 1979). We also have a tendency to remember more positive achievements than blame-

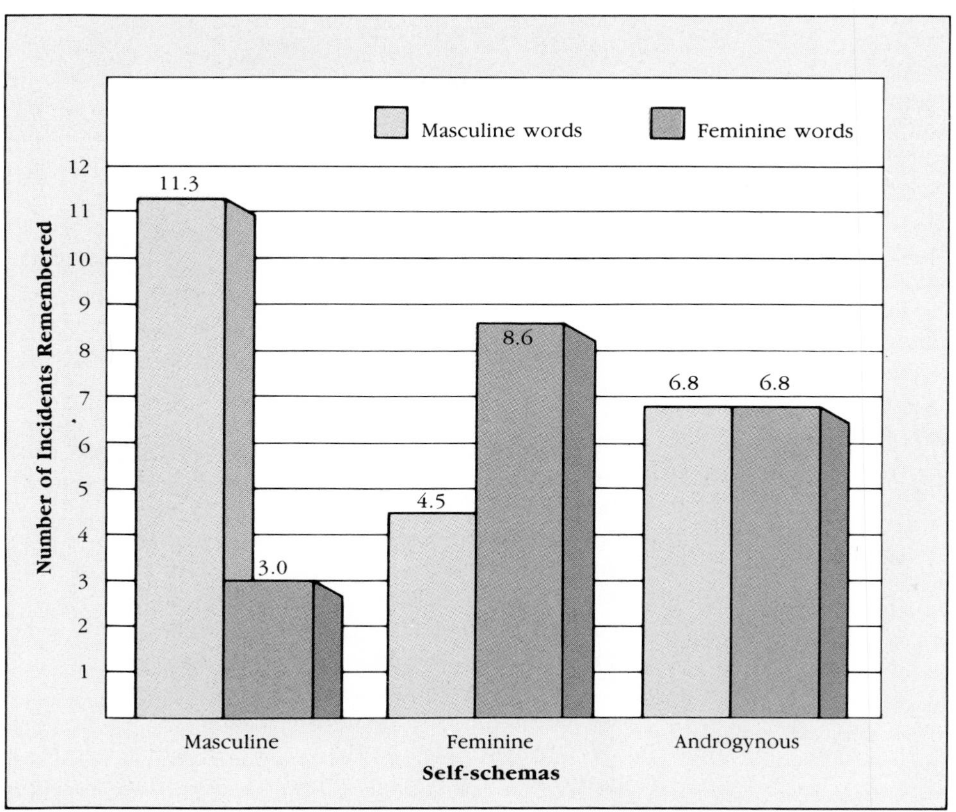

Figure 2-3 Self-schemas and recall of incidents related to male and female words.

Source: Based on "Self-schemas and gender" by H. Markus, M. Crane, S. Bernstein, and M. Siladi, 1982, *Journal of Personality and Social Psychology*, *42*, 38-50.

worthy incidents, probably because most of us tend to have positive self-schemas (Mischel, Ebbesen, and Zeiss, 1976). A summary of the functions of a self-schema is presented in Table 2-2.

Table 2–2 A summary of the Functions of Self-Schemas

Directs selection from available information: accepts congruent information and screens out incongruent information.
Organizes incoming information to be consistent with the self-schema.
Revises incoming information to fit the schema by adding information relevant to it and altering inconsistent information.
Speeds the processing of relevant information.
Facilitates the memory of schema-relevant information.
Reconstructs memory so events fit self-schemas.

Organizing self-relevant information

Nothing is greater than one's self is.
Walt Whitman, Song of Myself

The self is not just a set of disconnected self-schemas. The processing of self-relevant information is organized according to a hierarchy of categories and is systematized into a fairly integrated theory.

Hierarchy of information

Associated with maturity among children is the way they characterize themselves. When they are very young, they describe themselves in terms of physical attributes and group-related social identities. The movement along the hierarchy of self-relevant categories (shown in Table 2-3) as the child grows older is to social actions, abilities, and other more abstract characteristics, such as attitudes and personality traits (Rosenberg, 1979). The change in emphasis from concrete to abstract categories reflects the individual's ability to take the perspective of others, referred to as *decentering* (Piaget, 1966), to grow in the capacity to introspect, and to acquire more sophisticated linguistic concepts.

Comparisons of self-descriptions of younger children and adolescents revealed this movement from lower- to higher-level categories (Montemayor and Eisen, 1977). Adolescents revealed a more complex and differentiated structure of self-descriptions of themselves as unique individuals. Sex differences in the use of some categories of self-description also were found. For example, girls described themselves more in terms of their relationships with other people, especially family members, then boys did (McGuire and McGuire, 1982).

Self-theories

We hardly would have an integrated self-concept if it consisted of a set of unconnected schemas. Epstein (1973) has proposed that each person constructs a more or less integrated theory about the self. The process resembles that used by scientists in developing theories to explain a set of related phenomena. First, we make observations about ourselves either directly or through reflected appraisals. This is the information-gathering stage. Next, we make inferences about what we are like based on observations of our own behavior and reflected appraisals. We then derive how we should act if our self-theory is true. Finally, we test these deductions through observing our own subsequent behavior. If the observations are consistent with our expectations, we retain the self-theory. Behavior that is inconsistent with the self-theory can be rationalized as irrelevant to our self-theory or may lead us to review and perhaps revise our theory (see Box 2-5).

A self-theory serves three basic functions for a person: (1) it allows the person to view the self as consistent and predictable, hence the person can view himself or herself as capable of planning a way to maximize pleasure and reduce pain over the long run; (2) it helps the individual to organize complex experiences and information in order that he or she can deal effectively with the world (and other people); and (3) it provides the person with a basis for pride or disappointment, therefore giving him or her a sense of self-esteem (Epstein, 1973).

Table 2-3 Hierarchy of categories used to describe the self

CATEGORIES (YOUNGER TO OLDER)	EXAMPLES OF ATTRIBUTES
Physical and material	Body
Social identity	Sex, race, age
Social actions	Plays piano, dances
Abilities	Achievement, skills
Attitudes and interests	Likes sports and country music
Abstract	Personality traits

Biases involved in organizing information about the self

We lie loudest when we lie to ourselves.

Eric Hoffer

Greenwald (1980) has suggested that the way people organize a self-portrait fits a model of totalitarian information control like the one described in Orwell's *1984,* more than the more detached and objective process used by scientists. The organization of information about the self is designed to preserve the existing self-concept rather than to represent a balanced and accurate portrait. Three cognitive biases characterize the **totalitarian ego**, which is constantly engaged in the "fabrication and revision of personal

Box 2-5

Autophotography and measuring self-concept

A man never discloses his own character so clearly as when he describes another's.
Jean Paul Richter

A person's self-theory is difficult to measure scientifically. In many instances, people are not very articulate and cannot provide a verbal description of how they view themselves. Ziller and Lewis (1981) described an innovative technique for assessing a person's self-concept through the use of **autophotography**. A person is given an instamatic camera and told to take twelve photographs that reveal who they are. In an initial test of this procedure, juvenile delinquents took more pictures of peers and material things, while nondelinquents were more oriented to home, school, and aesthetics (i.e., plants, trees, art, flowers). These differences indicate that delinquent youths are influenced more by their peers than by institutional controls of home and family.

history": egocentricity, beneffectance, and conservatism.

Egocentricity

Events affecting the self are remembered better than information not relevant to the self. Actors take unwarranted credit for events in which they and other people are involved. In addition to these **egocentric** tendencies is the belief people have that they control events that occur purely by chance. This **illusion of control** was demonstrated when a series of coin flips were rigged. It was rigged so that in the first ten flips some subjects lost most of the flips whereas others won. At the end of the trials, regardless of how they fared in the first ten flips all of the subjects won and lost 50 percent of the time. Therefore, they all won over thirty flips. Those who won more often in the early trials predicted that they would do better in a hundred future flips while the early losers were less optimistic about future winnings. (Langer and Roth, 1975).

Egocentricity is also manifested by the belief that most people would act the way we do, a **false consensus effect**. Students who agreed to carry a large sign around campus saying, "Eat at Joe's," believed that most other students would agree to do this also. Yet, people who did not agree to carry the sign believed that fewer people would do it (Ross, Greene, and House, 1977). Still another form of egocentricity in self-knowledge is the belief most people have that they are better than average in any category or trait that is socially desirable (Felson, 1981; Myers and Ridle, 1979).

Beneffectance

In order to maintain a positive concept of the self, we claim credit for success and deny responsibility for failure. **Beneffectance** is a self-serving bias preserving our sense of competence. For example, when students do well on examinations, they say the tests are valid; but when students obtain poor grades, they question the validity of the tests (Arkin and Maruyama, 1979). This self-serving bias is discussed further in Chapter 4.

Cognitive conservatism

Once an organized self-theory has been developed, there is a conservative tendency to maintain and reinforce it and to resist change. This kind of **cognitive conservatism** was demonstrated by subjects, each of whom interviewed another person (Snyder and Swann, 1978). The way subjects asked questions allowed them to confirm prior hypotheses about the interviewee. For example, if a subject believed the interviewee to be an introvert, he or she asked questions like, "What do you dislike about loud parties" and "In what situations do you wish you could be more outgoing?" The answers then were interpreted, supporting the subject's prior belief that the interviewee was an introvert. In a similar way, information is selected to confirm expectations about one's self (Mischel, Ebbesen, and Zeiss, 1973). Furthermore, people reject arguments by those who disagree with them and are receptive of supportive arguments by those who agree (Cullen, 1968; Greenwald, 1968; Janis and Terwilliger, 1962).

Memories are reconstructed to fit an "I knew it all along" assumption. As compared to the number of correct answers actually obtained by people taking a test, more subjects claimed that they would have gotten the answers correct when they received the answers without actually taking the test (Fischoff, 1975). In addition, when subjects had acted in a way to contradict a prior attitude, they inaccurately recalled what that attitude was (Bem and McConnell, 1970). Memory appears to be malleable and is reconstructed to allow the person to maintain a consistent view of the self.

Self-Verification Processes

Self-verification theory assumes that people are strongly motivated to reaffirm some aspect of the self when they receive a challenge to their self-concept (Swann, 1984). If successful, this reaffirming action conserves the original self-theory. However, when people are prevented from making a confirmatory response following a challenge to self-concept, they will change in the direction of the disconfirmatory feedback.

In a test of self-verification theory, subjects were asked to describe themselves on a dominant-submissive dimension (Swann and Hill, 1982). In this way, subjects were separated into groups identified as dominant or submissive. Half of each group was given feedback that another perceived them as dominant, and the remainder in each group were told that they were perceived as submissive. As a result of this procedure, half of each group were provided with confirmatory information and half of each group were provided with disconfirmatory information. Some subjects were given the opportunity to respond to the feedback and some were not.

It was found that both dominant and submissive subjects who had been provided with disconfirmatory feedback, and also had an opportunity to respond to the feedback, maintained their original self-concepts; however, subjects who received disconfirmatory feedback and could not respond to it changed their self-concepts in the direction of the feedback. As can be seen in Box 2-6, if people can be led to predict an action, they probably will confirm their own predictions.

In order to produce long-lasting changes in self-concept, Swann (1984) proposed two necessary conditions: (1) there must be a change in self-conception and (2) this change in self-concept must be validated and legitimized by other significant people through social interaction. Although people go out of their way to sustain their self-concepts, reaffirming their beliefs through confirmatory actions, their inability to perform such actions will produce changes in their self-conception should disconfirmatory information be available. Any such changes will be brief with the individual reverting to the original self-concept unless social interactions confirm the new self-concept.

Self-evaluation and behavior

Remember, no one can make you feel inferior without your consent.

Eleanor Roosevelt

I have great faith in fools; self-confidence my friends call it.

Edgar Allan Poe

The self acts as a prime motivator of behavior. The evidence that people organize and bias information in self-serving ways implies that they have a need for positive self-evaluations. Positive and negative self-evaluations are based on internal comparisons of the real self with the individual's ideal self (Coppersmith,

Box 2-6

Self-erasing errors of prediction

Human participants in laboratory studies have been surprisingly compliant to requests to shock other people, to advocate positions contrary to their own private views, or to sing the "Star Spangled Banner" over the telephone. On the other hand, when people are expected to help others, they can be quite unhelpful. The degree of compliance to requests can be modified by first asking people to predict what they would do in certain situations (Sherman, 1980). Forty-eight percent of the subjects predicted that they would help and 31 percent actually did help; but if subjects did not predict their own behavior beforehand, only 4.2 percent complied to the request for help. Furthermore, thirteen of fourteen compliers predicted that they would comply, whereas twenty-two of thirty-one noncompliers predicted that they would not help.

1967). The ideal self is how the individual would like to be and the real self is how the person describes him or herself. **Self-esteem** is a general overall evaluation of real with ideal self. The larger the discrepancy, the lower the self-esteem, and vice versa.

Self-esteem is not affected by every possible yardstick. William James (1950) said:

> I, who for the time have staked my all on being a psychologist, am mortified if others know much more psychology than I. But I am contented to wallow in the grossest ignorance of Greek. My deficiencies there give me no sense of personal humiliation at all. Had I "pretensions" to be a linguist, it would have been just the reverse. (p. 310)

Almost a century later, evidence has been obtained for James's insight. Adolescents who did not consider themselves particularly likable did not suffer low self-esteem. They did not attach a great deal of importance to being liked (Rosenberg, 1982). Indeed, people may devalue attributes when others are discovered to be superior in some way. According to the evidence presented in Box 2-7, depressed people may be more honest than most people in the way they describe themselves. In another study, subjects who discovered a confederate to have performed better than they, later rated the relevant attribute lower in importance (Tesser and Campbell, 1980). An examination of the results in Table 2-4 shows that when the performance of both the confederate and the subjects was below average, few subjects devaluated the attribute.

Self-efficacy, mastery, and control

Bandura (1977a, 1977b) proposed that favorable self-evaluations become associated with other forms of reinforcement. The person develops a sense of **self-efficacy**, the feeling of being effective in coping with the environment. People who have a low sense of self-efficacy do not expect to be effective and may therefore avoid tasks or easily give up when attempting to solve problems.

Psychologists also have recognized individuals' perception of mastery and control or their opposites in numerous ways. Central to these overlapping theories is the common focus on the ability of individuals to reflect upon their own conduct, to evaluate it, and to use the evaluation as the basis of future behavior. Consistent with this general framework, Rotter (1954, 1966) proposed that individuals acquire expectancies about the future based on reflections about the past. In general, people learn that they are effective in gaining

Box 2-7

Is it depressing to tell the truth about ourselves?

People who are depressed generally do not have positive impressions of themselves. It is possible that they are just more honest about themselves than are nondepressed people. In an investigation of depression and self-perceptions three groups of people were examined: depressed, non-depressed but with other psychiatric problems, and a "normal" group having no psychiatric problems (Lewinsohn, Mischel, Chapline, and Barton, 1980). All subjects were provided an opportunity to interact with others, and then were asked to rate themselves and the other people.

Depressed subjects rated themselves as less socially skilled than members of the other two groups. This self-portrayal by the depressed subjects was accurate if we judge the way in which other people evaluated them. The self-ratings of the two nondepressed groups of subjects indicated that they rated themselves more favorably than others rated them. These findings indicate that depressed people have a better sense of how others judge them than nondepressed people have.

reinforcements for themselves or that they are not effective. Such self-evaluations lead to generalized expectancies regarding whether people control events or whether events exert control over them.

Defining an internal-external control orientation, Rotter (1967) refers to "the degree to which the individual believes that what happens to him results from his own behavior versus the degree to which he believes that what happens to him is the result of luck, chance, fate, or forces beyond his control" (p. 128). In other words, persons with an **internal control orientation** typically attribute their outcomes to the effects of their own behavior, while persons with an **external control orientation** attribute the causes of their outcomes to something outside themselves.

Research has established that "internals" are more achievement oriented (Lefcourt, 1972), develop more realistic aspirations based on past successes and failures, more actively seek information to help them solve problems (Seeman, 1967), and are better at delaying gratification than are "externals." As a consequence, people with an internal control orientation display greater success in giving up short-term satisfac-

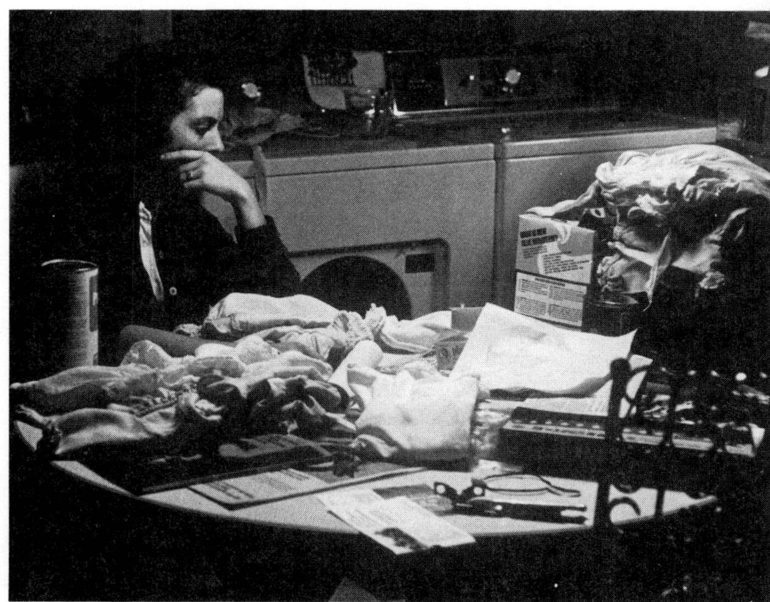

Through favorable self-evaluations, we develop the feeling of being effective in coping with our environment (self-efficacy). A person with a low sense of self-efficacy gives up easily when trying to solve problems.

TABLE 2–4 Change in rated importance of traits of social sensitivity and social judgment from first measurement to after test feedback

OTHER'S PERSONALITY	TEST FEEDBACK	
	Feedback that both subject and other person are below average on the traits	Feedback that subject is average but other person is above average on traits
Similar	−.06	−.42
Dissimilar	−.30	−.35

Source: Based on "Self-Definition: The impact of the relative performance and similarity of others" by A. Tesser and J. Campbell, 1980, *Social Psychology Quarterly, 43,* pp. 341-347.

Note: The negative scores indicate that the subjects rated the traits as less important on the second measurement as compared to the first measurement of how important the traits were.

tions for longer-term benefits. For example, "internals" have greater success in giving up cigarette smoking (James, Woodruff, and Werner, 1965).

In certain situations, a person may feel that nothing effective can be done to affect events. The person may feel impotent, depressed, and helpless (Seligman, 1975). Psychologists refer to such a pattern as **learned helplessness** and have demonstrated it in laboratory studies. Typically, subjects are presented with an insoluble problem; later they are presented with a soluble problem. The experience of being unable to solve the first problem tends to lead subjects to not try as hard on the second; hence these subjects do not perform the second task as well as those who had no experience with the insoluble task. For example, Hiroto and Seligman (1975) demonstrated that subjects who could not learn to control an unpleasant noise were slower to learn a response to control a similar noise in a later situation than were subjects who could control the earlier noise.

Learned helplessness is the self-perception of being unable to control events or to solve problems. The result is that the individual stops trying to solve problems, is debilitated, and suffers from depression (Seligman, 1975). Such people view their life circumstances in the following ways: "I give up." "What's the use of trying?" "I can't do anything." "Everything goes wrong for me." These kinds of self-descriptions strip people of all motivation to strive for achievement or to control their own reinforcements (see discussion of aging and control in Chapter 13).

Self-awareness

As he and others see me. Who chose this face for me? It asks me too.

James Joyce, Ulysses

Remember the jeans shopper gazing at the self in a full-length mirror. In this kind of mirror, the focus is on public appearance. The most evident aspects of appearance, particularly to strangers, are the physical aspects of shape, size, curvature, dress, and grooming. According to some social psychologists, the presence of a mirror can cause people to reflect about the self and their standards of conduct. Something like this happens in the opening section of James Joyce's famous novel *Ulysses.* It contains many pages reflecting the inner thoughts of the hero who looks into a cracked mirror at one point and reflects upon himself as others see him.

Wicklund (1975) has proposed that it makes a difference in subsequent behavior whether a person is focused on the environment or on the self. This theory of **self-awareness** presumes that when people are focused on the environment (are unself-conscious), their responses are apt to be determined situationally, but when people are self-focused, their responses probably will be principled and consistent with internal standards. More precisely, the major processes proposed by self-awareness theory are that self-awareness produces self-evaluation with respect to some standard of ability, performance, or other attribute; any discrepancy between action and internal standards produces discomfort for an individual. People are motivated to avoid discomfort either by escape from the uncomfortable situation or by some action that brings them into closer correspondence with their own standards.

Researchers directed toward testing self-awareness theory have used two basic procedures. One technique is to induce attention to the environment or cause the individual to be self-focused through some manipulation in the laboratory. Among the techniques employed are: having a small mirror in the research cubicle, having a video camera present, having the person hear his or her own voice on a tape, and so on. In a second approach, a paper-and-pencil measure of private or public self-consciousness (Fenigstein, Scheier, and Bass, 1975) is used to identify individuals as characteristically oriented to the environment and unreflective, or as distracted and introspective.

Manipulations of self-awareness

Duval, Wicklund, and Fine (reported in Duval and Wicklund, 1972) produced an example of self-focusing leading to escape behavior. Some subjects were told that they were creative and intelligent, others were told they were neither. After this feedback about their performance on a test, subjects were asked to wait for another experimenter. Subjects were free to leave if the experimenter did not show up within five minutes. Half of all subjects waited in front of a mirror and with a video camera pointed at them, while the remainder waited without such self-focusing stimuli present. Subjects who had been given the information that they had scored low on the test and who were self-focused left the laboratory sooner when the experimenter failed to show up than subjects who either believed they had performed well on the test or were not self-focused. This behavior was interpreted as showing that low scores were discrepant with self-standards and that the discomfort was more intense for those subjects who were self-focused. Since the latter subjects had no opportunity to act to reduce the discrepancy between performance and internal standards, they chose to escape from the situation.

Gibbons (1978) demonstrated a similar consistency effect by manipulating subjects' self-awareness with a mirror. Undergraduate women rated themselves on a test of sex guilt; included in the rating list were questions about their attitudes toward pornography. Several weeks later, the subjects were given a pornographic passage to read and then rated the reading on several scales, including how enjoyable it was. Subjects who read the passage and rated it in front of a mirror displayed a greater consistency between their pretested attitudes toward pornography and their later ratings of the passage than did those who were not in front of a mirror. A similar finding was obtained in the field study of trick or treaters described in Box 2-8.

Internal standards are derived from other people and are concerned with morality and achievement. A person who is aware of the self also may become more aware of the standards of other people. Three studies showed that self-focused subjects were better able to take the perspective of others (Stephenson and Wicklund, 1983). Subjects were less likely to display an egocentric bias in attributing responsibility for success to themselves or to others, and were better able to

The presence of a mirror and video camera leads an individual to self-awareness. Such self-focusing devices enable us to reflect upon our behavior and standards of conduct. Social psychologists are able to modify and change behavior by using self-focusing techniques.

Box 2-8

Cheating by trick or treaters on Halloween

Mirrors typically are used in research on self-awareness. The presence of a mirror should focus the individual's attention on an internal standard regarding morally appropriate behavior. Furthermore, the person should then act in a manner consistent with the standard. This theory was tested in a field experiment (Beaman, Klentz, Diener, and Svanum, 1979).

Trick or treaters entering a home on Halloween night were told that they each could take one piece of candy from a bowl on a table. The woman of the house then left the children alone with the goodies. Nearly half of those between nine and twelve years of age and almost three-fourths of those over twelve took more than one piece.

The researchers reasoned that by making the trick or treaters aware of themselves in this action, this self-awareness should cause them to focus on internal standards of honesty and make them less apt to violate the norm established by the woman of the house. A mirror was placed behind the table allowing the children to view themselves as they placed their hands into the candy bowl. The presence of the mirror was highly successful in reducing cheating. Less than 10 percent of the nine to twelve year olds and no one above the age of twleve took more than one piece of candy. Based on this finding it might be suggested that gigantic mirrors should be placed in all H and R Block offices where income tax forms are filled out.

estimate another person's liking for chocolate foods when they were self-focused. Similarly, subjects working in front of a mirror or an audience made more use of social comparison information when reproducing geometric figures where performance norms were available (Scheier and Carver, 1983).

Public vs. private self-consciousness

Scheier (1980) used the Self-Consciousness Scale to identify subjects who were either high or low in private **self-consciousness**. He found that there was strong consistency between attitudes and subsequent behavior by highly private self-conscious subjects who, according to the theory of self-awareness, should be guided by internal standards. Subjects who were low in private self-consciousness displayed little consistency between attitudes and behavior, presumably because their behavior was determined situationally rather than guided by principle.

People high in public self-consciousness have been found to be more concerned with fashions (Solomon and Schopler, 1982), better able to predict the reactions they will elicit from others (Tobey and Tunnel, 1981), and more conforming to social pressures (Froming and Carver, 1981) than are those low in public self-consciousness. On the other side of the scale, people who obtain high scores on the measure of private self-consciousness have finer taste discriminations (Scheier, Carver, and Gibbons, 1979), are more aware of their emotions (Scheier and Carver, 1977), and display a greater consistency between attitudes and behavior (Gibbons, 1978) than do people who obtain low scores. In addition, people high in private self-consciousness assign greater responsibility to the self for both positive and negative nonsocial events, such as, "The bus around which you are driving pulls out and runs right into you" (Fenigstein, 1979).

Summary

Contemporary approaches to the self focus on three general problems: (1) the origins of the self, (2) the self as organizer of information, and (3) the self as motivator of behavior. The development of the self is believed to be based on self-perceptions, comparative and reflective appraisals, and the various social and institutional attachments of the individual. As an organizer of information, the self-theory is believed to act as a selector of information and affects the ease of learning and remembering events. Without some overall self-theory, we might perceive the self as a set of disconnected experiences, traits, and dispositions. We hardly could function adequately, especially in dealing with other people, without some sense of integrity and one-ness.

The self is viewed as an important source of motivation. We develop a sense of competence or mastery, or a lack thereof, and this self-definition has an impact on our levels of aspiration, self-confidence, and assertiveness in behavior. Information contrary to a person's self-theory may serve to activate that person's attempts to reaffirm the possession of the traits in question. If this self-verification process is stymied because the relevant behavior is prevented from occurring, an individual may change his or her self-concept in the direction of the disconfirming feedback.

A theory of self-awareness proposes that when a person focuses inward, behavior will be consistent with internal standards. When the individual is focused on the environment (is nonaware or nonfocused), behavior will be more situationally determined. Thus, it is argued, human behavior could not be understood without a theory of the self.

Glossary

Beneffectance A hypothesis which asserts that people see themselves as unrealistically competent and good.

Cocktail party phenomenon Selective perception of self-relevant information wherever it occurs in a room full of people.

Cognitive conservatism A hypothesis that people maintain their image of the self by selecting information confirming the image and by rejecting contradictory information.

Comparative appraisal Assessment of the self is made by comparisons with the abilities, achievements, and motivations of other relevant people.

Consensual validation A process in which information indicates that others agree with our belief.

Egocentricity The hypothesis that events affecting the self are better remembered than those not relevant to the self.

External control orientation A general disposition to believe that our outcomes are a result of chance or fate.

False consensus effect An often erroneous belief that most people would act the way we do.

Homunculus A conception of the self as an inner creature who runs the outer person.

I and Me The *I* is the self as "knower," and the *Me* is the self as "known object" in the theory proposed by William James (1890).

Illusion of control The belief people have that they control events occurring purely by chance.

Internal control orientation A general disposition to believe that outcomes are under our own control.

Intrinsic motivation A person undertakes an action without clear external reasons, leading the person to infer that he or she must have values that led to the behavior.

Learned helplessness A perception of the self as ineffective, and a tendency to expend less effort in solving problems because of the belief that events are unpredictable and beyond one's control.

Looking-glass self Cooley's (1909) notion that our sense of what we are like is determined by how we imagine others perceive us; similar to reflective appraisal.

Material self According to William James (1890), that aspect of self-identity associated with our body, possessions, and so on.

Misattribution A mistaken belief regarding the cause of a reaction, particularly of sources of arousal and anxiety.

Physical reality World of material substances that can be perceived through our sensory systems.

Reflected appraisal An inference made about how other people perceive us; similar to looking-glass self.

Related ability hypothesis A person's choice of others for comparison is influenced by a specific ability being evaluated; this person then infers other abilities about these people he or she chose for comparison.

Schema A hypothetical cognitive structure representing associations among lower-level units of information; provides context for interpreting new information, allows predictions of future events, and serves as a guide for behavior.

Self Term referring to the capacity of humans to act and reflect on their actions, and to be simultaneously a knower and an object known.

Self-awareness State where attention is focused on the self as a result of social stimuli, such as seeing ourselves in a mirror, on television, and so on; is likely to produce behavior consistent with out internal standards.

Self-consciousness A personality trait reflecting the degree to which a person typically attends to either private (attitudes, motives) or public (appearances) aspects of the self.

Self-efficacy A person's self-concept of competence in effectively coping with the environment; similar to internal control orientation.

Self-esteem Overall evaluation of the self.

Self-perception theory According to Bem (1972), we draw inferences about our internal states from observations of our own behavior.

Self-verification theory When people receive a challenge to their self-concept, they will act to reaffirm the relevant identity; developed by Swann (1983).

Social reality Our perceived world of social meanings constructed from information transmitted by other people.

Social self The impressions others have of us; according to William James (1890), there is a separate social self for each significant person in our lives.

Spiritual self The processes that we use to experience and reflect upon ourselves, according to James.

Totalitarian ego The tendency of the individual, like authoritarian governments, to consistently fabricate and revise personal history to serve his or her own interests.

Two-factor theory of emotion Self-perception of an emotion requires both an experience of physiological arousal and a cognitive label for the arousal, which is drawn from prior learning or from information available in the current situation; developed by Schachter (1964).

Recommended Readings

Buss, A. H. (1980). *Self-consciousness and social anxiety,* San Francisco: Freeman.
A thorough and readable review of the origins of current investigations of self-awareness and self-consciousness, with implication for anxiety and shyness.

Percy, Walker (1983). *Lost in the cosmos: The last self-help book.* New York: Farrar, Straus & Giroux. A madcap review of the self and society by an eminent physician-novelist who is up to date on social theory.

Suls, J., & Greenwald A. G. (1980–1983). *Psychological perspectives on the self* (Vols. 1-2). Hillsdale, NJ: Erlbaum. A collection of articles, at an advanced level, by persons actively researching processes involving the self.

Wegner, D. M., & Vallacher, R. R. (1980). *The self in social psychology.* New York: Oxford University Press. Articles by theorists and researchers of the self that are written for the undergraduate reader; a suitable advanced introduction to the topic.

The face is the interface between the private person and the public life.

Margaret Mead

Things are seldom what they seem, skim milk masquerades as cream, highlows pass as patent leathers, jackdaws strut in peacock's feathers.

W. S. Gilbert

3
Identities and self-presentation

The human chameleon

Woody Allen's film *Zelig* tells the story of Leonard Zelig, a man who has no personality of his own. He takes on the physical and mental characteristics of those around him "In high society, he became a perfect socialite, with the plebes, a consummate plebeian. With Indians he became an Indian, with blacks a black, with psychiatrists, a close associate of Freud" (Simon, 1983, p. 950). In one scene, Zelig is shown singing one of Caruso's most famous arias. In another, the audience sees him getting ready to bat behind Babe Ruth and Lou Gehrig at Yankee Stadium. This ability to blend into the social background led to Zelig's fame as a "human chameleon."

Zelig eventually was institutionalized and treated by Doctor Eudora Fletcher (Mia Farrow). She discovered through hypnotizing Zelig that he experienced extreme rejection as a child. He evolved his chameleon ability because, as he said, "I want to be liked." The psychotherapy worked and Zelig eventually developed his own individualism.

To some extent, all of us act somewhat like the "human chameleon" in Woody Allen's satirical documentary. We want to be accepted, liked, and rewarded by other people. We manifest different identities for different audiences because we want to please others and have them think well of us. We do not change our

Zelig became an expert as a human chameleon because he wanted to be liked. He could assume the airs and demeanor of fashionable society, flaunt the macho image of a linebacker, sing the arias of Enrico Caruso, or stand humble like a red man.

appearances or behavior to the extent that Zelig did, but we do play a large variety of parts to produce specific reactions from audiences. Although the multiple identities assumed by Zelig originated in a severe psychiatric disorder, most people take on various identities as part of their normal pattern of social behavior.

Social psychologists use the term **self-presentation** to refer to the behaviors used by individuals to control the impressions they make on audiences. The idea that people are like actors or actresses in a theater performing before an audience is an old one but has only recently found a place in the scientific study of social behavior.

Life as theater

All men will see what you seem to be.

Niccolo Machiavelli

The comparison of everyday life to the theater is often referred to as the **dramaturgical perspective** (Burns, 1972). Greek philosophers and writers before the birth of Christ suggested the theater metaphor. The comparison is an important theme in the writings of Shakespeare. For example, in *As You Like It* Jacques says:

All the world's a stage,
And all of the men and women merely players:
They have their exits and their entrances;
And one man in his time plays many parts. . .

Above the Globe Theater in London, where Shakespeare's plays were performed, was the motto: *Totus Mundus Agit Histrionem* (All the World is a Theater).

Sociologist Erving Goffman has been most responsible for developing the dramaturgical perspective in social psychology. In his classic book, *The Presentation of Self in Everyday life,* Goffman (1959) interpreted social behavior in terms borrowed from literature and the theater. People are viewed as social actors or actresses who engage in performances. Just as a professional actor or actress is rewarded when the audience is pleased, most people discover that it is in their best interest to convey a favorable impression to others.

A superficial view of self-presentation, sometimes also referred to as **impression management,** is that it involves deceitful, manipulative actions by unscrupulous individuals. Goffman viewed self-presentation as a ubiquitous and necessary part of social life that helped to smooth and maintain routine social interactions. There is an unwritten rule called **working consensus** that governs social interactions. When individuals interact, the identity each projects will be accepted by the other. When a person makes a claim to be of a certain type, others have an obligation to accept this **definition of the situation** and to treat the person as if he or she has the qualities associated with the identity. On the first day of classes, a person walks into the room, assumes a prominent place in front of the room, and begins lecturing without any introduction. Such behavior represents a claim to an identity as the professor of the course, and seldom would anyone challenge this claim. The general acceptance of the professor's identity allows the class to continue without undue interruption.

When an actor's claim for an identity is challenged, the person experiences embarrassment and engages in **facework,** which consists of remedial actions directed toward saving or repairing the challenged identity. This process is depicted in Figure 3-1. If a student asks if the person in front of the room is really the prof, the person might indicate his or her name, office, and other indicators of an authentic identity. It is only when the rules governing social interaction break down, according to Goffman, that we notice them at all. Most of the time, reciprocal establishment of identities occurs smoothly and automatically and is a taken-for-granted aspect of everyday life.

Many social scientists agree that Goffman's work was path breaking. Nevertheless, his views have been criticized as almost entirely based on observation and analysis but lacking in "hard" scientific evaluation. The information in Chapter 3 shows that this criticism is probably no longer valid. Stimulated by Goffman's ideas, many social psychologists have investigated the kinds of self-presentational behaviors people use and the various identities they try to establish.

Negotiating identities

When we talk of negotiated identities, we are using a metaphor. It is not that we firmly present identities to others, who then counter with identities of their own. Rather, we tentatively put forth an identity, sometimes

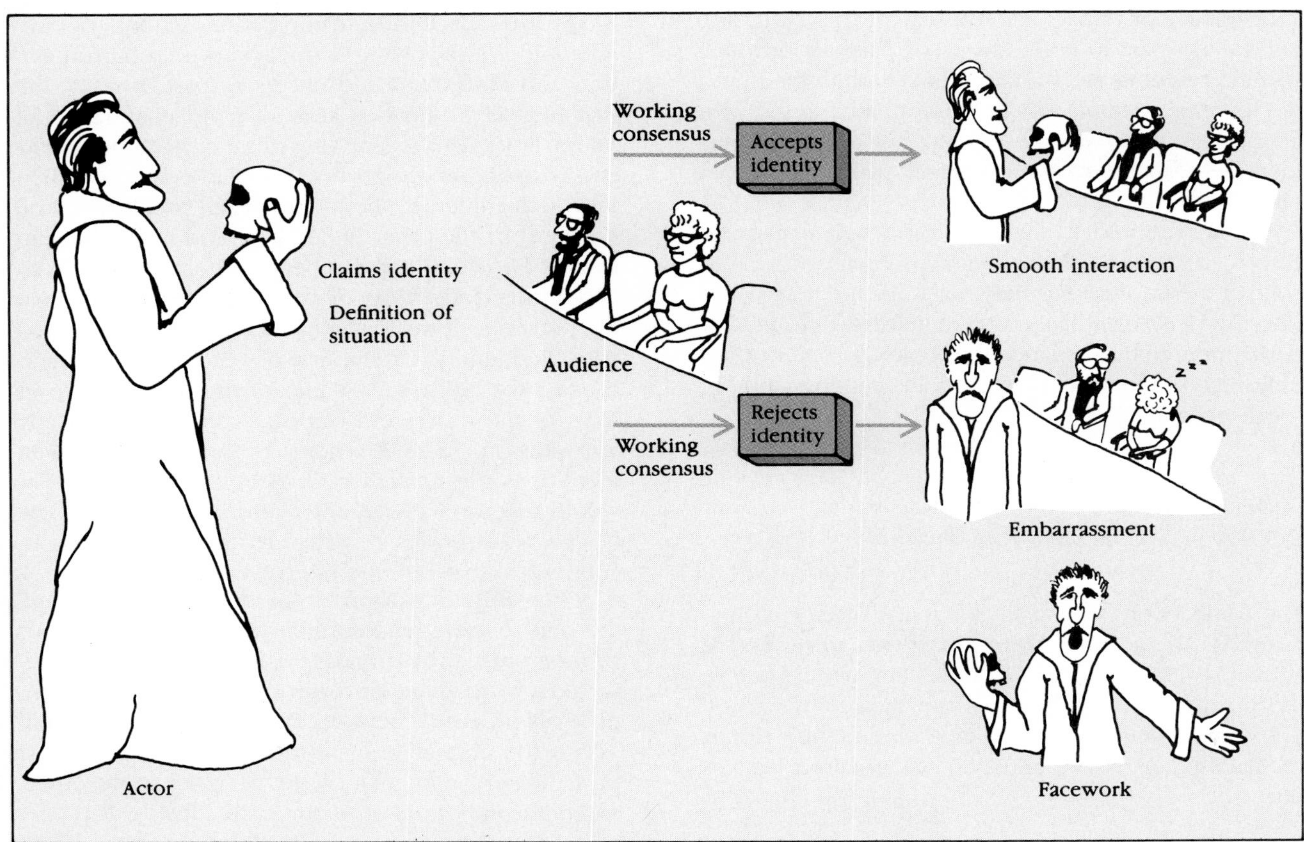

Figure 3-1 Goffman's view of self-presentation.

meeting resistance from others who ignore our tactic and present an identity of their own. This jockeying may go on for some time, or there may be an immediate acceptance of the proffered identity, and interaction smoothly continues. At a singles' bar, a person may attempt to create an identity as an interesting and desirable sexual partner; yet he or she may consistently be rebuffed by others. Or, a person may enter a classroom on the first day of the semester, go to the front of the room, begin to talk, and immediately gain an identity of "professor."

We can see from these two examples that identities tend to be *situated* (Alexander and Rudd, 1981); that is, identities often are appropriate as the basis for interactions only in certain situations. The professor-student relationship that works in the classroom is not appropriate when the two meet in the grocery store. Typically, some discomfort is felt until a variation of the respective identities are worked out for a new situation. It is in this sense that we talk about people negotiating identities with one another. If negotiation fails, the professor and student may avoid one another, recognizing that a social relationship involving them in that situation is just not going to develop.

Classification of self-presentational behaviors

Self-presentation consists of attempts by people to control the images or identities others have of them. Although some individuals may use deceitful methods in projecting false identities to others, self-presentation also entails making others aware of abilities or actions they may know nothing about, as when you call your parents and tell them you have made the dean's list at school. A person may not even be aware of self-presentational behavior. Small children engage in self-presentational behavior (Darby and Schlenker, 1982). We can assume that through the socialization process self-presentations are learned, like other habits, and may become automatic and nondeliberate responses triggered by various social cues (Jones and Wortman, 1973; Schlenker, 1980).

Although Goffman believed that we present a certain identity to facilitate social interactions, many social psychologists think that the reason why we engage in self-presentation is to control interactions and obtain rewards (Baumeister, 1982). Others are more likely to reward you if they have a favorable impression of you. Informing your parents that you made the dean's list may elicit financial support from them for that trip to Florida during the spring break.

Self-presentations are not always so straightforward and direct, but may consist of more indirect and subtle behaviors. An actor tailors a self-presentational behavior to his or her abilities, needs and goals, to the characteristics of the audience, and to the nature of the setting in which the behavior occurs. For sake of clarity, self-presentational behaviors can be divided into **assertive self-presentations**, which occur when a person actively tries to establish a particular identity, typically for purposes of gaining approval and rewards from others, and **defensive self-presentations**, which involve a person's efforts to protect, maintain, or reestablish his or her identity that others have challenged, threatened, or tarnished.

Self-presentational behavior can serve short- or long-term goals. **Tactical self-presentations** are actions taken to handle limited, spur-of-the-moment problems specific to particular situations. **Strategic self-presentations** refer to actions having important consequences across situations and time, thereby affecting the long-term identities of the actor. A television star who gets a zit before a performance can cover it with makeup, a tactical behavior. A television star who wants to continue a career as a youthful businesswoman on a soap opera may undergo cosmetic surgery, a strategic behavior.

These distinction yield four general classes of self-presentational behaviors, which are summarized in Table 3-1. We now examine each of these classes of self-presentational behaviors.

Small children engage in self-presentational behaviors to get reinforcement from adults. Through social interactions, people learn to present themselves to make others aware of their social identities. Some self-presentational behavior patterns may become automatic and nondeliberate.

Table 3–1 Classification of self-presentational behaviors

BEHAVIOR	TACTICAL	STRATEGIC
Assertive	Attempts to establish an identity for a particular situation. Example: entitlements	Attempts to establish a long-term identity. Example: attractiveness
Defensive	Attempts to protect, maintain, or defend threatened, challenged, or tarnished identity. Example: excuses	Life-long attempts to defend against threats to one's identity. Example: test anxiety

Assertive tactics of self-presentation

Praise yourself daringly, something always sticks.
Francis Bacon

Many of the behaviors people undertake to present an identity have the purpose of gaining rather immediate and foreseeable rewards. When assertive tactics are successful, an actor's social power is enhanced (Jones and Pittman, 1982). These assertive tactics typically have the purpose of establishing an identity for the actor, which arouses some emotion in the audience, such as love, fear, respect, or sympathy. These emotions, in turn, are expected to motivate the audience to undertake actions to benefit the initiating actor. A summary of assertive self-presentational tactics is presented in Table 3-2.

Although our description of self-presentational behaviors emphasizes their functions, it should be remembered that people probably do not always plan their actions in such a rational and somewhat Machiavellian manner. Instead, people more often imitate the behavior of others who have been successful or learn in other ways how to "get along" with people.

Table 3–2 Assertive self-presentational tactics

TACTIC	DESIRED IMPRESSION	IF BACKFIRES MAY CAUSE	SPECIFIC ACTIONS
Ingratiation	To be liked	Being viewed as a flatterer	Self and other enhancing communications; favor-doing
Intimidation	To be feared	Being viewed as impotent	Acting angry and threatening
Supplication	To be viewed as weak, dependent	Being considered a malingerer	Acting helpless
Self-promotion	To be respected for abilities	Being seen as conceited	Claiming entitlements, enhancements; BIRGing
Exemplification	To be respected for morality and worthiness	Being viewed as hypocritical	Acting as a social model

Source: From "Toward a general theory of strategic self-presentation" by E. E. Jones and T. S. Pittman, 1982, in J. Suls (ed.), *Psychological Perspectives on the Self* (Vol. 1), p. 249, Hillsdale, N.J. Erlbaum. Copyright 1982 by Laurence Erlbaum Associates, Inc. Adapted by permission.

Tactics of ingratiation

One of the most commonly used assertive self-presentation tactics is **ingratiation**, which consists of behaviors designed to gain the liking of the target audience. The ingratiator's purpose is to gain some advantage (Jones, 1964). Research evidence supports the belief that liking leads to more rewarding behavior by others (cf. Huston, 1974).

The ingratiator is often in a precarious position. To be effective, ingratiation must be well disguised. Behaviors that obviously are directed at manipulating others will certainly be detected as insincere. The more in need or dependent people are, the more likely they are to attempt to ingratiate themselves with a powerful person. As dependence increases, however, the chance that ingratiation will be viewed as manipulative will also increase (Jones, Jones, and Gergen, 1963). The **ingratiator's dilemma** refers to the fact that as the need for ingratiation increases, the probability of its success decreases. This relationship is illustrated in Figure 3-2.

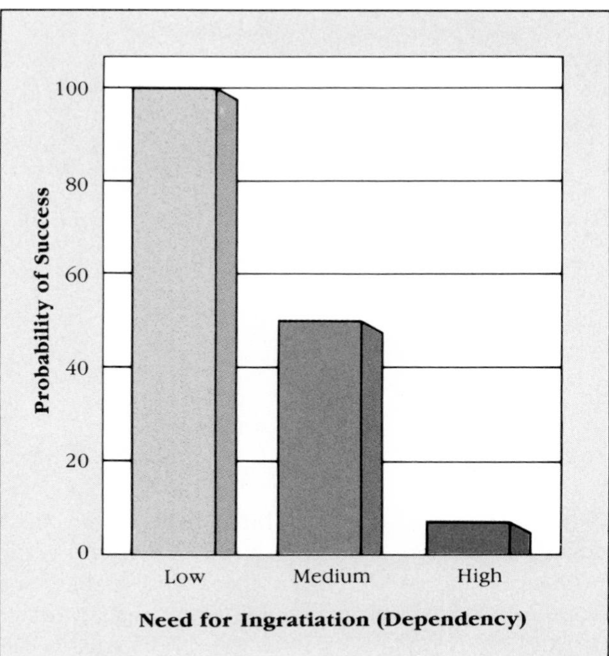

Figure 3-2 The ingratiator's dilemma. *Note:* Hypothetical values illustrating that as the need for ingratiation increases its chances of success decrease.

Four ways in which people may ingratiate themselves have been identified: self-enhancing communications, other-enhancing communications, opinion conformity, and favor-doing (Jones and Wortman, 1973).

Self-enhancing communications

Many situations require that we "put our best foot forward" and try to convince others that we are likable and worthy people. Perhaps you have had an interview for a job or maybe you have been evaluated by a teacher, a supervisor, or your father's or mother's boss. The task for the ingratiator in such a situation is to discover what the audience finds attractive or desirable and then behave in a positive way toward it.

Research has established that subjects tend to make self-enhancing statements in interview situations. For example, students who were told to pretend that they were interviewing for a free summer trip to Europe rated themselves more positively than did subjects who specifically were told to present themselves accurately to the interviewer (Jones, Gergen, and Davis, 1962). When actual job applications for a nurse's aide position were compared with the records of prior employers, it was found that over half of the applicants had exaggerated their salaries and length of service at previous jobs (Goldstein, 1971).

Self-enhancement is not always synonomous with bragging about our positive attributes. Perhaps a relevant audience would be more approving of a self-effacing, submissive, and modest person. Self-presentation of modesty was shown among Navy ROTC cadets who were told that they would be interacting in a decision-making group (Gergen and Taylor, 1969). Half of the cadets were told that their abilities were being judged, while the remainder were told that their social skills in getting along with others were being evaluated. Cadets manifested self-confidence and competence when they believed that was the appropriate identity to present; they projected an image of modesty and self-effacement when they believed sociability was the appropriate identity. In another study observers rate such self-effacing teachers very positively (Tetlock, 1980).

Preferences for egotistical versus modest identities may be due at least in part to cultural differences. The individualistic ideology of Western societies emphasizes achievement and focuses credit or blame for accomplishments or misdeeds on the individual. Among Eastern cultures, a collectivist ideology predominates and emphasizes the importance of the group. Individuals are expected to be modest in claiming responsibility for group accomplishments. Hong Kong Chinese college students exhibit modest self-presentations (Leung and Bond, 1981).

There may be occasions when an audience values a disagreeable identity. When subjects were told that an interviewer liked people to disagree with him, they presented themselves as having sharply different attitudes and opinions than he did (Jellison and Gentry, 1978).

Other-enhancing communications

But when I tell him he hates flatterers,
He says he does being then most flattered.
Shakepeare, Julius Caesar

In a famous book, *How to Win Friends and Influence People*, Dale Carnegie (1940) recognized the importance of praising others. He advised those seeking success to refer to people by their names as often as possible because a person's name is the "sweetest sound" to them. Carnegie cautioned that we should avoid insincere flattery while honestly emphasizing the positive qualities others have. Research has shown that people like others who bolster their self-esteem (Aronson and Linder, 1965). If the positive appraisals of others are perceived as insincere, however, these appraisals will not be effective in gaining the evaluation of attractiveness the ingratiator seeks (Dickoff, 1961; Jones and Schneider, 1968; Regan 1976).

Other-enhancing communications are most effective when target persons are unsure whether they have the relevant attributes (Schlenker, 1980). If people who are targets of praise are convinced that they do not have the attribute, they will doubt the evaluator's sincerity. If target persons believe they have the relevant attributes, they probably have received many previous compliments, reducing the value of the current one. For example, Finck (1902) argued that the "most common mistake of lovers is to compliment a woman on her most conspicuous points of beauty. This has very much the same effect as telling Rubenstein he is a wonderful pianist" (p. 245).

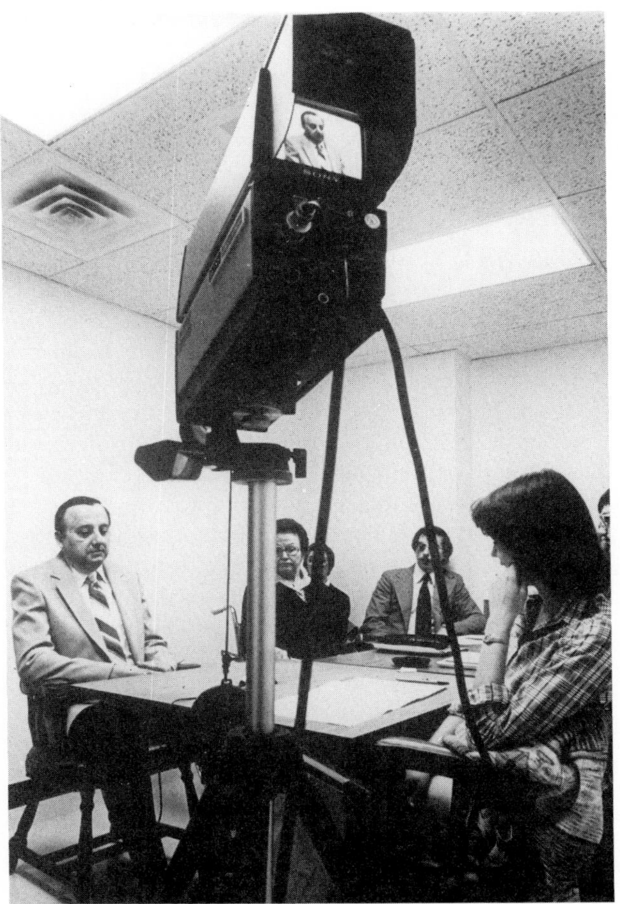

These people are being trained to improve their self-enhancing communication skills when they are interviewed and evaluated for employment. We use self-enhancing statements to convince others of our abilities and worth.

Opinion conformity

Imitation is the highest form of flattery.
Oscar Wilde

When Aristotle noted that "birds of a feather flock together," he was reporting an observation: people who are alike in significant ways tend to like one another. We have ample social psychological evidence to support Aristotle's observation (cf. Byrne, 1971). This general principle suggests a tactic of ingratiation: act as though you agree with the values, attitudes, and opinions of the target person.

Box 3-1

The female applicant and the male chauvinist interviewer

Sex-role identification historically has been a major factor in limiting opportunities for women in American society. Just as slaves ingratiated themselves with their owners, women similarly may attempt to manipulate men who hold traditional views of the female role in society. Chauvinistic men believe that women should be passive, nurturant, dependent, emotional, and physically attractive. "Liberated" men believe women should be assertive, independent, and given equal job opportunities in every area of employment.

Female applicants for jobs might use knowledge of a male interviewer's attitudes toward women as a basis for self-presentation. By conforming to the interviewer's opinions, the applicant presumably would stand a better chance of obtaining the job.

Von Baeyer, Sherk, and Zanna (1981) provided female subjects with information that a male interviewer had traditional or nontraditional views of women. As can be seen in Figure 3-3, this knowledge affected the subsequent interview behavior of the women. Although clothing for the interview did not differ, the women interviewing with the traditional male wore more cosmetics and accessories, looked at the interviewer less, talked less, gave more traditional responses to questions about marriage and the family, and were rated as more attractive by judges than women who interviewed with the nontraditional male. This conformity with the sex-related attitudes of males is presumably an effective ingratiation tactic.

Not only has such opinion conformity been demonstrated in laboratory studies, but the degree of opinion conformity has been found to increase when a person's dependence on another for rewards increases (Jones et al., 1963; 1965). This form of ingratiation is used frequently when a person is dependent on a punitive and unpredictable other person (Davis and Florquist, 1965). Slaves tended to agree with their masters by saying "yassuh" regardless of what the masters said. Prisoners in Nazi concentration camps during the holocaust often imitated the attitudes of their guards (Bettleheim, 1958).

As with other ingratiation tactics, overindulgence in opinion conformity can be conterproductive. Jones, Jones and Gergen (1963) had a dependent person either consistently or occasionally agree with the opinions of someone who controlled significant reinforcements. Observers liked the dependent person less when he always agreed with the powerful person than when conformity was infrequent. Also, indirect conformity is more effective than direct conformity (Jones, Gergen, and Jones, 1963). If your boss indicates support of increased defense spending, reduction of income taxes, and deregulation of controls on big business, an effective ingratiation tactic would be to say you voted Republican in the last election. (see Box 3-1).

Favor-doing

Favor-doers hope that by being kind to others, others will feel obligated to reciprocate. Favor-doing depends on the principle, "I will scratch your back and you should scratch mine." Cross-cultural research has shown that an unwritten universal rule, **a norm of reciprocity**, exists obligating people to return favor

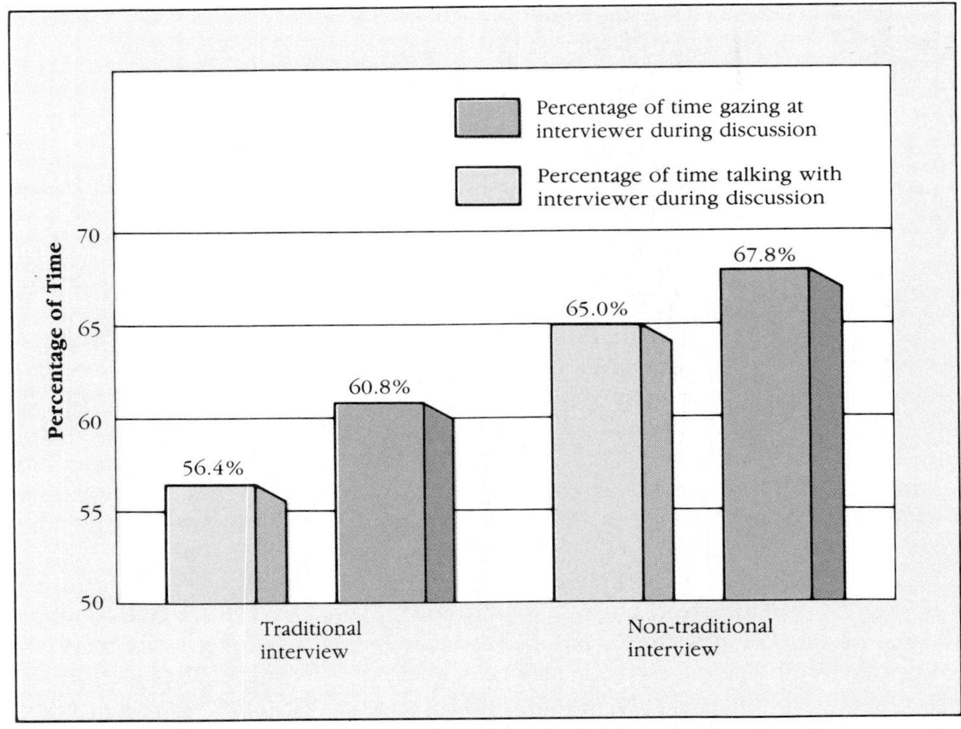

Figure 3-3 Conformity to sex-role stereotype.

Source: Based on "Impression management in the job interview: When the female applicant meets the male (chauvinist) interviewer" by C. L. von Baeyer, D. L. Sherk, and M. P. Zanna, 1981, *Personality and Social Psychology Bulletin*, 7, 45-51.

for favor (Mauss, 1967; Gouldner, 1960). It has also been established that people like those who reward them (Lott and Lott, 1974). By doing favors for others, the ingratiator can fulfill two important goals: (1) gain the liking of others and (2) create a sense of debt or obligation in the recipient.

The amount of gratitude and debt for a favor is proportionate to its value and the costs incurred by the benefactor (Tesser, Gatewood, and Driver, 1968; Muir and Weinstein, 1962). A recognition of these principles has led special interest groups to use favor-doing to sway the votes of persuadable politicians. By wining and dining candidates and contributing to their election campaigns, a lobbyist may engender a sense of gratitude and debt. The payoff may be a critical vote on legislation important to the lobbyist's organization.

Intimidation of others

The intimidator attempts to project an identity as a strong and dangerous person. By menacing looks, angry words, and threats of violence, intimidators try to gain acquiescence by inducing fear in others (Jones and Pittman, 1982). The class bully who pushes to the front of the lunch line, the hockey "goon" who menaces opponents, and the mobster who demands protection money from frightened businesspeople all use intimidation to gain advantages. Intimidation is not limited to threats of physical violence. In his interviews on "Sixty Minutes," Mike Wallace often uses an intimidating manner to coax people into revealing confidential or embarrassing information. His stern demeanor, steady stare, and courtroom-style questionning have the effect of eliciting unplanned and spontaneous comments from interviewees.

Intimidation tactics are commonplace in sports. Professional boxers may stare fiercely into each other's eyes during instructions from the referee just before the fight begins. There is evidence that staring does intimidate others. Ellsworth, Carlsmith, and Henson (1972) found that motorists sped away from red lights faster when scooter riders stared at them than when scooter riders did not look at them.

Supplication

Save me, Rick, save me!!
Peter Lorre to Humphrey Bogart, Casablanca

Supplication involves projecting an identity as a weak and dependent person with the goal of eliciting nurturant or protective behavior from the audience (Jones and Pittman, 1982). Supplication is similar to the principle of **secondary gain** popularized by psychotherapists. It has long been known that patients with psychological disorders often resist giving up their symptoms because of the attention, sympathy, and compassion they receive from others. Consider a child who complains about a terrible stomach ache. Look at all the benefits such a claim can bring. The child can stay home from school, there is no homework to do, mother provides a great deal of attention and concern, and there is unlimited television.

It is important for the supplicator to convey that a failing or dependency is uncontrollable (Barnes, Ickes, and Kidd, 1979). If the supplicator appears lazy, careless, or immoral, others will not provide help or succor (Jones and Pittman, 1982). Political debates regarding social welfare reflect candidates' concern for providing a "safety net" for dependent people, but citizens have different opinions about who genuinely deserves help and who are corrupt or lazy malingerers.

Self-promotion

Self-promotion involves attempts by an actor to achieve an identity as a competent and intelligent person. While both ingratiation and self-promotion involve self-enhancing communications, they differ in the identities that people seek to establish with each behavior. Ingratiators want others to like them, but self-promoters want respect for their abilities (Jones and Pittman, 1982). Self-promotion tactics are particularly important for the gaining of an immediate objective, such as admission to law or medical school.

There are four specific forms of self-promotion: entitlements, enhancements, basking in reflected glory, and blasting.

Entitlements

Verbal statements claiming credit for an individual's positive achievements are referred to as **entitlements** (D'Arcy, 1963; Schlenker, 1980). The world of scientific research is a frequent scene of entitlements. Well-known scientists have made competitive claims of discoveries or priority for ideas. The Nobel Prizes for research associated with the discovery of insulin by Banting and Best more than sixty years ago and the more recent discovery of the double helix structure of DNA by Watson and Crick have involved controversy about who should be considered more responsible for the monumental achievements.

Research indicates that entitlements may not always be effective in gaining approval from an audience. Students read a scenario in which a research team had just made an important medical discovery, and one of its members claimed credit for the breakthrough (Tedeschi and Giacalone, 1984). The individual's claim did not lead subjects to rate him more highly or to give him more credit than other members of the research team even when the project director confirmed the claim. An entitlement was effective when another member of the group made the claim for the person or when there was evidence that the group resisted the claimant's ideas, and the ideas led to the breakthrough.

Enhancements

Enhancements are verbal statements suggesting that the value of an outcome is greater than the audience might think (D'Arcy, 1963; Schlenker, 1980). For example, female college students who succeeded at a test rated it as more valid, accurate, and important than did women who failed (Rosenfeld, 1982).

Enhancement may be used to emphasize the difficulty of an accomplishment. When we overcome difficult obstacles in achieving a goal, our talent or motivation appears greater. (Jones and Davis, 1965). Riess (1982) found that successful members of a college ski team tended to emphasize how difficult the slalom course was. Quattrone and Jones (1978) had some students imagine themselves to be trying out for a desirable dramatic role for a director who had been favorably impressed with them in a previous audition. It was found that these students tended to present information that emphasized their difficulties in performing the part. For example, they said their performance in an earlier play required that they play a character opposite to the one they were auditioning for in the present play. By presenting obstacles to someone who already was convinced of their ability, the students may have been seeking to enhance the positive opinion the director already had of them as talented actors.

Social identity, BIRGing, and blasting

Tajfel (1971), a European social psychologist, has argued that identification with a group can have profound consequences for a person. Among such consequences is the way the person is perceived by others. Election to an honorary society or admission to a fraternity or sorority may strongly affect a person's social identity. A person may use even the most tangential relationship to celebrities or special events to indicate a positive aspect of the self. Obtaining autographs of celebrities constitutes proof of personal association. Schlenker (1980) referred to these attempts to gain a positive social identity as a more general **principle of association**. This principle states that people want to claim association with desirable events and disassociate from negative ones.

Cialdini and his colleagues (Cialdini, Borden, Thorne, Walker, Freeman, and Sloan, 1976) have referred to associations with positive groups as basking in reflected glory **(BIRGing)**. They demonstrated BIRGing in a clever field study. On Mondays following a football weekend when Arizona State University had won the game, more students were observed wearing something identifying them with the university, such as sweatshirts or jackets with the school logo, than when the university had lost the game. By being associated with a winner, people hope that some of the glitter will rub off on them.

Blasting involves an attempt by a person to enhance his or her identity by making negative evaluations of rival groups or persons (Cialdini et al., 1976). For years Texans and Oklahomans have traded insults before their annual football game. Most of us are familiar with American politicians who have enhanced their own careers by blasting the Russians.

Blasting was demonstrated among students who responded to a brief creativity test (Cialdini and Richardson, 1980). Some of the students were told that they were very creative and others were told that they were below average. When asked to evaluate their own university and a cross-state rival institution, students who believed they had failed the creativity test had a tendency to enhance the quality of their own institution and to derogate the rival school. This blasting did not occur among students who succeeded on the task.

President Ronald Reagan basks in the glory and honor of the U.S. Olympic team as the team lead the U.S. to victory in the 1984 summer events.

Exemplification

Exemplification consists of actions that a person uses to win the respect and admiration of others by projecting an image of morality, integrity, and worthiness (Jones and Pittman, 1982). The exemplifier has as an ultimate goal—modification of the behavior of the target audience. By acting admirably, a person emplifies a particular code, norm, or standard of conduct that, by implication, should guide the behavior of everyone.

A number of social roles carry with them responsibility to exemplify principles for others. Parents are models for their children, clergy for their congregants, and supervisors for their subordinates. A supervisor who shows up early for work, never takes more than an hour for lunch, and rarely misses a day due to illness is exemplifying a type of performance standard for subordinates to imitate.

Defensive tactics of self-presentation

Apologies only account for the evil which they cannot alter.

Benjamin Disraeli

When a desired identity is questioned or denied by others, the actor may act to defend or restore the spoiled identity. The goal of defensive self-presentation is to return to the status quo rather than to assertively establish a new identity. The actor is motivated to engage in defensive self-presentations because negative consequences are often associated with a spoiled identity. A marine sergeant who shows fear may lose the respect of the platoon; a college professor who makes errors of fact in lectures will lose the respect of the students. To prevent such negative reactions, people use defensive self-presentation tactics to avoid, defuse, or limit the damage associated with a spoiled identity. The marine sergeant may perform some heroic action and the professor may give some excuse for the errors he or she made in a lecture. A summary of defensive self-presentation tactics is presented in Table 3-3.

Predicaments and facework

We are placed in a **predicament** whenever others ascribe unwanted identities to us. A predicament may occur because of something a person did or allegedly did. A student who is accused of cheating will be concerned with restoring a positive identity as an honest person. Predicaments also may occur because others cast a person into a negative identity. Harold Washington was elected as the first black mayor of Chicago in the spring of 1983 despite a heated campaign during which the opposition tried to portray him as a dishonest, corrupt, and incompetent politician.

A person experiences shame or embarrassment when facing a predicament. **Embarrassment** is an emotion resulting from an actual or threatened disruption of a proffered identity (Modigliani, 1971). According to Goffman (1967), "Embarrassment occurs

TABLE 3-3 Defensive self-presentational tactics

TACTIC	DESCRIPTION	EXAMPLE
Excuses	Attempting to reduce responsibility	"Sorry, I bumped into you, I slipped on the wet floor."
Justifications	Accepting responsibility but provides overriding reason for behavior	"Sorry, I bumped into you, but I'm legally blind and can't see."
Disclaimers	Offering explanations before predicaments occur	"I don't mean to hurt you, but lets not see each other anymore."
Self-handicapping	Setting up obstacles to success	"I don't know if I can win the race today, my legs are sore."
Apologies	Admitting guilt and responsibility; expressing remorse and guilt	"Sorry I bumped into you, it was my fault and won't happen again."

Box 3-2

Some ways people avoid embarrassment

Sometimes people must do things in public that they consider embarrassing. For example, some people find it embarrassing to buy contraceptives at the pharmacy. Businesses may try to provide opportunities for people to avoid embarrassment as a way to encourage them to buy products. The *New York Times* (1981) provided useful information to cable television franchises. Oak Communications of Dallas, Texas, conducted a survey to find out what kind of services people in the community wanted and what kind they did not want. Adult programming, involving nudity and sex, "came off very low" according to the corporation's president, although 60 percent of the subscribers signed up to obtain the adult channel. Thus, when they made statements in public, subscribers indicated disapproval of adult programming; but when they could privately sign up for it, they did so. The same material they decry outside the home, they view within it.

Lewittes and Simmons (1975) found that college males tried to manage a casual impression when buying "girlie" magazines at a university bookstore. Those buying *Playboy, Penthouse,* and similar magazines, purchased more additional items, such as other magazines and candy, and more often asked for a bag for the items than those purchasing other magazines.

whenever the facts at hand threaten to discredit the assumptions a participant finds he has projected about his identity" (pp. 107-108).

Embarrassment may be perceived by others as a sign of naivete, inferiority, or weakness; hence it is an emotion we try to disguise or hide. People may experience greater embarrassment in front of strangers than in front of friends because friends know them better and are less likely to draw negative conclusions based on a single event. Generally, as is illustrated in Box 3-2, people try to avoid predicaments.

The ability to extricate ourselves from predicaments is a valued social skill. Such defensive tactics of self-presentation are sometimes referred to as **facework** (Goffman 1967). Facework need not always succeed in restoring a person's desired identity, but it may reduce or mitigate the negative reactions of others. Among the tactics used to mend a spoiled identity are excuses, justifications, disclaimers, and apologies (see Table 3-3).

Excuses

Freud (1938) noted that people tend to offer socially acceptable reasons for their conduct, no matter how strange or bizarre it may be. Such explanations of behavior may represent a concern for maintaining a positive self-concept, but very likely these offered reasons also serve to protect the individual's identity in front of audiences. A person's attempts to explain behavior when he or she is faced with a predicament have been referred to as **accounts** (Scott and Lyman, 1968).

Excuses are accounts that an actor uses in attempting to convince an audience that he or she was not responsible for what happened. An example was depicted in a *Peanuts* cartoon. Lucy was shown batting in a sandlot baseball game and she struck out. After each strike, she offered an excuse: dust was blowing in her eyes, the bat was too thin, the ball was too small, the catcher touched her bat with a glove, and so on. By offering these excuses, Lucy tried to avoid blame for striking out. The thrust of her excuses is to convince the audience that she does not usually strike out and that it could not judge her real ability under such handicapping conditions.

There are two broad categories of excuses: (1) those denying intention for negative consequences and (2) those claiming lack of control over our actions (Tedeschi and Riess, 1981). Intentional excuses include claims of accidents, ignorance, or honest mistakes.

Supervisory nurses demonstrated the effectiveness of an excuse denying intention (Wood and Mitchell, 1981). The supervisors read a description of a nurse who failed to carry out her duties properly. The excuse offered by the nurse was that a nurse's aide did not show up for duty. In the course of trying to do double duty, the nurse inadvertently ignored a patient. The excuse was effective. The supervisory nurses evaluated the offending nurse less negatively than did others who read the same incident without the description of the excuse included.

Excuses by which people can claim loss of control refer to some physical or psychological malfunctioning. Common forms of such excuses include, "I have a headache," "I am too tired," and "I was so angry I did not know what I was doing." Mental illness or insanity may be used to excuse people from responsibility for their actions. John Hinckley, Jr. was not convicted of attempting to murder President Reagan because the jury believed him to be insane at the time of the assassination attempt.

Some excuses involve a claim of ignorance (see Box 3-3). A driver may feign ignorance of the local speed limit when stopped by a police officer, or students may tell their professor they did not know the term paper was due on a particular date. The purpose of these excuses is to protect the identity of the actor as responsible and rule abiding.

People can use drugs or alcohol as excuses claiming that either impaired their judgment or diminished their control over behavior. Richardson and Campbell (1982) found that drunkenness may lead observers to attribute more responsibility to a person in one condition, but less to a person in another. Subjects read a description of a violent encounter in which a man physically abused a woman. The woman was considered more responsible for the incident when she was drunk, but the man was rated less responsible if he had been drinking before the incident. Apparently, when the woman was drunk, her condition was considered sufficient to provoke the man, so he would lose control in much the same was as when he was drunk.

Source: Reprinted with permission from the Saturday Evening Post Society, a division of BFL & MS, Inc. © 1984.

"They're making home computers more like humans everyday. This particular model blames its mistakes on another computer."

Justifications

Justifications are verbal statements by which we accept responsibility for what has happened, but we offer overriding reasons outweighing the harm we have done. A person using justifications wants others to believe that the ends justify the means. Such explanations are intended to help an audience place the event in a broader context and judge the situation in a new light. The purpose of justifications is to help people extricate themselves from predicaments and mend spoiled identities.

There are as many kinds of justifications as there are human values. Appeals to standards of justice, and humanistic values of beauty, truth, peace, and love are used for almost any conduct. For example, a large sign posted at the Homestead Air Force (SAC) Base in

Box 3-3

Playing dumb: a form of impression management

Playing dumb can serve as an assertive tactic to gain the liking of others. Very bright people may, through the process of social comparison, lead others to feel inferior and to experience low self-esteem. We tend not to like people who do not support positive self-esteem in us. In particular, we have often heard that men do not like women who are more intelligent than they.

A survey was carried out to assess whether people ever pretended to be less intelligent or knowledgeable than they thought themselves to be (Gove, Hughes, and Geerken, 1980). Over two thousand people were interviewed. Men reported playing dumb significantly more often than women. Contrary to the usual stereotype, men and women equally used the tactic of playing dumb on dates. The only instance where women played dumb more than men was in interacting with their spouses. Wives played dumb more often than did husbands.

Playing dumb tends to flatter the audience because it indicates that the audience is more intelligent; the actor feigns dependence upon the knowledge of the audience. People also may want to avoid being perceived as "too smart" or as someone who is apt to rock the boat. A person may have the primary goal of being accepted as "one of the gang" by others.

People may deliberately perform a task poorly if doing so will lead observers to evaluate them positively. This phenomenon might be called "taking a dive to make a point." In a demonstration of this tactic, subjects were told that they were expected to perform poorly because of one of their personality traits (Baumeister, Cooper, and Skib, 1979). For some subjects, this trait was portrayed as a desirable one, while for other subjects, it was presented as an unfavorable characteristic. Subjects who believed they had a favorable personality trait that would interfere with performance actually did worse in performing the task than those who were told that their personality trait was undesirable. These results indicate, paradoxically, that people do not mind "looking bad" if doing so will in some way make them also "look good."

Florida says, Peace is our Business. Acts of terrorism against innocent people are justified as furthering various doctrines, ideologies, liberation movements, or self-defense.

Effective justifications can save face and reduce the degree of negative reactions from others. Research has shown that acceptable justifications can defuse potentially violent situations (Cohen, 1955; Felson, 1982; Pastore, 1952).

In a study examining the relative effectiveness of excuses and justifications, introductory psychology students read fabricated newspaper descriptions about a fictional U.S. senator who was described as having taken a $1,000 bribe (Riordan, Marlin, and Kellogg, 1983). The senator offered either a denying intention excuse ("Just before I accepted the bribe, I had a big fight with my friend. I was so angry I wasn't thinking straight") or a justification ("Everybody takes small bribes at one time or another"). The results of the students' reactions showed that the excuse was effective in reducing the degree of responsibility attributed to the senator for taking the bribe, and the justification had the effect of reducing the perceived "wrongness" of the act.

Disclaimers

Excuses, justifications, or other explanations offered before a predicament occurs are called **disclaimers**. According to Hewitt and Stokes (1975), "A disclaimer is a verbal device employed to ward off and defeat in advance doubts and negative typifications which may result from intended conduct" (p. 3).

Disclaimers inform the audience about the purpose of some future behavior by a person with the hope that a negative impression, which might be created about the person, can be nipped in the bud and prevented. A reporter about to ask a senator a pointed question might first say, "With all due respect. . . ." Sometimes disclaimers are incomplete or vague, such as when a person says, "Don't get me wrong, but . . ." or "Try to understand what I am about to do." The implication is that there is a good explanation for the behavior even though the actor may not be specific about what it is. In general, disclaimers imply that the actor is basically good and is behaving properly, although the behavior he or she is about to perform may not be fully understood by observers.

Disclaimers also may be an effective way of allowing a person to explore the potential reactions of others when the person is contemplating future actions. If Jack tells his parents, "I hope you will understand. I am thinking about eloping with Juanita and joining the antigovernment terrorists in El Salvador next week," he can get an indication of what reactions his parents would have to him actually carrying out such plans (Schlenker and Leary, 1982).

Self-handicapping behavior

Self-handicapping refers to a tactic where a person sets up obstacles to successful performance on a task (Jones and Berglas, 1978). Why would someone want to increase the chances of failure? In order to understand such apparently self-defeating behavior, consider a situation where performance is believed to reflect a person's ability, and the person is apprehensive about what the audience will think. By setting up obstacles, the person makes it more difficult for the audience to judge ability from performance. If the person fails, it could be due to the obstacles. If the person succeeds despite the handicap, the audience will assume that he or she has great ability. By self-handicapping, the person renders failure nondiagnostic of abilities and defends the self against negative attributions made by others.

Self-handicapping rewards its users with a double payoff: failure is cushioned and success is enhanced (Goleman, 1984). Consider the case of Stan, who is a premed student about to take a crucial final exam in anatomy. He studies for a few hours and then goes on an all-night drinking bout. If he does poorly on the exam, he can claim it was a hangover and lack of sleep that interfered with his performance. If he performs well despite the adverse circumstances, his reputation will be enhanced. Stan's use of alcohol is a tactic aimed at solving an immediate problem. When this behavior becomes habitual, it is considered pathological.

In an experimental demonstration of self-handicapping, Berglas and Jones (1978) gave subjects two equivalent forms of an intellectual test. Subjects were told that they would be taking one of two drugs (actually placebos) between the two testings to determine whether the drugs affected intellectual performance. Half of the subjects were given solvable problems as part of their first test and the other half were given unsolvable problems. All subjects, however, were told that they had succeeded on the first test.

Subjects were then given a choice between ingesting "Actavil," which supposedly was used to facilitate intellectual performance, or "Pandocrin," which was said to impair performance. Subjects who had performed well with solvable problems should have been confident of future success. Subjects who had worked with unsolvable problems, however, could not be confident of future success and hence might be expected to engage in self-handicapping. The results supported these expectations, but only for male subjects. Significantly more males chose "Pandocrin" if they had worked with unsolvable problems on the first test, while those who had worked on solvable problems tended to choose "Actavil."

Although Berglas and Jones emphasized the role of self-handicapping in protecting a person's self-esteem, there is evidence that it is a defensive self-presentation tactic used as a disclaimer for an external audience. If self-handicapping is directed toward an external audience, then taking a drug that would hinder performance should not be an effective tactic when the experimenter scoring the second test does not know subjects had taken the drug. A test of this prediction showed that self-handicapping behavior occurred when the experimenter administered the "drug" and also scored the second test; but when the choice of drug was carried out privately, self-handicapping did not occur (Kolditz and Arkin, 1982). These results suggest that the subjects were more concerned about public identity than private self-esteem.

Apologies

Love means never having to say you're sorry.
Eric Segal, Love Story

In situations where a person cannot escape responsibility for undesirable behavior, defensive self-presentation can be used to soften or mitigate the negative reactions of others. A person may offer some form of **apology**, which may contain an admission of responsibility and blame, an expression of remorse and guilt, an offer of restitution for any harm done to others, and/or a promise to behave appropriately in the future (Goffman, 1971; Schlenker, 1980). If the apology is effective, it should leave the audience with an impression that the actor's undesirable action was atypical and is unlikely to recur. An apology divides the actor into a "bad me" who is responsible for the undesirable behavior, and a "good me" who realizes the wrongness of it and will not allow it to happen again. Apologies and justifications have in common people's attempts to realign themselves with the values, norms, or rules of society.

The complexity of apologies is associated with the severity of consequences of an action. This relationship was found among college students who were asked to imagine themselves in a situation where they bumped into someone in a shopping mall or crowded school hall (Schlenker and Darby, 1981). The severity of the consequences was varied. Some subjects were to imagine lightly bumping the victim. For others the victim was knocked to the ground but unhurt, while other subjects were to imagine they had hurt the victim's arm. The students were then given a list of apologies and asked to indicate which ones they would use. When no real harm was done, mild and automatic apologies, such as "Pardon me," were chosen. As the severity of the consequences increased, however, subjects chose more complex apologies containing statements of remorse and offers of help.

Apologies have been found to be effective in reducing negative evaluations by people. In one study, subjects read scenarios about two little boys who hid behind bushes in a park and tripped a little girl by pulling a rope taut between them (Schwartz, Kane, Joseph, and Tedeschi, 1978). When one of the boys expressed remorse, he was evaluated more positively and was considered less deserving of punishment than when he did not express remorse.

Apologies can help the actor avoid or limit punishment. The supervising nurses in the Wood and Mitchell (1981) study (see section on "Excuses") considered disciplinary action less appropriate for failure to perform duty if the offending nurse had apologized. There is considerable evidence that judges impose greater sentences on convicted felons if they do not express remorse (Ahleman and Walker, 1980). The nonpenitent harmdoer may be considered incorrigible and may require more severe punishment for rehabilitation.

Researchers have established that people make restitution to a victim even when they are not clearly responsible for the harm done to the victim. Berscheid and Walster (1967) created a situation in which another person's rewards depended on the ability of subjects to answer a quiz. Some subjects failed to provide satisfactory answers. Later, when provided with an opportunity to do so, the subjects compensated the other person and in an amount exactly equal to the missed reward.

This tendency by persons to engage in positive actions following transgressions may be restricted to circumstances where observers cannot be certain that a person intended to produce harm (Tedeschi and Riordan, 1981). From a self-presentational viewpoint, the positive action is interpreted as a tactic to convey the benevolent character of the person and to signal that the negative behavior was inadvertent or accidental. On the other hand, when it is unambiguous to everyone that a person meant to harm a victim, the tactic used by the assaulter may be to derogate the victim and thereby suggest that the harm was deserved (Lerner and Matthews, 1967).

Assertive self-presentation strategies

A gold plated thermos is man's best friend.
Michael Korda

So far in Chapter 3, we have considered the many specific tactics a person can use to present, protect, or restore identities for external audiences. These tactics refer primarily to actions that have immediate or short-term goals. Strategic self-presentations are focused on building a reputation for enduring and important identities that are relevant in many situations. The focus is on the identity to be created. An actor may use many different tactics in front of different audiences over a long period of time. He or she literally engages in **self-construction** and will often forgo expedient tactics and short-term gains in order to build and maintain a desired reputation (Baumeister, 1982). People may be tempted to lie, but the temporary advantage gained may damage their desired reputation as moral, honest, and sincere individuals. The use of intimidation tactics would detract from an identity as an attractive person. In such instances, the temporary advantage is like winning a battle, but the long-term damage to reputation is like losing the war. Self-construction is an investment in the future.

We generally desire to acquire reputations for possessing characteristics that will help us in getting along with and influencing others. Among the identities we seek to manifest are competence, attractiveness, status, prestige, honesty, trustworthiness, and moral integrity.

This actress flaunts the facade of a self-assured "lady," which leaves a lasting impression on the audience. People build reputations for enduring characteristics through assertive self-presentation strategies.

Competence or expertise

Self-promotion, entitlements, and enhancements are common means of advertising our abilities to others. Presenting positive information about the self is certainly not very modest, but perhaps it is a better strategy than not saying anything. One of the realities associated with being a new assistant professor at a college is that if you do not inform others of your merits (teaching, membership on committees, publications, research, directing thesis and dissertation projects, and so on), no one actually knows what you are doing. It will be assumed you are doing little or nothing, and you will be left out when salary increments and promotions are given out.

When others are aware of a person's competence, the person can choose a modest self-presentation. Ackerman and Schlenker (1975) had subjects perform successfully on a test and then provide self-ratings to a prospective interviewer. When the subjects believed the interviewer knew of their superior test performance, they presented themselves modestly; but when the interviewer did not know of their test performance, they presented themselves egotistically. Such aggrandizing self-promotion is more likely when people expect an audience to evaluate them (Schneider, 1969).

There are reality constraints against false egotistical self-promotion. When an audience already knows of a person's failures, it would be foolish to make egotistical claims about his or her relevant ability. A better strategy might be to admit the weakness and at the same time, to make some egotistical claims about other abilities. This kind of compensation process was found among subjects who had failed, but only when they believed the target audience knew about their failure (Baumeister and Jones, 1978). When their poor test results were said to be completely confidential and unknown to anyone, including the experimenter, subjects described themselves more favorably on the attributes relevant to the test performance.

Attractiveness

Most people have a strong desire to be liked by others, not just for some immediate tangible benefits that might be obtained through ingratiation tactics, but rather for themselves. There are many benefits associated with having lovers, devoted relatives, and good friends. They are often supportive of a positive image of the self, are unlikely to create predicaments for the person, provide rewards, and so on.

Blau (1964) has conceived of attraction as a type of power resource, like money, that can be accumulated until its expenditure will serve some useful purpose for the individual. Just as some people will expend great effort and time in seeking material wealth, others will concentrate on gaining social approval. Such socially oriented people manifest adherence to social norms, maintain a friendly demeanor, seek the companionship of others, and engage in nurturant behavior. As indicated in Box 3-3, people may play dumb in order to be liked.

People desiring to be attractive avoid actions that may convey emotional instability, unpredictability, and dishonesty (Tedeschi, Schlenker, and Bonoma, 1971). Inability to predict with any confidence what people will do is frightening, and observers may be motivated to find ways of controlling these people. A norm of consistency exists in social groups. People who do not abide by the norm are cast into deviant identities and are avoided or treated negatively by others.

Candidness and self-disclosure

Some people are secretive, revealing little about themselves; others "wear their hearts on their sleeves," telling people every little detail of their lives. **Self-disclosure** refers to "any information about self which Person A communicates verbally to Person B." (Cozby, 1973, p. 73). The self-discloser is typically selective, leaking information to others in a manner similar to the way press secretaries work to bolster a politician's public image.

An individual uses self-disclosure to build a reputation as a frank and trustworthy person. Two desirable interpersonal effects are often associated with self-disclosures: (1) the listener reciprocates the self-disclosure and (2) the listener likes the person making the original self-disclosure more. In a study of self-disclosure, an accomplice was rehearsed to reveal intimate or nonintimate information about the self to a subject. The interaction was controlled so that the accomplice and the subject took two-minute turns. Analysis of the content of the subject's conversation over a total of eight minutes revealed that when the accomplice's self-disclosures were more intimate, so were those of the subject. Thus, not only the amount but the kind of self-disclosure follows a rule of reciprocity.

Social norms guide the degree and kind of self-disclosure that is appropriate between two people. Too little self-disclosure or a disproportionate amount in relation to the length of association may lead listeners to form a negative impression of the self-discloser. Intimate self-disclosure to a complete stranger has been found to reduce liking for the self-discloser (Cozby, 1972). On the other hand, a refusal to reciprocate self-disclosure may be perceived as a form of rejection or refusal of friendship (Fitzgerald, 1963).

Listeners tend to imitate the form of self-disclosures they receive from others. The imitation of egotism or humility was found in a study where subjects exchanged self-ratings with a confederate (Gergen and Wishnov, 1965). The cover story for the study indicated that this procedure was intended to allow the two strangers to get to know one another. Subjects received self-ratings from their partners as either egotistical, humble, or average. The subjects then prepared self-ratings for their partners. The self-disclosures of subjects matched those of their confederates: they described themselves in the most positive way in the egotistical condition and in the least positive way in the humble condition.

Status and prestige

Most of us can empathize with Rodney Dangerfield when he says, "I don't get no respect." We realize the importance that respect and prestige have in interpersonal relations. Many Americans have a desire for fashionable clothing, expensive automobiles, and art objects. Status also is associated with rules of etiquette, choice of spouse, and church membership (Packard, 1966).

Symbols of status translate into instruments of authority and influence. For example, a field study showed that mode of dress elicited obedience from total strangers (Bickman, 1971). People in telephone booths at Grand Central Station in New York City were approached and asked if they found a dime that was left in the booth a few minutes earlier. When the male experimenter was dressed in working-class clothes and carried a lunch box, a little over a third of the people returned the dime. When the experimenter was dressed in a suit and tie, however, three-quarters of the people returned the dime. Perhaps the proverb that clothes do not make the person is true, but the apparel of the person does affect the reactions of others toward him or her. In *Hamlet,* Shakespeare had Polonius advise his son who was to embark on a journey:

> Costly thy habit as thy purse can buy; But not expressed in fancy; rich not gaudy; For the apparel oft proclaims the man!

This business man presents a sharp and well-defined image as a professional in order to command attention and respect from people with whom he will interact. Apparel often proclaims the status of a person.

Autobiography

Roy F. Baumaster

In high school I was a very straight, all-American boy. I did lots of homework, was on the swim team, and stayed away from drugs and sex and other delights. In college I grew a beard, played in a rock band, and in general became quite a different person. In graduate school I changed again. At that time, I noticed that it was annoying to interact with people who had known me as an undergraduate and downright irritating to meet people who knew me in high school. These people expected me to act the way I had acted when they had known me. This observation led me to realize how much the public self (the impressions others have of you) constrains behavior. My advisor, Edward E. Jones, showed me how to develop that idea into testable scientific hypotheses.

After receiving my Ph.D. at Princeton, I moved into my first academic position at Case Western Reserve University. Recently I have been investigating performance under pressure. How do professional athletes perform during the seventh game of the world series, the super bowl, or the deciding game of the NBA playoffs? What makes someone perform below their ability level? My main research interest in the next couple of years is to learn more about how the public self is related to the inner or private self, including emotions, attitudes, motivations, self-concept and self-esteem.*

* Personal communication, 2 July, 1984

Defensive self-presentation strategies

The assumption that the insane are not responsible for their actions provides the proper and indeed the perfect explanation.

Braginski and Ring, 1969

People who are ill and incompetent, overly anxious and shy, depressed, or out of control may escape responsibility for their actions, plea successfully for help from others, and be excused from obligations. When these reactions occur frequently during a person's life, they become part of a characteristic identity. For example, if a person often claims to be ill in order to avoid obligations, yet no organic problem can be found by a physician, the person may be considered a *hypochondriac.* Identities developed inadvertently from frequent and perhaps habitual use of defensive self-presentations tend to be negative.

Pathological use of excuses

As we indicated earlier, everybody uses excuses as a defensive tactic to extricate themselves from social predicaments. Excuses, such as "I have a headache" or "It was an accident," act as a "social lubricant" to help smooth over what otherwise might turn out to be conflicts between people.

A few people use excuses so frequently to avoid responsibility for their conduct that social relationships are frayed and psychological well-being may be impaired. **Pathological use of excuses** represents a strategic and desperate diversionary attempt by an individual in all situations where he or she might be considered responsible for negative behavior. The pathological use of excuses involves a distortion of facts and a fabrication of pretexts in order to avoid admission of fault or blame for any conduct (Snyder, Stucky, and Higgins, 1983).

The symptoms of a person who is a pathological user of excuses include (1) frequency: the person has an excuse for every action or failure to act; (2) extremity of the excuse: the reason given in the excuse is disproportionate to the action to be excused (e.g., someone who was late for a dental appointment would say, "My uncle just died," instead of saying "I had a flat tire" or "I overslept"; (3) excuses begin to have repercussions: when a particular form of excuse is used continually, the excuse maker may develop a self-schema consistent with the excuse, and a particular identity may be established in the eyes of others. For example, a person who often presents excuses of illness, may soon be perceived by others and by self as an unhealthy or sickly person.

Strategic self-handicapping

When a person occasionally sets up obstacles to make successful achievements more difficult, attributions regarding ability may be made more difficult both by the self and by others. When self-handicapping is used excessively by the person in every situation where judgments of competence, achievement, or ability might be made, we are no longer talking about a tactic but a strategic form of defensive self-presentation. Strategic self-handicapping takes the form of drug and alcohol addiction, test anxiety, and hypochondriasis.

Alcoholism and drug addiction

We associate the states of being "high" or "bombed" with the use of alcohol and drugs. In postpsychoanalytic Western civilization, the tendency is to view addiction to such substances as a form of illness. It is further accepted that sick people cannot be blamed for their condition, and they may be released from normal standards of responsibility, perhaps encouraging self-indulgence and lack of self-control. The loss of inhibitions when "high" may be due in part to the fact that others attribute less responsibility to those "under the influence."

Addictions provide people with an escape from the responsibilities and anxieties of everyday life and are forms of self-handicapping behavior. Although in Western society addicts are viewed as sick people, they are given negative labels.

Jones and Berglas (1978) have suggested that addictions may be a form of self-handicapping. Addictions represent an escape from responsibility and the stresses and anxieties of everyday living. There may even be a kind of sophistication or status in using certain kinds of substances, such as cocaine or scotch. Addictions are generally associated with stigma and negative identities, however. When life becomes unbearable, some people may prefer such negative identities to the problems and obligations facing them.

Test anxiety

Students reporting debilitating levels of test anxiety may be utilizing the symptoms in a self-handicapping manner (Smith, Snyder, and Handelsman, 1982). If these students do not perform well on tests, nothing can be concluded about their ability or knowledge because the anxiety has handicapped them. Students occasionally are heard claiming that they knew the material, but when the test began they could not remember a thing. They may prefer an identity of test anxious to one of dumb or lazy.

The hypothesis that test anxiety may be a defensive strategic form of self-presentation was examined among female college students who were identified as having high levels of text anxiety by a paper-and-pencil scale (Smith et al., 1982). These students were told that they would be taking an intelligence test in two testing sessions. After working on the somewhat difficult test in the first session, some of the students were told that anxiety would interfere with their performance, a second group was told specifically that anxiety would not interfere, and a third group was told nothing.

Before participating in the second testing session, the students were asked to describe their mood states. As can be seen in Table 3-4, the students who had scored high in test anxiety reported high anxiety, unless they had specifically been told anxiety would not interfere with test performance. In other words, as long as test anxiety could be used as an excuse for poor performance, high test-anxious students manifested anxiety. When the anxiety could serve no defensive purpose, these chronically test-anxious students did not report high anxiety.

Symptoms of mental illness

Once I was crazy and my ace in the hole
Was that I knew that I was crazy
So I never lost my self-control
I'd just walk in the middle of the road
I'd sleep in the middle of the bed

TABLE 3–4 Anxiety as a self-handicapping strategy in test taking

SUBJECTS	INSTRUCTIONS REGARDING EFFECTS OF ANXIETY		
	No Effect	Hurts Performance	No Instructions
High test anxious	28.0	29.8	31.6
Low test anxious	22.6	23.8	23.1

Source: "On the self-serving function of an academic wooden leg: Test anxiety is a self-handicapping strategy" by T. W. Smith, C. R. Snyder, and M. W. Handelman, 1982, *Journal of Personality and Social Psychology, 42,* p. 319. Copyright 1982 by American Psychological Association. Adapted by permission of the authors.

Note: Numbers represent self-reported anxiety scores. The higher the score the more anxiety. Statistical comparison showed that the "no effect, high test-anxious" group reported significantly less anxiety than the "no instructions, high test-anxious group".

I'd stop in the middle of a sentence
and the voice in the middle of my head said
Hey, Junior, where you been so long
Don't you know me
I'm your ace in the hole . . . .

Ace in the hole
Lean on me
Don't you know me
I'm your guarantee

Paul Simon, Ace in the Hole (1979)

Some investigators have interpreted the behavior of patients in mental institutions as a form of strategic self-presentation. For instance, it has been suggested that the abnormal behavior patterns of schizophrenics are aimed at gaining attention and sympathy from others (Watson, Daly, Zimmerman, and Anderson, 1979).

Once it is decided, usually by a physician, that a person is "mentally ill," the person takes on an identity as "patient." Patients adjust to the institution and assume the role by "acting sick," conforming to the rules, and settling into a lifestyle that is comfortable compared to the problems facing them in the outside world (Goffman, 1963; Rosenhan, 1973).

In their book *Methods of Madness,* Braginsky, Braginsky, and Ring (1969) report a number of experiments indicating that mental patients actively manipulate the way hospital personnel perceive and react to them. In one study, patients from the open ward of a hospital, which is the most desirable place in the institution, were told they would be given psychiatric interviews that would evaluate their mental health. Half of the patients were led to believe that those who were very sick would be placed in the undesirable back ward. The others were told the interview would determine their readiness for release from the hospital. Patients who thought they might be discharged reported many symptoms of illness, but the patients who feared transfer to the back ward revealed few symptoms. Clearly, these patients used symptoms as strategic self-presentations of identities as "sick" or "well" depending on their goals.

People may use neurotic symptoms to deny responsibility for inappropriate or troublesome behavior. This strategy was exemplified in the case of a woman married to a conservative European man. She was a housewife, and a servant to her husband. She developed an unreasonable fear of bacteria and, like Lady Macbeth, compulsively washed her hands. She could not do dishes because she was afraid of unscrubbed foods, and she could not cook. The husband took on these household chores because his wife was "sick." The identity as "sick" served to extricate the wife from a servile life and casted her husband into her former role as servant.

A study of strategic self-handicapping involving claims of illness was carried out with female college students who scored high on hypochondriasis on the Minnesota Multiphasic Personality Inventory, commonly referred to as the MMPI (Smith, Snyder, and Perkins, 1983). The women who scored high on hypochondriasis were told they would be taking a test of "social intelligence." Some subjects were told that illness would have no effect on performance, but nothing was said to the others.

When asked to fill out a questionnaire about their health, the women who were told nothing about a relationship between illness and performance reported more syptoms of illness than did women who specifically were told there was no effect of illness (see Figure 3-4). The women claimed symptoms only when they were convenient and could serve a defensive purpose for them.

There is no reason to believe the person is consciously aware of the function of such behaviors or that symptoms are a form of deceit. Rather, the use of illness as an excuse probably slowly becomes a way of life, one episode at a time.

Individual differences in self-presentation

Personality I now define . . . as the relatively enduring pattern of recurrent interpersonal situations which characterize the human life.

Harry Stack Sullivan

Everyone uses impression management tactics and strategies. There are important differences among individuals, however, in the kinds of tactics and strategies they habitually use. Certain traits of personality are associated with self-presentational styles. Among such traits are needs for affiliation and approval, self-

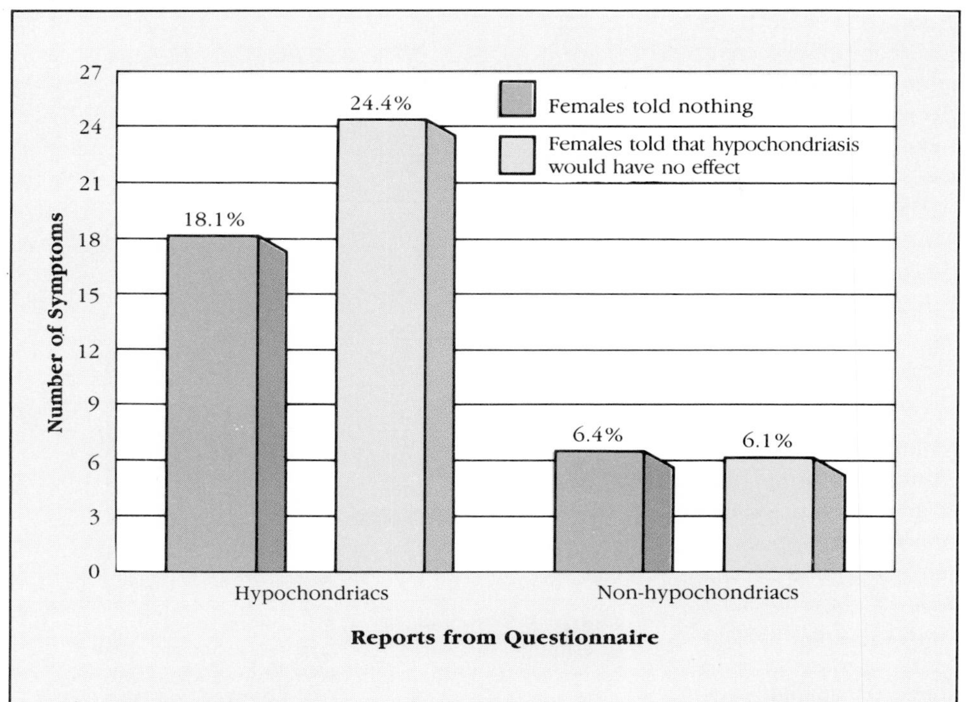

Figure 3-4 Symptoms of hypochondriasis as self-handicapping in female college subjects.

Source: Based on "The self-serving function of hypochondriacal complaints: Physical symptoms as self-handicapping strategies" by T. W. Smith, C. R. Snyder, and S. C. Perkins, 1983, *Journal of Personality and Social Psychology*, *44*, 787–797.

monitoring skills, Machiavellianism, and self-consciousness.

Needs for affiliation and approval

Crowne and Marlowe (1964) have developed a social desirability scale to measure a person's need for social approval. Items on the scale include, "I'm always courteous to people who are disagreeable," "I never hesitate to go out of my way to help someone in trouble," and "I have never intensely disliked anyone." People who agree with a large number of such items are concerned about presenting a socially desirable identity to others and will not admit to ever having the ordinary shortcomings virtually everyone else reveals. These people have a high need for social approval.

People who disagree with most such statements have a low need for social approval. People who obtain high scores on the social desirability scale behave differently in a variety of ways as compared to those who obtain low scores. People with high need for approval show greater conformity to peer pressure and are more responsive to social reinforcers in a verbal conditioning task (Crowne and Marlowe, 1964). Nevertheless, they are described by their peers as nontalkative, as not especially friendly, and as spending much of their time by themselves. Although people with high need for approval respond to praise, they apparently lack the desire or skill needed to assert themselves in obtaining it.

People with a strong need for affiliation, on the other hand, are more active in presenting themselves to others as friendly and likable. People with a strong need to affiliate with others often fill in "lone time" by turning on the television or by calling friends on the telephone. Both those with high need for approval and those with a strong need to affiliate tend to be conformists (McGhee and Teevan, 1967) and to experience low levels of self-esteem (Stang, 1972).

Self-monitoring

Some people are more socially skilled than others. The Self-Monitoring Scale, developed by Mark Snyder

(1974), measures the degree of control people have over their own verbal and nonverbal self-presentations. High self-monitors are keenly aware of how others perceive them and tend to regulate their own conduct to fit smoothly into the expectations and values of others. The characteristics of a high self-monitor are reflected by five basic tendencies: (1) concern for the social appropriateness of behavior; (2) very attentive to behavior of others as cues for own self-presentations; (3) skillful at modifying and controlling own self-presentations; (4) able to use self-presentational skills in a wide variety of situations; (5) has large repertoire of self-presentational behaviors (Gabrenya and Arkin, 1980).

At the other end of the continuum are low self-monitors who are much less concerned about the appropriateness of their behavior and the reactions of external audiences. Low self-monitors also appear to lack self-presentational skills. Their behavior is often a direct and undisguised expression of their internal feelings, and not specifically adapted to the situation (Snyder, 1979).

There is some evidence to suggest that high self-monitors more frequently engage in and are more effective in using assertive self-presentations than are low self-monitors. High self-monitors have been found to portray both introverted and extroverted identities skillfully and to practice deception in interviews (Krause, Geller, and Olson, 1976; Lippa, 1976, 1978). As compared to low self-monitors, those scoring high on the Self-Monitoring Scale more actively initiated conversations during an unstructured interaction (Ickes and Barnes, 1977). In addition, high self-monitors were more likely to reciprocate intimate self-disclosures.

If low self-monitors act on the basis of inner states, they should exhibit a greater correspondence between attitudes and behavior than high self-monitors, whose actions are more situationally determined. Confirmation of this hypothesis was obtained in a simulation of a jury trial. Subjects, whose attitudes toward affirmative action had been previously measured, were presented with a case involving purported sex discrimination. A female applicant for a faculty position was suing the university because it hired a male for the position. As can be seen in Figure 3-5, there was a positive correlation between attitudes toward affirmative action and degree of support for the

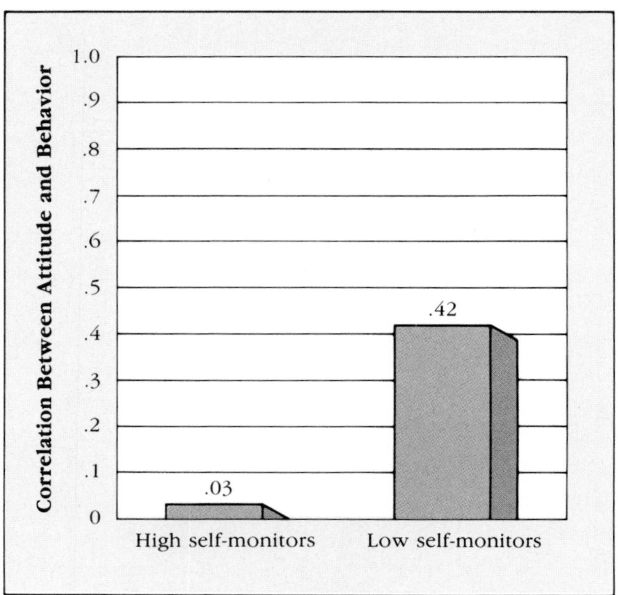

Figure 3-5 Self-monitoring involving a sex discrimination case. *Note:* Low self-monitors show a higher correspondence between attitudes and behavior.

Source: Based on "When actions reflect attitudes: The politics of impression management" by M. Snyder and W. B. Swann, Jr., 1976, *Journal of Personality and Social Psychology*, *34*, 1034-1042.

litigant among low self-monitors, but there was no relationship between attitudes and behavior of high self-monitors (Snyder and Swann, 1976). Like Howard Cosell, low self- monitors "tell it like it is."

In the future: a revised self-monitoring scale?

The concept of self-monitoring has provided a needed focus on individual differences in self-presentation. There have been some telling criticisms of the Self-Monitoring Scale, however, which contains twenty-five statements, such as, "At parties and social gatherings, I do not attempt to do or say things that others will like" and "When I am uncertain how to act in social situations, I look at the behavior of others for clues." A respondent marks true or false in response to each of the statements and a score is calculated. A basic assumption is that these items measure only self-monitoring and not some other personality characteristics that also might affect self-presentations.

Psychologists can examine the dimensionality of tests with a statistical test called "factor analysis." Analysis of the Self-Monitoring Scale has shown at least three dimensions of behavior: (1) extraversion, (2) other-directedness, and (3) acting ability (Briggs, Cheek, and Buss, 1980). Furthermore, the relationships among these dimensions were not consistent. For example, a person who scored high on extraversion did not necessarily score high in other-directedness. Thus, an extraverted person might be considered a high self-monitor in one study. A person high in other-directedness and low in extraversion might be considered a high self-monitor in another study.

Other research has confirmed the multidimensionality of the Self-Monitoring Scale (Gabrenya and Arkin, 1980) and has failed to support predictions of self-monitoring theory when subjects were selected based on scores obtained from the scale (Tobey and Tunnel, 1981). One group of researchers concluded: "The [self-monitoring] scale does not measure what it purports to measure. The construct cannot begin to fulfill its considerable potential until it is more adequately operationalized" (Wolfe, Lennox and Hudiburg, 1983, p. 1074). It is likely, given the complexity and inconsistency of the present scale, that a revised version will be developed in the near future.

Machiavellianism

The name of Machiavelli is associated with a cynical and manipulative view of life. In *The Prince,* the only things that matter are power and the gain of whatever objectives the prince desires. The prince discards morality as a weakness that only interferes with effective action. He practices truth and honesty only when it is useful to do so.

Christie and Geis (1968, 1970) developed a paper-and-pencil test consisting of items that more or less reflect Machiavelli's views. For example, "Anyone who completely trusts anyone is asking for trouble"; "Never tell anyone the real reason you did something unless it is useful to do so."

People who agree with items such as these are considered high "MACHs." Characteristics of high MACHs include a disinterest in obeying the moral rules of society, a desire and ability to manipulate other people, and a lack of emotion in interpersonal relationships (Alexander and Rudd, 1981). The high MACH may be characterized as an amoral manipulator who unscrupulously uses impression management tactics with little concern of their implications for long-term (strategic) identities.

Research using the MACH scale has shown that people who score high on this test receive low scores on tests of trustworthiness and altruism. High Machia-

Biography

C. R. (Rick) Snyder

Rick Snyder played organized baseball in his youth. However, Snyder realized while playing for Southern Methodist University that his pitching arm was not going to take him to the major leagues. So he began to study for a career in social psychology. Snyder's interest in social psychology was stimulated by the fact that he attended 10 schools in 12 years prior to college. He was always the new kid in class and was very much aware of how people behave in groups. In 1971 Rick received his Ph.D. in clinical psychology from Vanderbilt.

As director of the graduate training program in clinical psychology at the University of Kansas, where he has been since 1972, Snyder has studied coping strategies of psychiatric patients. He noticed how people in general respond to negative feedback. Typically, some form of excuse is offered to neutralize criticism and unfavorable evaluations. Since 1981 he has been developing a theoretical model of how excuse-making operates and has applied the model to laboratory research and to psychotherapy. These experiences are described in a book, *Excuses: Masquerades in Search of Grace,* coauthored by Snyder, Higgins, and Stucky.

Snyder indicates that in the future he intends to examine who uses what kinds of excuses in which situations. He wants to study the factors that make excuses effective for the person and acceptable to audiences. In general, Snyder will focus on excuse-making as a normal coping strategy.*

* Personal Communication, 1984.

vellians tend to come from large urban areas and frequently can be found among white male college students. There is a significant relationship between a father's score on the scale and his children's scores (Kraut and Price, 1976). There is no relationship, however, between intelligence, educational level, or political affiliation and scores on the Machiavellianism Scale. It is interesting to note that high scorers on the Machiavellianism Scale tend to choose professions in which they counsel, interview, supervise, and control other people, such as psychiatry, clinical psychology, and business administration (Kraut and Price, 1976).

We are less interested in what Machiavellians think than we are in how they act, although it seems clear that the two are related. Machiavellians do not hesitate to use devious tactics to gain their objectives. They lie, cheat, or steal whenever they believe such behavior serves their best interests (Bogart, Geis, Levy, and Zimbardo, 1970; Exline, Thibaut, Hickey, and Gumbert, 1970; Geis, Christie and Nelson, 1970; Harrell and Hartnagel, 1976). They stay within the bounds of appropriate conduct, however, when they believe little can be gained by immoral or unethical means or when they expect such tactics would be detected.

Some fifth graders demonstrated Machiavellian behavior (Braginsky, 1970). The children were asked to taste a cracker that had been soaked in quinine and had a bitter taste. Under the pretense that the experimenter was testing the crackers as a new product, the children were told they would be paid five cents for each cracker they could get another child to eat. Machiavellians manipulated other children to eat twice as many crackers as did non-Machiavellians. Machiavellian children were effective in using lies to persuade other children to eat the crackers. The skill of these children is revealed by the fact that onlookers evaluated the Machiavellians as more honest, innocent, and effective than they did the non-Machiavellian children.

Schlenker (1980) has depicted the characteristics of a Machiavellian person: "an ability to initiate and control the structure of interaction; ability to resist social influence when it is to their advantage; orientation toward a detached cognitive assessment of the situation; and willingness to employ 'unethical' methods to achieve goals" (p. 82). These attributes lead Machiavellians to be more successful in college and in professional advancement (Christie and Geis, 1968). Their cynical attitudes toward others make them less satisfied, more anxious, more suspicious about superiors, and more anxious than others with comparable job status (Gemmill and Heisler, 1972). Thus, they pay an inner price for their outward success.

Public self-consciousness

The Self-Consciousness Scale, discussed in Chapter 2, provides a measure of the degree to which people are aware of themselves as social objects (Fenigstein, Scheier, and Buss, 1975). People who are high in public self-consciousness are aware of their appearance in social situations and are concerned about making a good impression on others. People low in public self-consciousness tend to be unconcerned about aspects of the self that generally are open to public scrutiny.

The validity of the Self-Consciousness Scale was supported by a study examining how people react to being ignored by others (Fenigstein, 1979). A female student waited in a room with two other people who were actually accomplices of the experimenter. The two accomplices spoke only to each other and ignored the subject. In another condition, the accomplices were friendly and responsive to the subject. Subjects were informed that in the main experiment they would be in a three-person group and could choose to remain with the two people they had already met, or they chould choose a new pair of students. As you can see in Figure 3-6, about 50 percent of the subjects who were low in public self-consciousness chose to affiliate with a new pair when they had been ignored. Eighty-five percent of subjects high in public self-consciousness sought new affiliations when they had been ignored. When the accomplices had not ignored the subjects, the subjects predominantly chose to keep the same partners, whether the subjects were high or low in public self-consciousness.

Other researchers found a positive correlation between public self-consciousness and scores on a scale measuring subjects' interest in clothing. The relationship between public self-consciousness and interest in clothing was stronger among men than among women. One explanation for this sex difference is that almost all women are interested in fashion and clothing, while only men who are concerned about self-presentation maintain such an interest. In still another study subjects were asked to estimate from pho-

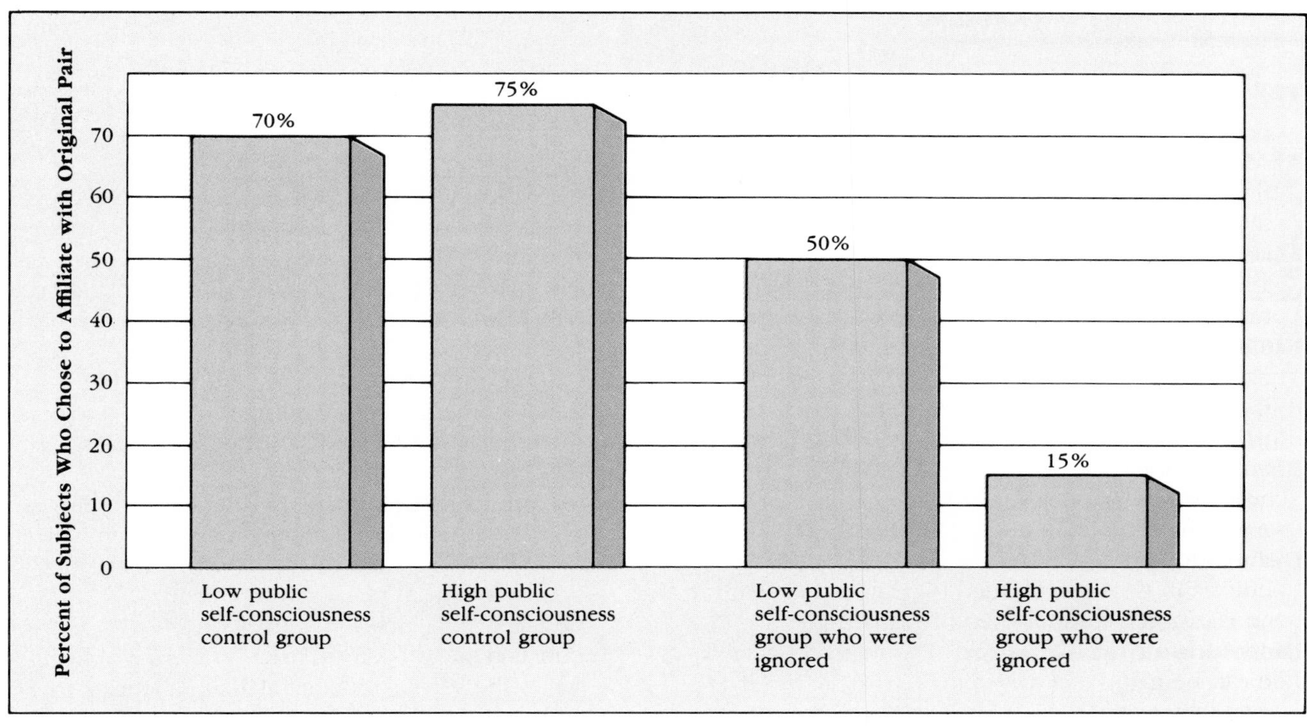

Figure 3-6 Study of public self-consciousness.

Source: Based on "Self-consciousness, self-attention, and social interaction" by A. Fenignstein, 1979, *Journal of Personality and Social Psychology*, *37*, 75-86.

tographs how much makeup each of forty-two women was wearing. These estimates were positively correlated with the public self-consciousness scores of the women in the photographs (Miller and Cox, 1982), and indicated that the higher the public self-consciousness exhibited by the women, the more makeup they wore.

Summary

The actions of people convey identities to audiences. Self-presentations are attempts to convey particular kinds of identities to specific audiences. Self-presentations can be assertive or defensive and tactical or strategic.

Assertive tactics of self-presentation include ingratiation, intimidation, supplication, self-promotion, and exemplification. These tactics are attempts to arouse some emotion from observers so that some short-term goals of the tactician can be achieved.

Defensive tactics of self-presentation include excuses, justifications, disclaimers, self-handicapping, and apologies. These tactics have the goal of protecting the reputation of a person and of restoring his or her face when predicaments occur.

Through their actions, people develop rather stable reputations in the eyes of others. These reputations may be constructed assertively or occur inadvertently through a person's habitual use of defensive self- presentational tactics. Defensive self-presentations may be used by people with alcohol and drug addiction and by those with symptoms of mental illness. Assertive actions may lead to styles of behavior perceived as personality traits, including needs for approval and affiliation, self- monitoring, Machiavellianism, and self-consciousness.

Glossary

Accounts Explanations offered by people for behavior following predicaments.

Apology An admission of responsibility for a negative outcome that has the goal of softening the reactions of others.

Assertive self-presentation A classification of behaviors that are intended to establish a desired identity.

BIRGing People "bask in reflected glory" by associating with other admirable people or events for the purpose of gaining a positive identity for themselves.

Blasting A person makes negative evaluations of rival groups or persons with the objective of making the self look better by comparison.

Defensive self-presentation A classification of behaviors that are intended to protect, maintain, or reestablish a threatened or spoiled identity.

Definition of the situation The interpretation of the meaning of a situation for a particular individual; as opposed to an objective description of a situation.

Disclaimers Explanations offered by people before they perform a behavior that might create a predicament; the explanations have the intention of avoiding or defusing the predicament.

Dramaturgical perspective Term referring to sociological theories that compare everyday life to theatrical performances.

Embarrassment An emotion that results from an actual or threatened disruption of an identity.

Enhancements Verbal statements exaggerating the value of positive outcomes.

Entitlements Verbal statements in which people claim credit for positive outcomes.

Excuses Accounts an actor uses in trying to convince an audience that he or she was not responsible for what happened.

Exemplification Behavior a person uses to project a moral and worthy identity in order to elicit similar behavior from others.

Facework Remedial actions undertaken to mend a spoiled identity.

Ingratiation An actor behaves in a particular way to induce liking by others for the purpose of gaining some advantages.

Ingratiator's dilemma As the need for ingratiation increases, the probability that the target person will perceive the actor as engaging in it increases.

Justifications Accounts in which an actor accepts responsibility for events; often by offering reasons that justify his or her actions.

Norm of reciprocity A universal rule obligating people to return favor for favor or harm for harm.

Predicaments An experience where people believe others ascribe unwanted identities to them because of something they did or allegedly did.

Principle of association People may establish a positive identity by claiming an association with desirable events and people and by dissociating themselves from negative events and people.

Secondary gain A term used by therapists to refer to the secondary benefits that patients gain from pathological symptoms.

Self-construction The attempted construction of a reputation for an enduring identity that is relevant in many social situations.

Self-disclosure Any information about the self that an actor communicates to another person.

Self-handicapping The setting up of obstacles to a successful performance so that subsequent failure will be excused and success will be enhanced.

Self-presentation Behaviors exhibited by people that allow others to ascribe identities to them: also called **impression management.**

Self-promotion Actions by which an actor intends to convey an identity as a competent and intelligent person, usually with some specific objective in mind, such as gaining employment or admission to college.

Strategic self-presentation Actions that affect the long- term identities of an individual.

Supplication Actions by which a person projects an identity as weak and dependent with the goal of eliciting nurturant or protective behavior from other people.

Tactical self-presentation Actions an individual takes to project, maintain or defend identities relevant to particular situations.

Working consensus An unwritten rule governing social interactions, specifying that identities projected by each person will be accepted by others.

Recommended Readings

Schlenker, Barry, R. (1980). *Impression management.* Monterey, CA: Brooks/Cole.
A well-written and comprehensive treatment of the entire self-presentation literature; appropriate for advanced undergraduates.

Snyder, C. R., Higgins, R. L., & Stucky, R. J. (1983). *Excuses: Masquerades in search of grace.* New York: John Wiley.
An important recent attempt to apply concepts, such as excuses and self-handicapping, to phenomena of concern to clinical psychologists.

Tedeschi, James T. (Ed.) (1981). *Impression management theory and social psychological research.* New York: Academic Press.
Aimed at a professional audience, this edited book contains original contributions from the leading impression management theorists.

Beware, as long as you live, of judging people by their appearance.

Jean de la Fontaine

4
Perceiving persons and explaining behavior

Appearances can be deceiving

Winston Smith worked at the Ministry of Truth. Each day at 11:00 A.M., the employees of the Ministry gathered around a giant telescreen for the "Two Minutes Hate." The employees shouted and screamed to denounce the voice of the "Enemy of the People." One day, Winston noticed a dark-haired, athletic, and attractive young woman in the audience. She wore a red sash about her waist, indicating she was a member of the Junior Antisex League. Winston disliked young women. They acted as amateur spies, eager to report anyone to the Thought Police. He remembered seeing her and the sidelong glance she had given him in the corridor. It had filled him with terror.

The next day in the dining room, Winston saw her seated at the next table. She was watching him! When he looked at her, she turned away. Why was she following him? Two days in a row! Later that day, after Winston left an antique shop, once again he saw the dark-haired girl. She looked at him directly in the face and walked on as though she had not seen him. There could be no doubt. She was spying on him. For a couple of minutes, Winston considered running after her and bashing in her skull with a cobblestone. But he did nothing.

The next day the two passed in the corridor. All of a sudden she stumbled and fell. She cried out in pain, and Winston helped his enemy up. She pressed something into his hand—a piece of paper. Was it a threat? An order to commit suicide? He delayed looking at it until he got back to his desk where he could conceal the act from the ever-present telescreens. When he gathered up his nerve he read the note. It said, "I love you."

What is a person?

The above episode from George Orwell's novel *1984* illustrates the problem we have of determining what other people are like. Surface appearances often do not reveal inner realities. We can attain some perspective on the problems of person perception by considering the ways in which people differ from things (Heider, 1958). First, people are believed to have a rich interior life consisting of beliefs, values, wishes, intentions, plans, and emotions. A sure tip-off that you are dealing with an android, a complex robot with an outward appearance of a real person, comes when you see that it is incapable of experiencing love, anger, or other human emotions. Moreover, androids are incapable of making their own plans. They are preprogrammed to speak. Although we might ask people what they are feeling or planning, we would ask an android how it was programmed.

This brings us to a second difference between humans and things. The behavior of people is perceived at times to be spontaneous and expressive of their desires. We perceive people to be agents or the origins of their own behavior. When things move or affect other things, we seek explanations in the environment for what happened. Things are the pawns of natural forces, and people are the origins of their own behavior (deCharms, 1968). If an android strikes at us, we blame the human who programmed it. When people strike at us, we hold them responsible.

A third difference is that people can plan to deceive, manipulate, and otherwise influence how others perceive them. In *1984* Julia later told Winston that she went along with the public requirements of the party, like wearing the sash, but she kept her private opinions to herself. Androids may be programmed to carry out such deceptive acts, but they cannot develop such strategies spontaneously. The origin of the manipulative process is human, and the android is just a tool.

Our goal of person perception is to gather information that allows us to predict and possibly control the behavior of other people (Heider, 1958). The historical continuity of behavior provides the basis for separate identities of persons. We hold people accountable for what they do and assign credit for positive behavior and blame for negative behavior. By rewarding desired actions and punishing undesired actions, we can control and change the behavior of others. Thus, because we desire some control over events, we act as moral accountants, judging over time how many debits and credits to give to others for their behavior. One way to define a **person** is as a locus of responsibility (Strawson, 1959).

People are not held responsible for everything they do. For example, a person could hardly be blamed for

Biography

Fritz Heider

Fritz Heider, who is widely recognized as the father of attribution theory, was born in Vienna, Austria in 1896. He received his doctorate in 1920 from the University of Graz in Austria. From the beginning of his career, he was interested in the problems of person perception. Before he published his famous book *The Psychology of Interpersonal Relations* in 1958, few psychologists paid any attention to the average person's common sense perceptions of other people.

Heider had an early interest in drawing and painting, and he believed it was necessary to approach the study of perception as an artist would. The artist paints the world as it appears, not necessarily as it really is. In painting an apple, the artist must create an illusion of three dimensions on a two-dimensional surface; he or she must create the illusion of light and shadow and provide perspective or else the apple would not look real. In the same way, persons form impressions of each other, not as they really are, but as they appear to be. Each observer fills in the picture to give it meaning. In a way, perceiving a person is to draw a picture in our mind.

Heider recalls that his experiences as a graduate student at the University of Graz underscored the importance of interpersonal perception for him. In 1918–19 immediately following World War I, conditions of privation existed in Austria. Electricity and heat were either absent or scarse. He wrote his thesis by an oil lamp, often wearing thick gloves because the room was unheated for much of the day. Under these conditions, people were tense and easily angered. In his efforts to mediate disputes between friends, Heider discovered great differences in their accounts of events. Tracking how they came to have such different ideas of the same events led Heider to the study of the attributions of cause and responsibility. He continued his work through most of his career at the University of Kansas, where at the age of seventy he retired in 1966 as a distinguished professor of psychology.

doing something at the point of a gun. Rewards and punishments are not effective in changing this kind of coerced or unfree behavior. It would serve little purpose to reward or punish an android because it is not free to choose any course of action other than the programmed sequences built into its tape. People typically are held responsible only for behavior that is perceived as freely undertaken.

Causes of and reasons for behavior

A cause-effect relationship is said to exist when one event, X, is always associated with another event, Y, such that when X occurs Y also occurs. If X occurs earlier in time, it is referred to as the *cause* and Y is the *effect.* If an air puff were directed toward your eye, you would blink. This is an uncontrollable reflex. The air puff is the cause, and the blink is the effect.

Our everyday explanations of the actions of people do not refer to physical causes, but instead refer to the intentions, motives, and goals of people or the social rules they follow. These personal or social factors are said to be the **reasons** for the behavior (Buss, 1978).

Behavior that is caused tells us little about individual people. Nearly everyone reacts in the same way to putting their hand on a hot stove or to a stomach virus. We are particularly attentive to information that tells us how one person is different from another. Behavior exhibited without strong environmental causes tells us the most about another person.

Making stable attributions

Heider (1958) portrayed the ordinary person as rather lazy in searching for the reasons for actions. Once a sufficient reason is found, a conclusion is reached without looking for further reasons (Kelley, 1973). We direct our everyday perceptions of people toward attaining stable and meaningful impressions of others. Once we achieve such stable attributions, we no longer need further information. On the other hand, we feel uncomfortable when confronted with strangers in unfamiliar situations and are uneasy around people who appear to be unstable and unpredictable.

Theories of attribution

In their attempts to explain behavior, ordinary people act as naive psychologists. An old story relates how one psychologist passed another in the hallway and said, hi. The second spent the rest of the day wondering what was really meant by that. Psychologists may have a tendency to overinterpret behavior (Wrong, 1961). Actually, most behavior does not require explanation. It is fairly obvious why people eat dinner or go to the movies. What are the conditions that lead an observer to seek an explanation for behavior? In trying to reconstruct the way the naive psychologist explains behavior, social psychologists have proposed a number of principles that appear to be used in attributing actions either to the environment or to the person.

Attributions based on a single observation

It is important to remember that attribution theories essentially are concerned with how individuals process information about other people. The most fundamental issue is the observer's decision whether to explain behavior in terms of situational factors or in terms of something about the actor. The observer witnesses an event and processes the information to seek an explanation for it. According to Jones and Davis (1965), the observer processes information backward from effects to dispositions.

The backward processing of information is illustrated in Figure 4-1. Suppose a man on a picnic reaches into a bag, pulls out an apple, inspects it, and then throws it toward the woods. Several effects may occur: a child is hit in the leg, the apple breaks into pieces, the child cries, and other picnickers yell at the man. As observers, what conclusions can we reach about this man?

Most people would evaluate the effects, shown at the right side of Figure 4-1, negatively. Should we blame the man and conclude that he just hates kids? Before making such judgments, observers first consider whether the actor had the ability to produce the observed effects intentionally. It is not easy to hit a moving target at a distance with an apple; perhaps the

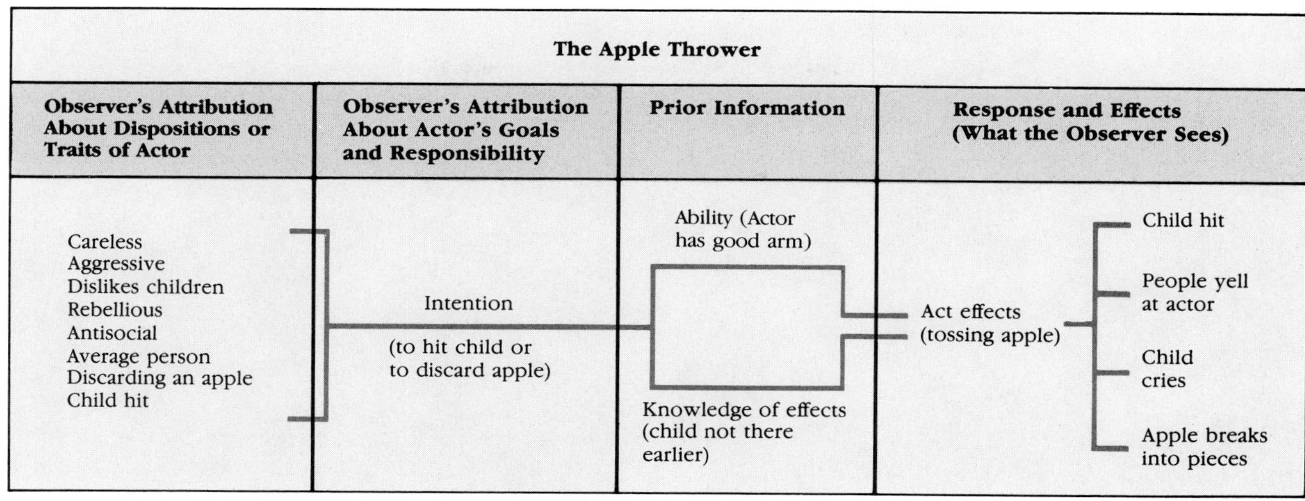

Figure 4-1 The process of making correspondent inferences by observer.

Source: Based on "From acts to dispositions: The attribution process in person perception" by E. E. Jones and K. E. Davis, 1965, in *Advances in experimental social psychology* (Vol. 2), L. Berkowitz (Ed.), New York: Academic Press.

man was observed playing softball earlier and displayed a strong and accurate throwing arm.

In addition to ability, the man must have had prior knowledge about the effects of his action, if we are to hold him responsible for it. If the child had just emerged from a cave or if the man did not look up when he threw the apple, we might conclude that he had no prior knowledge of the effects his action would have. If the man had both the ability and foreknowledge of effects, however, observers would conclude that he intentionally hit the child, and they would make inferences regarding negative traits, such as aggressiveness and hostility. Thus, the information-processing sequence is from observation of effects and acts to inferences about abilities, knowledge, intentions, and traits of the actors. In other words, the attribution process is from specific acts to inner dispositions.

Jones and Davis (1965) call this theory **correspondent inferences**. When someone's true personality is reflected in behavior, a high correspondence exists between acts and dispositions. If we perceive the apple thrower as intentionaly hitting a child, a correspondent inference would be that he is an aggressive and hostile person. Factors that lead observers to attribute effects to the person and to discount the enviornment contribute to correspondent inferences. We consider two such factors: social desirability and noncommon effects.

Social desirability

Most people act in a manner calculated to gain approval and rewards from others. High degree of conformity in actions gives us little information for making inferences that distinguish one person from another. If people act in unusual, risky, and costly ways when they appear to be free to act otherwise, observers attribute the actions to inner reasons rather than to environmental causes. Why should actors deliberately invite the disapproval of others? Perhaps this is why Confucious said we can know more about a person from knowing his or her enemies than from knowing his or her friends.

There are many occasions when a person must act to fulfill the expectations of others. A **role** consists of expectations by others about how a person is supposed to act. The traditional housewife role is bound

Can you tell how patriotic each member of this crowd is? Do their roles consist of actions that others expect from them? Are they trying to gain approval from each other and their teachers? Conformity to expected and in-role behavior yields little information about people.

up with expectations regarding chores around the house, including cooking, washing clothes, cleaning house, and catering to the needs of everyone else in the family (some equate this role with being a slave). When a person acts in role, approval and rewards usually are provided; however, when a person acts **out of role** by not conforming to expectations, others are likely to disapprove and punish the behavior. Thus, out-of-role behavior is low in social desirability because it is contrary to the expectations of others. Most people conform to role expectations, therefore their behavior reveals more about the situation than about their personal qualities. On the other hand, out-of-role behavior leads to highly correspondent inferences; that is, it suggests a personal rather than situational explanation for the behavior exhibited.

The informativeness of out-of-role behavior was demonstrated with subjects who were asked to evaluate a person interviewing for a job (Jones, Davis, and Gergen, 1961). Half the subjects first heard the job described by the interviewer as that of an astronaut whose most desirable characteristics were said to be inner directedness, self-reliance, and ability to work alone (these characteristics were necessary because early in the space programs astronauts flew alone). The other half heard the job described as that of a submariner whose ideal qualities were said to be other directedness, sociability, friendliness, and cooperation. Subjects then heard an applicant describing himself in a manner either consistent or inconsistent with the ideal qualities for the particular job. The results showed that subjects believed the applicants who presented themselves out of role (inner-directed submariner or other-directed astronaut) were most candid and possessed more of the traits they described themselves as having. Subjects were less confident they knew much about the job applicants who affiliated themselves with the job descriptions (i.e., presented themselves in role). These results are shown in Figure 4-2.

Kelley's (1973) **augmentation principle** states that the more effort, pain, embarrassment, or costs associated with performing an act, the more diagnostic it is of the person's dispositions. The willingness to perform an action in spite of risks or costs, tells us much about the actor's true nature. The "sincerity" of the out-of-role job applicants may be presumed to reduce their chances to obtain the jobs of submariner or astronaut, and this anticipated cost led subjects to a more confident impression of what the out-of-role applicants were really like than was the case for in-role applicants. Why else should a person act out of role in this kind of situation other than because of great honesty?

Kelley's **discounting principle** refers to the fact that when other plausible reasons for behavior are present, the belief in any single explanation is lessened (or discounted). In-role interviewees, who described themselves in a manner consistent with the attributes desirable for a successful applicant, could be perceived as acting expediently, thus the inference that they really were inner or outer directed was discounted.

Consider how you would react to flattery? You

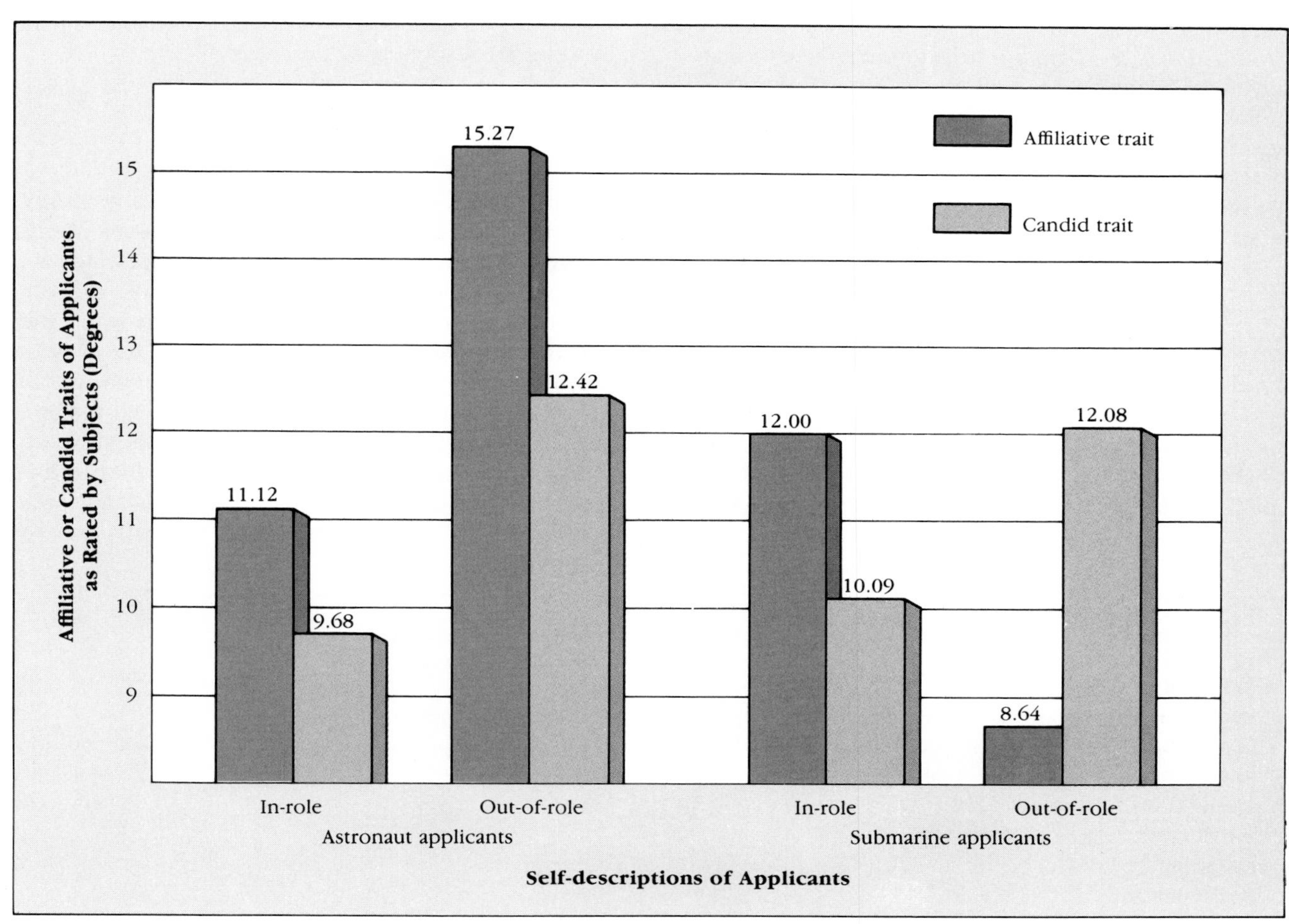

Figure 4-2 Ratings by subjects of their perceptions of the affiliativeness and candor of the job applicant. *Note:* The degrees of traits were rated on 15 pt. scales. In-role refers to self-descriptions coinciding with interviewer's descriptions and out-of-role refers to self-descriptions not coinciding with interviewer's descriptions.

might think it represents a sincere positive evaluation of your character. You might be less confident of the flatterer's sincerity, however, if the latter had something to gain. This kind of discounting was demonstrated in a laboratory study when a flatterer had something to gain from the target person (Dickoff, cited in Jones, 1964).

The degree of discounting is related to the importance or value of the alternative reasons and not just to the number of alternatives (Hull and West, 1982; Wells and Ronis, 1982). A student may be considered very committed to her studies if she gives up a relaxed summer at home and the chance to earn some money in order to stay on campus. She may not be considered so studious, however, if we also know that her lover had to stay on campus that summer. Even though staying on campus may both provide her the opportunity to do library research for her honors thesis due next year and permit her to be with two close friends also staying on campus, the fact that her lover is staying on campus is sufficiently important to discount her other reasons for staying.

Noncommon effects

Before choosing a particular course of action, a person usually considers a number of alternatives. The alternatives may lead to several common effects, but they also may lead to **noncommon effects**. Suppose Mary has been asked to go to a beach party by both Bruce and Tony. In trying to understand what her choice of Tony tells us about her personality, we need to consider the possible outcomes of dates with either young man. The effects of Mary making each choice are depicted in Table 4-1. Bruce and Tony are good looking, drive expensive cars, dress well, and have an excellent sense of humor. These common effects tells us nothing about why Mary chose one over the other. If, however, Tony is a religious Catholic while Bruce is Jewish, this noncommon effect could lead to a correspondent inference that Mary chose Tony because they are of the same religion. Catholicism could be an important value for her. If this were the only difference between the two men, we would be more confident of our attribution than if they differed in many ways. In general, fewer noncommon effects lead to more correspondent inferences.

Attributions based on multiple observations

Harold Kelley (1967, 1973) has proposed a model of the attribution process in which the observer uses a **covariation principle** in attributing cause for an actor's behavior. Over time and situations, the observer discovers what factors are present when the effects of interest occur, and what factors are present when they do not occur. If a factor is present in both instances, it cannot be a cause of the effect; but if a factor is present when the effect occurs and not when it does not occur, then the observer will infer that it is the cause. Two factors that co-vary over time and space

TABLE 4–1 Analysis of Mary's choice of a beach partner and what it reveals about her

PARTNER	COMMON EFFECTS	NONCOMMON EFFECTS
Bruce	Good looking Drives expensive car Dresses well Good sense of humor	Jewish
Tony	Good looking Drives expensive car Dresses well Good sense of humor	Catholic

allow for an attribution of cause to the one occurring first. It is as if the observer continually carries out social experiments to arrive at attributions of causes of behavioral effects.

Whereas the theory of correspondent inference is most conerned about attributions to dispositional factors in the actor, Kelley's theory seeks to answer the question about whether the observer will attribute the cause of behavior to the person or to the environment. Whichever attribution is made, we could ask further questions but Kelley's theory does not consider more than the initial step.

Distinctiveness, consistency, and consensus

Kelley applied three basic criteria to the attributions made by the naive scientist: distinctiveness, consistency, and consensus. **Distinctiveness** refers to whether a behavior occurs in response to a particular event and not others. If Marlene seldom watches television, but always watches "Hill Street Blues," her behavior has high distinctiveness. Darlene, on the other hand, is a television junkie. She watches many programs, therefore watching "Hill Street Blues" has low distinctiveness for her. The more distinctive a behavior, the more likely it is caused by specific environmental circumstances. We would attribute Marlene's behavior to the quality of the television program, but would attribute Darlene's behavior to a lack of discrimination in feeding her addiction to viewing television.

Consistency refers to whether a reaction occurs repeatedly over time and in different situations. Marlene always watches "Hill Street Blues," whether she is at school, home during vacations, or at her boyfriend's apartment. The high consistency of her reaction suggests that it is determined by some characteristic associated with the program being watched. Darlene watches a lot of television wherever she is and whatever the program. Darlene possesses some stable characteristic that leads to such consistent behavior.

Consensus refers to the behavior of other people. To what extent do other people display similar reactions in the same situation? The greater the perceived consensus, the more the observer will attribute a behavior to the environment. Marlene's parents, friends, and acquaintances all enjoy "Hill Street Blues"; the critics praise it, and the show won numerous Emmy awards. This consensus of reaction suggests that Marlene's positive reaction is attributable to the program and not to something about her. On the other hand, this consensus for a positive reaction serves as a lack of consensus for Darlene's lukewarm reaction to the program. Low consensus would suggest that Darlene's reactions are attributable to something about her and not the program. If Marlene watches and enjoyed "Hill Street Blues" part of the time, but sometimes does not like it, we cannot say anything confidently about her reaction to the program.

Table 4–2 Covariance principles and attribution to entities or persons.

PRINCIPLE	ATTRIBUTION
Distinctiveness	
High	Entity
Low	Person
Consistency	
High	Either entity or person
Low	Neither makes sense
Consensus	
High	Entity
Low	Person

In summary, as can be seen in Table 4-2, we can attribute a person's behavior to an entity when the behavior is distinctive, consistent, and has high consensus. Marlene was discriminating in her choice of programs, her reactions were consistent over time and situations, and ratings indicate consensus for a positive reaction to "Hill Street Blues." An attribution to the person will be made when there is low distinctiveness, high consistency, and low consensus. Darlene was indiscriminate in liking all television programs and reacted positively to all of them over time and situations. Judging from the ratings, few of the programs Darlene viewed received strong positive reactions from other people. These principles have been applied to the way juries reach verdicts of guilt and innocence, as is described in Box 4-1.

In general, when observers are provided with written information about the distinctiveness, consistency,

Box 4-1

Multiple observations and jury decisions

It generally is believed that knowledge of a defendant's previous criminal record will make a jury more likely to convict him or her. Current legal practice is for judges to instruct jurors to disregard a defendant's past criminal record; that is, jurors are to ignore consistency information in reaching a judgment of whether the defendant was the cause of a criminal action. Dana Anderson (1981) extended the reasoning in this matter by conceptualizing decisions of juries as essentially an attributional task that should follow the principles of Kelley's (1967,1973) model.

To examine this formulation of jury decision making, Anderson had subjects read a summary of a case involving a defendant who, it was alleged, had punched a victim and knocked him to the ground. High and low distinctiveness, consistency, and consensus information were manipulated, creating eight case summaries. Each of eight groups of subjects read only one summary. For example, a summary might contain high distinctiveness, low consistency, and high consensus information. In this case, the defendant was described as fighting only with the plaintiff, but no one else (high distinctiveness); the fighting occurred only once (low consistency); and other people also fought with the plaintiff (high consensus).

The judgments of subjects were predicted by Kelley's attribution theory. When subjects were presented with high distinctiveness, high consistency, and high consensus information, the attributions for the assault were to the plaintiff (the environment). On the other hand, when all three factors were low, the defendant was held responsible for the assault. It should be noted that in the high consistency case summaries, information was included that the defendant had a previous criminal record. Instructions to ignore the defendant's past record were disregarded by subjects in reaching their decisions.

and consensus for the reactions of a person (e.g., laughing, crying, getting angry, etc.), support has been obtained for Kelley's theory (Hansen and Stonner, 1978; McArthur, 1972; Wells and Harvey, 1977; Zuckerman, 1978). When observers were asked to evaluate people convicted of drug-related crimes, in support of Kelley's (1971) consistency principle, the observers were more confident in making dispositional attributions to repeated offenders than they were to first-time offenders, (Lussior, Perlman, and Breen, 1977). Furthermore, they recommended stronger punishment for the recidivists.

The underutilization of consensus

Research tends to show that consensus information has less of a role in the attribution process than distinctiveness and consistency information (Kassin, 1979; Nisbett and Ross, 1980). For example, McArthur (1972) asked subjects to attribute the cause of Ralph's tripping over Joan's feet while they were dancing. Information that Ralph always tripped over Joan's feet (consistency) and that Ralph tripped over other people's feet (low distinctiveness) had a greater impact on attributions than did information indicating that other men did or did not trip over Joan's feet (consensus).

In another study, subjects given a description of the procedures used in the Milgram study of obedience (described in Chapter 1) were asked to rate subjects who gave increasing levels of shock to a victim (Miller, 1975). Some subjects were provided with information that 65 percent of all subjects were obedient (high consensus), while others were given no information about other subjects (no consensus information). Attributions were strongly dispositional (to the person), and consensus information had no effect on the attributions made.

It should not be concluded that consensus has no affect on the attribution process, but the exact conditions under which it plays an important role and when it does not must be specified carefully. For example, people have been shown to utilize consensus information when there is little information about other factors (Read, 1983). When the cause of behavior appears complex, people tend to ignore information about the reactions of other individuals. They make judgments and generalizations about the individual case. One review of research on the impact of consensus on attributions concluded that consensus information is used only when prior expectations are neutralized and the consensus information is clear, strong, and relevant (Kassin, 1979).

Modifications of attribution theory

Lalljee (1981) has suggested a number of possible modifications of attribution theory. First, he noted a tendency of observers to assign responsibility when attributions are made to a person. Lalljee notes that responsibility also may be assigned to a person for getting into, creating, or allowing certain situations to happen. For example, a person may be held responsible for an automobile accident because of negligence. If the person does not properly maintain the automobile, it will not function properly, and accidents become more likely. Although the person does not intend to have an accident, and it is a result of mechanical or situational factors, the person is considered blameworthy.

Secondly, Lalljee argued that consistency is not just a matter of counting occurrences of a behavior. Obtaining four divorces in five years may be considered very frequent, but jogging four times in five years hardly would represent a steady habit. What represents "doing it often" depends on the kind of action under observation. People bring social schemata with them into any situation, which helps them explain the actions of others.

Similarly, although consensus sometimes may be important when we make attributions, such information may depend upon who the other people are. Social comparison theory suggests that we choose selectively when making comparisons of the self with others, and it seems plausible that we are likely to be selective in using consensus information in the attribution process. The relevant comparison group may be different for various classes of actions.

Lalljee suggests an alternative to the kind of information processing proposed by attribution theorists, where witnesses observe effects and, by an inductive process, go backward in the causal chain to discover the reasons for behavior. The person carries around a rich store of hypotheses about the reasons for various actions. When an observer witnesses an event, the attribution problem is one of choosing among alternative available hypotheses. The observer uses specific cues and items of information to distinguish among these alternative explanations for behavior.

Biases in the attribution process

When the preconceptions, expectations, and perspectives of observers have an impact on how they explain behavior, we call these **attribution biases**. As can be seen in Box 4-2, Americans tend to perceive themselves as desiring peace and the Russians as aggressive and warlike. In a mirror image, the Soviet people perceive things the other way around. These differences arise because each side has preconceptions about the other and about themselves, and because each has different national interests around the world. Similarly, when I fail, there are extenuating circumstances, but when you fail, it is because you are lacking in ability and motivation. It is important to understand attributional biases because they contribute to conflict between people.

Differences in attributions of actors and observers

There is a reliable difference in attributions made by people engaging in behavior (i.e., actors) and those who only observe the behavior. Actors tend to make attributions for their own behavior to the situation, while observers are more likely to make attributions to the actor (Jones and Nisbett, 1972). In a demonstration of this difference, college students were asked to write paragraphs explaining their own and their best friends' reasons for choosing a major and a girlfriend (Nisbett, Caputo, Legant, and Maracek, 1973). As can

Box 4-2

Mirror images in Soviet-American relations

The perceptions of nations appear to follow much the same kinds of principles as the perceptions of people. Nations, like people, gain reputations, are perceived as responsible for actions, and are evaluated positively or negatively. Leaders in both the Soviet Union and the United States have warned their citizens about the dangerous characteristics of the other. Each says about the other: "They are aggressive, warlike, expansionistic, and godless. We are good, they are evil." Each action taken by the Soviet Union is evaluated in the context of these moralistic preconceptions by many Americans. Most Americans responded with alarm when Soviet troops put down the Hungarian revolution and their tanks rolled through the streets of Prague; when the Russians carried out maneuvers on the borders of Poland, sold weapons and other supplies to North Korea, Cuba, Vietnam, and Nicaragua, and invaded Afganistan. To Americans, these actions represent a worldwide pattern of agression. Especially salient in the early 1980s is a large buildup of strategic weapons capable of destroying the United States.

What do the Soviet people think about the United States? They must know we would not start a war and that all we care about is protecting our own security. Right? So, if we send troops to Korea, Vietnam, the Dominican Repulic, Lebanon, and West Germany; station missiles and aircraft around the borders of the Soviet Union; have the CIA install friendly governments in various countries; and spend trillions of dollars for weapons systems, they must realize that we would never attack them without provocation. Right?

According to research carried out by social psychologists, the answers to our two questions are: *wrong*! On a visit to the Soviet Union in 1960, Urie Bronfenbrenner found that the Soviet people had attitudes toward Americans very similar to those Americans had toward them, a kind of mirror image. The Russians perceived Americans as aggressive and warlike, and were apprehensive about the possibility of a first-strike nuclear attack. They viewed our interventions into the conflicts of other countries as a pattern of worldwide aggression and expansionism.

White (1965) believes that the self-perceptions of both Americans and Russians depend on a fundamental premise that "Our nation is peace-loving." Suppose you were a Soviet citizen and you sincerely believed your nation to be devoted to peace in the world. How would you interpret American actions? Each side can maintain its belief in its peacefulness despite increasing the tempo of the arms race, issuing threats to the other side, and fighting proxy battles all over the world because such policies can be attributed to the aggressive actions of the enemy.

As George Kennan (1947), our former ambassador to the Soviet Union has said, "It is an undeniable privilege of everyman to prove himself in the right in the thesis that the world is his enemy; for if he reiterates it frequently enough and makes it the background of his conduct, he is bound eventually to be right" (p. 569).

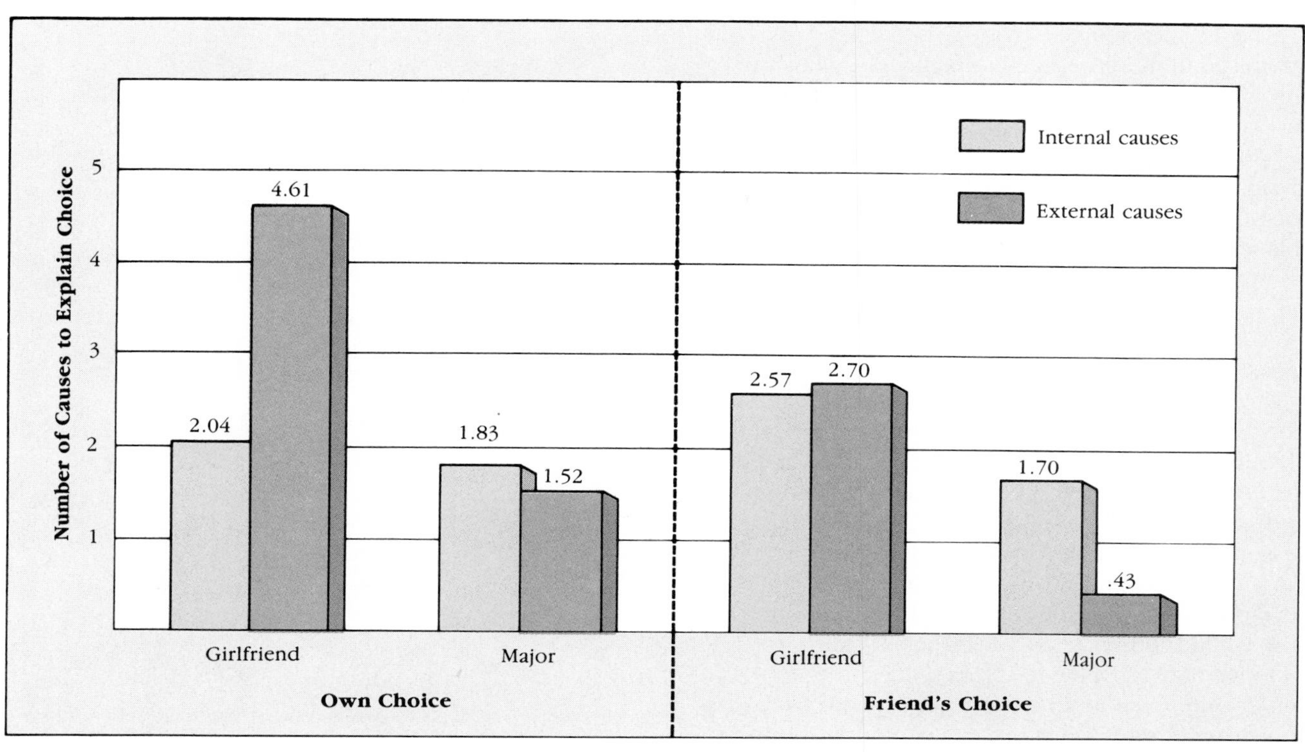

Figure 4-3 Attributions of cause for self and others in choosing a major and a girlfriend.

Source: Based on "Behavior as seen by the actor and as seen by the observer" by R. E. Nisbett, C. Caputo, P. Legant, and J. Marecek, 1973, *Journal of Personality and Social Psychology, 27*, 154-164.

be seen in Figure 4-3, the choices of the best friends were attributed to some personal quality, but attributions about their own choices were externalized as due to the qualities of their major or their girlfriends.

Storms (1973) was able to show both actor and observer biases by the same subjects. A two-person discussion involving the subjects was videotaped. At first, the actors tended to explain their behavior as responsive to the other person (i.e., a situational attribution). Later, however, when they viewed the videotape and had the perspective of a third-party observer, they made more dispositional attributions for their own behavior. Similarly, observers first made dispositional attributions, but when the videotape assisted them in seeing the situation from the actor's perspective, they made more situational attributions.

In the Watergate affair that brought about the resignation of President Richard Nixon, the participants (e.g., Hunt and Liddy) made situational attributions (following orders, national security) for their behavior, while the mass media made internal attributions (corrupt, power hungry) to explain the break-in and cover-up (Wegner and Vallacher, 1977).

A systematic study of a watergate-style burglary used a procedure to entice students to participate in a burglary. A private investigator presented undergraduate criminology students with a plan to break into a local business establishment and microfilm their records. Some subjects thought they would be paid $2,000 by a competing firm; others were led to believe the Internal Revenue Service (IRS) wanted the records in order to prosecute the company. Half of the students in the IRS burglary condition were promised immunity from prosecution if caught; the other half were not given this promise. After hearing about the plan, students were asked if they would agree to come to a final meeting. No meeting actually was held, and of course no burglary was attempted.

The results showed that 45 percent of students promised immunity agreed to come to the final meeting, while only 5 percent of those not promised immunity and 20 percent of those offered $2,000 did. In support of the divergent perspectives hypothesis, the students attributed their decision to agree or disagree to situational factors. Observers given descriptions of this experiment, on the other hand, attributed both compliance and noncompliance to the dispositions of the students.

It is common knowledge that criminals often attribute their illegal conduct to an unjust society and a lack of opportunity to "make it the straight way." Evidence for such situational attributions was found among prisoners at a medium-security Canadian penal institution (Saulnier and Perlman, 1981). The inmates and their social workers were asked to explain the reasons for the inmates' crimes. Although social workers are trained to recognize the situational causes of behavior, they nevertheless tended to blame the person, while the inmates blamed the situation.

Jones and Nisbett (1972) explained the actor/observer difference in terms of a **perceptual focusing hypothesis** stating that actors are poorly located to observe their own behavior. Their most important sensory mechanisms (the eyes) focus outward, and the situation is salient for them. When an outside person observes an action, the focus is on the actor and the actor's behavior "engulfs the field" of perception (Heider, 1958). Heightened attention to the actor obscures the contribution of situational factors. As a result of the perceptual focusing process, actors tend to make attributions to situational factors and observers tend to make attributions to the actor.

Another factor that might account for **divergent perceptions** between actors and observers is that actors simply have more information about themselves than do others. Actors are more aware of the demands placed on them and that their choices of what to do are based on the best alternative the situation will allow. Actors are also more familiar with their past than are observers, which gives them information about their typical behavior and how they have modified their plans according to circumstances. Actors perceive continuity in their behavior over time and situations, whereas observers tend to be limited to quick glimpses of behavior in specific contexts.

People tend to attribute their own behavior to external social situations. Slums usually breed poverty and lack opportunity. Criminals often attribute their conduct to social conditions such as these.

Finally, observers are more interested in gaining information that will allow predictions of future conduct by the actor. This goal motivates observers to look for stable characteristics of the person. Support for this hypothesis was obtained by Miller, Norman, and Wright (1978) who found that observers made more internal attributions about an actor when they expected to interact with the actor than when they did not. A summary of the factors accounting for divergences in attributions of actors and observers is presented in Table 4-3.

Table 4-3 Explanations for actor and observer differences in attributions

Perceptual focus: Observers concentrate their attention on the actor they are judging, while the actor is focused on the environment.

Self-knowlege: Actors know more about the pressures, demands, limitations, choices, and antecedent conditions for an action than do observers.

Different goals: Actors seek instrumental goals, while observers desire information to use in predicting actors' future behavior.

The fundamental attribution error

The relative tendency of actors to attend to situational factors when making attributions is an exception to a very pervasive bias. In general, people underestimate the importance of situational factors in explaining behavior. Both actors and observers give more importance to traits than to situations in explaining behavior (Watson, 1982). The tendency to personify historical forces, described in Box 4-3, is one manifestation of this bias. An exaggeration of the importance of personal factors is referred to as the **fundamental attribution error**. According to Ross (1977):

> He (the naive Psychologist) too readily infers broad personal dispositions and expects consistency in behavior or outcomes across widely disparate situations and contexts. He jumps to hasty conclusions upon witnessing the behavior of his peers overlooking the impact of relevant environmental forces and constraints. (p. 184)

In a demonstration of the fundamental attribution error, college students played a quiz game in which they were assigned randomly to either the role of questioner or contestant (Ross, Amabile, and Steinmetz, 1977). The questioners were told to make up tough questions that would show how much knowledge they had. The role of questioner gave a student an advantage because most of us know things others do not. Afterward, contestants and observers of the game rated the knowledgeability of the contestants. The results showed that contestants and third-party observers thought the questioner to be the more knowledgeable person. Although everyone knew that the questioner role was determined randomly and gave the questioner an advantage, observers nevertheless focused on the person and neglected the situation in making their attributions. It is a case of appearing "smarter" because of being in an advantageous position.

Biases in correspondent inferences

The theory of correspondent inferences (Jones and Davis, 1965), as described earlier, assumes that the observer is essentially a naive scientist rationally analysing the actions of others and drawing conclusions about the causes of their behavior. Sometimes, however, the self-interests of the observer become involved, and biases are introduced into the attribution process. Two such biases are hedonic relevance and personalism.

Hedonic relevance occurs when the actor's behavior has positive or negative effects on the observer (Jones and Davis, 1965). The more hedonically relevant the actor's behavior is perceived to be, the greater the likelihood the observer will perceive it as correspondent, that is, as reflecting some dispositional characteristic of the actor. This effect was shown in a study of problem-solving groups in which an accomplice of the experimenter was the only group member to fail (Jones and deCharms, 1957). The accomplice's failure either prevented the entire group from obtaining a reward or only affected the outcome of the accomplice. Although the behavior of the accomplice was exactly the same in both conditions, he was rated as more incompetent, a highly dispositional attribution, when his failure affected the interests of those who rated him.

Box 4-3

Personifying historical forces

The American people hold their president responsible for the performance of the economy and expect him to further their interests in the international arena. Can any one person have much impact on worldwide events? History books and biographies are filled with accounts of villains and heroes. Thomas Carlyle, a biographer, proclaimed that history is made by the acts of great people. Leo Tolstoy took the opposite view and proclaimed that all great people are the products of their times. These viewpoints reflect on such questions as: would the history of the United States be different if Abraham Lincoln never lived? One answer was provided by Lincoln himself. In a letter to A. C. Hodges on 4 April 1864, he wrote: "I claim not to have controlled events, but confess plainly that events have controlled me" (cited in Duschacek, 1971, p. 214).

Although our tendency is to view the president of the United States as the most influential man in the world, he is also the target of many influence attempts. He is seldom able to act according to his own prejudices and ideology. A nation's geographical location, its resources, traditions, and history will limit the power of even a powerful dictator. In an analysis of the contraints on the power of a president, Smith (1962) found the division of power to fragment responsibility so that committees of congress or departments of government can undertake actions undermining the patient development of positive relations with foreign countries. When Dwight Eisenhower became president, he was amazed because nobody followed his orders. Despite these examples, the fundamental attribution error is manifested by observers who frequently place responsibility on the apparently powerful person.

Personalism occurs when observers believe that the effects of an action were specifically targeted for them. Actions that are perceived as highly personalistic produce attributions about the dispositions of the actor. You would not be happy if your banker increased interest charges on a loan for all customers, but you would be furious if they were raised only for you. In the latter instance, you would be more extreme in characterizing the banker as mean, money hungry, and exploitative than you would be if all borrowers were affected similarly.

Self-serving biases

For what a man would like to be true, that he more readily believes.

Francis Bacon

To paraphrase a famous proverb, success has many fathers while failure is an orphan. A **self-serving bias** reflects the tendency of actors to attribute success to themselves and failure to situational factors. Seldom do tennis stars attribute victory to bad line calls against their opponents or to their own lucky shots. For example, after losing to Jose Luis Clerc of Argentina in a Davis Cup Match, John McEnroe was quoted as saying, "a few good games and some lucky shots" by Clerc led to his loss.

The tendency to make self-serving attributions was shown among subjects who were asked to take the role of teacher and instruct two elementary school students on multiplication problems (Johnson, Feigenbaum, and Weiby, 1964). The tutoring procedure required "teachers" to transmit their lessons in writing to the students, who were in another room. Feedback from the experimenter about the performance of the students was the manipulated factor in the experiment. In all cases, one student was represented as successfully having solved the problems in both sessions. In one condition, the second student performed poorly in the first session, but improved in the second. In the comparison condition, the student failed in both sessions.

Consistent failure by the student could be interpreted as either poor ability in the student or poor tutoring by the teacher. The results showed that the teachers attributed the failure to the student. On the other hand, when at first the student failed and then improved, the success could be attributed either to the increased effort or ability of the student or to the effectiveness of the teaching. The teachers attributed the success to their teaching. Thus the "teachers" attributed failure to the student but took credit for success.

The self-serving bias has been demonstrated in many experiments (cf. Bradley, 1978; Zuckerman, 1979). Not only does it occur in relation to observers' own behavior, but also to those with whom they associate. For example, fans of the Pittsburgh Steelers and Dallas Cowboys were interviewed after their teams met in the 1976 Superbowl game (which the Steelers won). While the Steelers' fans attributed their team's victory to the good play of their team, Cowboy supporters attributed their loss to bad luck and "the breaks" (Winkler and Taylor, 1979).

Taking credit for success and blaming others for failure is not only characteristic of Americans brought up in an achievement-oriented society. It has been found in collectivist societies also. Cross-cultural studies in Japan, South America, and Yugoslavia have shown that attributions to ability were higher following success than following failure (Chandler, Shama, Wolf, and Planchard, 1981). Even Nigerian tribespeople who highly value modesty, showed a self-serving attributional bias (Boski, 1983). Wan and Bond (1982) found that the powerful effects of outcomes on self-attributions "overcame" Confucious among Chinese college students from Hong Kong. Although Confucious said, "Haughtiness invites ruin, humility receives benefits," the Chinese students exhibited self-serving biases both when they could be observed personally by others and when they could not.

One explanation for the self-serving bias is that people have a need to maintain or enhance self-esteem (Greenwald, 1980; Hastorf, Schneider, and Polefka, 1970). Success and failure experiences are important in how people evaluate themselves (Strobe, 1980). Taking full responsibility for failure is tantamount to a negative evaluation of self and lowers self-esteem. Attributing the failure to the situation allows actors to protect their self-esteem and maintain a positive view of their own abilities. Implicit in this explanation of the self-serving bias is that people really see the world in a distorted manner. Their perceptions of causality are biased by the implications of outcomes for self-esteem.

A second explanation for self-serving attributions is that these attributions represent people's concern about how they look to others. This self-presentational view (Bradley, 1978; Riess, Rosenfeld, Melburg, and Tedeschi, 1981) contends that people want others to give them credit for success, and do not want others to attribute failure to some lack in their ability or competence. This self-presentation explanation is based on the assumption that actors' descriptions of causality, but not their actual perceptions, are biased. In other words, the attributional bias may reflect an insincere report used as a tactic of impression management (see Chapter 3).

Riess et al. (1981) conducted an experiment to examine whether self-serving attributions were sincere perceptual distortions or insincere descriptions. Subjects were given feedback that they had either succeeded or failed on a word association test. They then were asked to attribute their performance to luck, task difficulty, ability, and effort. The first two factors are external, and the second two are internal. Some of the subjects were asked to make their attributions on paper-and-pencil scales, while others were attached by electrodes to an apparatus identified as a kind of lie detector called the *bogus pipeline* (Jones and Sigall, 1971; Quigley-Fernandez, and Tedeschi, 1978). Participants in bogus pipeline experiments are convinced, through an elaborate set of ruses, that their responses are being monitored by a powerful and sophisticated lie detector. Riess et al. reasoned that if the self-serving bias were insincere, it would be reduced or eliminated by the bogus pipeline because fear of being detected as a liar (a very negative identity) would reduce self-presentational tendencies. If, however, the bias was an actual perceptual distortion, it should be unaffected by bogus pipeline measurement.

The results indicated support for both processes. The self-serving bias was obtained when subjects responded to paper-and-pencil scales and when they were hooked up to the bogus pipeline. Thus, even when there were constraints against descriptive bias, a self-serving bias occurred. The implication is that real perceptual distortion was involved. On the other hand, there was sufficient difference in the self-attributions of subjects in the two measurement conditions that some degree of descriptive distortion appeared also to occur.

A two-factor explanation suggests that the self-serving bias reflects both perceptual and descriptive distortions. The type and degree of descriptive bias depends upon the self-presentational goals of the actor. For example, when actors are fairly certain that others credit them with great ability, they might try to appear modest, although in their heart of hearts they think they are the best (Schlenker, 1980). There is evidence for such reverses of the self-serving bias (Ross, Bierbrur and Polly, 1974; Tetlock, 1980).

When people work together on group projects, there is a tendency for each member to claim disproportionate responsibility for success and to attribute responsibility for failure to others. This type of attribution bias in groups is called an **egocentric bias**. In a series of nine experiments in which problem-solving groups were provided feedback that they had succeeded or failed, an egocentric bias was found (Schlenker and Miller, 1977a, 1977b). When the group had succeeded, members claimed that they had contributed more than others did; but when the group failed, they attributed less responsibility to themselves and more to others.

The saliency bias

The tendency of observers to assign greater responsibility to individuals in a group who are distinctive in some way is called the **saliency bias**. For example, when a person was the only member of his or her sex or race in a group, subjects rated this person as more influential than other members of the group (Taylor and Fiske, 1978; Taylor, Fiske, Etcoff, and Ruderman, 1978). Because this phenomenon occurs when people make quick judgments about strangers, it sometimes has been referred to as the "top-of-the-head" phenomenon.

The saliency bias occurs when observers are not very involved, and the judgments appear to be unimportant. No saliency bias was found when subjects believed their judgments were important, but it did occur when they were little involved in the issue under discussion (Borgida and Howard-Pitney, 1983).

Forming overall impressions from trait information

I never forget a face . . . but in your case I'll make an exception.

Groucho Marx

There are many occasions where we must form a quick impression of someone we have never met before, as may be the case in an employment interview or a business deal. The perceptual task is to process whatever information is available, such as style of dress and the way a person treats the receptionist, and make attributions about that person's characteristics. The impression we form will help guide us through subsequent interactions with the person until we obtain further information.

Consider this description of a famous person: He was so conceited that "in his eyes he was the only person who existed," and so arrogant that "to hear him talk he was Shakespeare, Beethoven, and Plato rolled into one" (Taylor, 1966, p. 121). He violently attacked anyone who even slightly disagreed with him and had temper tantrums when frustrated by others. He had no sense of responsibility, often borrowing money but rarely paying it back. He rewarded the devotion and friendship of his closest admirer by stealing his wife.

This "monster" was Richard Wagner, one of the greatest composers of all time. Did Wagner's musical contributions outweigh the suffering he caused to those around him? Deems Taylor (1966) the music critic, has argued that the everlasting joy Wagner's music brought to the world more than offsets the short-term harm he did to his friends.

The Wagner example illustrates some of the principles of impression formation. Perhaps the negative information affected your reactions to Wagner more than it would have if you had been told who he was immediately and then had his negative traits described to you. Based on the details given, you probably concluded that he had other characteristics related to what you have learned so far. Furthermore, you were given contradictory information—he was a monster and a genius. How did this affect your overall impression of him?

Primacy and recency effects

In his pioneer research on person perception, Asch (1946) provided subjects a set of traits possessed by a hypothetical person. The subjects were asked to write a paragraph indicating their impression of the person. For example, one set of traits included intelligent, industrious, impulsive, critical, stubborn, and envious. A second group of subjects received the same list of traits but in exactly the opposite order. Asch found that the traits listed first had greater influence on subjects forming impressions than did the later traits regardless of the order of the traits. Subjects formed a more positive impression of the hypothetical person when intelligent and industrious were presented first. The disproportionate use of first impressions is referred to as the **primacy effect**. In the description of Richard Wagner, if we had given you information about his musical accomplishments prior to describing his personal life, you would most likely have had a more favorable impression of him.

Why do primacy effects occur? Asch offered a **trait-context interaction** hypothesis that the earlier traits form the context within which we interpret later traits. For example, to describe a person as undecided may mean that the undecided person is open minded and pays careful attention to all the evidence, or it may mean that he or she is wishy-washy and insecure. If the observer had learned earlier that the hypothetical person was shy and dependent on others, the more negative interpretation would be made. For example, a psychiatric patient was judged by observers to be more "sick" if the observers had evaluated persons with only mild pathology first, but as less "sick" if they had encountered more severe cases first (Bieri, Orcutt, and Leaman, 1963).

A second explanation suggests that people get tired, bored, or distracted after gaining initial information about a person. According to this **attention decrement** hypothesis, the primacy effect could be eliminated if observers could somehow be made to attend to all of the information provided to them. Support for this hypothesis was obtained in a study where subjects were given a list of adjectival descriptions of a hypo-

How do we form overall impressions of people we have not met previously? We process initial information and make attributions about a person's actions accordingly. What contributes most to your overall impression of John McEnroe? His negative demeanor on the court or his superior ability to play tennis?

thetical person (Anderson and Hubert, 1963). Half of the subjects were told they would later be asked to recall the list, and the remaining subjects were told nothing. The expectation that they would be asked to recall the list of adjectives should have caused subjects to pay attention to all of the information provided to them, and they did not display a primacy effect.

A **recency effect**, where later information has more impact than earlier information on forming impressions, rarely occurs. When information is presented over a substantial length of time, a "what have you done for me lately" effect can occur, and the latest information is more influential (Luchins, 1957). A recency effect also was found when subjects were asked to give their impressions after receiving each new trait description (Stewart, 1965). Primacy effects are the rule in everyday life because we rely on firm impressions already formed and discount subsequent information about someone we have judged already.

According to the **discounting hypothesis**, observers give reduced importance to information that does not fit into their original impression. The impressions of subjects have been shown to be less affected by each successive trait in a list of traits (Anderson and Barrios, 1961). Research has established that the primacy effect can be reduced, but not eliminated, if observers believe the judgments they make are important and if they have sufficient time to consider all of the information available. As can be seen in Figure 4-4 reliance of subjects on initial information in forming judgements was least when they believed their judgements reflected an important ability and when they were not pressured to reach their conclusion (Kruglanski and Freund, 1983).

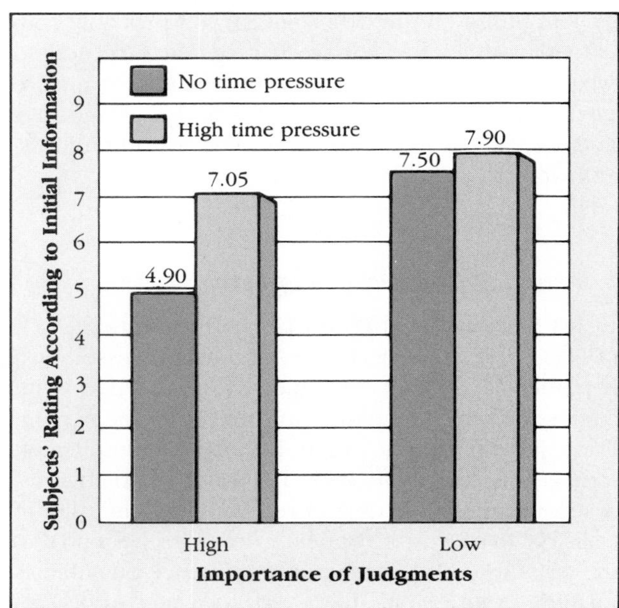

Figure 4-4 Factors affecting the impact of initial information on subjects.

Source: Based on "The freezing and unfreezing of lay-inferences: Effects on impressional primacy, ethnic stereotyping, and numerical anchoring" by A. W. Kruglanski and T. Freund, 1983, *Journal of Experimental Social Psychology, 19*, pp. 448-468.

Central and peripheral traits

Some traits are more important for observers in determining overall impressions, regardless of their order in the information flow. These influential trait descriptions are referred to as **central traits**. Less influential descriptions are called **peripheral traits**. Asch (1946) discovered that "warm" and "cold" are central traits. He provided subjects with a list of six adjectives to describe a hypothetical person. The adjective "warm" was presented in the list for half of the subjects, and the remainder had "cold" embedded in the list. While the group presented with "warm" in the list formed an impression of the stimulus person as humane, sociable, good natured, and generous, the group presented with "cold" in the list viewed the person as ruthless, unsociable, and ungenerous. When "polite" and "bold" were substituted for "warm" and "cold," no major differences in impressions were found. Thus, "polite" and "bold" were found to be peripheral traits.

The impact of central triats has been found also in a classroom setting (Kelley, 1950). Students were given a handout describing a guest lecturer. The descriptions were identical with the exception that for half the students the lecturer was described as "warm" and for the remainder the lecturer was characterized as "cold." Students who received the "warm" description participated more in postlecture discussion and rated the lecturer more positively than did students who received the "cold" description.

Observers tend to assume that people who are

We tend to assume that people who are outstanding in one trait are outstanding in many others as well. If you were told that this lecturer was "warm and caring," would you judge his teaching performance and other characteristics as positive on the basis of this given description?

outstanding on one dimension are positive on others (Thorndike, 1920). This overgeneralization from one positive aspect to the assumption that the person is positive in other respects is referred to as the *halo effect*. For example, a lecturer who was introduced to students in exactly the same way, except for being described as "warm" to half of them or "cold" to the other half, was rated "as more interesting" when he was believed to be warm (Kelley, 1950). Yet, the two groups of students were in the same classroom and heard exactly the same lecture.

Combining information

More refined models have been devised to represent how observers combine each piece of trait information to form impressions of a stimulus person. Through careful pretesting, a score can be given to each trait adjective. This score would indicate how much each trait contributes to an observer's judgment about the person, such as likeability. For example, "friendly" contributes more than does "skillful."

A **summation model** of impression formation

Box 4-4

Consumer advertising: adding or averaging?

Many advertisers bombard consumers with information about products and services. Support for these tactics could be drawn from the summation model of impression formation. The averaging model suggests, however, that more does not always mean better. Indeed, the averaging model predicts that additional positive information actually could produce a less favorable overall impression, if that information has a value less than the average of previous information.

In an examination of the applicability of these models, soon-to-be parents were given information about one very positive quality of a product or one very positive and one mildly positive piece of information associated with it (Troutman, Michael, and Shanteau, 1976). For instance, disposable diapers were described as having high absorbancy (very positive) or as having high absorbancy and above average durability (very and mildly positive information). The soon-to-be parents rated the diapers as a better product when they had been described by a single very positive trait than when the very positive trait was accompanied by a mildly positive trait. The clear implication is that advertisers should be guided by the averaging model.

predicts that from the summation of values for all adjectives used in a description, the overall likeability of a stimulus person can be determined (Triandis and Fishbein, 1963). Suppose a person was described as honest (+ 4), well-mannered (+ 1), and reliable (+ 1). The observer would simply sum up the values of the traits and give a likeability rating of 6 to the stimulus person.

An **averaging model** assumes that observers sum the values of all trait descriptions and then divide the sum by the number of traits (Anderson, 1962). The difference between the summation and averaging models can be illustrated by an observer who forms an impression of a person then receives additional information about the person. For the honest, well-mannered, and reliable person described above, the sum was 6, but if divided by the number of traits (3), the average is 2. Now suppose the observer discovered that the stimulus person was usually happy and that this trait by itself has a value of 2. In the summation model, this new value would simply be added to the prior sum (giving a value of 8), and would predict an increase in the observer's liking for the stimulus person. Adding another trait that has the same value as the prior average, however, would not lead to a change in the observer's liking for the stimulus person according to the averaging model because the average would not change in value.

A more sophisticated **weighted averaging** model was proposed by Anderson (1965) to account for the effects of primacy. Earlier traits are given more weight (an additional value) than later traits. The weighted averaging model is quite accurate in predicting ratings of likability. An application of information-processing models to consumer advertising is described in Box 4-4.

Implicit personality theories

Each person may be considered a naive psychologist. Each has a theory of what characteristics go with what other characteristics, so that given some information about a person, the observer will "flesh out" an overall impression of *that* kind of person. In other words, each person has an **implicit personality theory** and uses it as a guide for forming impressions of others (Bruner and Tagiuri, 1954). In the novel *1984*, Winston developed an elaborate theory about Julia based on her youthful appearance and the red sash she wore indicating her membership in the Junior Antisex League.

The effects of implicit personality theories on impression formation was demonstrated among children at a summer camp (Dornbush, Hastorf, Richardson, Muzzy, and Vreeland, 1965). Each child was asked to describe two other children at the camp. As is shown in Figure 4-5, there was more agreement in the way

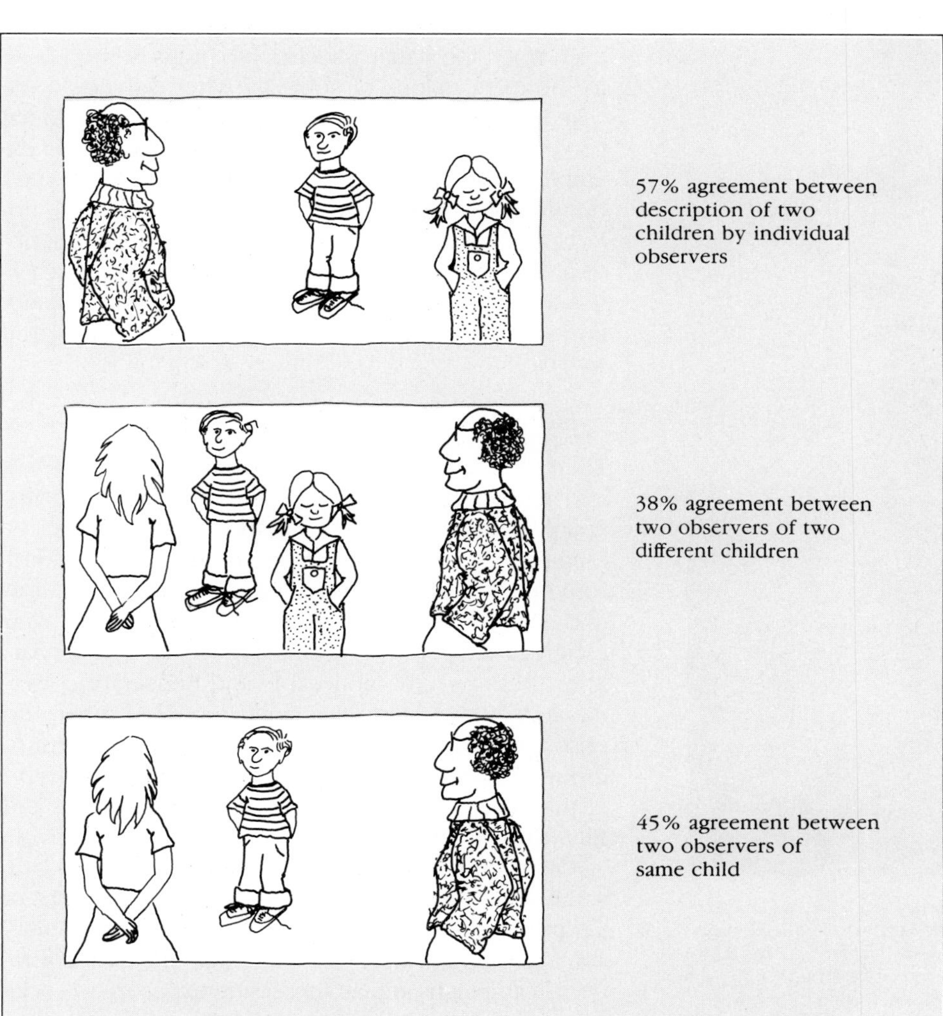

Figure 4-5 Drawing of agreement between children describing children.

one child described two other children than in how two children described the same person. The implication is that each person has an overall personality theory that provides a context for evaluating everyone.

We have noted that people have a tendency to classify or label others. Stereotyping results when people attribute a collection of traits to an entire group. If this person were labeled as a mental patient, would you stereotype him into a specific group? If he were identified as a job applicant, would you form a different impression of him?

Logical error

Often there is no logical reason why a person should believe that one trait invariably implies another trait (Bruner, Shapiro, and Tagiuri, 1958). For example, although people tend to believe that intelligent people are also responsible, there is not a shred of evidence that this is so. We may refer to the common assumption of an association of traits in the absence of any evidence as a **logical error**.

We may or may not actually associate traits with one another. In one study, traits were manipulated to be correlated, uncorrelated, or negatively correlated with one another (Berman and Kenny, 1976). The purpose was to see if the logical error type of bias would occur even when the actual association of traits was opposite to the expectations of subjects. When subjects were asked to describe the stimulus persons, their initial correlation biases affected their descriptions. For example, if the factual correlation between shyness and dominance was positive and the expectation of subjects was that they would be negative, then the description of the person reflected the initial bias as much as it did the factual description. The descriptions by subjects of the stimulus persons reflected a strong logical error.

Stereotypes

There is a tendency among people to classify others into ethnic, racial, religious, and gender categories. People could be classified into those with blue eyes or long finger nails. Indeed, there is a stereotype held by some people of blond females as "dumb." Classification is based usually on characteristics of people who congregate together in groups, however. These characteristics are often noticeable and hence are convenient as bases for classifying people. When an observer attributes a collection of traits to an entire group of people, the observer possesses a **stereotype** of the group (Lippman, 1922; Schneider, Hastorf and Ellsworth, 1979).

Over a thirty-year period, students at Princeton University have displayed stereotypes of various groups of people (Gilbert, 1951; Karlins, Coffman, and Walters, 1969; Katz and Braly, 1933). Although intensive educational campaigns and an increasing exposure to social science courses have softened students' stereotypes

Box 4-5

Poor is poor and rich is better

There is a tendency to assume that people from lower socioeconomic levels are poor because they lack intelligence. Some evidence of this stereotype was found among Princeton University students (Darley & Gross, 1983). One group of students watched a videotape of a fourth-grade girl in an unattractive playground in the middle of a run-down urban neighborhood. Another group of students viewed a tape of the same young girl playing in a tree-lined park connected with ball fields in an obvious affluent neighborhood. Fact sheets were handed out to the students describing the little girl's father and mother as high school graduates working as a meat packer and a seamstress, respectively (in the poor condition), or as college graduates working as an attorney and a free-lance writer, respectively (in the affluent condition).

All subjects then watched the same tape of the girl performing on a test. They could see the examiner, the problems, the girl's answers, and the correct answers. The girl's performance was average for her grade level. Yet, students who had information that the girl was from a lower socioeconomic class rated her abilities as below her grade level, and students who believed she was from a higher socioeconomic class rated her as above her grade level. In apparent justification for their ratings, subjects who were told of the girl in the affluent conditions judged the test as more difficult and estimated the girl to have more correct answers. These results show people's bias toward processing information to confirm existing stereotypes.

over time, they still hold widespread agreement about traits possessed by Americans (materialistic), Germans (industrious), Italians (passionate), and black Americans (musical).

Three explanations have been offered for stereotyping: psychodynamic, social learning, and cognitive-information-processing theories. The *psychodynamic view* derives from psychoanalytic theory and proposes that stereotypes satisfy unconscious needs of the individual (Allport, 1954). For example, people with low self-esteem may bolster their evaluations of themselves by derogating entire groups of other people. Then, by comparison, the individual can make a more favorable self-evaluation.

A *social learning* explanation of stereotypes contends that they are transmitted culturally through the socialization process (Hamilton, 1979). Parental models, a desire to display opinion conformity to gain group acceptance, and a desire to gain competitive advantage in economic and social life serve as a basis for people to learn stereotypes. Indeed, stereotypes may be based on observations taken out of context. For example, a high proportion of prison inmates in the United States are black (Silberman, 1978). This fact has contributed to a common stereotype of blacks as violent and antisocial (Hamilton, 1979). In countries where blacks predominate in government and business, this stereotype is nonexistant.

A *cognitive-information-processing* explanation for stereotyping suggests that there are just too many people for the individual to maintain an image of each one. The individual is motivated to form impressions of others, so their behavior can be anticipated and perhaps controlled or manipulated. When faced with information overload, the solution for the person is to chunk information into larger categories (Miller 1956; Hastie, 1981).

It is likely that all three views of stereotyping are correct. A more conspiratorial view also can be supported. A campaign can be deliberately waged to direct public opinion against a particular group. There are clearly very negative images of "communists" in the United States and of "capitalists" in Russia. These stereotypes often are used to support special interests or government policies. This raises an important question: what impact do stereotypes have on behavior toward the target group?

There is evidence that stereotyping may lead to negative reactions. Psychotherapists listened to a tape-recorded interview of a person who was labeled either as a mental patient or a job applicant (Langer and Abelson, 1974). The psychotherapists who thought the interviewee to be a mental patient viewed him as more disturbed than did the psychotherapists who thought him to be a job applicant. History provides many examples of cruelty toward and killing members of a stereotyped group. The Nazis exploited the stereotype of Jews as materialistic and money hungry, blaming them for Germany's economic woes and justifying their arrest, internment, and subsequent extermination. Described in Box 4-5 is a study showing that socioeconomic status affects evaluations of a person's performance.

A review of research on stereotyping concluded that "social stereotypes may affect judgments of individuals about whom little else is known beside their social category. But as soon as individuating, particular characteristics of a person are known, social stereotypes may have minimal, if any, impact on judgments about that person" (Borgida, Locksley, and Brekke, 1981, p. 167).

Research regarding stereotypes has too often taken an all-or-none approach (McCauley, Stitt, and Segal, 1980). When people hold a stereotyped belief, such as Germans are efficient, they do not mean that all Germans are efficient. Rather, the belief is that Germans as a group tend to be more efficient than other national groups, although any given German could be inefficient and lazy. Looked at in this way, stereotypes often may contain accurate information, which can be useful to people in making business decisions and in carrying on other kinds of interactions.

We can summarize the viewpoints on the effects of stereotypes by stating that when there is strong group consensus about them, people in the stereotyped group may act in a manner consistent with the stereotype. Without such social support, it is likely that stereotypes readily give way to information obtained about a specific member of the target group. Even when people are aware of stereotypes, including their own, they may remain unaware of the impact that stereotypes have on the way they form impressions of specific individuals (Hepburn and Locksley, 1983).

The absoluteness of stereotypes as applying to all members of a target group and their ambiguity have led to the use of another term. A **prototype** is an abstract example of a typical member of a group (Cantor and Mischel, 1979). When a person of the target group is encountered, perceivers will compare observations with the prototype. There is an attempt to find an appropriate prototype for the target person. Rather than forcing all members of a group into a given stereotype, observers find among a number of prototypes the one that fits the stimulus person best. The prototype used for a person may then be used to generate expectations about behavior. For example, a librarian may be expected to drink wine at dinner, but a waitress may be expected to drink beer (Cohen, 1977).

Summary

Attribution theory attempts to reconstruct how the average person explains behavior. A number of theories have been offered to explain how people assign causes to either the person or the environment. The correspondent inference theory of Jones and Davis (1965) maintains that socially undesirable and out-of-role behavior will convey more about someone's true character than actions that conform to social expectations. Kelley's (1967, 1973) theory of covariation claims that attributions are made to causes co-varying over time and situations along with particular behaviors.

People make characteristic errors in assigning causes for behavior. In general, actors perceive the environment as the cause of their behavior, while observers attribute the same behavior to the actor. There is a universal self-serving bits associated with the outcomes of behavior. Actors tend to attribute success to something about themselves, usually ability, while they attribute failure to external circumstances, often task difficulty or bad luck.

A number of factors are involved when we form overall impressions of strangers (see Table 4-4). We are influenced by both the type of information presented and the order of presentation. Central traits, such as warm and cold, have been shown to highly influence people in determining their impression of an actor's behavior. A primacy effect occurs when early information has more impact on impressions than later information. On occasion, the most recent information can have a disproportionate impact on impression formation. Although some theorists suggest that people simply sum the various bits of positive and negative information about a person when forming an impression, the evidence tends to support the more sophisticated averaging and weighted averaging models.

Forming impressions of others is not simply a matter of combining available information. Forming impressions may be influenced by preconceptions and implicit personality theories of observers. When these preconceptions are uniformly applied to all members of a group, a stereotype is said to exist. Stereotypes and prototypes are cognitive categories that help the individual classify others and develop expectations of how others will behave.

Table 4–4 Factors involved in our forming overall impressions of others

Primacy Effect
Trait-context
Attention decrement
Discounting
Recency Effect
Central and Peripheral Traits
Models of Information Processing
Summation
Averaging
Weighted averaging
Implicit Personality Theory
Logical error
Stereotype
Prototype

Glossary

Actor-observer difference Actors tend to attribute their own behavior to situational influences, while observers tend to attribute the behavior of others to internal factors, such as personality traits.

Attention decrement A hypothesis explaining the primacy effect stating that people get tired, bored, and distracted after gaining initial information about a person.

Attributional biases The distorting impact of preconceptions, expectations, and perspectives of observers on the way they explain behavior.

Augmentation principle The more risky or costly an act, the more confident are the observers that the act is consistent with the actor's intentions and dispositions.

Averaging model Observers sum the values of all trait descriptions of a person and then divide by the number of traits.

Central trait A single trait having a "spreading effect" so that all aspects of the stimulus person are affected: warm-cold is the clearest central trait in person perception.

Consensus principle The extent that other people display reactions similar to the actor in the same kind of situation; high consensus implies a situational explanation and low consensus implies a person explanation for behavior.

Consistency principle Behavior that occurs repeatedly over time and in different situations.

Correspondent inference Perception that an actor's behavior reflects his or her inner intentions and dispositions.

Covariation principle Model assuming that observers perceive factors co-varying with the effect of interest as causes of the effect; distinctiveness, consistency, and consensus are covariation principles.

Discounting hypothesis An explanation for the primacy effect stating that observers give reduced importance to information not consistent with their first impression of a person.

Discounting principle When there are other possible explanations for an act, the confidence of the observer in any single explanation is decreased.

Distinctiveness principle Refers to whether a behavior occurs in response to a particular event and not to others; a distinctive response implies an environmental explanation for the behavior.

Egocentric bias The tendency of each member of a group to claim disproportionate responsibility for success and to attribute responsibility for failure to others.

Fundamental attribution error The tendency of people to give more importance to personality traits than is warranted when explaining behavior; the importance of situational factors is underestimated.

Hedonic relevance When an actor's behavior is perceived as having potential consequences for the observer, the latter is more likely to make attributions to the actor's dispositions than to situational factors.

Implicit personality theory Each person tends to view others in terms of clusters of traits; learning that a person has one trait results in the unexamined assumption that the person also has the associated cluster of traits.

Logical error Assumption by observers that traits of a person are related in the absence of any evidence of such an association.

Noncommon effects An analysis of the effects of various alternatives available to an actor and the decision that is made; similar consequences reveal little, but noncommon effects are informative when observers make attributions about the actor.

Out-of-role behavior Behavior that is contrary to the expectations of others; suggests a personal rather than situational explanation for behavior.

Perceptual focusing hypothesis The tendency of actors to attend to situational factors and of observers to focus on the actor's behavior; one of the explanations for actor-observer differences.

Peripheral traits Characteristics that do not have much weight on observers who are forming overall impressions of people.

Person A human actor who is given an identity as a locus of responsibility.

Personalism A belief that an actor's behavior is directed toward producing effects on the observer leading the latter to make more confident and extreme attributions about the actor's dispositions.

Primacy effect Information received first about an actor often has more impact on observers' impressions than later information.

Prototype The abstract, typical member of a racial, ethnic, occupational or other social category.

Reasons Explanations for behavior that refer to intentions, motives, and goals of people or to the social rules they follow.

Recency effect Occasions when later information has more impact than earlier information on observers who are forming an impression of a person.

Role Expectations by others about how a person is supposed to act.

Saliency bias Cause is attributed to the most obvious and distinctive member of a group; also called the "top-of-the-head" phenomenon.

Self-serving bias A tendency to attribute successful outcomes to one's abilities and to attribute failures to situational factors.

Stereotype A picture in our heads about what a member of some social category is like; a collection of traits attributed to an entire group of people.

Summation model Observers sum the values of traits used to describe a person in forming an overall impression.

Trait-context interaction A hypothesis that presentation of earlier traits form the context within which later traits are interpreted.

Weighted averaging model Earlier traits are given more weight than later traits when an observer is forming an overall impression of a person.

Recommended Readings

Harvey, J. H., Ickes, W. J., & Kidd, R. F. (Eds.) (1976, 1980, 1984). *New directions in attribution research* (Vols. 1-3). Hillsdale, N J: Erlbaum.

A three-volume work that exhaustively treats the theory, research, and applications of person attributions.

Harvey, J. H., & Weary, G. (1981). *Perspectives on attribution process.* Dubuque, IA: Wm. C. Brown.

An introductory treatment of the basic principles of attribution with examples of how they have been applied to real-world problems.

Schneider, D. J., Hastorf, A. H., Ellsworth, P. C. (1979). *Person perception* (2nd ed.). Reading, MA: Addison-Wesley.

A comprehensive treatment of the major topics of person perception at a level appropriate for the advanced undergraduate student.

If men define situations as real, they are real in their consequences.

W. I. Thomas

We had the experience but missed the meaning.

T. S. Eliot

5
Social cognition: processing information

Flying saucers and Ouija boards

On Tuesday 24 June 1947 Kenneth Arnold, former all-state football player in the state of North Dakota, was flying a private plane over the Cascade Mountains of Washington. Ken was literally on top of the world. He was a handsome, athletic man in his middle thirties and owned a fire control supply company in Boise, Idaho. He used his plane to distribute and deliver fire-fighting equipment. On this day as he approached Mt. Rainier, he reported seeing nine circular objects in chain formation moving at high speed. They passed within twenty-five miles of his plane. The objects appeared to be slightly smaller than a DC-4, which also happened to be in the sky, and seemed to be linked together, swerving in and out of the mountain peaks with "flipping, erratic movements" (Gardner, 1957).

Ken told a reporter that the strange objects "flew like a saucer would if you skipped it across the water." Although Ken had not reported the objects as saucer-shaped, the newspaper stories that blanketed the country reported the first important historical instance of sighting of flying saucers. David Lawrence wrote in the *U.S. News* that the saucers were actually secret U.S. aircraft, "a combination of helicopter and a fast jet plane." Walter Winchell, a prominent columnist of the time, believed that the saucers were of Russian origin. Perhaps with tongue in cheek, Andrei Gromyko, the Soviet ambassador to the United States, conjectured that the saucers were coming from a Soviet discus thrower preparing for the Olympic games. Despite investigations that have accounted for almost all of the sightings of saucers over the years since Ken's first report, many people still believe that alien ships, perhaps from another galaxy, regularly visit the planet earth.

Fascination with exotic and mysterious events has produced a rather large industry in the occult. Did you know that in 1968 more Ouija boards were sold in the United States than Monopoly games? This piece of trivia is interesting because Ouija boards were used as early as 540 B.C. The modern Ouija board has the letters of the alphabet and numbers on it. Two or more people let their fingers touch and propel a piece of wood to point at letters in spelling out words. Some people believe the message of the Ouija is mediated by spirits moving the players' fingers. A little imagination on the part of one or both of the players coupled with the ability to imperceptibly move each other around the board provides an air of mystery and the occult.

Many people suspend customary reality checking and accept the more exotic and exciting world of the occult. Francisco Madero, the first president of Mexico following the 1910 revolution, strongly believed in the Ouija. He had been told by the Ouija that he would one day become president and it had come to pass. Careful examination of the occult by scientists typically provides a natural explanation and removes the mystery from the event. For example, sightings of flying saucers often turn out to be weather balloons, garbage can lids, astronomical phenomena, or experimental aircraft; and movement on the Ouija board results from subliminal muscular actions of either or both of the two players. Such explanations do not persuade many people, however. What matters for many is not what scientists think, but what they themselves believe to be true. Each person constructs a unique view of reality based on information, personal desires, and existing perspectives. In Chapter 5 we examine how the individual processes information in constructing reality.

Physical and social reality

In an attempt to understand how people form a picture of their world, a distinction has been made between physical and social reality (Festinger, 1954). **Physical reality** can be perceived directly through the various sensory modalities: vision, touch, audition, taste, and so on and can be measured through the use of various instruments, such as rulers, spectrographs, scales, and so on. **Social reality** is a construction of human experience and cultural products: economic conditions, political opinions, religious beliefs, history, science, philosophy, and art. These are unique human by-products, and although they may be par-

By processing and organizing information, we develop our view of reality. We perceive physical reality through our senses but construct social reality through our experiences and culture. Artists present their different views of social reality through their individual creations.

tially dependent upon physical reality, none would exist without our defining them, our providing categories and concepts to organize information, and our arriving at some degree of consensus about them. Even within a given culture, there can be sharply different views of social reality. Disputes on economic theory, the quality of a president's decisions, and the causes of a high divorce rate illustrate the uncertainties associated with complex judgments.

William James (1890) wrote a chapter on "The Perception of Reality" in his classic introductory psychology text. He avoided the philosophical problems associated with deciding just what the nature of reality is and instead focused on how people develop their various views of reality. Contemporary social psychologists have followed the example of James and continue to view the development of an individual's view of reality as a matter of processing and organizing information (Lauer and Handel, 1977).

Social filters of information

History's lessons are no more enlightening than the wisdom of those who interpret them.

David Schoenbrun

The individual is embedded in a set of groups and institutions and has a variety of relationships with other people. Almost everything we "know" about social reality is constructed out of information provided by other people. We read newspapers and books, talk to our friends, watch television, and attend lectures. The information gained from others is often obtained by them from still other people. If each person is considered a filter through which information passes, then most information is squeezed through many social filters on its way to us.

During the Middle Ages a few people traveled to distant lands. When they returned, listeners were held spellbound by the exotic tales that the voyagers told. The travels of Marco Polo are of interest even today. In modern societies, information can be transmitted instantaneously anywhere in the world. If governments do not restrict access, it is possible to acquire information from museums, scientific laboratories, concert halls, libraries, and through travel to remote deserts, mountain tops, and ruins of ancient civilizations.

Gatekeepers of information

A **gatekeeper** is a person who is a source of information about events that occur outside your own experience. Gatekeepers include family, friends, neighbors, tourists, news reporters, novelists, teachers, and anyone else who supplies information about events in the world.

A **two-step flow of information** has been found in the gatekeeping process (Katz and Lazarsfeld, 1955). Information from a primary group of gatekeepers, such as movie reviewers, columnists, and local cooperative extension services, is transmitted to a larger group of citizens. These primary gatekeepers or experts are called **influentials.** Interested people turn to these influentials when they want to know which is the best movie to see, what underlies the current conflict in the Middle East, or how to can tomatoes.

The two-step flow of information clearly was manifested among immigrants to Israel in the early years of that nation (Eisenstadt, 1952). The influentials were usually rabbis and teachers who kept close tabs on government regulations and procedures. The new immigrants went to them to find out how to make arrangements and to learn about the traditions of their new homeland. As they gained familiarity with the rules and customs of Israel, the immigrants depended less on the influentials.

Mass media

Without doubt the mass media constitute a powerful gatekeeping force in generating and maintaining images of reality. Television is the number one gatekeeper in American society with almost 100 percent of households having at least one television set. The average person views television almost thirty hours per week (*World Almanac,* 1982). People also spend a good deal of time reading newspapers, magazines, and books. These printed media are easily available in every grocery store and shopping mall.

A focus by the mass media on certain events has important effects on the reactions of people, including the setting of agendas for governmental policy making (Shaw and McCombs, 1977). As can be seen in Box

Box 5-1

Did you hear the news tonight?

Have you ever participated in passing a story around a circle? One person whispers a story to the next one, who passes it on to a third person, and so on until the last person receives it. Then the first and last persons tell the story to the group. Of course the two stories are usually quite different from one another. In much the same way, people have trouble remembering what they saw on the evening television news. They may have a difficult time remembering more than one or two stories.

What people remember from viewing thirty-second snippets on videotapes was investigated at twelve shopping malls in different parts of the United States (Jacoby and Hoyer, 1982). A total of sixty different snippets were used, including news, commercials, and dramas. Each of twenty-seven hundred people watched a tape in a private booth and were then asked to answer twelve true/false questions. Six of the questions were direct restatements from the videotape and six involved inferences that could be drawn from the material presented on the tape. Only 3.5 percent of the respondents answered all questions correctly. More than half of the respondents answered at least four questions incorrectly. Given the short duration of the film, the concentration by viewers on it, and the fact that testing occurred immediately after viewing, the rate of error is impressive. These errors did not depend upon content. This result can be interpreted as indicating that television has less impact on the cognitive structures of viewers than is popularly believed. Another possibility is that what the person remembers is simply not an accurate representation of the programs viewed.

5-1, however, the effects of television may be exaggerated by critics. The capture of hostages at the American embassy in Iran in 1979 stayed in the headlines of both print and electronic media until Jimmy Carter finally was defeated in a presidential election. A special late-night program, now called "Nightline," was created for the purpose of providing an update on events in Iran. Each night the program would begin with a dramatic statement of how many days the hostages had been in captivity. This spotlight on the government's impotency in doing something to rescue the hostages gave the matter a high priority in government policy making.

Exposure on the mass media may create instant celebrities or damage reputations. According to one study, almost any form of innuendo can have a damaging effect on a person's reputation (Wegner, Wenzlaff, Kerker, and Beattie, 1981). Subjects were presented headlines about fictitious people who were said to have been past candidates for the U.S. House of Representatives. The headline was alleged to have been printed by a highly credible source (*New York Times* or *Washington Post*) or a less credible source (*National Enquirer* or *Midnight Globe*). The headline represented an assertion (e.g., "Bob Talbert linked with Mafia"), a question (e.g., "Is Karen Downing Associated with Fraudulent Charity?"), or a denial (e.g., "Andrew Winters Not Connected to Bank Embezzlement"). A neutral headline was presented to subjects in a control condition (e.g., "George Armstrong Arrives in City"). Subjects then evaluated the person mentioned in the headline.

Every type of innuendo had a negative effect on impressions, although denial had the least negative effect. As can be seen in Figure 5-1, these effects occurred regardless of the source of the headline, even though separate ratings indicated a sharp difference in the perceptions of the credibility of the two types of sources used in the study.

The concern often expressed by people in the public eye about the way their names are bandied about in the press appears to be well founded because mention, even by less prestigeful magazines, can create a negative impression on readers. Stories in the newspaper about persons arrested for driving while intoxicated or alleged to have committed a crime may result in their remaining convicted in the minds of people in the community even though they are later acquitted in court.

Consider the problem facing reporters in gathering stories for the mass media. They must rely on informants because they cannot always directly observe newsworthy events. A reporter must attempt to reconstruct some happening from often conflicting accounts of informants. A story must be written or telecast to fit a restricted amount of space or time. News interview programs tend to develop favorite guests, such as Senator Robert Dole, because they have mastered the art of providing simple and short answers to complex questions. The story may be changed or omitted by an editor. Many reporters believe in providing an interpretative understanding of the event, giving the event historical context or analysis in terms of current policies. The resulting story is a neatly packaged, ideologically tinged view of social reality that can be readily adopted by the consumer without need of further analysis or thinking.

Propaganda

Through clever and constant application of propaganda, people can be made to see paradise as hell, and also the other way around, to consider the most wretched sort of life as paradise.
Adolph Hitler, Mein Kampf

The *Random House College Dictionary* (1973) defines propaganda as "information or ideas methodically

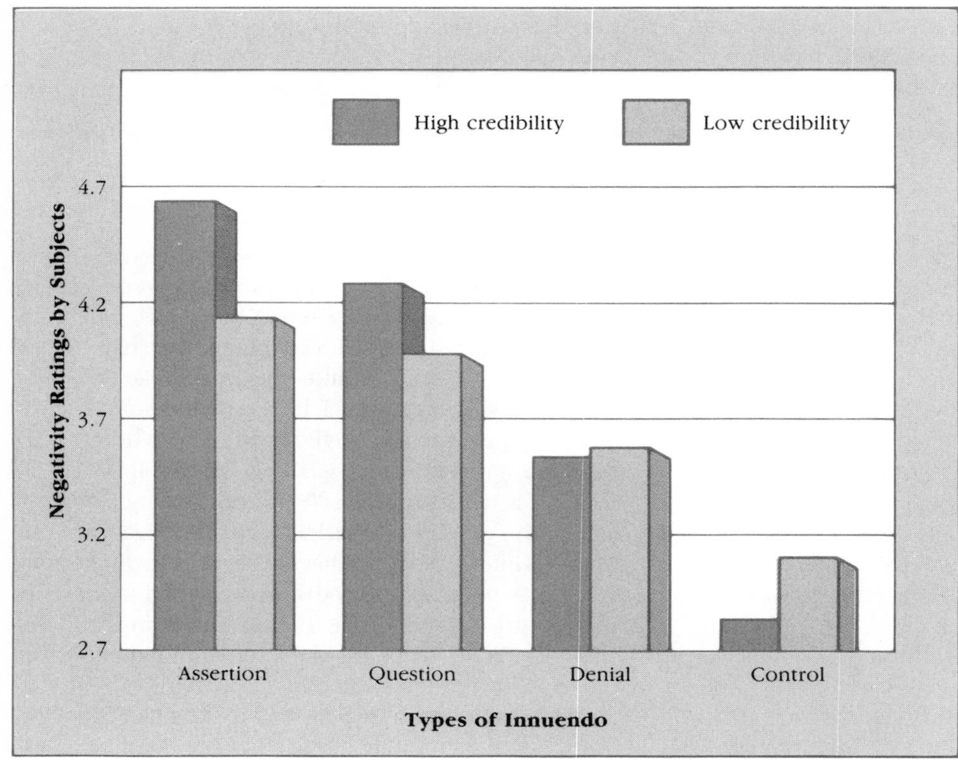

Figure 5-1 Effects of innuendos on subjects.

Source: Based on "Incrimination through innuendo: Can media questions become public answers?" by D. M. Wegner, R. Wenzloff, R. M. Kerker, and A. E. Beattie, 1981, *Journal of Personality and Social Psychology, 40*, 822-832.

spread to promote or injure a cause, group, nation, ..." In other words, **propaganda** is the use of information to achieve intended effects on other people. The information transmitted by a propagandist may be true or false (or just nonsense), and the effects intended may be benign or exploitative.

When the surgeon general of the United States issues a report on the harmful effects of cigarette smoking, one goal is to get people to stop smoking. This intention makes the report propaganda, but the justification is to prevent disease and death. The information transmitted is based on scientific theories and data. On the other hand, advertising meant to convince you to buy over-the-counter drugs may be false or misleading and devoted to making a profit for a manufacturer.

Not everyone who transmits false or incomplete information is a propagandist. Some people may simply be poor reporters or educators. As long as gatekeepers do not intend to produce any particular effect by transmitting information, it would be inappropriate to refer to them as propagandists. For example, educators are (at least ideally) supposed to be indifferent to the conclusions reached by students in political science courses. Thus, education and propaganda can be clearly distinguished from one another.

Education may function as prepropaganda when it prepares people to be receptive to persuasive communications (Ellul, 1965). Omissions of contributions by black people or women in history books, together with use of such language as "mankind" for human beings and "he" for any person, provide a cultural context within which racist and sexist propaganda are more likely to be effective. On the other hand, people can be educated to recognize propaganda techniques, use logic, and develop workable criteria for evaluating alternative views of reality.

Censorship

All censorships exist to prevent any one from challenging current concepts and existing institutions.

George Bernard Shaw

Censorship refers to the deliberate withholding of information or its restriction to a few privileged people. Censorship may be practiced by government, by judicial bodies, or by anyone in interpersonal relations. Although it is not the task of the social psychologist to study governments or courts, we must recognize that censorship has an impact on how an individual constructs reality from available information. In nations where the government controls all the media of mass communications and educational institutions, a more homogeneous view of reality exists among the populace than in nations where there is competition for control over images of reality. Censorship may be considered a form of "silent propaganda" and assumes that what you do not know cannot hurt the censor.

The impact of censorship is also felt in interpersonal relations. The unfaithful husband or wife may not inform the spouse of the adulterous conduct, and a person receiving a bonus at work may not tell a spouse about having extra money. Movies are rated PG, R, and X; some parents limit the kinds of television programs the children can watch and the magazines they can read. Department chairpersons do not tell the faculty about discussions held with deans and vice-presidents regarding promotions, tenure, and salary increases. The practice of censorship among people is widespread and is one of many techniques available to people or organizations in trying to gain control over the reactions of others.

A particular form of interpersonal censorship involves withholding bad news from a person. This form of censorship is referred to as the **MUM effect.** Tyrants have been known to cut out the tongues of messengers who brought bad news.

The MUM effect has been demonstrated in a laboratory study (Rosen and Tesser, 1970). Subjects were told that their partner was late in arriving. A person then entered the laboratory and told the experimenter that the late subject should call home immediately; the person mentioned either that the news was good or that it was bad. When the late person arrived, the waiting subject had an opportunity to pass along whichever message was given. Almost all waiting subjects mentioned the phone call and when there was good news, they also passed the news along. Waiting subjects who were told that the news was bad, however, mentioned only the phone call to their partners and remained MUM about the bad news.

People may feign ignorance when they possess bad news and are queried directly about what they know. For example, subjects were asked to assist in giving a test to a confederate and learned that the latter's performance was either good or poor. The confederate then asked the subjects for information about performance. When subjects believed the performance was poor, they often feigned ignorance and gave less information to the confederate than subjects who believed a confederate's performance had been good (Kardes, Kimble, DePolito, and Biers, 1982).

Rumor and gossip

Rumor is a pipe Blown by surmises, jealousies, conjectures, And of so easy and so plain a stop That the blunt monster with uncounted heads, The still-discordant wavering multitude, Can play upon it.

Shakespeare, King Henry IV

In 1888 the girls of North Hall, Newnham, debated the question whether life without gossip would be worth living. The vote was unanimously negative. . . .The principal defended this . . . decision. However, she understood gossip to mean ready, informed and piquant conversation.

Lumley (1925)

A **rumor** is information that is transmitted through a chain of people, requiring recall and retelling by each person in the chain. Rumors typically focus upon important events. **Gossip** is similar to rumors, except that the focus is on people and typically involves trivial personal circumstances (Rosnow and Fine, 1976). The frequency of rumors and gossip in the interactions of people underlines the importance of information exchange and the reliance people have on each other for constructing social reality.

The intensity of a rumor is a function of two factors: (1) the amount of interest people have in the relevant events and (2) the degree of uncertainty about what is happening (Allport and Postman, 1947). Rumors are common in wartime, during natural disasters, and on almost any day on Wall Street. Rumors may be considered adaptations to social disruption and may be associated with important events (Shibutani, 1966). Rumors and gossip serve the purpose of making sense of the social and physical environment, allaying anxieties, providing an outlet for the expression of hostility, and consensually validating and justifying people's shared beliefs, emotions and actions.

Rumors have been classified into three types: pipe dreams, bogies, and wedge-drivers (Knapp, 1944). Each type expresses desires or emotions of people. Pipe dreams express hopes and wishes; bogies fear and anxiety; and wedge-drivers hostility, aggressiveness, and hate. Examination of rumors during the early part of World War II revealed that less than 2 percent were pipe dreams, one-fourth were bogies, and more than two-thirds were wedge-drivers. Pipe dreams included reports of Hitler's death and of oil shortages in Japan. Among the bogies were stories that the disaster at Pearl Harbor was greater than was being admitted by the government or press, and that an invasion of California was imminent. Wedge-driving rumors of Jews or Catholics avoiding the draft also were circulated frequently around the general population.

Pipe dreams were found to be the most common type of rumors during the civil war in Nigeria (Nkpa, 1975). Long suffering and devastation may have made Nigerians strongly desire peace and normalcy. Divisions within families and institutions are very disruptive and demoralizing. Conversations reflected the desire to end the civil war. In contrast, Americans in the early days of World War II had little experience with armed conflict and were fearful and uncertain about the course of events. Thus, the conversation of Americans involved many bogies. As can be seen in Box 5-2, rumors are sometimes interwoven with superstitions in an individual's construction of reality.

There have been only a few controlled studies of rumor, but they generally show that interest, ambiguity, and anxiety are associated with the intensity of rumors. Conditions of interest and ambiguity were created in classes at a girl's preparatory school in order for researchers to observe if rumors would be fostered (Schachter and Burdick, 1955). In four classes, a student was removed from class, creating ambiguity about why she was removed. In two of these classes and in two classes where a girl had not been removed, students were interviewed and asked if they knew anything about examinations that had been

Box 5-2

Insecurity, rumors, and superstition

Superstition has been defined as "any belief or attitude that is inconsistent with the known laws of science or with what is generally considered in the particular society as true and rational; especially such a belief in charms, omens, the supernatural, ..." (Webster's New World Dictionary, 1966). Times of upheaval and crisis appear to breed superstition (Hofstader, 1963). For example, the black plague that killed almost one-fourth of the population of Europe in the twelfth century was explained as the wrath of God, the hand of the "evil one," the fumes from the earth's interior, and the result of titanic struggle between the planets (Tuchman, 1978).

One of the well-known, tragic chapters in American history involved the burning of witches at the stake in Salem, Massachusetts. It was assumed that the bizarre and "crazy" behavior of these women was due to their being possessed by demons. Recent advances in biochemistry have produced a more scientific explanation. There is a fungus called "ergot" that appears at times on rye and other cereal grasses. The weather conditions in the years of the witch burnings were conducive to the flourishing of ergot. Young women employed in handling the grain and flour would be particularly susceptible to ergot, which has peculiar biological and psychological effects including contractions of the uterus, asthma, deafness, general muscular spasms, and disruptions of cognitive processes. The women were indeed possessed, not by demons, but by a biochemical agent—ergot.

Fear, anxiety, lack of control over events, and ignorance regarding the causes of events appear to be associated with the development and acceptance of superstition. Padget and Jorgenson (1982) tested this hypothesis by examining the German equivalent of the *Reader's Guide to Periodical Literature* during the years 1918–1940. They counted the number of articles published dealing with astrology, mysticism, and cults. They also devised a measure of economic threat consisting of unemployment of trade union members, real wages of Ruhr miners, and the industrial production index for the preceding year. The proportion of publications in 1919 then could be compared with the economic index for the previous year and for a period covering over two decades.

Economic threat was correlated with interest in astrology and mysticism, but not with the emergence of cults or interest in topics not involving superstition (i.e., gardening). Publications of materials on astrology were very high in 1936 (invasion of the Rhineland) and 1939 (start of World War II), suggesting that political as well as economic threat produced interest in the occult. Similar findings were obtained in a study of the United States in the prosperous 1920s and the depression of the 1930s (Sales, 1973). A survey of mediums indicated that they believed wars, depressions, and disasters are associated with increased business for them (Keene, 1976).

taken from the office. In a control class, neither event occurred. Almost all students had heard a rumor that the girl removed from class had stolen exams. Students were more likely to transmit rumors, however, when a girl had been removed from their class and when she appeared to be under suspicion regarding stolen exams.

Hearing skepticism or resistance to a rumor discourages people from transmitting it. Inhibition of rumor transmission was shown among students who were exposed to a rumor from a confederate (Jaeger, Anthony, and Rosnow, 1980). A second confederate commented by saying, "I heard it. I don't know what to believe, but it is an interesting rumor." Or, the confederate said: "The rumor is absolutely false and I can prove it. I know the student who made it up." The rumor was transmitted less frequently by students who heard the discrediting comment. Furthermore, as can be seen in Figure 5-2, students who scored higher on a measure of anxiety more often said they repeated the rumor than did students with low anxiety.

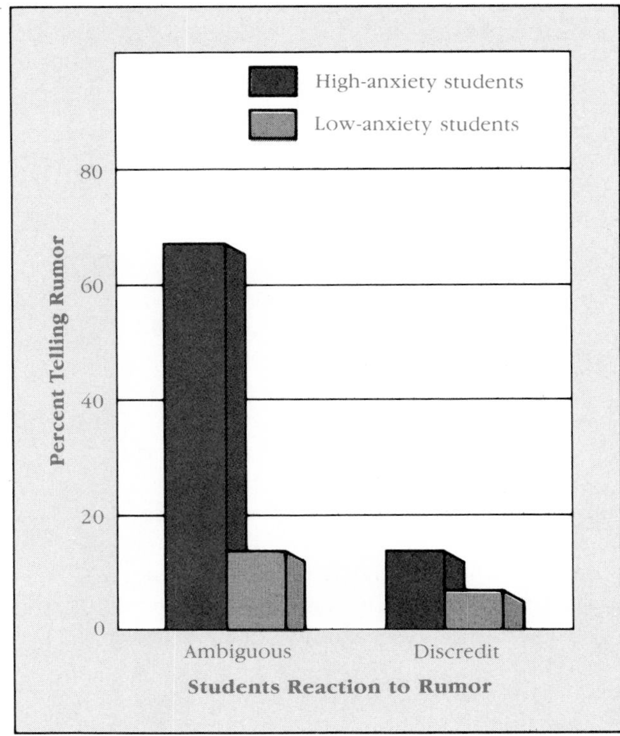

Figure 5-2 Anxiety, discrediting, and rumors among students. *Note:* Students with high anxiety more often said that they repeated the rumor than did low-anxiety students.

We cannot make any simple generalization about rumors. A review of the available research concludes that rumors may sometimes relieve anxiety and may at other times exaggerate threats or increase uncertainty (Rosnow, 1980). The distortion of information in rumors traditionally has been believed to be in the direction of simplification. One theory proposed three basic changes in information: leveling, sharpening, and assimilation (Allport and Postman, 1947).

Leveling is the dropping of certain details because they do not fit within the cognitive categories or values of the teller. **Sharpening** refers to the tendency to emphasize aspects of the story that are consistent with the values and interests of the teller. **Assimilation** involves the padding and organization provided by the teller to make the story better. Contrary to the expected shortening of rumors according to these three processes, most studies have shown that rumors become increasingly complex and disorganized with transmission (Rosnow, 1980).

Though rumors may defy prediction in some respects, they have real and disruptive effects. Residents fled from Port Jarvis, New York, in 1954 when they heard a rumor that a dam had burst and a typhoid epidemic was imminent (Rosnow and Fine, 1976). The New York Stock Exchange has a rule against circulating rumors on the floor, and rumor control centers have been established in cities, plants, and university campuses where people have experienced the disrupting effects of the spread of false information. Rumors are usually false and hence cannot be relied upon as a basis of action.

Summary of social filters of information

Figure 5-3 provides a summary of the social sources of information that serve as the basis for an individual's construction of social reality. While these social filters often change information in certain ways, they are ultimately the most important basis the individual has for forming impressions of events and of other people.

Figure 5-3 The social sources of information. *Note:* All sources stand between us and the actual event.

Personal filters of information

Skepticism is the chastity of the intellect.
George Santayana

In arriving at a personalized construction of reality, we must select from the information gathered through direct experience and through gatekeepers. Selection is affected by our biological capacities, acquired language, and prior beliefs and values. New information is interpreted in the context of old construction—new wine in old bottles. In a real sense, social psychologists have attempted to reconstruct how an individual processes information to develop and evaluate a particular view of reality. We have seen that information is changed as it passes through social filters. Examination of the way an individual changes the information after receiving it shows that further distortions occur as a function of personal filters.

Attention and the selection of information

An almost unlimited amount of information is available to the individual, but there are limits to how much a person can process. Almost a century ago William James (1890) observed:

> Millions of items of the outward order are present to my senses which never properly enter into my experience. Why? Because they have no *interest* for me. . . . Only those items which I notice shape my mind—without selective interest, experience is an utter chaos. Interest alone gives accent and emphasis, light and shade, background and foregound—intelligible perspective, in a word. (p. 402)

Just as a flashlight focuses on only some of the objects in the darkness, a person's perceptual apparatus ignores much and selects from what is available. **Attention** refers to our selectivity in processing information from the environment.

There are features of the environment that may attract the attention of an individual. A stimulus may stand out, as in the case of reflectors in the headlights of an automobile at night. Movement tends to attract the eye or a sound may reorient the perceiver toward the environment. The volume of sound on television commercials is louder than the program in an effort to attract the attention of the viewer. Other people may orient us to various aspects of a situation.

In a field study on the streets of New York City, groups of various sizes stood gazing up at a sixth-floor window across the street (Milgram, Bickman and Berkowitz, 1969). As can be seen in Figure 5-4, the greater the size of the group planted by the experimenter, the more passersby there were who looked up.

Each of us attends to and processes a selective amount of available information. People may serve to direct our attention to various aspects of our environment, as this crowd that gathers to observe an event attracts others to join.

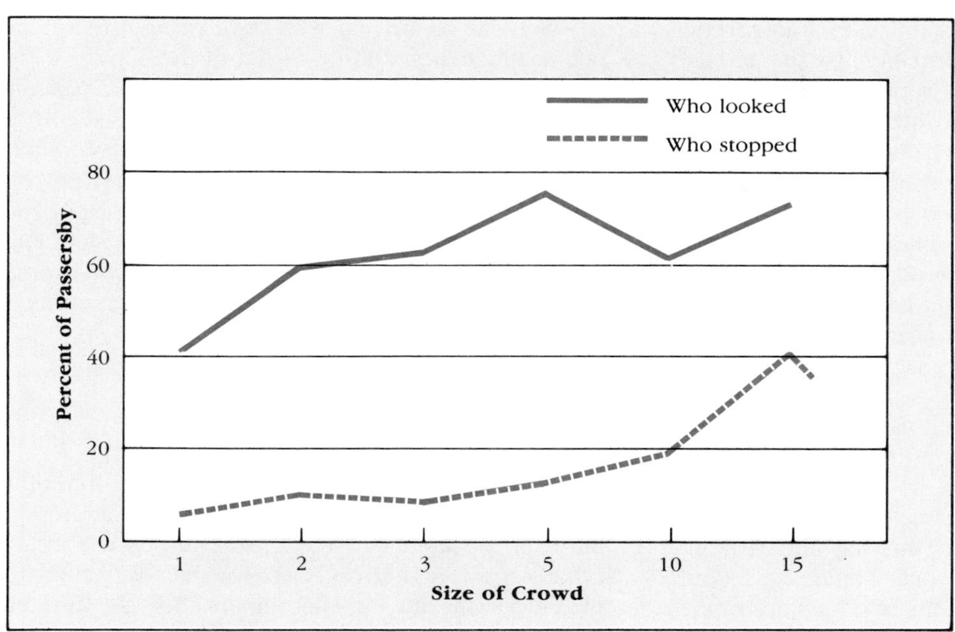

Figure 5-4 Size of crowd who stopped and who looked up.

The individual can process about seven (plus or minus two) chunks of information at any moment in time (Miller, 1956). Telephone numbers are limited to seven digits because most people can look at them once and then dial without having to look a second time. If a person is thinking about something else or experiencing strong emotions, however, the attention to internal stimuli will detract from the ability to process information from the environment. Under such circumstances, a person may have to look at a phone number two or more times before dialing is completed.

Although our sensory mechanisms allow us to make fine discriminations regarding external stimuli, we tend to aggregate information into larger units. This chunking of information allows an individual to ignore certain features of the environment and to attend to stimulus characteristics believed to be more significant. Consider the fact that humans can discriminate between seven million different colors (Nickerson and Newhall, 1943). If we paid attention to every variation of color we can discriminate, there would be no capacity to process any other kind of information. Most of us lump discriminable colors into larger chunks with the result that unless we are artists or designers, we form less than fifty categories within which we include the seven million possible discriminations. Social psychologists have proposed various ways in which individuals may chunk information. These categories represent the basic elements used in the construction of reality.

Cognitive units for the construction of reality

We have introduced several concepts representing basic elements used by individuals in constructing reality. For example, in Chapter 4 stereotypes and prototypes were introduced as cognitive categories for chunking individuals together in a group presumed to share certain characteristics. We now consider a number of other building blocks proposed as basic for an individual's understanding of the universe and the self.

Personal constructs

George Kelly (1955) assumed that people have a strong desire to develop an understanding of the world around them, so they can predict events and perhaps control them. According to Kelly, people form **personal constructs,** similar to transparent templates through which information passes and is organized. Personal constructs represent discriminations that a person makes regarding other people and the roles others assume in everyday life.

Kelly developed the Role Construct Repertory Test (Rep Test) to measure personal constructs. A respondent may be given a list of roles, such as employer, neighbor, lover, and friend, and may then be asked to think of a person to fit each of these roles. Similarities in the description of each of these people across different roles suggests that the respondent is using some personal construct to organize the information. Suppose the respondent uses the description of all of the imagined people in the various roles as cooperative or noncooperative and as intelligent or stupid. These two traits or characteristics would appear to be very significant in the way the person perceives other people. These traits would act as templates through which impressions of others are organized.

Kelly recognized that the same characteristic may not have the same meaning for two different people. For example, if two people were asked to provide antonyms for "kind," one may respond with "cruel" and the other with "selfish." Clearly, the personal construct "kind" would have different meaning for the two people.

People can be "primed" to use specific personal constructs to describe others. For example, subjects were given a task where they had to use "adventurous" or "reckless" and "persistent" or "stubborn" as cognitive constructs. They subsequently used the "primed" constructs to describe a character in a story. Although both groups read the same story, subjects who had been primed with favorable personal constructs described the character differently than did those primed with unfavorable ones.

Kelly's Rep Test was used in another study to measure the personal constructs of subjects. The Rep Test indicates how often various personal constructs are used by an individual. Frequently used constructs are assumed to be accessed more easily as templates for processing information. Two weeks later, subjects were asked to reconstruct a passage they had read. Impressions of the main character in these reproductions contained more references to accessible than to inaccessible constructs (Higgins, King, and Mavin, 1982).

Kelly was concerned with developing a theory of personality that would be useful in the clinical treatment of adjustment problems. He found that patients in therapy usually could act out the roles of other people. They could construct the world in ways different from their own. At times, if a depressed person could be induced to play the role of a happy person, remission of symptoms might occur for a considerable period of time. Taking a different perspective on the world may be an important way of changing our lives (Beck, 1970; Meichenbaum, 1977).

Actions, events, and episodes

Each of us has a set of concepts that serve as building blocks for constructing reality. Of particular importance is the ability to recognize various actions of other people. An **action** is a segment of behavior that has social meaning for observers. This is such an automatic and immediate process that we are usually not aware of doing it. We see two people reach out, grasp hands, and pump up and down, we call it shaking hands. "Shaking hands" is not a description of muscle movements but rather a social classification that includes the meaning of the act, given the rules and customs of social behavior in a particular culture (Harre and Secord, 1973). There are cultures in which people do not recognize this action and do not know what it means.

Our actions may have trivial, negative, or positive consequences. The organization of actions with consequences are referred to as **events** and may be evaluated as good or bad. For example, a person may punch another person and the victim may suffer some injury. The punch and injury may be characterized as an "aggressive event." Organizing experience into events requires the kind of causal analysis discussed in Chapter 4. The observer must attribute effects to actions (sometimes inappropriately) to arrive at the somewhat larger cognitive units referred to as events. Punching someone could be accidental, as when a person is demonstrating how he or she would do it and someone suddenly gets in the way. The event would be considered aggressive only if the observer attributes an intent to do harm to the actor.

An **episode** refers to a sequence of actions that have unity within an event (Harre and Secord, 1973). Consider what happens in a job interview. The first episode consists of actions of greeting, including shaking hands, saying names, smiling, nodding, and pointing to a seat. The second episode may involve small talk as the two people settle into their seats and into their roles as interviewer and interviewee. Next, an episode of questioning by the interviewer and answering by the interviewee may take place. The closing episode may include standing up, shaking hands, and making arrangements for future contacts.

People in the same society tend to divide behavior into the same units (Newtson, 1973; Newtson and Engquist, 1976). Research shows that breakpoints between units are more informative than actions within units. For example, we gain more information about people when we observe a change from greeting to questioning than when we view a handshake, statement of greeting, and settlement into chairs.

When people fail to follow conventions governing conduct, their behavior is difficult to classify. Episodes are recognized only when rules of social conduct apply and are followed by the actors. Some forms of violating rules, such as refusing to shake hands, may be rich in meaning precisely because they blatantly and obviously are meant to violate the rule.

Most people in our culture automatically process these hugging and hand-shaking actions as friendly greetings. Taken together, these actions form an event in which those who participate express positive behavior. The sequence of actions that comprise this convivial event are referred to as episodes.

Scripts

We organize actions and episodes of common events into cognitive structures called **scripts** (Abelson, 1981). Scripts are formed on the basis of repeated experiences and are similar to schemas (see Chapter 2). Once a script is activated, it influences expectations, interpretations, behavior, and recall.

Consider your script of what happens when you enter a restaurant. What sequence of episodes would you expect to occur? A maitre-d' will show you to a table, you will be given a menu, you will be asked if you want anything to drink; drinks will be served, and you will be asked to order your dinner. The meal will be brought in a specific sequence: salad and bread, soup and hors d'oeuvre, entŕee or dinner, dessert, coffee, and liquor. Then the bill will be given to one person at the table. The sequence is so invariant, we consider it a ritual (Goffman, 1967). If a waiter or waitress asked you to order dessert before the main meal, you would question his or her competence or sobriety.

Knowing the script permits the person to act appropriately and to have confident expectations about how others will behave. Abelson (1981) helps us to understand events in the restaurant so that we can see how expectations develop from scripts. "John was feeling very hungry as he entered the restaurant. He settled himself at a table and noticed that the waiter was nearby. Suddenly, however, he realized that he's forgotten his reading glasses" (p. 715). What is the significance of the reading glasses? Because you know the script, you probably have guessed that John needed the glasses to read the menu. But no one needed to mention the menu in the story for you to know why John needed his glasses. The script could lead to false conclusions. John could be at his favorite restaurant, could order without a menu, and could want his glasses to read the newspaper.

According to Abelson (1976), "Cognitively mediated social behavior depends on the occurrence of two processes: (a) the selection of a particular script to represent the given situation and (b) the taking of a participant role within that script" (p. 42). A person without a script for a given situation will be confused, disoriented, and unable to understand what is going on or what to do. In Box 5-3, an attempt to devise scripts for every eventuality in planning to wage war is described.

Box 5-3

Setting the stage for war

Contingency planning, war games, mock battles, and maneuvers help military tacticians prepare for future wars. Analysts of military strategy have observed that it is a Russian tradition to plan carefully and then proceed strictly according to plan. Russian maneuvers are planned so that each unit knows where it will encounter the enemy and which side will win each battle (Cockburn, 1983). Tanks will travel an assigned route and will destroy an enemy tank at point A; they will then be destroyed at point B. Each unit is expected to follow the script created for the battle, and each has little flexibility or initiative in adapting to unexpected events.

The historical record indicates that time after time in actual battles Russian troops have staged impressive advances only to lose the initiative in the midst of confusion because the troops did not know what to do next. Russian tacticians have responded to this apparent inadequacy of planning by providing more complex and complete scripts for future battles. They have analyzed every battle of World War II and have coded them, reduced them to mathematical models, and have provided a plan for each kind of situation. The commander's role is to determine which kind of situation confronts him, select the appropriate plan, and then implement it. Once the commander selects the "appropriate" script, he cannot take any unplanned initiative in the situation.

Veterans of the fighting in Afghanistan have complained in the Soviet military press of disasters attributable to inflexible adherence to textbook tactics. A prescription that has been offered by one analyst is for the Russians to develop "small, fast-moving units led by warrant officers and sergeants trained for independence in making decisions" (Cockburn, 1983, p. 173). Flexibility requires that commanders be able to discard one script in favor of some other tactics as the battle situation unfolds.

Constructed plans of action that lead people to perform certain events are called scripts. The battle scripts designed by Soviet tacticians are planned carefully and adhered to strictly. In this Associated Press photograph, Russian soldiers escort a convoy of supply trucks along the Salang Pass in Afghanistan. The commander of such an operation has little flexibility in adapting a rigidly designed script to a surprise guerrilla attack.

There is some preliminary evidence suggesting that the devising of scripts may encourage people to follow through with consistent behavior. In other words, constructing plans for action leads people to form the intention to carry out the action. This tendency was demonstrated among subjects who were asked to draw cartoons of themselves engaged in such activities as donating blood or not taking a trip during spring break. When they were asked subsequently about their intentions to donate blood or stay home during spring break, these subjects indicated they would act as shown in their cartoons (Anderson, 1983). Rehearsals may lead to performances.

Frames

We organize events into social contexts referred to as **frames** (Goffman, 1974). The same episode may be interpreted in a number of different ways depending on the frame we are using. One example is mouth- to-mouth resuscitation. One of the difficulties in training people in the use of this life-saving technique is that a well-established frame exists for the act of holding one's mouth to another person's mouth. The trainee must learn to give a life-saving frame rather than an intimacy frame for the behavior. In Box 5-4, a study suggesting that men and women have different frames for social behavior between the sexes is described.

Language as an information filter

Do not talk to me of Archimedes' Lever.
. . . Give me the right word and the right accent and I will move the world.

Joseph Conrad, A Personal Record

The beginning of wisdom is to call things by their right names.

Chinese proverb

The basic cognitive units we have been defining, such as actions, events, episodes, scripts, and frames would not be possible without language. We cannot provide a simple definition of language, but instead we will need to distinguish it from communication and note the differences among signs, signals, symbols, and meanings we assign to linguistic categories.

Signs, signals, and symbols

A **sign** is an environmental stimulus that leads an organism to expect some other experience. A snapping twig is a sign to a forest animal of the approach of potential prey or danger. Signs produced by living beings are called **signals.** The songbird's territorial call and the mating dance of the whooping crane are examples of signals among some animals. Humans may blow high-pitched whistles to summon dogs, operate traffic lights to regulate traffic, and learn complex hand signals to communicate nonverbally with one another. The capacity of chimpanzees to learn to communicate with signals has been demonstrated to be much greater than they usually display without human intervention (Premack, 1971).

A **symbol** is a stimulus that is given a shared meaning by a human group. Unlike a signal, which associates one physical stimulus with another (e.g., love song with mating), a symbol is a physical stimulus that can represent any human experience, including birth, love, death, freedom, and fantasy. An important characteristic of symbols is that they become detached from the physical world. Signals refer only to the present experience of the organism, but symbols are not bound by time or space; hence symbols can refer to what is happening many light-years away from earth, what happened thousands of years ago, and what may happen in the future. The ability to use symbols, which appears to be unique to humans, provides the imaginative capacity to create art, science, history, religion, and literature. The imaginative reconstruction of an entire culture by archeologists through the study of artifacts could not occur without the ability to use symbols.

An ape's ability to use hundreds of signals to communicate is impressive, but is limited to the existential moment and refers only to physical stimuli. An ape cannot communicate what happened yesterday or what is expected tomorrow. But science fiction writers can create imaginary worlds, as can film directors and artists. As the philosopher Cassirer (1944) has said:

> Man lives not merely in a broader reality; he lives so to speak in a new dimension of reality. . . . No longer in a merely physical universe, man lives in a symbolic universe. Language, myth, art, and religion are parts of this universe. They are the varied threads which

Box 5-4

Frames for heterosexual interactions

Antonia Abbey (1980) reported an incident when she and some female friends sat at a table with two male strangers at a crowded bar. The women and men engaged in a friendly conversation. The men interpreted the friendliness as a sexual invitation, and the women fled the bar to avoid attempts to move toward more intimate behavior.

This experience led Abbey to study the frames developed by male-female pairs of students at Northwestern University in Evanston, Illinois. The students were asked to talk for five minutes about their experiences during that year at school. Other male-female pairs observed the conversation through one-way mirrors. Both the male talkers and the male observers rated the female talkers as more seductive and promiscuous than did the female talkers and observers. In addition, the males rated the female talkers as more sexually attracted to and more willing to date their conversational partner than the females did. Male observers reported being more sexually attracted to and willing to date the opposite-sex talker than did female observers.

To some extent, the sexual frame given to heterosexual relations by the men may be due to their youth. The observation that men in bars attempt to move quickly to intimate relations may also be a function of a frame that bars are places to meet partners for sexual relations. There may be other situations where females give sexual frames for interactions and males do not.

> weave the symbolic net, the tangled web of human experience. All human progress in thought and experience refines upon and strengthens this net. No longer can man confront reality immediately; he cannot see it, as it were, face to face. Physical reality seems to recede in proportion as man's symbolic activity advances. Instead of dealing with the things themselves, man is in a sense constantly conversing with himself. (pp. 42-43)

Linguistic relativity

The **linquistic relativity hypothesis** asserts that the particular social reality constructed by a group of people is a product of their language (Whorf, 1956). Each language contains a set of symbols that provides the categories, schemata, actions, episodes, scripts, and frames an individual uses in interpreting events. Language serves as a gating mechanism, a filter through which a person apprehends the world.

Language is created out of experience and reflects what is important and valuable to a group of people. For example, among nomadic Arabs who live in a world of sun and sand, camels are important for transportation and survival. It is reported that there are six thousand Arabic words for camel, including fifty that describe various phases of camel pregnancy (Thomas, 1937). In contemporary economically developed societies, a new set of categories have been created to represent consumer items. It is an interesting experience for a novice to be introduced to all the nuances of designer clothing.

Languages in use are changing continually, reflecting the varying conditions of human experience. The language a person learns is a foundation that can be used to provide additional interpretations and discriminations. Poets, novelists, historians, and scientists continually invent new ways of expressing and catego-

Nomadic Arabs have six thousand words that refer to the characteristics and behavior of camels because camels mean survival to these nomads. According to the linguistic relativity hypothesis, the construction of a particular social reality depends upon the language of an individual society. Each language consists of symbols that a person uses to interpret events.

rizing experience. In everyday conversation, people can introduce changes in a language in the form of slang.

Symbols provide people with an ability to associate remote events with one another. A continuity of experience over time and situations gives rise to a self-concept. Sex-role identification, identification with national and ethnic groups, and occupations depend on symbolic categories used by people to define themselves. In a way, people "must talk about themselves until they know themselves" (Berger and Luckmann, 1966, p. 38).

Denotative and connotative meaning

As users of language, we need to know the referent of a symbol and be aware of our emotional reaction to it. The **denotative meaning** of a symbol is a definition that points to or implies a referent, and represents what we might expect to find in a dictionary. In everyday language, there are often a number of words that have the same denotative meaning, such as poet and bard.

The **connotative meaning** of a symbol is a person's emotional reaction to it. Researchers have established three dimensions of connotative meaning (Osgood, Suci, and Tannenbaum, 1957). The **Semantic Differential Scale** is a testing technique used to discover the complexity of connotative meanings. A set of scales anchored by polar adjectives, like those shown in Table 5-1 are given to subjects who are asked to rate a concept on each of these scales. In the example in Table 5-1, the concept is "comfort." Many people typically are asked to rate a number of concepts, and a statistical procedure (factor analysis) is used to determine which rating scales appear to be used in much the same way by most subjects.

The three basic dimensions used by subjects in rating concepts are: (1) an *evaluative dimension (E),* indicating a positive or negative reaction to a concept; (2) a *potency dimension (P),* representing how strong or weak the concept is perceived to be; and (3) an *activity dimension (A),* referring to how active or passive is the person who perceives the concept. In Table 5-1, "comfort" is evaluated positively (good, honest, wise, and kind), is perceived as weak (soft, cautious, weak, and lenient), and is rated as passive (passive, regressive, stable, and calm).

Words with the same denotative meaning may have different connotative meanings. For example, "whore" may be rated as more negative, potent, and active than "Lady of the night." Some concepts, such as justice, freedom, democracy, and racism, may be difficult to define with a precise denotative definition, but they may evoke immediate and definite connotative meanings for almost everyone. "Work" may have equal and opposite connotative meanings for different people. For some people, work provides a stable basis for self-identity, an opportunity for self-expression, and a source of economic security; but for others, it is demeaning, a source of physical agony and psychological boredom, and it does not provide sufficient income or security to overcome the other negative features. As is shown in Box 5-5, connotative reactions can be a product of deliberate manipulation and may be the source of conflicts between people.

Table 5–1 A hypothetical subject's rating on a Semantic Differential Scale

RATE THE CONCEPT "COMFORT"

	1	2	3	4	5	6	7		
P (+3) Hard							X	Soft	(−3)
P (−3) Cautious		X						Rash	(+3)
E (−3) Bad						X		Good	(+3)
A (+3) Active							X	Passive	(−3)
E (+3) Honest		X						Dishonest	(−3)
A (+3) Progressive						X		Regressive	(−3)
A (−3) Stable		X						Changeable	(+3)
P (−3) Weak		X						Strong	(+3)
A (−3) Calm		X						Excitable	(+3)
E (−3) Foolish					X			Wise	(+3)
E (+3) Kind			X					Cruel	(−3)
P (+3) Severe					X			Lenient	(−3)

Biography

Charles E. Osgood

Language has fascinated Charles Osgood since his childhood when his grandfather played word games with him. An aunt gave him a thesaurus for his tenth birthday and he spent hours thumbing through it. Charles attended high school in Brookline, Massachusetts where he became editor of both the weekly newspaper and the monthly short-story magazine. He pursued undergraduate studies in psychology and anthropology at Dartmouth College, and received his B.A. degree in 1939 and an honorary degree in 1962. After completing a Ph.D. in 1945 at Yale University, Dr. Osgood carried out research with the Air Force and Navy. His first academic position was at the University of Connecticut. He joined the faculty at the University of Illinois in 1949 and has been there ever since.

Professor Osgood has conducted research in 30 societies around the world. His books entitled "Method and Theory in Experimental Psychology" and "The Measurement of Meaning" coauthored with Suci and Tannenbaum are considered classic works in psychology.

In addition to research on language, Professor Osgood has been concerned with social conflict between persons and nations. He has published numerous articles and books (*Alternative to War or Surrender* and *Perspective in Foreign Policy*) proposing rational ways of reducing tension and reaching negotiated agreements between contending parties. He has served as a consultant to the Air Force, the Navy, and the Arms Control and Disarmament Agency. He is currently writing a book tentatively entitled "Mankind 2000??".

Professor Osgood has received wide recognition for his scholarship. He has been president of the American Psychological Association (1963) and received its award for Distinguished Contributions to the Science of Psychology (1960). In 1971 he received the Kurt Lewin Award for Contribution to the Solution of Social Issues. He was elected to membership in the National Academy of Sciences in 1972 and the New York Academy of Sciences elected him an honorary life member in 1977.

Box 5-5

Differences in meaning and interpersonal conflict

If two people give different denotative meanings to the same concept, discussions between them may appear on the surface to be about the same referent, but they really may be talking about two different things. Even if both share the same denotative meaning for a concept, they may disagree because of failure to recognize differences in connotative meanings given to the concept. A study carried out by Kuhlman, Miller, and Gungor (1973) demonstrated that conflicts between people occur as a function of different meaning structures.

Subjects were asked to rate the concepts "state control" and "elections" on a test of connotative meaning. Subsequently, subjects were given one of two forms of training regarding the denotative meanings of the terms. Half of the subjects learned that the degree of democracy in a nation could be predicted only from information about the amount of state control. The remaining subjects were informed that the presence of free elections was the most important factor in judging whether a nation was a democracy. Four conditions were created in which subjects were paired based on similar or dissimilar connotative meanings and the kind of training about the denotative significance of the key concepts.

Pairs of subjects were presented information about degrees of state control and free elections for twenty hypothetical nations and were given an opportunity to discuss how democratic they perceived each nation to be. As would be expected, people who had similar denotative and connotative meanings for the relevant concepts readily reached agreement on their judgments. Pairs who shared connotative meanings but had different training regarding denotative meanings had difficulty at first in reaching agreement, but as they continued through the list of hypothetical nations, there was less and less conflict between them. Pairs of subjects who had different connotative meanings for "state control" and "elections," whether or not they shared denotative meanings, continued to manifest conflict over all twenty judgments. Although conflict due to denotative differences may be resolved over time, connotative differences persist and maintain cognitive conflict between people. These findings are not optimistic in their implications, because many of the most important concepts in our political system tend to remain denotatively vague but are loaded with contradictory connotative meanings (e.g., welfare, socialism, arms control, and so on).

Summary of personal filters of information processing

Figure 5-5 provides a summary of the processes within the individual that filter, shape, and organize the information received from direct experience and from social sources. These processes and cognitive units are combined in ways not yet understood to form the individual's view of social reality.

Biased inferences in information processing

People gather information and use it to make inferences in constructing their views of social reality. People draw inferences from sampling opinions, much like scientists obtain responses through survey research. The layperson, however, does not carry out

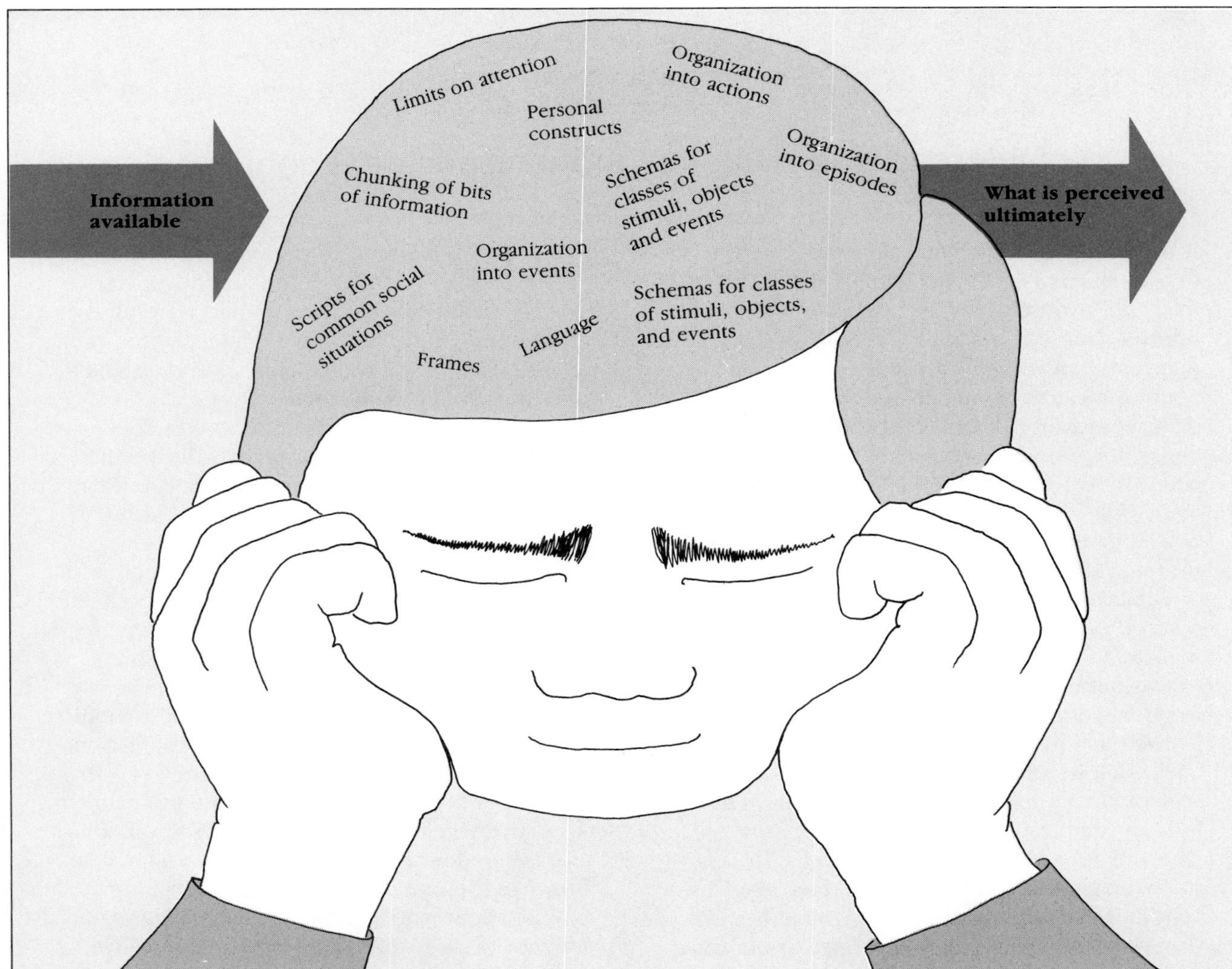

Figure 5-5 Each person's filters of information.

sophisticated sampling of respondents or use statistics to make inferences from data. As a result, most of us have a tendency to make inferences in a biased manner. Among the factors discovered to be associated with biased inferences are the tendency to ignore baserates, the vividness and availability of sources of information, the use of a single past incident or model to interpret the present, the tendency to confirm one's own predictions, and overconfidence. These cognitive biases contribute to the willingness of many people to accept occult explanations for natural phenomena (see Box 5-6).

Box 5-6

Magic, miracles, coincidence, and science

The mass media report that some psychics have the capacity to foresee the future, can help the police locate lost persons or murderers, and can use their powers to move physical objects. These processes of clairvoyance, telepathy, and psychokinesis have received worldwide attention. The United States Defense Department has shown concern about Russian scientists who may be gaining a lead in the race to dominate the world through paranormal power. A clairvoyance expert, for example, might be able to picture the exact coordinates of missile installations or nuclear submarines stationed underneath polar icecaps.

Some of the willingness to accept mystical explanations for events is due to the fact that events are often improbable. When an event is quite unexpected, its occurrence seems like a miracle. Yet, improbable coincidences do occur quite naturally and without divine intervention. Sometimes the vague predictions of your horoscope can be interpreted as accurate, and there are people who win state lotteries. One of the most improbable events of all is yourself. Your genetic makeup is determined by one combination of 23 maternal and 23 paternal chromosomes. The combination that turned out to be you is just one of 700 trillion equally probable combinations of those pairs of chromosomes (Guillen, 1983).

The current miracles of science and technology easily can lead people to believe in almost anything merely because it seems possible. Science is based on probability, not possibility, however. Scientific examination of the field of parapsychology has produced evidence of poor experimental procedures, inadequate use of statistics, misinterpretation of data, and fraud. Self-deception also may be involved among the few scientists who do believe in paranormal processes. James Randi, a professional magician, has demonstrated that he can fool even experienced scientists investigating the paranormal. The willingness to abandon a healthy skepticism about the occult may have tragic consequences. Fad foods and diets, the belief in fortune tellers, and membership in destructive and dangerous cults have in common people's hope of finding an answer to some problems of everyday living. A person's construction of reality provides the context for his or her behavior.

Ignoring baserates

Baserates refer to the frequency with which events normally occur. We use baserates as a basis for predicting future occurrences. Suppose you are betting on the flip of a coin and "heads" comes up ten times in a row. Would you be willing to give odds that a "tail" would come up next? If so, you would be a victim of the "gambler's fallacy." Actually, the probability of heads or tails on each toss is 50 percent, regardless of what has happened in the past. Because we know that heads and tails are equally likely, the occurrence of heads on ten consecutive coin tosses leads us to expect tails to catch up. We ignore the knowledge that the baserate is 50:50.

Baserates may be ignored when people believe they have representative information to use for making inferences. In one experiment, half of the subjects were told that out of one hundred people to be described, thirty were engineers and seventy were lawyers; and the remaining half of the subjects were told there were seventy engineers and thirty lawyers (Kahneman and Tversky, 1973). The 70:30 baserate could be used by subjects to judge the probability that any person described was either an engineer or a lawyer.

Representative information about a person was given to subjects in the form of a thumbnail sketch. For example, Kahneman and Tversky's (1973) description of one sketch was:

> Jack is a 45-year-old man. He is married and has four children. He is generally conservative, careful and ambitious. He shows no interest in political and social issues and spends most of his free time on his many hobbies which include home carpentry, sailing, and mathematical puzzles. (p. 241)

This description is representative of a stereotype that many people have about engineers. Engineers are apolitical, like mathematics, and have interest in concrete activities, like carpentry and sailing. Subjects virtually ignored the baserate information in favor of representativeness in guessing whether the person is a lawyer or an engineer.

The tendency of people to use representative information in drawing inferences occurs in primitive medicine. Substances with curative powers were believed to in some way resemble the disease to be cured. For example, tumeric is yellow, and its color was taken as a sign that it would cure jaundice. Because the fox has a strong respiratory system, it was believed that the lungs of a fox could cure asthma (Nisbett and Ross, 1980). An anthropological study of the primitive Azande culture shows that bird droppings were thought to cure ringworm because of the resemblance between the droppings and the lesion, and the burned skull of a red bush-monkey could be used to treat epilepsy because the wild antics of the monkey resemble an epileptic seizure (Evans-Pritchard, 1937).

Drawing inferences from a single past incident

Some experiences have such an impact on people that they use them to interpret subsequent events. For example, in the Vietnamese War Dean Rusk, the U.S. secretary of state at the time, justified participation in the conflict by comparing the situation to World War II. Just as Hitler might have been stopped by firm resistance before war began, China had to be discouraged from trying to conquer all of Asia. Mao Tsetung was perceived as the Asian Hitler.

This use of a past incident as a frame in which to interpret current episodes was found among sports writers and football coaches (Gilovich, 1981). In judging the potential of a player, they referred to resemblances with successful professional football players. A similar process was found among political science majors who were given information about hypothetical international crises. The descriptions were varied to suggest World War II, Vietnam, or neutral frames. For example, refugees were described as fleeing in boxcars or boats; a possible invasion was described as a blitzkrieg or quick strike. Except for the suggestive words, the descriptions received by all students were the same. The students more often recommended military intervention when a World War II frame had been elicited than when either a Vietnam or neutral frame was invoked.

The use of a representative past event to draw inferences about the present and future probably is encouraged by the absence of baserate information. Wars (or football players) are so different from one another, it is difficult to develop baserate information to use for purposes of making generalizations.

Vividness and availability

The more direct and dramatic a person's experiences, the greater their impact on inferences drawn from them. This principle has been supported in a study of physicians. There has been a decrease in smoking among physicians since the Surgeon General's Report detailing the dangers of cigarette smoking. The lowest rate of smoking has been found among radiologists and physicians who treat lung cancer (Borgida and Nisbett, 1977).

The vividness of experience makes schemas more available to use than more abstract knowledge (Kahneman and Tversky, 1973). Using information because it is there is a variation of a principle of least effort. It takes less cognitive work to make judgments with information that is readily available. Unemployed

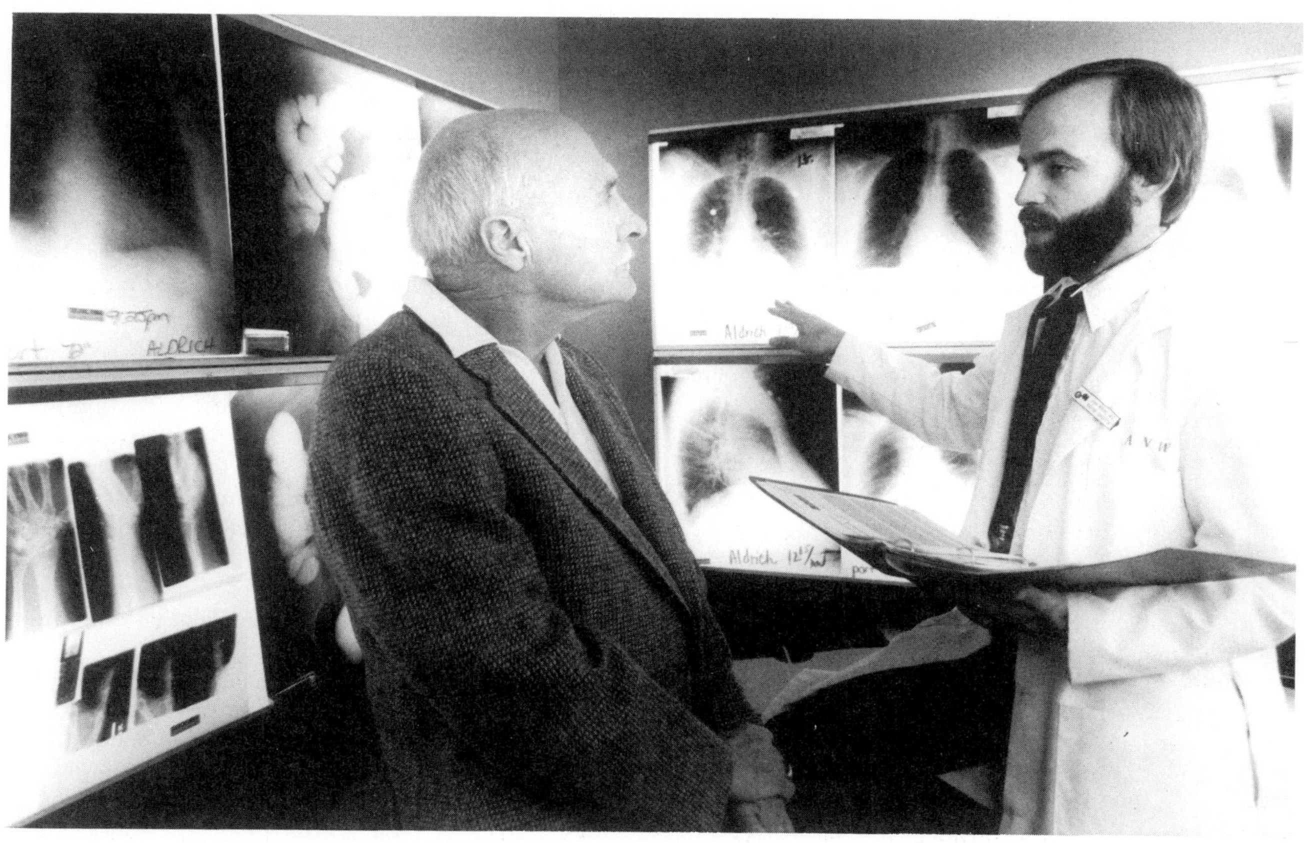

Surveys show that physicians who treat patients with cancer of the lung have the lowest rate of smoking because this group experiences more direct and vivid contact with these patients and with such pertinent diagnostic tests as x-rays.

workers, who probably encounter more unemployed workers at the state unemployment office, at the union hall, or on the street estimate that unemployment is higher than do people who have jobs (Nisbett and Ross, 1980).

Preference for confirming information

People prefer information that confirms rather than disconfirms their beliefs. This conservative tendency to resist change was demonstrated among subjects, half of whom had been provided information that high risk takers make good firefighters, and the remainder were informed that cautious people are more successful as firefighters (Anderson, Lepper, and Ross, 1980).

A subtle way of obtaining confirming information is to ask questions that are bound to elicit answers interpretable as supporting your prior beliefs. Suppose you have formed an impression of a person as an introvert, and you have a chance to ask questions to test your hypothesis. The evidence suggests that many people ask questions, such as, "What factors make it hard for you to really open up to people?" Any answer to this question would suggest that a person has trouble confiding in others and hence is likely to be an introvert. A hypothesis-confirming question that may be asked of someone you think is an extrovert would be: "What would you do to liven up a party?" (Snyder and Swann, 1978).

Hypothesis-confirming strategies are likely to be used when a person has impressions of others as extreme regarding some personality dimension. When others are believed to be less extreme, the person's preference is for information that is most diagnostic of personality traits (Trope and Bassock, 1982).

Individual differences in cognitive biases

Some people seem to be unjustifiably confident of having correct answers for questions of factual knowledge (Fischoff, Slovic, and Lichtenstein, 1977; Kahneman and Tversky, 1979). For example, if people on the average are about 60 percent correct, they will feel confident that they are 75 percent right. This overconfidence in one's judgments may represent a need for positive self-esteem and an impression management tactic of presenting a positive identity of competence to others.

Observation suggests that some people are more interested and energetic in seeking out information than are other people. People who are keenly interested in obtaining information and in thinking about events, who enjoy solving problems and are confident that cognitive work is the best way to achieve goals may be said to have a high *need for cognition* (Cacioppo and Petty, 1982). A paper-and-pencil test designed to measure this characteristic revealed that university professors scored higher than assembly line workers. Furthermore, college students who obtained high scores in need for cognition reported enjoying a complex cognitive task more than did low scorers. Just as people are more or less energetic in engaging in physical activities, there are individual differences in laziness in searching for information and in thinking about it.

Selective memory

Memory is not a static and perfect representation of past events. It is a selective process and one in which information undergoes change during storage. Leveling, sharpening, and assimilation, described in the discussion of rumors, distorts information stored in memory.

Memory is often a reconstructive process and not just a matter of recall (Loftus, 1980). When people are trying to recall an incident, they can be led by selective questioning into remembering what they did not experience. This reconstructive process was demonstrated among subjects who saw a movie of an automobile accident (Loftus and Palmer, 1974). Some of the subjects were asked, "How fast were the cars going when they hit each other?" Other subjects were asked, "How fast were the cars going when they smashed into each other?" Subjects estimated the speed as higher when the cars "smashed" rather than "hit" one another. Furthermore, although no broken glass was shown in the movie, twice as many subjects who were asked about the "smashed" cars reported seeing broken glass than did subjects who were questioned about the "hit" car.

Momentary states of emotion may reduce a person's capacity to store information in long-term memory. Indeed, traumatic events have been known to cause amnesia, a total loss of recall for events (see Box 5-7). Inducing the same mood or emotion that the individual was experiencing at the time an event transpired may elicit recall.

It has been found that subjects recalled the details of humorous or hostile short stories and editorials when the appropriate mood was induced (Laird, Wagener, Halal, and Szegda, 1982). The method used was to instruct the subjects to manipulate their facial muscles. For example, a happy mood was induced by telling subjects: "I would like you to contract the muscles near the corners of your mouth by drawing them up and back" (p. 649). Generally, the memories of people tend to fit the mood they are in. People who are happy and are asked to think of their childhood, remember happy times; while those induced to be in a more melancholy mood remember essentially sad events (Bower, 1981).

The study of memory is too complex for extended examination here, but enough has been said to indicate that a person's image of reality is not a photographic representation of an actual, perceivable world. Rather, it is an idiosyncratic **reconstruction** in which certain events were selectively noticed, categorized, and placed into a preexisting context. "There are no impartial facts. Data do not have a logic of their own that results in the same cognitions for all people" (Krech, Crutchfield, and Ballachey, 1962, p. 24).

The personal filter of memory explains why witnesses at a courtroom trial may represent very differ-

Box 5-7

You're crazy, I didn't do it

Sirhan Sirhan shot and killed Robert Kennedy in the kitchen of the Ambassador Hotel in Los Angeles in 1968. There was no question that Sirhan fired the fatal bullet. The event was witnessed by a crowd of people, and he was apprehended on the scene. Nevertheless, Sirhan denied guilt and seemed to have no recollection of firing the revolver. In response to the legal charges against him, Sirhan responded, "You're crazy, I didn't do it." Amnesia is not unusual under such circumstances. Sirhan was extremely agitated, wild, and emotional at the time of the shooting. Amnesia occurs in about one-third of violent and passionate crimes, such as assault and homicide.

Bernard Diamond, a forensic psychiatrist, was asked by Sirhan's attorneys to examine him. In an attempt to elicit recall of the assassination act, Diamond hypnotized Sirhan and gradually led him to a reconstruction of the event. While hypnotized, Sirhan became increasingly excited; the more excited he became, the more he remembered. On several occasions while under hypnosis, Sirhan reenacted the assassination—cursing, firing the shot, then choking as a Kennedy bodyguard almost strangled him. Sirhan, however, never was able to recall these events in a normal state of consciousness. (Bower, 1980)

ent versions of the same event (see discussion of eyewitness testimony in Chapter 13). As Senator Sam Ervin noted during the Senate Watergate hearings in the summer of 1973, contradictions in the testimony of witnesses does not necessarily mean that one of them is lying.

Summary

Each individual processes information in constructing a view of physical and social reality. Gatekeepers mediate the information and the cognitive units people use to process the information in a two-step flow of communications, the information passes through social filters, including the mass media, propaganda, and rumor and gossip. Censorship may be invoked to prevent information from being widely disseminated.

Once information becomes available to an individual, personal filters in the form of cognitive categories, limited ability to process information, and values and interests act to select, organize, and provide the basis for a person to interpret events. People literally are bombarded with information and, through the mechanism of attention, select from it according to their interests and motivations.

In the attempt to arrive at generalizations about the behavior of other people, an individual forms personal constructs that act as templates through which he or she draws inferences about their characteristics. The movements of others are organized into actions through attributions of intentions, knowledge of rules governing interpersonal interactions, and definition of the situation. We perceive actions and their consequences together as events. Within complex events, we may segment actions into different types, referred to as episodes.

People develop scripts, which are cognitive representations and expectations about the actions and episodes that occur frequently in their experience. Meanings are given to observations by frames, which are learned contexts allowing a person to interpret what is happening. Most of us do not invent these cognitive units, but instead acquire them through the language taught in our culture. Symbols allow a person to develop cognitive units for representing reality.

The inferences people draw from information are often fallacious or biased. People tend to rely on the representativeness of information rather than on baserates. Many people rely more on concrete experiences, including the use of a single dramatic past event, to interpret new events rather than on abstract categories or complex theories. When another is perceived as extreme on some characteristic, the observer seeks information to confirm the impression. When the other is not perceived as extreme in some way, however, the person prefers solid diagnostic information. Further bias may be introduced through the vagaries of selective memory, which is a reconstructive process that can be affected by present cues and queries. Memories associated with emotional experiences are more available to the individual than more mundane experiences.

Glossary

Action The meaning or social significance given to behavior.

Assimilation The process by which a person adds elements to fill in gaps and makes a smooth and comprehensive story in the reporting of an event.

Attention Our selective scanning of information available to the various senses.

Baserate information A statistical summary of expected frequency on some events, such as the proportion of engineers and attorneys in a given population.

Censorship Deliberate withholding of information or its restriction to a few privileged people.

Connotative meaning The emotional association attached to a symbol.

Denotative meaning The implied (points to) or dictionary definition of a word.

Episode A meaning given to a sequence of actions.

Event A sequence involving both actions (or episodes) and consequences.

Frame A context of norms that regulate people's actions and provides meaning for events.

Gatekeeper A social source of information about events outside the direct experience of the target person.

Gossip Information is typically about trivial circumstances of various people.

Influentials People who serve as experts for others about local and international happenings.

Leveling Details that do not fit the categories of the teller are omitted in a report of events.

Linguistic relativity hypothesis Because language provides the categories for interpreting experience, the construction of reality depends on the language a person has learned.

MUM effect A form of censorship by which people are reluctant to transmit bad news.

Personal constructs Cognitive categories that represent discriminations made about other people and the roles they assume in everyday life.

Propaganda Information is manipulated by a person to achieve intended effects on target people.

Reconstructive memory Instead of being a photographic representation of past events, memory is the product of selective perceptions and prompting through questions or other cues.

Rumor Information about important events is transmitted through a chain of people and typically undergoes substantial change.

Script A cognitive structure that organizes episodes into larger contexts and serves as a guide for predicting events and for actions.

Semantic Differential Scale A test consisting of a set of scales anchored by polar adjectives, measures the three dimensions of connotative meaning.

Sharpening An emphasis on details that are consistent with the values and interests of the teller in reported events.

Sign A stimulus that serves as a cue for the occurrence of a second stimulus.

Signal A sign produced by a living organism.

Symbol A stimulus that stands for or represents something else.

Two-step flow of information A frequent process of information flow from a primary gatekeeper, such as a movie critic, through a second person, referred to as an influential, to a third, target person.

Recommended Readings

Fiske, S. T., & Taylor, S. E. (1983). *Social cognition.* Reading, MA: Addison-Wesley.

A general introduction to this rapidly developing field of social psychology; well written and accessible for the beginning reader.

Loftus, E. F. (1980). *Memory.* Reading, MA: Addison-Wesley.

Written for the layperson, this is an entertaining and informative review of the mysterious processes of memory.

Nisbett, R., & Ross, L. (1980). *Human inference: Strategies and shortcomings of social judgment.* Englewood Cliffs, NJ: Prentice-Hall.

A technical, though readable introductory review of the biases and errors in cognition. This is must reading for any serious student of social psychology.

Rosnow, R. L., & Fine, G. A. (1976). *Rumor and gossip: The social psychology of hearsay.* New York: Elsevier North-Holland.

A highly readable review of the rather sparse literature on rumor and gossip.

After I saw the movie [*The Day After*], I thought to myself, "I am going to try and look at a flower and appreciate it more".

Maria Pepe, Age 17
USA Today, *(1983, p. 1)*

6
Attitudes and behavior

Seeing is not always believing

On 20 November 1983 almost 100 million Americans watched *The Day After*, a made-for-television movie. The film portrayed the effects of a nuclear attack on a midwestern city. Because the movie showed the horror of nuclear holocaust in a more detailed and explicit fashion than ever before attempted on commerical television, it became the focal point of heated debate between opposing factions on the issue of nuclear arms control. In the weeks preceding the airing of the movie, the media were filled with conjectures about the impact it would have on the attitudes and behaviors of viewers. The physicians for Social Responsibility predicted that many viewers would have feelings of helplessness and depression (Corry, 1983). The Federal Emergency Management Agency put on extra staff members to answer the phone calls of frightened viewers (*Newsweek*, 1983). A representative of the White House said the program was designed to propagandize people into supporting the nuclear freeze movement and to undermine the defensive strength of the United States.

There was no national outbreak of helplessness and depression, and the Federal Emergency Management Agency only got three calls related to the movie on the following day (*Newsweek*, 1983). A survey of nearly one thousand viewers showed little change in attitudes toward nuclear weapons issues (*USA Today*, 1983). Before watching the movie 46 percent of the respondents reported that they believed nuclear war to be likely within ten years, while 47 percent thought this afterward. Instead of shifting attitudes toward support of a nuclear freeze, the movie appeared to reinforce American's support of a policy to increase strength and deterrence. A larger percentage of viewers thought that the United States was doing all it could to avoid a nuclear conflict. After viewing the movie, they approved of defense policies and supported the reelection of incumbent President Ronald Reagan over his closest Democratic rival at the time, Walter Mondale. In comparison, in 1984 a total of ten studies involving 350,000 people indicated a profound, if delayed impact after viewing *The Day After* (Findlay, 1984). Eight months after the film was shown viewers reported a greater pessimism regarding nuclear war and voiced stronger support for a nuclear freeze.

This "happening" highlights two themes to be developed in Chapter 6: (1) attitudes are believed to be important for understanding behavior and (2) the conditions for changing attitudes or creating resistance to change are complex. We consider the nature of attitudes, their relations to behavior, and the factors that induce attitude change or resistance to change.

The nature of attitudes

Three things are necessary for the salvation of man: to know what he ought to believe; to know what he ought to desire; and to know what he ought to do.

St. Thomas Acquinas, Two Precepts of Charity

The concept of attitude has played a central role in the history of social psychology. Most early definitions of social psychology mentioned attitudes. A half century ago, attitude was considered "the most distinctive and indispensible concept in contemporary social psychology" (Allport, 1935, p. 798). Despite disagreements about the exact nature of attitudes and how to measure them, the study of attitudes continues to be of great interest to researchers. The extent of disagreement is indicated by one review of the literature, which indicates over five hundred different ways of measuring attitudes (Fishbein and Ajzen, 1972).

What is an attitude?

The word "attitude" first entered the English language around the beginning of the eighteenth century. It evolved from the Latin word *aptitudo* meaning "fitness" or "adaptedness" (Petty, Ostrom, & Brock, 1981). People used the term "attitude" to refer to the posture assumed by figures in statues and paintings. Charles Darwin used the term to refer to physical expressions of emotions. For example, a person crying expresses an unhappy attitude.

In 1918 Thomas and Znaniecki wrote a book about the difficulties encountered by Polish immigrants in the United States. They used the concept of attitude to refer to a feeling that people directed toward some object, such as money or dislike of work. This shift from a physiological to a psychological emphasis has had a profound effect on the social sciences. Most social psychologists have adopted the attitude construct as one referring to mental events.

An **attitude** is usually defined as a learned predisposition having three components: cognitive, affective, and behavioral (Fishbein & Ajzen, 1975). In other words, attitudes consist of thoughts, emotions, and actions, and tend to guide behavior in ways learned through experience (see Table 6-1).

The **cognitive component** consists of what we think about the item of interest, referred to as the **attitude object.** It refers to the positive or negative images and thoughts associated with the object (Cacioppo, Harkins, & Petty, 1981). Consider the cognitive appraisals of survivalists and preventionists who have adopted different positions on the issue of nuclear weapons. Survivalists have images of nuclear war as inevitable but survivable. They favor actions that would promote survival following the inevitable holocaust, such as stockpiling foods and building bomb shelters. Preventionists believe that nuclear war can be prevented but would not be survivable. The cognitive component of their attitude includes support for political and educational actions aimed at reducing the probability of nuclear war (Tyler & McGraw, 1983).

The **affective component** of an attitude refers to a person's feelings toward the attitude object. It consists of an emotional response or "gut feeling" associated with some issue, person, thing, or event. Surveys have been carried out in which measurements of affective responses toward the nuclear weapons issue were obtained. As can be seen in Figure 6-1, the percentage of people who indicated they were very worried about

Table 6-1 Three components of an attitude

Cognitive: What a person *thinks* about the attitude object.
Affective: What a person *feels* about the attitude object.
Behavioral: How a person *acts* toward the attitude object.

How has the women's liberation movement affected this man's attitude toward equality for all individuals? Why does his attitude provoke this behavior? Is his march for "husband's lib" a gut reaction against women's rights?

nuclear war has doubled in the past twenty-five years (Kramer, Kalick, and Milburn, 1983).

The **behavioral component** of an attitude consists of a person's tendency to act or desire to act in a positive or negative way toward the attitude object. In response to a question asking whether nuclear weapons should be used if the Russians attacked western Europe, respondents were much less favorable in 1982 than in 1958 and 1961 (see Figure 6-1).

Measurement of attitudes

The cognitive and affective components of attitudes are not part of physical reality and hence others cannot perceive them directly. The measurement of attitudes usually relies on inferences about these internal psychological states based on observations of what people say and do. In principle, this task is no different from that of the biologist who infers the nature and position of genes on a chromosome from reactions obtained in experiments. The most popular methods for measuring attitudes consist of paper-and-pencil scales. Three of the most frequently used methods for measuring attitudes are the Thurstone, Likert, and Semantic Differential Scales.

Thurstone Scale

Assessing the attitudes of people may seem simple enough. Why not just ask them what their attitudes are toward various attitude objects? Unfortunately, experience has shown that it is not so easy to construct questions that are unambiguous and neutral. The way a question is asked can affect the answer that is given. For example, people reported twice as many headaches when asked if they got headaches *frequently* than when asked if they got headaches *occasionally* (Loftus, 1975). Quite different attitudes would likely be obtained from the same person if the person responded to questions about "ghastly and destructive" nuclear weapons than when he or she responded to questions about "potentially dangerous" nuclear weapons.

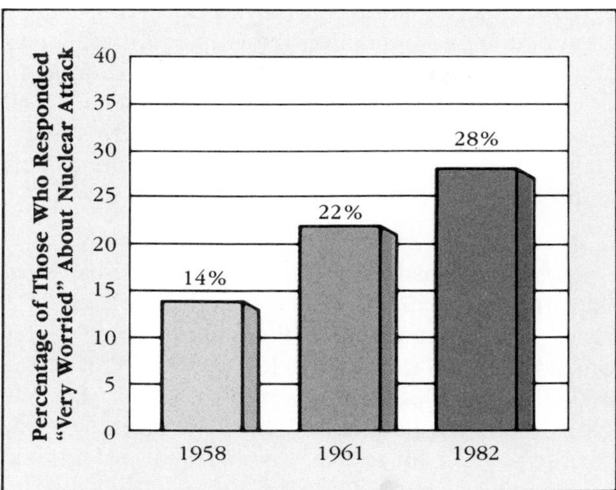

Figure 6-1 The affective component of people's attitudes towards nuclear war.

Source: Based on "Attitudes toward nuclear weapons and nuclear war: 1945-1982" by B. M. Kramer, S. M. Kalick, and M. A. Milburn, 1983, *Journal of Social Issues, 39,* 7-24.

Ambiguity within a question can cause people to interpret it differently. In effect, people would be responding to the same item but would be giving it different meanings. In such a case, it would not be appropriate to compare the scores of respondents because they actually were responding to different questions. Early attempts at attitude measurement indicated psychologist's awareness of these problems.

A laboratory was established at the University of Chicago in 1929 by Edward Thurstone, a former engineer, for the purpose of the development of precise, scientific measurements of attitudes. Thurstone's technique is called the **method of equal-appearing intervals** and typically involves the following seven steps:

1. A number of items related to an attitude object are constructed.
2. The items are evaluated by a set of judges who have characteristics similar to people who will serve as subjects.
3. The judges are asked to sort the items into 11 equal piles from most (1) to least favorable (11).
4. The items that the judges sort into the same piles are selected, and the items on which they disagree are thrown away.
5. Each of the items is given a scale value corresponding to the median value assigned by the judges. Thus, if all the scores, determined by the piles to which that item was assigned by all the judges, were arranged in order, the middle score would be used to represent the value of that item.
6. The actual subjects are given the items and asked to select the ones with which they agree.
7. A measure of the subject's attitude is calculated by the arrangement of the endorsed items according to their predetermined values and the selection of the middle score as representative of the strength of the subject's attitude (Cacioppo et al., 1981.).

A hypothetical Thurstone Scale for measuring attitudes toward nuclear weapons is presented in Table 6-2.

As you can see, each item provides the respondent

Table 6–2 Sample of Thurstone Scale measuring attitudes toward nuclear weapons

(1.6)	1. Until we reduce our supply of nuclear weapons, we cannot call ourselves civilized.
(3.1)	2. Mutual reduction of nuclear weapons should be a main goal of negotiations between the United States and the Soviet Union.
(7.3)	3. In an ideal world, nuclear weapons should be eliminated, but given the current world situation, the United States needs to continue production to maintain parity with the Soviet Union.
(10.8)	4. Individuals who advocate reduction of American nuclear weapons stockpiles are traitors.

Note: Subjects check all items with which they agree. Numbers in parentheses indicate the scale values assigned to the items based on the assessments of judges. These numbers do not actually appear on questionnaires given to subjects.

Source: Adapted from Petty, Richard E., and John T. Cacioppo, *Attitudes and Persuasion: Classic and Contemporary Approaches.*

the alternative to agree or disagree and each point on a scale represents a score. Summing scores over items provides a composite measure of the person's attitudes toward nuclear weapons.

Likert Scales

The construction of a Thurstone Scale involves a great deal of work and is expensive (Oppenheim, 1966). Easier methods of assessing attitudes have been sought by social psychologists. One such simpler scale, which is still frequently used, was developed in 1932 by Rensis Likert, a statistician for the U.S. Department of Agriculture. The steps involved in constructing a Likert Scale include these three:

1. A pool of items relating to various aspects of an attitude are selected by researchers based on past experience, intuition, or pretesting.
2. Subjects are given the items and asked to indicate their attitudes by making a checkmark along a 5-point scale, anchored at either end by the labels *strongly agree* (5) and *strongly disagree* (1). Researchers may vary the number of units used to measure the scale to any number, and 7-, 9-, and 11-point scales are often used.
3. The subject's attitude toward an object is determined by summing the responses on all items shown to correlate strongly with the entire scale. In other words, the items are combined to form a total scale and only those items that by themselves correlate strongly with the total scale are retained. This procedure is referred to as an **item analysis.**

To simplify matters even more, some researchers skip the item analysis in step 3 and give subjects a series of items referring to the attitude object along with a 5- or 7-point scale. This less precise technique is not a true Likert Scale and is referred to as a **Likert-type Scale** (Oppenheim, 1966). An example of a Likert-type Scale for assessing attitudes toward nuclear weapons is shown in Table 6-3.

The major advantage of a Likert Scale is that it requires less time and expense to construct than a Thurstone Scale. One concern might be that this savings would be associated with a lower quality product in terms of loss of precision and information. Research has shown this not to be the case. Attitudes obtained by the use of Likert Scales are highly correlated with those measured by the use of Thurstone's procedure (Edwards and Kenney, 1946).

Table 6–3 Sample Likert Scale measuring attitudes toward nuclear weapons

1. The United States should subscribe to a "doctrine of no first use" of nuclear weapons.

(5)	(4)	(3)	(2)	(1)
Strongly Agree	Agree	Undecided	Disagree	Strongly Disagree

2. Nuclear weapons reduction is one of the most crucial issues for the future of the world.

(5)	(4)	(3)	(2)	(1)
Strongly Agree	Agree	Undecided	Disagree	Strongly Disagree

3. Any discussion of nuclear weapons reductions by the United States without concessions by the Soviet Union are pointless.

(5)	(4)	(3)	(2)	(1)
Strongly Agree	Agree	Undecided	Disagree	Strongly Disagree

Note: Subjects circle the point on the scale that corresponds to their degree of agreement or disagreement with the statement.

Source: Adapted from Petty, Richard E., and John T. Cacioppo, *Attitudes and Persuasion: Classic and Contemporary Approaches.* © 1981, pp. 10-11. Wm. C. Brown Publishers, Dubuque, Iowa. All rights reserved. Reprinted by permission.

Semantic Differential Scale

As we learned in Chapter 5, the Semantic Differential Scale was developed to measure connotative meanings. The subject typically is given an object to rate, such as a nation, thing, event, or other person. The subject is given a set of bipolar adjectives separated by 7-point scales (see Table 6-4). Statistical analyses have shown that subjects' responses represent three dimensions: *evaluative,* representing a good-bad dimension; *potency,* representing a strong-weak dimension; and *activity,* representing an active or passive dimension (Osgood Suci and Tannenbaum, 1957). Often the evaluative dimension, which reflects positive or negative feelings about an object, is used as a measure of attitudes. An example of a Semantic Differential Scale for assessing attitudes toward nuclear weapons is presented in Table 6-4.

Physiological measures of attitudes

Making inferences about a person's internal states from interviews or responses to paper-and-pencil scales is at best an uncertain process. Suppose respondents are concerned about self-presentation and therefore give socially desirable rather than frank responses to questions about their attitudes? One suggestion for getting around this kind of problem is to obtain physiological measures of attitudes. The search for a physiological measure of attitudes, represented, for example, by the use of lie detectors, is based on the assumption that the affective component of attitudes produces a physiological reaction, which potentially can be measured.

One physiological measure capitalizes on a *galvanic skin response* (GSR). The skin conducts electricity. Perspiration increases the skin's ability to conduct electricity. This reaction is the GSR and can be measured by an instrument called a *galvanometer.* It is believed that the GSR reflects heightened physiological arousal associated with emotional reactions. Applied to attitudes, a heightened GSR has been interpreted by some researchers as evidence for a strongly held attitude (Cacioppo and Sandman, 1981).

It was found in one experiment that white subjects showed an elevated GSR in the presence of a black experimenter but did not in the presence of a white one (Rankin and Campbell, 1955). This result could be interpreted as indicating prejudice by the subjects to-

Table 6-4 Sample Semantic Differential Scale measuring attitudes towards nuclear weapons

1. Increasing stockpiles of nuclear weapons by the United States.								
Good	___	___	___	___	___	___	___	Bad
Harmful	___	___	___	___	___	___	___	Beneficial
Dangerous	___	___	___	___	___	___	___	Safe
Wise	___	___	___	___	___	___	___	Foolish
Sane	___	___	___	___	___	___	___	Insane
Rational	___	___	___	___	___	___	___	Irrational
2. Underground testing of nuclear weapons.								
Necessary	___	___	___	___	___	___	___	Unnecessary
Safe	___	___	___	___	___	___	___	Dangerous
Strong	___	___	___	___	___	___	___	Weak
Progressive	___	___	___	___	___	___	___	Regressive
Foolish	___	___	___	___	___	___	___	Wise
Active	___	___	___	___	___	___	___	Passive

Source: From *Attitudes and persuasion: Classic and contemporary approaches* (pp. 10-11) by R. E. Petty and J. T. Cacioppo, 1981, Dubuque, IA: Wm. C. Brown. Adapted by permission.

Note: Subjects respond by checking the place on the scales which correspond to their reactions to the attitude items.

ward the black experimenter. More recent evidence, however, has led to the conclusion that stimulus novelty and unexpectedness are causes of heightened GSRs (Cacioppo and Sandman, 1981; Petty and Cacioppo, 1981). The surprise at encountering a black experimenter may have produced the GSRs of subjects. This kind of interpretative problem lessens the value of the GSR as a physiological measure of attitudes.

Another physiological response that is associated with the autonomic nervous system is a change in the size of the pupil in the eye. Dilation (or expansion) has been interpreted as indicating a positive attitude, with constriction indicating a negative attitude (Hess, 1965).

In an attempt to validate a pupillary response measure of attitudes, students with liberal political views were exposed to photographs of Lyndon Johnson and Martin Luther King, Jr. There was evidence of pupil dilation. When these students were shown a picture of conservative Governor George Wallace, however, they experienced pupil constriction (Barlow, 1969). These pupillary responses are consistent with the expectation that liberal students would react positively to liberal public figures and negatively to conservative political personalities. Unfortunately, this relationship between attitudes and pupil size is difficult to replicate (Cacioppo and Sandman, 1981). Furthermore, it is known that the interest or attention-grabbing nature of stimuli may affect pupil size apart from the person's attitudes toward the stimuli.

You may recall from Chapter 2 that one theory about how people recognize their own emotions is through the muscles in their faces (Izard, 1977). If the muscle contractions in the face could be measured, then the affective component of the person's attitudes might be inferred directly. A machine that measures muscle responses is an *electromyograph* (EMG). A study using the EMG exposed subjects to a persuasive communication. When subjects were provided with information congruent with their beliefs, they showed a different pattern of facial muscle contractions than subjects who heard a message contrary to their original attitudes (Petty and Cacioppo, 1979). This preliminary study shows some promise, but much more work needs to be done before the EMG could be accepted as a reliable indicator of attitudes. In general, the efforts to find a physiologial measure of attitudes have not been successful.

Problems of attitude measurement

Paper-and-pencil techniques for measuring attitudes may suffer from an important weakness: people may be very hesitant to reveal attitudes that are socially undesirable. The bigot may be reluctant to express his hatred of black people, the chauvinist may lie about his attitudes toward women, and the teenage rebel may not want others to know about his or her patriotic zeal. A device called the **bogus pipeline** (BPL) has been used to reduce a person's reluctance to express socially undesirable attitudes (Jones and Sigall, 1971). The procedure consists of a series of ruses to convince subjects that a piece of sophisticated looking electrical machinery is really a new and powerful lie detector-type device that can accurately measure both the direction and intensity of their attitudes. If subjects are convinced that the BPL works, they are presented with a dilemma when their reaction to an attitude item would be considered socially undesirable. If they tell the truth about the way they feel, others may be offended and evaluate them negatively. If they lie by giving a socially desirable response, the subjects presumably believe that the BPL will detect the lie; therefore, they will be revealed as having a socially undesirable attitude *and* as being liars. It is assumed that subjects would prefer being perceived as honest than being revealed as liars, and this preference should lead them to tell the truth when their responses are being monitored by the BPL.

Subjects are hooked up to the BPL, which allegedly measures electrical impulses given off by implicit muscle responses. There are two meter dials encased in a box in front of them, identified by signs, such as Your Dial and Machine Dial. (See photo of BPL.) The machine dial is covered and the subject is asked to respond to an attitude item by turning a knob that moves the dial along a seven-point scale. The items used in a demonstration phase are ones given to subjects earlier in the procedures. The experimenter never actually looks at the subjects' responses, but a confederate surreptitiously copies them. Thus, the experimenter knows the subjects' previous responses, but the subjects are unaware that this is so. The machine dial can be manipulated without the subjects' knowledge. During the demonstration phase, the machine dial appears to "know" the subjects' true attitudes with an amazing degree of accuracy. When the experimenter begins to measure new attitudes, the

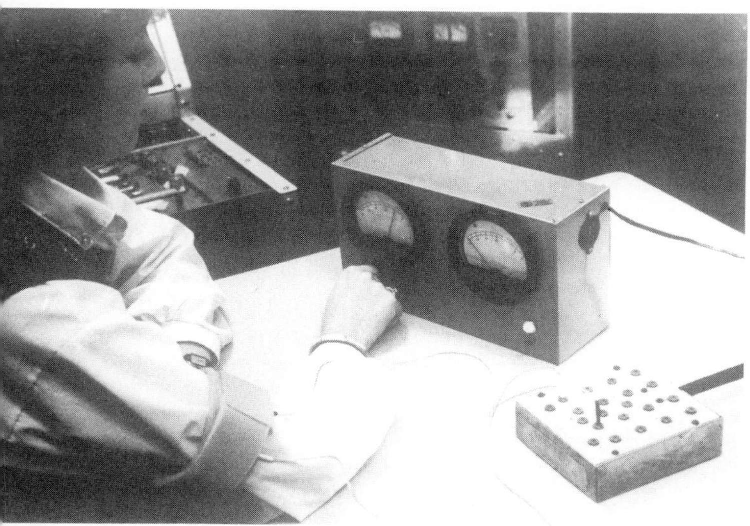

Psychologists have used the bogus popeline (BPL) to measure the direction and intensity of people's attitudes. A subject reveals a particular attitude by moving the dial on the left. An experimenter secretly manipulates the dial on the right, leading the subject to believe that the machine accurately knows her "true" attitude. Subjects hooked to the BPL find themselves in a catch-22 situation because they neither want to express socially undesirable attitudes nor do they desire to be detected as liars.

machine dial is covered and the subjects are led to believe that it continues to check against their attitude settings.

The BPL technique apparently does reduce the reluctance of people to express socially undesirable attitudes. In liberal northeastern universities, it is considered gauche to be prejudiced and to express strident nationalism, and consequently it might be expected that students would express more racial tolerance and muted nationalism in response to paper-and-pencil measures of attitudes, regardless of how they might really feel about these matters. Students expressed greater prejudice toward blacks and stronger patriotism when their attitudes were measured on the BPL than when they were quantified by paper-and-pencil measures (Sigall and Page, 1971).

Stronger support for the validity of the BPL was found when a confederate revealed to subjects how they could cheat on an experimental test. Although it was clear that the subjects used the information to do better on the test, they denied having any prior knowledge when specifically asked about it either in a face-to-face interview or on a paper-and-pencil questionnaire. When they were hooked up to the BPL, however, 60 percent of the subjects confessed to having had prior information (Quigley-Fernandez and Tedeschi, 1978).

The bogus pipeline is not a panacea for solving all the problems of attitude measurement. It is a cumbersome and time-consuming method as compared to a Likert or a Semantic Differential Scale. There are also ethical implications in using deception about powerful lie detector-type machines, both in forcing subjects to give socially undesirable responses and in inducing them to falsely believe that instruments with a great capacity for violating a person's right to privacy actually may exist in our society.

Learning attitudes

Where did you acquire your attitudes? There are such strong cross-cultural and historical differences among people that we can discount genetic determinants of attitudes. We acquire attitudes through experience. The principles of classical and operant conditioning may be used to explain the acquisition of attitudes.

Classical conditioning refers to learning by the association of conditioned and unconditioned stimuli. In the famous experiment by Pavlov, the dog learned to salivate at the sound of a bell. A dog salivates when meat is put in front of it, but not when it hears a bell. If a bell is rung repeatedly just before the meat is given to the dog, however, it soon will salivate at the sound of the bell.

Attitudes also may be acquired by classical conditioning. Objects and issues that become associated with already existing emotional responses acquire a similar emotional coloring. This principle was demonstrated by subjects who associated the words "black" and "white" with either the onset or termination of electrical shocks. The onset of shock is of course unpleasant, whereas the termination is pleasant. When "black" was associated with the termination of shock and "white" with its onset, later attitudes were more favorable toward "black" than toward "white" (Zanna, Kiesler, and Pilkonis, 1970). This kind of conditioning is illustrated in the classic movie described in Box 6-1.

Operant conditioning refers to stimulus-response associations that are formed as a function of

Box 6-1

Conditioning of attitudes in Clockwork Orange

The classical conditioning of attitudes is portrayed dramatically in Stanley Kubrick's movie *Clockwork Orange.* Alex, a young hoodlum in a futuristic society, is apprehended by the authorities after a spree of sexual and violent crimes. In prison he volunteers for an experimental procedure called the "Ludovecko Technique" that cures criminals in several weeks time.

Alex is injected with a drug making him so sick that he felt as if he was going to die. While under the influence of the drug, he is forced to view a series of films graphically depicting sexual and violent actions. After a number of pairings of the unconditioned stimulus (the drug) with the conditioned stimulus (sexual and violent movie), Alex comes to associate the effects of the drug (feeling like he is going to die) with the previously positive sexual and violent images. Soon, the mere suggestion of anything sexual or violent causes Alex to wretch. Thoughts, feelings, and behaviors associated with sex or violence make him ill. The Ludovecko Technique is simply an extreme form of classical conditioning that produces negative attitudes toward sex and violence.

reinforcements. Rewarded behavior is likely to recur under similar stimulus conditions, while unrewarded and punished responses are less likely to recur. If Johnny is given some M & Ms after finishing his homework, he should have a more positive attitude toward homework than if he was slapped while doing it.

The effectiveness of verbal reinforcements in shaping attitudes was demonstrated in a telephone study (Insko, 1965). Calls were made to college students who were asked a series of questions concerning an upcoming campus festival. For half of the students, whenever they agreed with a favorable or supportive statement regarding the festival, the experimenter said good. The remaining students received such social reinforcement whenever they expressed agreement with an antifestival statement. All of the students were later given an attitude questionnaire to fill out.

Attitudes toward the festival were found to be affected by social reinforcements. Attitudes were more favorable if the students had received verbal reinforcements for agreeing with profestival statements and more negative when "good" was made contingent on agreement with antifestival statements. By generalizing these findings to the question of how people acquire attitudes, we may conclude that when children are praised for expressing certain attitudes, they will continue to state those attitudes in the future.

Attitudes also can be acquired by *social learning* (Bandura, 1973). By observing the positive or negative consequences of an action preformed by a model, a person may acquire positive or negative attitudes. For example, it has been demonstrated that the attitudes of children toward particular behaviors became more positive after they had observed that their parents obtain rewards for performing the behavior (Petty and Cacioppo, 1981).

The relationship of attitudes to behavior

I don't believe in an afterlife, but I'm taking a change of underwear just in case.

Woody Allen

Social psychologists have been so interested in studying attitudes over the last half century because they believe that they can use attitudes to predict behavior.

Psychologists also are interested in indirectly changing behavior by affecting people's attitudes. Many of the traditional definitions of attitudes included the notion that an attitude is a "predisposition" to act in a certain way (Ajzen, 1982). If Lisa had procontraceptive attitudes, it was expected that she would use contraceptives, would support having a contraceptive clinic on campus, and would attempt to convince her undecided friends that contraceptive use would not take the spontaneity out of their sex lives.

Inconsistency of attitudes and subsequent behavior

It may surprise you to learn that attitudes by themselves are not very accurate predictors of behavior. A famous illustration of this lack of correspondence between words and deeds is a field study carried out in the 1930s. At this period in American history, there was widespread anti-Chinese sentiment. A sociologist named LaPiere (1934) took a Chinese couple on an extensive cross-country trip during which they stopped at several hundred restaurants and hotels. Only once were they refused service. After the trip, LaPiere wrote to the places they visited and asked if they would accept a Chinese couple. Over 90 percent of the replies indicated that the Chinese couple would not be provided service.

LaPiere's study has been criticized because he did not determine whether the people answering the written queries were the same as those who provided service for him and the Chinese couple (Dillehay, 1973). Nevertheless, the major finding of a lack of consistency between attitudes and behavior has been supported by the results of many later and more empirically sound studies. A review of these studies concluded that attitudes are at best only slightly related to subsequent behavior (Wicker, 1969). This review led some social psychologists to conclude that the concept of attitude was not a very useful one and had little utility for predicting behavior (Eagly and Himmelfarb, 1978; Jellison, 1981).

Global and specific attitudes

One analysis of why attitudes seldom predict behavior identified a **levels of correspondence** problem (Ajzen and Fishbein, 1977). Much of the research on attitudes shows that measures of general or global

Biography

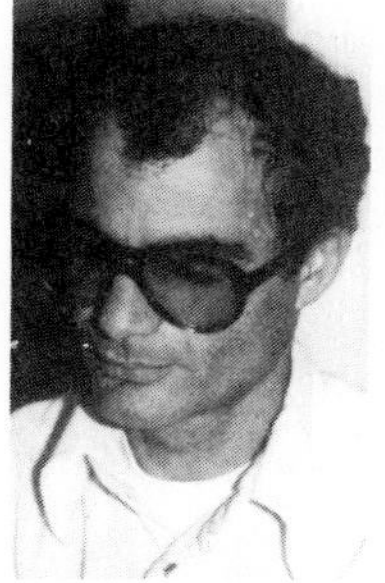

Icek Ajzen

Now a prominent scholar concerned with attitudes and behavior, Icek Ajzen received his undergraduate degree from the Hebrew University of Jerusalem, Israel, where he majored in psychology and graduated in 1967. As a boy, he was intrigued by the fact that the people he knew viewed the same issues in such different ways. He enjoyed participating in or simply listening to intellectual debates. Because he wanted to learn more about the way people think, how they influence the opinions of others through argumentation, and how these processes influence their behavior he decided to become a psychologist.

When Icek entered graduate school at the University of Illinois at Urbana, the attitude concept was under attack by contemporary social psychologists. It appeared that people said one thing (about their attitudes), but did something else. Together with his mentor, Dr. Martin Fishbein, Icek reconceptualized the relation between attitudes and behavior in what is now known as the "theory of reasoned action." This work appears to have rescued the attitude concept, which may now be considered alive and well in social psychology.

Dr. Ajzen has taught at the University of Illinois and Tel Aviv University and is now professor of psychology at the University of Massachusetts. He continues to be interested in attitudes, but believes they may not always predict behavior. According to Dr. Ajzen, attitudes are useful in predicting behaviors that are largely under voluntary control. Attitudes explain why a person choses one alternative course of action over another. Behavior is not usually completely volitional, however, and in such cases other factors influence achievement of the behavioral goal. Dr. Ajzen currently is developing and testing a "theory of planned behavior," which would extend the theory of reasoned action to behavioral goals, such as losing weight or discontinuing smoking, that are not completely under voluntary control.

attitudes are not a good basis for predicting very specific behavior. Any one behavior can be caused by many factors in addition to a person's attitude. Consider the problem psychologists have in trying to predict whether Tom will take part in a nuclear freeze rally (a specific behavior) from knowledge of his anti-nuclear weapons attitude (a global attitude). Tom may not attend the rally because he has to study for a chemistry test, or because he has been having problems with his girlfriend and is too depressed to do anything, or because he may not like being in crowds. If we want to predict whether Tom will attend the rally, we should find out what his specific attitude is toward attending a nuclear freeze rally.

Global attitudes are not consistent with specific behaviors, but they do predict global behaviors. A measure of global behavior can be obtained if we observe the person across a number of relevant situations. For example, global religious behavior can be measured if we develop an overall index of specific behaviors, including praying before meals, taking religion courses, attending formal ceremonies on holy days, and so on.

A survey of the religious attitudes and behavior of college students revealed little relationship between religious attitudes and any specific behavior, but there was a strong correlation between religious attitudes and an index of a number of religious behaviors (Fishbein and Ajzen, 1974). Another study showed only a slight relationship between global attitudes toward environmental conservation and any single related behavior. Global attitudes toward nuclear power, offshore oil drilling, and auto exhaust fumes were not related to such specific behaviors as participating in recycling programs, litter pickup, or petition signing. However, global attitudes were related significantly to a behavioral index composed of fourteen specific behaviors associated with the environment and conservation (Weigel and Newman, 1976).

A theory of reasoned action

In our example of Tom and his failure to attend a nuclear freeze rally (a specific behavior) we saw the need to measure specific attitudes and to take into consideration other factors that affect Tom's decision. Fishbein and Ajzen (1975) developed a **theory of reasoned action** by which we can predict specific behavior based on an analysis of factors that affect the way people make decisions. After considering a number of factors, a person arrives at a decision about what he or she intends to do. This **behavioral intention** usually leads to the intended specific action; that is, people will do what they say they will do.

The theory of reasoned action; is concerned with understanding the factors that lead people to form specific behavioral intentions. According to the theory, an intention to perform a specific action is a function of the person's **attitude toward the action** and the person's perception of how other people will evaluate the action, referred to as the **subjective norm.** Thus,

Intention = Attitude + Subjective Norm

Consider the case of Svenn, who is deciding whether to purchase a home computer. We could just ask Svenn what his intention is, but what if he has not yet made up his mind? We might be able to predict his intention by finding out his attitude toward buying a home computer. This attitude can be measured by any of the techniques discussed earlier.

Assume that Svenn has a mildly positive attitude toward the act of buying a home computer. In addition

What is this person's attitude toward the sinus relieving cold capsule, Contac? Is she deliberating about the effectiveness of this drug? What factors influence her decision to try this nasal decongestant?

to this personal factor, intentions are affected also by an interpersonal factor, the subjective norm. The impact of the subjective norm depends both on Svenn's perception of how others would view the act and on his motivation to gain approval from them. Suppose Svenn's family, friends, tax accountant, and coauthors would approve strongly of his action of buying the computer. The combination of a mildly positive attitude on the part of Svenn and a strong subjective norm to buy the computer should lead him form an intention to buy it.

Exposure to information leading to an even more positive attitude toward the action would strengthen Svenn's intention to perform it. On the other hand, anything that changes his attitude in a negative direction or weakens or shifts the subjective norm, would weaken or change Svenn's intention. For some behaviors, the attitude would be more important in forming intentions; in other instances, the subjective norm would have more impact.

As can be seen in the diagram of the theory of reasoned action in Figure 6-2, intentions usually lead to good predictions of specific behavior. For example, measures of intentions to diet and to engage in physical exercise were found to be correlated positively with the corresponding behaviors. A number of specific intentions were measured, indicated in Table 6-5. An overall index of these intentions provided an excellent basis for predicting actual weight loss (Ajzen and Fishbein, 1980).

Intentions do not always predict behavior. People may not carry out their behavioral intentions because they lack the necessary resources or have limited opportunities (Liska, 1984). Although Svenn may intend to buy a computer, unexpectedly large medical bills may leave him so broke that he cannot buy one. The greater the time interval between a measure of intentions and the relevant behavior, the less correspondence there will be. The reason for this effect of time interval is that other events transpire and people change their minds.

Evidence is generally supportive of the theory of reasoned action. In one field study, several hundred women filled out questionnaires measuring their attitudes about having a child in the next two years. They were asked to respond to items measuring subjective norms (Davidson and Jaccard, 1979). By considering both of these factors, Davidson and Jaccard made good predictions about which women actually would have a child in the following two-year period. Similarly, measurements of the factors specified by the theory of reasoned action accurately predicted the intention to have an abortion among women who were waiting to hear the results of a pregnancy test (Smetana and Adler, 1980).

Increasing attitude-behavior consistency

One factor that has been shown to increase attitude-behavior consistency is the degree of a person's direct

Table 6–5 Items measuring behavioral intentions to diet

1. I intend to adhere to a diet to reduce weight during the next two months.

   Likely ____ : ____ : ____ : ____ : ____ ____ : ____ Unlikely

2. I intend to engage in physical activity to reduce weight during the next two months.

   Likely ____ : ____ : ____ : ____ : ____ ____ : ____ Unlikely

3. I intend to avoid snacking between meals and in the evenings for the next two months.

   Likely ____ : ____ : ____ : ____ : ____ ____ : ____ Unlikely

4. I intend to do exercises, such as jogging or calisthenics, on a regular basis for the next two months.

   Likely ____ : ____ : ____ : ____ : ____ ____ : ____ Unlikely

Source: Adapted from Icek Ajzen and Martin Fishbein, *Understanding Attitudes and Predicting Social Behavior,* © 1980, pp. 107, 109. Reprinted by permission of Prentice-Hall, Inc.. Englewood Cliffs, NJ.

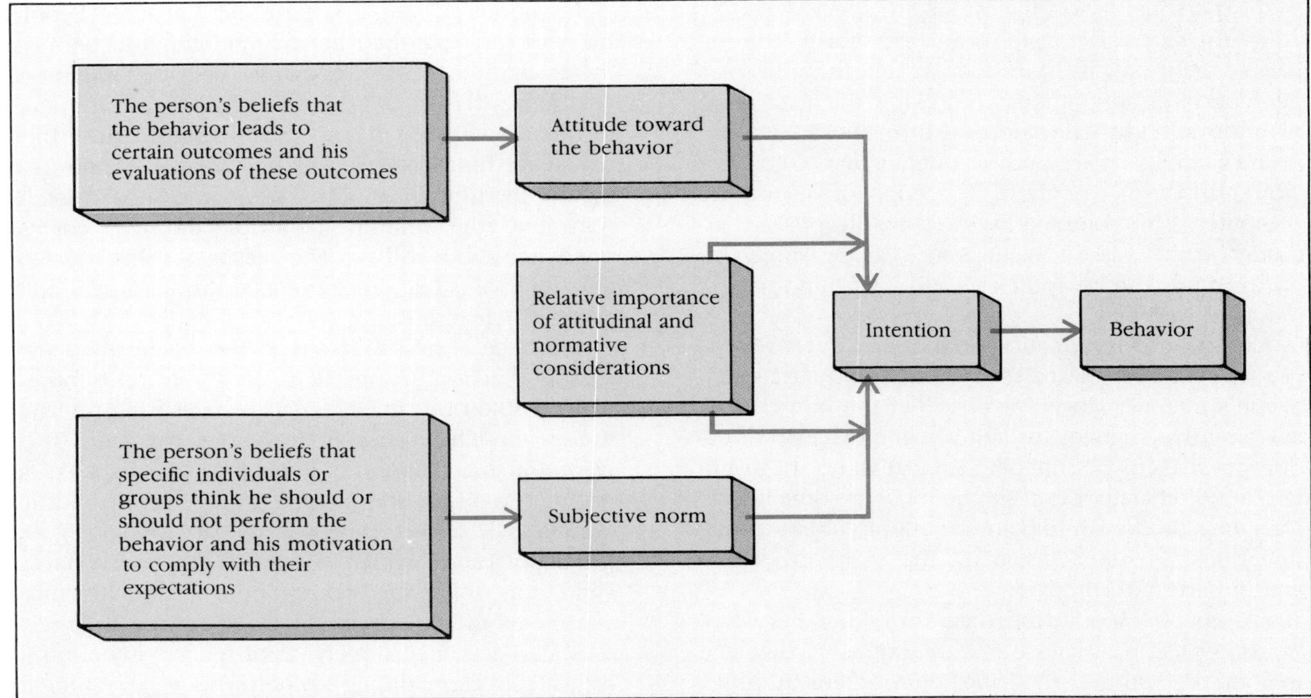

Figure 6–2 Components of the theory of reasoned action.

Source: From Understanding attitudes and predicting social behavior (p. 8) by Icek Ajzen and Martin Fishbein, 1980, Englewood Cliffs, N.J.: Prentice-Hall. Copyright 1980. Reprinted by permission of Prentice-Hall, Inc., Englewood Cliffs, N.J.

experience with the attitude object. The effect of direct experiences on attitude-behavior consistency was shown in an experiment conducted at Cornell University (Regan and Fazio, 1977).

When freshmen students were assigned temporary housing in the fall semester of 1973, they indicated strongly negative attitudes regarding their temporary quarters. In comparison to students assigned to permanent housing, who also had negative attitudes toward temporary housing, the disgruntled students were more likely to sign a petition or write a letter to the housing office asking for some remedial action.

The consistency between attitudes toward participating in experiments and volunteering to do so also was found to be a function of the related experiences of the subjects (Fazio and Zanna, 1978). Those students who had been in previous experiments were more likely to volunteer than students who had never been in a psychology experiment. Direct experience increases familiarity with the attitude object and probably affects its importance. These factors contribute to a feeling of greater vested interest in attitudes formed through direct experience and increase the likelihood of consistent behavior (Sivacek and Crano, 1982). A study of 2000 teenagers found that sex education classes affected knowledge regarding sex and birth control but had little effect on behavior. However, giving these students access to a health clinic dramatically reduced unwanted pregnancies over a two-year period. Thus, direct experience with a clinic increased consistency between attitude and behavior (Findlay, 1981).

Theories of attitude organization and change

Nothing is so unbelievable that oratory cannot make it acceptable.

Cicero

In addition to their interests in attitude formation and the relationship of attitudes to behavior, social psychologists have studied ways of changing attitudes. Change can occur as a result of the way attitudes are organized; that is, attitudes can change because of the presence of other attitudes and without the intervention of events outside the person. Three major theories of how attitudes change due to their relationships with each other are balance, social judgment, and cognitive dissonance theories.

Balance theory

Fritz Heider (1946, 1958) proposed that people are motivated to maintain a cognitive and emotionally harmonic **balance** between their attitudes and their relationships with other people. He conceptualized the organization of attitudes from the perspective of a person (P) and another individual (O), both of whom have an attitude toward some third object or issue (X). P, O, and X can have either unit or sentiment relations with one another. Positive **unit relations** exist when the elements are perceived as belonging together, such as a farmboy and a sheep or a police officer and a gun. Negative unit relations refer to cognitive elements that are perceived as dissociated or not belonging together, such as divorcees or Democrats and Republicans. **Sentiment relations** consist of positive or negative associations between the cognitive elements. Liking, cooperating, and endorsing are positive sentiment relations, while disliking, competing, and opposing are negative sentiment relations.

According to Heider, unit and sentiment relations can be balanced or unbalanced. What constitutes balance depends on the relationship. We expect people who like one another (positive sentiment relation) to like the same things (X). However, the discovery by P that O dislikes something P likes is disconcerting, produces psychological tension, and sets up strain toward changes that would restore balance. In such circumstances, there are two ways that balance can be achieved: P can change the sentiment toward O by disliking O, or P's attitude toward X can be changed to balance with O's attitude toward X.

Consider the relations between Seymour and Mary shown in Figure 6-3. If on their first date Seymour (P) takes Mary (O) to a Woody Allen movie (X) and they both like it, a balanced state exists (Figure 6-3*a*). The assumption is that there is a positive sentiment relation between Seymour and Mary. If Seymour liked the movie but believed that Mary did not, then Seymour's cognitions would be out of balance (Figure 6-3*b*). It seems wrong that people we like do not like what we like; so either we should not like them or we should change our attitudes.

In a balanced state, all three relations between P, O, and X are positive, or one is positive and the other two are negative. An imbalanced state exists if all three relations are negative or if one is negative and two are positive. The cognitive elements are all taken from P's point of view. Thus, Mary may like the Woody Allen movie, but Seymour may think she does not. It is what Seymour believes that is important in organization of cognitions into balanced structures.

Racial prejudice may be understood in terms of balance theory. Segregation, whether formal or informal, is a negative unit relation and implies incompatible attitudes. The assumption that members of a different racial group have different attitudes leads P to avoid them and engenders a negative sentiment relation. The cognitions involved may be: P and O are segregated from one another (a negative relation), therefore, P assumes that O's attitudes are different from P's attitudes. These relations represent a balanced cognitive state and lead P to maintain segregation and associated stereotypes about O.

According to balance theory, when prejudiced people learn of a successful member of a disparaged racial group, they will derogate the achievement of that person in order to restore cognitive balance. Confirmation of such a prediction occurred when white subjects were given descriptions of either a white or black successful bank manager who was said to be applying for a promotion (Yarkin, Town, and Wallston, 1982). Although the white manager's success was attributed to ability, the success of the black manager was attributed to luck.

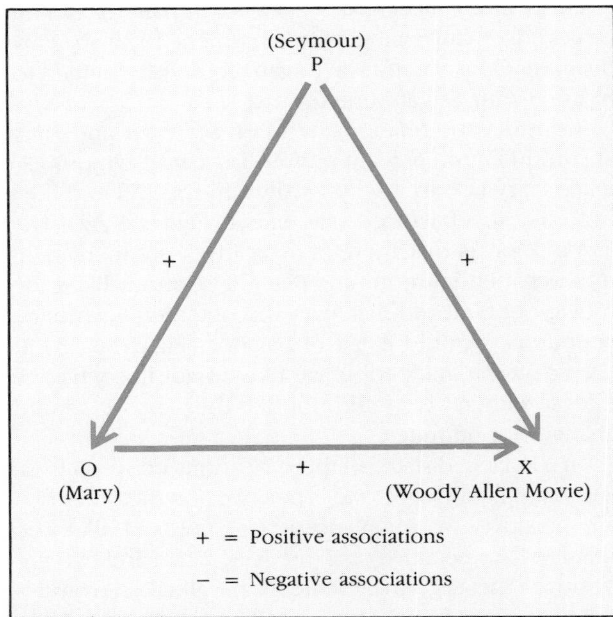

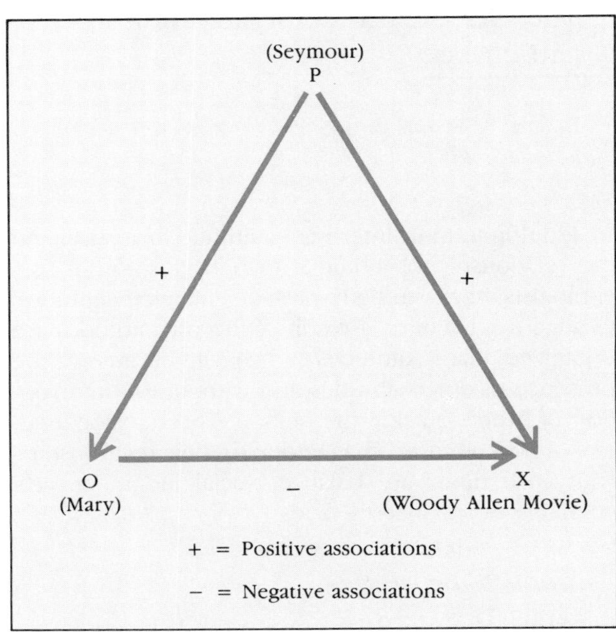

Figure 6–3a & b Balance theory and sentiment relations.

An implication of balance theory is that social contact would lessen prejudice if people discovered that they shared common attitudes; that is, it would create an imbalanced cognitive state if segregated people, P and O, discovered they shared similar attitudes. One way to restore balance would be to decrease support for segregation and to change stereotypes. In such cases, beliefs should be more important than race for producing social acceptance and rejection. Indeed, there is evidence that whites liked blacks with similar attitudes better than they did other whites who had dissimilar attitudes (Rokeach, Smith, & Evans, 1960). When relationships become more intimate, however, race is more important than attitudes in shaping social acceptance (Goldstein and Davis, 1972).

In general, when P's cognitions are out of balance, any of the relations may change. The weaker or less established of the unbalanced cognitions are most susceptible to change. If Seymour were highly attracted to Mary, he probably would be more willing to change his view of the movie to match with Mary's evaluation. If Seymour were president of his school's Woody Allen fan club, Mary probably would not have a chance with him.

Although balance theory has had great influence on the development of later theories, it has suffered from several defects. As we have seen, its predictions are far from firm because imbalanced states can lead people to change in a number of different ways. More damaging is the fact that the evidence for the theory is at best equivocal (cf. Zajonc, 1968c).

Social judgment theory

How much people will change their attitudes in response to others' attempts to influence may depend on where they currently stand on the issue. According to **social judgment theory,** attitude change depends on how people evaluate a persuasive communication within the context of their existing attitude structures (Sherif, Sherif, and Nebergall, 1965).

Consider the following demonstration: If you put your right hand into a bucket of cold water, your left into a bucket of hot water, then both into a lukewarm bucket, the water will feel hot and cold at the same time. The contrast of you moving your left hand from hot water to lukewarm water makes it feel cool, while moving your right one from cool to lukewarm makes this hand feel much warmer (Kiesler, Collins, and Miller, 1969). In an analagous way, the interpretation and effect of persuasive communications on attitude change depends on their relationship to existing attitudes.

People may perceive information that seems to be in substantial agreement with their attitudes as even more similar than it really is **(assimilation);** they may perceive contrary information as more in disagreement than it really is **(contrast).** The range of communications that people may assimilate is referred to as the **latitude of acceptance,** which consists of a range of positions they find acceptable. Communications that people contrast constitute a **latitude of rejection,** which consists of a range of positions they reject as incongruous with their current attitudes. There is also a neutral zone, the **latitude of noncommitment,** consisting of positions that people neither accept nor reject because they neither assimilate nor contrast information.

Persuasion attempts falling within the target person's latitude of acceptance usually will produce attitude change in the intended direction. If the persuasive communication is within the latitude of rejection, then it will be unsuccessful (Eagly, 1981). Suppose you are highly supportive of a bilateral freeze of nuclear weapons. An attempt to persuade you of the dangers of nuclear power plants probably would fall within your latitude of acceptance and would produce some attitude change. On the other hand, you probably would not change your attitudes in response to attempts to persuade you of the need for a buildup of satellite-based defensive systems (which has been advertised as President Reagan's "star wars" system) because a buildup of weapons of any kind falls within your latitude of rejection.

Involvement with a person, object, or event widens the latitude of rejection and decreases the latitude of noncommitment. For an involved person, the attitude is, "You are either for me or against me." If you are not very much involved in the issue of nuclear weapons, then you probably will be indifferent to most anything anyone says on the issue. If you are vitally concerned about it, then information is likely to be perceived as supporting or opposing your position on nuclear weapons.

Many of the expectations of social judgment theory were demonstrated in a study where women were exposed to a set of statements about alcohol, including a full range of positive and negative views (Hovland, Harvey, and Sherif, 1957). Women belonging to an antialcohol society, who by their membership indicated strong involvement in the issue, rejected more statements about alcoholic beverages than did nonmembers. This result indicates that involvement in an issue increases the latitude of rejection.

A contrasting effect was found among both the members of the antialcohol society and nonmembers. The members rated a moderately proalcohol message as being more in favor of alcohol, while women supporting the legal sale of alcoholic beverages viewed the same message as being more in favor of restricting alcoholic use. Assimilation affects also were found in each group of women. Mildly supportive statements were interpreted as strongly supportive of their initial views. Furthermore, as predicted, the more involved the women were in the issue, the more difficult it was to persuade them to change. When the women in the antialcohol society heard a proalcohol message, few changed in the proalcohol direction as compared to people in a control group (see Figure 6-4). Similarly, when women who had strong attitudes in favor of

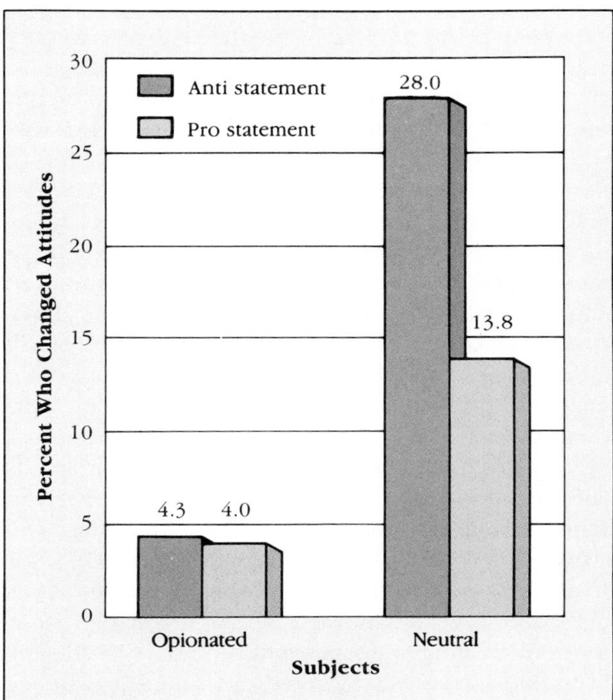

Figure 6–4 Social judgement theory involving women's views on statements about alcohol.

Source: Based on "Assimilation and contrast effects in reactions to communication and attitude change" by C. I. Horland, D. J. Harvey, and M. Sherif, 1957, *Journal of Abnormal and Social Psychology, 55,* 244-252.

liberalized drinking laws heard an antialcohol message, fewer showed attitude changes than did a comparison group in a control condition (Hovland, Harvey, and Sherif, 1957).

Cognitive dissonance theory

Of the many theories in social psychology, none has captured the interest and imagination of researchers as has Leon Festinger's (1957) theory of cognitive dissonance. The theory has generated more research and stimulated more debate than any other theory in social psychology (Eagly, and Himmelfarb, 1978; Petty and Cacioppo, 1981). Social psychologists have used cognitive dissonance theory as a framework for understanding a wide variety of situations involving attitude change and have applied it to psychotherapy (Cooper, 1980), moral development (Rholes, Bailey, and McMillan, 1982), and social drinking (Steele, Sothwick, and Critchlow, 1981).

A major premise of cognitive dissonance theory is that people are motivated to maintain consistency among cognitive elements (e.g., beliefs, attitudes). We are more relaxed when our attitudes and perceptions of our own behavior are in harmony **(consonant)** with one another. It is consistent to persuade others to desire the reduction of nuclear weapons stockpiles if you sincerely believe they should be reduced. When there is inconsistency between cognitive elements, a state of **dissonance** exists, involving mental tension and discomfort. A person would experience dissonance if he or she were opposed to the building of still more nuclear weapons but nevertheless supported legislation to increase expenditures for the construction of more.

Cognitive elements can have one of three relations with one another: dissonance, consonance, or irrelevance. People are motivated to reduce dissonance (inconsistency) and to attain a state of consonance (consistent cognitions). When a cognitive element is unrelated to our cognitive schemas, it is irrelevant in terms of creating or reducing tension states. Believing in tuition increases and perceiving yourself drinking from a water fountain are not relevant to one another; neither are they contradictory nor consistent with one another.

Contradictions among important beliefs produce more dissonance than inconsistency among relatively unimportant ones. In addition, the more cognitive elements that are contradicted, the greater the magnitude of tension or dissonance. If a devout Catholic plans to get an abortion, she probably would suffer from a great deal of dissonance; but thinking about going to the beach on a winter's day may create little tension within her because the beliefs are not that important. Planning an abortion may be inconsistent with prolife attitudes, positive evaluations of family life, and other important cognitions. The additional contradictions serve to heighten the degree of dissonance experienced by the person.

Methods for reducing dissonance

When dissonance is experienced, a person is motivated to change cognitive organization to reduce tension and bring about consonance. There are a number of methods available to a person for avoiding or reducing dissonance. Suppose someone is a heavy smoker and is exposed to information that cigarettes may be dangerous to health. It would be inconsistent both to smoke and to believe smoking is unhealthy. The smoker could avoid dissonance by denying that smoking is bad for health. He or she would accept research showing that rats smoking the equivalent of two packs a day have many health problems but would deny that such evidence has anything to do with humans. (So rats should not smoke.) If this sounds absurd, consider a survey taken soon after the Surgeon General's Report appeared in 1964 warning about the negative effects of smoking. Forty percent of heavy smokers denied any causal relationship between cigarette smoking and lung cancer (Kassarjian and Cohen, 1965). Presumably, it is more difficult to deny this association two decades later.

Another way of reducing dissonance is to change the importance of the conflicting cognitions. If planning to have an abortion produces dissonance, the person might reduce the importance of the decision by believing that life in a nuclear age is more expendable, that family life is not enduring, and that religious institutions are behind the times. The person also may acquire new beliefs as a way of reducing the contradictions. For example, joining an organization for planned parenthood reforms in the church would allow the person to believe in abortion, religion, life, and family without experiencing dissonance.

The most obvious form of dissonance reduction is to change one of the contradictory cognitions. If a person smokes cigarettes, has a corresponding belief ("I smoke cigarettes"), and also believes that smoking is harmful to health, one of the two cognitions can be changed. The person can stop smoking and thus arrive at the belief, "I do not smoke," which is consistent with the belief that smoking is harmful. The other alternative is to change the belief that smoking is harmful. The person may agree that smoking is harmful to many people, but there is no incidence of the relevant diseases in his or her family and the probability of smoking-related illnesses appears to be low.

It is usually more difficult to change a belief associated with a behavior than to modify an attitude that is largely evaluative or theoretical in nature. This may account for the persistent finding that behaviors predict attitudes better than attitudes predict behaviors. It is almost always easy to find attitudes that fit behavior but more difficult to change behavior to fit new attitudes. New Year's resolutions are not likely to bring about significant change in behavior. The ability of people to shift their attitudes to be consistent with their behavior is impressive, as is illustrated by the case of a religious sect in Box 6-2 on p. 176.

When does dissonance occur

A number of laboratory paradigms have been developed to study cognitive dissonance. Over a period of several decades, it has become clear that the phenomenon is more complex than Festinger (1957) assumed when he first theorized about it. The kinds of conditions that produce dissonance depend upon the situation used to study it. There are four basic research paradigms used to study dissonance: forced compliance, effort justifications, postdecision evaluations, and the forbidden toy paradigm.

Forced compliance paradigm

Dissonance is produced if people engage in behavior contrary to their beliefs. By inducing **counterattitudinal behavior,** people experience cognitive conflict between what they originally believed and knowledge about how they subsequently acted. This idea is at the basis of the **forced compliance paradigm.** Subjects are induced to make persuasive arguments or evaluative judgments that are contrary to what they really believe. For example, it can be assumed that most students will be against tuition increases and in favor of toothbrushing. When they come to the laboratory, these subjects may be asked to write essays in favor of tuition increases and against toothbrushing. A subsequent measure of the subjects' attitudes toward these issues typically shows an attitude change in a counterattitudinal direction after they wrote the essays; that is, students indicate more positive attitudes toward tuition increases and less favorable attitudes toward toothbrushing after making counterattitudinal arguments. This change in attitudes following counterattitudinal behavior is referred to as the **dissonance effect.**

According to Festinger, counterattitudinal behavior will induce dissonance only if a person has **insufficient justification** for performing it. If, for instance, subjects are ordered to write counterattitudinal essays, they will not experience dissonance because they have strong justification for performing the behavior. There is no contradiction between a belief that an individual was ordered to say something he or she does not believe and the fact that he or she believes it. The first experiment to test dissonance theory examined the role of insufficient justification in a forced compliance situation.

Subjects were asked to perform a set of repetitive and boring tasks for about thirty minutes (Festinger & Carlsmith, 1959). Afterward they were informed that the experiment was over but were asked to substitute for an absent confederate and tell a waiting subject that the task had been interesting, enjoyable, and important. Justification was manipulated by offering subjects money to engage in the counterattitudinal behavior. Students in the justification condition were offered $20 for saying the task was interesting, but subjects in the insufficient justification condition were only offered $1 to lie to another student. It was assumed that people cannot justify lying to other people for only $1. Dissonance should be aroused only in the insufficient justification condition where $1 was the reward offered.

A subsequent measure of attitudes revealed that subjects in the insufficient justification condition enjoyed the task more, said it was more interesting and important than did subjects in the justification condition. Assuming that both groups actually experienced

Box 6-2

When prophecy fails

There has been a number of historical occasions when a religious group has predicted the end of the world. When the designated date passes without the predicted occurrence, the followers are faced with a dilemma. They usually have invested time and made public commitments concerning their belief, then the event forecasted does not occur. According to dissonance theory, they should experience cognitive discomfort and change cognitions to reduce dissonance. Since they cannot take back their behavior, they may construe events as having reaffirmed their faith and as a result, their faith may be strengthened. Several social psychologists who joined an end-of-the-world group (given the code name, the Seekers) in a small town in the midwestern United States studied this process.

Mrs. Marian Keech claimed she had received messages from the Guardians, a group of outer space aliens from the planet Clarion. They asked her to act as their representative on earth and to warn the world of its impending destruction. The Guardians would save believers by transporting them from earth on a flying saucer. Mrs. Keech told several of her friends and neighbors about the messages and soon attracted a number of dedicated followers. The members of the Seekers began preparations to depart on flying saucers as the "target date" of 21 December approached. The Seekers received national publicity when one of their members, Dr. Thomas Armstrong, was fired from his job in a hospital.

On the evening of 21 December, the Seekers gathered to await the midnight arrival of the Guardians. But no saucers landed! By about 4:30 A.M., several people were crying and the group was bewildered. Mrs. Keech then gathered the group together and told them the message she had just received—the group's faith and goodness had saved the world from destruction. The members were elated. Despite undeniable evidence that Mrs. Keech's original prophesy had failed, her followers showed an increased fervor in proselytising to increase membership in the Seekers (Festinger, Riecken, and Schachter, 1956). The exposure to contradictory information generated dissonance, which members reduced by changing their beliefs to be even more supportive of their new religious affiliation.

While Mrs. Keech had predicted a worldwide flood, another fundamentalist group warned of a nuclear holocaust. Over one hundred of its members went into bomb shelters and stayed there for seven weeks. When they finally emerged from the shelters and found no signs of devastation, they did not conclude that they had been wrong. Instead, they experienced elation because in their minds faith and willingness to give up everything for their belief in God was responsible for saving the world (Hardyck and Braden, 1962). Once people publically commit themselves to a course of conduct, contradictory evidence only strengthens their original beliefs.

the task as very boring, those in the insufficient justification condition changed their attitudes in the direction of the counterattitudinal behavior and hence displayed a dissonance effect (Festinger and Carlsmith, 1959). A similar process may explain the effectiveness of the indoctrination procedure used by religious cults (see Box 6-3 on p. 178).

Hundreds of experiments using the forced compliance paradigm have now established that the dissonance effect occurs only under certain necessary conditions (cf. Collins and Hoyt, 1972). Subjects must have choice to perform the counterattitudinal behavior, which must have negative consequences either for the self or for others, and they must publically commit themselves to it. If any of these conditions are not fulfilled, subjects will not change their attitudes following counterattitudinal behavior.

Effort justification and dissonance

One implication of dissonance theory is that suffering leads to liking. Dissonance would be aroused if a person worked hard to attain a goal and the goal turned out to be trivial. It is contradictory to work hard for little reason. Such effort would be insufficiently justified. One way to reduce dissonance, if the goal is discovered to be less than was anticipated, is to enhance its attractiveness, a process referred to as **effort justification.**

Consider what happens when a college student endures a harsh initiation ritual in order to become a member of a fraternity or sorority and then finds the group to be less exciting than originally anticipated. The initiate already has made a public commitment to suffering to gain membership, and he or she would create cognitive conflict to believe the group was boring or worthless. The initiate cannot undo the behavior but can believe the group is more interesting and worthwhile than most people think. A study of the effects of the severity of an initiation demonstrated this kind of dissonance reduction (Aronson and Mills, 1959).

Coeds were recruited to participate in intimate discussions of sex and were led to believe they were being tested for emotional maturity. The coeds in a mild initiation group read aloud to a male experimenter a passage including some formal words referring to sexual behavior, such as petting and inter-

These pledges must suffer inane and harsh treatment in order to become members of a fraternity, but they expect the benefits of the fraternity to be worth the effort. Do you feel that the benefits of a fraternity membership justify their efforts to obtain it?

Box 6-3

Recruitment procedures of the "Moonies"

Dissonance theory offers an explanation for one of the most peculiar phenomena of our times: the conversion of ordinary, typical, "normal" young men and women into fervent devotees of religious cults, such as those ruled by Jim Jones of the People's Temple and the Reverend Sun Myung Moon of the Unification Church. These devotees can be seen in airports and bus terminals throughout the United States selling flowers and smiling when almost everyone tells them to "get lost." One student's account of his experiences at a weekend retreat for recruiting new members for the "Moonies" seems consistent with the tenets of cognitive dissonance theory.

Potential recruits were approached on the street or on college campuses in an apparently random selection process. A potential recruit would be invited to have dinner at a house in the neighborhood and to take part later in a weekend retreat in a secluded area. At the dinner and throughout the weekend retreat, the Moonies acted in a friendly, smiling, and caring manner. No overt physical or psychological coercion was used, but the recruit would be invited to take part in various communal activities, such as chanting or game playing. In the particular instance described here, a week-long retreat was announced at the conclusion of the weekend retreat. Gradually, individuals are led from one commitment to another until they are willing to give up their worldly possessions and drastically change their lifestyles.

One way for us to interpret this progression is to acknowledge that an individual can be led to agree to engage in a series of counterattitudinal actions (Zimbardo, Ebbesen, and Mashlach, 1977). The potential recruit almost surely has heard negative things about the "Moonies" and yet freely agrees to attend a weekend retreat. The lack of overt coercion by anyone leaves the potential recruit with insufficient justification for the counterattitudinal behavior. The recuit can reduce the unpleasant state of dissonance that occurs by changing attitudes in the direction of the counterattitudinal behavior. "Maybe there is something positive about the Unification Church" represents an initial cognitive change that may snowball until the recruit eventually becomes firmly committed. The process is similar to that described when Mrs. Keech's prophesy failed, but it strengthened her followers' belief in her. Just as members of the Seekers went out and tried to convert others to reduce their own dissonance, so too do new recuits to the Moonies soon become recruiters of new members.

course. In a severe initiation condition, the coeds read two pornographic passages and said aloud twelve dirty words that George Carlin says you cannot use on television. A control condition did not require the subjects to read anything to the experimenter.

After the initiation was over, all the coeds were placed in a cubicle and heard the group's discussion of a book on the sexual behavior of animals. The subjects believed they had been assigned to the group late and hence could not participate in the discussion, but they listened over earphones. They also were told that they had been placed in separate cubicles to decrease embarrassment and to encourage more frank discussions on sensitive topics.

The discussion that had been taped earlier was designed to be very boring. The young women who had experienced the most severe initiation indicated a more positive attitude toward the group and the discussion than did those who experienced a mild initiation. The boring discussion was dissonant especially to the coeds who had experienced the more severe initiation. It was they who evaluated the group most favorably. Similarly, subjects who experienced high levels of shock to join a boring group evaluated it more favorably than subjects who were exposed to an initiation of mild shocks (Gerard and Mathewson, 1966).

Postdecision dissonance

To be or not to be; that is the question:
Whether 'tis nobler in the mind to suffer
The slings and arrows of outrageous fortune,
Or to take arms against a sea of troubles,
And by opposing, end them?

Shakespeare, Hamlet

In Chaim Potok's novel *The Book of Lights,* the young protagonist encounters a number of difficult dilemmas involving his family, education, and career. Like Hamlet, he can never make up his mind. Rather, he lets events occur without actively making decisions. Dissonance theory points out the often painful consequences of making decisions. The alternatives available typically include negative as well as positive consequences. Decision making produces cognitive conflict between the positive aspects of the nonchosen alternatives and the negative features of the chosen alternative.

If a person chooses a stick shift for the new subcompact, the ease of having an automatic shift is lost, and continual use of clutch and shift is required in downtown traffic. A focus on the negative aspects of decision alternatives would leave the person in a state of regret for past choices. To make a choice but to believe a nonchosen alternative is superior would be contradictory and would produce **postdecision dissonance.** One way to reduce this dissonance is to enhance the evaluation of the chosen alternative and to derogate the nonchosen alternative. If your choice is superior to any alternative, then you suffer no cognitive inconsistency in having made that choice.

Postdecision dissonance was found among bettors at a race track (Knox and Inkster, 1968). Bettors at the $2 window were approached immediately before or just after they had placed their bets. Postdecision bettors expressed greater confidence in their horses than did predecision bettors. A similar process was found among undergraduate junior and senior students at preregistration (Rosenfeld, Giacalone, and Tedeschi, 1983). Students were interviewed just prior to registration or just afterward. They rated how good they expected their courses would be the next semester. Students who had already committed themselves to the courses rated them as significantly more attractive than did subjects who had not yet registered.

The forbidden toy paradigm

Studies of forced compliance, effort justification, and postdecision dissonance concentrate on the effects of active behavior on subsequent attitudes. Inaction also can produce dissonance. Not to do something desirable would be dissonance producing. If a child likes a toy, it would be inconsistent for the child not to play with it. One way to reduce dissonance in this type of situation would be to derogate the toy. Consonance exists for a person who does not play with an undesirable toy.

The effects of dissonance-producing inaction were demonstrated in children using a set of procedures referred to as the **forbidden toy paradigm.** Young children were asked to rank order their preferences of five toys. They were then left alone for a short while and told that they could play with any of the toys except the one they had ranked second in desirability. Before leaving the room, the experimenter issued either a mild or severe threat to a child. With the mild threat, the experimenter indicated that she would be annoyed if the child played with the (forbidden) toy. The rationale for this condition was that a mild threat would offer little justification to subjects not to play with a desirable toy, but would exert barely enough pressure to induce them not to play with it. The children in this situation would be left with insufficient justification for not playing with a desirable toy and should therefore experience dissonance. With the severe threat, the experimenter said that she would be very angry, take the toys away, and go home if these subjects played with the forbidden toy. It would not create dissonance for these children to not play with a desirable toy when they would face severe consequences for doing so.

Secret observation of the children during the experimenter's absence established that most children in both groups avoided playing with the forbidden toy. All children were asked once again to rank order their preferences of the five toys (Aronson and Carlsmith, 1963). Children in the mild threat condition rated the forbidden toy more negatively than those who heard a severe threat. Thus, dissonance theory has led to the conclusion that we not only find ways of justifying what we do, but we also rationalize what we do not do.

Alternatives to dissonance theory

Dissonance theory has been criticised on both methodological and theoretical grounds (Chapanis and Chapanis, 1964; Rosenberg, 1965). Current versions of dissonance theory are quite different from the early emphasis given to inconsistent cognitions by Festinger (1957). The changes in dissonance theory have been described by supporters as "a theoretical evolution" (Wicklund & Brehm, 1976) and by critics as "ad hoc modifications and reinterpretations" (Forsyth, Riess, and Schlenker, 1977). Dissonance theory has suffered from empirical shrinkage, particularly in the forced compliance situation where dissonance effects have been shown to occur under increasingly limited conditions (Smith, 1982). A number of alternative theories have been proposed to account for the results of cognitive dissonance experiments. Among the most important of these formulations are self-perception and impression management theories.

Self-perception theory

In Chapter 4 we describe Bem's (1967) self-perception theory, which focuses on the fact that people are observers of their own behavior. Often this behavior is undertaken without prior planning and appears to be spontaneous. When circumstances cause people to be concerned about their own internal states, people make attributions about their attitudes and emotions based on these self-perceptions. If the behavior is under the control of the environment, then people make no attribution to internal states. Because almost all college students were willing to write counterattitudinal essays when ordered to by the experimenter or when offered $20 for doing it, the behavior appears to be under environmental control. On the other hand, when people freely undertake a course of behavior without strong environmental pressure, they assume that the behavior reflects their internal attitudes. When subjects are given a choice to write counterattitudinal essays and agree to do it, they may later assume that the behavior reflects their true attitudes on the issue. Thus, while dissonance theory maintains that attitude change following counterattitudinal behavior represents a reduction of tension caused by cognitive conflict, self-perception theory claims that the attitude change is due to a person's attributions of his or her own internal states based on self-observation of the counterattitudinal behavior (Enzle, 1980).

If subjects perform counterattitudinal behavior without thinking about their attitudes and infer their attitudes from perception of their own behavior, then inducing them to think of their attitudes prior to performing the behavior should eliminate the dissonance effect. There is no need to infer attitudes from observations of our own behavior when the attitude is clearly in mind. According to dissonance theory, people who make initial attitudes salient should only increase cognitive conflict and dissonance. Initial salient attitudes should lead to even more attitude change.

These conflicting predictions of the two theories were tested in a study where in one condition subjects were asked to think about their attitude on the critical issue prior to being asked to perform counterattitudinal behavior (Snyder and Ebbesen, 1972). In another condition subjects were not asked to think about their initial attitudes. As predicted by self-perception theory, making people aware of their attitudes eliminated the dissonance effect (i.e., attitude change).

Another implication of self-perception theory is that subjects in forced compliance experiments may not remember their initial attitudes if these attitudes have not been made salient. When subjects in one experiment were asked to recall their initial attitudes at the conclusion of the forced compliance procedures, about three-fourths of them reported attitudes closer to their final attitudes than to their original ones (Bem and McConnell, 1970).

If people make attributions on the basis of behavioral observations, then self- and other perceptions ought to be quite similar. Observations of someone performing counterattitudinal behavior should lead to attributions of corresponding attitudes to the actor.

Dissonance theory assumes that the effects of counterattitudinal behavior only affect the actor because observers do not actually experience cognitive conflict. When observers were given descriptions of the procedures of a forced compliance experiment and asked to predict a subject's responses on an attitude scale, they predicted a dissonance effect (Bem, 1967). Other attempts to produce these results, however, have either failed (Jones, Linder, Kiesler, Zanna, and Brehm, 1968) or have been only partially successful (Bond, 1981).

Impression management theory

Private faces in public places are wiser and nicer than public faces in private places.
W. H. Auden

The description of impression management behaviors in Chapter 3 indicates that people often are concerned about maintaining a positive identity in public. In a forced compliance experiment, the individual who freely chooses to perform a behavior having negative implications for others is faced with a predicament. The only evidence the experimenter has about the person's attitude comes from observing the counterattitudinal behavior. If subjects argued against toothbrushing, the experimenter might believe that they really are opposed to toothbrushing. If the persuasive communication was directed to young people to convince them not to brush their teeth, potential harm is inflicted upon the audience (Hoyt, Henley, and Collins, 1972). If the subjects subsequently indicate they really believed toothbrushing to be good, then they look inconsistent (they advocated just the opposite view) and malevolent (they did so even though it would hurt other people). Very inconsistent people are perceived as emotionally unstable (Asch, 1946) and as lacking in credibility as communicators (Tedeschi, Schlenker, and Bonoma, 1971).

To avoid these negative identities, subjects express attitudes that are consistent with the counterattitudinal behavior. A belief that toothbrushing is to some degree harmful presents the subjects as more consistent and also denies that they did anything harmful. Arguing against toothbrushing when it *is* harmful is certainly not a malevolent action. According to impression management theory, attitude change in forced compliance experiments is a defensive and tactical behavior meant to maintain a positive identity and is not a real or permanent change in cognitions (Tedeschi and Rosenfeld, 1981). The dissonance effect is not a result of internal cognitive dynamics but is a manifestation of interpersonal dynamics where the person attempts to avoid looking bad in a situation contrived by the experimenter.

Attitude change may seem an unusual way to protect a positive identity, but it occurs because the experimenter blocks all other ways. When subjects overheard another person tell the experimenter that the essay did not represent her true attitude, they did not display attitude change because there was no longer any reason to defend themselves. (Joseph, Gaes, Tedeschi and Cunningham, 1979). When it was clear that the essay did not represent true attitudes, we can infer that the subjects held the experimenter responsible because he asked for the particular essay. This shift of responsibility helped subjects avert an impression management problem; they had no subsequent need to use attitudinal politics as a defensive tactic.

One implication of the impression management interpretation is that subjects do not really change their attitudes, but falsely tell the experimenters that they have in order to avoid looking bad. Some support for this view was found when subjects were hooked up to a bogus pipeline. The belief that the experimenter could detect lies eliminated attitude change (Gaes, Kalle, and Tedeschi, 1978). Furthermore, if no one knows the subjects performed the counterattitudinal behavior, they would have no impression management problem. From a dissonance theory point of view, however, they should still experience dissonance. When the anonymity of subjects was preserved and the experimenter was a temporary visitor to the campus and hence would not be likely to recognize the subjects by facial recognition later on, subjects did not display attitude change following counterattitudinal behavior (Malkis, Kalle, and Tedeschi, 1982).

Despite the results of these and other studies that claim the preeminence of one theoretical explanation over the others, there has been a recent trend to abandon attempts at determining which is *the* correct explanation for attitude change in the forced compliance situation. Some investigators contend that all of the theories may be partially correct. The focus should be on specifying where and when the processes postulated by each of the theories will apply (Baumeister and Tice, 1984; Fazio, Zanna, and Cooper, 1977; Paulhus, 1983). The future of research within the dissonance framework may be more a matter of experimenters mapping out "domains of explanation" for the various theoretical explanations (Tetlock and Manstead, in press 1985), rather than using the traditional scientific strategy of ruling out various theories through competitive experiments (Platt, 1964).

Resistance to attitude change

In theory it is easy to convince an ignorant person; in actual life, men not only object to offering themselves to be convinced but hate the men who convinced them.

Epictetus

Our discussion of attitude change may have led you to think that attitudes are in constant flux, changing as a result of the slightest intervention. Actually, it is often difficult to change attitudes. How influenced people are likely to be by persuasive communications is often a function of how involved they are in an issue and how much they know about it. For example, a survey of television viewers following the media coverage of the Watergate break-in and the subsequent resignation of President Richard Nixon showed little change in attitude among those who had a high interest in political issues, but viewers who had little prior interest in politics indicated rather strong attitude change (Kazee, 1981). Stubborn resistance to information was found also among a group of secondary school teachers who had taken part in a government-sponsored workshop on energy conservation (Page and Hood, 1981). The resistance phenomena we consider inoculation, anticipatory attitude change, and psychological reactance.

Inoculation to persuasion

Most of us are practiced in defending pet theories and cherished beliefs, particularly in such controversial areas as abortion, religion, and nuclear energy. But we have many beliefs, called **cultural truisms,** which seem so obviously true and have such overwhelming support we never have to defend them. When suddenly confronted with an argument against a cultural truism, we are not prepared to defend it and are likely to succumb to the persuasion attempt. An analogy can be made to the way contagious diseases are transmitted (McGuire, 1964). People who do not have the proper antibodies will contract a disease, but if they are inoculated against the disease, the chances are they will not get it. In the same way, resistance to persuasion can be increased by exposure to weak arguments and their refutations. **Inoculation theory** proposes that a person's defense against persuasion can be bolstered by exposure to counterarguments.

Support for inoculation theory was found when subjects who were exposed to arguments for and against a cultural truism displayed greater resistance to later persuasive attack than did individuals who were exposed only to prior supporting arguments (McGuire and Papageorgis, 1961). This initial research was followed by an elaboration of the theory to distinguish between two kinds of defenses. **Refutational defenses** are developed by exposing people to arguments and then offering rebuttals of them. Famed trial lawyer Louis Nizer described how he developed resistance to an opponents arguments by making a refutational defense. "Then, as I proceed to build my own case, I anticipate the contentions of my adversary. I announce his slogans and attempt to destroy them, asking the jurors to become my watchmen when they hear such sophistry and reject it as an insult to their intelligence" (Nizer, 1961, p. 434).

Supportive defenses provide favorable arguments in support of a particular position, bolstering the person for later attacks. Refutational defenses are superior when the issue is a cultural truism, but supportive defenses are equally effective on other types of issues (Cialdini, Petty, and Cacioppo, 1981). Inoculation theory is interesting, but research support has been obtained mostly in cases where cultural truisms are attacked. Because by definition, this seldom happens outside the laboratory, the theory has limited applicability.

Anticipatory belief change

In a study based on the assumption that forewarning of an impending persuasive communication would stiffen the target's resistance to influence, subjects

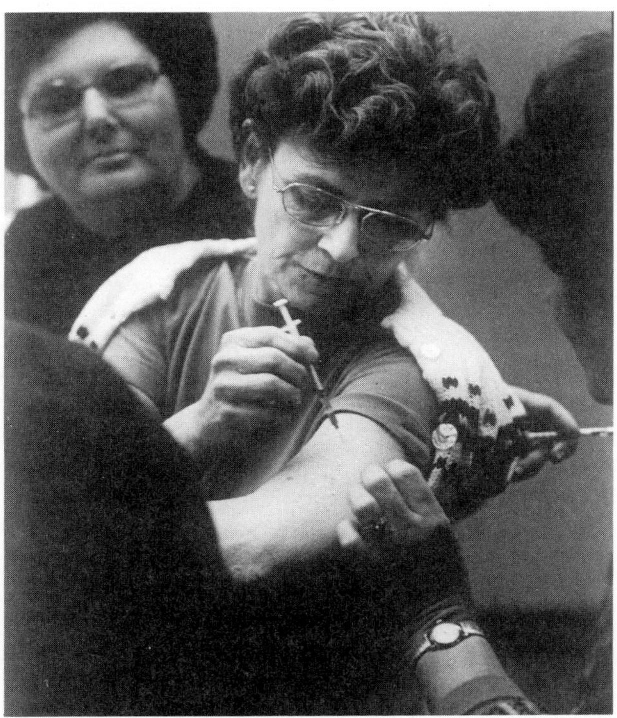

People can inoculate themselves against persuasion relating to cultural truisms as they can against certain contagious diseases. By exposure to arguments and counterarguments, they will maintain their beliefs and resist persuasive tactics.

manifested attitude change before they even heard the message (McGuire and Papageorgis, 1962). **Anticipatory belief change** occurs when subjects are pretested for their attitudes and then they are told that they will be exposed to a persuasive communication on the opposite side of the issue by an expert source. Before being presented with the communication, their attitudes are again measured. The anticipatory belief change effect is manifested when there is a change in subjects' positions from the first to the second attitude measurement. The change is typically in the direction of the expected position to be advocated by the expert source (Fitzpatrick and Eagly, 1981). The change appears to be somewhat "elastic" because when the subjects were told that the expert source would not be able to present the argument after all, they reverted to their original attitudes. Subjects stretch their attitudes to move toward the speaker but then contract back to the baseline attitudes when there is to be no persuasive communication (Cialdini, Levy, Herman, and Evanback, 1973; Hass and Mann, 1976).

Later research found a tendency among subjects to take a neutral stance when the issue was not very important or relevant to them. This effect is called **attitude moderation.** In contrast, subjects displayed extreme attitudes in the opposite direction to that of the prospective speaker, however, when the issue was important and relevant to them. This tendency is referred to as **polarization** (Cialdini, Levy, Herman, Kozlowski, and Petty, 1976).

Two explanations have been offered to explicate the moderation and polarization ABC effects. According to self-esteem theory (McGuire and Millman, 1965), people would evaluate themselves negatively if they were close-minded and not willing to listen to arguments by experts. Self-esteem also would be lowered if the person listened to arguments and was gullible enough to be persuaded by them. To avoid the horns of this dilemma, subjects moderate in anticipation of later belief change, so the conflict between them and the speaker is less and the need for later change is eliminated. It is not very clear how self-esteem theory explains the polarization effect.

Impression management theory (Gaes and Tedeschi, 1978; Hass, 1981) focuses on the concern of the individual not to look close-minded or be gullible to outside audiences. When an issue is not very important or relevant, the individual can appear fair-minded and reasonable by moderating in the direction of the expected position of a communicator. When the issue is important, however, other concerns become important. Polarization will let others know that you are committed and unlikely to be changed by persuasive communications. Some support for the impression management interpretation of moderation effects was found among subjects who indicated discomfort when with others (Turner, 1977). Socially anxious subjects showed greater anticipatory moderation than nonanxious subjects.

Psychological reactance

Have you ever noticed the tendency of some people to do just the opposite of what they are told to do? Prohibitions or rules against the performance of a particular behavior or the restriction of access to some commodity actually may make such alternatives even more desirable. The theory of psychological reactance postulates a need in people to maintain freedom of choice among behavioral alternatives (Brehm, 1966). When freedom is threatened, restricted or eliminated, an uncomfortable motivational state called **reactance** is aroused. By behaving in a manner designed to reaffirm one's freedom, reactance is reduced and cognitive comfort restored. If the restriction to freedom is perceived as legitimate and fair, reactance will not occur (Petty and Cacioppo, 1981). When a parent restricts television viewing because a child has misbehaved, the punishment may be experienced as justified. But if the restriction appears arbitrary or unfair, the child may have an increased desire to watch television and may find ways of doing so (e.g., visiting a friend's house).

Among the factors that have been found to affect the magnitude of reactance are the following:

1. *Expectancy of choice:* More reactance is aroused when a person expects to exercise control over the limited or threatened behavioral alternatives (Wortman and Brehm, 1975). In one study, subjects listened to and evaluated four record albums. Some were led to believe they would be able to choose one to be given to them, while others were told one album would be chosen at random and given to them. When subjects returned for a subsequent experimental session, they were all informed that the record designated to be given to them had been lost in shipment and would not be available. When asked to rate the four records again, subjects who could choose one album evaluated the record more favorably than those who believed they were to receive a randomly chosen record (Brehm, Stires, Sensenig, and Shaban, 1966). Not receiving something previously chosen made it more desirable.

2. *Strength of threat to freedom:* Stronger threats to freedom produce greater reactance. When in a voting situation, subjects were exposed to either a mild influence attempt, "Candidate A is the better advisor," or a strong one, "There is no question about it that A is the better advisor." The mild threat to freedom of choice had no impact on subjects' ratings of the candidates, but subjects exposed to the strong threat rated candidate A more negatively (Wicklund and Brehm, 1968).

This group of people are restricted from a certain area by police barricades. They are doing what is within their power to capture a part of the action, like standing on top of a barricade and shooting photographs. Rules that curtail freedom make the prohibited behavior more desirable.

3. *Similarity of alternatives:* Reactance will be lessened to the degree that similar alternatives exist to the person being restricted. This principle was illustrated among two-year-old children who were placed in a situation where one toy was in front of and another behind a barrier. The toys were equally attractive, but in one condition they were very similar and in another they were very dissimilar. The children showed more interest in the toy behind the barrier when it was dissimilar to the one they could easily reach (Brehm & Weinraub, 1977). We are less drawn to restricted alternatives when there are similar available alternatives.

4. *Importance of alternatives:* The more important a restricted or eliminated freedom is to an individual, the greater will be the amount of reactance (Wortman & Brehm, 1975). This process can lead

to unexpected results. For example, in one experiment, some subjects were told that the decisions they would make were important, and others were not given these instructions (Brehm & Mann, 1975). Half of the subjects were led to believe that other group members liked them, while the rest believed the group members did not like them. The group members then put pressure on the subjects to make a particular decision.

According to reactance theory, subjects would experience more pressure when they believed group members liked them, and this threat to freedom should be greatest when subjects thought that the decision was important. A prediction was made from these considerations: subjects who were told that their decisions were important and that they were liked would be most reactant (resistant to group pressures). As can be seen in Figure 6-5, subjects exhibited the least conformity to the group's pressures when their freedom to make an important decision was threatened by an attractive group (Brehm and Mann, 1975). Field studies described in Box 6-4 on p. 186, have also shown the tendency of people to do and to evaluate prohibited behaviors positively.

An impression management view of reactance

It has been suggested that some of the findings in reactance research may be interpreted as impression management tactics used by subjects. People do not want to be perceived as easily manipulated or susceptible to threats, perhaps because such perceptions invite others to use them. By reacting to threats, an individual presents an identity as a strong person—one who is not easily intimidated or coerced by others (Tedeschi, Schlenker, and Bonoma, 1971).

Several studies support this impression management interpretation. For example, when subjects were given a choice by someone they knew, they were later more compliant to a threat than when they had not been given a choice; that is, once freedom of choice was established, the subjects' identities were less damaged when they complied to a threat, but when the subjects did not have a choice and also were threatened, they exhibited reactant and noncompliant

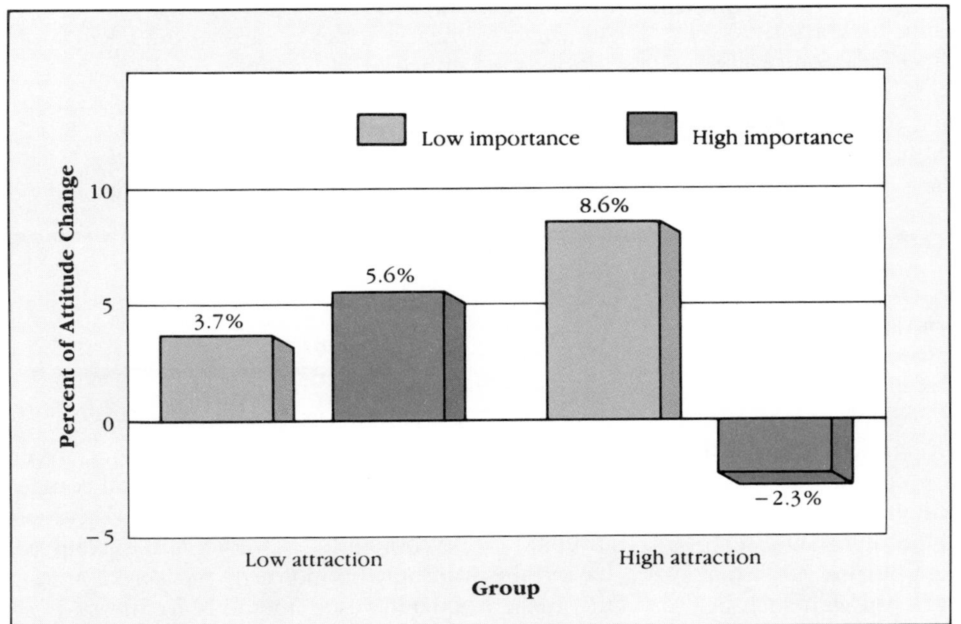

Source: Based on "Effects of importance of freedom and attraction to group members on influence produced by group pressure" by J. W. Brehm and M. Mann, 1975, *Journal of Personality and Social Psychology*, *31*, 816–824.

Figure 6–5 Importance of decisions and reactance of group members toward one another. *Note:* The higher percentages indicate the members who had greater attitude change in the direction of the group members. The negative percentages indicate the members who resisted changing their attitudes in the direction of the group, their attitudes becoming stronger in the opposite direction.

Box 6-4

Reactance, graffiti, detergents, and sexual attraction

Authorities represent rules and responsibility and hence may be experienced as restricting freedom to act. This reasoning was used in a field study of graffiti writing in a men's room. One of four signs was placed in toilet stalls, representing different levels of authority and magnitude of threat to freedom: (1) high threat/high authority—Do *Not* Write on Walls, J. R. Buck, Chief of Security, University Police; (2) low threat/high authority—Please Do Not Write on Walls, J. R. Buck, Chief of Security, University Police; (3) High threat/low authority—Do Not Write on Walls, J. R. Buck, Grounds Committeeman; (4) low threat/low authority—Please Do Not Write on Walls, J. R. Buck, Grounds Committeeman.

Based on reactance theory, we should expect more graffiti with the sign representing a strong level of threat to freedom and signed by a higher authority; that was the condition in which the most graffiti was written on the bathroom walls. The least amount of graffiti occurred when there was low threat to freedom and the person making the request was low in authority (Pennebacker and Sanders, 1976).

In another field study, residents in Miami and Tampa, Florida, were asked to evaluate detergents containing phosphates. A law had been passed in Miami prohibiting the sale of such detergents, while they were available to residents of Tampa. As would be expected from reactance theory, Miami residents rated the phosphate detergents more positively than did Tampa residents (Mazis, 1975).

Reactance is suggested by Mickey Gilley's famous line: "Don't the girls all get prettier at closing time." This is so because as closing time in a bar approaches, the opportunity to meet someone becomes increasingly constricted. Gilley's observation was confirmed when people were asked to rate members of the opposite sex in a bar that closed at 12:30 A.M. Ratings were taken at 9:00 P.M., 10:30 P.M., and 12:00 P.M. Members of the opposite sex were rated as more attractive the nearer it was to closing time. Ratings of the same sex did not show this increase of attractiveness over time (Pennebacker Dyer, Caulkins, Litourt, Ackerman, Anderson, and McGraw, 1979).

behavior. This pattern of behavior did not occur when subjects originally had been given a choice by an unknown source. Apparently it is important to establish freedom, especially in the eyes of strangers, to maintain a positive image as a strong and independent person. This is why reactance occurred only when attitudes were measured publically in another study (Baer, Hinkle, Smith, & Fenton, 1980). It would serve no useful impression management purpose to display reactance if no one could identify you with such behavior.

Summary

Attitudes are learned predispositions that enable us to respond positively or negatively toward some object. They have cognitive, affective, and behavioral components. Because attitudes are hypothetical constructs invented by psychologists to predict and explain behavior, they can only be indirectly measured. Among the most frequently used methods to measure attitudes are Thurstone, Likert, and Semantic Differential Scales. Although attempts have been made to develop physiological measures of attitudes, the reliability and validity of such measures have not been established.

Research showing inconsistency between attitudes and behavior raised questions about the utility of the attitude concept. One explanation for the inconsistency was that the attitude and behavioral measures were not taken at levels corresponding to one another. It now seems clear that universality or specificity of attitudes and behavior must be taken into account before consistency is assessed. A second explanation, provided in a theory of reasoned action, is that behavior is a function of other factors in addition to attitudes. Knowledge of a person's attitude toward an object, or an action and the perception of how people would evaluate the action (i.e., a subjective norm) provides the basis for social psychologists to predict behavioral intentions and actions likely to be performed.

A number of theories have been offered to explain why people change their attitudes. Balance theory contends that unbalanced unit and sentiment relations induce an unpleasant tension state that can be reduced by balance-restoring attitude change. Social judgment theory posits that the effectiveness of persuasive communications is associated with the relationship of their content to the existing attitudes of the target person. Messages that are too different from the person's attitudes will be rejected, but those that are sufficiently similar will be assimilated and will produce attitude change.

One of the most influential theories in social psychology over the past twenty-five years is cognitive dissonance theory. It maintains that a person experiences discomfort whenever there is a conflict between cognitions. When freely chosen behavior is inconsistent with previously held beliefs, dissonance is created and the person is motivated to change one or more behaviors to reduce cognitive conflict. The result is typically a change in attitudes in the direction of the counterattitudinal behavior. Competing theories have been offered for the abundant evidence supportive of dissonance theory.

Attempts to change the attitudes of other people sometimes meet resistance and may even have a boomerang effect. Inoculation theory proposes that people can be trained to resist influence, particularly on issues where little disagreement has been encountered in the past. There is also evidence to show that people display reactance when their freedom to make decisions is threatened. In this situation, they change their attitudes in a direction opposite to that of the persuasive communication.

Glossary

Affective component of attitude A person's feelings toward the attitude object.

Anticipatory belief change Attitude change that occurs when people are told to expect a persuasive communication; the change occurs before they actually receive the communication.

Assimilation Information that is within the latitude of acceptance and is perceived by people as closer to their own attitudes than it really is; a process assumed by social judgment theory.

Attitude A learned disposition by which we respond positively or negatively toward an object; has cognitive, affective, and behavioral components.

Attitude moderation People shift their attitudes to a more neutral position when the issue is not relevant to them.

Attitude toward the action How a person evaluates a specific action; a component of the theory of reasoned action.

Balance theory Heider's (1946, 1958) theory proposing that we are motivated to maintain emotional harmony between our attitudes and our relationships with other people.

Behavioral component of attitude A person's tendency to act in a positive or negative way toward the attitude object.

Behavioral intention What people say they will do; a component of the theory of reasoned action.

Bogus pipeline (BPL) A method of measuring attitudes designed to reduce the tendencies of respondents to lie, exaggerate, or otherwise provide insincere or socially desirable responses.

Classical conditioning We learn to associate previously neutral stimuli with an unconditioned stimulus because they are paired frequently with one another.

Cognitive component of attitude What we think about the item of interest, referred to as the *attitude object.*

Consonance A state of mental harmony that exists among cognitive units.

Contrast Information contrary to people's existing attitudes and perceived as more in disagreement than it really is.

Counterattitudinal behavior Behavior that is inconsistent with a person's existing attitudes.

Cultural truisms Beliefs that have overwhelming support, seem to be obviously true, and are never subjected to argument or disagreement.

Dissonance A state of tension or discomfort that occurs when there is inconsistency among cognitive elements.

Dissonance effect An attitude change in the direction of counterattitudinal behavior.

Effort justification When people are induced to work hard or suffer to attain a desirable goal and find it not to be very attractive after they obtain it, they exaggerate its attractiveness.

Forbidden toy paradigm A set of experimental procedures during which children are exposed to mild or severe threats admonishing them not to play with a desirable toy.

Forced compliance paradigm A set of laboratory procedures experimenters use subtly to induce subjects to engage in counterattitudinal behavior.

Inoculation theory A person's defense against persuasion can be bolstered by exposure to counterarguments.

Insufficient justification Performing a counterattitudinal behavior without any compelling reason for so doing.

Item analysis A statistical examination of items allowing selection of the most discriminative ones for construction of an attitude scale.

Latitude of acceptance A range of positions that a person finds acceptable; a component of social judgment theory.

Latitude of rejection A range of positions a person rejects as incongruous with his or her current attitudes; a component of social judgment theory.

Latitude of noncommitment A range of positions related to an attitude object that a person neither accepts nor rejects; a component of social judgment theory.

Levels of correspondence problem The argument that the generality or specificity of attitudes and behavior must be the same for consistency to be obtained between them.

Method of equal-appearing intervals A method of attitude measurement that uses judges to select and give scale values to items; subjects are asked to select items with which they agree and attitude scores are equal to the value of the middle score of the selected items; technique used to develop Thurstone Scales.

Operant conditioning Changes in cognitions, emotions, or behavior that occur as a result of the rewards or punishments associated with them.

Polarization People shift their attitudes to a more extreme position when an issue is very important to them.

Postdecision dissonance An inference made by dissonance theorists: when a person makes a decision between desirable alternatives, dissonance will be aroused due to a conflict between the positive qualities of the nonchosen alternatives and the negative features of the chosen alternative.

Reactance An unpleasant motivational state aroused by attempts that threaten or restrict freedom.

Refutational defenses A method used for increasing resistance to persuasion by exposing people to arguments and their refutations.

Sentiment relations Positive or negative affective associations between cognitive elements in Heider's balance theory.

Social judgment theory A person evaluates a persuasive communication in the context of existing attitudes.

Subjective norm A person's perception of how other people will evaluate a particular action.

Supportive defenses A method for increasing resistance to persuasion by providing arguments in favor of a particular position.

Theory of reasoned action Ajzen and Fishbein's (1975) theory specifying factors that predict behavioral intentions.

Unit relations The tendency we have to perceive some things as either belonging or not belonging together, according to Heider's balance theory.

Recommended Readings

Ajzen, Icek, & Fishbein, Martin. (1980). *Understanding attitudes and pedicting social behavior.* Englewood Cliffs, NJ: Prentice-Hall.

The most readable presentation of the theory of reasoned action and its many applications, including family planning, voting preferences, and consumer behavior.

Brehm, Sharon S., & Brehm, Jack W. (1981). *Psychological reactance: A theory of freedom and control.* New York: Academic Press.

This book offers the most recent and comprehensive review of research generated by reactance theory.

Petty, Richard E., Ostrom, Thomas, & Brock, Timothy (Eds.). (1981). *Cognitive responses to persuasion.* Hillsdale, NJ: Lawrence Erlbaum.

An edited volume containing contributions by leading scholars regarding the processes involved in influencing other people.

Zimbardo, Philip G., Ebbesen, Ebbe B., & Maslach, Christina. (1977). *Influencing attitudes and changing behavior* (2nd ed.) Reading, MA: Addison-Wesley.

A guide to using attitude change strategies in applied settings, written in a highly engaging style and especially accessible for undergraduate students.

The best audience is one that is intelligent, well-educated—and a little drunk.

Alben W. Barkley,
former vice-president of the United States

7
Social power and influence

Power of life and death over others

At Jonestown, Guyana, in November 1978 over nine hundred people committed mass suicide. They drank a strawberry flavored drink laced with cyanide and tranquilizers. Most people drank the poison brew willingly, but "nurses" grabbed babies from reluctant mothers and sprayed the poison down the infants' throats with hypodermic needles. Some adult resisters were shot.

There can be little question that the leader of the People's Temple, with the common American name of Jim Jones, exercised extraordinary influence over these people. As they approached the "death vat" containing the poison, they listened to Jim Jones say over a loudspeaker, "It's time to die with dignity." One man was recorded as saying, "We'll fall tonite, but he'll raise us tomorrow" (*Newsweek,* 1978).

The scene of nine hundred corpses lying on their faces in neat rows was a chilling sight. How could such a thing happen? How could one man have such powerful influence over others? As strange as these events may seem, Jonestown was not a totally unique historical event. Large numbers of zealots killed each other at Masada in A.D. 73 to avoid surrendering to Roman soldiers, and a thousand Japanese civilians jumped to their death from a cliff in Saipan to avoid capture by American forces occupying the island during World War II.

The dramatic impact of a single individual on the destiny of many others attracts a great deal of attention from both the average person and the historian. Most social influence, however, takes place in everyday interactions between ordinary people. Influence is seldom one way; people change each other through their contact with one another. Not only do parents exert great influence over their children, but children change the lives of their parents. The study of social influence among ordinary people has provided us with principles that can be applied in trying to understand more complex historical events, such as the mass suicide at Jonestown.

Influence is a central topic of social psychology. Tactics of impression management, described in Chapter 3, are attempts to influence the perceptions of other people. Aggression, leadership, conformity, and group decision making all involve social influence and are considered in some detail in following chapters. In Chapter 7, we focus on four basic topics: (1) types of social influence, (2) factors that increase the effectiveness of persuasive communications, (3) the gaining of obedience and behavioral compliance to requests, and (4) factors that affect the decision to attempt influence and the type of influence to be used.

Types of influence

Force rules the world—not opinion; but it is opinion that rules use of force.

Blaise Pascal

The actions of a person can be changed by the actions of other people. **Social influence** refers to the change in behavior, intentions, beliefs, or values of one person that can be attributed to the intervention of someone else. A classification of the various types of social influence is equivalent to the list of forms of such intervention. To paraphrase a love poem, "How many ways do I influence thee, let me count the ways." The types of influence can be classified into three broad categories: ecological control, reinforcement control, and information control.

Ecological control

Ecological control refers to an individual's manipulations of the physical environment that produce changes in the attitudes and/or actions of a target person. Prisons, mental hospitals, military academies, churches, and other institutions are arranged to affect the behavior and general values of people. Arranging soft lights and beautiful music may provide an atmosphere for romance. These manipulations of the environment may bring about changes in a target person without his or her awareness of the influence that has been exerted. On the other hand, people may seek out situations, like the honeymoon suite in a luxury hotel, to encourage desired behaviors.

Jonestown was physically isolated, constructed as it was in the jungles of Guyana. The population was

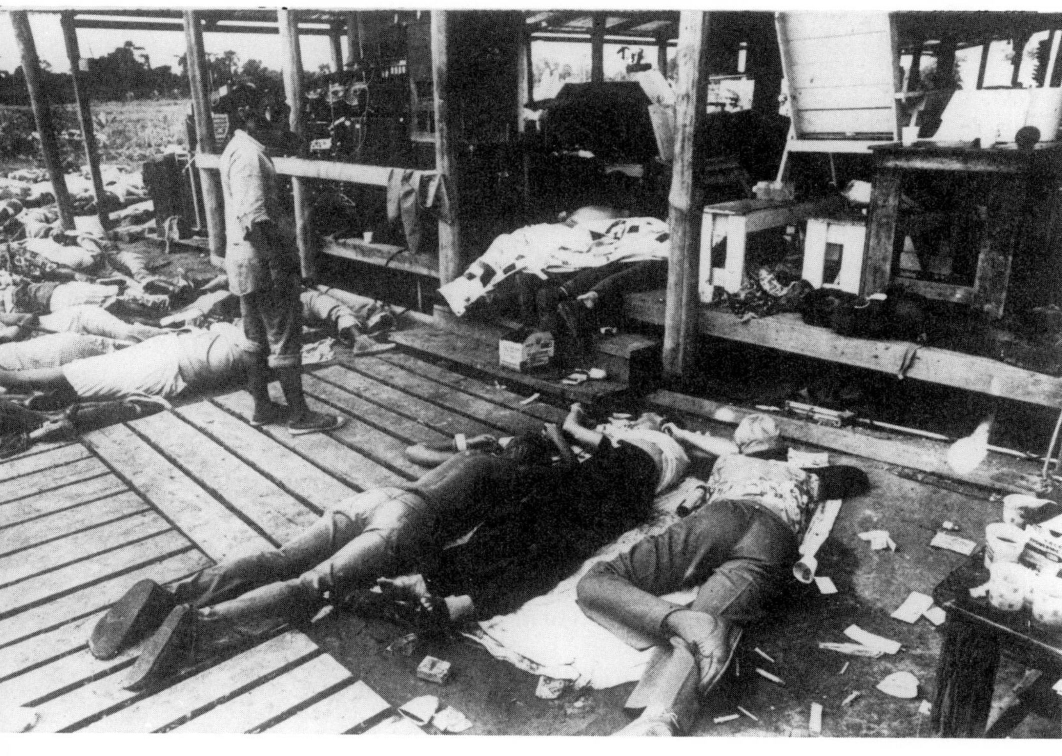

Dead bodies lie as they fell on the pavilion of the people's Temple in Jonestown, Guyana, while a person in a gas mask looks on. How did Jim Jones influence over nine hundred of his followers to commit mass suicide?

propagandized to believe that they were being persecuted by the United States government. They were dependent upon Jim Jones for their basic needs of food, shelter, and health care. They were surrounded by armed guards allegedly placed there to "protect them." The only information about the outside world was controlled by Jim Jones. A central authority maintained extraordinary ecological control over the entire village.

Reinforcement control

Reinforcement control refers to an individual's use of rewards and punishments to influence others. The individual can apply rewards and punishments directly or use them as incentives to gain compliance from a target person. One influential psychologist, B. F. Skinner (1974), believes that control is more successfully achieved through the use of positive reinforcements than through punishments.

In Jonestown Jim Jones had arbitrary control over rewards and punishments. Children who misbehaved were dunked in a well repeatedly until they satisfied Jones by crying loud enough, "I'm sorry, father, I'm sorry!" If children forgot to call him "dad" whenever they met him in the compound, they were blindfolded, tied to a stake in the jungle, and told that they would remain there until a poisonous snake bit them. Sexual relationships were governed by a relationships committee. Jones and his cadre of leaders imposed sexual intimacy of all forms on the members of the People's Temple. Jones also used scarce food and coffee as rewards for favored members (*Newsweek,* 1978).

People may use communications to set up rewards or punishments as incentives for others. The most important forms of such communications are threats and promises.

Threats

There are numerous ways of verbally stating threats, and the way the threat is worded may have a significant impact on how a person resonds to it. With a *contingent threat,* the source makes a demand of the target person and states that punishment will be administered for failure to comply. The goal of the source is to make the costs of noncompliance outweigh the costs of compliance and thereby induce the target to enact the desired behavior. When a source person makes a *noncontingent threat,* he or she states that a punishment will be inflicted. The punishment is not made contingent on any behavior of the target person.

There are two kinds of contingent threats: deterrent and compellent. A **deterrent threat** is a "don't do that, or else" communication. With a deterrent threat, a source person demands that a target *not* perform a specific action or else suffer punishment. The death penalty implies a deterrent threat. One argument in favor of capital punishment is that it deters homicide. The effectiveness of deterrence as a means of preserving world peace is discussed in Box 7-1.

A "do this or else" communication calling for a specific behavior from the target is a **compellent threat** (Schelling, 1966). With a compellent threat, a source demands that a target person peform a specific action or else suffer punishment inflicted by the source. Compellent threats are perceived as more offensive and aggressive than deterrent threats (Schlenker, Bonoma, Tedeschi, and Pivnick, 1970). The reason for this difference in perception is that a deterrent threat preserves the status quo and hence can be justified as defensive, while a compellent threat demands a change in the situation, and compliance by the target person would acknowledge the controlling power of the source.

Promises

With a **promise** the source person communicates an intention to provide rewards for another person. Just as with threats, promises may be verbal or nonverbal and contingent or noncontingent. A contingent promise represents an offer of exchange: "Do X for me, and I will do Y for you." A noncontingent promise may be made as a statement of intention to fulfill a formerly contracted obligation or to generate good will and earn a positive impression for the promisor.

A promisor incurs a moral obligation to provide the target with the promised reward. A failure to administer punishments would not lead others to accuse a threatener of being immoral, although others may perceive the one who threatens as weak (cf. Tedeschi, Schlenker and Bonoma, 1973). The moral quality of promises is translated into legal obligation in the form

Box 7-1

Deterrence theory

I'm not afraid to die. I just don't want to be there when it happens.

Woody Allen

A single death is a tragedy, a million deaths is a statistic.

Josef Stalin

A new military technology makes it imperative that a single failure of deterrence never should occur between the two superpower nations of the world. The cost of such a failure might be the discontinuation of the human species as we know it (Schell, 1982). An understanding of how people respond to threats is essential in the evaluation of deterrence theory.

It is difficult to determine when a deterrent threat is successful because the behavior at issue might not have occurred anyway. For example, the superpowers' claim that nuclear deterrence has worked for forty years in preventing world-wide conflict is about the same as you stating that your house has not been attacked by tigers because you have whistled *Tea for Two* each morning for the past twenty years.

A deterrent threat will not succeed if the target person does not believe the source will carry out the punishment. If the source has a history of bluffing or of not being honest in using other forms of communications, the end result may be the target's disbelief. (Schlenker, Nacci, Helm, and Tedeschi, 1976). The target will not believe a deterrent threat if there is some way to avoid the source's attempt to administer punishment. In the case of nuclear deterrence, if a first-strike attack would eliminate the ability of the target nation to retaliate, a deterrent threat, such as, "If you attack me, I will destroy your nation," would not be believed. For this reason, both superpowers have been concerned about developing "survivable weapons," such as nuclear submarines, so that after absorbing a first-strike attack, they would retain the capability of retaliating, making their deterrent threats believable. This feature of deterrence is referred to as Mutual Assured Destruction (MAD) and is required for a stable balance of terror.

It should be recognized that mentally disturbed or emotionally aroused persons may be at critical places in the decision structure during international crises and hence can contribute to accidental or unauthorized actions leading to an unleashing of nuclear destruction. A crisis does not allow much decision time for acting; if fear, anger, or anguish is associated with the fate of the earth (Schell, 1982), people may make decisions that they ordinarily would not make under calmer circumstances.

Diplomats who have responsibility for nuclear deterrence focus on (1) strategies designed to enhance the believability of deterrent threats; (2) management of international affairs to avoid crises; (3) development of contingency plans so that decisions are considered prior to crises; (4) development of arms control measures to assure stable mutual deterrence; and (5) creation of fail-safe methods to control unauthorized human actions and accidents.

of contracts and treaties, where all parties enter into formal agreements of exchange. The sense of betrayal and anger experienced by a target person when a source does not keep promises is not at all like the relief felt when the source does not back up threats.

Information control

As is documented in Chapter 5, a person's construction of social reality and available behavioral alternatives are based on processing information. To the extent that an influential person can control or channel communication to a target person, the latter's attitudes and behavior will be affected. Jim Jones gained control over the information available to commune members by cutting off all communications with the outside world. Letters were not delivered and the radio, which was available to leaders, was always swamped with static whenever others asked to use it. In the absence of contradictory information from the outside world, Jones could convince his people that the United States was their enemy. This function of censorship is recognized by all totalitarian regimes and by many parents, supervisors, and other people who are in a position to control information.

Forms of persuasion

Persuasion is the use of arguments, facts, predictions, and statements of value to change the attitudes, values, or behaviors of a target person. Generally, a persuader tries to change the target's decisions by showing that what is recommended is consistent with what the target wants. There are three major forms of persuasion: mendations, warnings, and activation of commitments.

A **mendation** is a persuasive communication predicting positive events. The statement that "an apple a day keeps the doctor away" is a mendation because it associates a dietary ingredient with the keeping of good health. A nonverbal but contingent form of mendation occurs in advertising. New automobiles are shown with sexy models implying that the buying of a particular type of car will make a male customer successful in attracting a beautiful lady.

Warnings are communications predicting negative events. They may be implicit, as in "Take your umbrella," "Steer clear of the boss today," or "You better lock your car." More explicit warnings specify the exact contingencies. For example, each pack of cigarettes states that smoking cigarettes can lead to several serious diseases and even death. This warning is intended to persuade people through fear to discontinue smoking.

Warnings and mendations, like threats and promises, predict punishments and rewards for the target person, and by so doing they are intended to change some target state or behavior. With warnings and mendations, however, the source of communication does not control the reinforcements predicted, although with threats and promises, the source person delivers the punishments and rewards.

Another form of persuasion is referred to as **activation of commitments** (Parsons, 1963). A source person communicates that what is being done or being proposed by the target is contrary to important moral values. As can be seen in the schematic overview of the types of influence shown in Figure 7-1, activation of commitments is a form of information control. Mahatma Gandhi campaigned for Indian independence by making it clear to Britain and the rest of the world that exploitative industrial practices and racism characterized Britain's colonial policies. Such actions were inconsistent with the belief of many British citizens that their country was the ultimate bastion of fairness and decency in the world. The unpleasant contradiction of valued principle and actual fact contributed to the eventual independence of India.

Enhancing the effectiveness of influence

The louder he talked of his honor, the faster we counted our spoons.

Ralph Waldo Emerson

Not all people are equally effective in using influence. There are essentially three reasons for differences; (1) characteristics of the people who influence can enhance or detract from effectivenes, (2) various tactics can be used to increase the probability of success, and (3) important factors associated with target people make them more or less acquiescent to influence

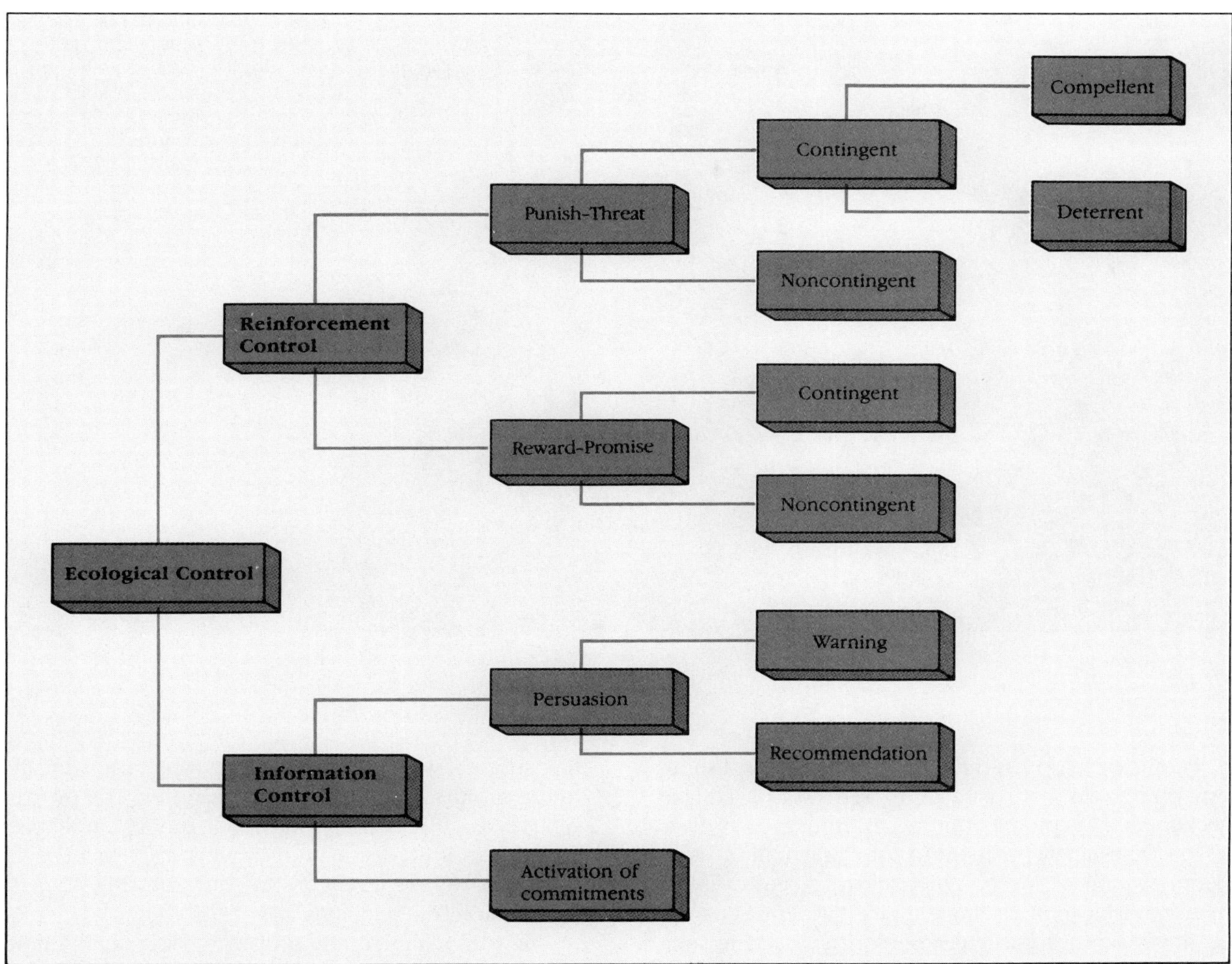

Figure 7-1 Types of influence.

attempts. Although all three of these factors can vary simultaneously, the tendency has been to examine them scientifically one at a time.

Source chracteristics as bases of power

Although control over environment, reinforcements, and information may yield power over others, characteristics of the source may enhance each of these types of influence. Those characteristics of the source that enhance the effectiveness of influence are often referred to as **bases of power** (French and Raven, 1959).

Truthfulness of the source

If someone is trying to persuade you to believe something that would affect your attitudes and behavior, you would probably ask youerelf: "Can I believe this person?" A very important determinant of the persuasiveness of a communication is the source's reputation for truthfulness.

Mahatma Gandhi took actions that focused attention on the contradictions between the valued principles of the people of Great Britain and their policies toward India. He committed himself to fasting and starvation in order to convince the exploitative British that he valued freedom and peaceful resistance more than survival.

People develop a reputation for honesty or dishonesty on the basis of past actions (see Table 7-1). Like accountants keeping a running inventory, each of us keeps an estimate in memory of the truthfulness of people we know. We combine all the pieces of information we have into a single index that represents for us how honest a particular person is (Becker, Dixit and Tedeschi, 1984).

In laboratory interactions involving strangers, the veracity of one of them (i.e., a confederate) can be manipulated. The probability and value of rewards were varied across certain conditions in one experiment (Zipf, 1960). Subjects were asked to estimate the probability that the promisor would reward compliance. We can interpret these probability estimates as an indication of the degree to which the subjects believed the promises. Subjects also had to indicate how valuable the reward was for them. Compliance to promises was shown to be a function of the product of the two manipulated factors (i.e., probability x value). Crosbie (1972) also manipulated the probability that a source would follow through on promises and found that subjects were more compliant when the veracity of the promisor was high rather than low. The probability that a threatener would punish noncompliance and the magnitude of punishments also have been shown to have joint effects on compliance by targets (Horai and Tedeschi, 1969).

The truthfulness of the source in using one kind of influence, say promises, affects the reactions of the target person to other forms of influence. Heilman (1974) told subjects that the person with whom they were about to interact had or had not kept either a threat or a promise sent to a prior subject. This information, establishing the reputation of the source for truthfulness, had a significant impact on the compliance of the subject to the opposite influence type. In other words, if the source was alleged to have kept a prior promise, subjects were more apt to comply to the threat sent them than if the source had not kept a prior promise. When a source's truthfulness was established through a history of direct interaction, researchers found a similar transfer from promises to threats in gaining compliance (Schlenker, et al., 1974).

Table 7-1 The contribution of different kinds of communications to an index of a person's truthfulness

INDEX OF TRUTHFULNESS
Threats: Does source back them up with punishments?
Promises: Does source keep them by providing rewards?
Warnings: Do the negative events predicted actually occur?
Mendations: Do the positive events predicted actually occur?
Reports of Past Events: Are they accurate?

Trustworthiness of the Source

When a source is communicating in a frank and honest manner *and* without the intent to mislead or exploit the target person, the source is perceived as trustworthy. (Hovland, Janis and Kelley, 1953). Perceived **trustworthiness** enhances the believability of promises, persuasive communications, and statements of fact or value. The consequence is that a trustworthy person is more influential than people without such a reputation. Trustworthiness is a power resource.

How does a person project an appearance of trustworthiness? A direct statement of "trust me" may induce suspicions of hidden intentions. A target person will perceive a source as more trustworthy when the source has no apparent association with the beneficiaries of a recommended action. For example, subjects were more persuaded to give blood to the Red Cross than to a private agency only if the speaker was a disinterested physician rather than a Red Cross official (Powell and Miller, 1967).

If speakers appear to give speeches against their self-interest, listeners are more likely to attribute trustworthiness to them. For example, a speech attacking a company for polluting a river was more persuasive when given by a businessman-politician to a company audience than when given by an environmentalist to a group of sympathetic supporters (Eagly, Wood, and Chaiken, 1978).

A person who directs communications at someone else is not apt to be perceived as trying to influence you. Overheard communications may therefore be perceived as nonexploitative. Audiences have been found to be more persuaded when an overheard conversation was relevant to their interests than when the same points obviously were intended to convince them (Walster and Festinger, 1962). If the topic of the overheard communication is not important or relevant to the interests of the listener, however, no influence will result even if the source is perceived as trustworthy (Brock and Becker, 1965).

Attractiveness of the source

People who are liked often serve as reference points for others who are forming opinions and making decisions. It is for this reason that interpersonal attraction has been considered a base of **referent power** (French and Raven, 1959). In addition to referent power, there are other reasons why attractiveness enhances the effectiveness of positive forms of influence. We are more attentive to what attractive people say, and hence are more apt to be influenced by them (McGuire, 1969). An attractive source of communications is perceived as trustworthy. As a result, the communications of an attractive source are generally more believable than those of strangers or unattractive people (Janis and Hoffman, 1971). Statements by a disliked source may cause a target person to take a more strongly opposite position on an issue—a *boomerang* effect (Abelson and Miller, 1967; Sampson and Insko, 1964).

There are occasions when dislike and even hatred can be a basis of power. It is easy to believe that a foe might relish the opportunity to punish us. Indeed, it has been found that dislike of a person who threatens does increase the probability of compliance by a target person (Tedeschi, Schlenker, and Bonoma, 1975).

Expertise of the source

Everybody is ignorant, only on different subjects.

Will Rogers

Knowledge is power.

Francis Bacon

The saying, "One man's expert is another man's fool," expresses the point that competence is a matter of perception and not just objective facts. In order for you to determine the expertise of another person, that

Box 7-2

The sleeper effect: who said that?

Sometimes a persuasive message appears to have little effect on attitudes, but after a period of time it has a delayed impact. For example, *The Battle of Britain,* a film developed by the U.S. War Department Information Office during World War II, produced more attitude change among audiences nine weeks after they saw the film than among audiences one week after viewing it (Hovland, Lumsdaine, and Sheffield, 1949).

Typically, communications from expert sources are more persuasive than communications from nonexpert sources. This effect of expertise was found when subjects were exposed to communications about juvenile delinquency either from a distinguished judge or from a man who had been arrested on a drug charge (Kelman and Hovland, 1953). Three weeks later, however, when subjects had forgotten who the source of the communication had been, the advantage of the expert source dissipated (see Figure 7-2) and a persuasive effect of the nonexpert's message emerged. When subjects were reminded of the identity of the source, the greater effectiveness of the expert source was reinstated. Instances where persuasive communications from noncredible sources have greater effect after a passage of time than immediately are referred to as the **sleeper effect.**

The sleeper effect is apparently a weak one. In one laboratory, there were seven failures demonstrating its weakness (Gillig and Greenwald, 1974). Research specifying the necessary conditions for obtaining a sleeper effect indicates that both the source and the message content must affect attitude change, and they must have their effects independently of each other. When these conditions exist, the effect of the message content can be retained when the identity of the source is forgotten (Gruder Cook, Henningan, Flay, Aiessi, and Halamay, 1978).

person's agreement with your point of view may be as important as his or her credentials. (Weiss, 1957).

Expertise, along with the other bases of power summarized in Table 7-2, is a power resource that enhances the effectiveness of warnings, mendations, aesthetic and moral judgments, and other forms of persuasion. Many studies have substantiated this principle—a radiologist was more effective than a nonexpert in persuading subjects that exposure to x-rays is dangerous (Johnson and Izzett, 1969); a professor of nuclear physics produced more opinion change regarding the consequences of nuclear war than did a high school sophomore who communicated exactly the same information (Miller and Hewgill, 1966).

Why is expertise a power resource? We have learned that competent people are more successful in manipulating the environment, in solving problems, and in predicting the future than people lacking in expertise. Following the advice or prescriptions of experts, therefore, is more apt to gain the target person favorable outcomes (Bandura, 1969). When a person is dependent upon the information or skills of an expert, the potential for influence is great. A person who knows nothing about automobiles may be susceptible to any recommendation by a garage mechanic. As is described in Box 7-2, we may be affected by the expertise of the source even when we do not recall who it is; even a nonexpert may have influence.

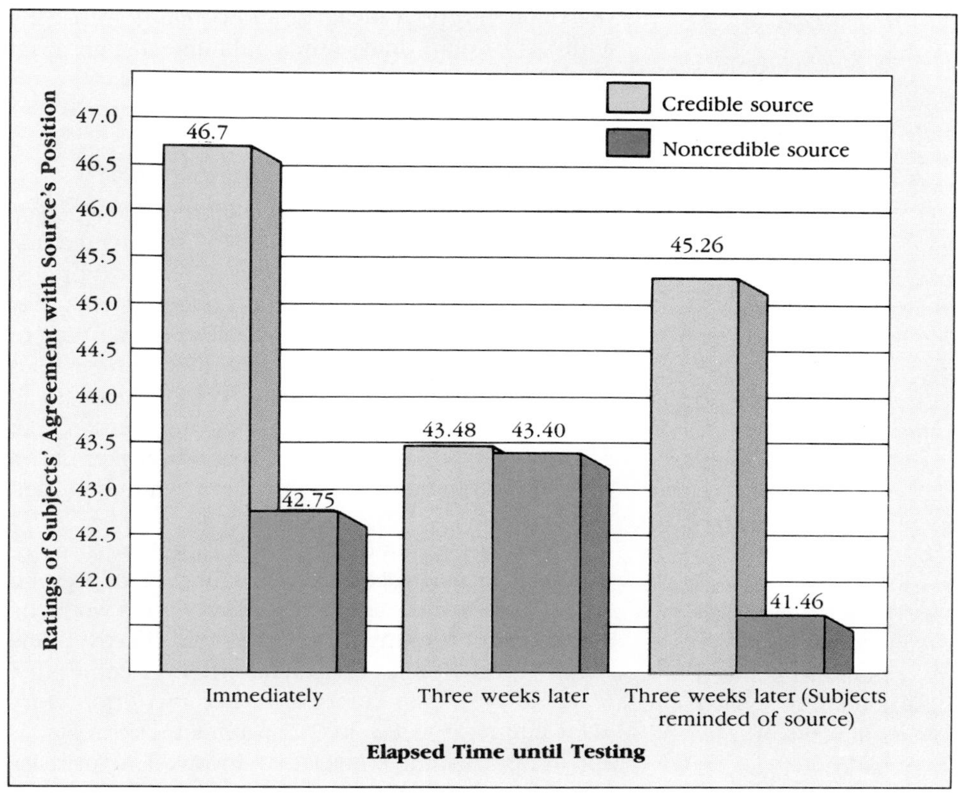

Figure 7-2 The sleeper effect—persuasion impact of a message after the passage of time. *Note:* Ratings were on fifteen-point scales that were summed up to obtain a measure of agreement.

Source: Based on "Reinstatement of the communication in delayed measurement of opinion change" by H. C. Kelman and C. I. Hovland, 1953, *Journal of Abnormal and Social Psychology*, *48*, 327-335.

Table 7-2 Source characteristics that enhance the effectiveness of influence

BASES OF POWER
Truthfulness
Trustworthiness
Expertise
Attraction
Legitimate Authority
Control over Resources

Tactics of persuasion

To treat your facts with imagination is one thing, but to imagine your facts is another.

John Burroughs

Most research on tactics of influence has focused on persuasion. What is the most effective way of persuading a target? How should information be presented in order to be most convincing? A number of principles have been found about factors that enhance the effectiveness of persuasion, but almost all of them require a consideration of who the audience is. There is no one effective method for all possible audiences. Let us consider some of the tactics of persuasion.

One-sided vs. two-sided communications

During World War II, the United States government was concerned that the defeat of Germany would lead the armed forces to be too optimistic about the length of time it would take them to conquer Japan. A one-sided propaganda message was devised for radio broadcast to convince the military forces that the war with Japan would be long and arduous. A second radio broadcast was two-sided because it included everything said in the first version and discussed the superiority of the U.S. Air Force and Navy in addition. A study of reactions to these two broadcasts showed that the one-sided appeal was most effective with those who had less than a high school education and who already believed the war with Japan would be prolonged. Personnel with at least a high school education were more convinced by the two-sided communication (Hovland, Lumsdaine, and Sheffield, 1949).

A similar finding was reported in 1953 when people were persuaded that the Soviet Union soon would develop atomic weapons (Lumsdaine & Janis, 1953). Those receiving the two-sided argument showed greater resistance to the opposing argument one week later. Apparently, a knowledgeable audience feels manipulated if a communicator does not acknowledge an opposing view about which they are informed. The source must acknowledge this opposing view and refute it to maintain a perception of trustworthiness. An uninformed audience would not react negatively if an opposing view were not mentioned because that audience would be unaware of its existence.

Drawing conclusions

If a persuasive communication is an interesting one for the audience and is not too complex to understand, letting the audience draw its own conclusions is an effective tactic (Cooper and Dinerman, 1951; Hovland and Mandell, 1952; Linder and Worchel, 1970). Such audiences might perceive sources as trying to think or draw conclusions for them, hence a source could be considered disrespectful. On the other hand, if the attention of the audience wanders or if the message is too complex to understand, then the source is more likely to be successful in influencing the audience by drawing a conclusion. If the audience does not process the information and if the source does not sum up a meaning and conclusion that the audience should draw, how could any change in attitudes be expected?

Order effects in presenting arguments

You may wonder if it makes any difference in a debate or in a jury trial whether an argument is presented first or last. When an audience expects to hear two opposing people and does not make any commitments after hearing the first, it will not be affected by order of presentation (Hovland, 1958). The first speaker does have an advantage if the audience commits itself to an opinion prior to hearing the opposing speaker, but this advantage disappears if the second speaker uses a two-sided communication (Hovland, Campbell, and Brock, 1957).

A **primacy effect** occurs when a speaker has more impact on an audience merely as a function of presenting arguments first. A **recency effect** occurs when the speaker who presents last is the most effective. One theory of order effects states that whoever comes first leaves more of an impression because *prior entry* gives emphasis to the initial argument. Prior entry is apparently not the only factor involved in primacy effects, however, because other investigators have not obtained a primacy effect when they presented two messages one right after the other (Insko, 1964; Thomas, Webb, and Tweedie, 1961).

Recency effects may be due to the fact that it is easier to remember the last argument better than the first one; that is, the first argument is subject to more *memory decay* than the last argument. Memory decay theory is supported by this finding: when two arguments were presented, one immediately after the other, a primacy effect was obtained, but when they were separated by a long time interval, a recency effect occurred (Miller and Campbell, 1959).

Number of arguments and repetition

Advertisers sometimes show the same commercials on television for months with little or no change in content. There is little doubt that repetition is associated with learning and remembering arguments (Hilgard and Bower, 1975). Repetition also can lead to more effective persuasion (Wilson and Miller, 1968).

Simple, repeated exposure of the same stimuli has been shown to be associated with positive attitudes toward them and is called the **mere exposure effect** (see Chapter 10 for more on this topic). If the stimuli consisted of words, subjects associated more favorable meanings to them; if the names of cities or countries were presented frequently to them, subjects would indicate a more favorable attitude toward living in those places (Zajonc, 1966). The mere exposure effect occurs only for complex stimuli (Smith and Dorfman, 1975), and there is clearly a limit to how much people can be changed through familiarization with stimuli. The effectiveness of repeated exposure as a way of influencing us can be observed informally when we find ourselves singing commercials. A study showing that famous political candidates (e.g., actors, athletes, etc.) spend the most on political campaigns, and that familiar and incumbent candidates are more likely to be elected to office confirms the effects of repeated exposure (Grush, 1980; Grush, McKeough, and Ahlering, 1978).

Redundancy also may lead to a loss of persuasiveness. In one study, the repetition of an argument five times decreased the effectiveness of persuasion (Cacioppo and Petty, 1979). Excessive repetition may become boring and cause the listener to "tune out." Continual presentation of the same message also may bring about increased resistance to what is perceived as explicit attempts at manipulation.

The annoying aspects of repetition can be reduced if a new point is made each time. Subjects who made more arguments won verdicts of either guilt or innocence in simulated jury trials (Calder, Insko, and Yandell, 1974). However, too many arguments presented in too short a period of time may exceed the audience's ability to remember or to think about what has been presented (Eagly, 1974).

The effectiveness of making a large number of arguments in enhancing persuasion depends to some extent on characteristics of the source. An attractive person was shown to be just as effective with no supporting points as with six, but an expert source was more effective when making more arguments (Norman, 1976). An attractive person may be effective because of perceived trust and may not need to provide many arguments. An expert is relied upon for information regarding an issue and is more persuasive when providing more arguments.

Number of persuaders

Several religious institutions send missionaries from door to door to seek converts. Typically, these missionaries travel in pairs. Experience may have convinced church officials that pairs are more effective than lone individuals. Research also supports this conclusion. Solicitors for the Leukemia Society went door to door alone or in pairs (Jackson and Latane, 1981). Larger average donations (88 cents vs. 62 cents) and more donors (58 percent vs. 46 percent) were obtained by the pairs. This "mild form of mugging" may gain its effectiveness through a kind of pressure toward conformity, an appearance of greater commitment on the part of pairs of solicitors, and perhaps a stronger concern about how generous a target person looks to others when the audience (e.g., solicitors) is larger.

Is the enhanced effectiveness of multiple persuaders due to their mere number, or to the distribution of arguments among them? Although no definitive answer has yet been given to this question, it has been found that three people giving different and reasonable arguments for the same position were more effective in persuading an audience than were three people giving the same argument, or one person giving all three arguments (Harkins and Petty, 1981). Receiving different arguments from different sources apparently causes target persons to think about each argument in greater depth than when receiving the same arguments from a single person.

Mode of communication

It is easy to turn off the television or radio, to fail to answer a letter, or even to say no on the telephone. It is more difficult to resist face-to-face persuasion. In the 1950s citizens of Ann Arbor, Michigan, received communications concerning proposals for revision of the city charter. One group received information via the mass media, a second group received four mailings, and a third group received face-to-face visits (Katz and Lazarsfeld, 1955). The percentage supporting the changes in the city charter were 19, 45, and 75, respectively. The effectiveness of direct face-to-face appeals also has been shown with people collecting money for crippled children on a street corner (Lindskold, Forte, Haake, and Schmidt, 1977) and with people gaining compliance to health measures to reduce the risk of heart disease (Maccoby, 1980).

An examination of audiotape,videotape, and written forms of communication has revealed that their effectiveness depends upon what kind of message is transmitted (Chaiken and Eagly, 1976). If the message is a simple one, video transmission has the most impact and written communication has the least effect. When the message is a complex one, written communications are the most effective; neither audio nor video transmission has much impact. Written communications can be studied, gone over again and again to derive their meaning, and one argument can be compared to another at leisure. Video may have more impact when simple messages are presented because nonverbal cues supplement verbal messages, and the viewer is more attentive to the speaker.

Arousing emotions and persuasion

An argument can be more effective if it is associated with a pleasant experience. Pleasant guitar music (Galizio and Hendrick, 1972), the availability of food and drink (Janis, Kaye, and Kirschner, 1965), and artistic slides (Biggers and Pryor, 1982) have been shown to improve the persuasiveness of communications. In recognition of this principle, many professional offices are provided with music and a full coffee pot. A great deal of business is conducted over a dinner table.

Fear-arousing communications also tend to enhance the effectiveness of persuasion. For example, in an effective campaign to convince drivers to wear seat belts, the danger of being thrown from a car was depicted by showing a pumpkin rolling down the road and an automobile running over it (Rochon, 1977). Arousing too much fear may increase the target's resistance to the message (Janis and Feshbach, 1953) unless instructions are given about how to avoid the danger (Bandura, Reese, and Adams, 1982; Beck and Frankel, 1981; Rogers and Thistlethwaite, 1970). People cut back on their smoking when told about its negative effects on health only if they also were given instructions about how to stop (Leventhal, Watts, and Pagano, 1967).

Not only is the magnitude of harm associated with the effectiveness of fear-arousing communications, but the probability of harm is also an important factor (Higbee, 1969). Little fear would be induced in a target person if the message seemed improbable (Katz, 1960). An antidrug campaign directed toward school children may not be effective when gangrene of the jaws, cancer, or brain damage are associated with the use of various kinds of drugs. Of course children are afraid of such disastrous consequences, but they are also 99 percent sure that the contingency specified in the message is wrong, and therefore disbelieve it.

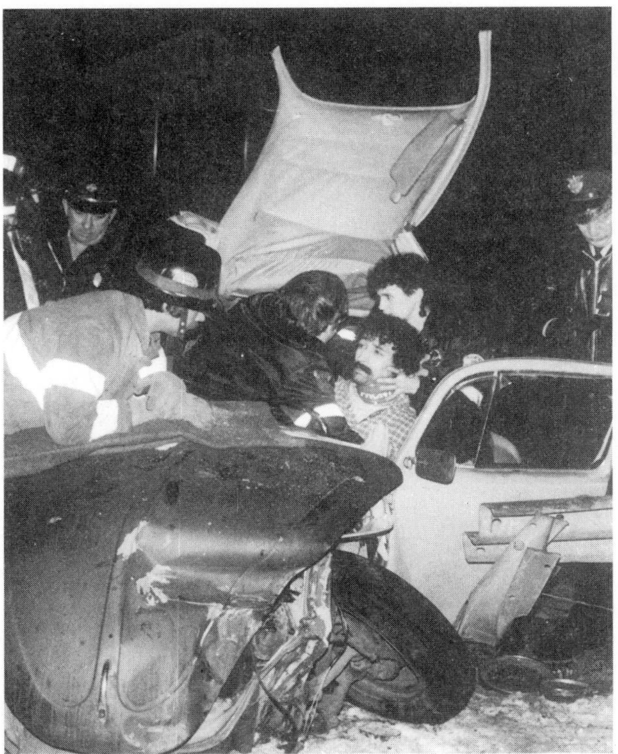

After viewing this fear-inducing auto accident, are you prompted to drive more cautiously?

Style of communications

In skating over thin ice our safety is in our speed.
Ralph Waldo Emerson

Among Americans, a fluent speaker is more persuasive than a slow or hesitant communicator (Miller, Maruyama, Beaber, and Valone, 1976). The speaker also will be more persuasive when directly gazing at the audience rather than when looking away (Hemsley and Doob, 1978). Rapid speech and direct gaze may give the appearance of knowledgeability and self-confidence, providing a basis for target believability in the message. When it comes to persuasion, how you say it is often just as important as what you say. The fluent style of Ronald Reagan, who has had life-long training in the use of the mass media, can be contrasted to the hesitant drawl of Jimmy Carter.

A tactic of the trial lawyer is to use rhetorical questions, such as: "Isn't it true, therefore, that Slippery Sam could not possibly have been present at the scene of the crime?" This tactic will work if the issue does not have high personal relevance for the target person and if the arguments offered appear strong (Petty, Cacioppo, and Heesacker, 1981). Even when no proof or support is provided for a rhetorical question, the listener is left with an impression that the conclusion was warranted. When the issue has high relevance for the target person, however, there is likely to be an extensive cognitive elaboration of arguments based on the question, causing disruption of any attempt to persuade and reducing the effect of the persuasive message. Perhaps the most effective rhetorical question of the last decade was the one asked by Ronald Reagan in the presidential campaign of 1980: "Are you better off now than you were four years ago?"

After-dinner speakers often begin their talks with a story or a joke. The idea is to relax the audience, gain its attention, and promote a positive impression. Yet, evidence does not indicate that humor increases the effectiveness of persuasive communications (Gruner, 1965; Lull, 1940). When people face each other in a competitive or hostile situation, however, humor may lessen the tension and allow them to make concessions without appearing weak or appeasing. Valeriani (1979) claims that Henry Kissinger

> made humor a tool of diplomacy. His banter inspired banter in others and usually led to a more relaxed atmosphere in the private, formal discussions or negotiations with world leaders. The humor opened the door to more frankness and less ritualized recitations as well. (p. 9)

A laboratory study of bargaining supports this journalistic observation (O'Quin and Aronoff, 1981). Subjects acted as buyers, and a confederate acted as seller of a landscape painting. The subjects were instructed to make a first bid of $10,000, and the seller began with a counteroffer of $70,000. When they were within $10,000 of one another, the seller made a final offer. In one condition he simply said, "My offer is ______ ," and in the other condition he added, "and I'll throw in my pet frog." Subjects offered more for the painting when the seller had a sense of humor.

Nonverbal tactics of influence

Facial expressions, body postures, interpersonal distance, gestures, and manipulation of artifacts and objects can all be used to increase the effectiveness of persuasion. Rights to approach and cues regarding status, dominance, and intimidation can be controlled and used to advantage by a person seeking influence over another.

There are a multitude of nonverbal tactics used to convey status. As shown in chapter 3, symbols of status, such as large office, private parking space, and other privileges, may be combined with control of access, including a closed office door and gatekeepers (receptionists or secretaries) stationed to guard access (Korda, 1975). Violations of interpersonal space connotes status. Men often feel free to reach out and touch women and adults often touch children (Henley, 1977; LaFrance and Mayo, 1978; Mehrabian, 1981). The posture of people with high status is more relaxed than that of those with low status (Mehrabian, 1981). An open posture adopted by a female persuader was shown to produce more influence than a closed posture by the same woman (McGinley, LeFevre, and McGinley, 1975).

A steady gaze conveys a stronger sense of dominance than does a gaze that is averted part of the time (Exline and Fehr, 1978). Being placed higher in elevation than others, whether standing or sitting, or being placed more forward of others is related directly to perceived dominance (Schwartz, Tesser, and Powell, 1982). The conditions under which various tactics enhance influence are summarized in Table 7-3. When serious conversation is ongoing, interruptions constitute a denial of speech and is a dominance-related pattern of action. It has been shown that people with higher status interrupt more frequently than people with low status, and that men interrupt women more than women interrupt men (Henley, 1977).

Nonverbal tactics of influence were used abundantly by Jim Jones at Jonestown. He sat in an elevated

"At least we always know who's in charge around here."

throne, had rights to touch anyone, (including any sort of sexual imposition) demanded obsequience in address ("dad"), and controlled conversation. The manner of his interactions with others conveyed to all onlookers who the dominant person was.

Table 7-3 Summary of influence tactics

One-sided communication—effective when audience is unintelligent, uneducated, or ignorant
Two-sided communication—effective when audience is intelligent, educated, or informed
Conclusion drawing—effective when audience is unattentive or message is complex
Repeated exposure—effective only for complex stimuli
Fear-arousing communications—effective only when recommendation is made for how to avoid danger
Rhetorical questions—effective when argument appears strong and issue has low relevance for audience
Nonverbal behavior—effective when body posture is relaxed, eye contact is maintained and personal space distances are optional

Target characteristics and acquiescence to influence

Man prefers to believe what he prefers to be true.

Francis Bacon

You probably have observed that some people are swayed easily by the influence of others, while other people have no trouble in saying no! Although there is no evidence for a general persuasibility characteristic of personality (Hovland and Janis, 1959), intelligence, competence, self-esteem, impression management concerns, and trust are associated with a target person's acquiescence to influence attempts.

Tailoring the argument for the specific target

Suppose you were trying to convince a lover of acid rock about the pleasures of listening to classical music, something the target would not do unless chained in place. You might begin by arguing about the superiority of classical music, the complexity of its structure, how it has maintained its popularity over centuries of time and over all age groups of people, and so on. This tactic almost certainly will fail in changing the rock lover's attitudes. Research indicates that you would be more effective by adhering to a basic tenet of social judgment theory (see Chapter 6), that is, tailoring your argument to fit within the latitude of acceptance of the rock lover (Atkins, Deaux, and Bieri, 1967; Peterson and Koulack, 1969). You might emphasize that classical and rock music have properties in common, and that understanding classical music can increase the appreciation of rock.

There are individual differences in how people make social judgments—some have a wide range of acceptance while others have a wide range of rejection. Open-minded people have a wide latitude of acceptance; they tend to be less certain and decisive about their judgments and more receptive to a wide range of arguments (Eagly, 1981; Eagly and Telaak, 1972). A person who likes all forms of rock would be open to a greater variety of arguments than a person who likes only acid rock.

Another target characteristic that is important to consider is ego involvement. A person who has a strong personal involvement in music, such as a musician or a vocalist, may have greater resistance to persuasion than a person whose ego is less involved (Sherif and Sherif, 1967). On the other hand, the weight of available evidence supports the conclusion that involvement fosters thinking about the arguments and that strong arguments combined with ego involvement can enhance persuasion (Petty and Cacioppo, 1979).

Intelligence and competence of the target

Intelligent people usually have more information and more training in logical thinking and hence can be expected to be more resistant to persuasion than less intelligent people. Evidence shows, however, that while less intelligent people are more persuaded by simple communications, more intelligent people are more persuaded by complex messages (Eagly and Warren, 1976). Perhaps low intelligence prevents people from understanding complex messages, and it is difficult to agree with an incomprehensible communication. On the other hand, highly intelligent people may consider simple messages to be too weak when unsupported by elaborate arguments or evidence.

A similar analysis applies to competence. It is unlikely that most of us would be persuaded by the calculations of a post-Keynesian economist to change our support of government economic policies because we would not be able to understand them. An economist may find the model interesting and, as a consequence, be influenced by it. Less competent people are more persuaded by simpler arguments and become more dependent upon directions given by others (Price and Garland, 1981).

Self-esteem of the target person

People with low self-esteem have been shown to be more yielding to influence than those with high self-esteem (Berkowitz and Lundy, 1957; Cohen, 1959; Janis and Field, 1959). On the other hand, people who evaluate themselves positively are less pessimistic and defensive than those with low self-esteem who are more likely to change their attitudes and behavior in pursuit of goals. Indeed, there is evidence showing that people with high self-esteem are more persuasible than those with low self-esteem (Cox and Bauer, 1964; Gelfand, 1962; Silverman, 1964).

McGuire (1968) tried to reconcile these contradictory findings by suggesting that successful influence is a product of two factors: comprehension of the message and degree of uncertainty in the target. While people with low self-esteem may be less certain (and thus more information-dependent on others), people with high self-esteem tend to be more intelligent and able to comprehend complex messages. A prediction of how people with high and low self-esteem would respond to persuasive communications would require an analysis of the importance of these two factors. Although lack of comprehension detracts from persuasiveness, uncertainty increases it.

Interpersonal trust

People who believe everything everyone says may be considered very gullible, but people who are suspicious of all communications from others may be perceived as cynical or paranoid. Rotter (1967) has developed a paper-and-pencil test to illustrate the tendency of people to believe the communications of strangers. He refers to this generalized tendency as **interpersonal trust.**

People who are high in trust assign greater legitimacy to government officials than do those who are low trusters. Furthermore, people scoring high on the scale of interpersonal trust are more cooperative in response to the noncontingent promises of another, but only when the promisor also possesses the capability of using threats and punishments against them (Monteverde, Paschke, and Tedeschi, 1974; Schlenker, Helm, and Tedeschi, 1973). The latter findings indicate that while high trusters find communications of strangers more believable than low trusters do, they may take advantage of the communicator when the costs of doing so are low. High trusters may believe others, but they are not gullible in the sense that others can easily take advantage of them.

Behavioral compliance

A coward is a hero with a wife, kids, and a mortgage.
Marvin Kitman

Most of the studies of persuasion have concentrated on attitude change. Nevertheless, there has been important research on gaining behavioral compliance from target persons. Primary among their research have been studies of individuals' obedience to authority and use of influence tactics, referred to as foot-in-the-door, door-in-the-face, and low-ball tactics that are used by highly motivated salespeople.

During surgery a nurse carries out whatever orders a doctor may give because the doctor is recognized as a legitimate authority. The nurse believes in and respects this authority because of the doctor's training and experience.

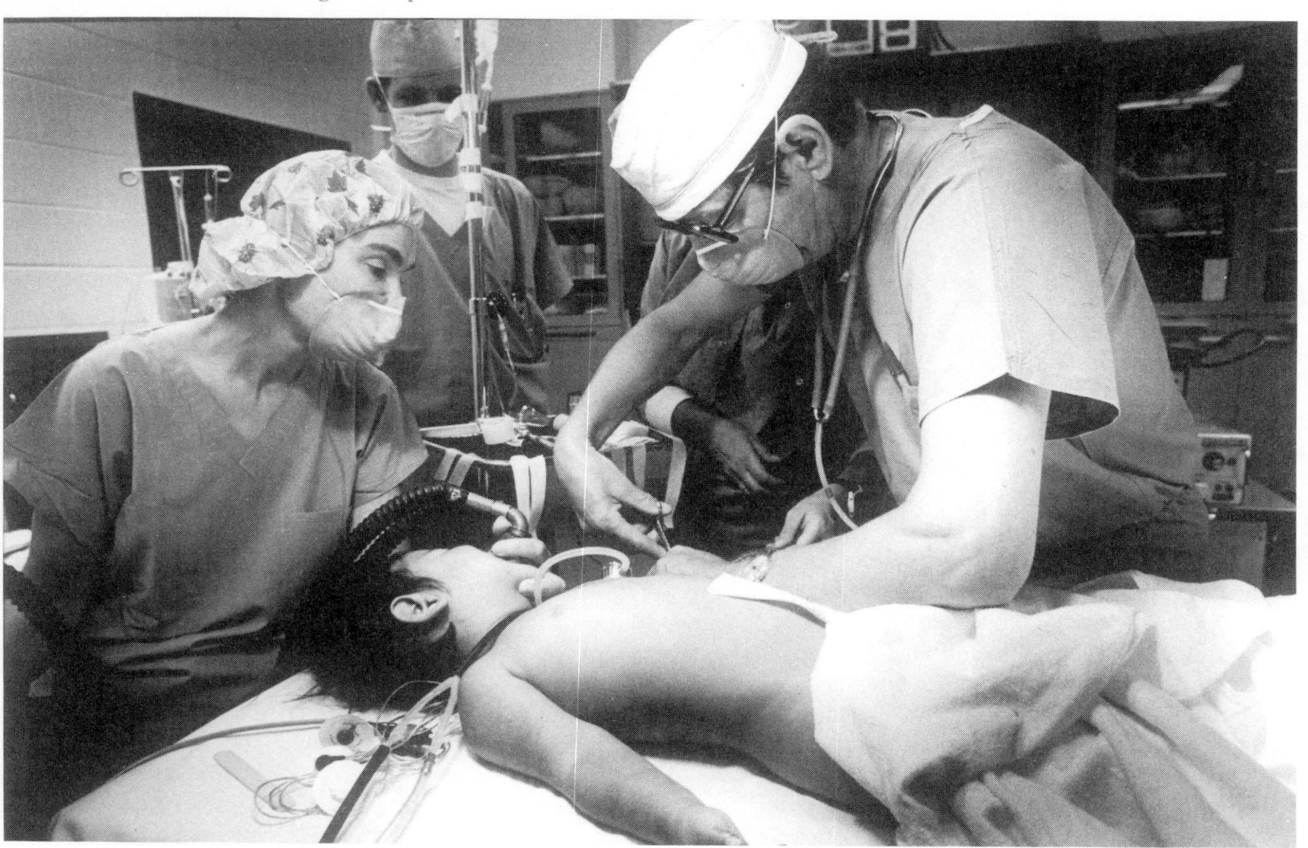

Legitimate power and obedience

If you wish to know what a man is, place him in authority.

Yugoslav proverb

The great majority of people have a strong need for authority which they can admire, to which they can submit, and which dominates and sometimes even illtreats them.

Sigmund Freud, Moses and Monotheism

Legitimate power has been conferred when members of a group or organization agree to defer to the decisions and preferences of another person. People in organized groups recognize the need for an authority to give direction and coordinate activities (Friedrich, 1963). Without leadership or directing authority, groups will fail to achieve important goals. A person's relative position of authority in a group is referred to as **status.**

There is a feeling that one *ought* to do as an authority orders. When people obey the orders of an authority, it is not because they are persuaded, threatened, or otherwise subjected to overt forms of influence, but because they believe they should do what is ordered (Gamson, 1968). If the president of the United States asks an army general to undertake a task, the general almost certainly will do as requested without question, even if that person does not understand or agree with the president privately. It generally is believed that legitimate authorities have good reasons for what they ask, even if followers are not told what they are. This principle is illustrated in surgery, where the head surgeon's orders are obeyed without question. In a relevant study, twenty-one out of twenty-two nurses complied with an order by an unknown doctor to administer an "unauthorized" medication that was excessive in dosage (Hofling, Brotzman, Dalrymple, Graves, and Pierce, 1966). Blind obedience to authority can produce the kinds of actions depicted in Box 7-3 on p. 211.

A series of studies by Stanley Milgram (1963, 1965, 1974) provided dramatic demonstration of the power authority figures have to command obedience from total strangers. Men, ranging in age from twenty to fifty and from a variety of occupations and educational levels, volunteered to participate in an experiment described as "interested in the effects of punishment on learning." A confederate, a middle-aged man, played the role of learner and was described in some conditions as having a slight heart condition. He made frequent errors on a learning task, and each time he made an error, the subjects were supposed to deliver an electric shock through an electrode attached to the confederate's finger. On each successive error, the level of shock was increased. Each subject sat in front of a shock apparatus with a meter showing the level of shock to be delivered. The shocks allegedly ranged from 15 to 450 volts, and labels indicated these levels as representing slight shock, moderate shock, strong shock, very strong shock, intense shock, extreme intensity shock, danger-severe shock, and XXX.

The confederate was seated in an adjoining room and was rehearsed to respond to the bogus shock. At 75 volts he began moaning. By 120 volts he was complaining that the shock really hurt. At 150 he mentioned that his heart was starting to bother him and that he wanted out. At 270 volts he was screaming. At 300 he was banging on the wall. At 330 he was screaming hysterically, and thereafter he remained silent.

The subjects gave visible evidence of being disturbed by the reactions of the learner. Whenever they indicated reluctance to continue delivering shocks, the experimenter authoritatively demanded they continue and prodded them with a series of commands: (1) "Please continue," (2) "The experiment requires that you continue," (3) "It is absolutely essential that you continue," and (4) "You have no other choice, you *must* go on." These remarks always were used in sequence with the more intense command being used when a more gentle prod failed. If the most intense prod (4) did not succeed in gaining obedience, the subject's participation was terminated.

The results showed that 65 percent of the subjects complied all the way to 450 volts (XXX). Only about 20 percent stopped after hearing the learner complain that his heart was bothering him. Many subjects said that they were very troubled by the experience. According to Milgram's report, the subjects perspired, trembled, and laughed nervously. Nevertheless, they agreed afterward that they were happy to have participated and to have learned much from the experience. Interviews by a psychiatrist a year later showed no long-term effects from their participation.

In a subsequent study, Milgram found that the immediacy of the victim was related to the obedience of

Stanley Milgram did a series of studies to demonstrate how authority figures can command obedience from total strangers. Photo I shows the shock generator that Dr. Milgram's subjects used to inflict punishment on someone who was described as a learner (a stranger).

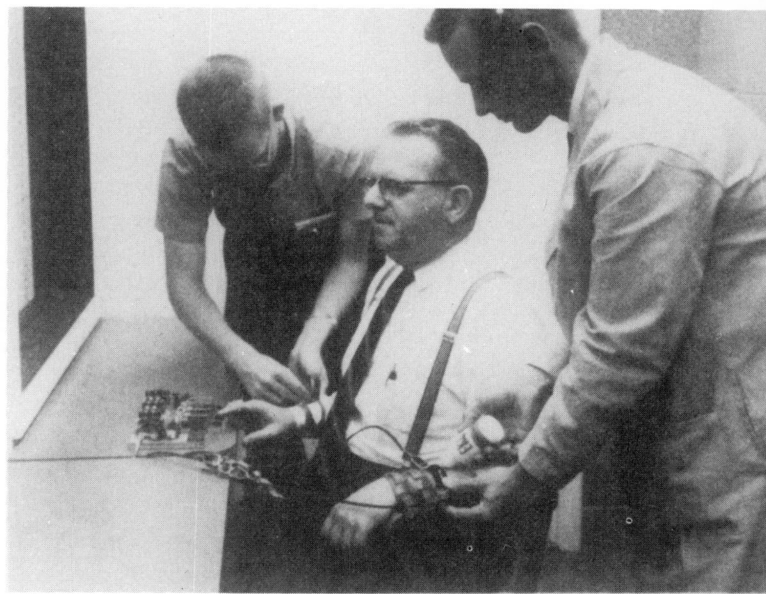

Photo II depicts a learner who was strapped into a chair with electrodes from the shock generator attached to his wrists. The learner provided answers to questions by depressing switches that lit up numbers on an answer box. When the learner answered incorrectly, the subjects were suppose to shock him with increasingly intensive voltage until the learner gave the correct answer.

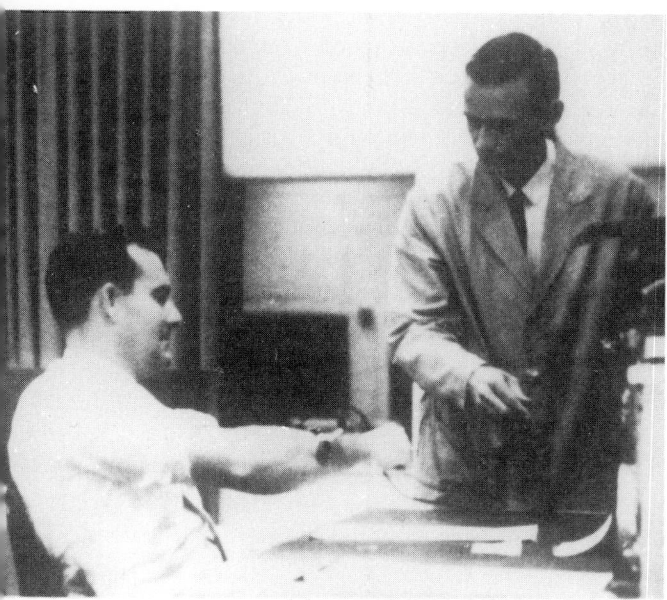

In photo III, a subject received a sample shock from the generator in order to experience the punishment he inflicted on the stranger.

Photo IV shows a subject who decided to quit the experiment because he was upset by the experience. Photographs were taken at the Yale Interaction Laboratory, Yale University. Copyright 1965 by Stanley Milgram. From the film *Obedience*, distributed by the Pennsylvania State University, PCR.

Box 7-3

Monstrous acts of obedience and personal responsibility

At the Nuremburg trials following World War II, war criminals were prosecuted on the grounds that individuals maintain their responsibility for crimes against humanity even when ordered to perform such actions by legitimate authorities. Although orders to murder large numbers of defenseless people should, as a moral and legal duty, be refused, in practice, this principle is very difficult to implement. Consider what happened at the small village of MyLai in South Vietnam on 16 March 1968.

The war was complex. It was not easy to discern who was an enemy and who was a friend. The people working in the rice paddies by daylight often became guerrillas by night, setting booby traps, sniping at government or U.S. forces, and engaging in surprise attacks. It was a total war in the sense that women, children, and old men as well as young men were involved in the fighting. Lieutenant Calley and his American company of soldiers believed they were occupying an enemy village at MyLai, and they were prepared to "waste" anything that moved. Unarmed villagers, including infants, women, and old people were shoved into a ditch and were shot to death systematically. The best estimate is that between 450 and 500 people were killed (Hersch, 1970).

Lieutenant Calley was tried and convicted for his actions at MyLai. He served three years in confinement and was then paroled. Calley stated that he was simply following orders and showed no remorse for the mass killings. Many Americans sympathized with Lieutenant Calley and thought it unfair of the government to send a man to fight in a foreign country then make him stand trial for doing his duty. In a survey, people were asked what others would do and what they themselves would do if ordered to shoot all inhabitants of a village, including women and children, suspected of aiding the enemy (Kelman and Lawrence, 1972). Sixty-seven percent thought others would obey orders, and fifty-one percent said that they would shoot if ordered to do so. What would you do?

---

subjects. In different conditions the learner banged on the wall, banged and made verbal protests, was in the same room with the subject, was seated next to the subject, or the subject was required to hold the victim's hand on a shockplate to deliver punishment. The more immediate the victim, the less compliant the subjects were to the experimenter's prods to continue to deliver increasingly intense shocks to him.

One possible implication of Milgram's studies of obedience is that much of the harm people do is not a function of some aggressive instinct but rather of their willingness to obey authorities. A bombardier peering through a bombsight does not see men, women, and children but only a physical target previously located on a map. The military personnel who launch missiles that may destroy entire cities will not see the results of their action and are only carrying out orders given to them by their superiors.

There is a tendency to exaggerate the degree of obedience obtained in Milgram's studies. We cannot draw a conclusion that the results demonstrate an "Eichmann effect." Adolph Eichmann was a German who claimed that he only obeyed orders by overseeing the extermination of Jews in concentration camps. The willingness of many Americans to give a dangerous level of shock to a total stranger suggests that they might act as executioners if ordered to do so by an authority. However, research has shown that subjects refused to give shocks unless they were reassured that the victim would suffer no harm (Mixon, 1972). Along with his prods, Milgram continually reassured subjects that the confederate would suffer no harm. Obedience to authority occurs only when the requests have been legitimized in the context of the rules and values of the group (Freidrich, 1963).

Control over resources—prestige of the source

Speak softly and carry a big stick.
Theodore Roosevelt

Prestige is the perception that another person possesses and is willing to use resources for purposes of social influence (Morgenthau, 1969). For example, a wealthy person is likely to have greater prestige than a poor person. A target person tends to believe influence communications from sources with great prestige because they obviously can provide rewards or administer punishments and are in better positions to obtain relevant information. Although people may feign having resources, as when bluffing in a poker game, actually possessing them offers a more secure basis of power in the long run.

A survey of nurses in hospitals revealed that supervisors who controlled greater resources to reward and punish nurses were more effective in gaining compliance to directives (Bennis, Berkowitz, Affinito, and Malone, 1958). Promises are more effective in gaining cooperation if the source threatens the target first (Lindskold and Bennett, 1973). The greater the ability to affect later evaluations of other ROTC cadets, the more a cadet tried to exert influence in five-man discussion groups and the more successful was the influence (Bass, 1963).

Foot-in-the-door and door-in-the-face

An important step in the success of a door-to-door salesperson is to get inside the customer's home. Once a simple request has been accepted ("May I

Biography

Herbert C. Kelman

Herbert Kelman was born in Vienna, Austria in 1927. In 1939 he fled with his family to escape Nazi persecution of Jews. The impact of the Holocaust and the horrors of World War II are reflected in his career choices. As a social psychologist he has studied the processes of influence, including conformity and obedience. He has been a leader among his peers in examining the ethics of social science research—concerned not just with how scientists should treat the subjects in their experiments but also with the broader question of whether the understanding of human relations ought to be founded on practices that involve deceit and the exploitation of the very humans being studied.

The disruption of his own life through war has also produced a career-long concern with international conflict. He was instrumental in founding the inter-disciplinary journal, *The Journal of Conflict Resolution,* and edited a landmark book, *International Behavior: A Social-Psychological Analysis,* published in 1965.

Dr. Kelman has been active as a concerned citizen in a troubled time. He helped to form the Baltimore Chapter of the Congress of Racial Equality in the early years of his career. He was a principal figure in forming the Research Exchange on the Prevention of War—one of the first groups formed to study war and peace in the nuclear age. In recent years Kelman has dedicated much of his private and professional energy to the discovery of means to resolve Arab-Israeli conflicts, traveling often in the region, meeting with officials at all levels, working as a visiting professor, and in general, serving as a model of the active scientist committed to the public interest.

Kelman earned his undergraduate degree in psychology at Brooklyn College. He obtained a Ph.D. in psychology at Yale. Most of his academic career has been spent at the University of Michigan and at Harvard University. He has been Professor of Social Ethics at Harvard University since 1968.

come in?"), then the salesperson can make a stronger request ("Buy my product!"). The **foot-in-the-door** tactic involves getting the target to comply to a small request for the purpose of inducing compliance to a later and larger request (Freedman and Fraser, 1966). For example, twice as many people gave to the Cancer Society if they had been asked the day before to wear a Cancer Society pin than if the donation request was made on the first contact with the person (Pliner, Hart, Kohl, and Saari, 1974). However, if the second request is too different from the first and hence perceived as too demanding, such as asking for increasing blood donations (Foss and Dempsey, 1979), then this influence tactic may be ineffective. Thus, foot-in-the-door may fail if the initial request is too small (Zuckerman, Lazzaro and Waldgier, 1979) or too large (Miller and Suls, 1977).

The foot-in-the-door technique was used by a group to collect money on the National Collection Day for the Rehabilitation of the Mentally Handicapped in Israel (Schwarzwald, Bizman, and Raz, 1983). Two weeks prior to collection day, half the subjects were asked to sign a petition to support a recreation center for the mentally handicapped. On National Collection Day subjects were asked to donate one of four amounts of money: 40, 50, or 60 Israeli pounds, or any amount according to the discretion of the subjects. As can be seen in Figure 7-3, the amount given at all levels of request was higher when subjects had first signed a petition.

A review of 120 attempts to demonstrate the foot-in-the-door effect indicates that it is a replicable but weak phenomenon (Beaman, Cole, Preston, Klentz, and Steblay, 1983). The probability of obtaining the effect is best when there is a time interval between the first and second request. This interval apparently allows

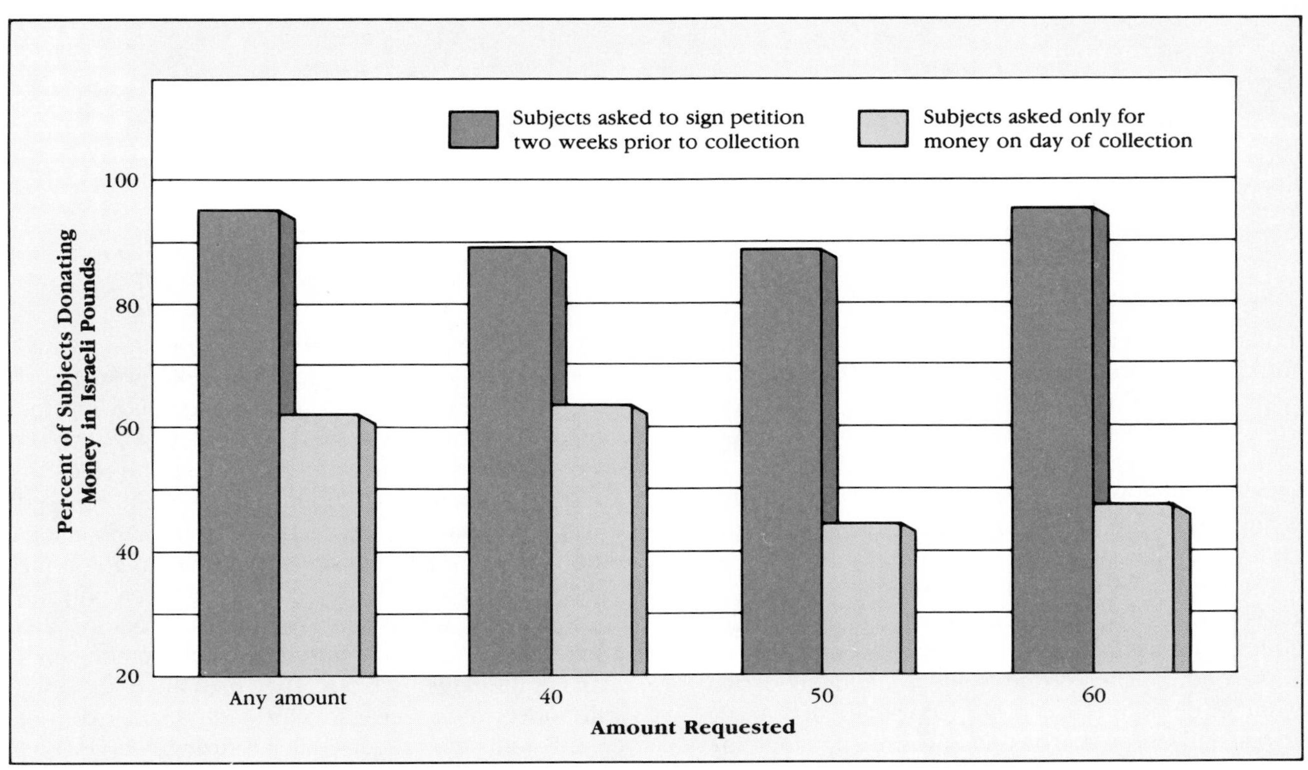

Figure 7-3 Foot-in-door technique used to collect money in Israel.

Automobile salespeople were once well versed in convincing buyers to agree on purchasing a car for a certain price before they allowed buyers to know other costs not stated in the original contract. By using this low-ball technique, salespeople had customers committed to the purchase, therefore, customers would often go along with the new, less favorable deal.

the target persons to think about themselves as the kind of people who would donate to the Cancer Society or who would donate blood (DeJong, 1979). Self-presentation concerns are almost certainly involved. Once people present themselves as cooperative, as they do for the small request, it is difficult to contradict the identity on a subsequent occasion even though the request is much larger.

The tactic of **door-in-the-face** involves making a large request, expecting refusal, then making a smaller request. The tactic is aimed at gaining compliance to the second, smaller request and is often quite successful. A demonstration of the door-in-the-face tactic was carried out at Arizona State University (Cialdini, Vincent, Lewis, Catalan, Wheeler, and Darby, 1975). In one condition, students were asked if they would serve as counselors for a juvenile delinquent for at least two years (a large request), and following the expected refusal, they were asked if they would go on an outing with the juvenile delinquents (a small request). In another condition, students were exposed only to the small request. In the door-in-the-face condition, 50 percent of the students agreed to go on the outing, but less than 17 percent agreed when only the small request was made. One explanation for this effect focuses on the impression management concerns of the target persons. They may worry that they will appear antisocial and unfriendly if they do not comply to a small request after refusing a larger one (Pendleton and Batson, 1979).

The low-ball tactic

A once widespread practice in the automobile business (which is now illegal) was for a salesperson to agree with a customer on the price of a car, seek approval from the salesmanager, and then return with the information that the price was disapproved or that some extras the salesperson was going to throw in for free would require payment. Once customers have been committed to a purchase, they often go along with the new, less favorable terms.

The **low-ball tactic** commits the target persons to an action or agreement before they are allowed to know there are costs not originally taken into account. For example, in one study students were asked to volunteer for an experiment that required a 7:00 A.M. appointment; only 25 percent volunteered (Cialdini, Cacioppo, Bassett, and Miller, 1978). In a low-ball condition subjects were first asked to volunteer and only subsequently were told to come to the laboratory at 7:00 A.M. In this case, 55 percent volunteered and almost all showed up for their appointments.

Why do people go along with the changed rules invoked after an agreement has been made? One hypothesis is that a sense of obligation associated with making an agreement with a particular salesperson leads the target person to go forth under less favorable circumstances. After all, the salesperson was agreeable; it was the (heartless) manager who killed the original agreement. A test of this unfulfilled obligations hypothesis showed that when the initial agreement was followed by a more costly request, more subjects complied if the second request came from the same rather than a different person (Burger and Petty, 1981).

The powerholder and the use of influence

When you have no basis for an argument, abuse the plaintiff.

Cicero

Theodore Roosevelt was notable for his inexhaustible energy and thirst for power. Joe Cannon, the old speaker of the House of Representatives in 1907 said: "Roosevelt's all right, but he's got no more use for the Constitution than a tomcat has for a marriage license" (Morris, 1979, p. 11). The old roughrider knew how to build the raw materials of power, who to influence, and what form of influence to use. Lee Iacocca, the corporate genius credited with saving Chrysler Motors from bankruptcy, not only has been effective in cutting costs, producing a new line of automobiles (K cars), and consolidating the company by selling off losing divisions and plants, but he has been effective also as the number one advertiser for Chrysler products on nationwide television commercials. These two holders of power acted as representatives of larger institutions, and had significant resources available for use in social influence.

In interpersonal relationships, we must rely upon resources we can accumulate as individuals. Nevertheless, like other powerholders, we seek to build reputations of attractiveness, prestige, status, trustworthiness, and/or expertise, and we must decide on whom to influence and how to do so. These latter decisions are affected by source characteristics, the nature of the situation, the relationship between the source and target, and the costs and gains associated with attempting influence.

Source characteristics and the use of influence

The possession of great resources encourages people to exercise influence (Kipnis, 1974). Research has shown that the person possessing the most reward power in a dyad used it the most (Molm, 1981), and subjects with the greatest ability to control precise punishments used their coercive power more often (Smith and Leginski, 1970).

People with high status in a group exercise the most influence (Hurwitz, Zander, and Hymovitch, 1968; Torrance, 1954). Similarly, people with expertise more frequently attempt influence (Shevita, cited in Hemphill, 1961) and are the most effective (Coleman, Blake, and Mouton, 1958; Luchins, 1945). People who consider themselves attractive transmit more communications in a two-person interaction (Back, 1951; French and Snyder, 1959). In Jonestown Jim Jones controlled resources and information, was held in high esteem, and had legitimate authority over the congregants. There was no doubt that he was the boss, the father, and the dominant power in the community.

Relationship to target and choice of influence

A friend in power is a friend lost.

Henry Adams

A father may be more likely to threaten his sons and offer rewards to his daughters in order to gain their compliance. A son may plead with his father but use coercion with his brothers and sisters. A mother may legitimately counsel her children about whom to marry, but their supervisor at a place of employment might arouse only their anger by broaching the topic. The relationship between the potential source of influence and the target plays an important role in determining who says what to whom about what.

Friendship implies equality of power. In laboratory games, people who like one another use fewer threats against one another (Krauss, 1966). When one person is clearly more powerful than another, however, it is difficult (although not unheard of) for them to be friends. It is difficult for the secretary to be a good friend of the boss or for the private to be friends with the general. Status differentials create responsibilities, obligations, and alliances that work against friendship.

The content of communications reflect status differences. Analyses of interactions of senior college students with freshmen and of professors with students revealed that the persons with higher status issued more commands, gave more advice, were more judgmental, and gave more clarifications and restatements (Cansler and Stiles, 1981). People with high status also maintain formality and social distance by disclosing fewer intimate details about themselves than do their counterparts with lower status (Earle, Giuliano, and Archer, 1983).

Threats and punishments are used frequently by authorities faced with insubordination. Some police officers use force against people who challenge the legitimacy of their actions (Kipnis and Misner, 1972; Toch, 1969). Supervisors are likely to admonish, penalize, or fire workers who openly resist their authority (Kipnis and Consentino, 1969).

Cooperative relationships encourage the use of promises and rewards (Miller and Butler, 1969) and the exchange of information. Deterioration of a relationship into a state of conflict brings about animosity and distrust of persuasive communications, promises, and other positive forms of influence. Each party senses a loss of control over the other as conflict intensifies, and at such times coercion provides them with the greatest sense of power (Kite, 1964).

As conflict intensifies, preference for the use of threats and force increases (Deutsch, Canavan, and Rubin, 1971). Conflict spirals get out of hand when each party has invested too much to quit (Teger, 1980). In a poker game in which the players have bet heavily, it is more difficult for any of them to drop out of the competition, especially when there is strong concern about losing face in front of others (Brockner, Rubin, and Lang, 1981). Once conflict gains momentum, it is very difficult to stop, but we examine several pacifying tactics in Chapter 13.

Self-confidence and the use of influence

Confident and self-assured people have a history of achievement and success, particularly in dealing with other people (Cialdini and Mirels, 1976; Hinkle, Corcoran, and Grene, 1980). Self-confidence is therefore associated with reputational characteristics that enhance positive forms of influence, such as persuasion and promises.

People who lack other reputational bases of power also tend to lack self-confidence and are not often successful in using most forms of influence. People with little education, expertise, wealth, or status have a last resort—the use of threats and force. Although the use of coercion brings resentment, rejection, and retaliation, the lack of other forms of power pushes some people into using them. It has been found frequently that people with low self-confidence are more likely to use threats and punishments against others than are more confident people (Goodstadt and Hjelle, 1973; Instone, Major, and Bunker, 1983).

The effects of costs on the use of influence

People use influence to gain some advantage in interactions with others. The "gain" may be positive or may represent an attempt to limit or reduce some negative state of affairs. For example, an attorney may try to influence a judge to give a guilty client a minimum penalty. Before attempting to influence a target person, the source tends to "size up the situation" by estimating how much there is to gain and how much the influence attempt may cost. An actual attempt at influence will occur only if the source calculates that a net gain is likely to be achieved by the action (Tedeschi, Schlenker, and Lindskold, 1970).

By acting to influence a target person, the source incurs **opportunity costs** that are dependent upon how the target responds. For example, if the source sends a promise to the target who complies to the request, the source must incur the cost of paying off the promised reward. Similarly, if a target does not comply to a threat, the source may incur the costs of carrying out the threatened punishment.

A source may be tempted to avoid incurring opportunity costs by not keeping promises or by not backing up threats. The probable loss of reputation for truthfulness, however, may be sufficient to encourage the source to absorb the opportunity costs. It has been found that subjects who were charged for administering punishments sent fewer threats than did those who had no opportunity costs (Tedeschi, Horai, Lindskold, and Faley, 1970). People estimate the opportunity costs of power before using it.

The target imposes **target-based costs** on the source. The use of threats by a source elicits the use of counterthreats by a target, and the use of punishment invites retaliation (Deutsch and Krauss, 1960). The use of threats and punishments also damages the positive reputation of the source. Lowered attraction and distrust and delegitimizing of the source's authority are costs imposed by the target. The source's ability to influence without maintaining constant surveillance over the target depends upon the source's bases of power and not on the use of coercion. The latter idea was not lost on the great French diplomat Tallyrand, who served under Napoleon. He once observed that governments can do everything with bayonets except sit on them. Force will not solve all problems of social order, and reliance upon it may be associated with high levels of target-based costs.

Summary

People can exercise influence by controlling the environment, reinforcements, and/or information. Ecological control, which includes all of these means of influence, is maintained in certain institutions and in authoritarian nations. Reinforcement control requires that a person who influences should give incentives or should provide rewards or punishments to bring about changes in a target person. A source may control information and persuade target persons through communications of warnings, mendations, and activation of commitments.

Characteristics of the source of influence can enhance or detract from the effectiveness of influence. The truthfulness, perceived trustworthiness, attractiveness, and expertise of the source directly increase the likelihood that persuasive influence attempts will be successful in changing the attitudes and behavior of a target person. Whether it would be better to transmit one- or two-sided communications and draw conclusions depends on the intelligence, knowledge, and education of the audience. A primacy effect typically is found when persuaders present opposite viewpoints, but recency effects are obtained when a long time interval separates the two presentations. Repetition, the presentation of more arguments, and the use of multiple persuaders also increases the impact of persuasive communications.

Characteristics of the target person affect the influence process. Uncertainty or low self-esteem makes a target susceptible to influence. A source will be more successful if arguments are tailored to fit within the latitude of acceptance of the target. The disposition of target persons to trust others is also directly related to how much they believe and are affected by persuasive communications.

Behavioral compliance to influence is strongly affected by legitimate authority and the prestige of the source and tactics, such as foot-in-the-door, door-in-the-face, and low-ball. The decision to attempt influence is associated with self-confidence and the possession of relevant power bases. What kind of influence will be attempted depends on the relationship of the source and target. The source will be more encouraged to make influence attempts, the greater the probability of successful influence and the more value such influence is expected to have. On the other hand, the anticipation of costs inhibits a source from trying to influence others.

Glossary

Activation of commitments A form of persuasion that relies on a source reminding targets of their commitments to values and moral principles.

Bases of power Characteristics of a source of influence, as perceived by the target, that enhance the effectiveness of influence.

Compellent threat A communication demanding that a target perform a specific action or else suffer a punishment to be administered by the source.

Deterrent threat A communication demanding that a target *not* perform a specific act or else suffer punishment by the source.

Door-in-the-face effect A source gains compliance by first making a very large request, getting a refusal, then making a somewhat smaller request to which the target agrees.

Ecological control A source arranges the environment to influence people in it.

Foot-in-the-door effect A procedure in which a person obtains compliance to a large request by first making a similar but smaller request that is easy for the target to agree to do.

Interpersonal trust A generalized tendency of people to trust or distrust strangers.

Legitimate power Deference given to a person because of his or her position within the group or organization.

Low-ball tactic A procedure (identified with but not limited to selling cars) by which a salesperson agrees to a price with the customer, alleges to seek ratification from a superior who vetoes the deal; the customer, having made a commitment to the purchase, is often more agreeable to pay a higher price for the commodity.

Mendation A persuasive communication predicting positive events not under the control of the communicator.

Opportunity costs The costs incurred by a source in acting to influence others, such as the cost of giving rewards or those associated with fulfilling threats.

Persuasion The use of arguments, facts, predictions and statements of value to change the attitudes, values, or behaviors of a target person.

Prestige The perception that another person possesses and is willing to use resources for purposes of social influence.

Primacy effect Early arguments are more persuasive than later arguments simply because of the order in which they occur.

Promise Source person communicates his or her intention to provide rewards for another person.

Recency effect Later or more recent arguments are more persuasive than earlier arguments simply because of the order in which they occur.

Referent power The tendency of people to be compliant as a way of fostering for themselves liking by an attractive other person.

Reinforcement control A person influences others through the use of rewards and punishments.

Repeated exposure effect A tendency for people to like frequently experienced exposure.

Sleeper effect Instances where persuasive communications from noncredible sources have greater effect after a passage of time then immediately: attributable to the failure of the target to remember that the communication was from a noncredible source.

Social influence The change in behavior, intentions, beliefs or values of one person that can be attributed to the intervention of another person.

Status A person's position of authority within a group.

Target-based costs Costs imposed on the source of influence by the target, as occurs in retaliation for punishment.

Trustworthiness The perception that another person is honest and not using communications for exploitative or self-serving purposes.

Warning A persuasive communication predicting negative events not under the control of the communicator.

Recommended Readings

Lips, H. M. (1981). *Women, men, and the psychology of power.* Englewood Cliffs, NJ: Prentice-Hall.
An innovative, interesting, and comprehensive review of the social research reflecting power differences between the sexes; may be read in order to learn about power and about sex-role differences in power.

Milgram, S. (1974). *Obedience to authority.* New York: Harper & Row.
This book is based on Milgram's classic research on obedience. It is an engaging report of some fascinating laboratory studies and an important basis for understanding social order (on the one hand) and legitimized violence by authorities (on the other).

Petty, R. E., and Cacioppo, J. T. (1981). *Attitudes and persuasion: Classic and contemporary approaches.* Dubuque, IA: Wm. C. Brown.
A current and comprehensive review of the topics of attitude change by active researchers in the field. This book is both entertaining and informative, is designed for the beginner, and emphasizes applied problems.

Smith, M. J. (1982). *Persuasion and human action.* Belmont, CA: Wadsworth.
This book clearly presents the various theories of social influence, including self-persuasion and resistance to persuasion.

Man, in contrast to virtually all mammals, is the only primate who can feel intense pleasure in killing and torturing.

Erich Fromm,
The Anatomy of Human Destructiveness

8
Human aggression

The concert was a riot

Diana Ross gave a free concert in the open air of New York City's Central Park on 22 July 1983. An audience estimated at 350,000 people gathered to hear her. Immediately after the concert, 1,000 youths traveled in a mob down Eighth Avenue to Times Square and on down to Fortieth Street. Along the way, they robbed and terrorized concertgoers, tourists, bystanders, and passersby. Members of the mob surrounded, robbed, and beat every person in their path. Among the victims was a family of French tourists, who had gold neck chains and watches literally torn off their bodies. They immediately decided to terminate their vacation and head back to the safety of France.

The city police described the incident by saying that the mob "struck like lightning." Nineteen blocks of Eighth Avenue were blanketed with the uncontrolled youths for almost two hours. Eighty people were arrested and arraigned under various charges, including robbery, assault, and inciting to riot.

This incident was a minor one in the scale of human history. The story of Cain and Abel may be accepted as symbolic of the fact that there has never been a society free of all human violence. It has been estimated that only 10 out of 185 generations have existed in peace during the past five thousand years (Baron, 1983). Individual acts of harm done to others include homicide, spouse abuse, rape, physical assault, child abuse, and verbal attacks upon the self-esteem of others. More organized forms of harm done to others include killing during time of war, terrorist activities, gang violence, and the use of force by police officers. Less organized acts by which groups of people do harm are lynchings, riots, and looting and burning during disasters. There have been several attempts to calculate the number of deaths brought about by the deliberate actions of people. One estimate is that there have been 14,500 wars since the year 3600 B.C. resulting in 3.5 billion deaths either directly through killing or indirectly through famine and epidemic disease (Beer, 1981).

Human aggression does not take a single form, such as striking with a clenched fist. A great variety of responses, not only by individuals but also by groups, organizations, and nations, can be called aggressive. There are many approaches to studying aggression, including those taken by scientists in biology, by psychologists in the social sciences, and by specialists in criminal justice and family violence.

Biological factors

The tendency to aggression is an innate, independent, instinctual disposition in man. . . . It constitutes the most powerful obstacle to culture.

Sigmund Freud, Civilization and its Discontents

On the one hand, man is akin to many species of animals in that he fights his own species. But on the other hand, he is, among thousands of species that fight, the only one . . . that is a mass murderer.

Niko Tinbergen

Thomas Hobbes (1909), a seventeenth century British philosopher, believed that people in a state of nature prior to the formation of organized societies were like wild animals. He referred to such primitive people as *Homo homini lupus*—human wolves. The lives of such people were "nasty, brutish, and short." From our vantage point almost three centuries later, such an analogy seems most inappropriate.

Hobbes failed to make a distinction between **predation,** where one species preys upon another in the food chain, and **agonistic behavior,** which has to do with threats and fighting typically within a species but also among species not linked in the food chain. Wolves are relentless and vicious when hunting prey (predation), but they are cooperative and gentle with each other, never killing one another (Gorer, 1968). Perhaps the human species should be renamed *Homo homini rattis*—man the rat—because rats do fight and sometimes kill one another. Actually, there are few species of higher animals that engage in frequent intraspecies killing.

Instincts

A biological approach to the study of aggression assumes that there is some internal, genetically determined basis for the behavior of those who do harm. The entire behavior pattern may be prewired in the nervous system of the animal and carried through the genes. Such prewired behavior patterns are referred to as **instincts.** Instincts have been defined as having five characteristics: (1) they are complex behaviors; (2) they occur automatically when certain releasing stimuli are present; (3) they are not learned; (4) all members of the species perform the behavior; and (5) the strength of instinctual behaviors is affected by biochemical factors.

There are many examples of instinctual behaviors among subhuman animals, including maternal behavior, mating behavior, migration, and dam and web building. Whether humans have instincts is a controversial one, but we restrict ourselves here to the question of whether humans have an instinct to be aggressive. Two forms of agonistic behavior—dominance hierarchies and territoriality—have been well documented to be instincts in lower organisms.

Dominance hierarchies

Almost all forms of animal life tend to congregate into groups, as flocks of birds, prides of lions, pods of whales, schools of fish, herds of grazing animals, and packs of wolves. In all of these groupings, a hierarchy of dominance and submission is established by fighting. The most dominant animal eats first and has first choice over mating partners. Biologically, the dominance hierarchy has the function of preventing fighting within the group and to assure that the genes from the strongest or best of the species are passed on to future generations.

Clearly, human groups also establish patterns of dominance and submission. There are leaders, presidents, dictators, and generals; people who are second in command, vice-presidents, aides, and colonels; and of course workers, followers, citizens, and privates. The status hierarchies in human groups, however, are different from dominance hierarchies in lower organisms in three ways:

1. The establishment of dominance hierarchies in lower animals is typically through physical characteristics, such as strength, speed, size, and even beauty; but position in human status hierarchies depends primarily upon psychological and social characteristics, such as competence, motivation, and leadership skills.

2. Animal dominance hierarchies serve the purposes of biological evolution. The strongest and best animals are more likely to survive because they have

first access to the available food, and they are first to mate and pass on their genes. In this way, dominance hierarchies contribute to the evolutionary principle of natural selection. Human status hierarchies are established to pursue group goals. People gain status and leadership in a group because members believe they can contribute to the achievement of collective goals. Group members would most likely perceive a leader's attempt to gain first access to food, territory, or mates, as illegitimate. Thus, animal dominance hierarchies serve a biological function and human status hierarchies serve social functions.

3. A human status hierarchy must be legitimized if members are to accept the pattern of dominance and submission in it. Legitimization may take the form of a charter, a constitution, a table of organization, or some other form of written or oral agreement. Legitimization is not a requirement of animal dominance hierarchies.

These three differences lead us to conclude that although animal dominance hierarchies and human status hierarchies appear on the surface to be the same, they are altogether different phenomena.

Territoriality

Adult males of some species choose, occupy, and defend fixed geographical territories. Such territorial behavior typically occurs during mating season, and the purpose is to protect access to one or more females. Territorial behavior is displayed by fish, birds, and mammals and has been shown to occur in organisms that were raised in isolation (Cullen, 1960; Tinbergen, 1955).

Territorial behavior serves the biological function of natural selection. Because each male has a fixed territory, the animals are distributed over a region with the "best" strategically placed to benefit should there be a scarce food supply. Dominant animals take the best territories to defend, mate with their choice of females, and thus pass on the best characteristics of the species to their progeny.

The concept of private property and its legitimation is a relatively recent social invention in human history. Eskimos had no concept of property or defense of territory (Montagu, 1968). Some tribes do not defend their territory even when invasions by outsiders may mean starvation and death. When primitive people followed migratory patterns in search of food, they did not defend fixed territories. In many modern Marxist societies, private property has been condemned and delegitimized. Thus, territorial behavior appears to be learned in humans and is neither automatic nor species specific; that is, territoriality is not an instinct in humans.

Brain structures

Investigations have shown that direct electrical stimulation to the lateral hypothalamus of cats induced them to attack rats (Sheard and Flynn, 1967). Similar studies have demonstrated increased aggression in other animals when the brain was stimulated directly. Conversely, stimulation of particular points in the caudate nucleus of the brain inhibits aggression among

A powerful bighorn ram chases off a more submissive one because his physical prowess enables him to capture and maintain his rights over other sheep in his domain. All social animals, except humans, establish dominance hierarchies biologically, that is, through strength, speed, agility, and size. Human hierarchial patterns reflect psychological and social factors, such as self-esteem, motivation, and leadership abilities.

uncontrollable monkeys (Delgado, 1960). Indeed, other monkeys soon learned that they could inhibit the aggressive behavior of the uncontrollable monkey by pressing a lever to deliver an electrical stimulus to its brain. Recent research indicates that there is no one brain center for all forms of aggression, but rather there are separate areas representing defensive, offensive, and predatory behaviors (Ursin, 1981).

There have been some reports of significant alteration in the behavior of persons who were extremely violent by brain surgery involving the amygdaloid region. Out of eighteen amygdalectomy patients, seven of nine who had been characterized as "interpersonally hostile" before surgery began to behave more positively following it. None of the other nine patients who were either self-destructive or self-mutilating showed persistent improvement, however (Kiloh, Gye, Rosenworth, and Bell 1974). In general, the nature of human aggression is so poorly defined and inadequately measured, and the amount of research is too sparse to draw any firm conclusions about the role of brain structures in its occurrence (Ursin, 1981).

The role of hormones

Males are typically more aggressive than females both in subhuman species and in human societies (see chapter 11). This sex difference has led biologists and physiological psychologists to look for underlying biochemical factors that might cause it. The male gonadal hormone, *testosterone,* has been linked to aggressive behavior among many species of male animals. On the other hand, castration of adult males lessens aggressive behavior (Moyer, 1976). Horses and bulls are sometimes castrated as a way of taming them.

Reviews of studies of the effects of androgens on human behavior, including injections and castration, conclude that as compared with subhuman animals, human behavior is relatively independent of hormonal influence (Beach, 1976; Benton, 1981).

Pain-elicited fighting

Exposure to painful electric shocks induces many species of animals, including rats, cats, and monkeys, to attack any nearby animal (Azrin, 1967). It has been suggested that suffering of any kind in humans facilitates aggression (Berkowitz, 1983). Human reactions to pain, however, are strongly affected by cultural factors. Although many people in American society withdraw from the source of pain, people do tend to react more negatively toward others when they experience unpleasant stimuli. Discomfort in the form of foul odors, heat, or disgusting sights have been shown to induce subjects to deliver shocks and unpleasant noise to other people (Baron & Bell, 1975; Griffitt, and Veitch, 1971; Jones and Bogat, 1978; Rotton, Barry, Frey, and Soler, 1978; White, 1979).

The association of discomfort with the onset of behavior by harmdoers probably is explained more thoroughly by social than by biological factors. To illustrate, let's examine one study in more detail. Subjects were told that the experimenter was interested in the experiences of people who had to work under harsh environmental conditions (Berkowitz, Cochran, and Embree, 1981). Subjects kept one hand in cold water (6° C) and served as teachers, using rewards or punishments to facilitate the performance of a confederate. As compared to subjects whose hands were in warmer water (18° C), those suffering from harsh conditions gave fewer rewards and more punishments, but only if the punishments had the effect of disrupting the learner's performance. The latter result suggests that the subjects were more interested in causing discomfort to the learner by preventing positive performance than by directly causing him pain. Rather than a reflexlike biological reaction to pain, this behavior appears to serve the social norm of equity, whereby there should be a sharing of discomfort among peers in the same situation.

Overview of biological factors

In support of the biological perspective, it has been reliably demonstrated that infrahuman animals have aggressive instincts, are propelled toward dominance and attack by hormones, and have brain centers that trigger aggressive behavior when electrically stimulated. Most researchers are very cautious about generalizing these findings to humans, however. Human aggressive behavior is more complex than that of lower animals and can serve diverse purposes, such as communication, punishment, and social influence. As one expert concluded: "It appears as if aggression were in animals more typically physiologically, and in humans, socially determined" (Lagerspetz, 1981, p. 395).

The behavioral perspective

The crucial issue is the nature of the reinforcing consequences that affect the occurrence and the strength of aggressive responses. In other words, what are the class of reinforcers that affect aggressive behavior?

Arnold H. Buss

Man is not born wicked: he becomes so as he becomes sick.

Voltaire

A behavioral definition of aggression is "a response that delivers noxious stimuli to another organism" (Buss, 1961, p. 1). A number of behaviorally oriented psychologists have found this definition too limited because it does not include behaviors that do indirect harm (e.g., to physical possessions) or psychological harm. A more general **behavioral definition** is that aggression is any behavior that does harm.

Both behavioral definitions have been criticized because they include behaviors producing unforeseen or inadvertent consequences, mistakes, accidents and uncontrolled bodily reactions. Would we want to label mistakes by the Internal Revenue Service in computing taxes or automobile accidents caused by mechanical failure as acts of aggression? Because each of these responses produces harm to others, the behavioral definition would identify them as aggressive.

To avoid including unintentional or inadvertant behaviors, an **attributional definition of aggression** has been offered: a behavior is aggressive if the actor intended to do harm to others. This definition does not include unintentional actions, but it does include inaction (i.e., passive aggression) and acts that do no harm (see Table 8-1). In Theodore Drieser's masterpiece, *An American Tragedy,* the antihero, Clyde, watches as his pregnant companion drowns when their canoe overturns on a lake. This inaction would be considered aggressive by the attributional definition because Clyde was a good swimmer, could have tried to save his companion, but wanted her to die. Actions that do no harm, such as a sniper shooting at a passerby but missing, are considered aggressive if there is intention to produce harm even though the attempt fails. Although the attributional definition has been criticized for failing to carefully define "intention" (Tedeschi, Melburg, and Rosenfeld, 1981), it is the most widely accepted definition of aggression.

Table 8-1 Behavioristic definition emphasizing harm done; attributional definition emphasizing harm intended

	HARM INTENDED	
Harm Done	Yes	No
Yes	Deliberate murder Armed robbery Burglary Drowning permitted through inaction Public insult Shooting of enemy soldiers	Mechanical failure causes accident Thrown baseball breaks window IRS makes mistake on tax computation Dentist causes pain and bleeding
No	Sniper misses target Insult sent but not understood Gun misfires	Threat is sent but is a bluff Insult represents a form of kidding Hits a punching bag

Frustration-aggression theory

More than four decades ago, five social scientists at Yale University proposed a learning theory of aggression (Dollard, Doob, Miller, Mower, and Sears 1939). This **frustration-aggression theory** postulated that aggression is always the consequence of frustration. **Frustration** was defined as any event that interferes with goal attainment. The emphasis of the theory is on the stimulus conditions that bring about aggressive behavior. Think of the many kinds of frustration you can experience. If you want to buy a car but have insufficient funds, you will experience the lack of a stimulus (i.e., money) as frustrating. If you aspire to get an A in this course but cannot develop an effective strategy for studying for the exams, you will experience the exams as frustrating. If you are accustomed to eating dinner at 5:00 P.M. and it is not ready until much later, you may feel frustrated. All of these sources of frustration may produce anger, hostility, and aggression. You may be angry at your boss or your parents for not giving you more money. You may show hostility to your professor because of "unfair" exams or say unpleasant things to the person responsible for getting dinner ready (see Box 8-1 on p. 229.).

According to frustration-aggression theory, frustration does not always lead to aggression. The organism may learn that it is costly to attack the frustrating agent. The withholding of an aggressive response because it is likely to be punished is called *learned inhibition.* When the organism inhibits an aggressive response, the frustration-produced aggressive energy is still present and seeks release. Under these circumstances, displacement of aggression may occur to allow release of aggressive energy, a process called **catharsis.** A schematic diagram of frustration-aggression theory is shown in Figure 8-1 on p. 228.

Displacement of aggression can take either of two forms. First, the organism inhibits the initial response toward the frustrating agent and instead takes some less direct action. For example, instead of saying or doing something face to face with the frustrator, a person may spread nasty rumors or perhaps withdraw support for the person in interactions with third parties. This form of displacement can be called *response substitution.* Second, inhibition of aggression against the frustrating agent may lead the organism to aggress against some third party. If you experience frustration on the job and cannot display aggression against your supervisor or boss, you may not be very pleasant to your roommates or to your family when you get home. This form of displacement can be called *target substitution.*

These people express anger and hostility because they are frustrated by social, racial, and political injustices in their town. Their frustration has led them to display aggressive behavior.

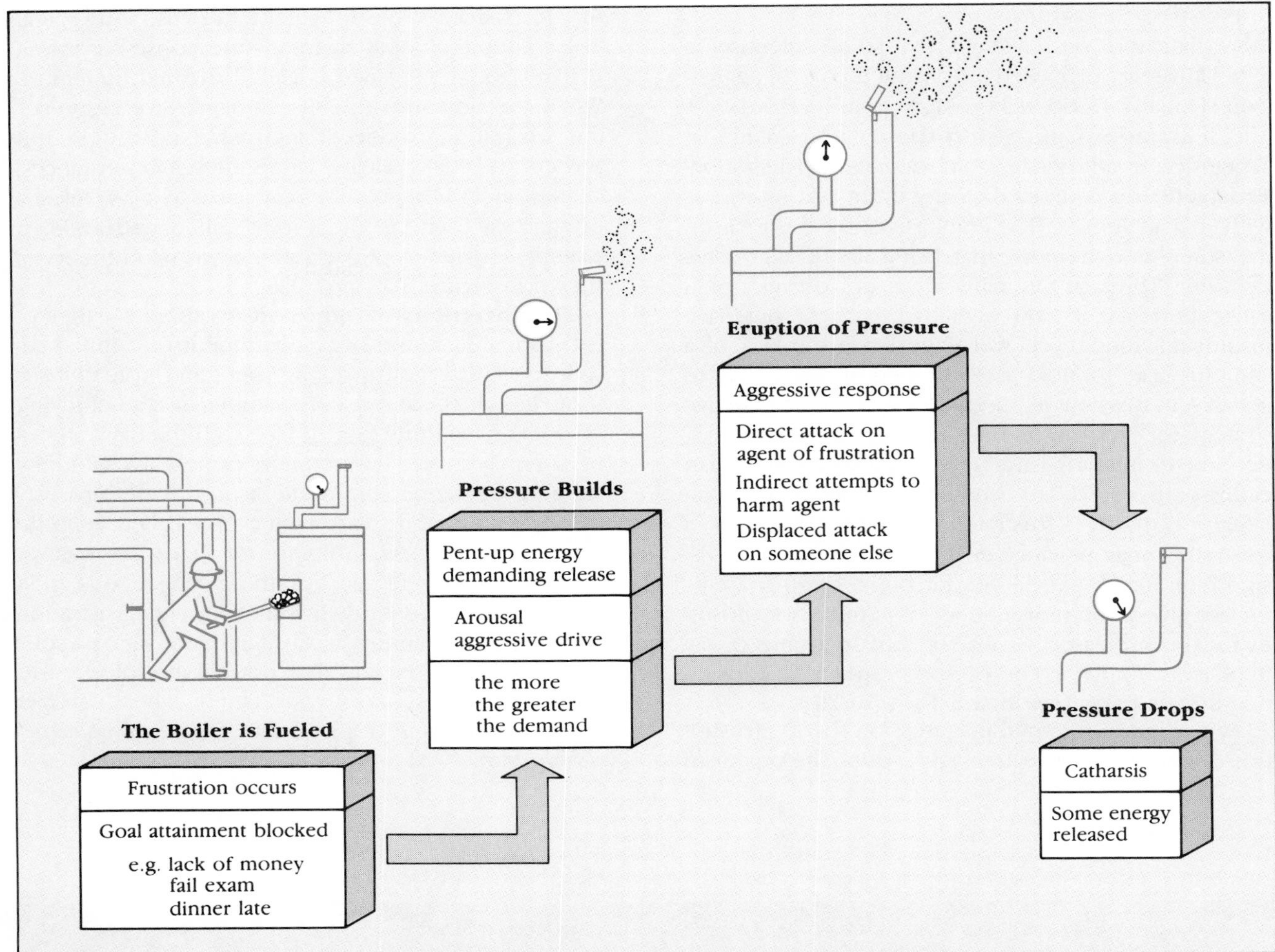

Figure 8-1 The build-up and release (catharises) of the tendency to aggress according to frustration-aggression theory.

Source: Based on "A reinterpretation of research on aggression" by J. T. Tedeschi, R. B. Smith, III, and R. C. Brown, Jr., 1974, *Psychological Bulletin*, *81*, 540-563.

Research on frustration

Frustration produced in the laboratory in the form of annoyance, insult, or attack by another person does increase aggressive behavior (Doob and Wood, 1972; Konecni and Doob, 1972). If unpleasant environmental conditions are interpreted as frustrating, we have seen that they often lead to more harm being done by an individual. In a classic study of the effects of frustration on behavior, some children were allowed to play with very attractive toys, while other children were only allowed to look at the toys (Barker, Dembo, and Lewin, 1941). The latter group of children acted more aggressively when later allowed to play with the toys (e.g., smashed them on the floor).

Just as not being allowed to play with attractive toys is frustrating to children, getting stuck at an intersection behind a stalled car is experienced as frustrating by many adults. In a field study testing the frustration-aggression theory, a car was driven down a small

Box 8-1

Anger and aggression

Anger is an emotion aroused by the individual's appraisal of events as illegitimate or unjustified. When frustrations are justified, the person does not get angry (Cohen, 1955). Some theorists believe that frustration only indirectly affects aggression and only when it makes the person angry (Berkowitz, 1962). In the typical social psychology experiment on aggression, there is an attempt to anger the subjects, usually by having a confederate attack or insult them. This anger-inducing procedure is meant to demonstrate a relationship between anger and aggression. This relationship has seldom been investigated outside the laboratory.

A survey of 160 college students and community residents showed that the most common response reported by people when they were angry was *nonaggressive* (Averill, 1983). In about 60 percent of the cases where respondents reported being angered, they said they had engaged in "calming activities"; that is, they talked over the incidents with the person who made them angry or with a neutral third party. Where anger-induced aggression did occur, it most frequently involved a verbal attack or the removal of some benefit from the other person.

In only 10 percent of the recalled incidents involving anger did respondents report an act of physical aggression. Even this statistic must be qualified, however, because one-third of the cases of physical aggression involved the punishment of children where the goal was to establish discipline or to teach the children. Although anger is seen by social psychologists as vital for inducing aggressive behavior from subjects, it may lead to aggression only in very special cases outside the laboratory.

street and stopped, making it impossible for the car behind to pass (Doob and Gross, 1968). The blocking car was either a fairly new or a rusty fourteen-year-old station wagon. It was assumed by the researchers that subjects stuck behind an old heap would experience more frustration than those blocked by a shiny new car. The measure of aggression was horn honking. It was found, as expected, that the most horn honking occurred when the old car blocked the road.

There also are many studies indicating that frustration may lead to nonaggressive responses. Task failure (Epstein, 1965; Gentry, 1970), receiving a lower grade than expected (Buss, 1966), and delay in obtaining reinforcements (Gentry, 1970; Jegard and Walters, 1960; Walters and Brown, 1963) did not lead to aggressive behavior. Continual frustration also has been shown to be associated with fixation, depression, and helplessness (cf. Seligman, 1975). Observation of mountain climbers and explorers indicates that some people experience frustrations as challenges to be overcome. Overall, the evidence suggests the conclusion that frustration *sometimes* leads to aggression (Berkowitz, 1969).

Research on catharsis

Catharsis or the reduction of aggressive energy also has been examined extensively in laboratory studies. According to frustration-aggression theory, "The expression of any act of aggression is a catharsis that reduces the instigation to all other acts of aggression" (Dollard et al., 1939, p. 33). Physiological arousal usually is assumed to indicate the level of aggressive energy.

Measurements of levels of systolic blood pressure immediately after subjects shocked a person who had attacked them revealed some reduction in the arousal of the subjects (Hokanson and Burgess, 1962; Hokanson and Edelman, 1966). Such autonomic recovery does not occur if the aggressive behavior is perceived by subjects to be unjustifiable or if the target person has high status and hence is perceived as threatening (Hokanson and Shetler, 1961). This finding must be qualified, however, because giving reinforcements to another person also leads to a reduction in arousal of subjects (Hokanson, 1966). It simply may be the case that the completion of any sequence of behavior where the goal is achieved leads to a reduction in arousal.

Is reduction of physiological arousal associated with less aggression? Several reviews of the relevant research conclude that the answer is no (Bramel, 1969; Geen and Quanty, 1977; Weiss, 1969). For example, in one study third graders were prevented from completing some tasks and were given an opportunity to aggress against the frustrating agent (a confederate). The children given the opportunity to aggress disliked the confederate just as much at the end of the experiment as did those not given the opportunity to aggress (Mallick and McCandless, 1966). Indeed, much of the evidence shows an effect that is the reverse of what is predicted by frustration-aggression theory. Angry children who pound on a box with a rubber hammer may be stimulated to become more aggressive (Hornberger, 1959).

Aristotle, the Greek philosopher, claimed that catharsis occurred when an audience watched a performance of tragedy on the stage. It is not actually necessary to perform an aggressive response to reduce arousal, but only to witness it. Accordingly, people who watch violence on television, attend wrestling and boxing matches, and spend Monday nights listening to Giff, O. J. and Don should be less hostile and aggressive afterward.

Several studies have reported that subjects who watched aggressive films were less aggressive subsequently than were subjects who watched neutral films (Feshbach, 1961; Feshbach and Singer, 1971). Juvenile delinquents who had been insulted, however, were even more aggressive after watching pain inflicted on another person (Hartmann, 1969).

Most of the available research indicates that violence stimulates aggressiveness in the observer rather than decreasing it, unless the violence is clearly described as illegitimate; in the latter case, aggression tends to be inhibited (cf. Goranson, 1970). When pain is observed and empathy is aroused in the observer, viewing violence may reduce aggression (Baron, 1977; Konecni and Ebbesen, 1976). Box 8-2 describes a field study of catharsis in which passengers were induced to have empathy for their taxi driver.

Much of the violence in the mass media appears to be antiseptic. People are shot, stabbed, and assaulted and seem to suffer very little. They either die instaneously or recover totally in a span of hours or days. As a consequence, viewing violence may desensitize viewers so that they feel no emotional reaction (Lazarus, Speisman, Mordkoff, and Davison, 1962). Just as medical students may feel squeamish with their first cadaver but later lose the emotional reaction, viewers of violence may lose their sensitivity to pain experienced by other people. We may hypothesize that desensitization contributes to aggression against others, but there is no research available to allow evaluation of this hypothesis. Alexander Pope cautioned about desensitization in his poem.

> Vice is a monster of so frightful mien,
> As to be hated need but to be seen;
> Yet seen too oft, familiar with her face,
> We first endure, then pity, then embrace.

Research on displacement

The usual way of studying displacement in social psychological research is to frustrate subjects, make the frustrating agent unavailable, provide a third party as potential victim, then give subjects an opportunity to harm or evaluate the third party. Again, as with the evidence regarding frustration-aggression and catharsis, the findings are somewhat inconsistent. Several studies have failed to indicate a relationship between task failure and displaced aggression (Cowen, Landes, and Schaet, 1959; Stagner and Congdon, 1955) but others have obtained positive results (Doob and Wood, 1972; Konecni and Doob, 1972). Overall, the evidence for displacement is probably stronger than for either the association between frustration-aggression or catharsis.

Box 8-2

Catharsis in a taxi

Applying Aristotle's notions concerning the catharsis of emotions to aggression suggests that viewing the aggressive behavior of others would make a person less likely to aggress themselves (Baron, 1983). The idea is that we can get it all out of our systems by identifying with someone else who is acting aggressively.

Evidence for this kind of catharsis was obtained in a field study using taxi cabs in a midwestern city. An experimenter, operating a cab, picked up a number of female passengers. In the middle of the ride, the male driver got out and left the cab for ten minutes with the meter running. It was assumed that the passengers would find this experience rather frustrating. Upon returning, the experimenter-driver read a letter he said he had just received. The letter either praised or derogated his work as an art student. Derogation is a form of social punishment. According to catharsis theory, the female subjects who heard the driver derogated in the letter should have experienced a degree of catharsis not felt by those who heard the favorable letter about the driver. It was expected therefore that the passengers who had heard the positive letter would be more hostile and aggressive toward the driver than those who had heard the derogatory letter. The results supported this expectation. Twenty percent of the passengers who heard the positive letter complained to the driver and 70 percent gave him a tip. None of those who heard the derogatory letter complained, and all gave him a tip (Fromkin, Goldstein, and Brock, 1977). Empathy for the driver had been aroused by the negative letter, and this positive emotion provided a catharsis of whatever anger the passengers felt.

Cue-arousal theory

Leonard Berkowitz (1969) offered a modification of frustration-aggression theory that is intended to account for why frustration only sometimes leads to aggression. Although frustration is assumed to produce arousal, this arousal is held inside the organism until appropriate environmental conditions (i.e., *cues*) occur for its release in the form of aggressive behavior. Aggressive cues, unlike releasers for instinctual behavior, are learned by an individual and are not the same for everyone.

Frustration causes arousal only when it is experienced as illegitimate or arbitrary in nature (Cohen, 1955; Pastore, 1952). People fined for a traffic violation do not feel frustrated unless they believe they are innocent. Students who receive poor grades do not get angry if they believe the grades were earned by inadequate performance on their part. Aggressive behavior occurs when the organism is aroused by arbitrary frustration, when an aggressive cue is available, and when inhibitions are weaker than the tendency to respond. A summary of **cue-arousal theory** is presented in Table 8-2.

The cue-arousal theory was demonstrated in a study where subjects were insulted by a confederate who was identified as either Kirk or Bob. They watched a violent film and were given instructions that legitimized aggressive behavior. When the film legitimized violence and when the actor in the film and the confederate's names were both Kirk, subjects delivered more shocks to the confederate than in the other

Table 8–2 Steps leading to aggression according to cue-arousal theory

1. *Frustration* occurs, creating a readiness to attack.
2. *Arousal* follows only if frustration is arbitrary or illegitimate.
3. *Dislike* of agent of frustration facilitates attack.
4. *Interpretation* of frustrating act as an intended attack provokes counterattack.
5. *Cues* in the environment may legitimize and therefore release aggressive behavior.
6. Heat, crowding, and other *unpleasant experiences* intensify arousal and aggression.

experimental conditions. If arousal was not present (no insult), or if no legitimization of violence in the film was given by the experimenter (lack of aggressive cue), or if the confederate's name was Bob and hence he was not associated with the legitimized violence in the film, fewer shocks were given by subjects (Berkowitz and Geen, 1966; Geen and Berkowitz, 1967).

Guns are certainly aggressive cues (see Box 8-3). That the presence of guns may encourage their use is suggested by a laboratory study. Some subjects were shocked by a confederate and subsequently were given a chance to retaliate (Berkowitz and LePage, 1967). Next to the shock apparatus were a revolver and a shot gun. Other subjects were shocked but did not see these weapons. When guns as aggressive cues were present, subjects retaliated with more shock than when guns were not present.

Caution must be exercised if generalizations of this finding are made to actual life situations because another study has provided evidence that the weapons-eliciting effect on aggression may be due to demand cues (Page and Scheidt, 1971). What would you think if you were about to give shocks to someone who had given you quite intense shocks and you saw guns near the shock apparatus? If you guessed the experimenter's hypothesis to be that the guns would lead you to give more shocks, and you acted to support that hypothesis, then it would not be cue-arousal but demand characteristics that would best explain why you acted as you did.

Cue-arousal theory has stood up well under empirical examination. Nevertheless, a major criticism has been offered. Laboratory studies almost always involve some form of insult or attack against subjects, who then have a chance to retaliate. Because self-defense and reciprocity norms legitimate proportionate retaliation, the harm done by subjects is legitimized (Kane, Joseph, and Tedeschi, 1976). The events of most interest to students of aggression, such as spouse abuse, rape, physical assaults, armed robbery, and homicide, are clearly illegitimate behaviors. Re-

Anthony Kiritsis held a mortgage banker hostage in Evansville, Indiana, claiming that he was cheated in a real estate transaction. Because Anthony felt frustrated by what he perceived as an unfair deal, he was unable to control his anger; therefore, he held a rifle to the banker's head. The high rate of violent crimes in the United States is related to the possession of guns, not only by hard-line criminals but by ordinary citizens who become uncontrollably angry.

Box 8-3

Possession of guns and incidence of violence

It is estimated that there are 250 million guns owned by private citizens in the United States—more than one gun for each person in the nation (FBI Uniform Crime Reports 1967). In the United States in 1979, 68 people were shot to death every day. There were over 10,000 homicides, 10,000 suicides, and 1,100 fatal accidents involving firearms. If the rate of homicides carried out with guns was the same in the United States as in Japan, the number of homicides each year would be less than 100. There are more guns in private hands in the United States than in any other country in the world.

Some guns are very inexpensive. Lee Harvey Oswald purchased the rifle with which he assassinated President Kennedy for $21.45 through a Chicago mail-order firm. Saturday night specials are believed by many, including the police commissioner of New York City, to be associated with violent crimes. People who are uncontrollably angry because of perceived injustice, loss of self-esteem, or drugs may use any weapon near at hand. If a gun is under the pillow, in the garage or barn, or in a drawer, the undercontrolled person might yield to momentary impulse and use it to shoot a victim. We know that guns were the weapons used in two-thirds of all homicides in 1979.

The prevalence of guns in the United States is correlated with the high rate of violent crimes. The homicide rate involving guns in the United States is thirty-five times higher than in England, Germany, or Denmark; thirty times higher than in Canada; and two hundred times higher than in Japan (*Information Please Almanac,* 1972; Johnson, 1972). Although the suicide rate in the latter countries is about 30 percent higher, the rate in the United States is higher than in many other nations. All of the statistics relating the prevalence of guns to the incidence of violence are impressive, but they do not justify a conclusion of cause and effect.

People who owned guns and had experience firing on rifle ranges delivered no more shocks in a laboratory study than nongun owners (Jones, Epstein, and O'Neal, 1981). On the other hand, examination of statistics in Jamaica both before and after a 1974 gun control law was passed showed a 50 percent drop in fatal and nonfatal shootings (Diener and Crandall, 1979). Other forms of homicide, however, increased so that the overall decrease in homicides was only 14 percent. Although this decrease is significant, it is interesting to note that few people actually turned in their guns. The legislation's effectiveness must be attributed to a heightened awareness of intensified law enforcement and more effective deterrence.

search that focuses on legitimized forms of aggression may not explain antinormative behavior. This criticism has broad application to all laboratory studies of human aggression, because subjects will not shock or otherwise harm others unless the experimenter legitimizes the behavior (e.g., Milgram, 1965). Perhaps antinormative harm done by people can be studied only outside the laboratory.

General arousal and aggression

A common theme of both biological and learning theories of aggression has been the presence of an internal state of tension, energy, or arousal that pushes the organism into performing aggressive behaviors. In general, it has been established that the greater the frustration, insult, attack, or anger experienced by people, the more aggression they display (Harris, 1974; White and Gruber, 1982). We can be aroused by a large number of environmental stimuli, including exercise, drugs and alcohol, sex, competition, and noise. Researchers have asked whether these apparently nonaggressive sources of arousal would add to the arousal associated with frustration to produce a greater overall state of arousal and therefore a stronger act of aggression.

When people feel aroused, Schachter's (1964) two-factor theory of emotion (see Chapter 2) assumes that they interpret the arousal in the context of the social cues available to them. Borrowing from this idea, Zillman (1971) proposed an **excitation-transfer theory.** People transfer residual arousal produced by one source to a new arousing condition; that is, arousal left over from a previous situation can be combined with arousal produced in a new situation. The result is a level of arousal higher than would occur otherwise.

A similar view proposes that all aversive feelings tend to instigate aggression automatically (Berkowitz, 1983). Not only anger, but depression, jealousy, envy, and other negative feelings whatever their source will make a person more aggressive.

Arousal from exercise

An early test of excitation-transfer theory had subjects ride an exercise cycle (an arousing task) or thread a disc (a nonarousing task). Some aroused and some nonaroused subjects were then insulted by a confederate, and some from each group were not provoked. Subjects who still were experiencing some of the physiological arousal from riding the cycle were more aggressive when provoked by the confederate than subjects who previously had the task of threading a disc. The level of previous arousal did not affect the behavior of subjects if they were not aroused by insults from the confederate (Zillmann and Bryant, 1974). The insult had made aggression the most dominant response, and the residue of arousal from riding the bicycle carried over and made the aggressive response even stronger (Tannenbaum and Zillman, 1975).

One assumption of excitation-transfer theory is that arousal produced by nonaggressive stimuli is misattributed and combined with arousal produced by aggressive stimuli. When a person had just dismounted from a bicycle, winded and perspiring from the exercise, the state of arousal (increased respiration, vasoconstriction, increased heart rate, etc.) was not misattributed to sources of anger, and excitation transfer did not occur. When there was greater delay and the only measurable sign of residual arousal was increased blood pressure, excitation-transfer occurred. Thus, subjects who waited for a while after exercising used more intense shocks than those who gave them immediately afterward (Zillman and Bryant, 1974; Zillman, Johnson, and Day, 1974). If this is the case and if the goal is to reduce angry outbursts, the worst thing a person can do when angry is to count to ten.

Arousal from noise, heat, and crowding

There are many aversive stimuli in the natural and man-made environments. Anyone who lives near an airport can testify to how annoying and tension-producing the noise is. Have you ever tried to study when a roommate was playing the stereo at full volume? One study has shown that subjects who are angered will use more intense electric shocks in retaliation if they also are exposed to unpleasant noise (Donnerstein and Wilson, 1976). The noise levels typical of urban areas may contribute to the higher level of violence occurring there as compared to the small amount of noise in quiet rural areas.

Uncomfortable heat can make people grumpy. The relationship of heat to aggression is not a simple one, however. Subjects who were angered and could retaliate while in a comfortable room retaliated with more shock than did angered subjects in rooms with temperatures above 90° F (Baron, 1972). Exposure to high temperature increased the use of shocks by nonangered subjects, but actually reduced the aggressiveness of angered subjects (Baron and Bell, 1975).

When a stimulus is too negative, a person has a tendency simply to try to escape from the situation. When a person is both angry and exposed to heat, this person tends to want to escape rather than to inflict harm on others; but when the person is not feeling particularly angry, the heat contributes to a moderate level of negative arousal and the person does become more aggressive. In other words, heat leads to arousal and aggressiveness, but if the person is experiencing too much discomfort, escape and not aggression is the most likely response (Baron, 1977).

There is statistical evidence showing a positive correlation between violence and temperature in American cities (Baron and Ransberger, 1978; Carlsmith & Anderson, 1979). A study of crime statistics for Houston, Texas, over the years 1980-1982 showed that increasing temperatures were associated with higher rates of such violent crimes as murder and rape. However, there was no relationship of heat with property crimes, such as robbery and arson (Anderson and Anderson, 1984).

Most days in the summer months, the daytime temperatures are typically in the 80° F range, but the probability of a riot is highest when the temperature is above 90° F. Again, you should be cautioned that correlation does not imply causation. On hot days, people stay up later at night because it is too hot to sleep, they are more likely to be outside, and they ingest more fluids, including intoxicating ones. Any of these factors or any combination of them may contribute to subsequent aggressive behavior. In addition, there is no evidence that people who live in tropical climates are more violent than those who live in temperate zones.

People may feel uncomfortable and experience negative arousal when placed in crowds. Furthermore, it has been found that there is more taunting and aggression in crowded preschool classes than in smaller classes (Loo, 1979). Violence also occurs more in crowded residential buildings (i.e., high rises) than where population is less dense (Scherer, Abeles, and Fischer, 1975). When income, educational level, and ethnic background are statistically removed, however, no relationship between residential density and social pathology is found (Freedman, Heshka, and Levy, 1975).

Laboratory research is similarly inconsistent. While one study showed that males (but not females) were more likely to reach a verdict of guilty in a jury simulation when they were in a crowded room (Freedman, Levy, Buchanan, and Price, 1972), a group of six children playing together in a very small area were not more aggressive than groups of six children playing in a much larger area (Loo, 1972).

A psychological factor that may be operating to produce mixed findings regarding crowding and aggression is the differing reactions of people to population density (Stokols, 1972; Worchel and Teddlie, 1976). The presence of a huge throng at an outdoor rock concert may produce exhilaration among members of the audience. Similarly, there is a sense of excitement when people participate together in public to protest or to advocate political viewpoints. At other times and in other situations, people may feel claustrophobic and closed in by crowds or may find crowds irritating when they interfere with desired activities. Standing in line for tickets, looking for a good seat at the movies, or trying to obtain a good bargain at a sale can be very frustrating if the crowds are large.

Arousal, drugs, alcohol, and aggression

The fact that pharmacological substances cause arousal is represented in slang terms, such as "turned on" and "high." Over 50 percent of victims of physical assault, homicide, suicide, and fatal automobile accidents had been drinking at the time of the negative incident (Wolfgang and Ferracuti, 1967). Other statistics indicate that 70 percent of stabbings, 65 percent of assaults, and 50 percent of shootings involved perpetrators who recently had been drinking alcoholic beverages (Moyer, 1976). Sensational accounts in the mass media often highlight the fact that a murderer was "high" on drugs. For example, J. D. Autry, who was executed in March 1984, murdered a convenience store clerk for a six-pack of beer while under the influence of beer and marijuana. This incident is of unusual interest to social psychologists because it generally is hypothesized that alcohol releases inhibition of aggression (Collins, 1981) and that marijuana makes the person more tranquil and passive (Baron, 1977).

Research has established that small doses of alcohol consumed in the form of either bourbon or vodka inhibits the use of shocks by subjects, but larger doses increase aggressiveness (Taylor, Gammon, and Capasso, 1976). Vodka was associated with greater aggressiveness than was bourbon, and subjects given large doses of alcohol were unaffected by the pain responses of the victim, while those whose consumption was low gave even lower intensities of shock when the victim indicated that the shocks were painful (Schmutte and Taylor, 1980). On the other hand, large doses of THC (the active agent in marijuana) led subjects to use lower shock intensities (Taylor et al., 1976).

The physiological reaction to alcohol consumption is complex to say the least (cf. Collins, 1981). Alcohol may produce stress to the body and activate certain biochemical processes that trigger arousal. Low levels of consumption produce physiological arousal, but higher levels act as a depressant. In the absence of an adequate physiological explanation of the effects of alcohol on aggression, there has been some attempt to find psychological explanations. It may be the case that there simply are more frustrations or stress in places where people consume alcohol. In addition, intoxicated people tend to interpret ordinary frustrations as direct personal rejections or insults rather than as normal everyday happenings (Blane, 1968).

Another hypothesis is that a person who has been drinking becomes less self-aware or less self-conscious and, as a consequence, is less regulated by internal standards for conduct (see self-awareness theory in Chapter 2). This hypothesis was tested with intoxicated and sober students (Bailey, Leonard, Cranston, and Taylor, 1983). Half of each group were asked their names, told their performance would be videotaped, and were seated in front of mirrors. The other half of the group were not asked their names and were not presented with self-focusing stimuli.

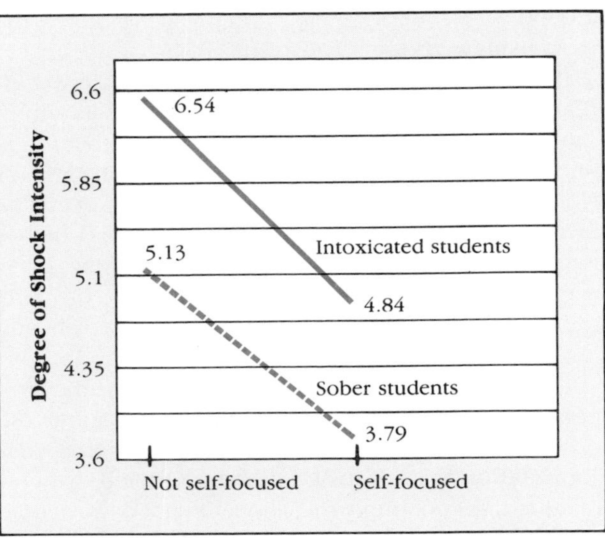

Figure 8-2 Self-consciousness and aggression in intoxicated and sober students. *Note:* Magnitudes of shock intensities available to subjects ranged from 1 to 7.

Source: Based on "Effects of alcohol and self-awareness on human physical aggression" by D. S. Bailey, K. E. Leonard, J. W. Cranston and S. P. Taylor, 1983, *Personality and Social Psychology Bulletin*, *9*, 289-295.

As can be seen in Figure 8-2, both intoxicated and sober subjects chose less intense shocks when they were self-focused. It is clear from these results that people who are inebriated can take the reactions of others into account and govern their behavior according to appropriate social norms. In the context of a loud party or a singles bar, however, where a person may be more anonymous and self-focusing stimuli may be absent, social standards may be less important in determining behavior.

Another suggestion is that the use of intoxicating substances is associated with impression management in two related ways: (1) drinking alcoholic beverages is associated with masculinity in men, a traditional sex-role stereotype (see Chapter 11) and (2) drinking serves as a self-handicapping tactic, lessening responsibility for subsequent actions (see Chapter 3). Males, who were heavy social drinkers and believed they were being evaluated in terms of personal attractiveness by a group of female peers, consumed significantly more alcohol than control subjects who did not anticipate evaluation (Marlatt, Kosturn, and Lang, 1975). Twelve-year-old children perceive male social drinkers as being meaner, braver, louder, stronger, and more aggressive than nondrinkers (Wanner, cited in McClelland, Kalen, Wanner, and Davis, 1972). In other words, heavy drinkers are perceived as "macho." Hypermasculinity may be associated with both drinking and aggressive behavior.

The expectation that a person should be less inhibited and more aggressive is associated with drinking. Subjects given a placebo alleged to be alcohol gave a confederate more shock in a teacher-learner situation than those given nothing to drink (Pihl, Zeichner, Niaura, Nagy, and Zacchia, 1981). Expectations also were shown to affect the previously established finding regarding the level of alcohol consumption. Two groups of subjects were given the same dose of alcohol, but one group was told it was a small dose and the other was told it was a large dose. Subjects were more aggressive when they believed it was a small dose. Apparently, *acting* drunk rather than *being* drunk contributes to such behavior.

Sexual arousal and aggression

If arousal produced by exercise, heat, and noise is associated with aggression, then it is reasonable to suggest that sexual arousal also might serve to increase aggressive behavior. According to excitation-transfer theory, residues from sexual arousal would increase aggressiveness if a person were subsequently angered because the arousal associated with anger would be greater than if no residue from other sources of arousal were present. In a demonstration of this principle, subjects watched one of three feature-length films: *Marco Polo's Travels,* an educational film of the famous adventurer's trip through China; *Body and Soul,* a prize fighting film with much violence; and *The Couch,* an erotic film containing nudity and precoital intimacy. Subjects then encountered a confederate who gave them shocks to indicate disagreements of opinion. When subsequently given the opportunity to shock the confederate, subjects who had seen the erotic movie delivered the most intense shocks, those who saw the fight film gave intermediate level shocks, and the nonaroused subjects who saw the adventurer's travels gave the mildest shocks (Zillman, 1971).

Subsequent research has produced contradictory findings. One set of studies has shown that the more erotic the stimuli, the greater the aggressiveness of subjects (Jaffe, Malamuth, Feingold, and Feshbach, 1974; Meyer, 1972), while others have shown that mild erotica in the form of nudes, such those shown in *Playboy* magazine, inhibited (i.e., reduced) aggression (Baron, 1974; Baron and Bell, 1973; Frodi, 1977). One explanation is that sexual stimuli can distract attention from preceding events. Thus, if a person is angered before being exposed to sexual stimuli, the latter will serve to distract attention, reduce anger, and inhibit aggression. If a person is angered after exposure to sexual arousal, the arousal from both sources will be combined, the person will experience greater anger than if sexual stimuli had not been encountered first, and greater aggressiveness will be displayed (Donnerstein, Donnerstein, and Evans, 1975).

Another explanation for the contradictory findings regarding erotica and aggression is that some sexual stimuli are pleasant and others are experienced as disgusting and unpleasant. Pleasurable stimuli inhibit or interfere with aggressive behavior, and unpleasant stimuli enhance aggressiveness (Zillman and Sapolsky, 1977). For example, sexual humor has been shown to reduce aggression (Baron, 1978). Assuming that mild erotica is experienced as pleasant by most people, but that hard core pornography is experienced as unpleasant, then mild erotica should inhibit aggression and strong erotica should enhance it. Although support for this explanation has been found when subjects experienced strong provocation (Ramirez, Bryant, and Zillman, 1982), the issue is yet to be resolved.

Given the present state of our knowledge, we can conclude that residual states of physiological arousal, whatever the source, are combined with the arousal produced by subsequent anger, and the result is more intense aggressiveness. Table 8-3 summarizes the sources of arousal that can intensify aggression. It must be remembered, however, that all of the laboratory research has been done in the context of first provoking the subjects and then giving them a legitimized opportunity (as teacher or evaluator of the other person) to deliver electric shocks to the provoker. In other words, arousal does not elicit aggression, but if aggression occurs, it can enhance it. When a person acts in accordance with social norms, such as self-defense, deterrence, punishment, or equity, residual sources of arousal may be associated with a tendency to overreact or to be more aggressive than the norms actually legitimize. On the other hand, arousal produced by nonaggressive stimuli may serve to inhibit aggression if these stimuli occur after the conditions that make the person angry.

Table 8–3 Sources of arousal shown to intensify aggressive behavior

Arbitrary frustration
Insult
Jealousy
Envy
Depression
Physical exercize
Uncontrollable noise
Excessive heat
Feeling crowded
Alcohol
Angel dust
Unpleasant sexual stimulation

Social learning theory

Although frustration-aggression, cue-arousal, and excitation-transfer theories examine the sources and outlets of internal arousal states, social learning theory emphasizes the social context in which people learn and exhibit behavior that causes harm (Bandura, 1973). Behavior patterns are acquired through direct reinforcements or by observation of others (i.e., models) who are successful in obtaining rewards and avoiding punishments. For example, a person may learn to box by watching others fight and by boxing. This acquired skill may be maintained by periodic training. Then, one day the person is angered and performs the learned behavior pattern to harm another person. This sequence of acquisition, maintenance, and performance must be studied to find all of the factors involved in aggressive behavior. Notably absent from this formulation is any reference to biological characteristics or physiological states of arousal.

Rewards and punishments

A community is infinitely more brutalized by the habitual employment of punishment than. . .by the occasional occurrence of crime.
Oscar Wilde

A fundamental law of learning is that whatever works in gaining rewards for the person is likely to be repeated in similar situations on subsequent occasions. This law of reinforcement applies to aggressive behavior. Children (Cowan and Walters, 1963) and adults (Geen and Stonner, 1971) have been shown to be more aggressive when rewarded for such behavior. Observation of the behavior of children in a playground indicated that the successful use of force in resolving conflicts encouraged more aggressive conduct (Patterson, Littman, and Bricker, 1967). By ignoring aggressive behavior and rewarding cooperative and peaceful behavior, the incidence of physical and verbal aggression in a nursery school was significantly reduced (Brown and Elliott, 1965).

Although direct punishment of aggression can reduce it in both children (Chasdi and Lawrence, 1955) and adults (Wilson and Rogers, 1975), learning theorists are hesitant to recommend punishment as a technique for controlling aggression. Punishing Johnny for shoving Richie does not teach Johnny appropriate behavior. The next time, Johnny may spit at Richie or throw something at him. Punishment may inhibit one response but may lead a person to do only more harm. Furthermore, there is sometimes a fine line between punishment and abuse (see Box 8-4).

Punishment may activate hostility toward the punisher and may be interpreted as a provocation legitimizing retaliation (Dyck and Rule, 1978; Harvey and Enzle, 1978; Taylor, Shuntich, and Greenberg, 1979). In other words, punishment may encourage and enhance aggressiveness instead of reducing it.

Parents who experience great stress may abuse their children because they were abused themselves as children, because they drink, and/or because they are troubled by problems associated with finances, sickness, or work.

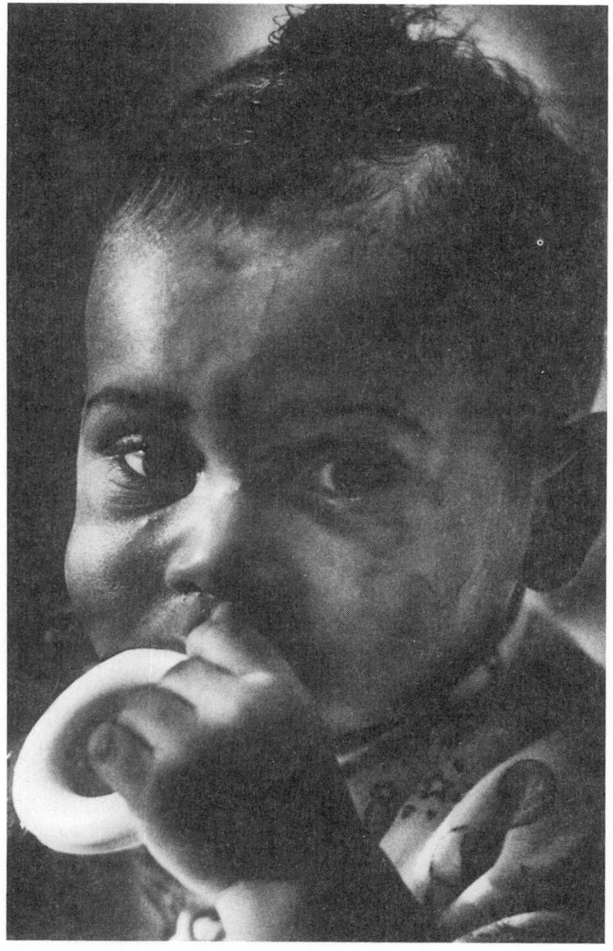

Box 8-4

Why do parents abuse their children?

Abuse of children is carried out by parents who were abused themselves as children (Gelles, 1979; Silver, Dublin, and Lourie, 1969). Child abuse tends to be an intergenerational problem. Each generation of children learns to use violence in the context of a conflict-filled home. Most abusive families are typified by a high incidence of unstable marriages, separations, and divorce.

The probability that a child will be abused increases with the size of the family. The highest rate of child abuse occurs in families with five children, but children are likely to experience less violence when there are more than five children. Abuse occurs in families with widely varying incomes. The use of alcohol and child abuse also are related statistically. Evidence suggests that between one-third and one-half of all child abusers also abuse alcohol (Shoredone, Gorelick, and Elliot, 1981). Handicapped and retarded children have a greater likelihood of being abused than normal children.

All of these factors together suggest that it is the amount of stress experienced by the parents that provokes violent outbursts against children (Straus, Gelles, and Steinmetz, 1980). Measures taken of stress, including items asking about troubles with the boss or other people at work, trouble with the law, financial problems, sickness or injury, and so on, established that among 2,143 abusive families, the greatest incidence of abuse occurred when stress was very high. The relationship between stress and child abuse is shown in Figure 8-3 on p. 240.

Modeling and imitation

It is organized violence at the top which creates individual violence at the bottom.

Emma Goldman

In a typical study of modeling and aggression, an adult is placed in a room with some props, including a large inflatable vinyl clown named Bobo, which when pushed, punched, or kicked falls over and bounces back. Coloring books, crayons, a rubber mallet, and dart gun (with rubber tips) are among the other props. The adult punches Bobo yelling, "Take that you bad Bobo." The person kicks, throws, shoots, and hits Bobo with the rubber mallet. This sequence either may be directly viewed by a child or it may be videotaped. An experimenter may be shown giving the model a candy bar as a reward for the behavior. As long as the model is rewarded, children perform many of the same behaviors when they are placed in the room with the same props (Bandura, Ross, and Ross, 1961, 1963). The more attractive and powerful the model, the more aggressive the behavior of the observer children (Bandura and Huston, 1961).

Not only do models provide an example of effective behavior in a particular situation, but they also serve to legitimize it. Subjects who observed a model receiving punishment for abusing Bobo displayed less aggression than control subjects who did not observe a model (Hicks, 1965). Based on this evidence, it might be expected that models of illegitimate violence on television would not be imitated because they almost always are punished for their behavior. According to critics of violence in the mass media, children often observe criminals gain short-term rewards for their behavior, and only later do they get their comeuppance. Small children are not believed to be capable of linking the original criminal conduct to the final outcome, but instead focus on the rewarding aspects of the behavior.

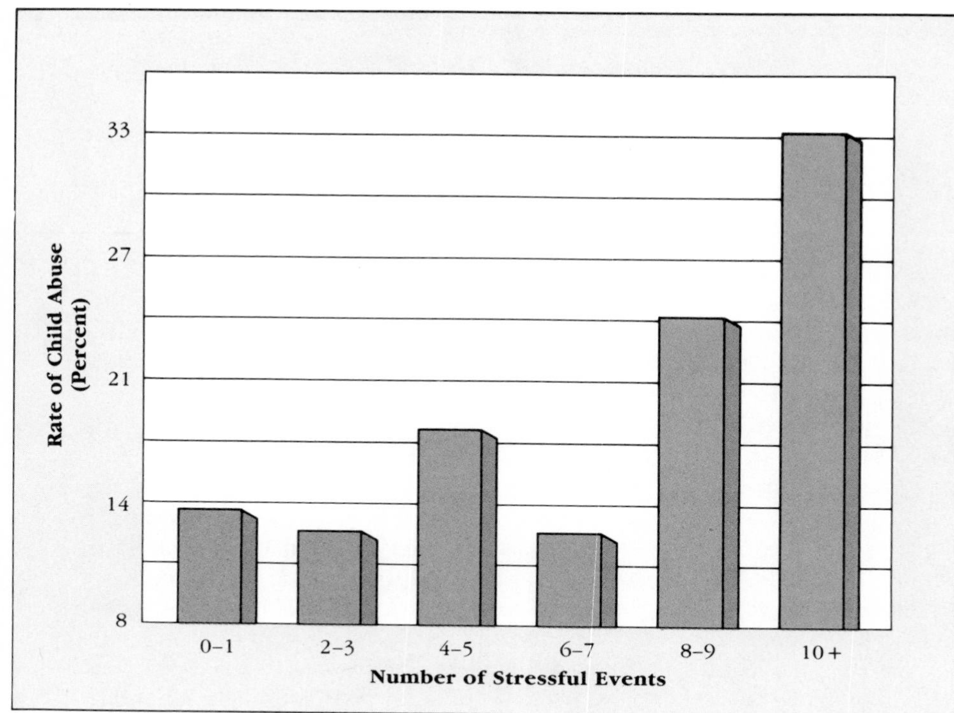

Figure 8-3 Family stress and child abuse.

The average high school graduate has spent twice as much time in front of a television set as in the classroom. Graduates will have seen 150,000 violent incidents and 25,000 deaths on television. Viewers of violent programs are apt to exhibit more fear and apprehension about their communities and to behave in more aggressive ways (Liebert, Sprafkin, and Davidson, 1982).

In a longitudinal study first begun in 1960, eight-year-old children rated each other's aggressiveness (Eron, 1980). In 1970 these same children were nineteen years old, and once again they rated one another. The best predictor of how aggressive the male teenagers were perceived to be by their peers was not how aggressive they were at the age of eight, but rather the degree of violence depicted in their favorite television show at that earlier age. The higher the aggressiveness ratings for male teenagers, the more television was perceived to be the cause. A number of other factors also are involved, including the age, intelligence, education, socioeconomic class, and sex of the viewer (Palmer and Dorr, 1980).

Females were rated less aggressive than males, and no association was found between the violence depicted in programs they watched on television and their rated aggressiveness. A positive correlation did exist, however, between the rated aggressiveness of the female teenagers and their tendency to perceive television programs as realistic (Eron, 1980).

Self-reinforcement of aggression

According to social learning theory, people are capable of monitoring their own behavior and evaluating themselves (Bandura, 1973). A person may feel bad (i.e., guilty) about harming a victim. On the other hand, if the doer of harm feels justified, there may be a bolstering of self-esteem for standing up and being counted. Members of violent gangs gain self-esteem from success in beating adversaries brutally (Toch, 1969). Commandants of Nazi extermination camps registered pride in surpassing their quotas and in performing better than officers of other camps (Bandura, 1973). Aggressive people may reinforce themselves by appealing to higher principles to justify their actions, and they may dehumanize and blame their victims, minimizing the consequences of their actions. These tendencies neutralize the effectiveness of social norms and internal standards in controlling the aggressive conduct.

Overview of social learning theory

The identification and emphasis on social factors, such as modeling and legitimation of aggression, has been an important contribution of social learning theory; however, it has not escaped criticism. The research on modeling has involved an inanimate object, and questions have been raised about why hitting Bobo is considered aggressive (Joseph, Kane, Nacci, and Tedeschi, 1977). No harm is done and it does not seem plausible to assume that small children intend to damage the inanimate object. There is also a question of whether imitation of a model hitting Bobo could be generalized to include that children would harm people (Bryan and Schwartz, 1971; Singer, 1971; Weiss, 1969).

Bandura (1973) interprets hitting Bobo as an aggressive act because it consists of a set of motor skills that *could* be used to harm people. The behavior is at the first stage of acquisition, and as a learned behavior pattern, it may later be performed to hurt others. The problem with this view is that almost any response can be used to harm others. The ability to talk allows a person to conspire against others, to spread vicious gossip, and to abuse a victim verbally. The ability to use the fingers permits people to fire guns and to push buttons controlling nuclear missiles. The answer to the question of *how* people hurt one another is not a satisfactory answer to the question of *why* they do so. If a person wants to inflict harm on someone, a way to do so can be found.

Social power and aggression

All cruelty stems from weakness.

Seneca

A social power perspective proposes that people threaten or administer harm as a means of gaining compliance or of carrying out retribution. The use of threats and punishments in pursuit of social power is referred to as **coercive power.** If the use of coercive power or the administration of punishment are justified in the eyes of observers, they do not perceive this power as aggression, but instead label it as defensive, correctional, or trainable. If the use of coercion is perceived as antinormative or illegitimate, the act and the performer will be labeled as aggressive.

Proponents of the social power theory have noted that most laboratory research legitimizes the use of shocks, irritating noises, or negative evaluations, thus subjects would not be labeled as "aggressive" by most observers (Kane, Joseph, and Tedeschi, 1976). In the arousal studies reviewed earlier, it was noted that arousal enhances retaliation but does not elicit or provoke a person to attack innocent victims indiscriminantly. The focus of social power theory is on why people use threats and punishments against one another and on the legitimations that encourage people to use coercive power.

Self-defense and the norm of reciprocity

How good bad music and bad reasons sound when we march against an enemy.

Nietzsche

In a national survey of adult American males, more than 60 percent considered it justifiable to kill to defend one's family, property, and self (Blumenthal, Kahn, Andrews, and Head, 1972). Many heroes of television and film intervene to kill a villain who threatens the weak, the women, and the aged. A claim of self-defense is used frequently by all nations to justify the use of armed force, which is perceived as legitimate by the United Nations if the facts substantiate a nation's claims. Providing cues that legitimize retaliation intensifies shocks used by subjects in laboratory experiments (Ramirez, Bryant, and Zillman, 1982), while instructions assigning full responsibility for attacks to the subjects reduces the intensity of retaliation (Diener, Dineen, Endresen, Beaman, and Fraser, 1975).

The **negative norm of reciprocity** prescribes doing harm for harm received and appears as a rule of conduct in all societies (Gouldner, 1960). The biblical rule of an eye for an eye and a tooth for a tooth stipulates that proportionality be observed in carrying out justifiable revenge. Subjects acting according to this largely defensive norm do tend to match the intensity of shocks delivered by an attacker (Berkowitz and Green, 1962; Helm, Bonoma, and Tedeschi, 1972; Taylor, 1967). There are times when it is difficult to determine how much punishment a person deserves for injuring others. For example, if a person humiliates you in public or causes you to lose a coveted objective, how much and what kind of retaliation would be justified? It is this kind of judgment, made in the throes of heated emotions, that leads to many acts of violence (Felson, 1982).

Punishment for disobedience to authority

Distrust all men in whom the impulse to punish is powerful.

Neitsche

Insubordination or failure to accede to the authority of another person may bring about coercive forms of behavior. Parents who abuse their children often explain their excessive use of punishment as an attempt to gain control over unruly and disrespectful children. When subjects were given supervisory authority over simulated workers, they chose to use threats and punishments rather than promises and rewards when the workers were noncooperative and nonproductive (Kipnis and Consentino, 1969).

A field study of assaults against police officers revealed a typical sequence of events (Toch, 1969). A police officer issues a command to someone on the street, perhaps telling the person to move along. The person replies that it is a free country, that he is not doing anything wrong, and that the police officer has no right to harass him. This response challenges the officer's authority. Before long there are angry words, shoving, fighting, and an arrest is made. The use of force may be a way of restoring authority and legitimacy by police officers. Interviews of police officers established that disobedience was an important cause of disorderly conduct arrests of male offenders (Kipnis and Misner, 1972).

Social influence

People use threats and punishments for purposes of social influence as is discussed in Chapter 7; people may use coercion to resolve conflicts over scarse resources, as an influence means of last resort or as a typical part of their influencing style (see Box 8-5). The source's goal is to gain compliance to some demand or to deter some behavior by the target person. When threats fail, the source may feel compelled to back them up with subsequent punishments. Otherwise, the threatener would be perceived as using empty threats, credibility would decline, and subsequent attempts to influence others would become less effective.

Self-presentation and self-esteem

Certain subcultures may perceive reluctance to fight or to use force as a lack of masculinity. A man may publicly advertise a willingness to fight anyone as a way of promoting a tough male identity (Toch, 1969). Such a person may provoke a fight with a total stranger and for no apparent reason. The self-promoter of an identity of toughness is like the fast gun depicted in western novels and movies. It is important to gain new conquests to keep one's reputation fresh in the minds of the intended audiences.

The person may be motivated to protect some positive identity. Consider what happens when someone insults you. Your identity as a person with positive

Fighting is one way to gain a tough and superior identity. By punishing others, people are able to restore or bolster their self-esteem and reputation.

Box 8-5

Fighting among children

The most frequent incidence of fighting in American society is between siblings (Felson, 1983). A common explanation for such fighting is **sibling rivalry.** Brothers and sisters are jealous over parent's attention. Because younger siblings often receive more attention from parents, older siblings strike out at their younger sisters and brothers.

The sibling rivalry hypothesis did not receive support in a study of college students who were asked to recall their relations with siblings and other children when they were in junior high school (Felson, 1983). The successes of younger sibs, the amount of jealousy, and the degree of parental favoritism did not correlate with the amount of fighting between siblings. Nevertheless, there was considerably more fighting between sibs than between nonrelated children. Furthermore, there was just as much fighting between opposite-sex siblings as between same-sex sibs.

The results supported a **realistic-conflict model** of aggression. Real disagreements about the use of property and the division of labor were the most frequent antecedents of fights. The single most important cause of fights was over which television program would be viewed. Access to the bathroom and disagreement about whose turn it was to perform some chore also served as bases for conflicts between children.

characteristics is challenged. Anger and retaliation often occur under these circumstances. Interviews of inmates convicted of physical assault and murder indicated that interpersonal conflicts escalated to the use of violence and the use of weapons when the convict and the victim began to challenge the identities of one another through disparagement and insults (Felson, 1978).

Punishing an offending person is a way for people to establish their superiority and restore self-esteem. Franz Fanon (1963), a black psychiatrist who was influential during the 1960s, argued that the colonized peoples of Africa could restore self-respect only by violently punishing those who had subjugated them. Research reported in Chapter 7 supports the hypothesis that people will punish others as a way of restoring positive identities for themselves (e.g., Brown, 1968).

A person with a poor self-image may be driven to an extreme action as a way of gaining the attention and respect of others. In many cases, men with no previous history of violence carry out extreme assaults (Megargee, 1970). Children who are ignored by family and peers may feel friendless and alone. They perceive the world as a hostile and rejecting place. By lashing out at others, the child captures their attention. Such actions may be resisted or punished, but at least the person will no longer be ignored. In this way, acts of violence reaffirm the person's existence (see Box 8-6).

Time perspective and expectation of costs

Social condemnation of aggression makes it costly. The ability to foresee future undesirable consequences helps people to resist momentary inclinations to threaten or harm others. This restraint may be lessened or removed if circumstances cause the person to disregard future consequences—such as guilt, remorse, and social disapproval. During intense and emotional conflicts, people focus on the present, perceiving their need to exert immediate control and

Box 8-6

The causes of political assassinations

After President McKinley was assassinated, John Schrank had a vision of the dead president rising from his coffin to accuse Vice-President Theodore Roosevelt for arranging his death (Taylor and Weiss, 1970). Eleven years later, the vision once again occurred and the unemployed Schrank interpreted it as a divine mandate to avenge McKinley's death and save the Republic from the new Caesar. Schrank waited for Roosevelt outside a hotel in Milwaukee and shot him in the chest. Fortunately, the bullet had to pass through a fifty-page speech and a metal glass case in the president's jacket pocket. Only a rib was broken. Among Schrank's personal papers, the police found a note that read: "Theodore Roosevelt is in conspiracy with European monarchs to overthrow the Republic. . . . We want no king. We want no murderer" (Taylor and Weiss, 1970, p. 296).

A more personal and less idealistic reason motivated Arthur Bremer who attempted to assassinate Governor George Wallace of Alabama. There was evidence that at one time or another Bremer had stalked Richard Nixon, George McGovern, and Hubert Humphrey before shooting Wallace. Bremer did not care whom he shot, as long as the victim was a nationally recognized political figure. The need to be noticed, to gain the attention of a national audience, appeared to be a dominant motive of this young man. As he was being escorted from the scene of the crime, Bremer asked the police officers how much they thought he would receive for his memoirs.

John Hinckley was infatuated with Jody Foster, a star of the movie *Taxi Driver*. Although he managed to contact her on several occasions, she would not see him. In order to impress her with the seriousness of his intentions and perhaps with his importance as a person who could affect national events, Hinckley shot President Reagan and several other people. His perception of events was so bizarre that a jury accepted his attorney's plea of insanity.

ignoring the needs and rights of others (Melges and Harris, 1970). The more egocentric and present oriented a person in conflict is, the less that person is concerned about future consequences; the result is a greater likelihood that he or she will use threats and punishments. One of the effects of alcohol intoxication is a focus on the present with the concomitant loss of long-term perspective that usually inhibits people from acting aggressively. The relationship of intoxication with violence is very strong.

A summary of the factors that lead a person to use threats and/or punishments is presented in Table 8-4. Although these sources of coercive means of behavior have been demonstrated in the laboratory, it is likely that there are many other factors not yet isolated scientifically that also induce people to harm one another.

Perceived aggression

The reason crime doesn't pay is that when it does it is called by a more respectable name.

Laurence J. Peter

An action is labeled as "aggressive" when observers believe the action is intended to harm someone, and there is no justification or excuse for doing so (Tedeschi, Smith, and Brown, 1974). We would not characterise as aggressive a fireman axing a door in the middle of the night, but someone who does so without justification would be perceived as aggressive. Similarly, a dentist does painful things to a patient, but justifies it as doing more good than harm.

The effect of justification on perceived aggression

was shown in a study where students watched actors perform on a stage. An actor who provoked conflict was perceived as offensive, aggressive, and illegitimate by the audience; but an actor who reacted to provocation by punching the other one in the stomach was perceived as defensive, nonaggressive, and legitimate (Brown and Tedeschi, 1976).

There are important consequences to being labeled as an aggressor. Subjects retaliate with higher levels of noxious stimulation when they believe the attack on them is intended rather than accidental (Dyck and Rule, 1978; Greenwell and Dengerink, 1973). We often are motivated to offer justifications for our actions as a means of removing the identity of "aggressor" and avoiding the negative reactions of others. Nations always justify their use of force, usually in terms of "defense."

It is almost axiomatic that people consider their own actions justifiable, otherwise they would not perform them. The tendency is to view other people as acting in offensive, illegitimate, and aggressive ways, but to view ourselves as defensive, justified, and nonaggressive (Tedeschi and Riess, 1981). For example, in the teacher-learner research paradigm, subjects who gave the highest levels of shock to the confederate-learner rated themselves as most altruistic (Baron and Eggleston, 1972). It is a case of "this is for your own good."

Subjects do not like to give shocks to strangers in the context of a laboratory while being observed by a psychologist, but they are told that their job is to help the learner perform better. The only means available is to give shocks, and presumably greater shocks have greater impact on the learning process. Thus, contradictory as it may sound, in order to help the learner, the subjects must deliver more intense shocks. Experimenters characterize such behavior as aggressive, however. This is a good example of the principle that the term "aggression" is a subjective one and depends upon the attributions and values of the observer. Aggression, like truth and beauty, involves a judgment; it is in the eye of the beholder.

Overview of the social power perspective

The social power perspective focuses on the question: why do people use threats and punishments? This is a broader question than typically studied by aggression theorists because it refers to legitimate and illegitimate uses of coercion, concerns itself with how legitimations increase the probability of coercion, and relegates the problem of when the use of threats and punishments are perceived as aggressive to the subfield of person perception. The emphasis of the power perspective is on the social and individual functions served by the use of coercion and on the situational determinants that elicit such behavior. A shortcoming of this perspective is that it is relatively new and has yet to be subjected to empirical testing to the extent that the biological and learning viewpoints have been. In addition, because threats and punishments include accidents and culturally approved behaviors, as well as antinormative ones, it seems unlikely that a single approach can explain such a wide range of phenomena. Some combination of factors drawn from each of the perspectives used by psychologists who try to understand human aggression will be needed to fully understand such behavior.

Table 8–4 Factors that encourage the use of threats and punishments

Norms of self-defense, reciprocity, and distributive justice
Challenges to authority
Intense conflict over resources
Self-presentation and face-saving
Need for attention
Desire to control immediate behaviors of others
Failure to consider future consequences

Biography

Richard Felson

Richard Felson comes from a family that includes four professors, a playwright, and a jazz musician. He was not a good student until he entered college at the University of Cincinnati, where he became interested in social psychology. He worked one summer helping his brother, who was conducting research for a doctoral thesis in sociology. These experiences as well as his curiosity about people motivated Rich to obtain a Ph.D. in sociology at Indiana University in 1977.

Dr. Felson read Erving Goffman (see Chapter 3) early in his career and has since combined an interest in impression management with a fascination for human conflict and aggression. As a child he fought frequently with his brothers, which may explain his interest in why siblings fight. As a graduate student he studied the psychology of aggression and was dissatisfied with the kinds of explanations that were offered for why people harmed one another. He became convinced that the study of human aggression required the examination of human conflicts in the real world. This orientation led him to study what happens during homicides and assaults, as well as less serious aggressive acts. He has found that many fights begin when a person is punished for an alleged violation of some rule. While the person who engages in punishment thinks his attack is legitimate, the target usually does not, and retaliates in order to save face.

Dr. Felson intends to continue his work on the sources of conflict and the factors that cause it to escalate. In the future he wants to develop a theory of punishment, since its use is widespread in society and since it may be considered an important aspect of human aggression.

Controlling aggression

With all the violence and murder and killing we've had in the United States, I think you will agree that we must keep firearms from people who have no business with guns.

Robert Kennedy (spoken five days before he was assassinated in May 1968).

Each of the perspectives described in Chapter 8 proposes ways of controlling aggression. The biological perspective suggests surgery, electrical control, and biochemical treatment as possible ways of reducing aggression. Because it views aggression as being ge-

Some psychologists believe that aggression can be channeled through social skills into nonviolent modes of conflict resolution. In competitive sports, such as racket ball, people can release aggression through strenuous physical exercise.

netically transmitted, however, the biological perspective tends to be pessimistic concerning the degree to which aggression can be eliminated or controlled. At best, natural aggressive tendencies can be channeled into socially acceptable outlets, like football, boxing, and business competition.

Learning theory proposes a number of ways of controlling aggression. One is to reinforce incompatible responses. If a person is rewarded for cooperative and friendly actions or is presented with humorous stimuli, an aggressive pattern of behavior is less apt to occur (Baron, 1983). A second way of controlling aggression is to provide people with nonaggressive models to emulate. A third technique is to increase inhibitions by punishing aggressive responses, but the punishments must be legitimized to the target person or else hostility may be increased. The effectiveness of deterrence also depends upon the probability and magnitude of punishment (Chambliss, 1966; Gibbs, 1968). A fourth control proposed by learning theorists is to remove aggressive stimuli, such as guns and violence on the mass media. A fifth and final control would be to delay the responses of individuals so that physiological arousal can decline, allowing the intensity of subsequent behavior to lessen.

Social power theorists agree with some of the proposals of learning theorists, but restate them in the language of social interactions rather than as reinforcement principles. If people use threats and punishments for purposes of social influence, then teaching them other effective means of influence should lessen their dependence upon coercion. Modeling, deterrence, and making weapons less accessible to impulsive action also are measures of control proposed by social power theorists (Tedeschi, Gaes, and Rivera, 1977).

It is important to foster empathy in people. There is a danger that exposure to a great deal of violence through the mass media desensitizes viewers to the pain and suffering of other people (Parke, Berkowitz, Leyens, West, and Sebastian, 1977). Finally and most importantly from a social power perspective, there is a need to change the bases of legitimation in people who use threats and punishments. Western culture justifies violence by armed forces, police, and parents; violence enacted in self-defense, in reciprocity, and in the establishment of equity is also lawful. A summary of the implications of biological, learning, and social power perspectives for controlling aggression is shown in Table 8-5.

Table 8–5 Steps proposed for controlling aggression

THEORETICAL PERSPECTIVE	STEPS TO TAKE
Biological	■ Use chemical or surgical therapy for individuals.
	■ Channel aggressive energy into acceptable outlets, like sports.
Learning	■ Reward response incompatible with aggressive behavior.
	■ Provide successful nonaggressive models.
	■ Punish aggressive behavior.
	■ Remove aggressive cues (e.g., guns, violent television programs, etc.)
	■ Delay action to permit arousal to subside.
Social Power	■ Teach nonaggressive social skills.
	■ Avoid desensitization and dehumanization.
	■ Develop norms that do not excuse or justify the use of threats and punishments.
	■ Develop nonviolent modes of conflict resolution.
	■ Use mediators to resolve conflicts.

Summary

A biological approach to the study of aggression focuses on evolutionary and genetic factors that contribute to behavior that does harm. Animal instincts for establishing dominance hierarchies and for defending fixed territories do not govern human behavior. Brain centers and hormones maintain strong control over aggressive behavior in animals, particularly in males. Although it is possible that similar physiological factors affect human behavior, there is no convincing evidence that they do. The inability to make generalizations from research carried out with subhuman animals limits the contribution of biology to the study of human aggression.

By far, the greatest amount of research on aggression by psychologists has been based on learning theory. Frustration-aggression theory has proposed how responses may be strengthened by rewards or inhibited by anticipation of punishments. It also has postulated processes of displacement and catharsis. The evidence indicates that frustration only sometimes leads to aggression, that catharsis as a release of aggressive energy probably does not occur, but that displacement of aggression is a reliable phenomenon.

Cue-arousal and excitation-transfer theories have focused on how increases in arousal from nonfrustrating experiences may be generalized to increase the arousal experienced from frustration. Arousal generated by exercise, by viewing legitimated violence on television or film, by discomfort experienced from noise, heat, and crowding, by drugs or low levels of alcohol, and by mild sexual stimuli has been associated with the use of increased levels of shocks or unpleasant noises by subjects against others in laboratory experiments.

Social learning theory focuses on the desire of people to obtain rewards and avoid punishments. An important way of learning what to do in various situations is to observe what others do and note what happens to them. When models are reinforced for aggressive behavior, observers imitate by performing similar aggressive responses. Whether observers will imitate illegitimate behaviors has yet to be established.

Social power theory focuses on a person's use of threats and punishments in interpersonal relationships. Self-presentation concerns, such as strength, courage, and toughness, may motivate people to engage in attempts to harm others. Norms of self-defense and reciprocity may require that people resort to the use of coercive power. There are many circumstances where a person, particularly one in authority, has the responsibility to administer punishments for misbehavior, disobedience, or as a form for training. Any event that decreases a person's ability to take into account the future consequences of behavior reduces his or her inhibitions to use threats and punishments against others. Finally, whether any use of threats or punishments will be perceived as aggression is in the eye of the beholder. An action is perceived as aggressive when the observer attributes to a performer an intent to do harm and considers the action to be unjustified and illegitimate.

Glossary

Agonistic behavior Threats and fighting that typically occur within a species, and also between species not linked in the food chain.

Attributional definition of aggression Any behavior where the actor intends to harm others.

Behavioristic definition of aggression Any behavior that does harm.

Catharsis A process by which aggressive energy is released when an organism performs an aggressive response, decreasing the probability of another immediate aggressive response.

Coercive power The use of threats and/or punishments for purposes of social influence.

Cue-arousal theory Frustration leads to aggression only when the frustration is arbitrary and an aggressive cue is available to suggest that an aggressive response is a legitimate way to behave in the situation.

Displacement of aggression A substitute aggressive response is used when a more prepotent response is inhibited; may be a less direct response toward the same target or an action directed against a third party.

Excitation-transfer theory Sources of arousal not directly related to aggression may combine with relevant sources to intensify aggressive responses.

Frustration Any event that interferes with behavior directed toward achieving goals.

Frustration-aggression theory Aggression is always a result of frustration, although organisms can learn to inhibit certain responses; catharsis and displacement are important processes postulated by the theory.

Instinct A behavior pattern having five basic characteristics: complexity, automatically elicited by releasing stimuli, not learned, species specific, and affected by biochemical factors.

Negative norm of reciprocity The widely accepted belief that people should harm those who harm them.

Predation Killing of members of another species for the purposes of feeding in the food chain.

Realistic-conflict model A theory that fighting among siblings is caused by real issues over the use of property and the division of labor.

Sibling rivalry A theory explaining that brothers and sisters fight because of jealousy over parental attention.

Recommended Readings

Brain, P. F., and Benton D. (1981). *Multidisciplinary approaches to aggression research.* New York: Elsevier.

A collection by researchers from different disciplines, ranging from endocrinology to psychiatry, summarizing work carried out with both animals and people. Some of the articles are technical but informative.

Geen R. G., and Donnerstein, E. I. (Eds.). (1983). *Aggression: Theoretical and empirical reviews.* New York: Academic Press.

A two-volume work that includes the latest versions of aggression theories and reviews of laboratory research.

Straus, M. A., Gelles, R. J., and Steinmetz, S. K. (1980). *Behind closed doors: Violence in the American family.* Garden City, NY: Doubleday.

An authoritative account of what social scientists know about spouse and child abuse; written at a level appropriate for advanced undergraduate students.

The worst sin towards our fellow creatures is not to hate them, but to be indifferent to them: that's the essence of inhumanity.

George Bernard Shaw, The Devil's Disciple

9
Prosocial behavior

The making of a hero

Forest Park in St. Louis is bordered by an expressway on one side and some of the finest homes and hotels in the city on the other. The park is a centerpiece of the city and contains a golf course, theater, art gallerys, and planetarium. There is also a pavilion fountain surrounded by a wading pool. In late July of 1983 at 5:00 in the afternoon while children were splashing around in the pool, two teenage youths raped a thirteen-year-old girl in waist-deep water. Although the girl screamed for help, no one responded. An eleven-year-old boy, who said four adults were watching the rape, took off on his bicycle to seek aid. He found a police officer three blocks away at the opera house. When the police arrived, the victim and another child were searching the pool for her clothing. The victim pointed out her attackers, they were arrested, and she was taken to a hospital for treatment. The hero asked not to be identified, but eventually he received public thanks by the mayor and appeared in New York on the "Good Morning America" television show.

Lennie Skutnik's name became a household word in the United States when television viewers watched him jump into the freezing Potomac River to rescue a passenger from an Air Florida plane crash. Lennie reported that he did not think about himself but only about the need to save the person in the water. The many people who stood on the river bank and watched the tragedy without acting believed there was little that they could do. Lennie received recognition for his heroism from the president of the United States and was a guest on network news shows.

Contrast the above instances of heroism to the inaction of people who witnessed the murder of Kitty Genovese in Queens (New York City) on 13 March 1964. Thirty-eight people witnessed part or all of three separate attacks by her assailant over the course of thirty-five minutes. Twice he had been frightened when lights came on, and witnesses yelled through open windows; but no one called the police and no one intervened to save the hysterical and screaming victim. This event captured the attention of social psychologists, who have examined the factors that contribute to bystander intervention in emergency situations.

Why do people sometimes help others, even at

great risk to themselves, and in other instances stand by and do nothing? The answer involves consideration of what the person is like, what the nature of the situation is, what the attributes and characteristics of the victim are, and how other people act. **Prosocial behavior** refers to helping, giving, caring, and other socially desirable responses an actor renders without apparent selfish motivation. Intervening to help others in life-threatening circumstances, giving gifts to others, stopping on the highway to aid people experiencing problems with their automobiles, and mailing a letter for someone are all instances of prosocial behavior.

Human nature and prosocial behavior

In heaven an angel is nobody in particular.
George Bernard Shaw

The observation that people often act to benefit others has raised a philosophical dispute regarding human nature. One view is that people are basically selfish and act only to minimize pain and maximize pleasure, a doctrine referred to as **hedonism.** The principle of hedonism does not assume that people never act to help others, but rather that such actions ultimately will benefit the helper. There is a difference between selfish behavior and acting in one's **enlightened self-interest.** A selfish person disregards the interests of others. When people act from enlightened self-interest, they are concerned about benefiting and not harming others. Enlightened self-interest, however, does include the expectation that helping others will bring benefits to the self. As you sow, so will you reap. A person may engage in philanthropic activities for tax write-offs, for self-satisfaction associated with positive self-regard, or to obtain respect and status in the community. The person thus gains tangible, social, or psychic rewards from the prosocial behavior.

Hedonists argue that concern about one's own interests is the basis for developing concern about the welfare of others. Enlightened self-interest recognizes that we often need the help of other people and that unless we show some concern for them, they will not care about us. This hedonist argument is meant to demonstrate that selfish motives provide the foundation for all moral conduct.

Another interpretation of prosocial behavior is that people may demonstrate unselfish concern for the welfare of others. Such unselfish behavior is referred to as **altruism.** A person acting to help someone in an emergency would be considered altruistic if the person did not anticipate social, material, or psychic rewards.

There has been some attempt to demonstrate the origins of altruism among lower organisms. For example, honeybees have a social organization with worker and soldier bees. These bees feed and protect the queen bee, who is capable of producing a prodigious number of offspring. The entire community of bees is dedicated to feeding and protecting the queen and the continuance of her genes.

Unlike the involuntary and genetically governed actions of bees, human society is affected strongly by learning and culture (Heelas and Lock, 1981). It is not clear how the great variety of human social behavior could be explained by a relatively homogeneous gene pool. Rats, which are mammals, have been shown to act to relieve the stress of other rats, but this apparently altruistic action is explained most easily in terms of reinforcement theory (Lucke & Batson, 1980); that is, it is the expectation of gaining rewards that leads rats to help other rats.

Sociobiologists (e.g., Wilson, 1978) have argued that if some members of primitive human groups were selfish and others were willing to sacrifice themselves for the group, the altruistic people (and their genes) soon would be selected out of the human gene pool. The remaining humans would be basically or entirely hedonistic. A different view is that enlightened self-interest could develop as people learned that cooperation and social exchange can benefit everyone (Dawkins, 1976). Indeed, the development of moral and ethical principles provides the basis for giving people credit and rewards for positive actions and blame and punishments for negative ones. In this way, people are socialized and must consider the welfare of others because it is coincident with their own.

Social psychologists acknowledge that although they use the term "prosocial," it is probably not possible to resolve the philosophical argument about the hedonistic and/or altruistic nature of the human species. A scientific investigation of prosocial behavior attempts to reveal the conditions under which people do or do not take actions that contribute to the welfare of others.

Bystander intervention

A person may cause evil to others not only by his actions but by his inaction, and in either case he is justly accountable to them for the injury.
John Stuart Mill

When bystanders encounter an emergency situation, like the young boy at the fountain in St. Louis or like Lennie Skutnik did, what factors lead them to intervene? Or conversely, what factors in the situation cause bystanders, like those who witnessed the murder of Kitty Genovese, to do nothing? A substantial body of research suggests a five-step process, involving a definition of the situation and a decision to act (Latane and Darley, 1970). At each step, if the bystander's answer is no, the process is aborted and no help is offered. If the answer is yes, there is progression to the next step until prosocial action is finally taken. The five steps are shown pictorially.

Notice

A person hurrying down a busy city street might fail to notice a person staggering with the first signs of heat exhaustion. On a quiet small-town street where distractions are fewer, these signs would be easier to notice. The rape in the St. Louis fountain occurred in waist-deep water among children who were splashing and screaming in play. Had the children not stopped and had the victim not been able to scream for help, passersby might not have had their attention directed to the scene.

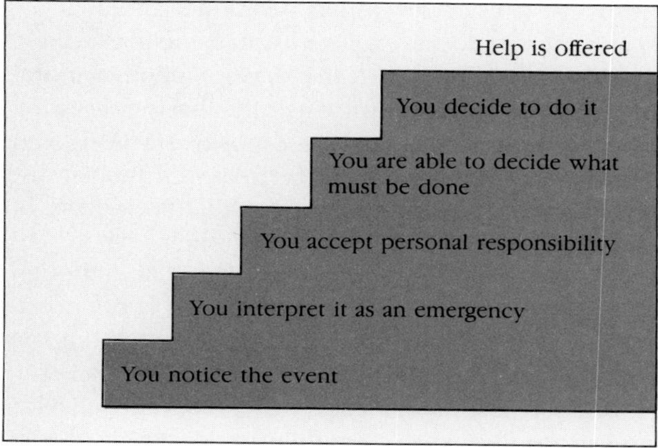

Figure 9-1 Scaling the steps to helpful action in an emergency.

People sometimes pretend not to notice a situation that may require prosocial action. They may lower their heads and walk straight ahead or walk around it. For example, in a field experiment passersby walked further away from a table where solicitors seeking donations were seated when the fund drive was advertised with a poster than when it was not (Pancer, McMullen, Kabatoff, Johnson, and Pond, 1979). The presence of other people affects this "staged nonnoticing." When smoke was pumped into a room where one or more subjects were filling out questionnaires, subjects continued to work and appeared not to notice the smoke for a longer period of time if they were with someone else than if they were alone (Latane and Darley, 1968).

Interpreting as an emergency

If you were a subject in a laboratory experiment and you saw smoke coming in the room, how would you interpret the situation? Actual subjects who left the room to report the event to the experimenter called it smoke, but those who did not report the event later told the experimenter they thought it was vapor from the air conditioning, steam, smog, or even a truth gas designed to make them answer their questionnaires truthfully (Latane and Darley 1968). In another study, subjects who responded to an experimenter's staged groans in the next room later said they thought help was needed. Those who did not respond said that they did not think anything serious had happened or that they thought other people would help (Latane and Rodin, 1969).

If the need for help is clear and if the situation is considered an emergency, it is likely that people will provide help. For example, when a fall by a window cleaner was staged (Yakimovitch and Saltz, 1971), subjects went to the window to see what had happened. Eighty percent went to his aid if he yelled for help but only 30 percent did when he held his ankle, screamed, and moaned. Similar findings were obtained when subjects heard someone fall in an adjoining room. The person who fell either did or did not cry out for help (Clark and Word, 1972). Only 30 percent of the subjects investigated the fall, but 100 percent answered the cry.

When researchers staged a fight between a man and a woman, 65 percent of the male passersby intervened if she yelled, "I don't know you!." Only 19 percent got involved if the utterances of the woman indicated that she knew the man (Shotland and Straw, 1976). Perhaps lack of clarity about her relationship with the attacker was a major reason why so many people failed to intervene when Kitty Genovese was attacked. Social custom tells us not to butt into the personal affairs of other couples.

The reactions of other bystanders help a person to interpret a situation as an emergency. In a study where pairs of subjects were seated back to back or face to face (Darley, Teger, and Lewis, 1973), a loud noise suggested the possibility of a fall by a construction worker, who subjects knew was working in the next room. Eighty percent of the subjects left the room to help when they had been seated face to face and could see one another's startle response to the crashing sound. Only 20 percent left the room to help when they had been seated back to back.

The nonverbal behavior of a victim can elicit bystander intervention. In the library at Dartmouth College, the following events were staged: In the clear view of others, a male student pulled a piece of folded paper from his pocket and a $10 bill fell to the floor. Apparently unaware of the mishap, the student moved to the reference desk. Another male student came along and picked up the bill, put it in his pocket, and walked on. The victim then turned from the reference desk and in different conditions he (1) walked away apparently unaware of his loss, (2) appeared puzzled and searched through his pockets, or (3) appeared puzzled, searched through his pockets, and made eye contact with an onlooker.

As can be seen in Table 9-1, the searching behavior of the victim was enough to energize about 40 percent of the onlookers to approach him and tell what they had seen. Eye contact in this case did not increase the number of people who intervened, although it sometimes does. When the victim was unaware of his loss, only 13 percent of the onlookers volunteered to tell him what they had witnessed (DeJong, Marber, and Shaver, 1980.)

Accepting personal responsibility

We have mentioned the tendency, shown in over fifty studies in many kinds of situations, for a lone person to respond more readily to help others in emergencies than for a person to react when other people are present (Latane and Nida, 1981). One explanation for this reliable finding is that each person feels less responsibility to act as the number of equally responsive people increases. This decreased sense of responsibility experienced by people in groups is referred to as **diffusion of responsibility.** All the responsibility falls on one person if that person is alone. If five other people are present, however, the responsibility to act is diffused among all six.

The effect of the number of bystanders on the likelihood of intervention was examined in a laboratory setting where subjects (students) were asked to take part in an in-depth discussion with strangers on

Table 9–1 Nonverbal behavior of victim and bystander intervention

VICTIM'S ACTION[a]	BYSTANDERS WHO INTERVENED[b]
Walked away unaware of loss	13%
Searched for lost $10	40%
Searched for lost $10 and made eye contact with bystander	37%

Source: Based on "Crime intervention: The role of a victim's behavior in reducing situational ambiguity" by W. DeJong, S. Marber, and R. Shewer, 1980, *Journal of Personality and Social Psychology Bulletin, 6* pp. 113-116.

[a]Victim accidentally lost $10 from his pocket onto the floor.

[b]Number of bystanders = 90.

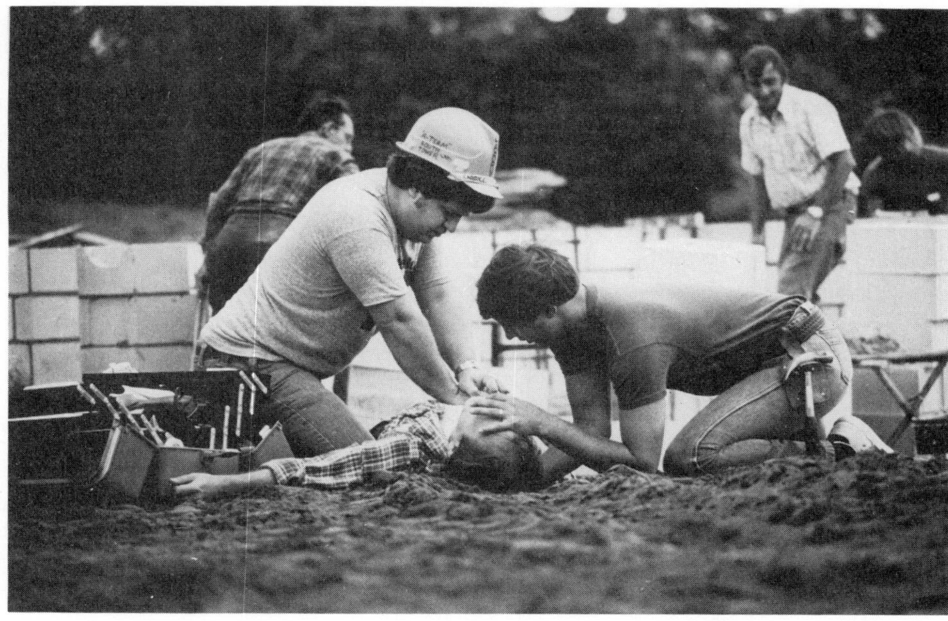

Co-workers give cardiac and respiratory resuscitation to a member of this construction team. In an emergency situation such as this, people will likely provide help especially when two or more face the problem together.

the personal problems faced by college students (Latane and Darley, 1968). The students were placed in separate cubicles supposedly to protect them from the embarrassment that they might experience in face-to-face discussions. Communications were transmitted over an intercom system, the discussants took turns, and only one microphone was turned on at any given time. The subjects were told either that one, two, or five other students were participating in the discussion. In each case, the first person who spoke mentioned having a history of experiencing seizures. Then on the second turn to speak, this person gasped and said that she was experiencing a seizure and was in need of help. The microphone went dead. As can be seen in Figure 9-2, the percentage of subjects responding to help the afflicted person was less when there was a greater number of other participants in the group. Correspondingly, the fewer the people in the group, the more quickly subjects responded in providing help. This hesitancy to provide help, presumably attributable to a diffusion of responsibility in groups, is considered a major contributing factor for the lack of response in the Kitty Genovese incident.

It has been established that people perceive themselves as less responsible when with others. This subjective component of the diffusion of responsibility hypothesis was found among witnesses to an emergency situation (Schwartz and Gottlieb, 1980). Interview responses from people who had been unaccompanied by friends or acquaintances at the time of the emergency indicated that 80 percent of them said they felt a personal responsibility to do something. Only 17 percent of the witnesses who were with someone else at the time felt a responsibility to intervene.

An appraisal of the competence of bystanders contributes to an individual's tendency to take personal responsibility in an emergency situation. When someone else in the group is perceived to be more competent to provide help, the individual will be less likely to volunteer. For example, in the laboratory situation where students discussed their personal problems and one had a seizure, some subjects learned that another discussant was a premedical student who worked three nights a week in the emergency ward of a local hospital. Fewer of those subjects left their cubicles to help the afflicted person than did the other discussants who were provided no information about a premed student (Schwartz and Clausen, 1970).

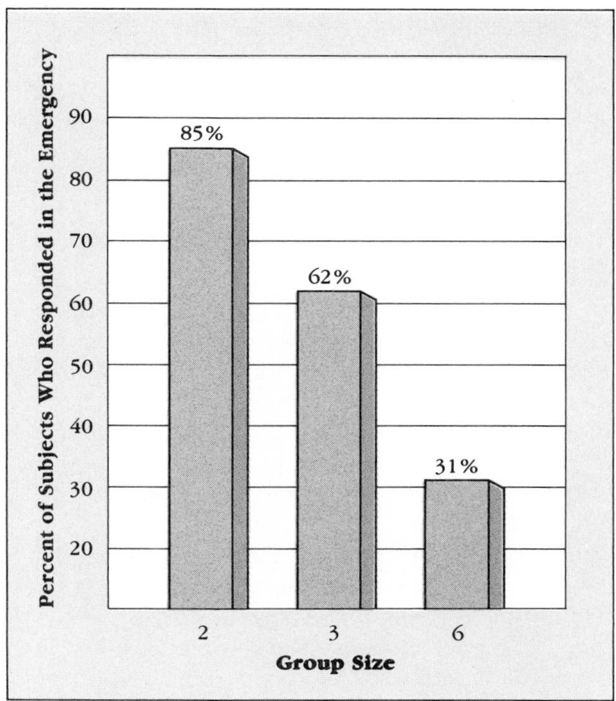

Figure 9-2 The effect of group size on intervention in an emergency situation.

Source: Based on "Group inhibition of bystander intervention in emergencies" by B. Latane and J. M. Darley, 1968, *Journal of Personality and Social Psychology, 10,* 215–221.

When a person perceives self as the most competent person in the group, that individual takes more personal responsibility to provide help. An investigation in support of this generalization placed students either alone in a cubicle, with two children aged four and six, or with two other adults. Subjects were more likely to report a possible emergency to the experimenter when they were in the company of children than when in the presence of adults. However, subjects were most likely to intervene when they were alone. Thus, even the presence of children contributes to a diffusion of responsibility, although less than when adults are present (Ross, 1971).

The relationship between perceived self-competence and compliance to requests for bone marrow donors has been investigated (Schwartz, 1970). Blood donors were interviewed and asked to place their names on a list of potential bone marrow donors. Prior to the request, some of the subjects were told that an appeal had been made to the people giving blood at donation centers and to the general public through newspaper ads. Other randomly selected blood donors were told that they were particularly suited to be on a list of bone marrow donors because their blood already was available for relevant tests. The percentage of people agreeing to sign their names to the bone marrow donor list was higher when the appeal was directed to their particular suitability.

Asking for a minimum amount of help avoids the problem of perceived competence and increases the probability that help will be given. There are times when a person may feel that the amount of financial aid they can give to a major institution would not really do much good. This may explain why only 29 percent of those approached for donations to the American Cancer Society gave a donation. These donors gave an average of $1.44. When told by the solicitor that "even a penny will help," 50 percent of the people donated. Their average donation of $1.54 was actually greater than when a plea for a penny was not used (Cialdini and Schroeder, 1976).

Responsibility can be assigned to others even when they are total strangers. A field study at a seaside beach established that such an assignment of responsibility can be accomplished with just a few words (Moriarty, 1975). The experimenter placed his blanket and portable radio next to another male sunbather. After a while he got up to leave, but before doing so, he made one or another of two requests: "Do you have a match?" or "Excuse me, I'm going to the boardwalk. Would you watch my things?" After the experimenter left, a confederate approached his abandoned blanket, took the radio and fled. When responsibility had been specifically assigned to a person on a neighboring blanket, 95 percent of them yelled or ran after the thief; only 20 percent took such action when they had not agreed to watch after the departed person's belongings.

In conclusion, available research has shown that the responsibility to act is influenced in many ways: the number of people who are witnesses, whether others present are perceived to be more competent to give the necessary aid, whether the individual is labeled as uniquely suitable for the needs, and whether responsibility has been assigned explicitly. Box 9-1 provides evidence of several other characteristics that may be added to this profile of the good samaritan.

Box 9-1

Profile of heroic samaritans

Several studies have provided enough evidence so that researchers can construct a profile of people who take risks to help others in emergency situations. For example, people who aided Jews to escape from the Nazis were interviewed (London, 1970). A consistent pattern showed that these people typically were adventuresome in many aspects of their lives, had a parent who stressed high moral standards, and lacked close relationships with other people.

In a more recent study people who had intervened in armed robberies, street muggings, and bank holdings were interviewed (Huston, Ruggerio, Conner, and Geis, 1981). Another sample of people who were similar to the heroic sample in terms of age, sex, education, and ethnic background were obtained, but these people had never intervened in such incidents. Although there were no personality differences between the two groups, they differed in abilities, training, and experience. The heroes had witnessed more crimes, had more often been victims themselves, and were taller and heavier than the nonheroes. The heroes had more training in lifesaving, medical practice, and police work, and they described themselves as physically stronger, more aggressive, more emotional, and more principled than did the nonheroes.

Knowing what to do

Sur Williams, the youthful hero at the St. Louis fountain, understood what was happening and knew what to do. He told reporters about the granddaughter of a woman who attended his church. The girl had been raped and, as a consequence, was injured so severely that she was unable to bear children. Sur's mother also had told him that if he ever saw a sexual assault, he should run to the police for help. These prior experiences prepared Sur so that when the event actually occurred, he knew what to do.

Studies show that people help more when they know *how* to help. Subjects instructed about what to do in case someone else should experience a seizure responded more frequently to provide help when a person actually had a seizure than did subjects who received no information (Schwartz and Clausen, 1970). In another situation, some subjects knew they could do something to alleviate the suffering of a victim who was experiencing electric shocks; others believed there was nothing they could do (Baron, 1970). Subjects acted more quickly to shut off the shocks when they knew what to do. Subjects who did not know how to help the victim tended to avoid watching the victim suffer. The tendency to avoid watching was greater with the intensity of the apparent suffering.

Deciding to act

A person may notice and interpret an event as an emergency, feel personal responsibility to do something and know what to do, but still not provide help. There are a number of reasons why a knowledgeable and moral person may not engage in prosocial behavior, and they all have to do with the costs associated with such actions. Some of these costs may be tangible, such as injury to self or monetary losses; some may be consequences of a social nature, such as embarrassment or negative reactions on the part of victims. Physicians may refuse to help someone injured in an accident for fear that a malpractice suit will be brought against them. On the other hand, Lennie Skutnik seemed oblivious to his own danger when diving into the icy Potomac River to save that air passenger, but many other onlookers probably thought that they would drown if they attempted to save her. People estimate the risks and costs of action differently and hence are more or less inhibited in their tendency to intervene in emergency situations.

People who are late for an appointment, for a class, or for a rendezvous with someone else, may use their own urgent interests as an excuse for not stopping to help another person. In a field study, a person was placed in a doorway, slumped over, coughing, and groaning (Darley and Batson, 1973). Passersby in a hurry to keep an appointment were less likely to stop and help than were people who were in no hurry. The people in a hurry were students at the Princeton Theological Seminary who were scheduled to give a talk on the parable of the good Samaritan! These students may have failed to interpret the situation as one requiring help because they were so preoccupied with preparing a speech and were pressed for time. A follow-up study showed that people in a hurry to make an appointment will stop to help if their mission is not very important (Batson, Cochran, Biederman, Blosser, Ryan, and Vogt, 1978).

Although many people feel responsible for helping others in emergency situations, some considerations must be given to the perceptions and desires of victims. For example, an aging person might resent help because it makes some age-related infirmity socially visible; hence, the good samaritan might be rebuffed and experience embarrassment. Students struggling to solve problems might resent attempts to help them. A reason why subjects paired together are less likely to respond to sounds of people falling outside a cubicle than are subjects who are alone might be the pair's concern about feeling embarrassed (Latane and Darley, 1968). Subjects might think that they would appear stupid if they left an experiment to help someone when other subjects in the same room did nothing and in fact no help was needed. Presumably, if subjects were friends who knew each other well, this sort of mistake would be much less embarrassing. Research has shown that pairs of friends did respond more quickly than pairs of strangers (Latane and Rodin, 1969). The study described in Box 9-2 suggests that where people live may influence how likely they are to help in emergencies.

Another study provides support for the suggestion that diffusion of responsibility may, to some extent, rest on impression management concerns of people in groups. Pairs of subjects who did not know each other and who wore costumes to disguise themselves helped more frequently than did pairs of subjects who were clearly identifiable (Becker-Haven and Lindskold, 1978).

A bystander's relationship with a victim is also an important factor in whether or not action is taken. Subjects in groups were less inhibited in trying to help a seizure victim if they had met the victim beforehand and if they had had a pleasant conversation (Latane and Darley, 1968). More subjects tried to help a victim who was choking when they expected to meet the person later on (Gottlieb and Carver, 1980). It would be potentially embarrassing to meet someone who knew you did nothing to help them in an emergency. Failure to respond to moral obligations and social expectations of others can bring embarrassment and condemnation from others (Schwartz, 1977).

Bystanders are reluctant to help victims who may react unpredictably, are dirty or unkempt, are of a different race, and are responsible for their own predicament. This reluctance was shown when black and white college students played the part of a victim on commuter trains in New York City (Piliavin, Rodin, and Piliavin, 1969). The victim was portrayed as either drunk or ill. A student portraying the role of a drunk smelled of liquor, carried a bottle wrapped in a brown bag, and staggered and collapsed to the floor of the subway. A student playing the role of a sick person was sober and carried a cane, then collapsed to the floor of the subway. More people helped the victim when he appeared to be sick rather than when he appeared to be drunk. The race of the victim did not influence helping if the victim was sick, but there was a distinct tendency to help the drunk only if he was of the same race. Bystanders were more likely to offer help if someone else did so first. Over 90 percent of the good samaritans were male.

People were more reluctant to help a victim who had blood trickling from his mouth (Piliavin and Piliavin, 1972), possibly because of their revulsion at the sight of blood or because blood signifies to them that the victim must be handled in an extremely careful way. On the other hand, bystanders were more apt to help a woman wearing a bloody bandage than one

Box 9-2

Bystander intervention by city slickers and by country folks

Kitty Genovese was killed in New York City. For many reasons, people who live in cities feel more anonymous and alienated from one another than do people who live in small towns who know one another and say hello to strangers. Based on these observations, it might be expected that residents of small towns would be more apt to help someone in distress than city dwellers would be.

McKenna (1976) tested this hypothesis using the *wrong number technique*. A female confederate called up randomly selected people, told them she was stranded, and asked if someone from "Ralph's Garage" could please come out and have a look at her car? When the subject said that it was a wrong number, the confederate said that it was her last dime and asked the subject if he or she could call Ralph's Garage for her. Ralph's Garage was actually just another phone number where a confederate was stationed to monitor incoming calls. Thus, the number of people who called "Ralph's Garage" was the measure of bystander intervention.

Over two-thirds of all subjects called the bogus garage. This positive response may be attributed to the ease and inexpense of carrying out the prosocial action. Nevertheless, place of residence did affect the willingness of people to help. While 67 percent of urban dwellers called "Ralph's," nearly 80 percent of people from small towns did so.

who simply held her hand (West and Brown, 1975). In the latter study, the form of help given to the woman with the bloody bandage was money for a tetanus shot; there was no requirement to touch the woman. Thus, the blood might have signified greater need and was effective in gaining more donations for the woman. We may conclude that cues indicating the need for help will facilitate it, but anything that makes the giving of help costly or difficult for the bystander makes it less likely that they will offer help.

Moods and prosocial behavior

A man's interest in the world is only the overflow from his interest in himself.

George Bernard Shaw

People experience a variety of moods. Sometimes we are happy and at other times depressed, up one day and down the next, full of energy or unwilling to move, sympathetic to the problems of others or absorbed in ourselves. We may feel guilty for having harmed or disappointed others or elated at our exemplary moral conduct. These moods and feelings affect the way we behave toward others.

Feeling good

When you're smiling, the whole world smiles at you.

Mark Fisher, Joe Goodwin, Larry Shay

Jean Paul Sartre, the French existentialist philosopher, has said that when we are feeling good, we make the best interpretation of circumstances, everything is rosy, and we act positively toward others. People who are made to feel good by performing a task successfully, by accidently finding some money, by receiving a gift, or by winning a competition have been shown to engage in prosocial behavior. Subjects who were told they had performed well on a task were more willing to donate blood (Kazdin and Bryan, 1971) and to help others with a task (Berkowitz and Connor, 1966) than were subjects who were told they had failed at the task. Students given a cookie while working in library carrels were more willing to volunteer to participate in an experiment than were students not receiving a gift. People who found a dime in a pay phone helped a stranger pick up papers dropped on the sidewalk more often than other people did (Isen and Levin, 1972). Professional football players have been observed to more often help other players to their feet when their team is winning the game than when their team is losing (Berg, 1978).

Inducing a pleasant mood increases the likelihood of prosocial behavior. Increased prosocial behavior has been induced in people when they hear pleasant music (Fried and Berkowitz, 1979), view a happy rather than sad movie (Underwood et al., 1978), listen to a comedy (Wilson, 1981), hear good news on the radio (Veitch, DeWood, and Bosko, 1977), and recall happy experiences (Rosenhan, Underwood, and Moore, 1974). People also provide more help on sunny rather than on overcast days (Cunningham, 1979). We should not assume from the latter that London or Seattle are unfriendly and inhospitable cities since a number of factors operating on a person may counteract the effects of any single factor. A research study described in Box 9-3 on p. 262 indicates that a smile from others may be all that it takes to increase the readiness of a person to be helpful.

The **glow of good will** that exudes from a happy person has certain limitations. People who feel good do not provide help if it disrupts their pleasant mood.

"Closing averages on the human scene were mixed today. Brotherly love was down two points, while enlightened self-interest gained a half. Vanity showed no movement, and guarded optimism slipped a point in sluggish trading. Over all, the status quo remained unchanged."

Biography

Alice M. Isen

While a graduate student at Stanford University, Alice M. Isen was impressed with the great amount of study social psychologists had given to aggression, conflict, deprivation, and prejudice. She was surprised at the lack of attention to kindness as a social phenomenon or happiness as a determinant of behavior. She received encouragement to pursue ideas about benevolence from her professors and began to test her ideas while on summer vacation at her home in Havertown, Pennsylvania.

In this initial study, Ms. Isen asked school teachers to perform some perceptual motor tasks. She either complimented them on their success or told them they had not done well. Subsequently, the successful teachers donated more money to a school air-conditioning fund and offered more help to a colleague who dropped a book while loaded down with cartons, notebooks, and books. After returning to Stanford in the fall, Ms. Isen found the same kind of "warm glow of success" among college students. Since then, Dr. Isen has found that good fortune in the form of finding a dime in a phone booth, being presented with a gift, or receiving a cookie increased the prosocial behavior of people.

Recently, Dr. Isen has been studying the impact of good fortune on cognitive processes. Pleasant events produce good moods, which in turn lead individuals to rate their possessions and neutral objects more favorably, to speed up their decision making and to enhance some forms of their creativity. The idea that someone must be miserable to be creative is not consistent with these findings.

Dr. Isen was an undergraduate student at the University of Pennsylvania where she majored in Russian Language and Literature. She was interested in psychology throughout her college career. In her senior year she applied for graduate study in psychology at Stanford, where she obtained a Ph.D. in 1968. Currently, she is a member of the faculty at Swarthmore College.

Box 9-3

Social cues that increase prosocial behavior

The final step that leads a person to perform prosocial behavior is a consideration of costs. There are many kinds of costs, including doubt whether the other person will welcome intervention; concern about appearing stupid in case help is not really needed; risks, time, and energy associated with performing the behavior; and so on. The expectation of costs may cause the person to stand by impassively and do nothing to help another person who is in distress. A report of three field studies showed that some social factors may temper such concerns and establish a readiness to help others (Solomon, Solomon, Arnone, Maur, Reda, and Roth, 1981).

The first study was carried out in a large department store in downtown Manhattan. A confederate was stationed near an elevator and either did or did not smile at women waiting for it. The confederate got on the elevator with the women and asked for information. Twice as many women responded to the inquiry when they had received a smile from the confederate.

It was not clear whether a smile induced a positive mood in the women or whether it established a sense of relationship or community. To examine which of these possibilities was more probable, a second study was conducted. This time a confederate made eye contact with individual women, walked up to each, and asked, "Excuse me, aren't you Suzie Spear's sister?" This reminder that it is a small world and a recognition of the relations between people were just as effective as smiling in inducing the women to be helpful.

A third study was carried out at a hockey arena. The experimenter feigned looking for a contact lens either in the stands or near the snack bar. It was found that more spectators were willing to help hunt for the lens if they were season ticket holders and were in their seats than if they did not have season tickets or if they were at the snack bar. Season ticket holders make up a small community in the stands. They sit in the same seats time and again, and they may become concerned about how others perceive them, just like people in a small town.

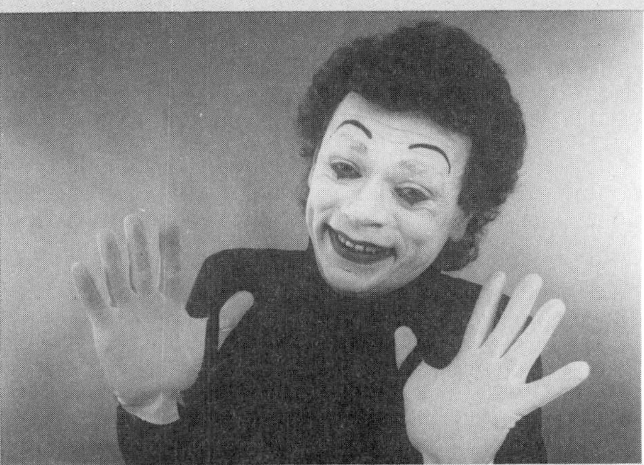

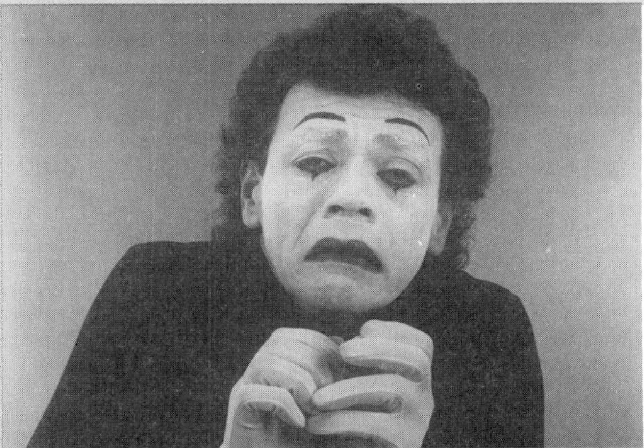

To ask for help is a difficult task. We may doubt whether anyone wants to assist us, or fear that we may appear stupid, or think the costs involved in accomplishing the task too great. So we look to those whom we feel will be most receptive and sympathetic to our plea. Which person would you ask for assistance?

People who found a dime were more willing to assist in an experiment, but not if they were asked to read material that would disrupt their pleasant mood (Isen and Simmonds, 1978). Actual disruption of a person's pleasant mood will decrease his or her proclivity to engage in prosocial behavior. For example, subjects are more helpful following success than following failure in performing a task, as we have seen, but this difference vanished when success was followed by an annoying noise (Yinon and Bizman, 1980).

Most of the available research has provided subjects with an opportunity to engage in prosocial behavior immediatley after a positive mood state was induced in them. Apparently, the lamp providing the "glow" has a rather short wick, dwindling in one experiment to just a flicker in in about twenty minutes. People who were given a free sample of stationery were then asked to assist another person by relaying a phone message (Isen, Clark, and Schwartz, 1976). The request was made at various times following the gift. As can be seen in Figure 9-3, requests made up to seven minutes after the gift was received were effective in gaining compliance. Even thirteen minutes later, more than half the people agreed to relay the telephone message; however, twenty minutes was sufficient to essentially eliminate the glow of good will. Prosocial behavior associated with a short-term relationship of feeling good also was revealed in a study where many subects volunteered to donate blood (Kazdin and Bryan, 1971). Few subjects actually kept their commitment to give blood. When the initial warm glow dissipated, the behavioral follow-through did not occur.

Feeling good because of something that happened to you has different implications for prosocial behavior than feeling good because of something that happened to a friend. This was demonstrated when subjects were asked to imagine a free trip to Hawaii given either to them or to their best same-sex friend (Rosenhan, Salovey, and Hargis, 1981). A control group heard a neutral tape and nothing was mentioned about Hawaii. All subjects were then asked to volunteer to answer test questions for an experiment regarding fairness in testing. Subjects induced to experience a good mood by imagining their own trip to Hawaii gave more help than control subjects. Subjects induced to experience a good mood by imagining the good fortune of their best friend however, were less helpful than control subjects. The glow of good will has a halo with a small circumference that does not extend beyond the good fortune of the self. As can be seen in Chapter 5, mood affects memory. A pleasant mood invokes pleasant thoughts and memories of positive and satisfying experiences. Such a positive overall cognitive set prepares the person to perform prosocial behavior (Isen Shalker, Clark, and Karp, 1978).

Feeling bad

If feeling good leads people to perform prosocial behaviors, then you might think that people would not help others when they feel bad. Indeed, this relationship was found with children who had been asked to sit quietly and think of a sad experience they had had (Rosenhan, Underwood, and Moore, 1974). These children put fewer pennies in a can marked "money for other children" than did children who had merely

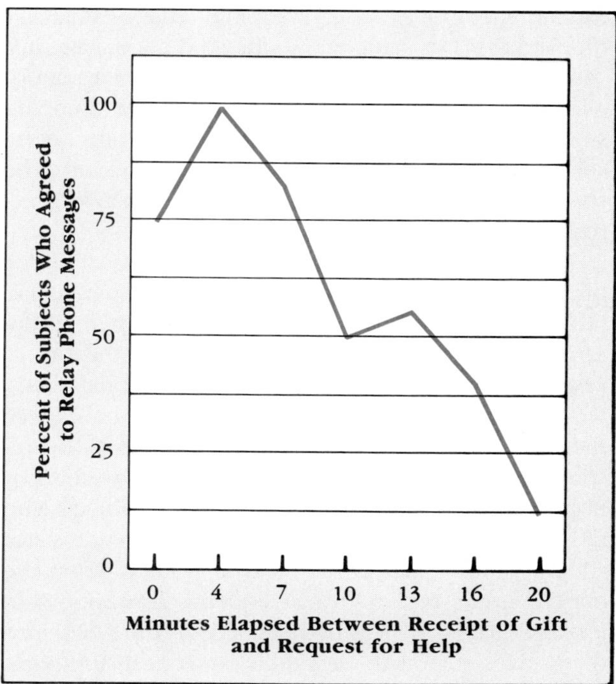

Figure 9-3 Prosocial behavior in subjects who received free stationery and were requested to relay phone messages.

Source: Based on "Competence and volunteering" by A. E. Kazdin and J. H. Bryan, 1971, *Journal of Experimental Social Psychology*, 7, 87-97.

counted slowly prior to the opportunity to donate. On the other hand, failure experiences do not decrease the probability of prosocial behavior as compared to the behavior of control subjects (Berkowitz and Connor, 1966; Kazdin and Bryan, 1971). Although success has the effect of producing a short-term increment in prosocial behavior, failure does not have a complementary negative impact.

A person in a bad mood may feel better after doing something positive for others, a kind of **negative state relief** (Bauman, Cialdini, and Kendrick, 1981). Engaging in prosocial behavior is self-gratifying and changes the mood of the person in a positive direction. Because people do not like feeling bad, they can do something positive and work their way out of the "funk." Consistent with this reasoning was the finding that subjects induced to be sad engaged in more self-reinforcement, but only if they had not been given an opportunity to perform prosocial behavior beforehand (Bauman et al., 1981). Thus, sad subjects acted to make themselves feel better either by reinforcing themselves or by helping others. Whatever they did first was sufficient, so they did not engage in a second positive behavior afterwards. A similar pattern occurs when people who feel bad go on a shopping spree, they may buy things for others or for themselves (prosocial or self-reinforcing behaviors). The shopping brings about relief from the negative affective state.

There are times when people are responsible for their own negative outcomes and times when bad things happen and there is little anyone can do about it. Subjects were or were not told that they were responsible for their own negative emotional states, which in fact had been induced subtly by the experimenter. Subjects who believed themselves to be responsible were not as likely to respond to subtle or nondemanding requests for help as were subjects who did not feel responsible for their own mood states (Rogers, Miller, Mayer, and Duval, 1982). When the experimenter made strong requests, however, subjects provided help whether or not they believed themselves responsible for their own negative moods.

Sadness can be oriented socially and outwardly or it can be a kind of self-pity. Research indicates that the direction of sadness affects prosocial behavior. Subjects either imagined observing a close friend slowly dying of cancer or they imagined a friend watching them dying (Thompson, Cowan, and Rosenhan, 1980). Measurements indicated that a sad mood was produced for subjects in both of these conditions. Subjects were more helpful, however, when their focus was on the dying person (empathy) than on themselves (self-focus). Similarly, when subjects were self-concerned in the sense of being apprehensive about failing on a test of an important characteristic, they were less inclined to be helpful (Aderman and Berkowitz, 1983; Gibbons and Wicklund, 1982).

Another source of bad moods is the guilt and remorse associated with harming other people. Performing good deeds may alleviate guilt, restore positive self-esteem, and demonstrate to others that

A person may feel better after helping another. Engaging in prosocial behavior is self-gratifying and can change the mood of a person in a positive direction.

we are really kind and responsible citizens. In a field study, women at a shopping center were approached and asked by an experimenter to take his picture with his camera (Regan, Williams, and Sperling, 1972). The camera was rigged so it would not work and the experimenter either blamed the women for breaking the camera or commented that the camera "acted up a lot." After the experimeter walked off, a confederate came along carrying a shopping bag with a hole in it and spilled candy on the sidewalk. While 55 percent of the women blamed for breaking the camera called the confederate's attention to the spilled candy, only 15 percent of the women not blamed did so. Prosocial behavior occurs when an opportunity presents itself and people feel guilty about some prior behavior.

It has been demonstrated that people will exhibit prosocial behavior when they do not feel responsible for a transgression, but are concerned that others will attribute responsibility to them. An experimenter rigged a machine to make a loud popping sound and to emit smoke when subjects touched it. More of these subjects volunteered to help the experimenter than did subjects who did not have this upsetting experience (Wallace and Sadalla, 1966), and the experimenter obtained more compliance from subjects when the amount of damage appeared to be greater (Brock & Becker, 1966). Of course subjects knew they had not sabotaged the equipment deliberately and that it was an accident at worst. Nevertheless, the experimenter might have doubts about the subjects' intentions. Thus, the willingness to help was a manifestation of their good intentions and lack of malevolence.

Empathy and prosocial behavior

Sympathy is defined as feeling sorry for others and wanting to relieve their distress. **Empathy** is an emotion where the other person's feelings are experienced as one's own (Stotland, 1969). An empathic person feels the same distress as the person who experiences pain and loss.

It has been suggested, as illustrated in Figure 9-4, that empathy is the basis of sympathy, which in turn induces the person to perform prosocial behavior (Aronfreed, 1970; Hoffman, 1981). The empathic person experiences the same stressful feelings as the victim, and by helping the victim, the person relieves the stress that both are feeling (Aronfreed, 1970). In this way, prosocial behavior is reinforcing to the empathic person who has helped, and therefore provides satisfaction to both self and victim.

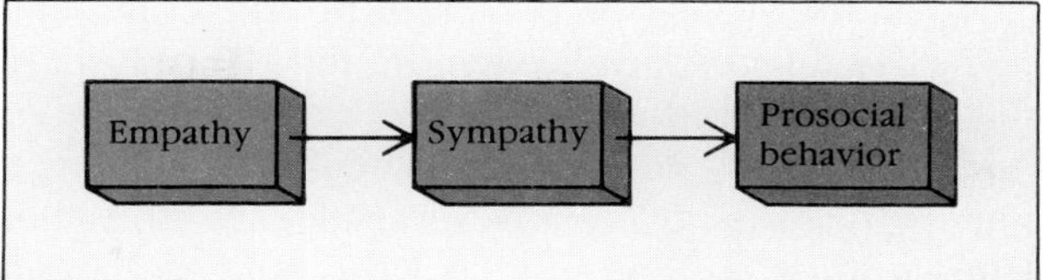

Figure 9-4 The relationships of empathy, sympathy and prosocial behavior.

Source: Based on "The socialization of altruistic and sympathetic behavior: Some theoretical and experimental analyses" by J. Aronfreed, 1970, in *Altruism and helping behavior: Social psychological studies of some antecedents and consequences*, J. Macauley and L. Berkowitz (Eds.), New York: Academic Press.

It is difficult to disentangle empathy and sympathy as emotional reactions. Sympathy is the more selfish motive and presumably could be relieved by turning away from distressing events, as might happen when a person leaves the scene of an automobile accident. People experiencing empathy can relieve their own distress only by helping the victim. If subjects are placed in a situation where they can choose to escape the disturbing feelings of sympathy or to relieve their empathic distress by helping the victim, their relevant motivational basis for the behavior may be inferred.

Subjects in a laboratory study were paired with a person who they knew had attitudes similar or dissimilar to their own (Batson, Duncan, Ackerman, Buckley, and Birch, 1981). In a rigged lottery, subjects were chosen to observe and a confederate was chosen to perform a task under aversive conditions (i.e., while being exposed to electric shocks). In an easy escape condition, subjects only had to observe two trials out of ten that the worker had agreed to undertake. In a difficult escape condition, subjects were told that they had to observe all ten trials. The female victim was observed by all subjects to suffer greatly from the shocks. After the second trial, she mentioned a childhood experience when she had been thrown from a horse onto an electrified fence, and she indicated an intense fear of even mild shocks since that time. After she asked for a glass of water, the experimenter asked the subjects if they would like to trade places with the victim for any of the remaining eight trails.

When the victim was perceived as similar and empathy could be experienced, more than 80 percent of the subjects agreed to take the victim's place whether escape was easy or difficult. When the victim was perceived as dissimilar, however, and sympathy rather than empathy was felt, subjects who could escape did so with only 18 percent agreeing to take the victim's place. Sixty-four percent of the sympathetic subjects volunteered to replace the victim when escape was difficult. Empathy evidently provides a stronger motivation for prosocial behavior than does sympathy. Furthermore, empathy is not an automatic reaction to the distress of all other people. The characteristics of victims and the circumstances leading to their distress affect whether onlookers will experience empathy.

The association of empathy with subsequent prosocial behavior apparently is learned. Children display empathy when observing an adult in stress, but they act to help the victim only after they are trained to do so (Aronfreed and Paskal, 1966). The two-stage process involving the experience of empathy and the motivation to provide help has been shown also among college students. They were exposed to radio broadcasts depicting the plight of another student who had experienced a tragedy in her family (Coke, Batson, and McDavis, 1978). More students who had been asked to take the victim's point of view later offered to help her with various chores than did students who had been told to listen to the broadcast objectively and to try to identify the techniques used by the producers to make it warm and personal.

Social norms and prosocial behavior

We could accept George Bernard Shaw's skeptical comment, "The golden rule is that there is no golden rule," and still admit that people are taught to be concerned about other people. Box 9-4 shows that some form of golden rule has existed in all great civilizations. Much human behavior is automatic and governed by rules once the individual interprets what rule should be applied to a specific situation (Harre and Secord, 1971). Whether people fulfill obligations set forth by rules because they wish to avoid the disapproval of others or because they are self-focused or concerned about their own self-esteem, there is little question that much prosocial behavior is rule governed.

The reciprocity norm

Most interactions between people involve exchanges of some sort (Homans, 1974). Sometimes these exchanges are worked out well before either party provides what the other wants, and they may be referred to as *economic exchanges* (Blau, 1964). *Social exchanges* occur when no agreements have been made beforehand, but one person takes an initiative and provides a reinforcement. We can expect the likelihood of this kind of initiative to be greater when the recipient of the gift can be counted upon to return the favor. The **norm of reciprocity,** which states that you should help those who help you, has the specific function of encouraging people to initiate positive exchanges with others (Gouldner, 1960). It acts as a "starting mechanism" for social exchange, providing the initiator with an assurance that anything offered will be reciprocated and not simply exploited by others. Positive social exchanges can provide the basis for friendship and alliances, and can allow conciliatory actions to break a cycle of conflict (see Box 9-5 on p. 268). It would be difficult to imagine an orderly society without a norm of reciprocity. Indeed, cross-cultural research has led to the conclusion that the norm of reciprocity is a universal rule of behavior (Gouldner, 1960; Mauss, 1967).

The obligation to reciprocate varies as a function of the perceived motives, resources, and costs of the donor. Whether the benefit was expected by the recipient also adds to the obligation. A person feels little sense of obligation if a gift is given reluctantly. Consider a child whose parents require a sharing of candy. The recipient may properly feel obligation to the parents, not to the child. Research has shown that subjects are more apt to reciprocate benefits when the benefits are given voluntarily rather than when they are a requirement of experimental procedures (Goranson and Berkowitz, 1966; Greenberg and Shapiro, 1971; Nemeth, 1970; Schopler and Thompson, 1968).

In laboratory situations, it typically is found that subjects provide help to others in proportion to the amount of benefits they receive (Wilke & Lanzetta, 1970). This is probably because the costs incurred in providing benefits is the same for donors and recipients. When costs were manipulated, gratitude was related to both the value of the benefit received and the costs incurred by the benefactor (Muir and Wein-

Box 9-4

The many forms of the golden rule

The universality of the golden rule suggests how difficult it might be to maintain social relations if you could not expect others to reciprocate positive actions. All the great religions of the world have some form of the golden rule.

Christianity	All things whatsoever ye would that men should do to you, do ye even so to them. Matthew 7.12.
Judaism	What is hateful to you, do not to your fellow-men. That is the entire law all, the rest is commentary. Talmud Shabbat, 31a
Brahmanism	This is the sum of duty: Do naught unto others which would cause you pain if done to you. Mahabharata 5.1517
Buddhism	Hurt not others in ways that you yourself would find hurtful. Udana-Varga 5.18
Confucianism	Surely it is the maxim of loving-kindness: Do not unto others that you would not have them do unto you. Analects 15.23
Taoism	Regard your neighbor's gain as your own gain, and your neighbor's loss as your own loss. T'ai Shang Kan Ying P'ien
Zoroastrianism	That nature alone is good which refrains from doing unto another whatsoever is not good for itself. Dadistan-i-dinik 94.5
Islam	No one of you is a believer until he desires for his brother that which he desires for himself. Sunnah

stein, 1962; Tesser, Gatewood, and Driver, 1968).

Unexpected benefits induce a person to return greater benefits. Subjects given unexpected hints about how to do well on a quiz and win a prize provided more help than did subjects receiving expected hints (Morse, Gergen, Peele, and van Ryneveld, 1977). Suppose you were in an experiment and another person was given ten dimes and told to distribute them anyway at all between the two of you. How many would you expect to receive?

This kind of situation actually was contrived so that subjects received eight of ten dimes or eight of forty dimes from a confederate (Pruitt, 1968). In both cases, subjects received eighty cents. The recipients were then given ten dimes to distribute. The dimes were divided not on the basis of the absolute amount subjects had previously received, but on how benevolent the other person had been proportionate to the wealth possessed. Furthermore, expectations that the other party would distribute even more money in the future induced subjects to give even more to the other person, presumably in an attempt to induce greater reciprocity from the partner. Not only does unexpected generosity induce greater reciprocity, but

Box 9-5

Giving and receiving gifts

Most of us have become accustomed to giving and receiving gifts. We give gifts on special holy days, such as Chanuka and Christmas, on birthdays and name days, when a person is sick or hospitalized, on wedding anniversaries, on mother's and father's days, at showers celebrating weddings and births, at housewarming parties, and on many other occasions. To whom do we give gifts: members of our family, friends, lovers, employees and employers, new acquaintances, and even total strangers.

In some societies, it is customary for strangers to bear gifts for the head man of a village (Mauss, 1967). Such gift giving communicates good will and the desire for friendship. In American society, most of us would be wary of a stranger who wants to give us a gift, and folk wisdom tells us to "watch out for strangers bearing gifts." The presumption is that the stranger wants something from us, and we are unwilling to be placed in debt before knowing what it is.

There are many reasons for giving gifts other than as gestures of good will and as means of manipulating others for your own advantage. People may gain status in a community by their philanthropic activities. For example, in many hunting and gathering societies, cooperation and sharing is obligatory. Nevertheless, conflicts among hunters may arise as to who can claim credit for a kill, not because of the desire for the slain animal, but to establish who has the right to give it away. This right is desirable because it gives status to a hunter in the community (Dowling, 1970).

Gifts may be given to others in order to humiliate them. The Kwakiutl Indians of the Pacific Northwest hold potlatches, consisting of ceremonies during which a person gives gifts to an enemy. If more is given to the enemy than can be returned, the enemy is humiliated and the donor gains status in the community (Cohen, 1972). It is sometimes said that people on welfare are humiliated by the experience because there is little they can do to pay the government back for what they have received.

Many gifts are given out of a sense of obligation. You cannot forget a birthday without fear of giving offense to someone. Gift giving shades into a version of looting on the island of Nauru in the Pacific Ocean. This is the wealthiest nation per capita in the world because of its valuable deposits of guano (bird droppings). Whenever someone experiences good luck, attains position, or acquires a large sum of money, people are free to help themselves to a share. For example, the fire chief lost all his belongings on his fiftieth birthday. When the president was elected, a friend slid into the driver's seat and drove his car away—legally! Well wishers stripped the president's house within hours (*Miami Herald,* 1978).

greater reciprocity may be used to induce others to be more generous, a kind of upward spiral of generosity.

Folk wisdom states that "if you want to make an enemy, loan your brother-in-law money." A person actually may resent receiving a gift because of the obligation it incurs. A cross-cultural study in the United States, Sweden, and Japan established that a donor was liked more if a loan of money in a gambling game specifically required repayment, than if it was considered a gift. The vague obligation incurred by such a gift was apparently onerous and avoided when possible (Gergen, Ellsworth, Maslach, and Seipel, 1975). It has been observed in prisons that old inmates find ways of placing a gift in the cell of a new prisoner (McCorkle and Korn, 1954). The newcomer must then find the giver of the gift and insist on returning it, otherwise the recipient may be forced to submit to the donor's wishes.

Norm of social responsibility

The expectation that advantaged people *should* help those more needy than themselves is referred to as the **norm of social responsibility.** In feudal societies, people of high station were expected to act according to a principle of *noblesse oblige* and to display charitable behavior. This moral obligation was sometimes met by the feudal lord when he invited all the peasants up to the castle for Christmas dinner. After dinner the peasants were sent back to the fields for another 365 days of serfdom. The exhortation that we are our brothers' keepers helps socialize us to act according to a social responsibility norm. On the other hand, as Box 9-6 indicates, some people may appear to be helpful in order to take advantage of other people.

Behavior governed by a norm of social responsibility is most apt to occur when the disadvantaged person is highly dependent upon the advantaged person. This principle was demonstrated in a situation in which subjects built paper boxes for a supervisor. The subjects' production either could contribute to the winning of $5 by the supervisor or it could have no consequences for the supervisor. Subjects made more boxes when the outcomes for the supervisor were dependent upon them than when little dependence on them existed (Berkowitz and Daniels, 1963). In another study, subjects offered more help when the beneficiary's opportunity to get a job clearly depended on help being given right away. When there was no urgency of time, subjects gave little help (Schopler and Bateson, 1965). There is a lessened sense of social responsibility, however, if people bring about their

A person who is more able helps a little boy who is less able. According to the norm of social responsibility, independent people are more likely to help those who are more dependent or less fortunate.

Box 9-6

Bad samaritans and the costs of being helped

On 20 January 1983 in Baltimore, Maryland, a sixty-three-year-old woman was arrested and charged with robbing elderly men. It was alleged that she would lure men, ranging in age from seventy-five to eighty-six years, into her car with offers of rides. Often these men had just left a bank. The lady would then drug them with spiked drinks and rob them. She would dump them unconscious in ditches and unfamiliar neighborhoods in the winter weather. The men described her as an apparent good samaritan and as a very outgoing and kind person. She was arrested when she picked up an undercover agent posing as an elderly man at a bus station. The bad samaritan was charged with robbery, kidnaping, and assault with intent to murder (*Albany Times-Union,* 1983).

own problems and misery through their own irresponsible conduct (Gruder, Romer, and Korth, 1978; Meyer and Mulherin, 1980).

Among people who request help from others, those who lack ability are more likely to gain compliance than those who lack motivation. Such differential helping was shown when phone calls, allegedly from a classmate, were made to members of an introductory psychology class (Barnes, Ickes, and Kidd, 1979). These calls were made just three days before an examination. The caller always (or sometimes) claimed to lack the ability to handle course material or always (or sometimes) indicated to be unmotivated to take good notes. The caller then made a series of requests, each contingent on gaining compliance to the one previous to it:

1. "Do you think I could look at your notes?"
2. "Can I come by tonight?"
3. "Could I borrow them for a day?"
4. "But I can't make it tonight. How about tomorrow night?"
5. "Could you pick them up when I'm finished?"

When the caller always claimed to lack the ability to take class notes, classmates on the average were willing to go at least as far as stage four, and some even agreed to pick up their notes. Classmates were least willing to help the caller who only sometimes claimed to lack motivation to take notes; they tended to be unwilling to lend their notes, although they agreed to let the caller come by to look at them.

There is some evidence that conspicuously dependent people are more likely to receive help than are less obviously dependent people. In a field study, an Australian and an American couple traveled about the United States on Greyhound buses (Pearce, 1980). In bus terminals, they would ask people for information about the time, about where to mail a postcard, and about where they could stay overnight. Fellow passengers were more likely to help the female supplicants and the male foreigner, presumably because they were perceived as more dependent on others for help. Total strangers who had not been passengers on the couples' bus were less apt to help and were less dependent on these differences among supplicants. Dependent people also may be vulnerable to exploitation, as in the case of the bad samaritan described in Box 9-6.

The norm of social responsibility has its strongest impact on governing behavior when the dependency is obvious, when it is not the fault of the disadvantaged person, and when the costs to the benefactor are low. The detrimental impact of costs was shown in a field study carried out in exclusive women's shoe shops in Chicago (Schaps, 1972). The experimenter walked into the stores with a broken heel on one shoe or she acted like a normal customer. The dependent variable included measures of the number of shoes tried on, the number of trips the salesperson made to the stockroom, and the time he or she spent with the experimenter. The customer received more help when she was most dependent. When there were other customers waiting and the cost of helping was therefore higher, salespeople gave less help, and a dependent customer received no more help than a nondependent one.

Distributive norms of equity and equality

From each according to his ability, to each according to his need.
Karl Marx, Communist Manifesto

The amount of benefits people are given is often influenced by social rules that specify fairness of distribution. An **equality norm** stipulates that each member of a group should be benefited equally to any distribution of rewards. This rule applies to the baseball team that wins the World Series. Each player receives the same amount of bonus dollars, whether they are regulars or substitutes, as long as they have been with the team most of the season. The equity norm takes into account the inputs of the person to the group's efforts to accumulate resources and the outputs in terms of rewards distributed to them. Groups might assess the value of inputs in different ways but could give credit for contributed resources, effort, time, seniority, and amount of responsibility. The **norm of equity** states that a person should gain a share of rewards in proportion to his or her relative input to the group; that is, given their inputs, members of the group get what they earn or deserve.

The temporary (ad hoc) groups formed by experimental social psychologists for purposes of laboratory study often ignore inputs and distribute rewards according to the norm of equality. For example, 30 to 90 percent of ad hoc groups of college students preferred an equal distribution in spite of ample information regarding different inputs by members (Harris and Joyce, 1980). These students also allocated expenses equally, although doing so actually contributed to unequal net outcomes. Even in negotiations, there is a tendency to settle for some compromise between equality and equity distributions (Komorita and Chertkoff, 1973).

It may be the case that people are more apt to use equality as a principle when they are chosen to allocate rewards, but expect equity when they have rewards allocated to them. Without specific instructions about how they should distribute rewards, members of ad hoc groups may be concerned about how other members will react to them. They all spend about the same amount of time serving as subjects in an experiment. Much of equity theory concerns the reactions of recipients to nonequitable distributions of rewards (Adams, 1965; Walster, Walster, and Berscheid, 1978). Equity theory is discussed further in Chapter 12.

Social and personal norms

There are two great rules of life, the one general and the other particular. The first is that everyone can, in the end, get what he wants if he only tries. This is the general rule. The particular rule is that every individual is, more or less, an exception to the rule.
Samuel Butler, Note-Books

We have seen in Chapters 4 and 6 that stereotypes and attitudes may be too general and abstract as bases for predicting behavior of an individual in a specific situation. The use of social norms to predict behavior is similarly ambiguous (Krebs, 1970; Latane & Darley, 1970). How does a person act if norms are contradictory? What if one norm tells us not to butt into other people's business and a second prescribes that we should intervene to prevent a woman from being beaten by a man?

It is plausible to suggest that norms not only cause behavior but also are used to justify behavior. Thus, a young assistant manager may be in favor of equality in distributing bonus money from exceptional profits earned in the last fiscal year, but an experienced and veteran manager may be in favor of equity. Because of less seniority, the young person would profit more from an equal share, but a senior person would profit more from an equitable distribution. Thus, each is pursuing selfish interests and rationalizes them in terms of social norms.

One proposal is that prosocial behavior can be better understood by an examination of **personal norms,** which represent an individual's values, principles, and feelings of moral obligation to help others in specific situations (Schwartz, 1977). Exhortations of people to act according to general social norms, such as the Ten Commandments, are generally ineffective in changing behavior. Most psychotherapists recognize the futility of exhorting their patients to change their behavior. Reminding a person about the expectations of others also does little to activate a sense of personal obligation. If psychologists are to use personal norms in predicting prosocial behavior, it is necessary to know what kinds of factors interfere with activating them, such as the costs of helping, the availability of more competent people, and so on.

Modeling and prosocial behavior

Social learning theory assumes that children learn a great deal just by observing the behavior of other people (Bandura, 1969). We show babies how to wave bye-bye and how to say "mama." Children imitate models whose behaviors are reinforced. A model's behavior and its outcomes are associated cognitively and can serve as a source of expectations about what will occur if the observer acts in the same way. In the absence of tangible rewards, some indication of pleasure by the model following the relevant behavior will elicit imitation from children. For example, children gave a greater share of their rewards to others when a model had displayed happiness following her own charitable behavior (Aronfreed & Paskal, 1966). The child should expect that his or her charitable behavior should lead to a feeling of happiness, and intrinsic

These children are sweeping fallen leaves because they observed this behavior in their parents. When children engage in prosocial behavior, they need to be recognized and rewarded.

Box 9-7

The addiction to helping others

There is a close analogy between the reactions of a parachutist and a blood donor. Prior to the first jump, parachutists typically are terrified. When the jump is completed, they appear emotionally stunned and display little emotion. After a few minutes, their emotional reactions return to normal. As training continues, the emotional state prior to a jump is described as a form of anxiety or eagerness rather than terror. The experienced jumper reports feeling exhilaration that may last for several hours after a jump.

Blood donors reveal a similar pattern of reactions. There is typically a good deal of apprehension prior to a first donation. With subsequent donations, the person gradually experiences strong positive feelings and a sense of self-satisfaction. These good feelings reinforce and tend to increase the probability of future donations.

An **opponent process theory of emotion and motivation** has been proposed to explain addiction to actions that frighten most people (Solomon, 1980). Two basic processes are involved: (1) the person's first experience produces a sharp, negative emotional response to an aversive event and (2) the human organism's emotional system produces an opposite reaction in order to prevent panic-type responses. Thus, an early negative response is countered and controlled by a positive response. The latter builds slowly but persists longer than the negative response. With continued experiences, the positive emotion becomes stronger than the originally powerful negative one. This process not only helps us to understand why people take risks to help others, but it also contributes to our knowledge about people who seek thrills, smoke tobacco, and engage in other forms of addiction (Piliavin, Callero, and Evans, 1982).

reward. Mere exhortations by adults do not elicit self-sacrificial behavior in children (Bryan and Walbek; Grusec and Skubiski, 1970; Rettig, 1956). Children do as we do, not as we say! The ideal condition for eliciting imitative prosocial behavior is for a model to state a personal norm of social responsibility, act charitably, and subsequently reinforce the child's imitative behavior. This sequence of actions elicits strong charitable behavior in children (Bryan, Redfield, & Mader, 1971).

The effectiveness of modeling among adults has been demonstrated on the nation's highways. A young lady was positioned by an automobile with a flat tire and a spare leaning against its side (Bryan and Test, 1967). In a modeling condition, a man was busy changing a flat tire for a woman just a quarter of a mile before the motorist encountered the stranded lady. When there was no model, thirty-five cars stopped and offered help; when there was a model, fifty-eight cars stopped out of two thousand that passed by. This modeling effect may be attributed to an activation of a personal norm, may reduce concern about embarrassment, or may call attention to the person in distress. Whatever the reason, people have been shown to be more charitable in dropping coins in a Salvation Army kettle (Bryan and Test, 1967; Macaulay, 1970), in agreeing to donate blood (Pittman, Pallak, Riggs, and Gotay, 1981; Rushton and Campbell, 1977), and in pledging donations to the United Way campaign (Catt and Benson, 1977) if they observe models engaged in such behavior. As is detailed in Box 9-7, once the individual engages in an act of charity, the good feelings experienced may become addictive.

Models who are extremely virtuous and take on

saintlike qualities no longer can be considered as relevant comparisons for others and hence do not stimulate imitation. Florence Nightingale, Albert Schweitzer, and Sister Teresa do not inspire imitation because they are believed to be too different from the rest of us to provide a basis for our own behavior.

Reactions to being helped

Reactions to being helped depend on the social and psychological implications of receiving it. Help from a wealthy person may imply a recognition of and/or acceptance of the existing social distance between the donor and the recipient. In addition, the debt created by the acceptance of a norm of reciprocity could be paid more easily to a poor person who needs it than to a wealthy person who does not need it. Given these considerations, it should not be surprising that people appreciate help from a relatively poor person more than they do from a relatively wealthy person (Fisher and Nadler, 1976; Gergen et al., 1975).

In some circumstances, help lowers the self-esteem of the recipient, while in other situations there are no psychological costs. For example, getting help for repairing your television set may not imply anything negative about your abilities, since few people have the requisite training for the task. On the other hand, it may threaten your ego if one of your parents tries to help you solve school problems. These generalizations were supported when students were asked to solve problems reflecting either their creativity and intelligence (ego involving) or their luck and momentary moods (not ego involving). The task was in fact unsolvable, and the subjects received help from a friend or from a stranger.

Subjects helped by a friend on a task that was not ego involving expressed a positive feeling about it and rated themselves positively. When help was received by a friend on an ego involving task, subjects expressed a more negative mood and rated themselves negatively. Help from strangers had less of an impact on the subjects, and the nature of the task was not important (Nadler, Fisher, and Ben-Itzhak, 1983).

People with high self-esteem should have stronger resistance to being helped than people with low self-esteem. Indirect support for this proposition was shown when people with high self-esteem performed better than people with low self-esteem after both received a hint from another person (DePaulo, Brown, Ishii, and Fisher, 1981). When no hint had been given, no differences between the two kinds of people were found. The implication is that people with high self-esteem were more motivated to prove to others that they were competent and that they did not really need the help when they had received a hint.

Seeking help

Although we have been considering who gives aid to others, it is also a valid question to ask who seeks help from others. In one study, when same-sex students were paired to perform on problem-solving tasks, they sought less help from physically attractive than from unattractive partners (Nadler, Shapira, & Ben-Itzhak, 1982). In cross-sex pairs, more males asked for help from the unattractive than the attractive female partner. This finding can be interpreted as indicating a desire by supplicators to avoid making a negative self-presentation to a target possessing a valued characteristic. Females in mixed-sex pairs more often asked for help from the attractive male partner, however. The reason offered for the latter finding is that traditional values allowed females to display dependency without creating a negative identity. Supplication by a female may therefore be displayed before attractive audiences.

It is easier to ask for help if only the potential benefactor is present. A reticence to ask for help in front of an audience was shown when it was arranged that the microcomputers of students jammed while they were taking an exam (Williams and Williams, 1983). The students were more reluctant to ask for help when there were three experimenters present than when there was only one. It is more embarrassing to display incompetence by asking for help in front of several people rather than in front of just one.

Attributions of altruism

Ordinary people distinguish between hedonistic and altruistic behaviors whether or not social scientists do. An attribution of altruism to the self or to others may be considered misattribution, self-deception, or illusory by skeptics, but people do label some actions as altruistic. Self-perception of altruism is less likely when norms are salient in a situation that requires

This couple is waiting for assistance but is reluctant to disturb the store attendant. People's tendencies to seek help are related to their self-esteem and to their social and psychological circumstances.

prosocial action in some sense. For example, subjects who helped another person perceived themselves as less altruistic if the other person had helped them first; that is, the reciprocity norm required them to give help (Thomas and Batson, 1981). Comparative appraisals were also important in this experiment, however. When subjects observed that four other people refused to give help, they perceived themselves as altruistic whether or not the recipient had given them prior help.

When people are pressured to engage in prosocial behavior or are compensated for it, they view themselves as less altruistic. Paradoxically, rewarding people for helping others may make them less rather than more helpful.

Correspondent inference theory (see Chapter 4) proposed that when environmental causes for behavior can be discounted, the behavior and the motive for it may be given similar descriptions. This implies that perceptions of prosocial behavior will be attributed to altruistic motives when no environmental causes are apparent for explaining it.

Even a suspicion of underlying selfish goals for performing prosocial actions may lead observers to discount an altruistic motive. In one study, observers read about either a person who responded to an appeal for a loan of money or one who offered a loan without solicitation (Ackerman, Rosenfeld, and Tedeschi, 1981). Offering the loan without a prior request for it led observers to perceive the giver as less altruistic than was the case when the loan offer was in response to a specific request.

When helping constitutes out-of-role behavior, altruistic motives are attributed to the one who helps (Fisher, DePaulo, and Nadler, 1981). A person who helps often is perceived as more altruistic than someone who seldom does, and providing help to many others is perceived as more altruistic than frequently helping only one other person (Ackerman, Rosenfeld and Tedeschi, 1981).

Summary

Prosocial behavior may be altruistic or hedonistic. There are numerous examples of such behavior among subhuman organisms. There is little evidence, however, that biological factors are involved in a decision by humans to intervene and help others in an emergency. Instead, there is a sequence of steps, including noticing and interpreting an event as an emergency, accepting personal responsibility to intervene, knowing what to do, and deciding to act which leads to prosocial behavior in humans. An important factor that people must consider when deciding to act is the material, social, and psychic costs associated with the action.

The emotional states of people affect their readiness to help others. When people feel good, they are more likely to engage in prosocial behavior. When people are in a bad mood, they will do something positive to make themselves feel better, particularly when they attribute responsibility for their mood to their own past conduct. Assuming responsibility for feeling bad leads people to reward themselves or to help others. Whichever behavior people carry out first will detract from the likelihood of them performing the other. Experiencing empathy and sympathy for others also induces people to engage in prosocial behaviors.

Social norms encourage and sometimes require prosocial behavior. The norm of reciprocity dictates that people should return benefits for benefits received. A norm of social responsibility encourages advantaged people to help less fortunate and more dependent others. Distributive norms of equality and equity prescribe how benefits achieved collectively should be distributed in a group. A personal norm of responsibility may be as important in the person's decision to act to help others as the prescriptions of social norms.

A person's reactions to being helped depend on a number of factors. In general, if the help has negative implications for the self-esteem of the recipient, there may be some resentment felt toward the benefactor. There may be some reluctance to ask for help if doing so reveals the incompetence of the person or is embarrassing to the recipient in other ways.

Glossary

Altruism Helping other people without expectation of social, material, or psychic rewards.

Diffusion of Responsibility Responsibility to act, or responsibility for an act already performed, is spread among members of a group so that each feels less responsible than if alone.

Empathy An individual experiences another person's feeling as his or her own.

Enlightened self-interest Recognition that it is often in one's self-interest to help others because of the increased likelihood of their favorable reaction in the future.

Glow of good will A generalization based on the finding that people in a good mood are more likely to help others, unless doing so will destroy the good mood.

Hedonism The doctrine that each person selfishly seeks to maximize pleasure and to minimize pain.

Negative state relief People who feel bad or guilty will help others in order to attain positive emotional states.

Norm of equality A rule of distributive justice that each member of a group should receive the same benefits.

Norm of equity A rule of distributive justice that each person should receive benefits in proportion to contributions made to the group.

Norm of reciprocity A social rule dictating that people should return help for help received.

Norm of social responsibility A social rule stipulating that advantaged people should provide help to disadvantaged and dependent people.

Opponent process theory An initial strong negative reaction to an aversive event is accompanied by a weaker positive reaction to prevent panic; the positive reaction builds slowly, while the negative reaction dissipates rapidly; explains why people obtain pleasure from taking risks.

Personal norms A concept representing individual differences in values, principles, and felt obligation to help others.

Prosocial behavior An action intended to benefit another that has no apparent selfish motivation.

Sympathy Experience of compassion and concern aroused in a person by witnessing the suffering of another person.

Recommended Readings

Dawkins, R. (1976). *The selfish gene.* New York: Oxford University Press.
A biological analysis of altruism that has earned a solid reputation. An excellent presentation of the sociobiological approach to explaining human social behavior.

Piliavin, J. A., Dovidio, J. F., Gaertner, S. L., and Clark, R. D., III. (1981). *Emergency Intervention.* New York: Academic Press.
A comprehensive discussion of the many perspectives offered for understanding the willingness or hesitation of people to give aid in emergency situations.

Rushton, J. P., and Sorrentino, R. M. (1981). *Altruism and helping behavior.* Hillsdale, NJ: Erlbaum.
A collection of articles by investigators who discuss their current theories and research. A source for the serious student looking for up-to-date and detailed information about particular topics within the scientific literature on prosocial behavior.

Every person, experiencing as he does his own solitariness and aloneness, longs for union with another.

Rollo May, Love and Will

10 Interpersonal attraction

What attracts people to one another?

This is the story of two men. One was from an impoverished black family in Omaha, Nebraska. His family was so poor that one winter he and his brothers survived starvation by eating birds they shot with a BB gun. He was very shy, quiet and introverted. The other was white and grew up in a middle-class family in Fort Lauderdale, Florida. He was outgoing, full of life, and always cheerful.

In 1965 while both were rookies trying to make the Chicago Bears football team, these two men competed for the same position. Given their immense racial, geographic, economic, cultural, and personality differences, and the fact that they were intense rivals for the same job, Gayle Sayers and Brian Piccolo surely were destined to become enemies. Yet, despite these obstacles, they became the best of friends, a friendship that was portrayed in a television movie, *Brian's Song*.

As depicted in *Brian's Song,* the Sayers-Piccolo friendship flourished after they became the first black-white roommates on the Bears' team. When Sayers became depressed after suffering a serious knee injury, Piccolo cheered him up and supported him through physical therapy. At the start of the 1969 football season, they were the regular running backs for the Bears. It was then discovered that Piccolo had cancer. He died in 1970 at the age of twenty-six.

Social psychologists are interested in studying the formation of friendships, such as the one between Sayers and Piccolo. What attracts people to one another? Attraction may be superficial and maintained to avoid loneliness, or it may be in the form of friendship or passionate love. In Chapter 10, we examine the scientific study of the antecedents of attraction, the development of friendship, and the nature of passionate and romantic love.

Affiliation

Everybody needs some loving sometime.
Irving Taylor

Are there times when you want to get away from it all—from home, from other people, from the stress and trials of everyday life? At such times, a walk in the

Box 10-1

Isolation in prisons

Humans are social animals. As infants they have the longest period of helplessness of any primate and require nurturance from others in order to survive. Long periods of social isolation during infancy may have profound negative effects on a human's later development. There is good reason to believe that humans need to affiliate with other people.

Some people are dangerous to others and are placed in prisons as a measure of social control. The profound impact of being isolated from other people has been described by Jack Abbott (1981) who has been in prisons most of his life:

> A man is taken away from other prisoners, from his experience of other people, when he is locked in solitary confinement in the hole. Every step of the way removes him from experience and narrows it down to only the experience of himself. . . . When a man is taken farther and farther away from experience, he is being taken to his death. (p. 62)

Given this description of the inhumane nature of solitary confinement, it may surprise you to Pennsylvania Quakers advocated such treatment as a measure of social reform. They opposed public whippings and executions and believed that criminals could be rehabilitated with the proper treatment. The Quakers believed that fraternization among prisoners encouraged further criminal conduct. Prisons were constructed, providing each criminal with a solitary cell where, with a Bible as a companion, they could reflect upon their lives.

The Quaker system was soon abandoned as impractical. Prisoners found ways to communicate with one another, for example, through the ventilating systems. Also providing single cells for prisoners was prohibitively expensive (Sommer, 1976). Socially, the extreme isolation was associated with an increase in insanity and death among prisoners (Mitford, 1973). Perhaps the most important lesson learned from this social experiment was that there is a vital human need for affiliation and that even criminals need somebody sometimes.

woods, a swim in the lake, a jog along the beach, or a quiet place to read a good book provides relaxation and enjoyment. Prolonged isolation from other people, however, creates psychological stress. In his autobiography, Admiral Richard Byrd (1938) recounted his experience of spending six months alone at a weather station in the Antartic. He anticipated enjoyment of solitude and had abundant food, books, and a radio to communicate with other people. In a couple of weeks, however, he began to feel lonely and depressed. He then sank into a state of apathy and experienced hallucinations. Somehow Byrd managed to remain physically healthy and suffered no permanent impairment of his mental faculties. There are other cases, however, suggesting that prolonged isolation may have deleterious effects on health (see Box 10-1).

There is evidence that people vary considerably in their reaction to social isolation. For example, one of five male students who had volunteered to remain in a small chamber without windows felt an uncontrollable desire to leave after only twenty minutes, three remained in the room for two days, and one stayed alone for eight days (Schachter, 1959). Some of these college students reported feeling uneasy and said they would not want to participate again, while two of them were not particularly affected by the experience. This difference among people in their need to affiliate with others is manifested in living patterns. For example, you probably know students who prefer to live alone and others who prefer to have several roommates. In order to avoid the feeling of being alone, many people turn on the television set or make frequent telephone calls.

Affiliation with others may indicate a desire to make social comparisons, to obtain rewards others control, or to form friendships or other more intimate relationships.

Affiliation and social comparisons

The feeling of anxiety reported by explorers, meteorologists at isolated weather stations, and prisoners in solitary confinement suggests that **affiliation,** or interacting with others, serves to reduce anxiety. In a series of classic studies, Schachter (1959) tested the hypothesis that heightened anxiety would cause people to affiliate with others. One group of undergraduate women were induced to experience high anxiety by a bearded male experimenter dressed in a lab coat who spoke in unnerving tones. He told them they would receive powerful shocks that would be quite painful, although no permanent physiological damage would occur. A condition of low anxiety was created by having the same experimenter tell undergraduate women that they would experience low-level shocks giving them a tingle but no pain or unpleasantness. Women in both conditions were told that it would take about ten minutes to set up the experimental equipment and that they could wait by themselves or with other women in the same study in another room.

In support of the hypothesis that people affiliate to reduce anxiety, about 66 percent of the women who expected high-level shocks chose to affiliate, but only 33 percent of those who expected mild shocks chose to wait with other subjects.

In a second study, it was found that anxious people had a clear preference for affiliating with people who faced the same danger as themselves (Schachter, 1959). Given a choice between waiting with others in the same experiment or waiting simply to be advised by their professor, subjects anticipating high shock unanimously chose to wait with people who could be assumed to share anxiety similar to their own. "Misery doesn't just love any kind of company, it loves only miserable company" (Schachter, 1959, p. 24). Furthermore, subjects preferred being with people who were anticipating the danger, like themselves, rather than those who had already experienced it (Zimbardo and Formica, 1963).

To some extent, affiliation can be encouraged by the moods induced through reading. Undergraduate students who read a depressing passage expressed a greater desire to affiliate and work with a person who had been similary depressed than did students who had read a happy passage (Bell, 1978). Contrary to Schachter's theory, however, both groups of students preferred affiliation with a happy rather than an unhappy person. These results are shown in Figure 10-1. Thus while misery likes miserable company more than happiness does, misery also prefers happy companions.

Figure 10-1 The affiliation choices of depressed and happy subjects and the mood of the available person.

Source: Based on "Affective State, attraction and affiliation: Misery loves happy company, too" by P. A. Bell, 1978, *Personality and Social Psychology Bulletin*, *4*, 616-619.

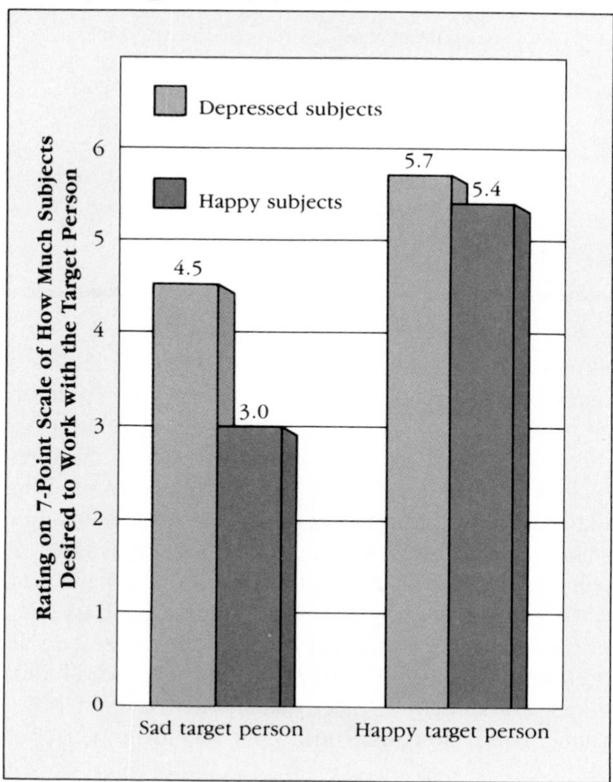

The desire to make social comparisons, not the social comfort of being with others, appears to be the primary basis of the fear and affiliation relationship. Consider the plight of the college students who were told by an experimenter that they would receive a strong shock. How afraid would you be? People are not often exposed to electric shocks, but they are taught to be fearful of them. Most people have no objective criterion and little past experience to evaluate the amount of pain the electric shocks may cause.

One way to gauge the appropriate level of fear is to gather information about the reactions of other people facing the same predicament. Evidence shows that if an experimenter provides subjects with information about the level of emotion experienced by others in the study, the desire to affiliate with others is greatly reduced (Gerard, 1963; Gerard and Rabbie, 1961). People who anticipate engaging in somewhat embarrassing behavior, such as sucking on a nipple, also tend to avoid being with others even if others anticipate the same experience (Sarnoff and Zimbardo, 1961). We may conclude that people want to make social comparisons and gain information relevant to how they should feel in an anxiety-producing situation, but not if sharing such information with others would heighten embarrassment.

People apparently seek some degree of social comfort through affiliation and social comparisons. You may join a group of fellow students immediately before taking an exam to discuss how prepared you are, what kinds of questions to anticipate, how fair the professor is, and how anxious you feel, but you probably would prefer not to do so if everyone is panic stricken. If given a choice to be with very fearful other people or to remain alone, subjects prefer to avoid affiliation (Rabbie, 1963).

Loneliness

All the lonely people, where do they all come from?

The Beatles, "Elinor Rigby"

It is not good that man should be alone.

Genesis

Loneliness is not simply the absence of affiliation. Despite the dictionary definition of loneliness as a lack of companionship, a person can feel lonely in a crowded stadium or not feel lonely on a deserted island. We should distinguish between being alone and feeling lonely (Rubenstein, Shaver, and Peplau, 1982). **Alone** is an objective term; it is defined by absence of other people and may or may not be experienced as unpleasant. **Loneliness** is subjective; it refers to a person's dissatisfaction with the quality of relationships with others and is *always unpleasant.*

People feel lonely when there is a discrepancy between the pattern of social relationships they desire and those they actually have (Peplau and Perlman, 1982). People who have a few very close friends might still feel lonely because they desire a wider range of friends, a situation referred to as **social loneliness.** On the other hand, a person who has many friends might feel lonely because the relationships lack depth and intimacy—an example of **emotional loneliness** (Weiss, 1973).

College students living in dormitories suffer more from emotional rather than social loneliness. A survey showed no differences between the number of best friends listed by lonely and nonlonely students (Williams and Solano, 1983). However, students identified as lonely by their responses to the UCLA Loneliness Scale were more likely to report that their relationships with best friends lacked intimacy. When the friends who were listed actually were contacted, their responses confirmed the perceptions of the lonely students.

Correlational studies investigating the relationships between loneliness and other psychological characteristics have shown that loneliness is associated with shyness, low self-esteem, and feelings of alienation (Jones, Freemon, and Goswick, 1981). Lonely people often feel depressed, bored, helpless, rejected, and dissatisfied with their lives.

Lack of social skills may produce the circumstances leading to loneliness. In group discussions, lonely people talked more about themselves, changed topics more frequently, and asked fewer questions than did their discussion partners (Jones, Sansone, and Helm, 1983).

The loner has been glorified as a cultural ideal in America. Literature and popular culture extol the virtues of characters such as the lone cowboy working the fences out on the prairie, self-sufficient private detectives, trail blazers like Daniel Boone, and the Lone Ranger. Being alone, independent of others, and content with one's lot in life is made to appear desirable (Bernikow, 1982). Nevertheless, loneliness appears to be a serious and growing problem in the United States. Although Americans typically appear to be friendly and outgoing, a number of writers have noted that this congeniality is rather shallow and that Americans are reluctant to let down all barriers to self-disclosure (Lewin, 1946). More than a century ago, de Tocqueville (1961) observed that Americans were "locked in the solitude of their own hearts." The breakdown of the family, increases in the rate of divorce, and the highly mobile character of contemporary society exacerbate the problem of loneliness.

An extensive survey of loneliness uncovered that much of common wisdom about who is lonely is incorrect (Rubenstein and Shaver, 1979). A rather low rate of loneliness was reported by senior citizens, but a high rate was discovered among young people between the ages of eighteen and twenty-five. A 1981 Harris Poll showed a divergence between young and old people in their perceptions of loneliness in elderly people (Bernikow, 1982). While 65 percent of the young thought that loneliness was a serious problem for old people, only 13 percent of the elderly thought so. Perhaps this divergence of perception is caused by a confusion between being alone and loneliness. The elderly may be more self-contained and less dependent on others for their satisfaction. They therefore experience less loneliness even though they may spend more time alone than younger people.

In a survey of young people carried out by the National Institutes of Mental Health, a sex difference was found. Sixty-one percent of female adolescents reported feeling lonely, while 47 percent of male teenagers said that they were lonely. This difference may reflect the traditional child-rearing patterns that en-

A person may experience emotional loneliness even in the midst of a crowded bar. When people are unhappy in their relationships with others, they may often feel depressed, rejected, and dissatisfied with their own lives.

courage nurturance and social skills in females and independence in males. In addition, the cultural ideal of a rugged individualist most often is identified with males; as a consequence, males may develop different attitudes about being alone than may females.

Interpersonal attraction

I like Ike.

Campaign button for President Dwight D. Eisenhower

I never met a man I didn't like.

Will Rogers

Of all the four-letter words in the English language, "like" may have more meanings than any other. We talk about "liking" ice cream, Porsche automobiles, cats, the Beach Boys, other people, and movies. We "dislike" organic chemistry, dentists, war, and obnoxious people. In the most general sense, "like" means a tendency to be attracted to or have a favorable evaluation of an object, event, or person. The scientific study of interpersonal attraction focuses on positive evaluations of other people, what produces them, how liking affects interaction between people, and theories about why people are attracted to one another.

Antecedents of attraction

We sometimes speak of the "right chemistry" when two strangers meet and immediately develop a liking for one another. Of course it is psychology and not chemistry that is involved, but exactly what factors cause people to like one another? Much of what psychologists have learned about this question has simply confirmed what social philosophers and great poets have written throughout recorded history. This should not be surprising because it is important for all of us to understand why people like or dislike us. Among the antecedents of attraction are physical proximity and familiarity; similarity of attitudes, values, and personality; physical and social desirability; reinforcements; and complementary characteristics. Let us examine each of these factors in more detail.

Physical proximity

When I'm not near the one I love, I love the one I'm near.

E. Y. Harburg, Finian's Rainbow

Reach out and touch someone.

AT&T advertisement

We know most of the people we like. We have interacted with them on a face-to-face basis. It is possible to like someone we have never met, such as a pen pal, a Prince or Princess Charming of our dreams, a movie star or some other celebrity we would like to meet, or a hero or heroine we have seen merely at a distance. But we cannot avoid developing attitudes toward people we are near because they affect the experiences we have in some measure.

A positive relationship between physical proximity and liking has been demonstrated frequently. As is documented in Chapter 13, architectural designs that arrange the spacing between people can have an important effect on their social relations. Work settings similarly affect who will be friends. For example, members of a bomber crew in the U.S. Air Force and clerks in a large department store liked those who worked next to them more than others who were separated by more space (Gullahorn, 1952; Kipnis, 1957; Zander and Havelin, 1960). College students who shared classes, dormitories, and apartments developed stronger friendships than those not in such proximity (Byrne and Buehler, 1955; Maisonneuve, Palmade, and Fourment, 1952; Willerman and Swanson, 1953).

Have you ever been assigned seats in class according to the alphabetical order of the first letter of your last name? If proximity is associated with liking, alphabetically determined seating arrangements should lead to the development of friendships among people whose last names begin with letters close together in the alphabet. A study of the development of friendships among trainees for the Maryland State Police force supported this expectation (Segal, 1974). Seat and dormitory assignments were determined alphabetically. After the six-week training period, the trainees were asked to name their three closest friends in the program. The closer together the first initials of their last names, the more likely it was that trainees became friends.

Geographical location has been shown to be an

important determinant of mate selection. There is a tendency to marry the girl or boy next door. An examination of five thousand marriage licenses in Philadelphia many years ago indicated that one-third of the newlyweds lived within five blocks of one another, and 12 percent indicated that they were living at the same address before being married (Bossard, 1932). Twenty years later, a similar relationship between physical proximity of geographical location and marriage was found in Columbus, Ohio (Clark, 1952). Almost half of the newlyweds lived less than sixteen blocks from each other at the time of their first date.

We usually like the people we are near and stay near to those we like. There exists a positive correlation between physical proximity and liking because we interact more frequently with people to whom we are near.

Familiarity

One reason why proximity may be related to attraction is that we interact more frequently with people who are near. Although "familiarity breeds contempt," frequent exposure has been shown to be related to more positive ratings of stimuli. This phenomenon is referred to as the **mere exposure effect** (Zajonc, 1968).

Experimenters have observed the mere exposure effect in a variety of situations. For example, students were exposed to photographs from a college yearbook (Zajonc, 1968b). Some of the faces were presented as many as twenty-five times, while others were presented only once or twice. When asked how much they liked the people in the pictures, the students reported greater liking for those they had seen more frequently.

Frequent exposure to photographs also is associated with more favorable personality and social appeal ratings (Wilson and Nakajo, 1966). The mere exposure effect is not limited to photographs of others, but also occurs when strangers meet face to face. Female subjects, who participated in a study represented as concerned with taste, moved from cubicle to cubicle in a laboratory and passed each other a controlled number of times (Saegert, Swap, and Zajonc, 1973). No matter whether subjects had tasted pleasant or bitter substances, they liked each other more the more frequently they had seen each other. Familiarity is apparently a factor in the public relations of promoting celebrities. Liking for presidents and actors or actresses has been found to be positively correlated with how often they appear in the mass media (Harrison, 1977). Indeed, as is described in Box 10-2, the familiarity of inanimate objects also may be a determinant of our attitudes toward them.

Similarity

Birds of a feather flock together.

Aristotle

In physics we learn that particles with opposite charges attract one another, but in social psychology

Box 10-2

Mere exposure and the Eiffel Tower

It has been established that liking for meaningless stimuli, such as nonsense symbols, unfamiliar words from foreign languages, and Chinese characters, is related to frequency of exposure (Zajonc, 1968). One implication is that frequent exposure may be important for people in developing a taste for various works of art. Historians of music are apt to recall that the audience stormed out of the concert hall during the world premiere of Stravinsky's *La Sacre du Printemp (The Rite of Spring),* a work that is much admired by contemporary audiences. Repeated performances over the years has lent familiarity to this once strange piece of music, and with familiarity has come more enthusiastic audience responses.

A very similar process may have occurred with the Eiffel Tower, a structure visible from most places in the city of Paris. When it was first built in 1889 for a World's Fair, the Eiffel Tower was met with widespread criticism. Many French people objected to what they perceived as a cheapening of the arts and as a detriment to the reputation of France as a cultural leader in the world. As they go about the routines of everyday life, Parisians often see the Eiffel Tower. Their familiarity with its presence has been associated with a growing admiration for this architectural structure (Harrison, 1977).

we find that among people similarity breeds attraction. Think of your own attitudes toward nuclear power plants, a nuclear weapons freeze, an increase in expenditures for defense, punk and funk, big band and country, Johnny Carson, quiche Lorraine, and the New York Yankees. Suppose you dated someone who had attitudes exactly the opposite of your own. How well do you think you would get along? A refrain of a newly infatuated couple often is: "We have so much in common!" An interaction will flow more smoothly if each person does not have to defend every attitude or value that is expressed.

Numerous experiments, interviews, and field and correlational studies firmly have established that the more similarity there is in the attitudes of two people, the more they will like one another (cf. Byrne, 1971). In one of the first systematic studies of this principle, transfer students to the University of Michigan were offered free housing for a semester in exchange for their time in filling out questionnaires each week (Newcomb, 1961). Transfer students were selected because it was unlikely that they would have known one another prior to arrival on campus and because they would have settled on a subject major in most cases. The questionnaires assessed the attitudes of the transfer students and their perception of each other's attitudes and indicated how much they liked one another.

At first, proximity was the factor most associated with liking; students liked their roommates or near neighbors in the rooming house. As time went on, attitude similarity turned out to be the best single predictor of longer-term attraction. These students chose as friends others who were similar in political and religious views, college major, urban or rural background, and so on. Even though perceptions of the attitudes of others became more accurate over time, there was a tendency by students to overestimate the degree of similarity of their friend's attitudes. This exaggeration of similarity also has been found with married couples (Byrne and Blaylock, 1963). Indeed, the greater the similarity assumed by married couples, the more satisfied they were with their marriage (Levinger and Breedlove, 1966).

The most rigorous, precise, and voluminous research program demonstrating the similarity-attraction relationship has been carried out by Donn Byrne and his colleagues (cf. Byrne, 1971). This research program used a standard set of procedures. Subjects filled out a short attitude questionnaire asking them to indicate their attitudes toward religion, music, drinking, and so on. Their attitudes were expressed on six-point scales. The subjects were then told that the study was concerned with how people form impressions of one another when the only information they have is an expression of some of the attitudes of the other person. A questionnaire identical to the one subjects had filled out was then given to them. It was alleged to have been filled out by the "other subject"—sometimes referred to by social psychologists as the "phantom other" because there is really no one else. Actually, the experimenter, who can present the other person in different degrees similar or dissimilar in attitudes to the subjects, fills out the questionnaire. The subjects' impressions of the phantom other are obtained on an Interpersonal Judgment Scale, which contains a measurement of how much subjects think they would like the other person.

It was established that it is the proportion of attitudes people have in common and not the absolute number of agreements that affects attraction (Byrne and Nelson, 1965; Gonzales, Davis, Loney, Lukens, and Junghans, 1983). Suppose Louise and Gordon have positive attitudes toward mud wrestling, beer drinking, and Monday night football, but disagree in their attitudes toward weight lifting, the value of subhuman research for understanding people, and apple strudel. The proportion of agreement is 50 percent, but the number of consonant attitudes is three. Louise and Gordon will like each other less than another couple sharing similar attitudes in just two areas but disagreeing in only one;—that is, the latter couple are 66 percent in agreement although they agree on only two attitudes. By varying both the number and proportion of similar attitudes, a precise mathematical relationship was obtained between proportion of sim-

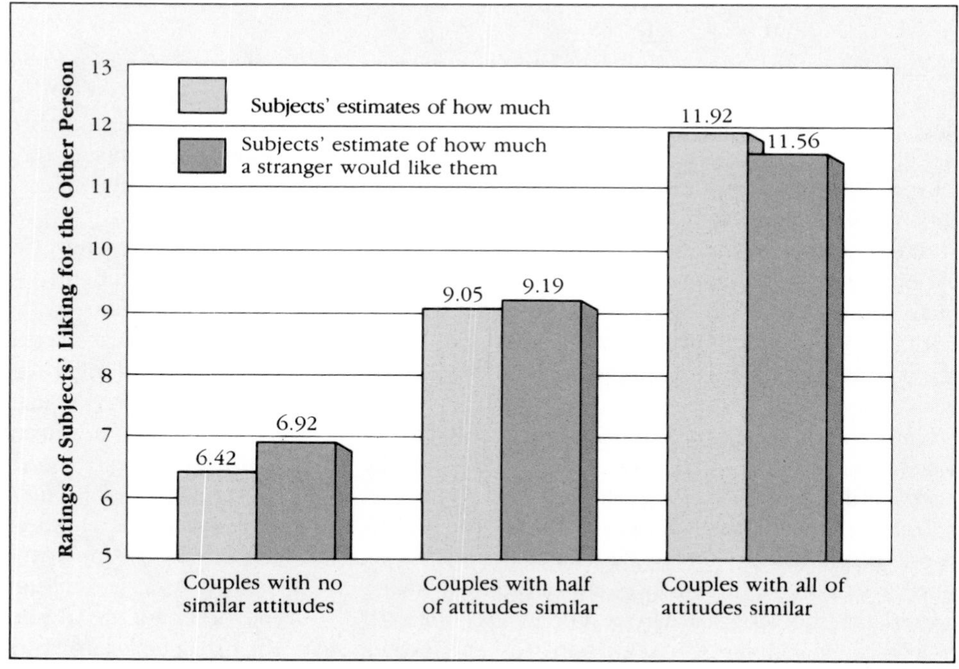

Figure 10-2 Attitude similarity and attraction. *Note:* Ratings were a sum of two 7-point scales indicating subjects' liking for and desire to work with the other person.

Source: Based on "Interactional approach to interpersonal attraction" by M. H. Gonzales, J. M. Davis, G. L. Loney, C. K. Lukens, and C. M. Junghans, 1983, *Journal of Personality and Social Psychology, 44.*

Box 10-3

Choosing companions in a fallout shelter

Debates on the effectiveness of fallout shelters during and after a nuclear war often ignore the social psychologial factors in such a situation. Many people would arrive at the shelter wounded or with radiation sickness. There would be little or no professional medical assistance. If people die in the shelter, it would not be possible to remove the bodies. Many would be suffering from shock and would be extremely anxious about the welfare of friends and family members. Unlike other disasters where help could be expected from outside, those inside would be trapped perhaps for a long period of time with little likelihood of receiving help from others. Under such stressful circumstances, how would these people get along with one another?

In a simulation study, thirteen male volunteers spent ten days together in a 12-by-24-foot room designed to reproduce as closely as possible the conditions of a fallout shelter (Griffitt and Veitch, 1974). Their diet consisted of 1.25 quarts of water per day, 8 civil defense crackers four times a day, and 4 sugar candies four times daily. Each volunteer had a bunk bed; there were chairs, a table, and a television set in the room. The toilet facilities were partitioned by a hanging cloth.

Before entering the shelter, the volunteers completed an attitude questionnaire. During their stay in the shelter, they were asked to indicate whom they would most want to leave the shelter and whom they would like to keep as companions. The volunteers chose as companions others who had attitudes most similar to their own, and they wished to remove those who had attitudes divergent from their own. We must recognize that this simulation does not capture the degree of stress that would occur in real crisis conditions. It might be expected that stress would only exacerbate the problems between people with dissimilar values, backgrounds, and attitudes.

---

ilarity and liking (see Figure 10-2). This relationship may be referred to as Byrne's **law of attraction** and states that attraction toward another person is a positive linear function of the proportion of similar attitudes (Clore and Byrne, 1974). Byrne's law of attraction is often used by computer dating services to pair people for blind dates. There is evidence that pairing people who have similar interests and backgrounds does lead to liking. Thirty-minute coke dates were arranged between similar and dissimilar pairs of male and female college students at the University of Texas (Byrne, Erwin, and Lamberth, 1970). Following these dates, similar pairs reported greater attraction for one another than did dissimilar pairs. As is indicated in Box 10-3, the law of attraction may also have implications for the way people would react to one another in a fallout shelter in the event of nuclear war.

Complementarity

Although the evidence is overwhelming that similarity is a basis of attraction in superficial contacts between strangers, it has been claimed that complementarity of needs may be more important in establishing long-term relationships, such as the one between Gayle Sayers and Brian Piccolo (Winch, 1958). **Complementarity** exists when the dispositions of one person fulfill the needs of the other and vice versa. A domineering person may seek out a dependent partner, or a talkative person may become attached to someone who is quiet and listens well. The relationship of complementarity and the meshing of needs to attraction is congruent with the notion of people seeking a quality in a friend or a lover that they perceive lacking in themselves. (Reiss, 1960). We can speculate that complementarity was the basis of attraction between Bud Abbott and Lou Costello and between Laurel and Hardy.

An interview study of 100 couples who had maintained romantic relationships for less than eighteen months showed that the most important factor in determining whether they thought the relationship would continue to develop was similarity in attitudes regarding family values (Kerckhoff and Davis, 1962). For couples who had been going together for longer than eighteen months, however, the best predictor of progress in the relationship was need complementarity and not attitude similarity. These results indicate that in the development of a relationship, complementarity is not very important at first but becomes the necessary cement for keeping people together in the long run (Campbell, 1980).

Complementarity also has been shown to be an important factor in the formation of friendships among camp counselors (Wagner, 1975). A psychologist interviewed the counselors to assess their needs and to measure their liking for one another. In two of the three camps studied, there was a significant relationship between complementarity of needs and attraction. People with aggressive needs tended to form friendships with those who had abasement needs. Dependency needs were associated with needs to provide succorance. Extreme instances of these tendencies may occur in sadomasochistic pairs or between people who seem to form a kind of surrogate parent-child relationship.

Not all of the available research is supportive of complementarity theory. A study of 66 couples who had been married for five years or less showed no relationship between their needs and their degree of marital adjustment (Meyer and Pepper, 1977). In fact, just the opposite pattern was found. Couples who had similar needs experienced positive marital adjustment, but couples who had dissimilar needs experienced more marital difficulties. The happiness of 108 Australian couples was found also to be associated with similarity but not with complementarity of needs (Antill, 1983).

Differences in populations of subjects, measures of needs, and other procedures may be involved in the contradictory findings obtained in the studies of complementarity. It also may be the case that some dissimilar needs are complementary and some are not. Research that does not distinguish between complementary and noncomplementary needs may fail to show support for complementarity theory. It is a task for future researchers to specify precisely when and how complementarity influences attraction.

Physical attraction

Regard not the vessel but what is in it.

Talmud

A cynic familiar with the research literature might think that the person who first said that "beauty is only skin deep" must have been quite ugly. Despite the lip service that people give in American society to the importance of character over looks, people often do judge a book by its cover. There is a wealth of evidence showing that people who meet the cultural standards of physical attractiveness are liked more than those who do not (Berscheid and Walster, 1974).

There is no universal standard about physical attractiveness. In some cultures, scarification of the body or placing large wooden plugs into lips to make them protrude may be carried out as cosmetic aids to make a person beautiful. While it may be desirable to be fat in one society, to be thin may be preferred in another. Within a culture, however, there is usually a great deal of agreement about what is beautiful (Kopera, Maier, and Johnson, 1971). Box 10-4 describes a standard of height that people in American society call beautiful. Consensus about the standards of physical attractiveness may be less when the age, sex, and racial characteristics of the people rated and the judges are different (Cross and Cross, 1971). Table 10-1 summarizes the antecedents of attraction.

Table 10-1 Antecedent factors leading to attraction

Proximity We like those who are physically close to us.

Familiarity We like people we see frequently.

Similarity We like people who share our attitudes, values, and other characteristics.

Reinforcements We like those who reward us.

Complementarity We like those who have opposite traits that support our needs.

Physical attractiveness We are attracted to people who meet cultural standards of beauty.

Box 10-4

Tall is beautiful

Height is an important standard of attractiveness at least for men in American society. An important principle of date selection is that the man should be taller than the woman (Berscheid and Walster, 1974). Among teenagers who are concerned about their heights, girls are afraid of growing too tall and males are worried about being too short (Stolz and Stolz, 1951).

A man's height may be related to occupational success. A survey of graduates from the University of Pittsburgh revealed that male students who were six feet two inches or over garnered starting salaries 12.4 percent higher than graduates who stood less than six feet tall (Feldman, 1971). When presented with information about two job candidates who were equivalent in all respects except that one was six feet one inch tall and the other was five feet tall, only about 1 percent of college recruiters would have hired the shorter man.

The amount of time and money spent on cosmetics, clothes, aerobics, sweat suits, running gear, Nautilus equipment, and other health and beauty aids indicates the degree of importance that people place on physical attractiveness. Diet and exercise books are regularly among the top ten bestsellers on the nonfiction book charts. Large numbers of people, especially college students, regularly "pig out" on junk foods, pizza, and beer, then make themselves regurgitate to avoid gaining weight. A health hazard for ballerinas is anorexia nervosa. Richard Simmons and slim, vigorous females grace the television screen. The ideal female figure has changed from hourglass to athletic, slim, and rather straight. Middle- and upper-class college females appreciate men with tight buttocks (Beck, Ward-Hull, and McLear, 1976). The youthful look is the standard of beauty even for older people who, like the hero of Oscar Wilde's *Picture of Dorian Gray,* may try to look young all their lives. Surgery may remove wrinkles, uplift breasts, tighten buttocks, remove fat, or do almost anything else to help a person achieve a desired physical appearance.

Self-perceptions of physical attractiveness

Are people generally egocentric about their attractiveness? Do physically attractive people perceive themselves as more attractive than other people? Are females more concerned about physical attractiveness than males?

Tentative answers to these questions were obtained from a survey of undergraduates attending Johns Hopkins University (Rand and Hall, 1983). Coeds were found to be more sensitive about their physical attractiveness than were male students. Furthermore, the self-perceptions of coeds corresponded closely to ratings by judges, while the self-perceptions of males were unrelated to the perceptions of judges.

Another survey of college students indicated that they thought physical attractiveness was not important in forming friendships but was important for serious romantic relationships (Miller and Rivenbark, 1970). Yet, when college students were asked to rate the most important factors in choosing a date, they chose personality and character over "looks" (Tesser and Brodie, 1971).

Freshmen at the University of Minnesota were rated by other students for physical attractiveness. In addition, measures were obtained of their attitudes, intelligence, and personality (Walster, Aronson, Abrahams, and Rottman, 1966). These students were then randomly paired and attended a "welcome week" dance. The students thought they had been paired by a computer dating process. At intermission students were

People spend effort, time, and money to enhance or maintain their physical attractiveness. How does physical attractiveness relate to self-image and cultural standards. Are you more attracted by a beautiful person than by one that is less so?

asked to indicate how satisfied they were with their dates. It was found that the sole determinant of how much students liked their dates was physical attractiveness. Examination of social skills, intelligence, personality, and attitudes indicated that these had no relationship to the Minnesota students' desires to date their partners again or to how much they liked their dates.

If everyone desires a physically attractive romantic partner, do you think a person given a choice would always approach the most attractive other person for a date? Or, do you think that people tend to match up so that they are about equal in attractiveness? In an investigation of this question, a laboratory version of the "Dating Game" was devised (Huston, 1973). College students were given pictures of several students of the opposite sex and were asked to choose which one they would like to ask for a date. Although flashbulbs simulated picture taking in another part of the laboratory, the pictures actually used had been previously taken and rated for physical attractiveness by judges. The subjects also were rated for physical attractiveness. When students were assured that whoever they chose would agree to a date, they tended to choose the most attractive partner, irrespective of their own attractiveness. When subjects were assured whether their offer of a date might be accepted, however, they chose members of the opposite sex who matched their own level of attractiveness.

The **matching principle** is supported also by field studies. For example, a positive correlation was found between increasingly deeper romantic involvement and similarity in physical attractiveness among sixty-seven couples first paired by a Los Angeles dating service (Folkes, 1982). Judgments of the physical attractiveness of married couples indicated greater matching than would be expected by chance (Price and Vandenberg, 1979). The matching principle also extends to same-sex friendships. Ratings of photographs of twenty-four pairs of male and female friends indicated a significant matching in terms of physical attractiveness (Cash and Derlega, 1978).

Figure 10-3 Ratings of mental adjustment and prognosis of future adjustment of physically attractive and unattractive patients. *Note:* High numbers (on a 7-point scale) indicate better evaluations.

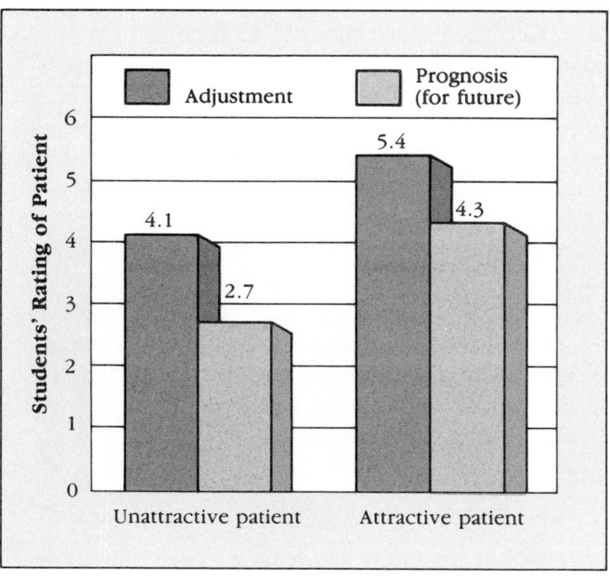

Box 10-5

Physical unattractiveness and psychopathology

Indirect evidence linking mental illness to appearance was obtained by comparing a sample of female psychiatric patients with coeds on a college campus and women at a shopping mall. The patients were less attractive on the average than were the other women (Farina, Fischer, Sherman, Smith, Groh, and Mermin, 1977). Negative correlations were found between the attractiveness of hospitalized female mental patients and the severity of their symptoms, their length of stay in the hospital, and the number of visits by outsiders. A second study showed that ratings of photographs from high school yearbooks of psychiatric patients established that they were less attractive than others of the same sex directly adjacent to them in the yearbooks (Napoleon, Chassin, and Young, 1980).

Not only are people who are unattractive more likely to have some diagnosed psychiatric disorder, but they are also more likely to be perceived as psychologically disturbed whether they are or not. Students listened to a taped interview between a psychologist and a person alleged to be a patient. They also were shown a slide of the patient, who was either physically attractive or unattractive. As can be seen in Figure 10-3, students rated the unattractive patient as more disturbed and less adjusted, and as having a poorer prognosis than the attractive patient (Cash, Kehr, Polyson, and Freeman, 1977).

These findings are only suggestive, but their implications, if confirmed, appear to contradict a major conclusion reached by researchers of attraction: "Physical attractiveness is an important variable only in the initial stages of interaction and its influence decreases rapidly with the weight of additional information about the person" (Berscheid and Walster, 1974, p. 205). For some people, their lack of attractiveness or some form of physical stigma may keep other people at a distance so that normal relationships never get to the point where other factors become more important.

Consequences of physical attraction

In general, people react positively to physically attractive people (Berscheid and Walster, 1978). On the other side of the coin, however, is the evidence that physically unattractive people may be treated negatively or shunned altogether by others (Goffman, 1963; Jones, Farina, Hastorf, Markus, Miller, and Scott, 1984). Unfavorable reactions from others can be psychologically disturbing, particularly when the individual has done nothing to deserve such treatment.

In the job market, personnel consultants recommend higher starting salaries for physically attractive interviewees (Jackson, 1983). Although attractiveness may help men in their climb up the organizational ladder, it helps women only to an intermediate level of management and thereafter is a hindrance to advancement (Lips, 1981). Unattractive people have been rated as less suited for jobs of high status (Unger, Hiderbrand, & Maden, 1982). The evidence examined in Box 10-5 also indicates that unattractive people are perceived as more apt to display pathological symptoms.

Stereotypes of physical attractiveness

There is a general stereotype about physically attractive people, at least among college students. Attractive people of both sexes are believed to have happier marriages and to be kinder, more interesting, more sexually responsive, and better in character than less attractive people (Dion, Berscheid, and Walster, 1972). Teachers perceive attractive children as more intelligent, expect them to perform better (Clifford and Walster, 1973), and give them higher grades (Felson, 1980) than children who are not as physically attractive. The relationship between physical attraction and the attribution of desirable traits is shown in Figure 10-4.

Does the stereotype that to be beautiful is to be good have any truth to it? Like most stereotypes, there is a tendency for the group typified to fit the overall picture generally, although any particular individual may not. Expectations of success in social situations are positively correlated with the physical attractiveness of a person (Abbott and Sebastian, 1981). In other words, the more attractive people are, the more self-confidence they manifest. Physically attractive females report having more dates than unattractive ones, but the same relationship was not found among men (Berscheid, Dion, Walster, and Walster, 1971). Attractive college coeds report being in love more often, engaging in more petting, and experiencing more sexual intercourse than less attractive women (Kaats and Davis, 1970). Spontaneous phone conversations with a stranger showed that physically attractive people are perceived as more likable and socially skilled even when no visual information is available to the judges (Goldman and Lewis, 1977).

Figure 10-4 Ratings of the personality characteristics of persons of varying physical attractiveness present to subjects in photographs.

Source: Based on "What is beautiful is good" by K. Dion, E. Berscheid, and E. Walster, 1972, *Journal of Personality and Social Psychology*, *24*, 285-290.

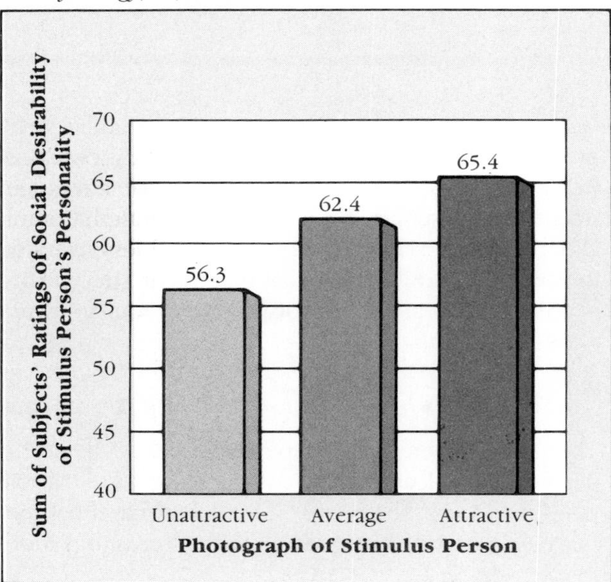

A self-fulfilling prophecy appears to be responsible for the above behavioral differences (Sussman, Mueser, Grau, and Yarnold, 1983). Physically attractive people are approached more frequently by other people; this social experience allows physically attractive people to gain social skills and bolster their self-esteem through positive interactions. Less attractive people may have fewer social contacts, and relative isolation may prevent them from developing social skills.

There is a kind of irradiation that flows from a physically attractive person. To be seen with a beautiful woman or a handsome man increases the romantic partner's social desirability ratings. In one demonstration of this radiating effect of beauty, subjects were briefly introduced to a young man who was sitting next to a female (Sigall and Landy, 1973). The female was either attractive or unattractive and the man was said to be linked romantically to her or not to be associated with her at all. The subjects were then asked to rate the man on a series of personality characteristics in terms of how much they thought they would like him. When the man was romantically associated with the woman, an attractive partner led to more positive impressions of him but an unattractive one detracted from his social desirability to the subjects. When the woman was a stranger, however, her physical attractiveness had no effect on the social desirability ratings of the man. Essentially the same results were obtained in reactions to a woman accompanied by an attractive or unattractive male companion (Sheposh, Deming, and Young, 1981). As is described in Box 10-6 on p. 296, women may suffer from comparison with a strikingly beautiful other woman, however. Table 10-2 summarizes the many effects that physical attraction has on the reactions of people.

Theories of attraction

A number of minitheories have been offered to explain why people like or dislike one another. Among these explanations are reinforcement, exchange, gain-

Table 10–2 The effects of physical attraction on the reactions of others

BENEFITS OF BEING ATTRACTIVE	COST OF BEING UNATTRACTIVE
1. Get more dates	1. Has fewer dates
2. Perceived as successful	2. Has fewer friends
3. Seen as emotionally stable	3. Seen as more maladjusted
4. Receive better grades in school	4. Seen as more responsible for accidents
5. Receive higher starting salaries	5. Perceived as less suitable for high status jobs
6. Less likely to be found guilty in jury trials	6. Receive less sympathy from others after a misfortune
7. Believed to be happier than other people	7. Perceived as more depressed than other people
8. Believed as children to be more intelligent than other children	
9. Believed to have more socially desirable personalities	

loss, depth, and balance theories. These theories are not mutually exclusive, and each may be partially correct.

There is some evidence in favor of and against each of these theories, suggesting that a better, more integrative theory is yet to be developed.

Reinforcement theory

We like those who reward us. A **principle of secondary reinforcement** states that we like people who are associated with pleasant events and dislike those who are connected with unpleasant events (Lott and Lott, 1972). On the basis of this principle, if on a first date the restaurant is terrific and the movie is fantastic, your partner would have to be a complete clod not to produce a favorable impression.

Research has demonstrated that when good things happen to people they like others more than when bad things happen (cf. Byrne, 1971). For example, when subjects were given extra credit for an experiment, they liked their partner better than when they were not (Griffitt, 1968). A benign cycle of interactions may occur. Rewards induce liking, liking leads to expectation of rewards, which in turn encourages frequent interaction; if further rewards are obtained, further increments of attraction are probable. Research has shown that more frequently rewarded children liked their two companions more than children rewarded less often (James and Lott, 1964). An adult who provided reinforcements when expected was liked more than one who delayed in providing them (Lott, Aponte, Lott, and McGinley, 1969). Thus, people associate magnitude, frequency, and immediacy of rewards with liking.

Feeling uncomfortable in the presence of a stranger also may generate dislike. College students, who had been asked to volunteer to help a doctoral student finish his dissertation, were placed in small cubicles controlled for temperature and humidity (Griffitt, 1970). Students in comfortable cubicles indicated more liking for the doctoral student than did students in hot and humid cubicles.

Consistent with the notion that "when you smile the whole world smiles with you but when you cry, you are alone," is a study that manipulated the moods of subjects by showing them a movie (Gouaux, 1971). *Good Old Corn,* a Warner Brothers comedy, produced laughter, positive feelings, and liking for a stranger, but *John F. Kennedy 1917-1963* by Twentieth Century Fox produced sadness, depression, and less liking for a stranger. These findings indicate that strong emotional states create at least temporary liking or disliking for any stranger who is nearby. Whether someone likes or dislikes you may have nothing to do with your behavior, but rather may be a matter of coincidence.

Exchange theory

The principle of reinforcement has been integrated with concepts from economic theory as a general model of human social behavior (Blau, 1964; Homans,

Box 10-6

Contrast effects: the Farrah factor

What effect does watching a very beautiful woman have on judgments of the attractiveness of other women? In one study bearing on this question, some male students at Montana State University watch an episode of "Charlie's Angels", a popular television show at the time. There were three beautiful actresses featured in the program, including Farrah Fawcett. A control group of students did not watch the show.

The interviewers then asked all of the men to rate the attractiveness of a woman whose photograph had been rated previously as average (4.1 on a 7-point scale). The men who had viewed "Charlie's Angels" rated the woman as less attractive than did the subjects in the control group. This contrast effect, where viewing beautiful women leads to judgments that others are less attractive, has been referred to as the "Farrah factor" (Kenrick and Gutierres, 1980).

A second study also showed an impact of the Farrah factor. Men who had just seen a slide of Farrah Fawcett rated a photograph of a female in a yearbook as less attractive than did men who were not shown the slide. Perhaps women should avoid movie dates or watching television programs that feature beautiful women if they want to appear beautiful themselves to their male friends.

1974). The metaphor of the marketplace is used to explain social behavior, including interpersonal attraction. In the old marketplaces of the Middle East and on New York City's Lower East Side, people would argue, haggle, and barter with merchants to get the best deal possible. In order to obtain something desired, the buyer had to give up something that the merchant desired, usually money. In the social marketplace, we exchange all kinds of values.

What trading rules apply to the marketplace of romantic relationships? In the United States, there are changes occurring in the primary rule that a man will provide security or prestige to a woman in exchange for her physical attractiveness and her provision of a home support system. In the 1960s, the dating attitudes of Iowa State undergraduates were in accord with this rule (Coombs and Kenkel, 1966). Males were most concerned about the physical attractiveness of their dates and coeds desired males who were intelligent, socially skilled, and had status on campus. An examination of females who were judged for their physical attractiveness from their high school yearbook pictures indicated that the more attractive women married men of higher status than did their less attractive classmates (Elder, 1969).

Huston and Cate (1979) have summarized the major principles of exchange theory. First, people are rational and hedonistic. This means that people make decisions based on both the probability and value of outcomes, and that they seek pleasure and avoid pain. Secondly, in the pursuit of reinforcements, people seek to maximize their rewards and minimize their costs, a tendency referred to as the **minimax principle.** Finally, people are interdependent for their outcomes and thus must exchange rewards to obtain them. If in these exchanges the rewards exceed the costs, each person will perceive the relationship as profitable and will like the other. If the result of social exchange is a net loss, then each will dislike the other (Jones, 1974). If someone takes something away from us by use of threats or force, then we gain nothing and what has been taken from us is a cost. We would dislike the coercive other person.

Thibaut and Kelley (1959) and Kelley and Thibaut

(1978) have grafted social comparison and exchange theories together. According to these theorists, each person develops an expectation for what he or she can gain from interaction with other persons. The level of outcomes that individuals feel they should receive in a relationship is referred to as the **comparison level** (CL). When a social exchange provides benefits exceeding the CL, a positive increment in liking should occur; but if benefits fall below the CL, there will be a decrease in liking. A person who has a history of positive relationships with others, and hence has been rewarded frequently, will have a higher expectation for rewards (high CL) than someone with a history of poor relationships with others (low CL). The result is that what is reinforcing for one person is not satisfactory to another.

People always are comparing their existing relationships to alternative possibilities. The **comparison level for alternatives (Clalt)** refers to the amount of reward available to the person from the best alternative to the current relationship. If current rewards exceed the Clalt, the relationship should be experienced as satisfying and it should be stable. If, on the other hand, a present relationship provides less profit than a person could expect from someone else, that person will leave the existing relationship. In the social marketplace just as at the shopping mall, we tend to seek the best bargain available. On the other hand, people often stay in what appear to be unsatisfactory and highly unrewarding relationships. According to Thibaut and Kelley, this "loyalty" can be understood as indicating that these people do not believe they could have more satisfactory exchanges with any other alternative people. We "settle" for the best we think we can get in terms of social relationships.

Exchange theory offers plausible explanations for why physical attraction and proximity are associated with attraction. Beauty is exchanged for other benefits,

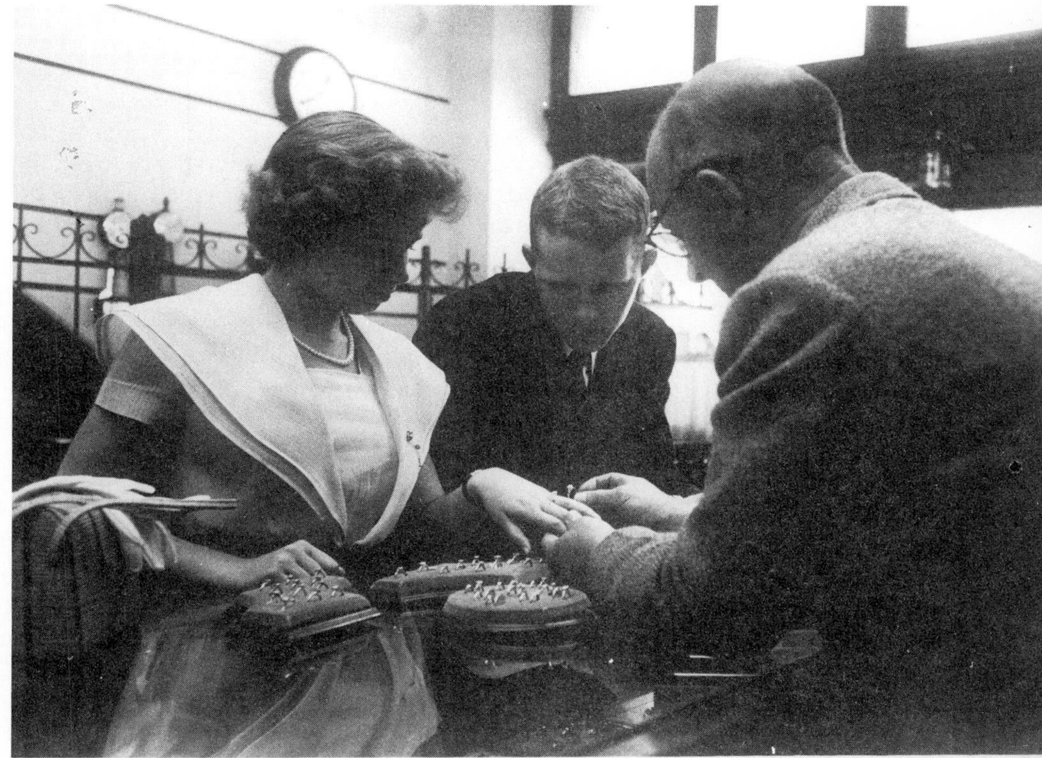

In the 1950s, a woman was expected to be physically attractive and to provide a home for her husband and children; a man was looked upon as the bread winner of the family. The couple was in love and their exchange was balanced. In Western culture today, our image of expected roles and balance of give and take is changing as women have moved into the work force, but romantic love is still the predominant basis of marriage.

and proximity provides opportunities for exchange. In addition, relationships can be examined for the ratio of rewards to costs. For example, married couples were asked how often they argued and how often they had sexual intercourse (Howard and Dawes, 1976). Twenty-eight out of thirty happily married couples reported making love more than they argued, while twelve unhappy couples reported fighting more often than engaging in sexual intercourse. When rewards exceed costs, people have good relationships. The slogan Make Love, Not War apparently has marital as well as political ramifications.

Kelley and Thibaut (1978) have argued that the more positive available alternatives a person has, the more control he or she will have in any particular relationship. Another way of saying this is that the more dependent a person is on another because of lack of available alternatives, the less power that person will have in the relationship. Thus, power is the opposite of dependence (Emerson, 1962). One way to achieve power in a romantic relationship is to try to induce the partner to become jealous by indicating the availability of alterative partners. A survey established that 31 percent of women and 17 percent of men reported inducing jealously (White, 1980). Furthermore, the more involved women were in a relationship, the more likely they were to try to induce jealousy. Perhaps the disadvantages women experience with regard to access to power resources in American culture (see Chapter 11) leads them to use this tactic for the purpose of redressing the balance of power.

Gain-loss theory

Never saw the morning till I stayed up all night.
Never saw the sunshine till you turned out the light.

Tom Waits

Staying up all night is exhausting and may be considered a cost, but the gain of seeing something beautiful is appreciated even more than if one had simply gotten out of bed early one morning. In the same way, we appreciate a sunny day after a week of rain. A **gain-loss theory of attraction** refers to the fact that people like someone more who provides positive evaluation if that person provided a negative evaluation beforehand (Aronson and Linder, 1965). A constant admirer may be taken for granted, but people who are selective in administering "strokes" are admired and liked. Social approval and bolstering of self-esteem are more valuable if given sparingly (Homans, 1961). Undiscriminating approval implies that the evaluator is not hard to please. The praise of a discerning judge is more rewarding. Getting an A from a tough professor is experienced as more rewarding than getting an A in an easy course.

In a demonstration of the gain-loss theory, students heard seven evaluations of themselves by a confederate (Aronson and Linder, 1965). These evaluations were either all negative, all positive, first negative and then positive, or first positive and then negative. The students liked the confederate least when evaluations shifted from positive to negative; they liked the confederate most when there was a shift from negative to positive evaluations. One implication is that we would strongly dislike a former friend who now criticizes us, and may develop a strong liking for a former enemy who now sings our praises.

It has been pointed out that we seldom actually experience a series of evaluations by a single person in everyday life (Berscheid, Brothen, and Graziano, 1976). Instead, we typically receive evaluations from two or more people more or less at the same time and about the same kinds of things. When students received a positive evaluation from someone who had previously provided negative evaluations, and a positive evaluation from someone else who had consistently given the students a positive one, they liked the consistent evaluator more than the inconsistent one. Although gain-loss theory may apply to situations where a single evaluator provides a set of evaluations, it does not apply to social triangles.

Development of relationships

One of the most powerful criticisms of research on attraction in social psychology is that it primarily focuses on attraction to or rejection of strangers. First impressions are important in the desire to affiliate and they may be a building block for the development of attraction, but development of a relationship takes time, experience, and a variety of interactions before a strong attachment occurs. **Depth theory** views attraction as a developmental process where two people engage in give-and-take and self-disclosure. They take on complementary roles and become increasingly involved in each other's lives over a period of time (Levinger and Snoek, 1972).

The first stage of a relationship is *unilateral awareness,* where each person is aware of the other but there is no interaction. You may judge that someone across the room looks interesting and worthwhile to approach, but that person may not appear to notice you. Some form of affiliation may then occur, but this second stage is one of only **surface contact.** Interaction between the two people exists only on a superficial level and behavior is guided by general social norms. A chat with a stranger on a bus, train, or plane tends to be fleeting, superficial, and predictable, but such surface contact provides information about whether we would like to know a particular person better.

Attraction research tends to focus on the level of surface contact. For example, you could reword the typical question used to measure liking by asking, "How much do you think you *would* like the other person?" The question well might be rephrased as, "Would you like to get to know the other person better?" Depth theory suggests that such antecedents of attraction as proximity, attitude similarity, and physical attraction may be important for the stages of unilateral awareness and surface contact, and hence are crucial in the development of relationships; but these initial factors recede and become less important as the relationship evolves into a deeper one.

Although many of our relationships will remain on a surface level, a few may evolve to a third level of **mutuality.** People share mutual self-disclosures of an intimate level not shared with others. This display of trust induces reciprocal disclosures by the other person in a spiral of increasing intimacy. During mutuality, the partners exhibit shared responsibility and concern of each other's welfare. In close relationships that have reached the stage of mutuality, both parties tend to be empathic with the feeling and reactions of the other, and they make accommodations for the needs and desires of the other person. In everyday language, we say the two people are committed to each other.

A related theory emphasizing the gradual deepening of relationships is **social penetration theory** (Altman and Taylor, 1973). According to their theory,

Biography

George Levinger

George Levinger, perhaps more than anyone else, has made researchers interested in attraction aware of the need to study the nature of deep relationships between people. His work on attraction began after he received degrees from Columbia University (B.S.), University of California at Berkeley (M.S.), and University of Michigan, (Ph.D.). He first became interested in deep relationships in the late 1950s when he was teaching at Western Reserve University in Cleveland. A local judge required couples with young children who were seeking a divorce to see a marriage counselor before finalizing their divorce. Dr. Levinger studied these couples and found that 20 percent of those who had counseling dropped the divorce petitions. Follow-up interviews indicated that most of the couples from these "saved" marriages were happy with their relationships a year after reconciliation. An account of this research and others can be found in *Divorce and Separation,* a book edited by Levinger and Moles (1979).

Dr. Levinger has continued to probe the dimensions of deep relationships at the University of Massachusetts in Amherst, where he is currently a professor of psychology. His research has convinced him that similarity or complementarity of attitudes and personality, factors that many social psychologists who study the development of liking between strangers in brief encounters consider to be the prime determinants of interpersonal attraction, are not so important. The factor that seems to be most important in the formation or dissolution of deep relationships, such as marriage, is the degree of commitment the partners make to each other. Lack of commitment is often associated with the dissolution of a relationship. Dr. Levinger presented his perspective on relationships in an influential book, *Attraction in Relationships,* coauthored with J. Snoek. In the future, Dr. Levinger desires to extend his research on attraction and conflict between people to an understanding of the relationships among nations.

our personalities can be conceptualized in terms of a series of circles within larger circles. The outermost circles contain information that is accessible to many other people, such as a person's age, profession, religion, and so on. The innermost circles contain private and sensitive information known primarily to the individual and not easily obtained by others. The deepening of a relationship involves the joint penetation of each other's innermost circles. The disclosure of intimate information cements the relationship and increases attraction. Table 10-3 provides a summary of theories of attraction.

Table 10-3 A summary of four major theories of attraction

Reinforcement theory: We like those who reward us, and the greater the frequency and amount of reward, the more the liking.

Social exchange theory: People exchange values with one another. If values received are greater than costs, then we will like the other person; but if costs are greater than rewards, we will dislike the other person.

Gain-loss theory: We like those who bolster our self-esteem. Liking will be greater if positive evaluations follow negative or neutral evaluations than if they are constantly positive.

Depth theory: Relationships evolve from superficial to deep attachments. Mutual self-disclosures involve increasingly intimate information as people move toward increasingly deep relationships.

Love

Love is.

Gertrude Stein

Consider the multitude of ways the word "love" is used. "God is love" (I John 4.8). We "love" our parents, siblings, friends, animals, and humanity; yet, we have our "one true love." Solomon (1981) noted the extraordinary ways in which people think of "love."

> Adults dismiss it as adolescent. Adolescents are embarrassed by it and deride it as childish. Children are bored by it. Therapists try to cure it. "True" men regard it as feminine. Feminists attack it as oppressive. Radicals demean it as frivolity. Frivolous people see it as absurdly serious. Christians call it "profane." Libertines mock it as "pious." Biological realists accept it as "Nature's way of telling us what to do." Social realists tolerate it as Western society's slippery slope to marriage. Businessmen sell it. Consumers voraciously buy it. (Master Charge and Visa are not accepted.) Cynics sneer at it, a nasty gloss over timid sexual lust. Puritans are appalled by it, a timid gloss over nasty sexual lust. Self-styled romantics, of course, think it's "divine," but they make such fools of themselves that they only confirm what everyone else suspected all along—that romantic love is like a disease, perhaps "incurable." (p. xix)

The complex and mysterious nature of love and the associated taboos related to sex have until recently deterred social scientists from its scientific study. Even politicians have expressed skepticism about the ability of science to understand this phenomenon. In 1975 Senator William Proxmire of Wisconsin conferred a Golden Fleece Award, symbolizing a waste of federal tax dollars, to the National Science Foundation for issuing an $84,000 research grant to Elaine Walster and Ellen Berscheid to study love. The senator expressed that no amount of investigation could lead to an understanding of love, and even if it could, it would be undesirable because the mystery of love is essential to it. As he said in a press release, the "National Science Foundation (should) get out of the love racket. . . . Leave that to Elizabeth Barrett Browning and Irving Berlin" (Walster and Walster, 1978, p. viii). Many social psychologists disagree with Senator Proxmire and think the study of love can add much to our understanding of human behavior.

Measuring Love

How do I love thee? Let me count the ways.
Elizabeth Barrett Browning

Rubin (1970) developed a paper-and-pencil scale that has gained general acceptance as a valid measure of love. He asked students at the University of Michigan to respond to thirteen items related to various aspects of love. Some of these items are shown in Table 10-4. A second scale designed to measure how much they liked others also was given to these students. Although this study indicated that liking and loving are on a continuum of some sort, they are clearly distinguishable by people. Liking represents a less intense feeling of similarity with another person than does loving, and

Table 10–4 Sample items from Rubin's Love and Like Scales

Love Scale
1. I would do almost anything for ________ .
2. It would be hard for me to get along without ________ .
Like Scale
1. Most people would react very favorably to ________ after a brief acquaintance.
2. ________ is the sort of person whom I myself would like to be.

Source: From "Measurement of romantic love" by Z. Rubin, 1970, *Journal of Personality and Social Psychology, 16,* pp. 265-273. Copyright © 1970 by the American Psychological Association. Reprinted by permission of the author.

admiration and respect are more typical of liking than of loving.

Three components of love were measured by the thirteen-item scale: (1) caring, (2) attachment-dependency, and (3) intimacy. **Caring** refers to the desire to help the other person, particularly when it is needed. **Attachment** refers to the desire to affiliate or be with the other person, a kind of emotional dependence. **Intimacy** consists of empathy, trust, self-disclosure, and interpenetration with the other person.

The dating couples who had scored high on Rubin's Love Scale were more likely to gaze into each other's eyes, and to say that they were in love and that they would get married someday than did couples who had scored low on the scale. Six months later, it was more likely that couples were still together if they scored high on the Love Scale and if they strongly believed that love conquers all (romanticism). It is not surprising to most of us that respect, trust, caring, attachment, and intimacy should be related to commitment, love, and marriage, but the first stumbling steps in our scientific examination of this complex human relationship have been taken at least. Surely we will find out more about the nature of love and how to measure it in the future.

Passionate and companionate love

In Western cultures where romantic love has emerged historically as the predominant basis of heterosexual mating and marriage, it is common for young people to experience "puppy love," infatuations, and passionate love. This experience includes strong physiological arousal, an idealization of the partner, and passionate sexual attraction. Observations of other cultures indicate that passionate romantic love does not exist everywhere. Indeed, marriages are often arranged by families or as a form of barter (Lévi-Strauss, 1967). These marriages involve all the ingredients of love, including caring, attachment, and intimacy. Passionate love would be too exhausting for a long-term relationship, and successful marriages occur when passionate love evolves into a more stable but less intense form. A distinction can be made then between passionate and companionate love (Berscheid and Walster, 1978).

Passionate love "is a wildly emotional state: tender and sexual feelings, elation and pain, anxiety and relief, altruism and jealously coexist in a confusion of feelings" (Berscheid and Walster, 1978, p. 177). The Latin origins of the word passion (*(passio)* carried the meaning of agony. Popular music also notes that passionate love is not always pleasant as in Joan Baez's rendition, "Love is just a four letter word." Typically, the object of love is idealized as Mr. or Ms. Wonderful. However, passionate love diminishes over time. "The history of a love affair is the drama of its fight against time" (Geraldy, 1939, p. 7). The day by day routine of

Relationships evolve from initial attraction to mutuality. When two people become mutually involved, they share in each other's lives. They grow together, are concerned for each other's welfare, and are committed to each other.

After passionate involvement has disappeared in a relationship, do people become bored with each other? The answer is sometimes, as with the couple here. But often passionate love evolves into companionate love in a marriage, the couple becomes good friends and feels comfortable with one another even in performing mundane activities.

living and the compromises that must be worked out between people whose lives are intertwined bursts the fantasy bubble that lovers have constructed. The idealized picture of the other is flawed by dirty socks, warts, and clashing interests.

Schachter's two-factor theory of emotions (see Chapter 2) has been applied to the understanding of passionate love: "To love passionately a person must first be physically aroused, a condition manifested by palpitations of the heart, nervous tremor, flushing and accelerated breathing" (Berscheid and Walster, 1971, p. 47). Once this complex of feelings is labeled as passionate love, the person will have an authentic experience of love. Arousal may be triggered by any number of environmental events but usually will be attributed to the heterosexual partner. People whose lives contain a rich variety of adventures might therefore be expected to be more romantic because they would experience more arousal than those of us who live more placid lives. Perhaps this is one reason why so many love affairs seem to characterize the lives of celebrities.

In the movie *My Dinner with Andre,* the title character states that two strangers traveling on a plane might mistake their fear of a crash with love. Some indication of this kind of misattribution process, which is the basis of a theory of passionate love, has been demonstrated in an experiment (Dutton and Aron, 1974). Males crossing a swaying suspension bridge above a 250-foot gorge in British Columbia were interviewed by an attractive female as they stepped off the bridge. The respondents were shown a picture of a young woman, who was covering her face with one hand, and asked to make up a story about her. They were then given a questionnaire to fill out. The female interviewer gave each respondent her name and phone number and invited them to call if they were interested in learning more about the study. As compared to a control condition where respondents were obtained after they crossed a concrete bridge just a few feet over a stream, the men crossing the suspension bridge made up stories with more sexual imagery and were more likely to call the female interviewer. These differences did not occur if the interviewer was a male. Although these results suggest support for the misattribution theory of passionate love, we must exercise caution in interpreting them because in subsequent studies, the same results have been difficult to obtain.

One group of researchers reported four successive failures to replicate Dutton and Aron's results (Kenrick, Cialdini, and Linder, 1979). In another study, results opposite to what a misattribution theory would predict were obtained (Riordan and Tedeschi, 1983). Male undergraduates were told that they would receive high or low shocks. This information was intended to arouse high or low levels of fear. Either a female was present when fear was induced or the subject was alone. According to misattribution theory, the presence of a female when the male subjects were aroused should lead to an enhanced judgment of her attractiveness. However, as is shown in Figure 10-5, the female confederate present in the high fear condition was rated as less attractive than in the other conditions. This finding is consistent with the reinforcement theory; that is, we tend to dislike those whom we associate with negative experiences (Riordan and Tedeschi, 1983).

Although people often think that love is forever, the evidence regarding the time span of passionate involvements is sobering. A survey of college students who had been dating for more than six months, 75 percent on a "steady" basis, showed that two years later almost 45 percent of the couples had parted company (Hill, Rubin, and Peplau, 1976). The major

Box 10-7

Women and men in and out of love

There is a commonly held stereotype that women are more romantic and emotional than men. If this common belief is correct, we might expect women would fall in love sooner and suffer more from the dissolution of a relationship than men would. The evidence indicates that just the opposite is true. Men report falling in love faster than women (Kanin, Davidson, and Scheck, 1970). Twenty percent of males as opposed to 15 percent of females reported falling in love by their fourth date. By their twentieth date with the same partner, over 40 percent of the women but only 30 percent of the males were still unsure about whether they were in love.

A similar pattern exists for ending relationships. While males tend to remain in deteriorating relationships, females are more apt to terminate affairs (Hill et al., 1976). Men report feeling more lonely, unhappy, and depressed than women when affairs terminate. Men are three times as likely as women to commit suicide following the termination of a passionate love affair (Walster and Walster, 1978).

Men have a more idealistic view of love while women are more realistic. In a survey of college students, men more often agreed with such sayings as, "True love lasts forever" and "True love leads to almost perfect happiness," and women more often subscribed to statements such as, "It is possible to love two people at the same time" and disagreed with "There is only one real love for a person" (Dion and Dion, 1973).

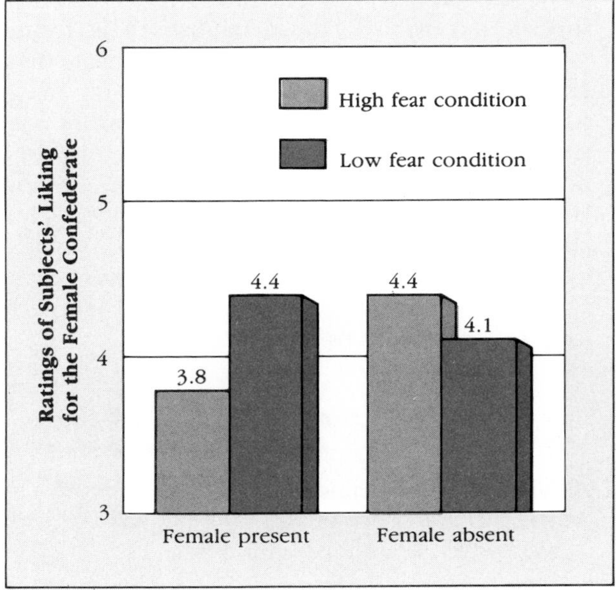

Figure 10-5 Attraction of subjects to female confederate in high and low fear conditions. *Note:* A female confederate was liked least when she was with a subject experiencing a high level of fear.

Source: Based on "Attraction in aversive environments: Some evidence for classical conditioning and negative reinforcement" by C. A. Riordan and J. T. Tedeschi, 1983, *Journal of Personality and Social Psychology*, *44*, 683–692.

reason given for the dissolution of relationships was boredom. Differences in approach to romanticism between the two sexes are described in Box 10-7.

Companionate love is an affectionate, caring relationship involving warmth, empathy, and shared experiences. The two people feel quite comfortable with one another (Berscheid and Walster, 1978). They have an intimate relationship in terms of the intensity of their feelings for one another and the degree of their attachment, but most of the time they are good friends and companions.

Permanent attachments between heterosexual couples typically evolve from passionate to companionate love. A survey of married couples suggests this kind of change over time (Cimbalo, Faling, and Mousaw, 1976). Rubin's Liking and Loving Scales were given to these couples. The love scores were negatively correlated with length of marriage, indicating that romantic love declines with years together. The liking scores, however, did not diminish with time. Although passion appears inevitably to decrease with length of attachment, affection need not decline (Walster and Walster, 1978).

The Romeo and Juliet effect

The more the flame is covered up the hotter it burns.

Edith Hamilton

In Shakespeare's *Romeo and Juliet,* two teenage lovers desire each other even though their families are engaged in a feud. Parental rejection of suitors may serve only to fan the flames of passionate love. Because of their unpredictable nature, affairs often meet with resistance from those who think one or the other of the lovers, blinded by passion, is acting irrationally. In addition, young people often ignore differences in religious or ethical beliefs by falling in love with someone from a very different family background.

Research indicates that parental interference may be counterproductive (Driscoll, Davis, and Lipetz, 1972). Couples who were either dating seriously or who were married were interviewed regarding parental interference and also were asked to respond to the Love Scale. The intensity of reported love was found to be greater the more parents tried to intervene. In other words, parental interference does not quench the flames of love, but instead fans them. This "Romeo and Juliet effect" still was present several months later in follow-up interviews. A finding from another study indicated that mixed-religion couples who had been going together less than eighteen months had higher love scores than couples from the same religious background (Rubin, 1974). For couples going together for more than eighteen months, the pattern was reversed, however. Thus, the Romeo and Juliet effect may be restricted to short-term relationships.

Summary

Humans are social animals who need the company of others and who suffer when isolated for extended periods of time. The need to affiliate with others is heightened when the person experiences anxiety. People who are anxious apparently need to make social comparisons with other people facing similar situations. Loneliness occurs when a person feels dissatisfied with the quality of his or her interpersonal relationships.

Many factors are involved in the development of attraction between two people, including proximity, attitude similarity, physical attraction, and complementarity of needs. People like those who are nearby and with whom they frequently interact, who share similar attitudes and who are as physically attractive as they are, and who have interests, abilities, and values that complement their own.

Several minitheories have been offered to explain why people are attracted to one another. Reinforcement theory states that we like those who reward us. Social exchange theory proposes that interactions involve costs and gains and that we like other people when our exchanges with them yield "profits," that is, where rewards exceed costs. Gain-loss theory contends that positive evaluative feedback from others, especially when it is discerning rather than indiscriminate, bolsters self-esteem and increases liking. Depth theory emphasizes the evolution of relationships from superficial contact to intimate mutual self-disclosures.

Liking and loving appear to be qualitatively different. Love may be a many splendored thing, but research has begun the task of trying to measure it and subject it to scientific scrutiny. A distinction has been made between passionate and companionate love. Passionate love is intense, turbulent, not always pleasant, filled with idealism, and rather short. Companionate love is less intense, but involves caring, attachment, and intimacy and is a more stable basis for long-term relationships.

Glossary

Affiliation Interacting with other people.

Alone The absence of other people; may be experienced as pleasant or unpleasant.

Attachment A strong desire to be with another person.

Caring A desire to help another person, especially when it is needed.

Companionate love A long lasting form of love based on companionship; involves mutual admiration and caring rather than the stronger emotions associated with passionate love.

Comparison level (CL) The level of outcomes people expect in interactions with others; outcomes greater than the CL lead to liking and outcomes below the CL lead to decrements in liking.

Comparison level for alternatives (Clalt) The amount of reward available to a person from the best alternative to the present relationship.

Complementarity A principle of attraction based on the idea that opposites attract; the traits of each person in an intimate relationship are different and fulfill the needs of the other.

Depth theory Liking is a gradually deepening process as people over time become increasingly involved in each other's lives.

Emotional loneliness A type of loneliness that occurs when existing relationships lack the depth and intimacy a person desires.

Gain-loss theory of attraction Providing positive evaluations gains more liking from target people if positive evaluations follow negative ones than if they are consistently positive.

Intimacy A deepening mutual feeling of trust, empathy, and self-disclosure between two people.

Law of attraction A precise mathematical relationship indicates that as the proportion of similar attitudes between two people increases, the more they will like one another.

Loneliness An unpleasant feeling resulting from a person's dissatisfaction with the quality of his or her relationships with other people.

Matching principle The hypothesis that people choose dating partners who match their own level of physical attractiveness.

Mere exposure effect The reliable finding that people like a stimulus the more often they are exposed to it.

Minimax principle A major assumption of exchange theory that people always act to maximize rewards and to minimize costs.

Mutuality A deep level of attraction in which reciprocal intimate self-disclosures are made.

Passionate love A highly volatile form of romantic and sexual love characterized by extremes of emotion, ambivalence of feelings, and unpredictable shifts in moods.

Principle of secondary reinforcement A well-established principle of learning; as applied to attraction, it states that we like people who are associated with pleasant events and dislike those associated with negative events.

Social loneliness A type of loneliness that occurs when a person has a few very close friends but desires a wider range of friends.

Social penetration theory A view that intimacy increases with gradual mutual penetration of each partner's personality.

Surface contact Interaction is often guided by social rules and constraints rather than by personal feelings.

Recommended Readings

Hendrick, C., & Hendrick, S. (1983). *Liking, loving and relating.* Monterey, CA: Brooks/Cole.
A recent review of research on all aspects of attraction written in a style appropriate for undergraduate readers; also contains material on in-depth relationships and sections on marriage, separation, and divorce.

Huston, T. (Ed.). (1974). *Foundations of interpersonal attraction.* New York: Academic Press.
This has remained the most readable and comprehensive source book of theories of attraction for the last decade; required reading for all serious students of attraction.

Walster, E. H., & Walster, G. W. (1978). *A new look at love.* Reading, MA: Addison-Wesley.
A highly readable treatment of this most elusive of topics.

We are all partly male and partly female.

Virginia Woolf

The woman's cause is man's. They rise or fall together.

Alfred Lloyd Tennyson

11
Male and female: social and sexual behavior

The challenge of equality for women

In June 1983 a crew of five astronauts were rocketed into orbit aboard the space shuttle *Challenger*. After thirty-six manned American space missions, including six shuttle flights, the launching of yet another shuttle would hardly seem special. Yet, there was something different about this thirty-seventh flight that became the focus of intense international media attention. One of the astronauts was a thirty-two-year-old former child tennis prodigy who had a doctoral degree in physics. The young physicist-astronaut was a woman. As the first female American astronaut, Sally Ride became a symbol of feminine emancipation and a model of achievement for all females in society. Her success in a predominantly male-oriented program was testimony to how much progress women have made in a male-dominated society. Some of the other pathbreaking women of the past fifteen years are listed in Table 11-1.

There were times when the press appeared to hold on to traditional stereotypes about women, but reporters and commentators treated Sally Ride as an exception. It was as if she was not really a female, at least not like most other females. For example, in various interviews Ms. Ride was asked if she planned to wear a bra in outer space and if she cried when she had personal problems (*Newsweek,* 1983). No one asked the male astronauts whether they wore jockey shorts in space

Table 11–1 Some recent firsts for women in the United States

1971	First Women Senate Pages
1972	First Woman Rabbi
1973	First Women Miners
1976	First Woman Episcopal Priest
1981	First Woman Supreme Court Justice
1983	First Woman Astronaut
1984	First Woman to Graduate First in Class at U.S. Naval Academy
1984	First Woman to be nominated as Vice-President

Source: Based on The longest war: Sex differences in perspective by C. Tavris and C. Wade, 1984, San Diego, CA: Harcourt Brace Jovanovich.

Sally Ride and fellow crew members posed aboard the shuttle *Challenger* in space. As the first female American astronaut, Ms. Ride symbolized women's progress toward equality in a male-dominated field. Do you think there are inherent differences between men and women or are observed differences attributable to sex-role stereotypes?

or whether they ever shouted in anger at their loved ones when facing personal problems. Obviously for Sally Ride and for each and every one of us, being male or female has a profound influence on the way people perceive and react to us.

In this chapter we will focus on the impact that being male or being female has on our social and sexual encounters. When psychologists discuss a person's awareness of being either female or male, they use the term **gender identity.** Most cultures have developed different expectations about how males and females should act. The appropriate actions prescribed for the sexes are referred to as **sex roles.** When individuals accept the sex roles their society prescribes and the belief that the sexes are different in fundamental and perhaps unchangeable ways, they are exhibiting **sex-role stereotypes.** Although sex-role stereotypes are pervasive in American society (as well as most other places in the world), the degree of documented differences between males and females is small.

Sex-role stereotypes

Women are wiser than men, because they know less and understand more.

James Stephens

Charm is a woman's strength, just as strength is a man's charm.

Havelock Ellis

Can you solve the following riddle? A father and son are driving down the road when all of a sudden the father loses control of the car and it crashes into a telephone pole. The father is killed instantly and the son is severely injured. The young man is rushed to a hospital where the emergency medical team determines that he will require immediate surgery. A well-known surgeon is called in to perform the operation. Upon arrival at the operating room, the surgeon looks at the boy and says in anguish, "I can't operate on this boy. He is my son!" Who is the doctor?

If you guessed the surgeon was the young man's stepfather, godfather, or natural father who had given him up for adoption, your answer is incorrect, and you do not win the trip to Hawaii. When fifty college students were given this riddle, only seven guessed the correct answer (Goldberg, 1974). The surgeon was the injured youth's mother.

The reason many people find this riddle difficult is that the role of surgeon (at least in the United States) is almost always associated with being male. Most cultures stereotype males and females in particular roles and behaviors. People have preconceptions about how a member of each sex expresses emotions, the values that guide their behavior, and how they relate to other people. These preconceptions can serve as guides or scripts for people about how they *ought* to behave. A cycle develops in which stereotypes become prescriptions, and members of each sex actually may come to act in the expected ways (Skrypnek and Snyder, 1982).

Research indicates that men and women often are perceived as typically at opposite extremes on many dimensions. Men are perceived as strong, independent, objective, logical, ambitious, competitive and strong, while women typically are characterized as passive, submissive, dependent, illogical, gentle, and weak (Broverman, Vogel, Broverman, Clarkson, and Rosenkrantz, 1972; Rosenkrantz, Vogel, Bee, Broverman, & Broverman, 1968). These sex-role stereotypes were similar for groups of people differing in religious, economic, and educational backgrounds.

In addition to showing that most people shared stereotypes of men and women, there were differences in overall evaluation of the sexes. Characteristics associated with the masculine sex-role stereotype were rated more positively than traits associated with the feminine sex-role stereotype. It is more positive to be strong, logical, and independent than to be weak, illogical, and dependent. In general, the traits rated most positively for men were those related to competence, while positive traits associated with women included warmth and expressiveness.

Mental health practitioners might be expected to be more enlightened than the general population and hence less likely to form stereotypes based on sex. Yet when psychiatrists, clinical psychologists, and social workers were asked to choose traits that characterize a healthy adult male and a healthy adult female, they stereotyped each sex just as nonprofessional people did (Broverman, Broverman, Clarkson, Rosenkrantz, and Vogel, 1970). A healthy male was described as independent, logical, and competent; a healthy female was described as emotional and submissive. When another group of mental health practitioners were asked to characterize a healthy adult without reference to gender, the traits chosen were those used in sex-role stereotypes of a healthy male. In contrast, the traits chosen to describe a mentally ill person were quite similar to those typically included in stereotypes formed of women.

Are sex-role stereotypes changing?

During the 1970s and 1980s, the women's movement has been and continues to be a powerful political and social force in the United States. With the widespread publicity obtained by advocates of women's rights and equality of the sexes, do you think that sex-role stereotypes have diminished in recent years? The answer provided by research is both yes and no. Some features of the traditional stereotypes have moderated, but others still persist.

One study comparing the attitudes of individuals in 1964, 1970, and 1973-1974 indicated a sharp decrease in acceptance of the traditional role given to women in American society (Mason, Czajka, and Arber, 1976). Over the ten years surveyed, subjects expressed an increasing belief in equal opportunities for men and women in the workplace and an equitable division of labor in the home. This "raised consciousness" may have leveled off, however. Students at the University of Texas in Austin had their attitudes toward women measured in 1972, 1976, and 1980 (Helmreich, Spence, and Gibson, 1982). Although there was a liberalization of attitudes toward women between 1972 and 1976, there was little further change between 1976 and 1980. Indeed, there was a slight shift toward more traditional beliefs among women between 1976 and 1980.

Another recent study showed the surprisingly strong degree to which people believe that there are fundamental personality differences between males and females (Ruble, 1983). Subjects rated fifty-four adjectives in terms of how much each applied to the typical male and the typical female. For fifty-three out of the fifty-four items, the ratings of the typical male (e.g., active, aggressive, dominant) were different than the ratings of the typical female (e.g., emotional, un-

Box 11-1

Changing sex-role stereotypes in popular magazines

An indirect method of determining whether the way people perceive the sexes has changed over the years is to examine how portrayals of males and females have changed in popular magazines. A **content analysis** was carried out on a sample of nonfiction articles published in two popular women's magazines: *Redbook* and *Ladies Home Journal* (Geise, 1979). Content analysis is a research technique by which the frequency or patterns of particular words are measured in written publications. Articles appearing between 1955-1965 were compared with those published during the period 1966-1976.

The comparison of articles failed to show an abandonment of the traditional sex role, but it did indicate that the articles written between 1966-1976 exhibited an increased tolerance for alternative, nontraditional roles, such as full-time careers for women. As compared to the 1955-1965 period, which portrayed women in a traditional fashion, the 1966-1976 period showed less discussion of women who needed to be sheltered or protected, an increase of emphasis on the importance of careers for women, and a greater acceptance of the idea that husbands and wives should share similar roles. Thus, two magazines that many people associate with unequivocal support for the traditional female sex role have shown significant liberalization in the way they portray women.

derstanding, gentle). This stereotyping occurred in both sexes with 85 percent agreement between male and female subjects.

Given the mixed nature of the evidence, we cannot safely conclude that sex-role stereotypes have diminished during the last fifteen years. Although the degree of acceptance of sex-role stereotypes apparently did diminish during the 1970s, the most recent evidence suggests a trend toward tolerance of both traditional and liberated roles for women in the 1980s. This acceptance of different lifestyles is reflected in the mass media (see Box 11-1).

Psychological differences between the sexes

Man differs from women in size, bodily strength, hariness . . . as well as in mind.

Charles Darwin

Unquestionably there are physiological differences between males and females. Men tend to be taller, heavier, and stronger than women; women may have more endurance than men and are less likely to suffer from physical disorders, disease, and death. There is some tentative evidence that the brains of women and of right-handed men may be organized differently, perhaps because of hormonal differences that occur early in life (Bryden, 1979). These biological factors may contribute to variations in abilities and behaviors of the two sexes.

There is controversy surrounding the identification of **sex differences.** In what actual ways, if any, do the sexes differ? Those who wish to break the chain of domination by men over women are motivated to deny that there are any sex differences. In addition, there is scientific dispute about conclusions reached on the present state of evidence. One very influential review of thousands of studies concluded that only four differences have been strongly established (Maccoby and Jacklin, 1974): females were superior to males in verbal ability, and males were superior in quantitative and visual-spatial abilities. Males also have demonstrated to be more aggressive than females.

A decade later, evidence continues to support the

four differences between the sexes. It now seems clear, however, that there are also differences in attributions of success and failure, in conversation patterns, and in nonverbal behavior.

The sexes and cognitive abilities

A review of studies examining the performance of males and females on standardized intelligence tests indicated no difference between the sexes (Maccoby and Jacklin, 1974). Although there is no overall difference in global intelligence, significant differences in types of specific abilities have been found. Females are often superior in verbal and linguistic ability, and males usually perform bettter than women on quantitative and spatial-perceptual tests. These differences are established in adolescence and continue throughout the adult years.

If you are planning to go on to graduate or professional schools, you will in all likelihood have to take an aptitude test called the Graduate Record Examination (GRE). A survey of the verbal GRE scores for 1973-1974 showed that females scored about ten points higher on the average than did males (Hoyenga and Hoyenga, 1979). The reverse pattern was true for quantitative scores during the years 1969-1972 with males outperforming females by a substantial margin. Males attained an average score of 545 out of a possible 800, while the average for females was 468. These latter results are consistent with similar sex differences established on a wide range of standardized math tests. Again, we advise you to be cautious when using such information to make judgments or decisions about any single individual. The differences between the sexes typically are smaller than those within each sex (Frieze, Parsons, Johnson, Ruble, and Zellman, 1978).

The catch-22 facing females is well illustrated by reactions to their performances in language use. Despite the fact that females have a demonstrated superiority in verbal ability, the identification of a female with a piece of writing leads observers to rate it less positively than if the same writing was identified with a male. This was demonstrated in a study where students were asked to evaluate the writing style, persuasiveness, and competence of journal articles (Goldberg, 1968).

Identical articles were presented for evaluation to all students; however, half of the students were told that the authors were male and the other half were told that the authors were female. Subjects perceived the author as more competent and evaluated the articles more positively when they believed the author to be a male. Just another example of male chauvinism? Not in this case! The subjects were female college students. The experimenters did not investigate whether the female subjects' biases were greater, lesser, or the same as those of males.

In another study, both male and female college students evaluated the quality of an article allegedly written by a male, a female, or an author whose sex was not identified (J. T. McKay). The article was evaluated less positively when the students believed it to be written by a female than when they believed it was written by a nonfemale (male or unidentified) author. There were no differences between male and female students in this evaluative bias against females (Paludi and Bauer, 1983). Sexism is not manifested only among males.

The sexes and perceptions of success and failure

In Chapter 4 we learn that there is a widespread tendency for people to claim credit for successful performances and to deny responsibility for failure. Comparisons have shown that the sex of subjects affects the magnitude of these self-serving biases. Males more strongly attribute success to their own ability, but females tend to view success as due to luck, an external factor. Females interpret failure as due to their lack of ability, but males view failure as due to bad luck (Wallston and O'Leary, 1981).

These differences in attributions for success and failure established among college students also exist among school children (Nicholls, 1975). When girls failed, they said it was because they lacked ability, but males attributed failure to bad luck. Boys also tried harder after failure than did girls.

These sex differences in attribution biases may explain why women feel less competent than men and appear to be less concerned about achievement than men. Indeed, it has been reported that females have lower self-esteem and are less confident about being successful in the future than are men (Maccoby and Jacklin, 1974). A vicious cycle may be involved. Women are socialized to believe that they are inferior in ability to men. They are uncertain about their ability to be successful, so when they fail, they assume it is because of their poor ability, and so on. Men are socialized to be confident of their abilities, and when they fail, they assume it must be due to something beyond their control, hence they remain confident and continue to strive for success.

If women are not confident that they can perform successfully because they believe they lack the required abilities, they might prefer situations where the outcomes depend upon chance or luck. Men, on the other hand, would prefer situations requiring skill. These hypotheses were investigated in a field study at state and county fairs in Indiana (Deaux, White, and Farris, 1975). People were observed playing games that primarily involved skill or chance. The skill games required players to throw a coin in a dish, toss a ring on a bottle, and stand a soda bottle up with a fishing pole. The luck games were bingo, bouncing ball (where the player guessed on which color a bouncing ball would land), and a mouse game. In the latter game, a live mouse was released on a spinning roulette wheel. When the mouse eventually escaped through a hole, the wheel came to a halt and the person who bet on that color was the winner.

Observation established that more males than females played the skill games. The greatest difference was noted in the bottle game, which was rated as requiring the most skill. Furthermore, males tried harder and played longer on the ring toss and coin dish games than did females. More women than men played bingo, indicating that females have some preference for games of chance. However, equal numbers of both sexes played the bottle or mouse games.

The "what is skill for male is luck for the female" principle extends to observer perceptions of performance. Subjects rated the performance by either a male or a female who did well on either a masculine or feminine task (Deaux and Emswiller, 1974). For the masculine task, both male and female observers attributed the male's success to his ability and the female's success to luck. Female observers subscribed to these perceptions just as strongly as male observers did. These sex differences were eliminated (but not reversed) for the feminine task.

Fear of success

There are two tragedies in life. One is not to get your heart's desire. The other is to get it.

George Bernard Shaw

One of the factors that may affect how women perform in achievement situations where success is involved is **fear of success.** According to this hypothesis, women in competitive situations experience anxiety about the negative consequences of success. There is a price for success, including jealousy and envy of others, social rejection, and loss of a feminine identity (Horner, 1968). These potential results of success are so unpleasant that many women may avoid those situations where they can achieve success.

In an influential dissertation study, Horner (1968) had undergraduate college women write stories about a first year medical student named "Anne," who found herself at the top of the class after first term finals. Horner also asked a group of male students to write stories about a male medical student named "John," whose credentials were identical to Anne's. While less than 10 percent of the stories written by males contained negative themes, almost 65 percent of the stories related by females had negative themes.

The fear-of-success concept has been criticized extensively and has not been supported by more recent studies. In one review of the fear-of-success literature, Zuckerman and Wheeler (1975) concluded that fear of success was unrelated to later academic performance or career choice. Even more damaging to Horner's theory was a follow-up study done with the subjects who had participated in Horner's original experiment. No differences in either educational or professional achievements were found between subjects originally classified as having great or little fear of success (Hoffman, 1977).

Another criticism of Horner's study is that the profession (medical) used in the story was male dominated. When students were merely told that a person (Judy or Joe) had succeeded in accomplishing a goal, there were no significant differences between males and females in fear-of-success imagery (Gravenkemper and Paludi, 1983; Tresemer, 1974). The balance of evidence indicates that there is no deeply ingrained fear of success among women. Rather, the level of fear of success among both men and women depends on the situation, with both sexes avoiding success if the consequences are sufficiently negative (Schaffer, 1981).

One of the more important effects of Sally Ride's achievement in being the first American woman to rocket into space is to reduce the fear in women of succeeding in male-dominated professions. Sally Ride may be represented as the **talking platypus phenomenon:** "It matters little what the platypus says, the wonder is that it can say anything at all" (Abramson et al., 1977, p. 123). When a female unexpectedly succeeds on a clearly masculine task, observers may view her as more competent than a male in the same situation (Abramson et al., 1977).

Sex differences in the ability to influence

The courage of a man is shown in commanding, of a woman in obeying.

Aristotle

A widely shared component of sex-role stereotypes is that men are more persuasive and influential, while women tend to be more conforming and easier to influence. Such a stereotype was revealed in a study where subjects read descriptions of attempts to influence made by a male directed toward a female or made by a female directed toward a male. The descriptions concerned either the female or the male trying to persuade the other to work overtime at a supermarket during the Christmas season (Eagly and Wood, 1982). Subjects expected that the female target would be more compliant to the male's influence attempts than the male target would be to the female's.

Research, carried out mostly by male social psychologists, frequently showed that females were influenced more in persuasion and conformity situations than were males. Many social psychology textbooks written in the 1960s and 1970s stated as fact that the sexes differed in their ability to influence and to be influenced (Tavris & Wade, 1984).

Alice Eagly and her associates have challenged this conclusion in a number of influential papers. A statistical analysis of a large number of previous studies did uncover a reliable difference between males and females. Although females were sometimes more likely to change their attitudes in persuasion and conformity studies than were males, the differences were often quite small or did not exist at all (Eagly & Carli, 1981). For example, in one study females were more influenced by a group's opinons than were males, but only when the members of the group maintained surveillance over the individual's opinions (Eagly, Wood, & Fishbaugh, 1981). This result suggests that females may be more socially concerned about the opinions of others in some situations.

The validity of research on sex differences in the ability to influence has been questioned because it has been discovered that the studies carried out by male researchers have showed women to be more conforming than the studies carried out by female psychologists (Eagly and Carli, 1981). Given that about 80 percent of this type of research has been carried out by men, there remains a real question of experimenter bias by researchers, perhaps by members of both sexes. It is likely that men are more easily influenced in some situations and women in others. Future researchers will need to establish the conditions and situations in which sex is associated with the ability to influence and susceptibility to influence.

Sex roles, dominance, and social power

The hand that rocks the cradle rules the world.

Old saying

The roles they played were based upon a script constructed around a few basic axioms. One was that men were created dominant and would always remain so because of their superior strength and superior wisdom, and because it was the will of God.

Elaine Morgan

It is difficult to measure dominance-submission patterns of behavior objectively. One reason is that a person may be relatively weak in one situation or group, but more powerful in another group or situation. Although a husband might have great influence at his place of business, he might be quite submissive to his wife at home. These difficulties notwithstanding, males score higher on paper-and-pencil measures of dominance than do females (Hoyenga and Hoyenga, 1979).

Both sexes perceive males as more powerful than females. Among 562 college students asked to identify the most powerful person they knew, 91 percent of the males named a male and 30.6 percent of the females listed a female (Lips, 1981). About one-fourth of each sex named their fathers as powerful people. Only 2.2 percent of the males identified their mothers as powerful, however, while 17.9 percent of the females did so. Indeed, the stereotypes of the male sex role involves traits instrumental in gaining influence and power—independence, self-assurance, competence, aggressiveness, and competitiveness. On the other hand, the stereotype for the female role includes traits related to submissiveness—warmth, nurturance, generosity, social sensitivity, and responsiveness.

When men and women were placed in a leadership position in a group and provided with six influence messages to persuade group members to work faster, striking differences were found (Johnson, 1974). Males frequently sent messages reflecting competence, essentially saying, "Here is the way to do it." Females tended to avoid competence messages and instead used persuasion based on helplessness or dependence, such as "Help me because I don't know how to do it." It was also found that supplication was associated with a loss of self-esteem, but influence based on competence raised self-esteem.

Dominance patterns also may be inferred from control over space. A survey established that fathers are more likely to have a special room in the home than mothers are (Altman and Nelson, cited in Frieze and Ramsey, 1976). The mother's room, if she has one, is more apt to be violated by others than is the father's room. Although fathers often have a "special chair" (like Archie Bunker), mothers seldom do.

Surveys asking who makes decisions in the home indicate a rather democratic process. For example, self-reports by 731 women from Detroit indicated that husbands make decisions about their jobs and the automobile, wives make decisions regarding their own work and the food, and the couple shares decisions regarding insurance, vacation, house, and doctor (Blood and Woolfe, 1960). In general, however, wives perceive themselves as having somewhat more power to make decisions in the home (even when the husbands think they themselves made the decision), and husbands believe power is equally distributed (de Lenero, 1969; Safilios-Rothschild, 1969). The catch seems to be that while husbands may make fewer decisions, they tend to make the decisions about more "important" family matters. Women, on the other hand, prevail when the task is repetitive, time consuming, and "unimportant," such as in the purchase of food and in the daily care of a child.

Factors that contribute to a man's power outside the home also increase his influence within it. Education, occupational status, and income are related significantly to the degree of control husbands have over decisions made in the home (Blood and Wolfe, 1960). As more and more women enter the job market and compete with men, they should have more resources to bring into the power struggle that takes place in every home. Women may therefore be required to take submissive roles less often than in the past.

The sexes and aggression

The emphases on commercials directed toward men during television presentations of boxing matches and professional football games imply that men enjoy watching these events more than women. Newspaper and television stories frequently have described a "football widow syndrome" as a cause of marital stress. Hubby watches football on weekends and Monday nights, a sport involving fierce body contact and many injuries to players, while his wife broods from boredom and lack of attention.

This differential interest in watching violence is matched by evidence that men also behave more aggressively than females. In ninety-two studies in which the two sexes were compared, males were more aggressive in fifty-two, females were more aggressive in five, and there were no differences in the remaining thirty-five studies (Maccoby and Jacklin, 1974). The tendency of males to be more aggressive than females emerges about the age of two and is reported widely across cultures. One anthropologist has been quoted as saying: "I don't know of any society where females do more aggressive acts than males or any society where females commit as much aggression" (Nelson, 1983, p. 6).

In the United States, males perform more acts of antisocial violence then females. Nine times more men than women are arrested for violent crimes. Men commit more murders, physical assaults, rapes, and armed robberies, but women are more abusive of children (Hoyenga and Hoyenga, 1979; Nelson, 1983).

Society has more tolerance for aggressiveness in males than in females. Aggression is appropriate or at least expected behavior by males, but it is inappropriate and punished when performed by females. Females may have the same degree of inherent aggressiveness as males, but such behavior is suppressed or inhibited because of the negative reactions of others. In other words, females must at least appear to be nonaggressive.

This impression management view of sex differences in aggression was supported when females displayed just as much aggressiveness as males in private, but not in public (Mallick and McCandless, 1966). In a competitive situation, females who were targets of aggression by males retaliated with weak shocks when an observer was present, but used stronger shocks when there were no witnesses present (Richardson, Bernstein, and Taylor, 1979).

The universality of sex differences in aggression suggests a biological explanation. As we conclude in Chapter 8, however, there is no solid evidence for biological roots to human aggressiveness. Although hormones, brain centers, and instincts account for much of the predatory and agonistic behavior of subhuman animals, the evidence that such findings can be applied to human beings is slender indeed. It is more likely that there are social and cultural reasons for those occasions when humans try to harm one another.

Some researchers have disagreed, however, with the suggestion that males are *always* more aggressive than females. A review of seventy-two studies that measured aggression showed that 60 percent failed to find sex differences in aggression (Frodi, Macaulay and Thome, 1977). The most reliable sex differences found were that males consistently admitted to being more aggressive than females and that males engaged in more physical aggression without anger. Males, it appears, are only *sometimes* more aggressive than females; the degree of difference in aggression exhibited by the sexes, when there is one, is small. That difference is related to environmental factors.

Heterosexual conversation patterns

The classic American male hero is depicted in popular fiction and in the movies as strong and silent. A Gary Cooper or Clint Eastwood gets the job done without saying much. Women are typically portrayed as more verbose and as having a natural penchant for endless talking and gossiping. Research on heterosexual conversations has not substantiated these stereotypes.

Analyses of male-female conversations in laboratory settings and in everyday life revealed that it is men who talk more often and for longer periods of time, while women frequently adopt a listening role and smile and laugh more often (Francis, 1979). A study of conversations in drug stores, coffee shops, and other public places revealed that in male-female conversations, males interrupt females more often than females interrupt males (Zimmerman and West, 1975).

These sex differences in conversation patterns may be explained in terms of a dominance hypothesis. By talking, interrupting, and choosing topics, males maintain control over conversations with females. Support for this dominance hypothesis was found in an analysis of the content of male-female conversations. Heterosexual conversations tended to focus on such "male" topics as the men themselves, sports, cars, and current events. Conversations between women tended to focus on topics such as relationship problems, food, clothing, children, and weight (Sherman and Hass, 1984).

Sex and personal space

Individuals maintain a *space bubble* around their bodies, and they keep all but their most intimate acquaintances outside this boundary. Approaches that violate this space bubble make the person feel uncomfortable. One study of personal space showed that male subjects reported feeling more uncomfortable at the approach of a male confederate than did female subjects who were approached by a female stranger (Barnard and Bell, 1970). Women tend to allow both male and female invaders to approach closer than males allow them (Harnett, Bailey, and Gibson, 1970).

The sexes also react differently to invasions of their space bubbles. When approached on a sidewalk, women move out of the way more frequently and sooner than men (Dobbs, 1972). Across a number of situations, women choose body postures that take up a minimum of space, while men tend to spread out their arms and legs (Frieze and Ramsey, 1976; Henley, 1973). One commentator summarized the findings by stating that "women contract and men expand!" (Lips, 1981, p. 98). In general, these findings tend to support a dominance hypothesis with men as more assertive and women as more deferent when interacting with the opposite sex. These behavior patterns presumably are based on socialization practices that focus on traditional norms about the proper sex roles of men and women.

We should emphasize that sex differences in the use of personal space have been found in only a minority of studies. One review of research (Hayduk, 1983) found clear sex differences in only 27 out of 110 studies (see Figure 11-1).

Sex differences in touch

Nancy Henley (1973) conducted a field study in Baltimore, Maryland, and observed who touched whom in naturally occurring interactions. Figure 11-2 shows that the greatest percentage of observed touches involved males touching females. Males were observed also to be the initiators of touch in intersex interactions at an airline terminal (Heslin and Boss, 1980).

What accounts for the greater tendency of males to initiate touch? Touching others can have many meanings, including affection, intimacy, and sexual interest. According to Nancy Henley (1973), touching others communicates status, power, and dominance. The greater tendency of males to initiate touching is reflective of the status and power that males exert in American society. It is the prerogative of individuals with higher status to initiate touch, but it is taboo for lower status persons to touch people with higher status without permission. In a description of behavior in hospitals, it was reported that "the doctors touched other ranks as a means of conveying friendly support and comfort, but other ranks tended to feel that it would be presumptious for them to reciprocate a doctor's touch, let alone initiate such contact with a doctor" (Goffman, 1967, p. 74).

Evidence supporting the hypothesis that touch frequently indicates a status differential includes data showing that older people initiate touch more than younger people (Heslin and Boss, 1980), that people in a higher socioeconomic bracket more frequently touch people who are in a lower bracket (Henley, 1973), and that people report being touched more by their bosses and co-workers than by subordinates (Henley, 1977).

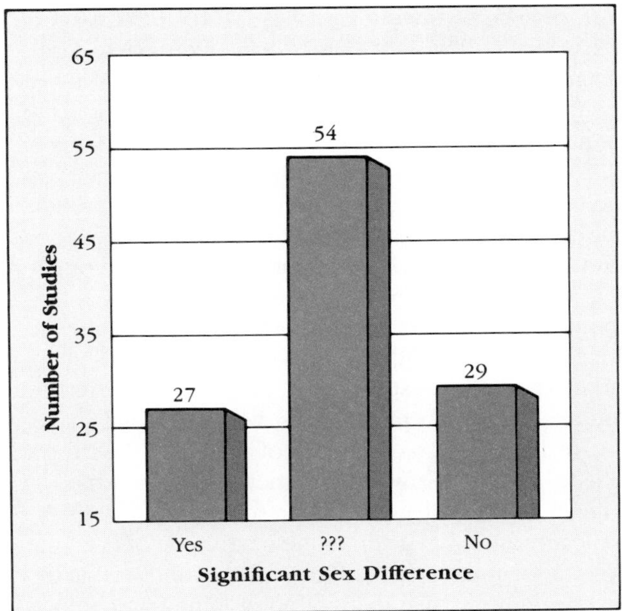

Figure 11-1 Sex differences in personal space.

Source: Based on "Personal space: Where we now stand" by L. A. Hayduk, 1983, *Psychological Bulletin*.

Evidence shows that men more often touch women than women touch men. Desire for affection, intimacy, sex, status, or social power can motivate someone to touch another.

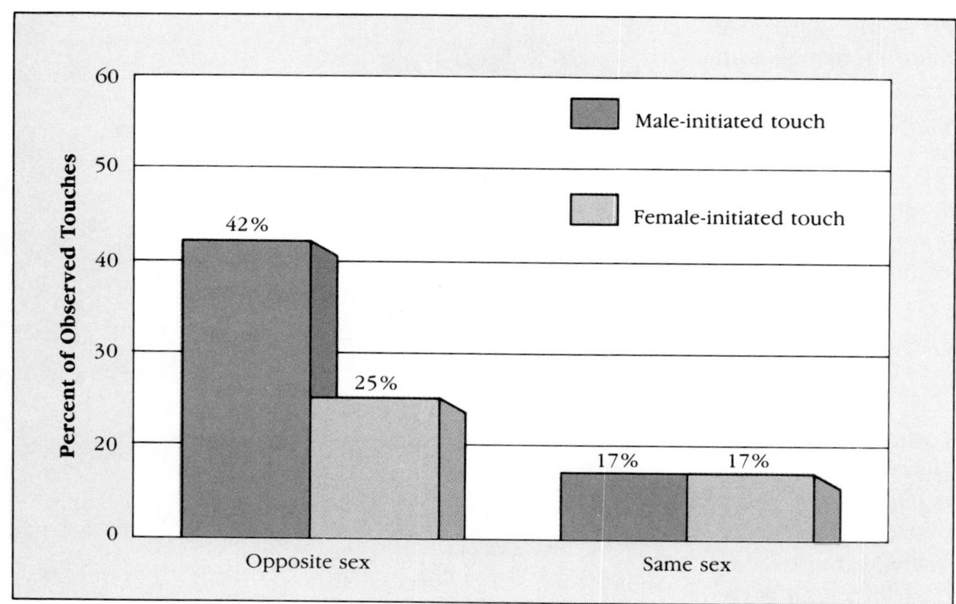

Figure 11-2 Sex differences in touch.

Source: Based on "Status and sex: Some touching observations" by N. M. Henley, 1973, *Bulletin of the Psychonomic Society*, *2*, 91-93.

Touch may have little to do with sex and may only appear to be sex linked because sex masks the more important factor: status differences. Indeed, some researchers have gone so far as to maintain that it is the lower status of women in American society that account for many of the sex differences we have discussed (Deaux, 1984; Eagly and Steffen, 1984; Eagly and Wood, 1982). The relatively higher status that males enjoy in a variety of situations gives them more self-confidence that leads them to be more aggressive, interrupt conversations, take up more space, exert more influence, resist pressures to conform, and initiate touch (Eagly, 1983). If the status and power interpretation of sex differences is correct, then we can expect that they will diminish as women gradually place themselves into more roles with greater status and social power.

Sex differences: conclusions and a word of caution

The findings of many studies indicate differences in behavior between the two sexes. We should exercise caution in interpreting sex differences of traits or behaviors. The differences found between males and females were based on group averages and not on the performance of any individual. A **fallacy of the average** refers to the mistaken tendency of people to make assumptions about particular individuals based on group averages without taking into consideration the number of people who fall above or below the mean.

Consider the example of height. Although males on the average are taller than females, there are numerous instances where a woman is taller than the average man and a man is shorter than the average woman. Just ask Susan Anton and Dudley Moore. Caution about making a fallacy of the average also applies to the psychological differences we present in this chapter. Madame Curie surely was more success oriented and analytical than most males, while William Shakespeare had greater command of language than most females. Talent of any kind has never been reserved as an exclusive privilege of either sex.

Recent attention given to the magnitude of even the best of documented sex differences has shown that the sexes are more alike than different in any psychological characteristic. The differences *within* the sexes on any given dimension are greater than the reported differences *between* the sexes. A reanalysis of data from experiments originally establishing sex differences in verbal, mathematical, and visual-spatial abilities showed that the sex of subjects accounted for under 5 percent of the variation in behaviors (Hyde, 1981). Indeed, the curves showing male and female performance in these dimensions greatly overlap, as can be seen in Figure 11-3. Although sex differences do exist, their size is very small and most probably attributable to cultural rather than biological factors.

Nonbiological explanations for sex differences

No convincing evidence exists to substantiate that biological factors account for the psychological differences found in experiments. The origins and nature of sex differences appear to be a product of culture, and anthropologists rather than psychologists probably will obtain answers about them. Nevertheless, some studies carried out by social psychologists indicate that gender identification may be affected by stereotypes conveyed in the mass media. These stereotypes are learned as a result of socialization practices of parents and other adults, and are quite variable across cultures. A proposal advocating a unisex personality, referred to as androgynous, having traits associated with stereotypes of both sexes has also been made.

Sex-role stereotyping in the mass media

Since the invention of writing, the printing press, and the electronic media, men have controlled mass communications for the most part. During the nineteenth century, some women adopted male pseudonyms in order to get their work published. For example, George Eliot, who wrote *Adam Bede, Middlemarch,* and other great novels, took a man's name, dressed as a man, and smoked cigars. Her real name was Mary Ann Evans. The bias is still so strong that Mary Shelley is more likely to be remembered as the wife of the poet than as the author of *Frankenstein.* When Barbara Walters became a co-anchor of a network television news program, the reaction was much the same as when Sally Ride rocketed into space.

Gender stereotypes are perpetuated and reinforced by the print and electronic media. Examination of children's books has uncovered that males are portrayed typically as active leaders, while more dependent females rely upon the braver, stronger masculine sex for their welfare (Weitzman, Eifler, Hokada, and Ross, 1972). While males strive to become president, females aspire to become mothers. Pictures of males were ten times more frequently seen than pictures of females. Even when animal pictures were seen, there were nearly one hundred times more male than female animals. Boys are depicted as doers and in-

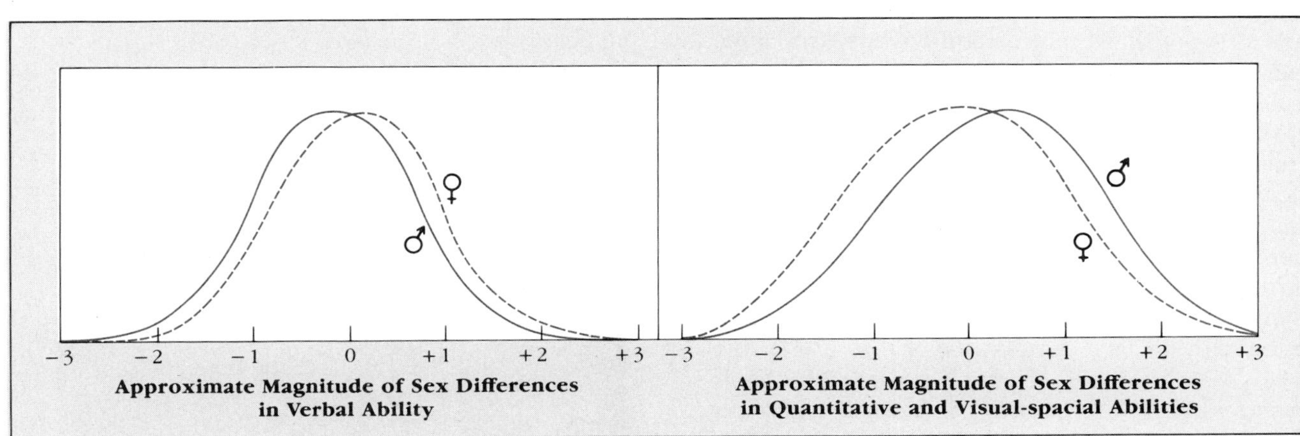

Figure 11-3 Magnitude of cognitive sex differences. *Note:* The mean for females is greater by .25 of a standard deviation. The mean for males is greater by .50 of a standard deviation.

Source: From "How large are cognitive gender differences? A meta analysis using ω and δ" by J. S. Hyde, 1981, *American Psychologist, 36,* p. 899. Copyright 1981 by American Psychological Association. Reprinted by permission.

"Will you have the babies now, too?"

ventors, while girls are observers and users of male inventions (Key, 1975). Although publishers are trying to change such stereotypes, a study conducted by the National Organization for Women showed a continuing bias (Unger, 1979). Children's books portrayed boys as strong, brave, and assertive, while girls lacked ambition, were fearful, and had interests in domestic activities, such as cooking and child care.

The full impact of electronic media on formation of attitudes and behavior is not known, but surveys have shown that children spend more time watching television than they do in school (Schaffer, 1981). Furthermore, television clearly presents traditional sex-role stereotypes in children's programs. There were twice as many male as female characters in these programs in the early 1970s (Sternglaz and Serbin, 1974). The males were assertive, effective and helpful; female characters tended to be weak, passive, and not very effective at getting things done. A similar pattern was found five years later (Feshbach, Dillman, and Jordan, 1979).

Traditional sex-role stereotypes are reflected also in commercial messages accompanying children's television programs. Boys appeared in more commercials advertising toys than did girls. There were more boys than girls in commercials representing both sexes, and girls typically were presented as more passive than boys (Feldstein and Feldstein, 1982). We might expect, given this differential treatment of the sexes, that children would internalize these implicit stereotypes and develop preferences for toys associated with their own gender. Some support for this expectation is presented in Box 11-2.

Adult television programs also present traditional sex-role stereotypes. Three-fourths of all leading characters are male (Schaffer, 1981). Males actively play sports, work hard, and assertively pursue the opposite sex, while females stay home, react to dominant males, and focus on seduction. When females do get out of the house, it is usually to shop, to eat dinner, or to visit a friend.

In sum, research on the mass media indicates that the portrayals of males and females are nearly identical to the widely accepted sex-role stereotypes that we discussed earlier. Whether mass media portrayals cause or just mirror existing societal attitudes is unclear from the evidence we have considered. Given the powerful influence that the media have in our

Children learn sex roles by observing adult models. Boys identify with men who lift weights because this is a predominately masculine activity. Women usually care for the family and home, therefore, girls identify with this feminine role.

Box 11-2

Letters to Santa Claus

The strength and pervasiveness of sex-role stereotypes among adults suggests that they originate in the socialization process. Examination of children's letters to Santa Claus revealed sex-related preferences for toys (Downs, 1983). During early December, grade school children between the ages of six and eight were asked by their teachers to write letters to Santa Claus telling him what they wanted for Christmas. As determined by personal interviews, only the letters of children who said they believed in Santa Claus were included as data. Boys requested masculine and neutral toys in about equal frequency, but they almost never chose feminine toys. Girls had a greater preference for neutral toys, a lesser preference for feminine toys, but they least desired toys stereotypically associated with boys. Sex-role stereotypes were apparently stronger for boys than for girls, but even at this very young age, most children showed a greater preference for toys stereotypically associated with their gender—guns for boys, dolls for girls.

daily lives, however, it would not be surprising if future research showed the media to shape the attitudes of the audience and also to reflect them.

Socialization and gender identity

The expectations and reactions of parents clearly are associated with the sex of a child. Parents perceive a day-old infant differently depending on whether the newborn is a male or female. Thirty, first-time parents were interviewed twenty-four hours after their children were born (Rubin, Provenzano, and Luria, 1974). Half of the infants were male and half were female. Physical examinations of the infants revealed no differences between males and females in muscle tone, color, reflex irritability, or size. Nevertheless, the parents, especially the fathers, perceived the boys as stronger, more alert, larger, hardier, and better coordinated than the girls. Dependent behavior is encouraged in infant girls but discouraged in infant boys (Lewis, 1972). Boys are also more often left alone than girls, even at eighteen to twenty-four months of age (Fagot, 1974).

Because play occupies such an important place in the lives of children, it has a critical role in the development of gender identity. Parents encourage different forms of play in girls and in boys. A study demonstrating this was carried out with six mothers who said they believed the following: At six months of age boys and girls are the same, and they would treat their own sons and daughters exactly alike (Will, Self, and Datan, 1976). They said they gave their sons dolls to play with and engaged their daughters in rough house play. These mothers were presented an opportunity to play with a six-month-old infant, who for half of them was identified as a boy (Adam) and for the other half as a girl (Beth). A doll, train, and fish were available as props. The mothers handed "Beth" a doll, but gave the train to "Adam."

A survey conducted in 1975 revealed that although mothers buy more toys than fathers, the purchases of both parents are equally likely to be associated with the gender of their child (West, 1976, cited in Cairns, 1979). Such differential treatment continues throughout childhood (Rothbart and Maccoby, 1966). The case study reported in Box 11-3 suggests that gender identification is more influenced by social than by biological factors.

Inappropriate sexual behavior by boys is more strongly discouraged than this behavior is in girls

Box 11-3

Sex change surgery and gender identification

An otherwise physically healthy male infant accidentally had his penis amputated during surgery when he was seven months old. After much soul-searching and consultation with medical authorities, the parents agreed to a plastic surgeon's recommendation that the child be "redesigned" as a girl. When the child was seventeen months old, his name, clothing style, and hairdo were changed to reflect a feminine gender. Several months later, surgery was performed to give the child female genitalia, but she was not given any special hormone treatments (Money and Ehrhardt, 1972).

The medical authorities, who monitored the child's progress and compared her behavior to that of an identical male twin, examined her annually. The little girl showed a preference for dresses, liked long hair and ribbons, and was tidier than her identical male twin brother. For Christmas presents one year, she said she wanted dolls and a doll house, while her twin brother wanted cars, a garage, and a gas pump. By age five (which is the last reported information), the little girl and her twin brother had different career aspirations. The girl wanted to be a teacher or doctor, and the boy wanted to be a policeman or fireman. Although the girl had been the dominant twin prior to the accident, by age five the boy had assumed dominance in their relationship (Money and Tucker, 1975). Given that the girl and her twin brother had identical genetic backgrounds, the conclusion we can draw from this case study is that social factors exert a powerful influence on the formation of gender identity.

Parents channel children's behavior in masculine and feminine directions. Boys are encouraged to play with toy guns, and girls are given dresses, makeup, and dolls.

(Fling and Manosevitz, 1972). Parents are more disturbed by sons who put on lipstick or dresses than by daughters who wear toy guns and cowboys hats. One explanation for these reactions is that homosexuality is much more common among males than females; therefore, parents believe it is necessary to channel boys' behavior in clearly masculine directions (Maccoby and Jacklin, 1974).

Segregation by sex is practiced widely in school and neighborhoods. Physical education classes and community sports activities separate boys and girls. For example, Pop Warner football, Little League baseball, and All American Girls softball teams recruit all males or all females. On the rare occasion when a girl joins a boys' team or vice versa, it generates enough interest to be reported by the national news media. Customs of dress, cosmetics, body posture, way of walking, and many other factors continue to emphasize differences between men and women. Jeans and other unisex fashions allow women to dress more in the custom of men, but men who wear dresses are still believed to be transvestites, unless they are from Scotland or dance for the New York City Ballet.

The sexes—cross-cultural evidence

Every culture makes some distinction between the roles of males and females. It makes a difference everywhere which gender identity you have. Just about all societies are patriarchical in structure. Men maintain dominance over women. In many instances, women are treated as property owned, used, and dispensed with or sold by men. The prestige associated with being male is transferred to the tasks they perform. If males do the weaving, then weaving is prestigious, but if women do the weaving, it loses importance (Tavris and Offir, 1977). In a New Guinea tribe in which women grew potatoes and men grew yams, yams were always chosen for important occasions (Mead, 1935). If, as it is sometimes said, women's work is never done, it is also the case that such work is usually thought to be tedious and beneath the dignity of men. A study of thirty-one societies showed that males dominated in domestic affairs in twenty-six. In all thirty-one of them, males had higher status and dominated in public affairs (Stephens, 1963).

In general, cross-cultural research has established that sex-role behaviors may vary considerably across societies, but men are given more importance than women and have greater power. Variations in gender identity and behavior suggest that sex roles are learned within specific cultures. The general dominance of males, however, may be associated with biological characteristics, particularly with respect to size, strength, and speed.

Sex-role styles and androgyny

It is not necessary to view gender-related traits of men and women as mutually exclusive. A person may learn to manifest feminine traits in some situations and masculine traits in others. A person who maintains flexibility of behavior, regardless of sex-role prescriptions is considered **androgynous.** An androgynous person may play an aggressive game of tennis, be competitive in business, yet display nurturance with a baby and tenderness with a lover. Androgyny combines the instrumentality of the traditional male role with the expressiveness of the female stereotype (Bem, 1974).

Biography

Sanda Lipetz Bem

Sandra Lipetz Bem was born in Pittsburgh, Pennsylvania, in 1944. Her early career aspiration was to be a clinical psychologist because she wanted to help parents to avoid making mistakes in raising their children. However, while taking courses at Carnegie Mellon University (CMU) aimed at fulfilling her desire to be a clinical psychologist Bem first became exposed to research. As a senior she took a psychology laboratory course and discovered that she liked designing and carrying out research so, she changed her career direction and obtained her Ph.D. in child psychology at the University of Michigan in 1968. She has since held faculty appointments at CMU and Stanford Unviersity and is now a professor of psychology at Cornell University.

Dr. Bem traces her interest in the psychology of women and adrogyny to her marriage to Daryl Bem in 1965. Before her marriage she really was unaware of "women's issues", but they became salient as the Bem's worked out the compromises of a two career marriage. She was surprised to discover that people assumed she would not attend graduate school when they heard she was getting married. Many people cast her into the role of "Sandy, the wife."

Dr. Bem became politically involved in feminist issues and devoted a great deal of time to making speeches about them. She soon realized that she could merge her political and scientific interests. The result has been Dr. Bem's pioneering research on adrogyny. The importance of her work was recognized when Dr. Bem was awarded the 1976 Early Career Achievement Award by the American Psychological Association.

In the future Dr. Bem is interested in investigating how children in American society come to view the world in terms of the dimensions of masculinity and femininity, a process she calls gender schema processing.

Box 11-4

What's in a name?

Labeling theory, discussed in Chapter 2, proposes that names, categories, or labels given to people may provide them with identities. Labeling someone as "crazy" may lead that person to act "crazy." Of course one label given to us sometimes before we are born is our name. Names are linked typically to gender identification. So, John is male and Jane is female. Some names, however, are ambiguous with regard to gender, such as Jamie, Robin, and Marion. One wonders whether Marion Morrison would have enjoyed such phenomenal success in his movie career if his name had not been changed to John Wayne.

Applying these considerations regarding names to the concept of androgyny led some psychologists to the hypothesis that people with non-ambiguous names or nicknames with respect to gender would be more likely to be androgynous.

There are three reasons why names might affect gender-related identities: (1) people with non-ambiguous given names or nicknames develop self-concepts skewed in the direction indicated by the label; (2) parents who give their children these names might raise them in a way reflective of the name they chose; and (3) other people may act toward the person in a manner suggested by the name.

The above reasoning led to a study of college students, who were given the BSRI (Rickel and Anderson, 1981). Their scores indicated no difference in percentages of androgyny between those with ambiguous (21 percent) and those with names clearly associated with gender (25 percent). More students with gender-ambiguous nicknames were androgynous (43 percent) when compared to students with nonambiguous nicknames (24 percent), however. What accounts for androdyny more in people with nicknames than in people with given names? One suggestion is that nicknames are *self-selected,* while given names usually are not. In other words, gender identity does not appear to be affected strongly by given names, contrary to expectations of labeling theory, but rather the individual adopts a name to fit his or her gender identity.

Bem has attempted to measure the degree to which people identify with a masculine, feminine, or androgynous sex role. The Bem Sex-Role Inventory (BSRI) contains twenty adjectives classified as masculine (e.g., independent, ambitious), twenty classified as feminine (e.g., compassionate, gentle), and twenty adjectives that can be identified with either sex (e.g., happy, truthful). Respondents are asked to indicate the degree to which each adjective describes them. People who score high in both masculine and feminine traits are considered androgynous. Testing of more than fifteen hundred Stanford University students indicated that about 50 percent conform to sex-role stereotypes, 15 percent were cross sexed, and 35 percent were androgynous (Bem, 1979). Research described in Box 11-4 suggests that a person's name may affect his or her gender identification.

Research has established that men sometimes display greater independence than women (Eagly and Carli, 1981). Although these differences are quite small, we might expect that people who measure high in masculinity or androgyny, regardless of actual gender, would display more independence when pressured by a group to conform than would people measuring high in femininity. In an investigation of this hypothesis, male and female subjects pretested on the BSRI were asked to rate the funniness of cartoons. The cartoons were selected on the basis of previous reactions by other people. Before rating each cartoon, subjects heard what they believed to be the ratings of other members of their group. These ratings were contrived to indicate that cartoons either were or were not funny, and were sometimes associated with a cartoon previously established as funny or not funny. Consistent with expectations, people of both sexes who scored high in masculinity or androgyny displayed greater independence of judgment than did subjects who scored high in femininity (Bem, 1975).

Androgynous people also can display behavior considered appropriate for females. Subjects who scored high in femininity or androgyny on the BSRI were more nurturant toward a baby and more sympathetic to a lonely college student than were subjects who scored high in masculinity (Bem, Martyna, and Watson, 1976).

Contradictory evidence also has been obtained. In a survey of over fourteen hundred college students, it was found that individuals scoring high in masculinity were more flexible, adaptable, and competent than students scoring high in androgyny (Jones, Chernovetz, and Hansson, 1978). Other contradictory findings may be attributable to some imperfections in the BSRI, which has been found to be more complex and to measure something other than the three sex types it was designed to identify (Hoyenga and Hoyenga, 1979). There also may be a bias built into the test, because men more often characterize themselves as androgynous than females do (Ruble and Higgins, 1976). In response to criticisms of the BSRI, Bem (1979) revised the scales to eliminate those items that were correlated with sex. She also removed several feminine items that had been found to be low in social desirability. This revised BSRI contains twenty items reflecting highly desirable characteristics of males and females, along with ten filler items not linked to sex-role stereotypes. It is too soon to evaluate the validity of this revised androgyny scale.

There is much debate about the ideal of androgyny and the apparent desire by some to eliminate gender differences completely in favor of a unisex society. The concept of androgyny appears to carry the burden of specifying what an ideal individual in American society should be like (Sampson, 1977). "Thus, it was good and wise and liberal to be androgynous and mental health was proposed to be synonomous with androgynous scores" (Deaux, 1984, p. 109). The proposal of personal ideals as scientific theory violates the traditional rules of scientific investigation discussed in Chapter 1. Although the notion of androgyny is provocative and challenges common sex-role stereotypes, the evidence frequently has failed to support Bem's theory (see Taylor and Hall, 1982 for a review).

Sexual behavior

There may be some things better than sex, and some things may be worse. But there is nothing exactly like it.

W. C. Fields

Sexual intercourse is clearly one of the most intimate and important of social behaviors. Yet, until relatively recently, it was considered taboo to study sexual behavior scientifically. Astronauts were circling the earth several years before Masters and Johnson (1966) described the physiology of the sexual orgasm. With no objective standards to judge their own behavior, people were left with unsystematic and oftentimes secretive ways of obtaining social comparison information. The taboos against studying sexual behavior were so strong that several college professors in the 1920s were dismissed for asking their students questions about their sexual experiences (Walster and Walster, 1978).

The controversial and pioneering work of Kinsey and colleagues gave scientific respectibility to the study of sexual behavior (Kinsey, Pomeroy, and Martin, 1948; Kinsey, Pomeroy, Martin, and Gebhard, 1953). Many long-held popular myths about sex have been exposed by this research. For example, a Victorian view was that males were driven by strong biological urges and needed frequent outlets for these powerful desires. It commonly was believed that women did not possess as strong a sex drive as men. Women were presumably more motivated by a desire to please men, participated in sexual relations out of a sense of marital responsibility, or wished to become pregnant (Hyde and Rosenberg, 1980.). The "discovery" of the female orgasm and the development of reliable birth-control devices not only has dispelled the Victorian view but, if anything, has revealed the female as having greater sexual capacity than the male.

The Kinsey studies

In the late 1930s Alfred Kinsey, a biologist at Indiana University, was assigned to teach a course in human sexuality. He immediately ran into a formidable problem; there was almost no good scientific evidence about human sexuality. To satisfy his own keen curiosity, Kinsey began an investigation of the sexual attitudes and practices of more than ten thousand people over a period covering more than two decades. Psychiatrists and sociologists carried out most of the previous scientific work on the topic, focusing their research on the various forms of pathology through case studies.

The detailed interviews with thousands of volunteers from the general population documented the practice of many "taboo" sexual behaviors, such as masturbation, extramarital sex, and homosexuality (Kinsey et al., 1948, 1953). Great care was taken to protect the anonymity of the respondents. To some extent, common sexual beliefs about differences between the sexes were substantiated. Men reported higher rates of premarital sex, extramarital sex, masturbation, and arousal as a response to viewing explicit erotic material. On the other hand, the data also served to dispel the myth that women are basically asexual. Although their activities were less frequent than men, the percentage of women who engaged in diverse sexual behaviors was much higher than anyone expected.

Nearly half of the women said they engaged in premarital sex compared to 85 percent of the men. Twenty-five percent of the women said they engaged in extramarital sex compared to 50 percent of the men. Nearly two-thirds of the women and 90 percent of the men said they had masturbated.

Many women reported failure to achieve orgasm during sexual intercourse, although those who masturbated said they could reach orgasm within three to four minutes. The problem seemed to be that about 75 percent of the men said they reached orgasm in less than two minutes after initiating coitus.

The data on homosexuality were little short of sensational, given the "closet days" of prewar America. Males had far more homosexual experience than did females. Four percent of the men and 1 percent of the women admitted to having a sexual preference for members of their own sex. More shocking to the general public was the fact that almost half of the men reported having experienced homosexual arousal at one time in their lives, and over a third reported one or more homosexual experiences.

The Kinsey studies received extensive criticism (cf. Hyde and Rosenberg, 1980; Rohrbaugh, 1979). It should be remembered that the respondents in these surveys were volunteers. In the 1940s people did not talk openly about their sexual experiences. It is likely that people who volunteered to disclose their most intimate experiences to a stranger (even though a scientist) were not representative of the general population. Indeed, critics contended that volunteers probably were more sexually active than the general population. As a result, the statistics may have vastly overestimated the frequency of many forms of sexual behavior. The respondents were overly representative of the middle and upper economic classes. The critics believed that biased sampling overestimated the degree of preference for partners of the same sex. Despite these real shortcomings, later studies tended to confirm the "ballpark figures" obtained by Kinsey (Rohrbaugh, 1979).

Have sexual practices changed?

The 1960s saw much ferment in America. The civil rights movement, demonstrations against the war in Vietnam, the widespread experimentation with psychodelic drugs, and changes in lifestyles represented what was called the "greening of America" (Reich, 1970). It was also generally believed that significant changes occurred in patterns of sexual behavior, sometimes referred to as the "sexual revolution."

The Playboy Foundation sponsored an extensive survey of sexual behavior in the United States almost thirty years after Kinsey's pioneering work (Hunt, 1974). Virginity among women prior to marriage declined over the three decades from 50 to 25 percent. While 85 percent of the men told Kinsey that they had engaged in premarital sex, almost all the men of the next generation said that they had lost their virginity before marriage. The overall rates of extramarital sex, reported by Kinsey as 25 percent for women and 50 percent for men, remained about the same. There was a significant change for women under twenty-five years of age, however. The extramarital rate for married women under twenty-five was about 10 percent in 1940 and 25 percent in 1970. There was a slight increase in the number of women (from 58 to 63 percent) and men (from 92 to 94 percent) practicing

Box 11-5

Perceptions of sex and aging

The youth orientation of America has perpetrated the myth that older people rapidly lose both their sexual interests and capacities. The view of older people as asexual beings is particularly true when people are asked about the sexual behavior of their parents. College students were asked to estimate how often their parents engaged in a variety of sexual activities, including intercourse and premarital and extramarital relations (Pocs and Godow, 1977). Their responses were compared to the data gathered by Kinsey about the generation of adults who were representatives of the students' parents.

Only 10 percent of the female students believed their mothers had experienced premarital sexual intercourse, but Kinsey's figures indicated about 50 percent. Fifty-five percent of the male students believed their fathers were virgins when they married, but according to Kinsey about 85 percent of married males reported having premarital sexual relations. Although the exact reasons for these sizable underestimations are not known, the researchers suggested that the incest taboo causes children to repress notions of their parents as sexual beings. Parents, in turn, avoid acting in an overt sexual manner in front of their children. This hypothesis leads to the expectation that children would underestimate the sexual activities of their parents as compared to other couples of the same age as their parents. Research has confirmed this expectation (Zeiss, 1982).

There are some physiological changes in the sexual organs with aging (Masters and Johnson, 1966), but there is no known age limit for people engaging in sex. Recent research on the sexual activities of senior citizens leads to three general conclusions: (1) sexual behavior among the elderly is a continuation of life-long patterns; (2) both sexes retain the capacity for sexual pleasure throughout life; (3) a decline in sexual activity among the elderly, especially females, is more often due to the lack of availability of a suitable partner because of death or illness than because of lack of interest or capacity (White, 1982).

We tend to underestimate the sexual activity of our parents and elders. Because we retain the capacity for sexual pleasure throughout life, sexual behavior among older people is a continuation of life-long patterns that they have established.

masturbation. The average duration for coitus had increased from two to ten minutes. The rate of homosexuality had not changed. These data indicate a significant change in sexual behavior, particularly by women, and might well be characterized as a "revolution." The evidence reported in Box 11-5 also dispels the myth that people lose interest in sex when they grow older.

Physiology of sexual responses

Freud's theory of psychoanalysis emphasized the central role of sexuality in human behavior and helped give respectability to the future scientific study of human sexuality. Freud claimed that women were capable of two kinds of orgasms—clitoral and vaginal. He indicated that clitoral orgasms occurred first and were associated with immature sexual functioning. As a woman matures and reproductive concerns become paramount, vaginal orgasms are experienced. These early pronouncements about female sexuality have incurred the wrath of feminist writers. Many women suffered from feelings of inadequacy because of their failure to attain Freud's standard of sexual maturity—vaginal orgasm (Hyde and Rosenberg, 1979; Unger, 1979).

A male physiologist and a female psychologist carried out a controversial research program to investigate the physiology of sexual responses (Masters and Johnson, 1966; 1970). Hundreds of couples engaged in a number of sexual behaviors in the controlled conditions of the laboratory. Precise measurements were obtained regarding physiological changes that occurred at all phases of sexual relations. Perhaps the most dramatic finding contradicted psychoanalytic theory. There was no vaginal orgasm! The evidence showed that orgasms are indistinguishable as to the source of sexual stimulation. Although the clitoris is the most sensitive part of the female anatomy to stimulation, many women can reach orgasm through the stimulation of other sensitive or erogenous zones, such as the breasts and the buttocks. Indeed, orgasms can be experienced through fantasy or dreams.

Masters and Johnson found that the stages of sexual arousal are similar in the two sexes and can be divided into four phases. During an initial *excitement phase,* there is increased blood flow to the genitals, erections of the penis and clitoris, as well as lubrication of the penis and vagina. In the *plateau phase,* muscle tension builds, heart rate increases, breathing quickens. The climax is reached during the *orgasmic phase* during which a rapid, extremely pleasureful discharge of tension is experienced. The heart rate increases dramatically, blood pressure goes up, males ejaculate seminal fluid, and women typically experience muscle contractions. The orgasmic experiences of men and women are different. Most men experience a single orgasm, after which they require some rest (called a *refractory period*) before they can achieve erection again. Women may experience several orgasms in a relatively short period of time. The *resolution phase* completes the sexual arousal cycle. The bodily processes gradually return to their quiescent states (Basow, 1980).

Reactions to erotica

Almost every major city in the world has a "porno" district. There are rows of triple "X" movie houses on Forty-second Street in Manhattan, peep shows and sex shops abound in Boston's "combat zone," and the "porno flicks" of Copenhagen are as famous as the "red light district" in Amsterdam. Sex is big business. The consumers of commercial sex are primarily males. Although male strippers have been popular among females, the reaction is not sexual arousal so much as amusement and hilarity. The popular view is that men are aroused sexually by viewing erotica, but women are not. Indeed, in Kinsey's studies, only 15 percent of women said they had been aroused by viewing erotica, while 50 percent of men reported erotica-induced arousal.

The sexual revolution of the 1960s apparently has changed the way women respond to erotica. In a laboratory study, male and female college students were shown slides and movies of explicit sexual behavior, including heavy petting and sexual intercourse (Schmidt and Sigusch, 1970). The majority of both sexes reported being aroused by the stimulus materials, and there were no sex differences in levels of arousal. A study obtaining both self-reports and physiological measurements showed that females were more aroused by material taken from pornographic books than were males (Heiman, 1975). While physiological indicators revealed this difference, self-reports did not. Perhaps women are less in touch with their sexual responses than males, or maybe they are more reluctant to admit experiencing arousal, particularly to male interviewers.

Do women respond most to erotica with themes of romantic love, and do men respond most to visual stimuli and casual sex? According to the available evidence, the answers to both of these questions is no. In a study examining these questions, male and female college students were shown erotic movies involving a couple engaging in oral sex and intercourse (Fisher and Byrne, 1978). Although all subjects saw the same film, descriptions about the nature of the relationship between the two people in the film were manipulated.

"Porno" flicks, peep shows, and sex shops line Manhattan's famous Forty-second Street. Commercial sex is a big business primarily attracting males, although females admit to being as aroused by such erotic material.

One group was told that the film was of a married couple having sex as an expression of love. A second group believed they were watching a film of a prostitute and customer. A third group of subjects were told that the couple had met at a party and were engaged in a casual sexual encounter. Both sexes were most aroused when they believed the film represented a casual sexual encounter, and there were no differences between the sexes in level of arousal.

Rape

Rape is a crime against the person, not the hymen.

Deena Metzger, The Rape Victim

Rape is defined legally as sexual relations without the consent of one of the participants. There were 81,000 reported forcible rapes in the United States in 1981 (Tavris and Wade, 1984). This is a underreported crime, however. The rate may be anywhere from three to ten times as large as indicated by official statistics. According to a recent FBI report, rape is the fastest growing violent crime. In 1979 there were nearly eighty-thousand rapes reported, an increase of 13 percent over the year before (Strong and Reynolds, 1982). Increased education about rape, feminist groups organized to facilitate the reporting of rapes (rape crisis centers), and changing attitudes among law enforcement officials may be a factor in the increase of *reported* rapes.

Although we tend to think of rape as an individual crime, about one-third of the rapes reported in United States cities (Amir, 1971; MacDonald, 1971), and in Denmark (Svalastoga, 1962) involved at least two rapists. In the United States, minorities are overrepresented among rapists who tend to be young and poor. Victims are usually of the same ethnic background as the rapists. Almost half of all rapes involved people who knew each other and occurred in the victim's place of residence. In a survey of more than a thousand rape victims, it was found that 41 percent of the rapists were strangers, 5 percent were relatives, 23 percent were acquaintances, 12 percent were dates, 3 percent were ex-lovers, 1 percent were lovers, and .4 percent were husbands (Bart, 1975). Attempted rapes are often carefully planned beforehand. Thus, the belief that most rapists act alone in a fit of lust is revealed largely as a myth.

The element of power and domination is present in most instances of rape (Brownmiller, 1975). Several anthropologists have documented cultures in which women sexually attack men in a hostile and violent manner with the apparent goal of establishing domination (Malinowski, 1929; Mead, 1935). To use the bodies of other people without their consent is to take away their freedom and to submit them to the rapist's will; that is, it enslaves the victim. By hurting victims, by making them cry in pain, and by humiliating them with sexual assault, the rapist establishes who is powerful and good and who is weak and bad. The rapist may achieve this power goal in heterosexual or homosexual rapes, inside or outside of prisons.

Some may view rape against women as a brutal way of maintaining a stereotype of women as inferior, weak, and helpless creatures (Strong and Reynolds, 1982). Eldrige Cleaver wrote a book in prison entitled *Soul on Ice.* In this book, he tells why he raped women:

> Rape was an insurrectionary act. It delighted me that I was defying and trampling upon the white man's law, upon his system of values, and that I was defiling his women. . . . I was very resentful over the historical fact of how the white man has used the black woman. I felt I was getting revenge. (p. 14).

Consistent with the power and humiliation view is the fact that rapes occur frequently in times of war and have become a mode of political torture (Mahoney, 1983; Strong and Reynolds, 1982).

Rapes sometimes occur during heterosexual dates. There are probably occasions when there is failure of communication or where no is believed to mean yes. Rapists commonly believe that women secretly enjoy rape (Gager and Schurr, 1976). None of the women surveyed on a college campus believed they would experience rape as pleasurable. Many believed, however, that some other women could be turned on by forced submission (Malamuth, Haber, and Feshbach, 1980).

Courtship practices in America apparently produce some confusion regarding cues indicating consent. A survey of 190 male students found that 53 percent had kissed a woman against her will, 61 percent placed a hand on a knee or breast despite protest, 42 percent removed or disarranged clothing of a resisting woman, and 15 percent reported engaging in intercourse without consent (i.e., technically committing rape). When asked what kind of coercion they had used, 70 percent said they used verbal persuasion, 11 percent used physical restraint, 35 percent ignored protests, and 3 percent said they had used physical aggression (Rapaport and Burkhart, 1978).

When sexual intercourse occurs during a date, it is sometimes a matter of subjective perceptions whether or not rape has occurred. When given a description of such an incident, college students related three factors regarding their judgment of rape: how much force was used, the degree of resistance offered, and when protests began. The greater the force used and the stronger the resistance, the more likely observers are to perceive the intercourse as a rape. If protests were made at the level of a French kiss, subsequent intercourse was more likely to be perceived as rape than if the protests did not begin until after all clothes had been removed (Shotland and Goodstein, 1983).

Common rape myths lead some people to believe that "only bad girls get raped" and that many women "ask for it" (Burt, 1980). Cashing in on these rape myths, defendants try to bring into court irrelevant information concerning the complaining victim's prior sexual history. Indeed, these defendants are often successful in reducing their own guilt in the eyes of judge or jury (Burt and Alben, 1981; Kalven and Zeisel, 1966; Pugh, 1983). A woman who was gang raped by four men in Boston was quoted as saying, "Everyone blamed me, even my boyfriend. They said, 'what did you do to cause it'." (Hirschfeld, 1983, p. 15).

While both sexes make attributions to the rape victim, the specific reasons for doing so tend to be different. For example, in one study men blamed rape victims for wearing provocative clothing and behaving in a seductive way, while women blamed the victims for being in the wrong place at the wrong time. In support of a **just world hypothesis,** which assumes that people believe in a world where all outcomes are deserved, Jones and Aronson (1973) found that a respectable rape victim was blamed more than one who was not respectable. The reasoning appears to be that respectable people suffer more, and the more people suffer, the more they must have deserved what happened.

There is no profile of a rape victim. Any female from the ages of three to ninety is a potential rape victim regardless of ethnic background, physical attractiveness, or mode of dress. Although the public often has images of rape occurring in back alleys or in remote and abandoned lots, the assault most often occurs in the victim's home or apartment (Chapman and Gates, 1978). There is no evidence to support the contention that rape is a victim-induced crime.

Summary

There is a widespread acceptance of stereotypes reflecting differences between males and females. Males are believed to be aggressive, dominant, independent, and logical, while females are frequently perceived as nurturant, dependent, and emotional. Actual sex differences are relatively few and small in magnitude. Although the similarities far outweigh the differences, researchers traditionally have focused on the differences between the sexes in cognitive functioning, causal attributions, ability to influence, aggressiveness, and nonverbal behavior. Biological factors may contribute to these differences, but cultural and social factors appear to be more important.

If the sexes are really not all that different, what accounts for widespread sex-role stereotypes? The mass media probably both cause and reflect cultural stereotypes regarding the sexes. The prevalence of women in jobs with lower status, as opposed to men, may also lead observers to conclude that gender, rather than the underlying variable of status, accounts for sex differences in behavior. One way to reduce belief in sex-role stereotypes, according to advocates of the status hypothesis, is to eliminate the status differences between males and females.

The pioneering work of Kinsey and Pomeroy and of Masters and Johnson has dispelled the myths and conceptions about sexual behavior. The belief that women are essentially asexual and cannot experience orgasms has not only been emphatically shown to be wrong, but the new knowledge has had a revolutionary impact on the sexual relations between men and women. In addition, scientific surveys established that although males more frequently engaged in behaviors such a masturbation, premarital, and extramarital sex, females engage in them at a rate much higher than researchers believed previously. More recently, researchers have focused on responses to erotica and factors associated with rape.

Glossary

Androgyny A construct advocated by Sandra Bem (1974) referring to a person who displays behaviors associated with both male and female sex-role stereotypes.

Content analysis A research technique by which the frequency or patterns of particular words in documents are measured.

Fallacy of the average The tendency of people to make assumptions about particular individuals based on group averages and to ignore deviations from the average.

Fear of success A construct proposed by Horner (1968) to explain the alleged poor performance of females in achievement situations; anxiety generated because of the negative consequences associated with success, such as jealousy or loss of femininity, is hypothesized as interfering with performance.

Gender identity A person's awareness of being male or female; typically the same as biological gender.

Just world hypothesis People believe in a world where all individuals deserve what happens to them—positive outcomes occur for good people and negative outcomes occur for bad people.

Sex differences Actual ways in which the sexes differ.

Sex roles The behavior patterns that society prescribes for males and females.

Sex-role stereotypes Widely accepted beliefs that the sexes differ in fundamental ways.

Talking platypus phenomenon A woman's successful performance on stereotypical male tasks is to some observers as unexpected and wonderous as a platypus talking; this success places the woman in a different category than other women.

Recommended readings

Henley, Nancy M. (1977). *Body politics: Power, sex and nonverbal communication.* Englewood Cliffs, NJ: Prentice-Hall.

An extensive treatment of the author's provocative hypothesis that nonverbal communication can serve as a potent indicator of power and status differentials.

Tavris, Carol, and Wade, Carole. (1984). *The Longest war: Sex differences in perspective* (2nd Ed.). San Diego: Harcourt Brace Jovanovich.

An exceedingly well-written, up-to-date treatment of a complex topic; includes coverage of the anthropological and biological perspectives, as well as social psychological research on sex differences.

Zilbergeld, Bernie. (1978). *Male sexuality.* New York: Bantam Books; Barbach, Lonnie G. (1985). *For yourself: The fulfillment of female sexuality.*

Two well-written guides to male and female sexuality; worthwhile readings for both sexes.

I'd never join a group that would have me as a member.

Groucho Marx

12
The individual in groups

The "Third Wave"

Ron Jones was teaching his high school history class about the holocaust in Nazi Germany. He wanted to explain how ordinary people can be led to participate in genocide. The idea was to demonstrate to the students how groups can be powerfully attractive to individuals. Mr. Jones introduced his students to discipline, an important concern of the Nazis. The class was to assume a new seating position: feet flat on the floor, hands on the small of the back. New rules were introduced. Students were to be seated before the bell rang, and they were to carry pen and pencils for note taking.

Instead of rebelling, the students appeared to enjoy the new discipline. Soon Mr. Jones had them repeating slogans: Strength Through Discipline, Strength Through Community. A class salute was instituted. All students in the class were required to salute each other whenever they met outside the classroom. Membership cards were issued to all those who wanted to be identified with the group. By the third day of the classroom experiment, forty-three students had joined the "Third Wave" group.

Members were told to memorize the name and address of every other member, and active recruitment for new members was undertaken. The membership of the Third Wave swelled to more than two hundred in twenty-four hours. It was announced that a rally would be held and that the members were to see a national press conference on closed-circuit television announcing the formation of a Third Wave National Youth Program.

When the students showed up at the auditorium for the rally, the television set was turned on, but there was only a white test pattern. The students soon realized that they had been misled and that there was to be no press conference, no national youth movement, and no Third Wave. They sat in stunned silence as they viewed a film of a Nazis rally at Nuremburg. The students left the auditorium, and many later denied that they had ever intended to take part in the rally (Jones, 1984).

Membership in a group affects the person's identity, provides rules of conduct and expectations about "proper" attitudes, establishes obligations and privileges, and defines how the person should act toward members of other groups. You can know a lot about a person by knowing what books that person reads, but you can gain more knowledge by identifying the groups to which the individual belongs.

There must be at least two people to make a group, and their interactions involve communications, influence, and exchange. The most important defining characteristic of a group is that its members share common goals. To some extent, the achievements and failures of the group reflect on each of its members. In short, **groups** consist of two or more people who communicate with one another to coordinate activities directed to achieving common goals. In Chapter 12, we explore the many effects that membership in groups has on the attitudes and behavior of individuals.

The effects of others on the behavior of the individual

When people are free to do as they please, they usually imitate each other.

Eric Hoffer

The actions of other people might stimulate individuals to do things they otherwise would not do. On the other hand, it is also possible to hide in groups, to be nondescript or anonymous, and to avoid responsibility and work. The presence of others sometimes contributes to better task performance by the individual, but also may interfere with or disrupt performance. The conditions under which each of these responses occurs is being studied currently by social psychologists.

Social facilitation

Have you ever studied in the library or tried to read on a crowded beach? Do you think you can learn as effectively under such conditions as when you are alone in your bedroom? Some activities apparently are facilitated by the presence of others. For example, most people report that they find jogging easier if they run with someone than if they run alone. The enhancement of performance by the presence of other people is referred to as the **social facilitation** effect.

It has been shown that subjects learn nonsense syllables (Pessin, 1933) and finger mazes (Husband, 1931) better when alone than when in front of an audience. The latter findings can be called a **social impairment** effect. An individual's performance on well-learned tasks seems to be facilitated by the presence of a group, but his or her performance on complex or unlearned tasks appears to be impaired by a group's presence. Scientific research has been directed toward understanding when to expect either social facilitation or social impairment effects and what causes them.

Arousal hypothesis

Basketball superstars, like Larry Bird and Julius Erving, play their best when the stakes are high, the game is close, and the crowd is all but hysterical. Playing at home is considered an advantage in most sports because of the social facilitation created by enthusiastic and loyal fans (see Box 12-1), but some participants might display social impairment under such conditions. A study of pool players at the Student Union on the campus of Virginia Polytechnic Institute first identified good and poor players through observation (Michaels, Blommel, Brocato, Linkous, and Rowe, 1982). Then a staged audience arrived. The good players got better and the poor players performed even worse than before.

Zajonc (1965) noted that the presence of others appeared to produce a social facilitation effect when the task was simple or when the individual was skilled in performing the task; the social impairment effect occurred when the task was complex or novel. According to Zajonc, the presence of others caused the individual to experience physiological arousal. Athletes talk about adrenalin flowing. The arousal energizes the individual, and when the task is simple or the correct response is well rehearsed, this energizing helps to facilitate performance. When the task is novel or complex, however, the tendency of arousal to energize dominant or well-rehearsed responses causes social impairment in individuals, because triggering of well-learned responses interferes with learning new responses.

Box 12-1

The home court advantage

Statistical analyses have established that playing at home correlates with winning in competitive sports (Schwartz and Barsky, 1977). This advantage is greater in indoor sports where the crowd noise is greatest. The performance of basketball players at the University of Illinois and Kansas State University was observed for fifteen seconds following noisy demonstrations by the spectators. Turnovers and scoring favored the home team regardless of crowd noise, but the number of fouls called against the visiting team increased following noisy crowd demonstrations. Without crowd noise, the fouls were distributed equally between home and visiting teams (Greer, 1983).

When the outcome is most important to it there is evidence that a team is more likely to "choke" in front of a home crowd. For example, in major league baseball, the home team clearly has an advantage in the early games of a World Series but tend to lose the final game if it is played at home (Baumeister and Steinhilber, in press). The same pattern was found when the playoff games of the National Basketball Association were examined. Concern about looking good before the home crowd apparently interferes with the players' optimal performance when the stakes are very high.

Distraction-conflict hypothesis

If you find it difficult to read at the library or on the beach, it may be because other people distract you. Distraction from a buzzer and a flashing light produces the same kind of impairment effect as does the presence of an audience (Pessin, 1933). A distraction-conflict hypothesis does not deny that the presence of others produces arousal in the individual, but states that the person may experience conflict between attending to the other people who are present and attending to the task (Jones and Gerard, 1967; Sanders, Baron, and Moore, 1978). Performance on simple tasks may be possible without much concentration; an individual often can carry on routine tasks while daydreaming about something else. Under such circumstances, the arousal produced by the presence of others, as suggested by Zajonc (1965), may create a social facilitation effect. When the task is sufficiently novel or complex and others serve to distract the individual, however, a social impairment effect may occur.

Evaluation apprehension hypothesis

If the mere presence of others produces arousal, as Zajonc (1965) proposed, then who the audience is and what its function is should be relatively unimportant. No social facilitation of dominant responses exists when the audience is uninformed about the task, however (Henchy and Glass, 1968). This finding suggests that evaluation apprehension is a key factor in producing the social facilitation effect (Cottrell, 1972). Concern about being approved or disapproved, praised or blamed, and rewarded or punished by audiences causes the individual to be aroused by their presence. Muhammad Ali, when he was heavyweight champion of the world, had a reputation as a terrible gym fighter (i.e., when no audience was present). In the arena, however, when the crowd was chanting, "Ali! Ali!" he would display his considerable boxing skills. An individual's embarrassment about making errors and his or her inability to demonstrate mastery of a complex task was shown to contribute to the social facilitation effect (Bond, 1982; Knowles, 1983). Furthermore, size of the audience is related directly to the magnitude of the effect. Social facilitation cannot be totally explained by an evaluation apprehension hypothesis, however. Studies have shown that social facilitation enhances people's performance even when the audience was blindfolded or had their backs turned to the performer (Haas and Roberts, 1975; Markus, 1978; Rittle and Bernard, 1977).

Conclusions regarding social facilitation

A statistical analysis of 241 studies has established that the presence of others facilitates performance of individuals on simple tasks and impairs their speed of performance on complex tasks (Bond and Titus, 1983). Although the effects are small, they are reliable. None of the theories proposed to explain these effects is sufficient to explain the findings of these experiments. Arousal, distraction, and evaluation apprehension all contribute to social facilitation and impairment effects.

Social loafing

The comic strip character, Beetle Bailey, a private in the United States army, has refined "goldbricking" or loafing into an art. **Social loafing** refers to the decrease in effort of an individual within a group when his or her behavior is not under surveillance. Social loafing takes place in the context of group activities, particularly when members are working on an **additive task** where productivity is a sum of all their work. Social loafing has been found in a tug-of-war. Measurements showed that individuals pulled twice as hard when alone than when part of a team of eight (Ringelman, cited in Moede, 1927). When individuals' efforts in tugging alone were compared to their participation in groups with two to five members, it was found that even in the smallest group, individuals exerted only 80 percent of the force they exerted when alone (Ingham, Levinger, Graves, and Peckham, 1974).

Research shows that social loafing occurs at tug-of-war games. A person tugs with greater force when alone than when participating in a group because the group masks the individual's effort.

Box 12-2

The year the Beatles were goofing off

An analysis of the quality of the songs written by Paul McCartney and John Lennon during their years with the Beatles showed some interesting changes over time (Jackson and Padgett, 1982). Their songs were of higher quality early in their careers, as measured by the charts and sales of their records, when they wrote together, but they declined in quality in the middle of the Beatles's career. In the final years of the group (1967–1970), each wrote better songs alone. This change in quality from working together to working alone reflected the relationships of the young men over the years. There was movement away from the spirit of group cohesiveness captured in *I Am a Walrus* ("I am he as you are he, as you are me, and we are all together") to a more egocentric "I, me, mine."

It is known that less loafing occurs among friends than among strangers (Williams, 1981). We may conjecture that the cohesiveness of the Beatles deteriorated as time went on. In addition, the intrinsic interest of the task produced higher quality at first, but later the individual concern for fame and fortune became more important. The lower quality of the songs written in the middle years may have reflected a kind of social loafing in their efforts to collaborate in songwriting.

The belief that one's efforts can be monitored eliminates the social loafing effect. When asked to shout as loud as they could, subjects were less exhuberant when in a group than when alone. Shouting by oneself in front of a scientist is probably somewhat embarrassing, while doing so in a group should be less so. When subjects in groups believed their shouts to be monitored by the experimenter, social loafing was eliminated (Williams, Harkins, and Latane, 1981).

Some football coaches attempt to eliminate social loafing by linemen who tend to gain little recognition for their efforts. The coaches watch films of the game, give grades to each player, and have them wear stars on their helmets proportionate to their game ratings. Social loafing may partially explain why agricultural output in the Soviet Union is higher on individual plots than on large, government-regulated collectivist farms (Smith, 1977).

The ability of others to monitor an individual's performance is not the only factor that eliminates social loafing. Intrinsic interest in a demanding or challenging task may motivate group members. It has been demonstrated that social loafing occurs on simple or repetitive tasks, but not when the task is complex and interesting or when each member has a unique subtask to perform. As is indicated in Box 12-2, some social loafing may have occurred among the Beatles when they became successful.

Social loafing by people performing additive tasks, such as clerks stuffing envelopes, gardeners landscaping an estate, or painters applying a new coat to a building, may be eliminated by separating each member of the group or by giving them subtasks to perform. Clerks may be given a set of envelopes, perhaps with names A through G to stuff; painters may be given different sides of the house to trim; and gardeners may be given subtasks, such as hedge trimming, grass cutting, and so on. If social loafing is due to an individual's lack of recognition and lack of intrinsic interest in the group task, then anything that will provide personal rewards or increase the challenge of the task should help eliminate it.

Social conformity

I conform in all the little ways, so that I can nonconform in the important things.
George Bernard Shaw

Many teenagers in American society feel pressured by their peers to experiment with drugs and sex. Many people buy clothing that is "in fashion." Some of us cannot make up our minds about what to order at a restaurant, so we order whatever others do. All of these examples represent conformity with social groups, but they differ in the degree of pressure felt by the conformist.

Normative and informational conformity

A distinction has been made between normative and informational conformity (Deutsch and Gerard, 1955). **Normative conformity** occurs when an individual fears punishment or desires to gain approval from group members. More generally, **social conformity** is defined as an individual's change in behavior or belief in a direction favored by a group that occurs as a result of real or imagined group pressure (Kiesler and Kiesler, 1969).

Compliance refers to an individual's public behavior that conforms to the group, but the individual maintains differing private attitudes. For example, during the Spanish Inquisition many Jews were forced to convert to Christianity under penalty of death. Although many did comply, they secretly continued to practice their Jewish faith. Normative conformity usually takes the form of compliance.

Normative conformity was demonstrated in the classic studies of Asch (1956). Subjects were shown two cards like those illustrated in Figure 12-1. Their task was to decide which of the three lines on one card matches the length of the single line on the standard card. When judging alone, subjects were correct about 95 percent of the time because the task is simple and unambiguous.

Conformity pressure was evident when seven confederates announced their unanimous but incorrect judgments, then publicly the subjects made a judgment regarding the same lines. For example, if given the comparison shown in Figure 12-1, the confederates would all say that line *c* on Card II was the same length as the standard line on Card I. Sometimes the

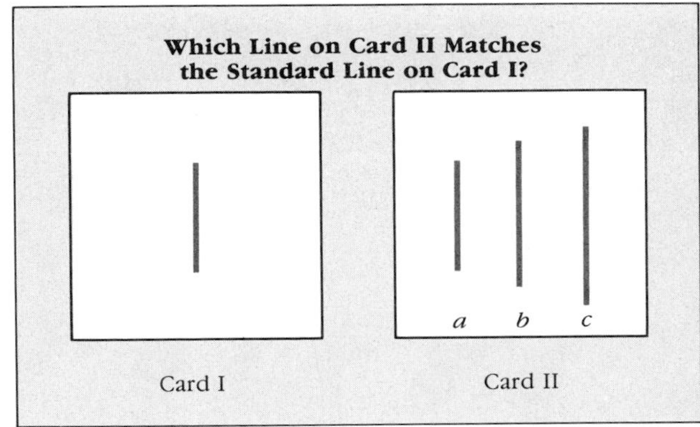

Figure 12-1 Asch line-matching task.

Source: Based on "Studies of independence and conformity: A minority of one against a unanimous majority" by S. E. Asch, 1956, *Psychological monographs*, *70* (9).

confederates indicated that a much longer line was equal to the standard line, and sometimes they all said a much shorter line was. It was found that subjects agreed with the erroneous judgments of the group about one-third of the time.

Informational conformity involves the resolution of personal uncertainty by following the example of others. Pressure is at a minimum, and the group's example resolves an individual's indecision rather than imposing normative pressure on the individual. A second task typically used in conformity research, called the **autokinetic effect,** illustrates informational conformity. When a pinpoint of light is presented in a pitch-dark room, it gives the illusion of movement because of the side-to-side movements of human eyes. Since the movement of light is an illusion, judging the distance of movement is difficult at best. When individuals are alone, their judgments tend to converge on a range of distances, such as one to two inches or seven to eight inches. But when individuals make judgments along with other people, their judgments converge with the range of judgments made by the others. Subjects conformed about 80 percent of the time when judgment ranges of distance were manipulated in experiments (Sherif, 1936).

The research clearly indicates that people conform more to the group when they are uncertain than when they disagree with the group and are pressured to

These privates stand at attention in a prescribed manner because military regulations dictate that they obey commands without question. Why do they conform to the rules? Are they compelled by a sense of duty, by fear of punishment, by pressure from peers and superiors, by public approval, or by all of these factors?

comply. In informational conformity, there is **internalization** of beliefs; that is, people conform with group norms either in private or public as a result of their internal (private) acceptance of group standards. In normative conformity, people outwardly comply with group norms, but they do not internally accept the group's standards (Kelman, 1958). The behavior of members of the "Third Wave" illustrates internalization. After they experienced the disciplinary training procedures by their high school teacher, many students accepted the group's beliefs and made them a part of their beliefs.

Group attraction

As you may expect, the more attractive the group and the more the individual desires to stay in the group, the greater is the tendency to conform to group judgments. People want to remain in groups because "they enjoy the activities, desire the wages or other tangible payoffs they hope to receive, wish to satisfy ego needs, avoid boredom, alleviate uncertainty and fear, or escape the more oppressive social restrictions imposed by other groups" (Steiner, 1972, p. 161). The strong positive relationship of group attraction to conformity has been demonstrated both in the laboratory (Back, 1951) and among teachers in a school setting (Rasmussen and Zander, 1954).

Ambiguity

There are many issues for which there is no possibility of finding out what the truth is. When the truth is not or cannot be known, the impact of the group on the individual is greater than when clear criteria are available (Sherif and Sherif, 1956). In that situation the confidence of the individual is reduced because judgments are more difficult, thereby the individual is more likely to conform to the group. (Colman, Blake and Mouton, 1958; Deutsch and Gerard, 1955; Kelman, 1950). The individual is likely to conform to the group if he or she perceives other members as very competent (Mausner, 1954), but only if the competence is relevant to the task at hand (Croner and Willis, 1961). Under conditions of ambiguity, lack of confidence, and presence of competent other people, the individual is dependent on others for information, and internalization is most likely to occur (Moscovici and Faucheux, 1972).

Information dependence often involves social comparison processes. Social consensus may be the most important way of determining the truth of some aspects of social reality. In evaluating our abilities, opinions, and attitudes, we compare them to relevant other people; agreement suggests that our judgments are correct. In this way, social comparison processes are related to internalization and conformity (Festinger, 1954; Suls and Miller, 1977).

Size of group and unanimity

The size of the group and the degree of unanimity within it affects the amount of conformity exhibited by each member. Little conformity occurs when subjects are paired with only one other person, but three confederates produce as much conformity as sixteen (Asch, 1951). If a member disagrees with one other member, this hardly constitutes deviant behavior. If a member opposes the unanimous judgments of three other people, this behavior appears to be idiosyncratic; but if one other person in a group goes against the majority, pressure to conform greatly diminishes (Asch, 1951). Concern about public ridicule and negative evaluation by audiences are reduced in this instance, and the individual gains the courage to assert private judgments.

Reactions to deviance

Conventional people are roused to frenzy by departure from convention, largely because they regard such departure as a criticism of themselves.

Bertrand Russell

Judgments about physical reality are less ambiguous than judgments about social reality. Viewing the stationary and clear lines in the Asch (1956) task provides a person with an external reference for making judgments, but the illusion of a moving light, as in the Sherif (1936) task, makes the person more dependent on the judgments of others. The tendency of many people to conform to incorrect aspects concerning physical reality is exceeded by their conformity to group consensus regarding social reality. Conformity to a group's accepted view of social reality is protected by the punishment a group can give to anyone who opposes it. In a classic study, Schachter (1951) demonstrated what happens to individuals who go against the group. A group was formed to discuss what action should be taken against Johnny Rocco, a juvenile delinquent. The tendency of college students was to be quite lenient with Johnny. Three confederates were planted in the group: one argued for leniency, thereby aligning himself with most of the subjects, and the other two took a hard line, arguing for strong disciplinary action.

Observation showed that subjects directed their arguments toward the two nonconformists. One of the latter, a *slider,* allowed himself to be convinced that more lenient action should be adopted, but the *deviate* held firm to the more punitive position. Eventually, the group began to ignore the deviate, and when asked whom they would exclude if the discussion group became too large, the deviate was most often chosen. The next time you are with your friends, advocate an unpopular position just to see what their response is.

Influence of a minority

Not only can a group influence an individual, but the individual can change the group. History is filled with examples of artists, scientists, theologians, and politicians who have contributed to revolutionary changes in many aspects of life and beliefs. Consider the impact of a Newton or Michelangelo or Shakespeare on the beliefs of people. Dissent in a group encourages minorities to resist pressures to conform, and dissent is an important factor in democratic societies.

Research has shown that minority influence in a small group is effective only if the minority is consistent in arguing for its position (Moscovici, 1976, 1980). Minority influence is greater as the size of the majority decreases and when the minority is made up of two rather than just one person (Tanford and Penrod, 1984). The influence of a majority is greater when deviant behavior is public because the deviant individual can be identified and punished. Minority influence tends to manifest itself in the private behavior of individuals or on different but related issues because deviance will remain undetected. In such cases minority influence may be indirect or delayed. For example, when a minority argued for much lower compensation in a personal injury case, there was no immediate effect on the majority who decided to make a generous award. The members of the majority, however, voted for less generous awards in subsequent cases (Nemeth and Wachtler, 1983).

Social contagion

On occasion, a behavior appears to be transmitted in a social group like a disease. The laugh tracks on television sitcoms are designed to induce humorous responses from viewers. **Behavioral contagion** occurs when a person first observes and then imitates an action performed by someone else (Wheeler, 1966). Examples of behavioral contagion are described in

Box 12-3

Watching arm wrestling isn't that easy

Good old Uncle Ed used to sit in his armchair watching ice hockey after it was introduced to television. He had been a hockey fan since he was a small boy in Canada, and it showed. He twisted and fidgeted in his chair as the teams skated furiously up and down the ice. The way he moved you would think he was out there on the ice, stick-handling his way through the defense, slapping in a shot, throwing his body into a hard check along the boards. When the game got close and the tension was high, we all hoped old Ed's heart would hold out until the end of the period.

Arm wrestling fans are like Uncle Ed. Two researchers at the University of Massachusetts monitored muscle movements of their subjects' right arms with electronic instruments while they watched thirty-two seconds of an arm wrestling match on television (Markovsky and Berger, 1983). As the contestants strained and the crowd noise got louder, there was more nonvisible activity in the arm muscles of the students, but when the crowd noise diminished, the level of subliminal muscle movements also declined in amplitude. This activity never got translated into visible arm movements. However, the researchers commented that the presence of another person might have inhibited the students from making visible movements, or else they might have looked like Uncle Eds, pressing their imaginary foe into submission.

Box 12-3. **Social contagion** occurs when a person who wants to do something that is socially prohibited, observes another person engage in the action, making it much easier for that person to do the same thing; that is, the person is much less reluctant to inhibit his or her socially undesirable behavior (Wheeler, 1966).

Behavioral contagion is a form of imitation, but social contagion requires that a person overcome inhibitions against performing the behavior. For example, if a lecturer is a bit long winded, you might be reluctant to get up and leave the room; but if others do so, you would be much more likely to leave also. Social contagion tends to eliminate pressures toward conformity, lessens inhibitions and concern about censure, and facilitates the relevant behavior.

Social contagion has been demonstrated by having a confederate cross an intersection against a light (Lefkowitz, Blake, and Mouton, 1955). Pedestrians were more likely to cross against the red light once someone else had done so. A contagion effect was found also with trick or treaters on Halloween. Children were left alone with candy but told to take only one piece. (Beaman, Klentz, Diener, and Svanum, 1979b). When one child took more than one, most of the others also broke the rule. Without the example of another person, however, the children took only one piece of candy. In other words, either no children in a group took more than one piece of candy or almost all of the children did.

Deindividuation

Every man has a mob self and an individual self, in varying proportions.

D. H. Lawrence

Individuals might undertake harmful and antinormative actions in groups when they would not perform such actions if they were alone. A social psychological explanation of destructive and antisocial behavior associated with groups contends that these effects are due to **deindividuation.** According to deindividuation theory (e.g., Zimbardo, 1970), people in a group experience a loss of personal identity. When individuals are not identifiable and cannot be held responsible by other people, they lose their abil-

Box 12-4

We had a smashing good time

Living in large cities increases the resident's feeling of anonymity and deindividuation. This may be one reason why there is so much more antinormative behavior in urban areas. As a demonstration of this principle, Zimbardo (1970) purchased two 1959 Oldsmobiles. One was placed in the Bronx in New York and the other in the small town of Palo Alto, California. The hoods on the two cars were raised and the license plates were removed, indicating that the cars had been abandoned. The researchers than observed the behavior of passersby.

Within ten minutes of abandonment in the Bronx, a family began to strip the car. In less than three days, the car was reduced to a useless wreck. There were twenty-three recorded instances of vandalism, some carried out by well-dressed adults who appeared to be law-abiding citizens. Photographs were obtained showing a person swinging a sledge hammer and smashing the car. In Palo Alto, the car was untouched. Indeed, when it began to rain one day, a concerned motorist stopped and lowered the hood of the abandoned car so that the motor would not get wet!

ity to restrain themselves against violent and aggressive actions. The "animal" in all of us becomes unleashed, and the behavior satisfies our primitive urges.

In a classic study demonstrating the effects of deindividuation, groups of college students were formed to discuss their parents. These groups were encouraged to make hostile and unfavorable statements about their parents. They were told of surveys in which 87 percent of college students held deep-seated hatred for one or both of their parents. They were also told that those who were most unwilling to express their hostility actually felt the most hatred (Festinger, Pepitone, and Newcomb, 1952). Twenty-three groups of four to seven students held discussions in a regular classroom. It was found that the students who were identified by a paper-and-pencil test as deindividuated rated their group as more attractive, suggesting that a loosening of restraints against antisocial behavior was experienced as enjoyable. A demonstration that destructiveness could be fun is described in Box 12-4.

"So anyway, I thought, you won't be back for 10 minutes. I'll grab a hot dog."

There have been a number of occasions when a suicidal person threatened to jump off a building and a crowd below began to chant: "Jump! Jump!" An analysis of twenty-one of these incidents, including ten where the crowds baited the victims and eleven where they did not, revealed that two factors were associated with baiting: crowd size and darkness (Mann, 1981). Both of these factors contribute to a loss of individuality and accountability by crowd members. This kind of incident also indicates a tendency of deindividuated people to dehumanize others. The potential suicide victim is cast into the role of a crazy and weird person not at all like members of the crowd.

Deindividuation may have played a role in lynchings of blacks by sheet-covered members of the Ku Klux Klan. A hood and a flowing robe creates anonymity, at least in the eyes of out-group members (Mann, Newton, and Innes, 1982). A loss of individual identity may loosen the normal constraints on behavior. Some support for this conjecture was provided in a laboratory study in which college students, who wore large labcoats and pillow slips for hoods to disguise themselves, delivered longer duration shocks to a victim than students who could be identified clearly (Zimbardo, 1970). A summary of the hypothetical features of deindividuation is presented in Table 12-1.

An individual might not vent his prejudice by lynching black people if he were not a member of the well-disguised Ku Klux Klan. Through the deindividuation process, KKK members relinquish their personal identity to the unrestrained spirit of this destructive group.

Table 12-1 An analysis of the deindividuation process

CONTRIBUTING FACTORS
Being in a group
Anonymity
Diffusion of responsibility
Intense activity, overload of sensory stimulation
Physiological arousal
Focus on present to exclusion of past and future
Altered consciousness due to alcohol, drugs, and so on
EFFECTS WITHIN THE PERSON
Minimized concern about self-evaluation
Lowered concern about the evaluations of others
Release of restraints against normally inhibited actions
Liking for group associated with pleasurable release
EFFECTS ON SUBSEQUENT ACTIONS
Antinormative behavior performed
Intense, emotional, and self-intensifying action
Once begun, behavior difficult to direct or stop
Behavioral contagion and conformity to group pressures
Insensitive to normal reference groups
Perceptual and memory distortions

Source: Modified from "The human choice: Individuation, reason, and order versus deindividuation, impulse, and chaos" by P. G. Zimbardo, 1970, in W. J. Arnold and D. Levine (Eds.), *Nebraska Symposium on Motivation* (Vol. 17), Lincoln: University of Nebraska.

Research demonstrating the decivilizing effects of deindividuation has not escaped criticism (Dipboye, 1977; Lindskold and Propst, 1981). Because college students are usually reluctant to engage in antinormative behavior in the laboratory, such behaviors as delivering an electric shock to another person or hitting someone with a styrofoam bat are usually legitimized by the experimenter to make them seem part of a worthy scientific endeavor. Under these conditions, it is questionable whether the deindividuated behavior observed in laboratory experiments is either antinormative or antisocial.

Polarization of opinions in groups

Assume that you are an electrical engineer, married with one child, working for a large corporation since graduating from college five years ago. You can be fairly certain of a secure future with modest financial benefits through retirement. Then suppose you are offered a job wth a new and small company at a higher salary with the promise of a share in the company if it does well. Would you accept the offer if you thought the chances were one to ten that the new company would succeed? How about if the odds were three in ten or seven in ten? As you might expect, some people are willing to take greater risks than others. Contrary to the belief that people in groups are more conservative and conforming than when alone, Stoner (1961) found that individuals who were alone made more conservative decisions (i.e., involving less risk), than when they discussed the matter with others. This shift toward taking risks following discussion represents a **polarization** in individuals by which they become more extreme in making decisions. This is often referred to as a **risky shift.**

Polarization toward risk is of great interest to social psychologists because of the potential implications of such a process. Consider the joint chiefs of staff at the Pentagon. Would they make more risky decisions after discussing the matter than when alone? Would organizations and governments that are run more democratically make more risky decisions than authoritarian ones?

It is now clear that the direction of polarization depends on the values or original preferences of the group members and their degree of unanimity. For example, shifts toward caution (i.e., less risk) occurred within groups as opposed to lone bettors at a race track where the risk was real rather than hypothetical (Knox and Safford, 1976; McCauley, Stitt, Woods, and Lipton, 1973; Sanders, 1978). Shifts toward risk were found in people who made decisions that had real consequences for friends (Runyan, 1974) and in people who had to choose a date whether the conditions were real or hypothetical (Spector, Cohen, and Penner, 1976). A shift toward caution typically occurred on two of the original twelve items constructed by Stoner (1961). As is described in Box 12-5 on p. 346, polarization effects also occur in the courtroom.

Explanations of polarization in groups

An important feature of polarization in groups is that subjects subscribe to a particular position prior to discussion, and upon hearing the discussion, they adopt a more extreme position. Such a shift toward risk is depicted in Figure 12-2. Subjects who were originally neutral on an issue heard a discussion indicating that others had made more risky choices than themselves. The subjects then shifted and made riskier decisions.

Cultural similarity among people gives them a tendency to agree on many attitudes and values. Group discussion provides each person with an opportunity to discover that most other people hold the same basic position. Indeed, when discussion groups were constituted deliberately so that half favored one position

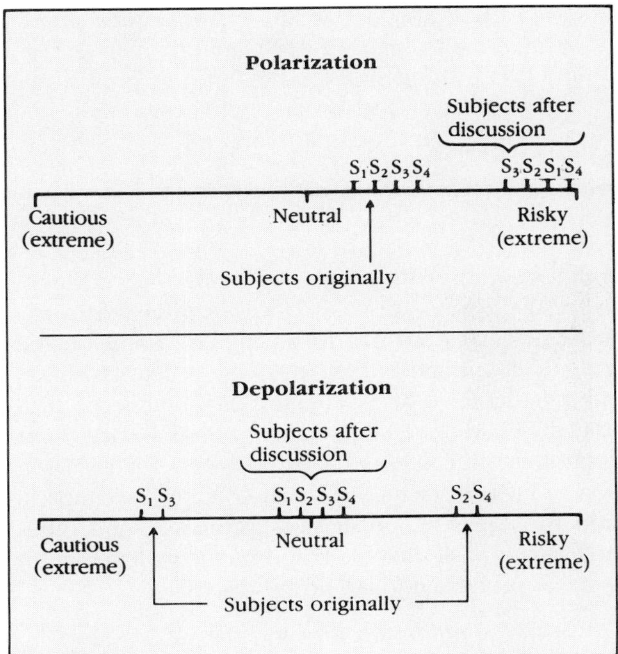

Figure 12-2 Group polarization and depolarization after discussion.

Source: Based on "Depolarization of attitudes in groups" by A. Vinokur and E. Burnstein, 1978, *Journal of Personality and Social Psychology*, *36*, 872–885.

Box 12-5

Group shifts and the courtroom

Legal judgments are often made by juries or by groups of judges (e.g., the Supreme Court). These judicial groups typically hold discussions about their opinions prior to reaching decisions. It is reasonable to ask whether polarization effects occur in the courtroom.

The available evidence suggests that the deliberation of juries and judges does reflect a polarization effect. In laboratory experiments, simulated juries, consisting of college students who rendered decisions regarding hypothetical defendants, had stronger opinions concerning the defendant's guilt or innocence after they held group discussions than before they did (Kaplan, 1977; Kaplan and Miller, 1977; Myers and Kaplan, 1976). The jurors apparently form an initial weak opinion regarding a person's guilt or innocence, and group discussion tends to strengthen this initial tendency and make it more extreme than when no group discussion takes place.

Knowledge and sophistication regarding the law does not eliminate the polarization effect. Comparisons of decisions made in civil liberties cases by individual judges and by panels of three judges indicate that panels made decisions more in favor of civil rights than did individual judges. Since the initial views of judges tended to be mildly pro-civil rights, the effect of group discussion made their positions more extreme (Kaplan and Miller, 1977).

Although polarization in judicial decisions may appear to be an unwanted departure from standards of impartiality and fairness, research has shown that subjects adhered more strictly to a norm of equity in dispensing rewards following group discussion than did individuals acting alone (Greenberg, 1979). The implication is that polarization in the courtroom may produce decisions that are more fair and responsive to the law than those rendered by a single judge.

and the other half favored the opposite position, the result of group discussion was **depolarization**—movement by each half to the neutral point on the scale (Vinokur and Burnstein, 1978). A depolarization effect is depicted also in Figure 12-2. Subjects, who originally had extreme positions shifted toward more neutral ones. The current explanations for polarization in groups, including social comparison, impression management, persuasive arguments, and diffusion of responsibility, are based on the general agreement of subjects prior to group discussion.

Social comparison and impression management

When asked to indicate a decision, attitude, judgment, or value publically, people may not know how other people will respond to their position. In group discussion, people are given an opportunity to compare their views with those of others. A person's viewpoint is validated when general agreement is expressed by others. Social consensus indicates a shared cultural value. A person may try to gain approval of others by indicating a stronger position in the favored direction than other group members may indicate (Brown, 1965; Jellison and Arkin, 1977).

There are four essential steps involved in a social comparison and impression management explanation of group polarization: (1) members are like-minded but do not know that they share a common cultural value; (2) members regard their values, including the value of risk taking as better than the relevant cultural values of most other people (Levinger and Schneider, 1969); (3) members make social comparisons and discover during discussion that others' hold positions very much like their own; and (4) members indicate a more extreme position in the culturally valued direction in order to make themselves more distinctive and to gain approval from others (Baron, Sanders, and Baron, 1975; Jellison and Arkin, 1977).

Persuasive arguments and information

Polarization has been found when subjects were asked to write arguments in favor of their position rather than to participate in a discussion. On the other hand, merely hearing the choices of others did not produce a shift in these subjects unless they had time to think about arguments in support of their position (Burnstein and Vinokur, 1975; Vinokur and Burnstein, 1974, 1978). These studies suggest that polarization is dependent upon the number, type (pro or con), and perceived persuasiveness of the arguments. For example, as can be seen in Figure 12-3, when individual subjects heard a taped group discussion the degree and direction of their shift from prior opinions was affected by the proportion of risky to conservative arguments that they heard the group express (Ebbesen and Bowers, 1974). More risky decisions were made only when risky arguments were preponderent in the group discussion.

Persuasive arguments affect a group in three ways: (1) Like-minded members generate more arguments favoring the valued side of the controversy; (2) arguments favoring one's own views are considered more persuasive than opposing arguments; and (3) members may hear new points to add to their prior store of favorable arguments during discussion. The result of this information exchange is to persuade a member to take a more extreme view on the issue than he or she did prior to hearing the arguments of others. Self-persuasion may occur when an individual is encouraged to generate arguments for a position that has not been expressed previously.

Diffusion of responsibility

Most group polarization effects can be explained by the principles already discussed. Yet, it is also true that

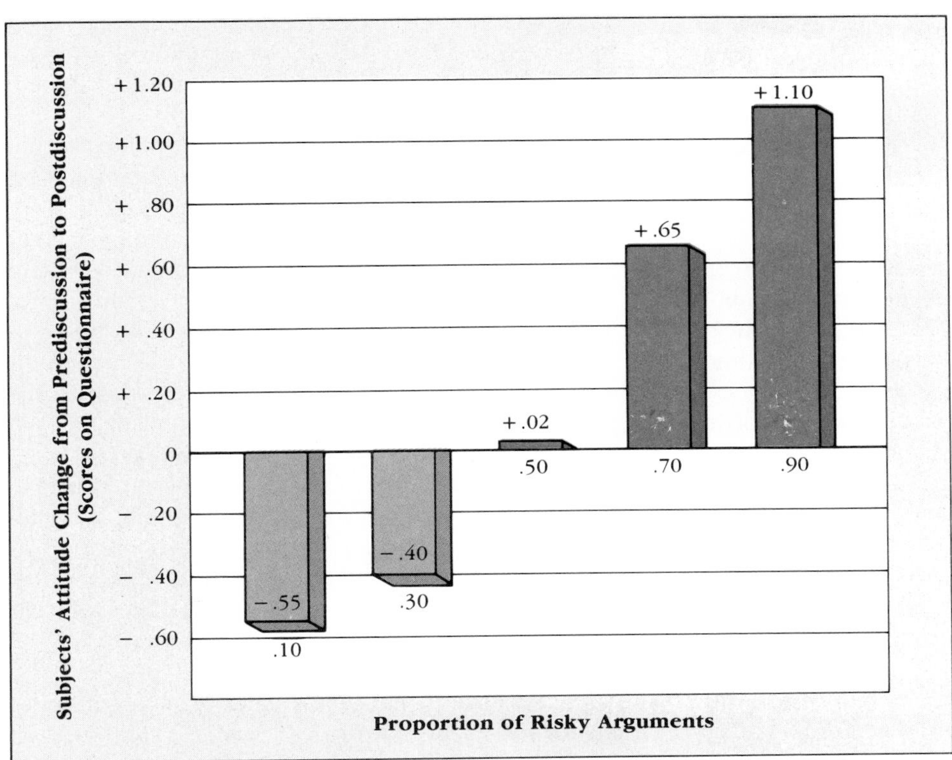

Figure 12-3 The effect of persuasiveness on polarization. *Note:* Minus numbers indicate depolarization and plus numbers indicate polarization.

Source: Based on "Proportion of risky to conservative arguments in a group discussion and choice shifts" by E. G. Ebbesen and R. J. Bowers, 1974, *Journal of Personality and Social Psychology*, *29*, 316-327.

group decisions differ from individual decisions in that no one member typically can be singled out and held responsible for a group decision. In Chapter 9 we examine evidence indicating that an individual is less likely to help another in an emergency when other people are present than when alone. If diffusion of responsibility occurs in decision-making groups, individual members may be encouraged to agree with more extreme, more risky, or more costly actions. We can attribute this diffusion of responsibility effect to the fact that the individual cannot be held accountable for what the group does and therefore can escape any negative consequences for making poor decisions.

Kogan and Wallach (1967) found, for example, that groups were less inclined to recommend risk on risk dilemma items when the responsibility for the decision would fall on a single group member. Moreover, there is evidence that groups are more likely to engage in acts bringing censure, such as administering punishments and sending threats, than individuals are (Bem, Wallach, and Kogan, 1965; Lindskold, McElwain and Wayner, 1977; Mathes and Kahn, 1975; Mynatt and Sherman, 1975). It is thus plausible that a diffusion of responsibility based on the difficulty of assigning blame to a single individual for a group decision may sometimes be the basis of polarization effects.

Ethnocentrism and bias against outsiders

Membership in a group affects an individual's perceptions and attitudes toward members of other groups. Three cognitive effects associated with group membership are: (1) homogeneity bias, (2) group ethnocentrism, and (3) group-serving bias.

A **homogeneity bias** is manifested when individuals perceive people in other groups as more similar or homogeneous in characteristics and opinions than people in their own groups (Linville and Jones, 1980; Park and Rothbart, 1982; Quattrone and Jones, 1980). This homogenization of members of other groups is not due to the fact that members of one's own group are better known. A study of large clubs at Princeton University showed that the homogeneity bias still was present even when people were unacquainted with most of the members of their own group (Jones, Wood, and Quattrone, 1981). The tendency is to form stereotypes of out-group members and to refer to them as "they." For example, Americans frequently view Communists as if *they* are all alike (Bronfenbrenner, 1961).

Another tendency is to form negative impressions of out-group members (Brewer, 1979; Howard and Rothbart, 1980; Tajfel, Billig, Bundy, and Flament, 1971). Group **ethnocentrism** is a bias in favor of one's own group and against other groups. In all likelihood, it contributes to prejudice and discrimination (Giles, 1977). Many years ago, fans who had attended a Princeton-Dartmouth football game that was quite rough and resulted in an injury to a star player were interviewed (Hastorf, and Cantril, 1954). As might be expected, fans of each team perceived the other team as having committed the most infractions. There is a corresponding willingness to treat out-group members unfairly. For example, when no conflict of interest existed, and members of the out-groups were anonymous, in-group members allocated more rewards to their own group than to the out-groups (Tajfel et al., 1971). This unjust behavior toward out-groups has been demonstrated frequently in experiments (Turner, 1981). Outsiders are evaluated negatively and assumed to be competitors; hostile actions frequently are directed toward them (Jaffe and Yinon, 1979).

The quality of the product of out-groups is unjustifiably evaluated as inferior to that of the in-group (Blake and Mouton, 1961; Ferguson and Kelley, 1964; Hinkle and Schopler, 1979). This group ethnocentrism is more pronounced in groups with low status where members are more insecure about the evaluation of their own group (Amabile and Glazebrook, 1982).

Group ethnocentrism is stronger when there is competition with an out-group, especially when the in-group wins (Worchel, Lind, and Kaufman, 1975). If the out-group wins, however, the in-group is devaluated. An evaluative bias against competitors can lead to overconfidence, which in turn can lead to upset victories in professional sports. Coaches of superior teams constantly fight battles against overconfidence, especially when their own teams are heavily favored to win a particular game.

Social identity theory (Tajfel and Turner, 1979) proposes that group membership helps a person to define his or her individual identity. We are motivated to maintain positive self-esteem and perceive ourselves in positive or negative ways depending on how we evaluate our groups as compared to other groups. To enhance our own social identity, the difference between the in-group and the out-group may be exaggerated. The tendency to attribute positive characteristics to in-group members and negative characteristics to members of out-groups is an extension of a self-serving bias and is called a **group-serving bias** (Bond, Chin, and Wan, 1984).

If members make unfavorable comparisons of their own group relative to other groups, they experience a negative social identity. In such instances, an individual may attempt to join a more positive group by adopting whatever characteristics are valued in the positive group. This kind of intergroup mobility will occur when boundaries between groups are easy to cross. When an individual cannot transfer into a more favored group, a cognitive reevaluation may occur. A selection of some less positive members of the out-group may be chosen for comparison or other characteristics may be chosen so that the in-group appears more positive to a dissatisfied member. When unfavorable intergroup comparison occurs, another response by a member or members is to compete with the out-group in order to produce change and promote a positive evaluation of the in-group (Tajfel, 1978).

An in-group bias against out-groups can be reduced if the in-group members provide information about differences of judgment among out-group members, thereby reducing the homogeneity bias (Wilder, 1978). Creating superordinate goals to be achieved by cooperation of an out-group and an in-group also breaks down the hostilities between both (Sherif and Sherif, 1953; Wilder, 1978). When the out-group provided rewards to the in-group, ethnocentrism and discrimination was lessened, especially when members of the in-group did not provide rewards for one another (Locksley, Ortiz, and Hepburn, 1980).

Group dynamics—achieving group goals

Technically speaking, we have not as yet considered group activities in Chapter 12. Groups consist of two or more people who coordinate their activities to achieve group goals. The impact of other people on the individual, whether it is social facilitation, conformity, deindividuation, or group ethnocentrism, does not help achieve group goals. Performance within a coordinated group depends on many factors, including the size of the group, the skill and style of leaders within the group, and the dynamics of interaction that characterizes group members.

Group size

The effect of group size on task performance depends on the type of task. Where the quality of performance depends on the most talented member, as for example in a scientific research team, the larger the group the more likely it will contain a member with the relevant talent. On the other hand, increasing the size of the group also will create problems of coordination and morale (Frank and Anderson, 1971). The tendency to rely on the most competent person makes the addition of more and more members superfluous to task solution.

With a task that requires the joint actions of group members, like the playing of softball, increasing group size is likely to include even less competent members, hence the quality of the group's performance may be decreased (Frank and Anderson, 1971). This negative result is not inevitable, however, because careful recruitment practices or rules of inclusion can be used to screen out less competent people. Rookie players do not necessarily decrease the quality of performance of professional football teams. Scouting and computer analysis of skills, size, speed, and reactions are scrutinized before a team decides on the desirability of various potential players.

When the group must deal with tasks that have no obvious correct solution, such as when an investment club buys stocks, increasing group size can have seriously disrupting effects. Members of large groups feel that they have less influence than members of smaller groups (Golembiewski, 1962), are less satisfied (Slater, 1958), participate less in group activities (Bales, Strodtbeck, Mills, and Roseborough, 1951; Gibb, 1951; Indik, 1965), and tend to be more antagonistic toward one another (O'Dell, 1968).

Group cohesiveness

The sum of all the members' attraction to the group and their desire to remain in it constitutes group

Productivity and morale are greater in cohesive groups because every member works toward shared goals and mutual respect.

cohesiveness. Cohesiveness is a result of shared goals, experiences of success, competition with out-groups, and enhanced self-esteem. Interaction among members is smoother, occurs more frequently, and is more pleasant in cohesive groups (Back, 1951; Lott and Lott, 1961; Shaw and Shaw, 1962). Conflicts among members are resolved more easily (Shaw, 1981). Cohesiveness has been found to increase the productivity of army field teams (Goodacre, 1951), of bomber crews (Hemphill and Sechrest, 1952), and of workers in a steel mill (Speroff and Kerr, 1952). Member satisfaction with the group and its progress has been shown to be related to cohesiveness in different kinds of groups, for example, in work teams, in decision groups, and in artificial groups formed for laboratory study (Exline, 1957; Gross, 1954; Marquis, Guetzkow, and Heyns, 1951; Van Zelst, 1952b).

Given the desirable effects of group cohesiveness, it is important to understand the factors that create this social glue. There are essentially five factors that produce group cohesiveness: (1) attraction of members toward one another as individuals (Davis, 1969); (2) esteem of each member for the group as a source of social identity (Tajfel, 1978); (3) shared common values and goals (Davis, 1969; Schachter, Ellertson, McBride, and Gregory, 1951); (4) success in attaining goals or making progress toward them; and (5) a common threat or an out-group enemy (Shaw, 1981; Steiner, 1972). For example, associations of small, independent grocers were more interested in having further meetings when they perceived a threat of supermarkets moving into their areas than when they perceived no outside threat (Mulder and Stemerding, 1963). Sharing a common threat and having common goals motivated members to seek further contact with other group members.

Communication networks

Groups often are organized formally, and **communication networks** represent the distribution of tasks and responsibility. The chain of communications linking one person to others affects the quality of a group's performance in solving group tasks. Researchers have examined the various communication networks shown in Figure 12-4. Note that these net-

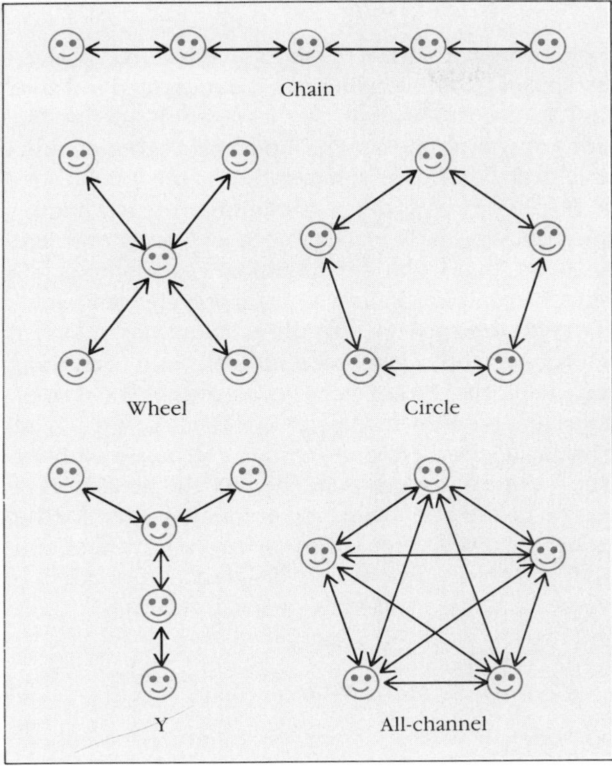

Figure 12-4 Types of communication networks in five-member groups.

works are centralized and decentralized. The *wheel network* requires all communications in a five-person group to be channeled through member *C,* therefore it is highly centralized. The *Y network* is the next most centralized, allowing communications to be directed to either of two central members. The *all-channel network* is the most decentralized, as each member can communicate directly with any of the other four members of the group. The *chain* and *circle* networks are less centralized than the wheel but more centralized than the all-channel network.

Early research employed the procedure of giving each of five subjects a card containing five of six possible symbols (Leavitt, 1951). All subjects held only one symbol in common. The group's task was to ascertain which was the common symbol. The fewest errors and the fewest communications occurred in the most centralized network (the wheel), where it was relatively easy to channel information to a "key person" who could make the necessary comparisons and transmit the information back to each group member. On this kind of simple task, a completely decentralized communication network represented by the circle was the most inefficient organization.

Biography

Marvin E. Shaw

Marvin E. Shaw was a navigator in the Eighth Air Force, flying missions over Europe in World War II, when he became fascinated with groups. Because of varying assignments and changing personnel, he was a member of many groups during those years. A different kind of social chemistry existed in all of these groups, and Shaw was interested in finding out what produced this variation.

After the war, Shaw completed his undergraduate degree at Arkansas College and obtained a Master's Degree in psychology at the University of Arkansas, where he taught for several years and collaborated with Dr. Jack Gilchrist in doing group research. When Dr. Gilchrist moved to join the faculty at the University of Wisconsin, Shaw joined him there and completed his Ph.D. At Johns Hopkins University and subsequently at MIT, where Shaw was also a faculty member, he carried out many studies on groups. Since 1959 Dr. Shaw has been professor of psychology at the University of Florida.

Shaw's most recent research has focused on exploring techniques for learning in groups. The questions asked by students and interaction among them produces as much of the learning in a classroom as the lectures of an instructor. More importantly, students learn more when they work in groups than when they work alone. Dr. Shaw's book on *Group Dynamics* has been a standard text for many years; it is now in its third edition and has been translated into Spanish and Japanese.

A review of eighteen studies (Shaw, 1964) established that when a group must work on a complex task, a decentralized network is most efficient. The key person in a centralized network may suffer from information overload, referred to as **saturation** (Gilchrist, Shaw, and Walker, 1954). Furthermore, when information is widely distributed, as in decentralized networks, each member of the group can check for errors and add their special knowledge and expertise to the task. Even when the task is relatively simple, if the key person happens to be incompetent or irresponsible, a centralized network will not function well.

A major strength of decentralized communications is the high morale of group members (Shaw, 1981). The more each member can contribute to group task performance, the greater the experience of satisfaction (Gilchrist et al., 1954). In a classic study of employee relations in a factory, it was found that the more involvement employees had in decisions regarding work assignment, the more cooperative and satisfied they were (Coch and French, 1948). Whenever morale or satisfaction is important to group achievement, effective leaders should take measures to decentralize communications.

Leadership in groups

Most tasks in groups are divisible, and specific subtasks generally are assigned to different people. The distribution of duties and responsibilities to members of the group is referred to as *role differentiation*. A wide variety of roles may exist in a group: secretary, treasurer, president, jokester, messenger, and sergeant at arms. An important role in many groups is that of the leader.

Biographers, historians, and laypeople have long been fascinated by the lives of individuals who have had great influence over events. We think of such historically important people as "leaders," and when studying them, we are keenly interested in what it is about these leaders that placed them at the center of events. Are they more intelligent, articulate, persistent, or just more lucky than others? It has been said that dying at the right time can salvage a hero's mantle and make the person a historical figure. For example, what would Abraham Lincoln's reputation be if he had to preside over the reconstruction period following the Civil War?

What is leadership?

Social scientists disagree about the nature of leadership. Six different definitions are presented in Table 12-2. As you can see, whether leadership is defined in terms of contributions to group goals, degree of influence over other members, various kinds of behaviors or whether it refers to an attribution process whereby a person acquires the label of "leader," some problem has been found with the definition. Leadership is obviously a complex phenomenon, involving some or all of the features provided by these definitions. A leader is a person who occupies a central position in a group and helps the group achieve its goals. The leader holds that position and uses it to influence, direct, and coordinate the behaviors of other group members. One political scientist has viewed the leader as a beacon giving orientation and pointing the way for the group (Lasswell, 1966). The "what, how, when, and why" of group actions are developed through the prisms of the leader's view of social reality.

Characteristics of leaders

Do leaders have special traits or abilities that put them in the forefront of their groups? There is evidence that a person who gains acceptance by the group as a leader also tends to attain that identification in other groups (Bell and French, 1950; Carter, Haythorn, Shriver, and Lanzetta, 1951). Apparently, there is something about the person that is associated with leadership potential, yet a long and arduous examination of personality characteristics has failed to uncover any leadership traits (Gibbs, 1969).

Factors associated with leadership are the ability to help groups attain their goals, self-confidence, assertiveness, persistence, sociability, and acceptance by followers. (Carter, 1954). The assertive ability to talk more than others leads members to perceive a person as contributing most to solutions of group problems even when others offer more useful information (Bass, 1949). Members may perceive a talkative person as interested in the group and the task, as motivated to work on it, and as having some ability to make an important contribution. Give little other information about group members in artificial laboratory groups composed of strangers, the group will nominate the assertive person as the leader. When a laboratory

Table 12–2 Central features that have been used to define leader and leadership

DEFINING FEATURES OF A LEADER	PROBLEMS IN DEFINING LEADERSHIP
Center of attention	Group often focuses attention on a deviate or weak member.
Moves group toward goals	Goal is not always obvious, and strong leader may divert group from original goals.
Acquires label as leader	Actual leader may be someone else.
Most influential	A person may influence group by causing members to react negatively to all suggestions.
Clarifies, decides; suggests alternatives	Usually these behaviors are carried out by several group members and not just one person.
Appointed by a higher authority	May be given a title, but may not win acceptance or legitimation of members.

group is given information about a less talkative member who has expertise relevant to the group task, however, the expert and not the talkative person is chosen as the leader (Gintner and Lindskold, 1975).

There are various ways of asserting oneself. A person can volunteer to gather information, carry out a task, perform in a particular role, such as treasurer, and so forth. There are certain people who automatically take the end seat at a conference table, and such a position may bring that person into leadership (Korda, 1975). Observation of 20 five-person groups with three people seated on one side of a table and two on the other revealed that the leader emerged from the two-person side of the table in 14 out of the 20 groups. (Howell and Becker, 1962). In a centralized communication network, the individual may attempt to gain a central position, which would automatically confer the leadership role on him or her.

Certain leaders appear to have charisma, a kind of hypnotic, heroic, larger-than-life quality that electrifies and excites followers. Charisma is not a trait of born leaders, but rather a relationship between the needs of a disoriented group and the assertive self-confidence of a recognized leader (Gerth and Mills, 1953). Although Adolph Hitler mesmerized the German people with his speeches in the 1930s, would his shrill and raspy voice attract many followers now? What has changed are the conditions of the German people.

Transactional theory of leadership

Those who try to lead the people can only do so by following the mob.

Oscar Wilde

Hollander (1958, 1960) has proposed that leadership involves a transaction between members of the group and a leader. It is a process of social exchange. The leader performs some necessary functions for the group, and the group rewards the leader with status and esteem.

The transactional theory of leadership proposes that leaders begin by conforming to group norms, perhaps more strongly than other members, and assertively make contributions to achieving group goals. The group assigns **idiosyncrasy credits** to the leader in proportion to the leader's contribution to the group. Idiosyncrasy credits allow the leader to deviate from group standards, values, and actions. Innovation and the ability to take new directions depends on the accumulation of idiosyncrasy credits. An established and successful leader accumulates enough idiosyncrasy credits to allow innovation and the development of new standards.

The legitimacy of the leader as an authority in the group is based on two factors: endorsement and normativity (Michener and Burt, 1974). **Endorsement** is the degree of support that members of a group give its leader. Elections in a democratic society provide one way of assessing endorsement. Obviously, elections do not provide a measure of the degree of endorsement of an autocratic leader. It should not be assumed that autocratic leaders receive less endorsement than democratic ones. Lenin and Mao Tse-tung are just two examples of modern autocratic leaders who reached almost godlike status in their nations. Research indicates, however, that group members make greater demands and have higher expectations of success from an elected leader than from a person appointed to a position of leadership (Hollander and Julian, 1970). Whether the leader is elected or appointed, endorsement depends on three characteristics in a leader: competence, success, and assertiveness in pursuing group interest.

Normativity refers to a leader's scope and limits of action that group members consider legitimate (Michener and Burt, 1974). Three factors contribute to normativity: the range of activities giving the leader authority to control, the right to reward and punish group members, and group consensus about these rules.

What made Abraham Lincoln one of the greatest leaders in history? Did his self-confidence, assertiveness, and persistence contribute to maintaining the union of the United States?

The leader's scope of action always is limited to some degree. There are definite constraints on the actions of a president of the United States determined by the Constitution and the balance of power among the institutions and groups in the society. When a leader goes beyond the scope of authority allowed in the group, there is a loss of endorsement. The resignation of Richard Nixon from the presidency of the United States was brought about by allegations that he obstructed justice in covering up an attempt to bug the Democratic campaign headquarters at the Watergate Apartments in Washington, D.C. The president of the United States is not above the law, but like every other citizen is expected to obey it.

The fairness with which a leader exercises the right to reward and punish group members is related directly to endorsement. In some groups where power is not distributed equally, a leader may selectively reward those followers whose endorsement is most necessary for the leader to maintain or augment his or her authority. If consensus in support of rules is low, little obedience to authority will occur, and there will be group resistance to a leader's attempts to enforce the rule. A leader who would be too diligent about punishing all users of marijuana would soon create great resistance and lose the endorsement of many Americans.

According to the transactional theory of leadership, strong endorsement of a leader should provide the leader with leeway to deviate from group standards (Hollander and Julian, 1970). The principle is: The stronger the endorsement, the greater the temptation to violate normativity. Some political commentators have interpreted Lyndon Johnson's commitment to the Vietnam War as being without the consensus of the American people and triggered by his landslide re-election victory.

Contingency theory of leadership

Early researchers on leadership assumed that there was one best type of leadership style. Several studies indicated that democratic leadership, involving the offering of suggestions and help but not the giving of directions, was more effective than authoritarian leadership in respect to both quality of the group product and group morale (Kahn and Katz, 1953; Lewin, Lippitt, and White, 1939). Other research showed that autocratic leadership was more effective, however (Hare, 1962; Meade, 1967). Apparently, the impact of leadership style was dependent upon a number of factors; one style might be more effective under some conditions and another form of leadership would be better in other circumstances.

Most researchers agree that leaders perform two primary activities: they carry out group tasks and deal with the socioemotional factors associated with morale in the group (Halpin, 1955, 1956; Halpin and Winer, 1952). To be more specific, a leader may emphasize production goals or may spend more time working out harmonious relations among workers and improving morale.

Whether a leader is task oriented or focused on a group's socioemotional needs, Fiedler (1964, 1978) proposed that the leader's effectiveness is contingent upon three situational factors: (1) *leader-follower relations,* involving endorsement and loyalty; (2) *task structure,* including the specificity of the goals and methods and the availabilty of standards to assess performance; and (3) the *power position of the leader,* involving normativity and control over resources. Each of these factors can be favorable or unfavorable for the leader, and there are eight possible combinations. Leader-follower relations can be good or poor, task structure can be high or low, and leader power can be strong or weak. The contingency theory specifies which kind of leadership will be most effective in each of these eight possible situations.

When all three situational factors are favorable, a task-oriented leader can focus on maximizing performance. The morale of a well-functioning group is apt to be high, and there is no need to focus on human relationships. When situational factors are unfavorable, the group needs a strong task-oriented leader to define goals, specify methods, and organize members to improve group performance. Focus on socioemotional relationships would not be an effective way to improve the functioning of the group under such poor circumstances. A socioemotional leader will be most effective when situational factors of intermediate favorability prevail. Under these conditions, cultivation of better relationships in the group, particularly leader-follower relations and improved cooperation among group members, can enhance group performance. These predictions are summarized in Table 12-3.

In order to test the contingency theory of leadership, it was necessary to develop some measure of the task or socioemotional orientation of potential leaders. Fiedler (1971) reasoned that such a measure could be developed by asking subjects to think of all the people they had ever worked with and, on rating scales, to describe the one co-worker they thought had been most inadequate. Thus, respondents rated their **least preferred co-worker** (LPC). The assumption is that task-oriented people will rate the least preferred co-worker more negatively than relationship-oriented people will because task-oriented people do not weigh the positive aspects of personal contact but focus only on production. Thus, high scores (i.e., more favorable evaluation) on the LPC indicate a socioemotional orientation and low LPC scores (i.e., very unfavorable evaluation) indicate a task orientation.

Table 12–3 Effectiveness of leadership style based on contingency theory

	SITUATIONAL FACTORS		
LEADERSHIP STYLE	Very Favorable	Moderately Favorable	Very Unfavorable
Socioemotional Orientation (High LPC)	Ineffective	Effective	Ineffective
Task Orientation (Low LPC)	Effective	Ineffective	Effective

Source: Based on "The contingency model and the dynamics of the leadership process" by F. E. Fiedler, 1978, in L. Berkowitz (ed.) *Advances in experimental social psychology* (Vol. 11), New York: Academic Press.

Researchers testing the predictions of contingency theory have encountered problems of measuring situational factors, and the LPC Scale is at best an indirect way of assessing leadership orientation. Nevertheless, studies in the laboratory, among military groups, and within organizations tend to support the theory (Bons and Fiedler, 1976; Strube and Garcia, 1981).

Fiedler (1978) suggested that when a group is performing successfully and socioemotional relations are good, both low and high LPC leaders have their primary needs satisfied. Under these conditions, each may spend some time with the opposite orientation. A tendency of leaders to adopt an opposite leadership orientation under favorable conditions has been shown in a laboratory study, but when conditions became unfavorable, leaders adopted the primary orientation indicated by their LPC scores (Green, Nebeker, and Boni, 1976).

Groupthink

People don't mind if you betray humanity, but if you betray your club, you are considered a renegade.

Arthur Koestler, The Age of Longing

Successful, long-standing, and cohesive groups may adopt a number of mechanisms that become counterproductive for effective functioning. Janis (1972) proposed that such groups reach decisions in characteristic ways, which he called **groupthink.** He analysed historical foreign policy decisions by the United States that have been typically judged as poor ones, including the Bay of Pigs invasion of Cuba, the failure to anticipate the surprise attack by the Japanese on Pearl Harbor, the decision to invade North Korea, and participation in the Vietnam War. None of these policies were based on false or inadequate information. Rather, the decision groups had all the information needed to anticipate the failure of the policies adopted. So why did they adopt those policies?

Janis found eight factors contributing to groupthink that fit all the cases he examined: (1) the prior successes of the groups led them to think that destiny was on their side, and excessive optimism made them believe they were invulnerable to failure; (2) the groups tended to rationalize warnings that would require a reexamination of the fundamental assumptions of their policy; (3) the groups' members were inclined to ignore the ethical and moral consequences of their decisions because they believed in the inherent morality of their group; (4) the groups imagined enemy leaders as too weak or stupid to counter risky U.S. policy, or as too evil to allow negotiation; (5) group members exerted pressure against any "deviate" who questioned the group's policy and treated dissent as disloyalty to the group; (6) group members were reluctant to voice dissent (because of self-cen-

Because the National Security Council is a long-established, cohesive group, its members are susceptible to functioning in specific modes that may have detrimental effects on the group's ability to make sound decisions. Irving Janis referred to such a counterproductive process as groupthink.

Box 12-6

The Bay of Pigs disaster

The processes of groupthink appear to have occurred in Kennedy's decision to help Cuban exiles invade the Bay of Pigs. John Kennedy had just been elected president, and his euphoric group of intellectuals felt that they were on the crest of historical currents and destined for great achievements. They discounted the odds that faced the fourteen hundred Cuban exiles as they confronted the two hundred thousand soldiers of Cuba. The implication of these numbers was denied by assuming that the Cuban army was badly trained and suffering from low morale. Both of these assumptions clearly were wrong.

Black-and-white simplistic thinking occurred among the advisors who assumed that they were strong and wise and that the enemy consisted of weak and stupid bad guys. Two mind guards emerged in the group, Secretary of State Dean Rusk and Attorney General Robert Kennedy. They defused criticisms and doubts by arguing that the decision to go ahead already had been made and that the requirements of secrecy would not allow for actions to check the underlying assumptions of the policy to invade. Arthur Schlesinger, Jr., an advisor to the president, said later that he did not voice objections because he thought others would consider him a nuisance. He felt that nothing would be accomplished anyway. No one raised a strong voice in opposition to alter this policy at any of the key meetings. Schlesinger later said, "Had one senior advisor opposed the adventure, I believe Kennedy would have canceled it. No one spoke against it" (Janis, 1972, p. 39).

Whether or not these processes operate frequently in cohesive groups, the knowledge that they can happen alerts members to avoid them. Eighteen months after the Bay of Pigs disaster, President Kennedy and his advisors faced the Cuban missile crisis. A number of procedures were adopted to avoid the groupthink processes that had occurred earlier. The president stayed away from some meetings so that advisors would not be inhibited in their discussions. He encouraged all members to question all facts, assumptions, and opinions, and to be devil's advocates. Outside experts were brought in, and a conscious effort was made to develop a set of possible alternatives. Robert Kennedy argued that a sneak attack against Cuba would be immoral and compared such an attack to the bombing of Pearl Harbor. The preferred policy at the beginning of discussions was not the policy adopted (Schlesinger, 1965; Sorenson, 1966).

sorship) and discounted the importance of any members' doubts about their policy; (7) no members spoke forcefully against their policy so all of the above factors contributed to an illusion of unanimity; (8) *mind guards* emerged who protected the leaders from contrary information and demanded that "nervous nellies" get behind the leader. The operation of these processes at the Bay of Pigs is described in Box 12-6.

Summary

Participating in groups affects the cognitions and behavior of individuals. Performance of simple tasks is facilitated and performance of complex tasks is impaired when an audience is present. Social facilitation occurs when audiences cause arousal in individuals and energize their dominant responses. Audiences can serve to distract individuals and interfere with their solving of complex tasks because individuals become concerned about how audiences will evaluate them. When individual members cannot be identified by others, as occurs in group activities, they tend to engage in social loafing.

People have a tendency to conform to the attitudes and values of groups to which they belong. The probability of conforming, including compliance and internalization, is greater when a person who is attracted to a group experiences ambiguity in making judgments and there is no dissent in the group. Groups isolate and punish deviant members, but the presence of one dissenter significantly decreases the perceived pressure to conform among other group members. The behavior of others often leads to behavioral and social contagion. The example of one member decreases others' inhibition and concern about negative evaluations from others. Deindividuated behavior may occur in groups because of lessened responsibility associated with anonymity.

People make more extreme choices after hearing group discussions than before. With such polarization, people may take greater risks or they may become more cautious. The direction in which people change or shift is affected by cultural values, social comparisons on the valued dimensions, a desire to project a positive impression in the eyes of others, and the number of persuasive arguments. A member may shift toward risk in groups because of diffusion of responsibility that makes the individual less concerned about the possibility of failure. To some degree, people gain their identities by membership in groups. Such membership has an impact on how the individual perceives members of other groups. Out-group members are perceived as more homogeneous in characteristics than in-group members. Group ethnocentrism is exhibited in the evaluations of the activities, products, and performances of in-groups and out-groups with more positive evaluations of the former and more negative evaluations of the latter. A group-serving bias is also exhibited, whereby negative traits are more apt to be attributed to out-group members and positive traits are attributed to in-group members.

The group dynamics associated with collective problem solving requires coordination and leadership. Increases in the size of the group may have positive or negative effects on group problem solving, depending on the nature of the task. Leaders provide orientation for the group, help coordinate activities, and contribute to solving tasks for the group. In a form of transaction, the group gives rewards, status, and idiosyncrasy credits to the leader. The legitimate authority of a leader is based on normativity and consensus. The effectiveness of task-oriented and socio-emotional leadership is contingent on the type of situation.

Glossary

Additive task Productivity in working on a task is a sum of all those who work on it.

Autokinetic effect A pinpoint of light gives the illusion of movement in a dark room.

Behavioral contagion An individual performs a normally inhibited behavior after observing another person perform it.

Cohesiveness The sum of attraction members have for a group as a result of shared goals, experiences of success, competition with out-groups, and significance of the group for personal identity.

Communication network A pattern of person-to-person communications in a given group that varies from centralized to decentralized.

Compliance An individual conforms in public in order to gain rewards and/or avoid punishments.

Deindividuation A state of lessened responsibility produced by loss of individual identification, which leads to antinormative behavior.

Depolarization An individual's movement from an extreme to a more neutral position on an issue following group discussion.

Endorsement Support given a leader by group members, as in voting; depends on leader's competence, success, and interest in the group and its goals.

Ethnocentrism Bias favoring one's own group that contributes to prejudice against an out-group.

Group Two or more people who communicate with one another to coordinate activities directed toward achieving shared goals.

Group-serving bias The tendency to attribute positive characteristics to in-group members and negative characteristics to members of out-groups.

Groupthink Premature consensus seeking in cohesive groups.

Homogeneity bias Members of an out-group are perceived to be more alike than individuals in one's own group; contributes to ethnocentrism.

Idiosyncrasy credit Hypothetical credit earned by a leader through conformity to the expectations of followers and through contributions to group goals; these credits can be expended in proposing innovations.

Informational conformity An individual yields to group judgments when the individual is uncertain or when the task is ambiguous.

Internalization Conformity with group norms either in private or in public as a result of private acceptance of group standards.

Leader An individual who occupies a central position in a group and is labeled as a leader; one who influences, directs, and coordinates the behavior of other members to achieve group goals.

Least preferred co-worker (LPC) A person who is rated the most inadequate co-worker in a rater's work history; the rating provides a measure of task vs. socioemotional orientations of leaders; more negative ratings indicate a task-oriented leader.

Normative conformity An individual alters his or her behavior or belief out of desire to gain approval from group members or out of fear of punishment.

Normativity Limits on a leader's actions in terms of range of activities, rights to reward and punish group members, and group consensus on limits.

Polarization A member's shift in attitudes from more moderate to more extreme positions following group discussion.

Risky shift An increased tendency by individuals to make more risky or extreme decisions following group discussion.

Saturation A key person experiences information overload in a communication network.

Social conformity Changes in an individual's behavior or belief in a direction favored by a group that occurs as a result of real or imagined group pressure.

Social contagion The example of another person encourages an individual to perform a socially prohibited action.

Social facilitation An individual's performance on a well-learned task is expedited by the presence of others.

Social identity theory Self-esteem depends on how we evaluate our groups as compared to other groups.

Social impairment An individual's performance on tasks that require learning is impeded by the presence of others.

Social loafing Decrease in the effort of an individual member particularly when the group is working on an additive task and when behavior is not under surveillance.

Recommended Readings

Austin, W. G., and Worchel, S. (1979). *The social psychology of intergroup relations.* Monterey, CA: Brooks/Cole.

The authors concentrate on intergroup perceptions and actions. The emphasis is on the development of conflict between groups and techniques of conflict resolution.

Forsyth, D. R. (1983). *An introduction to group dynamics.* Monterey, CA: Brooks/Cole.

An up-to-date review of topics, such as conformity, social facilitation, and leadership, from the perspective of a relative newcomer to the study of groups.

Janis, I. L. (1983). *Groupthink* (2nd ed.). Boston: Houghton Mifflin.

A very successful, widely read book that presents the theory of groupthink and supporting evidence from an analysis of major political events; written for the general reader and of special interest to those who enjoy political history.

Shaw, M. E. (1981). Group dynamics: *The psychology of small group behavior* (3rd ed.). New York: McGraw-Hill.

One of the classic texts on group dynamics for the serious, technically oriented reader.

There is nothing so practical as a good theory.

Kurt Lewin

13
Applying social psychology

The case of the "Harrisburg Seven"

At the height of domestic turmoil over the Vietnam War, the federal government accused Father Philip Berrigan and six other antiwar protesters of conspiring to raid draft boards, kidnap Henry Kissinger, and blow up heating tunnels in Washington, D.C. Although the trial could have taken place in any number of different cities, the government chose Harrisburg, Pennsylvania, a city where the population was known to be conservative and progovernment (Saks, 1976).

A group of social scientists volunteered to aid the defense for the "Harrisburg Seven" in selecting a jury (Schulman, Shaver, Colman, Emrich, and Christie, 1973). They gathered data about the characteristics of the general population of Harrisburg and about the pool of potential jurors. The scientists discovered that the pool of jurors was older than the general population. When the defense presented this information to the judge, a new jury pool was created to make it more representative of the community.

Education was found to be associated with conservative attitudes among the potential jurors. College educated people over the age of thirty tended to be conservative business people, and could be assumed to have a tendency to be biased against the defendants. A profile of the kind of juror most likely to be sympathetic to the defendants was constructed. The "perfect" juror would be a female Democrat who had no religious preference and who worked in a white-collar job. The defense adopted the tactic of disqualifying as many jurors as possible who did not fit the "perfect" profile constructed by the social scientists. Over a three-week period, 465 potential jurors were reduced to the required number of 12 people.

The actual trial began on 24 January, 1972. The prosecution called 64 witnesses, but the defense, led by former Attorney General Ramsey Clark, called no witnesses. After two months, the jury began deliberation but was unable to reach a unanimous decision on the conspiracy charges in seven days. Ten members favored acquittal and two held out for a guilty verdict. A mistrial was declared. Although we will never know whether the intervention of social scientists affected the final outcome, the case is a dramatic example of the use, and some would say abuse, of social psychology in an applied setting—the courtroom.

Social psychologists increasingly are turning their

attention to research that has some practical application. For example, they carry out research to find the best ways to encourage people to conserve energy and to discover methods of reducing conflicts between people and nations. In Chapter 13, we explore some of the contributions social psychologists have made to law, health, environment, and social conflict.

A perspective on applying social psychology

We shall never succeed in changing our age of iron into an age of gold until we give up our ambition to find a single cause for all our ills.

Aldous Huxley

Kurt Lewin was an early advocate of conducting research in applied settings. He believed that behavior was not just a set of learned habits, but that it was often developed in the context of an individual's social and physical environment. If this is true, then we could not develop an adequate theory of social psychology only from research in laboratories. Lewin argued for **action research,** which is devoted both to scientific knowledge and to social action. In his own research, Lewin (1948) examined social conflicts in marriages, in organizations, and in majority and minority groups. While recognizing that the goal of science is to develop coherent theories to explain behavior, Lewin (1948) also believed this: "Research that produces nothing but books will not suffice" (p. 203).

Not every social psychologist agrees with Lewin. There are real conflicts between the goals of pure and applied researchers. The **pure scientist** desires to understand social behavior, devises elegant theories, and evaluates them in controlled experiments. The **applied scientist** is a kind of engineer, more concerned with finding solutions to practical problems and applying them to real-world situations than with discovering the basic principles of social behavior. Generally, however, the work of pure and applied scientists is useful to social psychologists.

The more complex the situation, the less control researchers have over the variables operating on human actors, and the less confident we can be about any generalizations drawn from research. On the other hand, one can adopt Lewin's notion that "sloppy validity is to be preferred to strict reliability." There is obviously a trade-off between the scientific concern for control and manipulation of variables and the applied concern for studying people in the natural world where a set of uncontrolled and complex events transpire. In Box 13-1 on p. 364, a strategy for breaking large problems into simpler and more controllable ones is described.

We must remember that social psychology is concerned with a limited range of human behavior (see Chapter 1) and focuses mostly on the face-to-face interactions of individuals. Social problems always involve economic, political, geographical, and sociological factors. The social psychologist is seldom sufficiently knowledgeable to undertake a study of an entire problem area, but instead concentrates on various psychological aspects. Just as an accountant does not tell the engineers at General Motors how to design cars, any single social scientist is poorly positioned to make recommendations on overall solutions to social problems.

Applying science can be difficult, but we need not throw up our hands in despair. The skills and tools of social scientists are invaluable aids in coming to grips with apparently intractable social problems. The first stage is to analyze a problem. The social scientist is skilled in breaking down a problem into component parts, looking for relations among the parts and devising methods of measuring and studying the hypothesized relationships. If potential solutions to problems are recommended, the social scientist also has the tools to evaluate the impact of those policies. As Lewin suggested, action research asks three basic questions: what is the situation, what are the problems, and what are the solutions? In addition, **evaluation research** can determine if the solutions are having the intended effects.

Social psychology and the law

Jurymen seldom convict a person they like or acquit one they dislike.

Clarence Darrow

The case of the Harrisburg Seven is just one instance where research carried out by social psychologists has been applied to the law. Among the many research areas undertaken by social psychologists in addition to

Box 13-1

Small wins

Many social problems, such as poverty, air pollution, and racial prejudice, are so complex that researchers may feel they are unsolvable. The immensity of the problems may produce feelings of helplessness and frustration, interfering with the researcher's ability to plan a research strategy systematically. Researchers may free themselves from the burden of trying to solve massive social problems all at once by attempting to gain *small wins* (Weick, 1984). By segmenting social problems into clearly defined smaller ones, a researcher can achieve tangible solutions that may stimulate others to achieve further small wins until ultimately the larger problem is solved.

Weick provides several interesting examples of small wins by political groups fighting for social change. For example, advocates of gay rights are strongly in favor of equal treatment of homosexuals in every facet of society. Although this goal may seem remote at present, members of the Gay Liberation Movement realized a small win in 1972 when they persuaded the Library of Congress to change the way it classified books on homosexuality. Before 1972, books concerned with homosexuality were classified under the topic of abnormal sexual relations and perversions. After a protest by gay rights activists, the classification system was changed so that these books were catalogued under "varieties of sexual life." The long-term goal of equal rights for gay people ultimately may be achieved by a series of such small wins. It will be interesting to see if an analogous strategy of small wins will be adopted by applied social psychologists in their attempts to eventually find solutions for complex social problems.

Believers in gay rights rally for homosexual equality and against discrimination. The Gay Liberation Movement has made slow but small wins in advancing its goals as have other minority groups throughout history.

jury selection are eyewitness testimony, factors affecting jury decisions, and attitudes of jurors toward the death penalty. This research increasingly has captured the attention and respect of members of the legal community. Historically, the first major recognition of the research of social scientists was in the *Brown v. Board of Education* case in 1954. In a footnote to their landmark ruling that "separate but equal" education was unconstitutional, the Supreme Court of the United States cited a number of research studies, including those of social psychologist Kenneth Clark, indicating that segregation had deleterious psychological effects on children.

Eyewitness testimony

In 1908 Professor Munsterberg of Harvard University wrote a book entitled *On the Witness Stand.* This book constituted the first attempt to apply the principles of psychology to the evaluation of courtroom testimony (Tapp, 1976). Munsterberg contended that eyewitnesses were highly unreliable informants about events. Little research was carried out to substantiate his hypothesis. A resurgence of interest has occurred, however, with the emergence of cognitive social psychology (see Chapters 2, 4, and 5) and the discovery of a number of perceptual and cognitive biases.

Professionals working within the American legal system regard the testimony of eyewitnesses as the most influential evidence that can be presented in court (Hosch and Cooper, 1982). It is considered more valid and accurate than either alibi testimony or circumstantial evidence. In one study, subjects who acted as mock jurors heard one of four forms of testimony: eyewitness, fingerprint expert, polygraph expert, or handwriting expert. As can be seen in Figure 13-1, the highest rate of convictions occurred when subjects were presented with eyewitness testimony (Loftus, 1983).

Even when eyewitness testimony is later discredited, research indicates that it continues to have an impact upon decisions of mock jurors. Subjects acting as jurors read a scenario depicting a robbery of a grocery store and the murder of the store owner and his five-year-old granddaughter (Loftus, 1974). Some of the subjects read that the prosecution's case was based primarily on physical evidence: the defendant was found with a large sum of cash in his possession, and traces of ammonia used to clean the grocery store were on his shoes. In addition to this evidence, other subjects read about a store clerk who testified that he had seen the defendant shoot the victims. In a third condition, subjects were presented with both physical evidence and eyewitness testimony, then they were

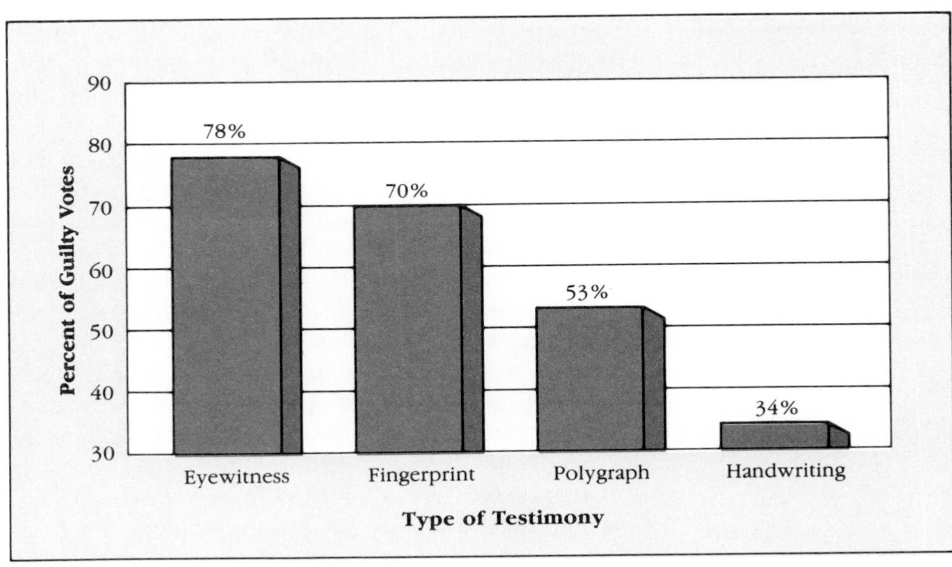

Figure 13-1 Disproportionate influence of eyewitness testimony.

Source: Based on "Whose shadow is crooked?" by E. Loftus, 1983, *American Psychologist, 38,* 576-577.

told that the eyewitness had poor vision and was not wearing his glasses on the day of the crime.

The results showed that eyewitness testimony, even when it was discredited, strongly influenced jury decisions. Eighteen percent of the jurors voted for conviction when presented only with physical evidence, but 72 percent believed the defendant to be guilty when they also heard eyewitness testimony. Even when the eyewitness testimony was discredited, 68 percent of the subjects voted for conviction.

Given the importance of the testimony of eyewitnesses on jurors' decisions, it would be desirable to evaluate the accuracy of eyewitness testimony. Researchers have found that eyewitness testimony is often unreliable, and results have contradicted popular beliefs about eyewitness testimony many times (see Table 13-1). An appropriate depiction was presented in the Japanese movie *Rashomon,* in which four travelers described the same occurrence. Although they witnessed the same event, their stories were all different. Like these Japanese travelers, eyewitness testimony for the courtroom tends to be idiosyncratic and error prone (Monahan and Loftus, 1982).

Although there is no doubt that a good deal of lying takes place in a courtroom, despite the oath witnesses take to tell the truth, the inaccuracy of eyewitnesses is not only a matter of deliberate deception. As we see in Chapters 2,4, and 5, perception and memory are constructive (or reconstructive) processes and not videorecorded playbacks of events. Self-interest and self-esteem, impression management concerns, expectations, perspective, and cognitive and perceptual biases affect the accuracy of eyewitnesses in criminal cases. As in the case described in Box 13-2, one consequence is that people can be convicted for crimes they did not commit.

The Jackson case illustrates the fallacy associated with the belief that victims remember the details of violent crimes better than nonviolent crimes. If there is an association between accuracy of memory and emotional arousal, it may be in the opposite direction. The increased stress and anxiety induced by violence, as in a rape, may produce distortions and biases in a victim when he or she later tries to reconstruct what happened.

A sure-fire, attention-grabbing classroom demonstration is to have someone enter the room during lecture and fire a starter's pistol at the professor. After the cheering dies down, the students can be asked to report what they have witnessed. In one such demonstration, marked disagreement was found between what the eyewitnesses reported and what a videotape of the incident showed (Buckhort, 1979). Although the actual incident took just thirty-four seconds, the 141 eyewitnesses estimated the duration at eighty-one seconds. They overestimated the suspect's weight (on the average) by about twenty-five pounds, slightly overestimated his height, and thought he was several years younger than his actual age. Seven weeks after the incident occurred, students were asked to identify the attacker from a set of six photographs. Only 40 percent of the students were able to correctly identify the attacker, and 25 percent identified an outsider who just happened to be in the classroom at the time of the incident. Even the professor who had been attacked was unable to identify the actual assailant correctly, but instead chose the innocent stranger.

The tendency for victims to be just as inaccurate as other observers was demonstrated in a more systematic laboratory study. Subjects interacted with a female confederate, observed the confederate steal another person's calculator, or had their own watches taken. When later asked to identify the confederate from among six photographs, subjects were more accurate when a theft had taken place. There was no difference

Table 13-1 Common misconceptions about eyewitness testimony

Misconception: Eyewitnesses remember the details of a violent crime better than one that is nonviolent.
Actuality: The opposite is true, violence-produced stress distorts perceptions and recall.

Misconception: Eyewitnesses typically underestimate the duration of a crime.
Actuality: Eyewitnesses usually estimate that a crime takes longer than it really does, with the amount of overestimation increasing as the degree of violence and stress increases.

Misconception: The more confident eyewitnesses are, the more accurate their reports.
Actuality: There is no relationship between confidence and accuracy.

Source: Based on "Essential but unreliable" by E. F. Loftus, February, 1984, *Psychology Today*, pp. 22-26.

Box 13-2

Five years in jail for a crime he did not commit

The unreliability of eyewitness testimony led to tragedy for William Bernard Jackson. He spent five years in jail for a conviction on several counts of rape. Jackson was released when a person who looked like him confessed to the crime. Eyewitness testimony had led to Jackson's conviction. Two of the rape victims positively identified him as the man who had assaulted them. During testimony, one of the rape victims was asked whether she had any doubt that Jackson was the man who raped her and whether there was any chance that she could be mistaken. She confidently answered no to both questions. Although several witnesses for the defense testified that Jackson was at his home during the time of the rapes, the jury chose to believe the eyewitness testimony of the rape victims. (Loftus, 1984).

in subject accuracy when the subject had or had not been the victim (Hosch and Cooper, 1982).

It also has been found that the accounts of eyewitnesses can be distorted by the way in which they are asked to recall what they saw. In one study, subjects were shown a film of a car crash and then were asked how fast the cars were going (Loftus and Palmer, 1974). For some subjects, the word "hit" was used to describe the accident, for others the word "smash" was used. Subjects who were asked how fast the cars were going when they "hit" each other estimated slower speeds than those who estimated how fast the cars were going when they "smashed."

One week later the same subjects were asked whether they had seen broken glass in the filmed incident. Actually, no broken glass had been shown. Only 14 percent of the subjects who heard the word "hit" said they had seen broken glass, but 32 percent of the subjects who heard the word "smash" responded affirmatively to the question. The latter subjects apparently incorporated the term "smashed" into their reconstruction of the accident and, as a result, remembered it as more serious than those who heard "hit."

There are ways of training people to be more accurate as eyewitnesses. In one demonstration of training people in observational skills, students were shown a videotape of a purse-snatching incident (Boice, Hanley, Shaughnessy, and Gansler, 1982). They then either had a difficult or easy observational task to perform. When later asked to identify the perpetrator from a lineup, subjects who had completed the difficult observation task were more accurate. Police academy training programs often include courses that aid rookies in observing and remembering details of events they witness.

Jury decisions

Social psychologists cannot carry out experiments in courtrooms. As an alternative, subjects are instructed to act "as if" they are jurors judging the guilt or innocence of a defendant in actual trials. This role-playing technique is often referred to as **mock jury research.** Results obtained from mock jury research can then be compared to natural observations of actual jury trials. When the data obtained from the two sources are sufficiently similar, we may tentatively conclude that factors affecting jury decisions have been found.

In Chapter 10, we saw that the physical attractiveness of a person affects others' judgments about the

Biography

Elizabeth F. Loftus

Although she is now one of the best-known psychologists in the world, Elizabeth Loftus had other career aspirations in her younger years. At different times in her childhood she wanted to be a doctor, a private eye, and a stockbroker. Her medical interests came from her father who was a general practitioner in southern California. Spy novels generated her aspiration to become a private detective. Loftus's interest in a career as a stockbroker came after she used her high school graduation money to buy Comsat at $20 per share and watched it double in a short period of time.

Despite these diverse early interests, Loftus majored in mathematics at UCLA. She had won a high school mathematics prize; but about halfway through college, she became somewhat bored with math, because it "seemed so dry." She happened upon a few psychology courses and loved them. After hearing about "mathematical psychology," she decided to enroll in graduate school at Stanford University to combine her math and psychological interests.

When Loftus was at Stanford she combined her research on traffic accidents for the government with a study on how we remember words. The end result of this work has produced much of the research on eyewitness testimony and reconstructive memory reported in Chapter 13. Dr. Loftus' book entitled *Eyewitness Testimony* (1979) won the National Media Award from the American Psychological Association in 1980. Now a professor of psychology at the University of Washington in Seattle, Dr. Loftus has written numerous articles and books relating to the areas of cognitive psychology, memory, and psychology and the law.

As to the future of eyewitness testimony, Dr. Loftus notes:

> The reason that this area is such a wonderful one to research is because it has both theoretical and practical implications. Theoretically, there is the issue of memory and when and how it changes. I see more work occurring here. From a practical standpoint, the work tells us something about how to interview people so as to get more accurate and complete information from them. The next few years should show an increase in the number of studies that are done to develop ways of improving the information that we obtain from witnesses. (personal communication, July 30, 1984)

person's responsibility for his or her action. A review of mock jury studies shows that attractive defendants are less likely to be found guilty and are given lighter jail sentences when found guilty than unattractive defendants (Perlman and Cozby, 1983). We know that similarity is related to attraction, so we might expect that jurors would be lenient toward those with whom they share similar attitudes. Indeed, this was the assumption of the social scientists aiding the Harrisburg Seven. In confirmation of this hypothesis, mock jurors who had favorable attitudes toward the use of drugs recommended more lenient sentences for accused drug offenders (Lussier, Perlman, and Breen, 1977).

In an examination of actual courtroom decisions, judges were asked to recount decisions made by juries, the judgments they would have rendered, and their reasons for disagreements (Kalven and Zeisel, 1966). Of the 962 criminal trials where the judges disagreed with the juries' decisions, the judges indicated that 11 percent could be attributed to the positive or negative impressions that the jury formed of the defendant.

Attractiveness of the defendant does not always affect the decisions of jurors. For example, attractive defendants were judged as deserving less punishment for traffic violations than those who were less attractive, but subjects saw no difference in defendant attractiveness when the crime was vehicular homicide (Piehl, 1977). In general, the more severe the crime, the less the influence of the defendant's attractiveness on a jury's verdict (Carol and Wiener, 1982).

Attractiveness also has less impact on a jury's decision when the evidence in the case is unambiguous. This result was found when college students acting as mock jurors were provided with information about a hypothetical case in which the defendant was accused

"Too bad! If you had shaved and worn a tie, I could probably have gotten you off with life."

of driving while intoxicated. The driver was described as attractive or unattractive and was said to be drunk, but the speed of the car was either known to have been excessive or was not known. The attractive defendant was judged less severely than the unattractive one when the jurors did not know the actual speed of the automobile, but this bias diminished when the speed was known to have been excessive (Baumeister and Darley, 1982).

Where the attractiveness of a defendant is perceived as having aided the crime, it may become a liability in the courtroom. Mock jurors were less likely to convict an attractive defendant in a theft case; but when the crime was swindling, a crime aided by an attractive appearance, the unattractive defendant was treated more leniently (Sigall and Ostrove, 1975). We can conclude from these studies that attractive defendants generally do get the benefit of the doubt in simulated jury studies. This benefit, however, decreases in instances where the evidence is unambiguous or where the defendant's good looks appear to have helped in committing the crime.

Race and jury decisions

Statistics show that over 50 percent of the population in American prisons are nonwhite (Silberman, 1978). Minority group members are more likely to be charged with crimes, to be convicted, and to receive greater sentences than other citizens (Stark, 1975). These data do not necessarily imply a pattern of discrimination, but could indicate that members of minorities are more likely to be criminals and to commit serious crimes. Laboratory studies suggest that racial bias does occur in courtroom decisions, however. White mock jurors were more likely to find a black defendant guilty than a white defendant charged with the same crime (Foley and Chamblin, 1982). Black mock jurors did not show any bias in reaching decisions about black and white defendants. The tendency of white jurors to be biased in reaching verdicts for black defendants is particularly serious because blacks typically are underrepresented on juries (Silberman, 1978).

Some research indicates that the race of a victim has a greater impact on jury decisions in cases where the evidence against the defendant is equivocal or ambiguous than when the evidence is clear cut. A simulation of a rape trial was acted out and recorded on videotape. White college students watched the trial, heard the testimony, and saw the defendant and victim. The victim was either white or black. When the evidence was strongly in favor of the defendant or the prosecution, the race of the victim did not affect the mock juror's judgments. When the evidence was less clear, however, the jurors tended to perceive the defendant more guilty if the victim had been white rather than black (Klein and Creech, 1982). When uncertainty is greatest, other characteristics of the defendant and victim become more important for jurors in reaching a judgment about the defendant's guilt or innocence.

Attitudes of jurors toward the death penalty

The attitudes and values of potential jurors may prompt attorneys to dismiss them during the jury selection *(voir dire)* phase of a trial. We have seen in the case of the Harrisburg Seven that jurors were selected on the basis of their liberal political attitudes. A common basis of exclusion in trials involving capital crimes is the citizen's attitude toward the death penalty. It seems reasonable to exclude from jury duty people who are opposed to the death penalty. Such people might acquit a guilty person rather than contribute to a form of punishment they oppose. On the other hand, excluding such people from jury duty could mean that the defendant would be faced with a "hanging" jury more likely to reach a guilty verdict.

A survey of eight hundred eligible jurors in California revealed that 17 percent would not vote for a death penalty (Fitzgerald and Ellsworth, 1984). More women than men, and more blacks than whites opposed the death penalty. In addition, those people who would be dismissed systematically from jury duty in capital cases were more concerned with due process, less favorable to punishment of all kinds, and more open to the arguments provided by defense attorneys than citizens who favored the death penalty.

In a follow-up study, potential jurors were recruited to participate in a mock jury trial in which they watched a videotape of a murder trial (Cowan, Thompson, and Ellworth, 1984). One twelve-person jury consisted only of people favoring the death penalty, and a second type consisted of at least two people who opposed the death penalty. As might be expected, the homogeneous juries were more likely to reach a guilty verdict than were the mixed juries. In addition, mixed juries were more critical in the evaluation of testimony and recalled evidence better than did homogeneous juries. The clear implication of these findings is that exclusion of people from jury duty because of their opposition to the death penalty makes it more likely that a defendant in a capital case will be found guilty. This has led some to seek change in the judicial process.

Social psychology and the law: some limitations

The use of role-playing in mock jury studies has been criticized. People in hypothetical situations may behave differently from people in courtrooms where significant consequences occur. This difference between the imaginary and the real was shown in a study in which undergraduate students were provided with information about another student who was alleged to have stolen an examination (Wilson and Donnerstein, 1977). Some of the students were told that the case was only hypothetical and that they were to act "as if" they were jurors; other students were led to believe their decisions would have real consequences for the alleged test thief. Students who believed their decisions would have real consequences were more likely to convict the accused student than were those who believed they were making a decision about a hypothetical case. This finding suggests that psychologists should be cautious in interpreting mock jury studies.

Although we have concentrated on eyewitness testimony and jury decisions, social psychologists also have carried out studies on the setting of bail bonds, the effects of instructions by judges on jury decisions, such as the charge to the jury by the judge, the size of the jury, sentencing, rehabilitation, and parole. This is a rapidly expanding area of research and can be expected to generate many interesting findings in the future.

Social psychology applied to health and aging

Every affection of the mind that is attended with either pain or pleasure, hope, or fear, is the cause of an agitation whose influence extends to the heart.
William Harvey (1628)

For many centuries, it has been believed that psychological factors are important to the biological health of the person. In the nineteenth century, these beliefs entered the field of medicine under the name of psychiatry. Freud and his contemporaries developed the notion of psychosomatic medicine, which focused on how psychological problems were converted into physiological symptoms of illness. In the 1980s, it is recognized that the habits of a person may contribute to physiological states, which in turn, create health problems. For example, smoking, poor diet, and lack of exercise are associated with various symptoms of disease. The person also may experience a great deal of psychological stress in modern society, and learning to relax or to control sources of stress may be important to the maintenance of health. Some of the sources of stress are described in Box 13-3. These concerns have led to a new field in applied social psychology: **health psychology.**

The field of health psychology is already too large for us to describe in one section of this textbook (Gatchel and Baum, 1983). As a consequence, it will be necessary to present only a few selected areas of research to illustrate the contribution that social psychologists are making to health care.

Box 13-3

Stressful life events: the eruption of Mount St. Helens

Tragic life events, such as separation, divorce, and death, have been associated with increases in physical illnesses (Vinokur and Selzer, 1975). It is not just the **stressful life event** that causes health damage, but a feeling that the calamity is uncontrollable. A feeling of control over unpleasant events decreases the amount of stress experienced by the person (Rodin, Bohm, and Wack, 1982).

The stress associated with natural disasters may have a negative impact on the health and adjustment of entire communities. There is some evidence that citizens of Othello, Washington, may have suffered long-term health problems as a result of the volcanic eruption of Mount St. Helens on 18 May, 1980 (Adams and Adams, 1984). Data were obtained six months after the eruption and compared with information from an equivalent period before the disaster. It was found that the eruption significantly affected the health of the citizens of Othello. The postdisaster community records indicated a 21 percent increase in emergency room visits, a 19 percent death rate increase, and over a 200 percent increase in psychosomatic and mental illnesses.

The researchers concluded that the psychological and physical harm caused by an uncontrollable natural disaster, such as Mount St. Helens, is not just a temporary dislocation, but it induces stress that continues to have detrimental effects on health long after the immediate physical damage has been repaired. This conclusion must be accepted with caution, however, because we must recognize that other factors occurring in the world at large and in Othello following the volcanic eruption, and not the eruption itself, might have caused the increase in health problems.

Cigarette smoking

It is better to be without a wife for a bit than without tobacco for an hour.

Estonian proverb

Warning: The Surgeon General has determined that cigarette smoking is dangerous to your health.

Inscription on all cigarette packages

In 1979 Joseph Califano, Secretary of the U.S. Department of Health and Welfare, called cigarette smoking the largest preventable cause of death in America and referred to smoking as "slow motion suicide" (Gatchel and Baum, 1983). Despite these stern warnings, people continue to smoke. More than 600 billion cigarettes are smoked each year in the United States (Oskamp, 1984). It is estimated that 80 million workdays are lost each year due to the deleterious effects of smoking on health (Parkes, 1983). Smoking has been linked to heart disease, cancer, and stroke, the three leading causes of death, as well as to other diseases.

Of course smoking is a behavior pattern, a habit, that is very difficult to break by all accounts. Indeed, evidence points to a physiological addiction in heavy smokers not unlike other forms of drug addiction. A dependence on nicotine was investigated among light and heavy smokers (Schachter, 1977). Heavy smokers compensated for a reduction in the nicotine levels in cigarettes by smoking more cigarettes. This kind of compensation did not occur among light smokers. Like other forms of addiction, smoking is not reduced or terminated easily through therapeutic intervention (cf. Lichtenstein, 1982). It might be easier to prevent people from developing a smoking habit than to get them to stop once they have it.

Most people who have a smoking habit developed it when they were adolescents. Knowledge of this fact has led to the widespread use of informational and educational campaigns in schools to deter young people from smoking. The word has gotten across. Most school children know full well the dangers of smoking by the time they are twelve (Evans, Rozelle, Mittlemark, Hansen, Bane, and Havis, 1978). Yet, they still develop smoking habits. Why?

Someone once said that youth is wasted on the young. They typically are concerned only with the here and now and pay little attention to far-off consequences of their actions. The long-term effects of smoking on health are sufficiently remote for young people who feel indestructable and immortal to ignore them. Young people who smoke simply do not feel they are endangered by the habit (Henderson, Hall, and Lipton, 1979).

Another reason why adolescents continue to smoke is that there are very powerful social factors motivating them to smoke, and these factors overwhelm their knowledge of its dangers. Many adolescents smoke for self-presentational reasons. They believe that smoking makes them appear sophisticated, mature, successful, and attractive to others (Barton, Chassin, Presson, and Sherman, 1983).

Most people establish smoking habits when they are adolescents. Strong peer pressure and self-presentational factors can motivate adolescents to indulge in cigarettes and alcoholic beverages. Once these behavior patterns are well developed, they are difficult to change.

Adolescents who begin smoking may perceive peer pressure to continue because they think "everyone else is doing it." In Chapter 4, we learn that people sometimes exhibit a **false consensus effect** whereby they think that what they do is done more by other people than is actually the case. A survey of adolescents found a false consensus effect among smokers (Sherman, Presson, Chassin, Corty, and Olshavsky, 1983). The 25 percent of the adolescent population who are regular smokers made higher estimates about the number of adolescents who smoked than did nonsmokers.

Recognition of the tendency of young people to ignore remote effects of smoking led some researchers to emphasize more immediate negative outcomes. In one study, young people were shown a videotape depicting the immediate effects of smoking, such as carbon dioxide entering the body. Others were exposed to a message from the American Cancer Society that emphasized the long-term dangers of smoking. The group exposed to the message about immediate negative outcomes expressed less desire to begin smoking and indicated a greater awareness of smoking as an immediate risk to their health than the group given the educational message about long-term effects (Mittelmark and Evans, 1978).

An even more sophisticated approach is to present adolescents with information from peers about immediate consequences of smoking and to include advice about strategies that can be used to resist peer pressures and modeling by parents (cf. Evans, 1980). Seventh graders in Houston, Texas, were shown videotapes depicting the social pressures on them to smoke and the various ways of resisting the temptation to smoke. To drive the message home more effectively, the actors and actresses in the movies were similar in age to the students. A follow-up several months later showed that only 10 percent of the students had begun smoking. This number was significantly less than the 18 percent among students not presented with this information. A follow-up three years later showed that 80 percent of the students said the tapes influenced their decision not to smoke. Only 20 percent said that the information had no impact on whether or not they chose to smoke. These data suggest that the antismoking commercials by Brook Shields shown on national television are probably effective.

Although this research is encouraging it must be

placed in the context of the immense pressures on young people to begin smoking. The cigarette industry is the leading advertiser in the United States in terms of dollars spent (Liebert, Sprafkin and Davidson, 1982). Attractive adult and peer models are presented to young people. These models are portrayed as sexy, sophisticated, and macho. Smoking is associated with independence, rebellion, and maturity. These are potent images and have magnetic power in inducing teenagers to begin smoking.

Coronary heart disease and personality

The reduction of starvation and malnutrition and the development of medicine in modern industrialized societies have extended the life span of the average person. It is difficult to believe that life expectancy for the average person in ancient civilizations was less than thirty years of age, and that even today in countries like Brazil and Bangladesh the average person will die before the age of forty. The extension of life into old age is associated with an increase in coronary heart disease. Diseases of the cardiovascular system are the leading causes of death in industrialized societies (Dembrowski, MacDougall, Herd, and Shields, 1983). One-half of all deaths in the United States are due to cardiovascular diseases (Krantz, Baum, and Singer, 1983). Approximately six hundred thousand Americans die from coronary heart disease annually and more than one-third of them are under sixty-five years of age (Suinn, 1982).

Smoking, diabetes, high levels of blood cholesterol, genetic background, obesity, and environmental stress are all associated with heart disease. Even combining these risk factors does not yield very good predictions about who will experience a heart attack (Glass and Carver, 1980). Recent research suggests that a particular lifestyle is a good predictor of the coronary-prone person. A person who adopts this pattern of behavior has come to be known as the ***Type A personality.***

The Type A personality shows a tremendous concern about the pressures of time, is very competitive, tends to be hostile and aggressive, and suppresses physiological symptoms. People who do not fit this description are referred to as **Type B personalities.** People with these two types of personalities can be identified by stressful interviews or by a paper-and-pencil scale called the Jenkins Activity Survey for Health Predictions. Both techniques are used to question respondents about behavior patterns relevant to the identification of a Type A personality (Cohen, 1980). It has been found that people identified as Type A personalities are twice as likely to have heart attacks as individuals identified as Type B personalities (Rosenman, Brand, Jenkins, Friedman, Straus, and Wurm, 1975).

Just as a professional football team rushes through its plays in the last two minutes of a game, the Type A personality lives life as a perpetual two-minute drill (see Box 13-4 on p. 374). There is a continual struggle to do more and more in less and less time. When asked to estimate a one-minute interval, Type A personalities thought the time period elapsed faster than the more laid-back Type B personalities (Carver and Humphries, 1982). Type A people also show up earlier for appointments (Gastorf, 1980). This concern for time, although adaptive in many situations, can lead to impaired performance when patience or delayed responses are required (Carver, 1980).

When Type A personalities work with others who work more slowly than themselves, they exhibit impatience and irritation (Matthews and Siegel, 1982). In such circumstances, the Type A personality is apt to use threats and punishments to make the other person work more quickly or efficiently. One study showed that Type A personalities gave more shocks to a confederate who was interfering with their completion of a difficult puzzle than did Type B personalities (Carver and Glass, 1978). The Type A personality is more achievement oriented and receives more honors in college. Type A personalities who become social scientists have their work cited more frequently in professional journals than scientists with a Type B personality (Glass, 1977; Matthews, Helmreich, Beans, and Lucker, 1980).

Since illness and fatigue interfere with achievement, Type A personalities tend to suppress physiological symptoms that would interfere with their urgent need to accomplish tasks. When asked to walk uphill on a moving treadmill, Type A men, women, and children maintained a pace closer to their maximum capacities and reported begin less fatigued than other subjects (Carver, Coleman and Glass, 1976; Matthews and Carra, 1982). Ratings by football coaches indicated that among injured players, those identified as Type A continued closer to the limits of their abilities than those identified as Type B (Carver, DeGregorio, and Gillis, 1981). Similarly, Type A women

Box 13-4

Living life on the edge of their seats

In a highly successful television commercial for Federal Express, an extremely agitated harrowed-looking executive speaks at incredible speed to one person after another while a paper machine goes out of control in the background. The idea created is that this executive is busy, has no time to waste, and has a lot to do. He needs to choose a company that can ensure delivery anywhere when "it positively, absolutely has to be there overnight." This tendency to behave at "full speed ahead" was associated with heart disease as early as 1892 (Osler, cited in Dembrowski et al., 1983).

An incident that occurred in the late 1950s led to a "discovery" of this time-pressured component of the Type A personality (Friedman and Rosenman, 1974). An upholsterer had been called to mend some chairs in the waiting room of some doctors' office. He asked what kind of doctors Friedman and Rosenman were. They told him they were cardiologists, but wanted to know why he asked. The upholsterer replied that he had mended chairs in many doctors' offices before, but that the chairs here were unusual because they were worn out primarily on their edges. This image of living life on the edge succinctly characterizes the behavior of the Type A personality.

suppress symptoms of menstrual distress more than their Type B counterparts (Matthews and Carra, 1982). A summary of differences between Type A and Type B personalities is presented in Table 13-2.

Table 13–2 Characteristics of Type A behavior pattern

Time urgency: Type A people constantly struggle to do more and more in less and less time. Type B people are more relaxed and less time conscious.

Aggressiveness and hostility: In response to frustrating events, Type A people react more aggressively than do Type B people.

Competitive achievement striving: Type A people typically work hard to win and succeed. They often will work at maximum capacity even in the absence of pressing deadlines.

Symptom suppression: Type A people suppress physical symptoms, such as fatigue and illness, that interfere with maximum achievement.

The push to do many things quickly places great stress on the body. Even among individuals as young as nineteen, those identified as Type A were found to have higher levels of serum cholesterol (Glass and Carver, 1980). A review of the relevant research sponsored by the National Heart, Lung, and Blood Institute and carried out by a panel of experts concluded that a significant association exists between Type A behavior patterns and heart disease (Suinn, 1982). Prevention of coronary heart disease may require some modification of Type A behaviors. The task is difficult because American society rewards those who get the job done in a quick and aggressive fashion. Preliminary results from a study of patients who had suffered a heart attack revealed that those who were undergoing behavior modification of their Type A characteristics had a 50 percent less chance of having a second attack than a control group (*USA Today,* 1984).

Institutionalization of the elderly

An important process associated with aging is a loss of control over aspects of the environment (Rodin, Bohm,

Elderly people lose a sense of how to regulate and manage their lives when they are institutionalized. Research studies have shown that those who are given an opportunity to exercise some control over their destiny in confined settings enjoy better health and contentment.

and Wack, 1982). Loss of job through retirement, reduced income, physical impairment, and loss of family, spouse, and friends are common occurrences as people grow older. The confluence of these factors can culminate when a once self-sufficient individual is no longer able to control his or her life. The result may be an increasing dependency upon family, friends, or institutions.

A feeling of loss of control over one's own life can induce stress and anxiety, and ultimately have a negative impact on both physical and psychological health even among young people. The loss of control experienced by elderly people when they are institutionalized can have catastrophic effects on their health. Research has shown that elderly people within an institution who have more control over their lives have better health. Even limited amounts of control may be important. For example, residents on one floor of a nursing home were encouraged to take responsibility for themselves, were given a plant to care for, and were given a choice of movies to watch. Residents on another floor were told that their needs would be taken care of by the staff, were given a plant that was watered by the staff, and had no choice of which movies they would view (Langer and Rodin 1976). Physical checkups six months later by doctors who were unaware of the psychological intervention showed that residents who were given more responsibility were more active, happier, and healthier than those with less responsibility. Eighteen months after first starting the study, it was discovered that 30 percent of the residents with low responsibility had died, while only 15 percent of those with high responsibility had died (Rodin and Langer, 1977). An apparently minor intervention, such as giving someone a plant to care for, dramatically affected both the quality and duration of the residents' lives.

Giving people control and then removing it may have deleterious effects on the health of the institutionalized elderly resident. In a field study done by Schultz (1976), four conditions were established regarding the residents' ability to control or predict the length and duration of visits from a college student: (1) control was given to the resident; (2) the resident knew when the visits would occur but could not alter them; (3) the resident could not control and was unable to predict when the visits would occur; or (4) the residents were not visited by a college student.

The immediate impact was that residents who could control the visits were happier and healthier than those in the other conditions. However, follow-up observations in twenty-four, thirty, and forty-two months, respectively, showed that residents in both the control and predictable visit conditions suffered deteriorating health. This treatment outcome is directly contrary to the earlier findings by Langer and Rodin (1976). The reason appears to be in the duration of control. Although the visits from the college student terminated after two months, the control given to residents to take care of their own plants was a permanent change. Apparently, those who had tasted the pleasure of control suffered when deprived of it.

Social psychology applied to the environment

Each of us inhabits an environment consisting of other people, noise, light, heat, architectural structures, and much else. Variations in these factors have noticeable effects on human behavior. Social psychologists who study the environment must first ascertain what its effects are and then if desired, find out how to change behavior by changing features of the surrounding environment. Among the more interesting factors under contemporary study are the individual's maintenance of personal space, the utilization of social space, crowding, and architectural design.

Personal space

There are cultural differences in postures, physical contact, and use of interpersonal distance (Hall, 1959). Those cultures that maintain small interpersonal distances when interacting have been classified as **contact cultures.** Included among contact cultures are the Mediterranean, Moslem, and Latin American cultures. **Noncontact cultures,** such as North Americans and Northern Europeans, prefer greater interpersonal distances (Hall, 1959). **Personal space** refers to an invisible and variable amount of space around a person's body that is guarded against intrusions (Sundstrom and Altman, 1976).

Invasions of the individual's personal space usually are experienced as unpleasant. When students in class were asked to talk to an acquaintance and to bring their faces close to the other person's, they caused the other person to become confused and embarrassed (Garfinkel, 1964). The person whose personal space had been invaded attributed sexual intentions to the intruder. Personal space and touch are so tied to sex and intimacy that it is difficult for people to disassociate them.

People's reactions to invasions of their personal space include reducing eye contact, turning away from the intruder, building a barrier and withdrawing from the invasion (LaFrance and Mayo, 1978; Sommer, 1969). Studies of personal space invasions in libraries have shown that people used books to build barriers and leaned away from intruders. They also left the library sooner than people whose space was not invaded (Patterson, Mullens, and Romano, 1971; Sommer, 1969). The people who stayed longest in the libraries were those who were seated alone at reading tables (Becker, 1973).

The interpersonal distance maintained by a person while interacting with another person is affected by considerations of status and social power. Historically, people maintained a respectable distance from the rich and the powerful. Confirmation of this relationship has been seen in studies of invasions of the space of women and blacks, two groups occupying inferior status positions in the United States. At a shopping mall, two people were positioned at some distance from one another and carried on a conversation. The pair consisted of two black people, one black and one white, or two white people. More people walked between the black-black pair than the other two pairs. Also, when people walked around the black-white pair, they more frequently walked in back of the white person (Brown, 1981). Similarly, when a male or a female was stationed two feet away from an airport water fountain, passersby were inhibited from drinking only when they would invade the space of the male (Riess and Salzer, 1981). In another variant of the drinking fountain procedure, it was found that fewer people drank when a confederate dressed in a suit and tie stood nearby than when one dressed in jeans and T-shirt stood there (Rosenfeld and Hessel, 1983).

Seating arrangements

In medieval times, kings seated themselves at one end of a long table with the court jester at the opposite end. Knights were seated along the two sides. A knight's importance was signified by how close he was seated to the king (Winick and Holt, 1961). A similar principle has been incorporated into modern rules of etiquette: "The guest of honor is always she who is taken in to dinner by the host and placed on his right. Whether she is the one for whom the dinner is given or merely selected at random, this place at the table

Box 13-5

The Paris peace talks for ending the Vietnam War

After years of fighting, the parties to the Vietnam War reached a snag in arranging a peace conference in Paris. Disagreement about the size and shape of the negotiating table and seating arrangements took several months to resolve. The negotiators for the United States and South Vietnam wanted a rectangular table with opposite side seating. This appearance of a two-sided negotiation was to prevent the National Liberation Front (NLF), believed to be sponsored by the North Vietnamese, from being recognized as an independent party to the conference. The North Vietnamese wanted a square table with the negotiators seated on all four sides. This would give the appearance that four equal parties were negotiating—the Americans, the South Vietnamese, the North Vietnamese, and the NLF.

A compromise was finally worked out. A round table was to be used with no dividing lines. This arrangement allowed the North Vietnamese to claim that all four parties were negotiating at the table, while the American side could argue that the lack of identifying physical dividers and a rule that both members of a side had to speak consecutively indicated that there were two main parties to the negotiations. During the eight months it took to resolve the dispute over the shape of the table and the seating arrangements, thousands of people on both sides were killed (Knapp, 1978).

makes her the guest of honor" (Post, 1960, p. 352). In his memoirs Henry Kissinger, former secretary of state, recalled how he and Alexander Haig fought for a room next to President Nixon on a visit to the Soviet Union. Both recognized that the perception of their status and power was directly related to their physical nearness to the president.

These historical and anecdoctal observations suggested the possibility that in situations where people can choose where to sit, their choices may imply their desire for power and influence (Korda, 1975). People who sit closer to one another tend to like each other (Byrne, 1961). Indeed, the nearer two people are in a seating arrangement, the more likely it is others will perceive them as liking one another (Rosenfeld, 1965). In mock jury deliberations, a person who was seated at the head of the table was most likely to be chosen foreperson (Strodbeck and Hook, 1961).

Evidence has been gathered indicating that college students are aware of the implications of seating arrangements and seat themselves according to their desired standing in a group. Subjects were instructed to imagine that they were taking part in a small group discussion around a rectangular table. They were asked to take a seat to convey an impression of leadership and dominance, attractiveness or hostility, or disinterest. Subjects systematically placed themselves at the head of the table to assume leadership, seated themselves close to the head of the table to induce liking from the leader or far away to indicate their dislike of the leader, and took positions of maximum distance and limited eye contact to indicate nonparticipation in the group (Riess and Rosenfeld, 1980). Seating arrangements can have international significance, as is indicated in Box 13-5.

Crowding and social behavior

By the year 2000, a large part of the world's population will live in densely populated urban areas (Davis, 1978). Mexico City and Bombay, for example, may each exceed 40 million in population. What effect does aggregating large numbers of people in limited geographical regions have on their behavior?

A series of studies have established statistical relationships between population density and deviant behavior patterns. Juvenile delinquency and adult crimes were found to be correlated with population density in the city of Honolulu. Similar findings were reported for Seattle and Minneapolis, along with evidence of fewer social problems in the less-populated suburbs (Schmid, 1969). The incidence of mental illness also was found to be higher within the cities than in the suburbs (Faris and Dunham, 1965). Sailors on more densely populated ships contracted more illnesses, and inmates of crowded prisons more frequently complained of illness (Dean, Pugh, and Gunderson 1975; McCain, Cox, and Paulus, 1976). The effects of density are even felt in college dormitories. Students living in three-person suites had lower grade point averages than those with only one roommate (Karlin, Rosen, and Epstein, 1979).

Crowding also has been associated with depression. In a survey of over sixteen hundred residents of the southeastern United States, it was found that the 8 percent who lived in densely populated areas scored higher on a scale measuring depression than did the 92 percent who lived in less densely populated areas (Schwab, Nadeau, and Warheit, 1979). When examining all of this evidence, we must remember that correlation does not imply causation. Successful and wealthy people can afford to buy ranches or farms and live in the suburbs, while poor people may have little choice but to remain in crowded low-rent tenements located in the inner city. Lack of education and economic and cultural deprivation could be the real causes of these social maladjustments (Altman, 1975).

Several laboratory studies have shown that crowding is an aversive state of negative arousal interfering with performance. A group of subjects placed in a small room exhibited increased physiological arousal, such as more rapid heart rate, and indicated that they felt more stressed, uncomfortable, had a lower tolerance for frustration, and were generally in a more negative mood than did subjects in groups of the same size in a larger room. Furthermore, subjects in the crowded condition performed more poorly on a complex task (Epstein, Woolfolk, and Lehrer, 1981; Karlin and Epstein, 1979).

This person looks out over a densely packed city of buildings and people. Research studies have revealed that depression can be associated with crowding.

Architecture and social behavior

We shape our buildings and afterwards our buildings shape us.

Winston Churchill

The design of a man-made structure can be cold and alienating or it can be warm and comfortable. The constructed environment can facilitate social relations or inhibit them. In a housing project, the closer the apartments of the residents, the more often the residents socialized with each other (Festinger, Schachter, and Back, 1950). Similarly, the architectural design of college dormitories has been shown to have an impact on the social relations and task performance of the student residents.

Comparisons were made between students at the State University of New York at Stony Brook who lived in corridor-style dorms and those living in suite-style dorms (Baum and Valins, 1977). Residents of the corridor-style dorms lived two to a room in a double-loaded corridor where they shared a rest room and lounge with thirty-four other students. Suite-style living arrangements consisted of two or three double rooms in which four to six students shared a common bathroom and lounge area. Other than these architectural variations, there were no major differences between these groups of students. The physical space per person and the number of residents per floor were virtually identical for both groups. Furthermore, students were assigned randomly to each of the two living conditions. We can safely assume they were essentially the same in terms of social skills, intelligence, and other characteristics.

The design of the dormitories in which they lived affected the behavior of the students. Corridor residents reported feeling more crowded and said they often avoided other people on their floor, while residents in the suites did not feel as crowded and reported that most of their friends lived on the same floor. Laboratory experiments revealed that corridor residents performed better on competitive tasks where there was little interpersonal contact, but suite residents performed better on cooperative tasks requiring interaction with others (Baum and Valins, 1977, 1979). Corridor residents waiting with an experimental accomplice to participate on a cooperative task were observed to sit further away and to avoid eye contact with the accomplice, while suite residents sat closer to and had more eye contact with the accomplice.

One hypothesis for the effects of crowding is that people may experience **social overload,** an excess of stimulation from interacting with many other people (Milgram, 1970). People suffering from social overload seek relief by reducing their contacts with others. The corridor residents coped with their more crowded living conditions by socially withdrawing, by being less cooperative, and by acting in a less altruistic and socially responsible manner (Saegert, 1978; Valins and Baum, 1973). Because aggression typically involves social contact, we might expect people living in crowded conditions to be less aggressive toward one another. Indeed, one study has shown that crowded subjects involved in a competitive task were less aggressive than subjects who competed under less crowded conditions (Matthews, Paulus, and Baron, 1979).

Another hypothesis offered to explain the impact of crowded living conditions on the social and task behaviors of residents is that they experience **loss of control** (Rodin and Baum, 1978). The loss of control hypothesis maintains that it is the loss of perceived control and not the number of people in a limited geographical region that produces in people a feeling of being crowded. According to one variant of this theory, losing control in a densely populated environment is a negative experience because people who are crowded feel that they have lost their ability to control the nature of their interactions. The unpleasant sensation is attributed to the number of people in the situation, therefore a person "feels crowded" (Burger, Oakman, and Bullard, 1983; Schmidt and Keating, 1979).

If this attribution theory of crowding is correct, then people who feel they are in control of events should feel less crowded than people who believe they have little control, even though both are in densely populated environments. This hypothesis was supported in a field study. People who were asked to push buttons in a densely packed elevator felt less crowded than people who did not have an opportunity to exert control (Rodin, Solomon, and Metcalf, 1978).

Aversive environmental conditions: noise

Among the more aversive conditions of the environment are excessive noise, uncomfortable temperatures, air and water pollution, and unaesthetic environments due to deterioration, lack of control over city zoning and design, and vandalism. Of these conditions, social psychologists have learned most about the effects of noise. It has been estimated that over 70 million Americans are exposed to substantial amounts of noise in their day-to-day lives (Cohen, Krantz, Evans, and Stokels, 1981). The levels of noise in some metropolitan areas is so excessive that the average city dweller has lost the ability to hear half of the range of sounds available to the unimpaired person according to research estimates.

Psychologists make a distinction between sound and noise. *Sound* is a physical concept and refers to changes in air pressure. *Noise* is a psychological concept and refers to sounds that are experienced as unpleasant and interfere with various activities (Cohen and Weinstein, 1981). People exposed to excessive noise show less patience and less tolerance for frustration than other people. For example, children from schools exposed to loud airplane noises from the regular flight patterns of Los Angeles International Airport became frustrated easier, gave up sooner, and performed more poorly on problem-solving tasks than a matched sample of children from schools in quieter neighborhoods (Cohen et al., 1981). Furthermore, the children did not adapt to the noise and continued to display decrements in performance.

The deleterious effect of noise on performance may be due to its unpredictability rather than to its aversiveness. College students exposed to high or low levels of noise performed equally well under either condition on a simple task, such as crossing out letters. When the noise was loud and unpredictable, subjects experienced higher levels of frustration and did more poorly than subjects exposed to predictable loud sounds (Glass and Singer, 1972).

Noise also reduces the frequency of prosocial behaviors. For example, people were found to be less helpful when in the presence of a noisy lawnmower than when in the presence of a rather quiet machine (Matthews and Canon, 1975). Noise may cancel out conditions that would ordinarily produce helping behavior in people. This cancelation effect was found after female undergraduates had been given feedback that they had either succeeded or failed in performing an intellectual task. The usual finding is a "glow of success" (see Chapter 9). People who succeed are more generous in helping others. When the successful students were asked to volunteer to provide help in conditions with high noise, however, they volunteered no more often than students who had failed (Yinon and Bizman, 1980). Perhaps the often reported lack of concern for the welfare of others in large cities is due to some extent to the epidemic of noise pollution in our high-tech society.

Conflict and its resolution

Conflict, like sex, is an essential creative element in human relationships. . . .Conflict, like sex, is to be enjoyed.

John Burton, World Society

It seems foolish for people to argue, fight, and go to war. If everyone would just mind their own business and avoid antagonizing others, the world would be a better place. Right? Children need not fight with one another over which television show they will watch or which computer game they will play. Roommates could work out problems associated with keeping the suite clean and could schedule the visits of their friends. Great Britain and Argentina could have worked out something mutually satisfactory in order to avoid their 1982 war over the Falkland Islands. All of these observations have a common assumption: conflict can be avoided and people of good will can always find a solution to their problems. Unfortunately, things are not this simple. Social psychological research has shown that conflicts may be inevitable in human affairs, and there often appears no peaceful solution to them.

Conflict may be said to exist "whenever persons, groups, or nations engage in incompatible activities" (Deutsch, 1973, p. 10). It is important to distinguish between competition and conflict. **Competition** exists when two or more parties pursue mutually incompatible goals. Conflict can occur even when the parties have common objectives and would like to cooperate. For example, both parents may want to help their child develop better learning skills, but one may emphasize punishment and the other may favor mixing recreation with study to make it more fun. The parents are not in competition, because they favor the same goal, but they are in conflict because they are engaging in incompatible activities.

The usual evaluation of conflict is that it is undesirable. It may serve some useful and creative functions, however. Conflicts may unify groups or nations, encourage alliances between former enemies, nudge competitors into a severe crisis and recognition of a need for compromise, and stimulate ideas, inventions, and art (Coser, 1956, 1967). As the famous American philosopher, John Dewey (1922) argued: "Conflict is the gadfly of thought. It stirs us to observation and memory. It instigates us to invention. It shocks us out of sheeplike passivity" (p. 300). Most social psychological research has focused on destructive forms of competition and conflict, however.

Competitive forms of conflict

When two suitors want to marry the same person, they are competitors in a state of conflict. Short of a three-way living arrangement, no compromise can be reached. The success of one of the suitors means the failure of the other. This type of interaction structure is referred to as a **zero-sum conflict situation.** A poker game illustrates the basic idea. What one player loses is the amount the other player wins; so the sum of the losings and winnings is zero. If you lose one dollar, the winner gains one dollar. The Super Bowl is a zero-sum situation because only one of the two teams can win. There can be no tie and no compromise about the outcome.

There are times when people perceive their conflicts as zero-sum in nature when they are not. Most conflicts can lead to win-win or lose-lose, as well as to win-lose outcomes. Conflicts that can lead to any of these outcomes are referred to as *nonzero-sum conflicts.* Bargaining between labor and management is typically a nonzero-sum conflict because if both deadlock and there is either a strike or a lockout, management loses profits and workers lose income—they both lose. On the other hand, a compromise agreement may lead to fewer profits for the corporation and perhaps less income than the workers desire, but each is better off than if no agreement is reached—so both win.

Research on competitive conflicts

An important determinant of competition and conflict is struggle for scarce resources (Kuhn, 1963). In management-labor negotiations, the two parties are usually competing for a share of the profits. In examining the basis for fights between children in families, Felson (1981a) found that the most important factor was disagreements about which television programs would be viewed. The solution to this kind of conflict is to have more than one television, have the children reach agreement through compromise, or have an authority impose a solution.

Compromise requires that the conflicting parties receive less than each might desire, but both avoid a loss-loss outcome by so doing. If children continue to fight about television viewing, their parents may prohibit them from watching any programs. If they can agree to some schedule so they can each see some (but not all) of their favorite programs, they are better off than if they cannot watch any of them.

A competitive orientation of one or both of the parties interferes with compromise solutions. Laboratory studies have shown that either competitive instructions, in which each subject is asked to gain more than the other person, or the occurrence of one or both parties with a competitive personality, cause less chance for compromise, and the likely outcome is that both parties will lose (Deutsch and Krauss, 1960; Kelley and Stahelski, 1970).

Conflict tends to feed upon itself. Those engaged in competition tend to perceive each other as hostile, rigid, selfish, unwilling to compromise, and evil (Deutsch, 1980; Pruitt and Gahagan, 1974). In response to perceived threat from the other party, each party uses threats and force in self-defense. That which is considered self-defense by the actor is perceived as offensive and hostile by the other party. A conflict spiral of increasing use of threats and force may result. The hostility that fuels the arms race between the United States and the Soviet Union appears to follow these fear-inspired perceptions (see Box 4-2 on "Mirror Images" in Chapter 4).

Subjects in laboratory experiments report that their responses in nonzero-sum situations are based on their expectations about what the other person will do. Subjects who expect the other person to compete are initially quite competitive, and if the other person competes, an impasse occurs resulting in a loss to both in the interaction. On the other hand, people who expect others to cooperate will initially offer conciliatory behavior, and if reciprocation occurs, both will continue to cooperate. Cooperators will switch to competitive behaviors if the other person attempts to exploit their attempts to be conciliatory (Dawes, McTavish, and Shaklee, 1977; Kelley and Stahelski, 1970; Kuhlman and Marshello, 1975; Maki and McClintock, 1983). Thus, people with a competitive view of others may bring about a self-fulfilling prophecy and induce someone who would like to cooperate to be competitive.

Box 13-6

The dollar auction

An economist on the faculty of Yale University invented a little game for use at cocktail parties to illustrate how people can become entrapped by their investments in conflict situations (Shubik, 1971). This dollar auction game has become a research tool in the study of conflict by social psychologists (Teger, 1980; Rubin, 1981). A dollar bill is auctioned to the highest bidder. There is one important difference from most auctions, however. Both the highest bidder, who gets the dollar, and the second highest bidder who does not, must pay the auctioneer.

The authors of this text have carried out dollar auctions in classes. Students are encouraged to bid a nickle or a dime for the dollar, which is held high in the air for all to see. Typically, someone will start at some absurdly low level, like 2 cents. Students will titter, then someone else bids 5 cents, and so on. When the bidding reaches 50 cents, it begins to dawn on everyone that the bidders are trapped.

At this point, all but the top two bidders stay out of it. If one of the bidders offers 25 cents and the other 50 cents, neither can quit without losing what was bid. Even a bid of $1 would allow the winner to split even. But if one person bids $1 and the other had bid up to 75 cents, it would be better for the lower bidder to up the ante to $1.74. If that bidder won the dollar, his or her loss would be 74 cents instead of 75 cents. Each is trapped into this kind of thinking, and it is not unusual for bids to reach $4 or $5 before the game is called off. Having too much invested to quit often leads people into an escalation of conflict and far more losses than if they had cut losses earlier in the auction.

Parties to conflict may suffer greater costs than necessary because they invest so much in a particular line of behavior, and do not feel that they can withdraw or seek conciliation without losing their investment (Teger, 1980). Once the United States committed large number of troops to Vietnam and lives were lost, too much had been invested to withdraw. This principle is illustrated by the dollar auction game described in Box 13-6.

Social dilemmas, traps, and fences

In his theory of capitalism, Adam Smith assumed that if each individual pursued selfish interests, an invisible hand of economic processes would work out to the benefit of all; but in real life, what one person does in self-interest may be detrimental to all. When short-term and rewarded actions of individuals lead to long-term losses for many people, a *social dilemma* is created. A conflict exists between people who may not even be aware of their interdependence and the impending problems they are creating by pursuing their individual interests.

Social traps refer to situations where independent actions benefiting persons lead to outcomes detrimental to a larger group of persons (Platt, 1973). This form of social dilemma has been illustrated by the **commons dilemma.** In historic New England communities, the residents constructed their houses in a circular configuration around a meadow used by all for cattle grazing. This central area was the commons. It was in the interest of each family to increase its herd of cattle, but as each added to the stock, the commons became overgrazed and all suffered losses (Hardin, 1968). More contemporary forms of the commons dilemma include the air we breathe, the rivers and lakes we use for recreation and fishing, the limited supply of electric power and natural resources. Social traps, such as water shortages and "brown outs," result from the single-minded pursuit of self-interest by individuals and nations.

A laboratory situation was created to study a commons dilemma in which each person could benefit in the long run if everyone restrained the desire for immediate gains. Subjects were informed, either individually or in groups of three or six, that they could withdraw points from a pool. They were to obtain as many points for themselves as possible without depleting the pool, and everytime they withdrew points, the pool would be replenished by one-third of its original size. There were 10 points in the pool for individuals, 30 points for three-person groups, and 60 points for six-person groups. Subjects in groups were not given the opportunity to talk to one another, but they did know that overuse of the pool would cause a collapse of the commons pool. On each trial, subjects simply held up a card indicating how many points they would withdraw from the pool. None of the groups and only two of six individuals maintained the pool for as many as fifty trials (Messick and McClelland, 1983).

A **social fence** is a situation in which each person acts to avoid immediate costs, but the long-term consequence is a greater loss to the group (Dawes, 1980). If public television depended entirely upon voluntary contributions, it could not survive because most people avoid the costs. The maintenance of roads, bridges, military bases, and public parks cannot rely upon voluntary contributions by citizens but instead is based on taxation. The extra effort required to place trash in available receptacles is a cost some are not willing to assume, and as a consequence, public parks and streets are filled with litter.

Free-riding occurs when people fail to assume the costs but still take advantage of an available public resource. People may free ride when they believe some other able person in a group will take remedial action. In the context of a laboratory experiment, subjects were less motivated to work when they had information that other group members were making successful contributions to the group. A sucker effect was also found; subjects did not work as hard when they believed other group members were able but were not making successful contributions to the group (Kerr, 1983). The concern about being exploited kept subjects from contributing to the public good.

Research on social dilemmas is in an early stage of development (Edney, 1980). The greater the number of people involved and the less they trust one another, the more difficult it is for them to recognize and solve the dilemma. There also may be disagreements about the size of the commons pool. For example, the amount of crude oil reserves in the world estimated by various groups can be radically different. Even if the reserves are thought to be small and easily exhaustible, people may believe that other forms of energy will be available when the oil runs dry. This kind of thinking, if wrong, can lead to the collapse of the commons pool.

Another problem may be one of trust. While I may be willing to conserve, what use is it for me to do so, if you will not conserve. Perhaps it is necessary for powerful groups or for the government to impose solutions to social dilemmas. Lobbying by conservation groups and government regulations are two kinds of political solutions to social dilemmas. Still another approach is to establish smaller commons pools (Edney, 1980). For example, smaller utility districts allow people to recognize their interdependence more easily and to build the trust necessary to resolve the commons dilemma.

One study has indicated that modeling may be used to increase water conservation. A large sign was placed near the shower facilities in a college field house. The sign asked people to turn off the water while soaping up. In a second condition, a student model turned off the water while soaping. In a third condition, two models turned off the water while soaping. As can be seen in Figure 13-2, the sign had some impact on compliance, but modeling had a much stronger effect particularly when two models were present (Aronson and O'Leary, 1982-1983).

Simply making people aware that they are wasting energy can result in some savings. Many people use air-conditioners during warm weather and leave it running even when the weather outside turns cooler. By opening the windows when it is cool, people could take advantage of "natural air-conditioning," a fact they might not recognize if the windows are shut and the air-conditioner is on. Becker and Seligman (1978) attempted to reduce excessive air-conditioner use by attaching a flashing blue light to the cooling unit that would signal the owner when the outside temperature was below 68° F. They found that after one month, people who had been given the signalling devices

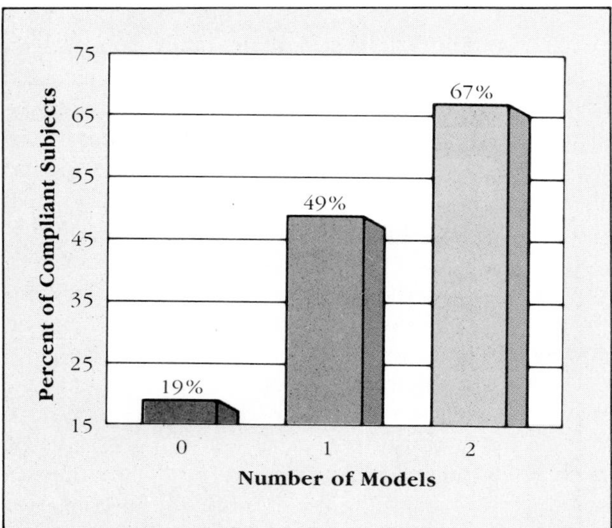

Figure 13-2 Modeling used to increase subjects' conservation of water.

Source: Based on "The relative effectiveness of models and prompts on energy conservation: A field experiment in a shower room" by E. Aronson and M. O'Leary, 1982, *Journal of Energy Conservation, 12,* 219-224.

used 15.7 percent less electricity than people who did not have the signal lights. Furthermore, there were no major differences in electrical usage between the two groups at times when the temperature was above 68° F, indicating that the increase in electricity saved was due to the installation of the signalling devices.

Conflict resolution strategies

There are many strategies available to those who strive to resolve social conflicts. These range from proposals to change the perceptions that opponents have of one another, to increasing opponents' trust in one another, to formal bargaining between them. Of course one way to resolve a conflict is to impose a solution favorable to the self. War may be considered an institutional response to conflict that has a long history of success in resolving conflicts. Today, although many nations around the world continue to war against one another, war can no longer be used to resolve conflicts between superpowers armed with nuclear weapons. We will restrict our discussion in this section to several strategies of conflict resolution that have been studied by social psychologists.

Graduated reduction in tensions (GRIT)

There are three alternatives available to a person locked in a competitive conflict: (1) give in to the other person, (2) impose a solution on the other person, or (3) work out some form of compromise. Surrender or appeasement often only encourages the adversary to become more demanding (Oskamp, 1971). Attempts to impose solutions may escalate conflict, generating high costs to both parties. Yet, hostility and distrust may be so high that neither party believes that a compromise can be worked out. A strategy proposed for this kind of situation is for one of the parties to initiate a series of actions directed toward reducing tensions and induce the opponent to reciprocate conciliatory gestures (Osgood, 1959, 1962). This strategy for a graduated reduction and reciprocated initiatives in tension reduction (GRIT) has been summarized in a series of ten steps outlined in Table 13-3 (Lindskold, 1981).

Subjects placed in nonzero-sum conflicts tend to exploit the conciliatory responses of their opponents,

Table 13-3 Ten steps to be followed in a GRIT strategy

1. Make general announcement emphasizing common interests and need to reverse the escalating course of conflict.
2. Announce conciliatory initiative.
3. Carry out promised initiative exactly as promised.
4. Invite reciprocation, but do not demand it.
5. Continue initiatives even in the absence of immediate reciprocation.
6. Allow inspection and verification that initiatives are being carried out.
7. Maintain defense and retaliatory capacity.
8. Retaliate if exploited, but do not escalate conflict by overreacting.
9. Diversify conciliatory initiatives.
10. Match any reciprocation with additional initiatives.

Source: Based on "Trust development, the GRIT proposal, and the effects of conciliatory acts on conflict and cooperation" by S. Lindskold, 1981, *Psychological Bulletin, 85,* pp. 772-793

Is it easier to wage war or to fight for peace and resolution of conflict? Social psychologists have proposed ways in which opponents can gradually reduce tension and reciprocate initiatives to promote peace.

but if a prior announcement of cooperation is made, the likelihood of positive outcomes for all parties is enhanced (cf. Tedeschi, Schlenker, and Bonoma, 1973). These promises and conciliatory behaviors must be unilateral and cannot take the form of "I will be cooperative, if you will." Such a statement essentially turns over the initiative for reducing conflict to the opponent and has been shown to be relatively ineffective in a laboratory study in which the general announcement, "I'll be making a cooperative choice; it's what we have to do to get the most points," was compared to, "If you cooperate, so will I" (Lindskold and Finch, 1981).

Concern about being exploited or being perceived as weak and appeasing the opponent often prevents a person from initiating conciliatory actions. To avoid such a reaction from the opponent to unilateral conciliatory actions requires standing firm in areas not associated with the conciliatory action. If the opponent tries to take advantage in some other way, the party engaged in a GRIT strategy should take defensive action. If some form of threat or force is used by the opponent, the initiator should employ appropriate levels of counterthreats or force to deomonstrate his or her resolve not to be intimidated or exploited.

The opponent should be invited to reciprocate conciliation, but the initiator would be unreasonable to demand it given the level of distrust that probably exists between the two parties. When the opponent does reciprocate, the initiator should recognize and match it. To fail to do so would raise questions of the genuine intentions of the initiator. A GRIT strategy was found to be successful in a laboratory study even among subjects who previously had been consistent competitors (Lindskold, Walters, and Koutsourais, 1983). Retrospective analysis suggests that GRIT was followed systematically by President Kennedy in reducing tensions with the Soviet Union and in obtaining agreements regarding the testing and deployment of nuclear weapons (see Box 13-7).

Box 13-7

Seeking tension reduction with the Russians

The language of conflict is dramatic and attention grabbing; it therefore commands much more space and time in the mass media than quiet forms of diplomacy and attempts at peaceful resolution of conflict. One historical sequence that appears to fulfill the steps proposed by the GRIT strategy was initiated in a speech by President John F. Kennedy at American University in Washington, D.C., in the summer of 1963. He announced a "strategy for peace," asked Americans to reexamine their attitudes toward the Russians, and put forth a policy designed for coexistence and to further the mutual interests of the two contending superpowers. President Kennedy announced a first conciliatory action, a unilateral cessation of nuclear tests in the atmosphere.

The Russians unjammed the Voice of America and printed Kennedy's speech in full in *Pravda* and *Izvestia,* their two major national newspapers. Several days later Premier Khrushchev announced a halt in the production of strategic bombers. This reciprocation of conciliatory behavior led to a series of positive actions by both sides. A communications link between the two nations was established in Geneva, a proposal for both superpowers to cooperate in space exploration was made, the first in a long series of wheat sales from the United States to the Soviet Union was arranged, embassies were set up in Leningrad and Chicago, air travel was increased between the two countries, and a ban on the test of nuclear weapons in the atmosphere and against placing such weapons in space was signed (Etzioni, 1970). A considerable reduction in tensions was achieved and a period of *detente* ensued, lasting almost two decades.

Surveys have shown that the American people have become increasingly reluctant to make unilateral conciliatory gestures toward the Soviet Union. While 68 percent favored a declaration of a "no first use" of nuclear weapons in 1949 and 74 percent of the respondents were favorable in 1955, only 34 percent supported this policy in 1982. On the other hand, 74 percent of Americans in 1982 were in favor of a bilateral freeze in nuclear weapons between the two superpowers (Kramer, Kallick, and Milburn, 1983).

Setting up superordinate goals

Conflict often can be resolved by appealing to common goals that the adversaries share. An example of the effects of **superordinate goals** was the financial crisis faced by Chrysler Motors in the late 1970s. Management asked labor to give up benefits and take reductions in pay so that together they could save the company and jobs. A representative of labor was placed on the board of the company. In the crisis facing the company, the common goal of both management and labor was the priority of returning the company to solvency. This pulling together blunted the usual adversary relationship between the two sides.

A field study conducted at a boys summer camp illustrates the use of superordinate goals for conflict resolution. Boys were organized into two groups and were placed in competitive interactions. The result was hostility and conflict between the two groups. They traded insults and fought with one another. The camp counselors then created a superordinate goal for the two groups. The water supply to the camp deliberately was disrupted, and it took the collective efforts of all the boys to restore it. A series of incidents requiring the cooperative efforts of the two groups of boys led to a dramatic change in the way in which they related to one another. By the end of the camp season, all the boys were friends and the insults and fighting had stopped (Sherif, Harvey, White, Hood and, Sherif, 1966). Common goals and a coincidence of interests reduce conflict and induce cooperative relations between former adversaries.

Bargaining and conflict resolution

Bargaining involves communications between people directed toward reaching a compromise agreement about how to resolve conflicts between them. There is a give and take character to the process, and each party may receive less than desired. In order to strike an agreement with my roommate so that I can watch "Hill Street Blues" on our one television set, I have to agree to let him watch "The David Letterman Show."

Typically in bargaining there is a great deal of probing. Offers, refusals, and counteroffers provide information to each party about the kind of agreement that can be obtained (Liebert, Smith, Keiffer, and Hill, 1968). When subjects in experiments knew the least their bargaining opponent would accept in advance, they stood firm to reach an agreement at that point. When subjects had no idea about what their adversary would settle for, however, they were much more responsive to the bids and offers made to them. Because bargainers are aware that offers and concessions communicate to their opponent something about what they would settle for, they use these bargaining ploys as ways of disguising their true preferences.

A person who makes great demands but few offers is said to be using a *tough bargaining strategy*. A tough and unyielding bargainer offers two choices to an opponent: drop out of bargaining and forgo reaching an agreement or make large concessions to reach an agreement. Research indicates that a tough bargaining strategy may yield an advantageous agreement, but it also materially reduces the chances of reaching an agreement (Bartos, 1966, 1970). "Tough but fair" involves making a few concessions and is the most profitable approach to distributive bargaining (Chertkoff and Esser, 1976).

Sometimes there are time pressures in bargaining situations. A baseball player may be holding out for a better contract, but the season is fast approaching, or a strike deadline has been set by labor in negotiations with management. A tough bargaining strategy maintained under the pressures of time is likely to lead to failure. In laboratory studies, subjects under time pressures settled for less in bargaining, reduced the degree of bluffing, and made fewer demands from their bargaining adversaries (Pruitt and Drews, 1969).

A team of social scientists at the Harvard University Negotiation Project has summarized an overview of bargaining strategies. (Fisher and Ury, 1983). Four

Postal workers threatened to strike immediately if their demands for job security were not met. The time pressures imposed by their tough bargaining strategies forced President Carter to make a quick settlement with the postal workers' union before a large disruption of mail deliveries occurred.

major principles should enhance the likelihood of reaching agreements by adversaries at the interpersonal, intergroup, and international levels:

1. Separate the problem from the people involved. Avoid a contest and the need to save face. Try to appreciate the opponent's point of view. One way to avoid misunderstanding is to state the opponents' point of view to their satisfaction.
2. Focus on real interests, desires, and concerns, rather than on attacking the other's position or defending one's own position. The focus on old commitments gets them frozen in place and distracts bargainers from the real issues.
3. Create options that lead to gains for both sides. A realistic appraisal of preferences and a creative set of means for achieving them will move the bargaining process forward.
4. Insist on using objective criteria when they are available. In the absence of objective data and clear standards of fairness, a fair procedure can still be adopted. For example, a fair way of dividing a piece of cake between two children is to have one cut it and the other to choose first.

Summary

The methods and theories of social psychologists have been used to help solve social problems. Research on psychology and the law has shown that eyewitness testimony is often unreliable, that jurors disproportionately weigh extraevidential factors, such as attractiveness, status, and race, in reaching verdicts, and that the size and attitudes of jurors are important factors in jury deliberations.

Research on health and environment has documented the importance of perceived control in human behavior. The Type A coronary-prone personality is immersed in an unending and frantic attempt to control an environment that is perceived as hostile and dangerous. For the elderly, loss of control often is an inevitable by-product of diminishing physical capabilities and reduced economic resources. The additional loss of control associated with institutionalization can have catastrophic health consequences for the elderly. Loud noise may impair intellectual functioning, but only when it is uncontrollable. Similarly, the negative reactions of people to invasions of their personal space may be due to the uncontrollable nature of their social interactions, such as those that occur in college dormitories.

Research on social conflicts suggests that they are an inevitable feature of human interaction, but conflicts can often be resolved peacefully and through bargaining. An analysis of social traps provides an insight into the problems associated with inducing people to engage in conservation of such vital resources as oil, electrical power, and water.

Glossary

Action research Research that is concerned both with gaining scientific knowledge and with solving social problems; advocated by Kurt Lewin.

Applied scientist Someone who applies the principles developed by pure scientists to real-world situations and problems.

Bargaining Communications of offers and concessions used to reach a compromise agreement to resolve a conflict.

Commons dilemma A situation in which selfish pursuit of individual interests depletes needed and shared resources.

Competition A state that exists when the goals pursued by two or more parties are incompatible.

Conflict A state that exists whenever people engage in incompatible activities.

Contact cultures Those cultures that maintain small interpersonal distances when people interact.

Evaluation research Research techniques by which policy changes that have been implemented are studied to gauge their effectiveness.

False consensus effect An attributional bias, also discussed in Chapter 4, where people overestimate the prevalence in the general population of behaviors they themselves perform.

Free-riding People take advantage of an available public resource but fail to assume the burden of responsibility for maintaining that resource.

Health psychology A rapidly emerging discipline that investigates the role of psychological factors in health and illness.

Loss of control A hypothesis contending that the reason people who are crowded or institutionalized suffer negative psychological consequences is that they have lost the ability to control the nature of their interactions.

Mock jury research Research typically using college students who role play jurors while taking part in simulated trials.

Noncontact cultures Those cultures in which people prefer large interpersonal distances when interacting.

Personal space An invisible and variable amount of space around a person's body, invasions of which are usually experienced as unpleasant.

Pure scientist Someone who desires to accumulate scientific knowledge without regard for its practical applications.

Social fence A situation in which each person acts to avoid immediate costs, but the long-term consequence is a greater loss to the group.

Social overload A hypothesis offered as an explanation for the negative effects of crowding contending that too much stimulation from others is unpleasant.

Social trap Actions that benefit an individual can ultimately lead to harm for many people.

Stressful life events Tragic events in a person's life, such as divorce, death, or separation, that are associated with an increase in physical illnesses.

Superordinate goals General shared goals that may be used to help resolve conflicts between adversaries.

Type A personality A behavior pattern consisting of time pressure, competitiveness, hostility, and symptom suppression that is associated with a higher rate of coronary heart disease.

Type B personality A behavior pattern exemplified by a lack of type A characteristics and a lower rate of coronary heart disease.

Zero-sum conflict situation A situation where a victory by one party inevitably means a loss by the other.

Recommended readings

Gatchel, R. J., and Baum, A. (1983). *An introduction to health psychology.* Reading, MA: Addison-Wesley.
The first major textbook of a rapidly emerging and developing field. Written by two leading health psychologists, this book provides an up-to-date review of research, theory, and application.

Loftus, E. F. (1979). *Eyewitness testimony.* Cambridge, MA: Harvard University Press.
This award-winning book provides a readable account of the many studies documenting the foibles of eyewitnesses.

Mehrabian, A. (1976). *Public places and private spaces.* New York: Basic Books.
A highly readable book written in nontechnical language exploring the effects of various environments, such as offices, schools, dormitories, and prisons, on behavior. A wonderful book for those seeking an introduction to environmental social psychology.

References

Abbey, A. (1980). Sex differences in attribution for friendly behavior: do males misperceive females' friendliness? *Journal of Personality and Social Psychology, 42,* 830-838.

Abbott, A. R., and Sebastian, R. J. (1981). Physical attractiveness and expectations of success: *Personality and Social Psychology Bulletin, 7,* 481-486.

Abbott, J. H. (1981). *In the belly of the beast, letters from prison.* New York: Random House.

Abelson, R., and Miller, J. (1967). Negative persuasion via personal insult. *Journal of Experimental Social Psychology, 3,* 321-333.

Abelson, R. P. (1976). Script processing in attitude formation and decision making. In J. S. Carroll and J. W. Payne (Eds.), *Cognition and social behavior.* Hillsdale, NJ: Erlbaum.

Abelson, R. P. (1981). Psychological status of the script concept. *American Psychologist, 36,* 715-729.

Abramson, P. A., Goldberg, P. A., Greenberg, J. H., and Abramson, L. M. (1977). The talking platypus phenomenon: Competency ratings as a function of sex and professional status. *Psychology of Women Quarterly, 2,* 114-124.

Ackerman, B., and Schlenker, B. R. (1975, September). Self-presentation: Attributes of the actor and the audience. Paper presented at the meeting of the American Psychological Association, Chicago.

Ackerman, L. J., Rosenfeld, P., & Tedeschi, J. T. (1981, April). *Principles of attribution and altruism.* Paper presented at 52nd annual meeting of the Eastern Psychological Association, New York.

Adair, J. (1973). *The human subject: The social psychology of the psychological experiment.* Boston: Little, Brown.

Adams, P. R., and Adams, G. (1984). Mount Saint Helen's ashfall: Evidence for a disaster stress reaction. *American Psychologist, 39,* 252-260.

Adams, S. (1965). Inequity in social exhange. In L. Berkowitz (Ed.), *Advances in experimental social psychology* (Vol. 2). New York: Academic Press.

Adelson, J. (1982). Still vital after all these years. *Psychology Today, 16,* 52-59.

Aderman, D., and Berkowitz, L. (1983). Self-concern and unwillingness to be helpful. *Social Psychology Quarterly, 46,* 293-301.

Ajzen, I. (1982). On behaving in accordance with one's attitudes. In M. P. Zanna, E. T. Higgins, and C. P. Herman (Eds.), *Consistency in social behavior: The Ontario Symposium* (Vol. 2). Hillsdale, NJ: Erlbaum.

Ajzen, I., and Fishbein, M. (1977). Attitude-behavior relations: A theoretical analysis and review of empirical research. *Psychological Bulletin, 84,* 888-918.

Ajzen, I., and Fishbein, M. (1980). *Understanding attitudes and predicting social behavior.* Englewood Cliffs, NJ: Prentice-Hall.

Staff. (1983, January 21). Bad Samaritan arrrested. *Albany Times-Union,* pp. 1.

Alexander, C. N., Jr., and Rudd, J. (1981). Situated identities and response variables. In J. T. Tedeschi (Ed.), *Impression management theory and social psychological research.* New York: Academic Press.

Allport, F. H. (1924). *Social psychology.* Boston: Houghton Mifflin.

Allport, G. W. (1935). Attitudes. In C. Murchison (Ed.), *Handbook of social psychology* (Vol. 2). Worcester, MA: Clark University Press.

Allport, G. W. (1954). *The nature of prejudice.* Reading, MA: Addison-Wesley.

Allport, G. W. (1968). The historical background of modern social psychology. In G. Lindzey and E. Aronson (Eds.). *The handbook of social psychology* (2nd ed.). Reading, MA: Addison-Wesley.

Allport, G. W., and Postman, L. J. (1947). *The psychology of rumor.* New York: Holt, Rinehart and Winston.

Altman, I. (1975). *The environment and social behavior.* Monterey, CA: Brooks/Cole.

Altman, I., and Taylor, D. A. (1973). *Social penetration: The development of interpersonal relationships.* New York: Holt, Rinehart and Winston.

Amabile, T. M., and Glazebrook, A. H. (1982). A negativity bias in interpersonal evaluation. *Journal of Experimental Social Psychology, 18,* 1-22.

American Psychological Association. (1981). Ethical principles of psychologists. *American Psychologist, 36,* 633-638.

Amir, M. (1971). *Patterns in Forcible rape.* Chicago: University of Chicago Press

Anderson, C. A. (1983). Imagination and expectation: The effect of imagining behavioral scripts on personal intentions. *Journal of Personality and Social Psychology, 45,* 293-305.

Anderson, C. A., and Anderson, D. C. (1984). Ambient temperature and violent crime: Tests of the linear and curvilinear hypotheses. *Journal of Personality and Social Psychology, 46,* 91-97.

Anderson, C. A., Horowitz, L. M., and French, R. (1983). Attributional style of lonely and depressed people. *Journal of Personality and Social Psychology, 45,* 127-136.

Anderson, C. A., Lepper, M. R., and Ross, L. (1980). Perseverance of social theories: The role of explanation in the persistence of discredited information. *Journal of Personality and Social Psychology, 39,* 1037-1049.

Anderson, D. D. (1981). *Defendant's past criminal record: Effects of attributional information and judicial instructions on verdict-related judgments.* Unpublished Ph.D. thesis, Ohio State University, Columbus.

Anderson, N. H. (1962). Application of an additive model to impression formation. *Science, 138,* 817-818.

Anderson, N. H. (1965). Averaging versus adding as a stimulus combination rule in impression formation. *Journal of Experimental Psychology, 70,* 394-400.

Anderson, N. H., and Barrios, A. A. (1961). Primacy effects in personality impression formation. *Journal of Abnormal and Social Psychology, 63,* 346-350.

Anderson, N. H., and Hubert, S. (1963). Effects of concomitant verbal recall on order effects in personality impression formation. *Journal of Verbal Learning and Verbal Behavior, 2,* 379-391.

Antill, J. K. (1983). Sex role complementarity versus similarity in married couples. *Journal of Personality and Social Psychology, 45,* 145-155.

Arkin, R. M., and Maruyama, G. M. (1979). Attribution, affect, and college exam performance. *Journal of Educational Psychology, 71,* 85-93.

Aronfreed, J. (1970). The socialization of altruistic and sympathetic behavior: Some theoretical and experimental analyses. In J. Macauley and L. Berkowitz (Eds.), *Altruism and helping behavior: Social psychological studies of some antecedents and consequences.* New York: Academic Press.

Aronfreed, J., and Paskal, V. (1966). *The development of sympathetic behavior in children: An experimental test of a two-phase hypothesis.* Unpublished manuscript, University of Pennsylvania, Philadelphia.

Aronson, E., and Carlsmith, J. M. (1963). Effect of the severity of threat on the devaluation of forbidden behavior. *Journal of Abnormal and Social Psychology, 66,* 584-588.

Aronson, E., and Carlsmith, J. M. (1968). Experimentation in social psychology. In G. Lindzey and E. Aronson (Eds.), *Handbook of social psychology* (Vol. 2, 2nd ed.). Reading, MA: Addison-Wesley.

Aronson, E., and Linder, D. (1965). Gain and loss of esteem as determinants of interpersonal attractiveness. *Journal of Experimental Social Psychology, 1,* 156-171.

Aronson, E., and Mills, J. (1959). The effect of severity of initiation on liking for a group. *Journal of Abnormal and Social Psychology, 159,* 177-181.

Aronson, E., and O'Leary, M. (1982-1983). The relative effectiveness of models and prompts on energy conservation: A field experiment in a shower room. *Journal of Energy Conservation, 12,* 219-224.

Asch, S. E. (1946). Forming impressions of personality. *Journal of Abnormal and Social Psychology, 41,* 258-290.

Asch, S. E. (1951). Effects of group pressure on the modification and distortion of judgments. In H. Guetzkow (Ed.). *Groups, leadership and men.* Pittsburgh: Carnegie Press.

Asch, S. E. (1956). Studies of independence and conformity: A minority of one against a unanimous majority. *Psychological Monographs, 70,* (9, Whole No. 416).

Atkins, A. L., Deaux, K. K., and Bieri, J. (1967). Latitude of acceptance and attitude change: Empirical evidence for a reformulation. *Journal of Personality and Social Psychology, 6,* 47-54.

Averill, J. R. (1981). A constructivist view of emotion. In R. Plutchik and H. Kellerman (Eds.), *Emotion: Theory, research, and experience.* New York: Academic Press.

Averill, J. R. (1983). Studies on anger and aggression: Implications for theories of emotion. *American Psychologist, 38,* 1145-1160.

Azrin, N. H. (1967, May). Pain and aggression. *Psychology Today,* pp. 27-33.

Back, K. W. (1951). Influence through social communication. *Journal of Abnormal and Social Psychology, 46,* 9-23.

Baer, R., Hinkle, S., Smith, K., and Fenton, M. (1980). Reactance as a function of actual versus projected autonomy. *Journal of Personality and Social Psychology, 38,* 416-422.

Bailey, D. S., Leonard, K. E., Cranston, J. W., and Taylor, S. P. (1983). Effects of alcohol and self-awareness on human physical aggression. *Personality and Social Psychology Bulletin, 9,* 289-295.

Bales, R. F., Strodtbeck, F. L., Mills, T. M., and Roseborough, M. E. (1951). Channels of communication in small groups. *American Sociological Review, 16,* 461-468.

Bandura, A. (1969). *Principles of behavior modification.* New York: Holt, Rinehart and Winston.

Bandura, A. (1973). *Aggression: A social learning analysis.* Englewood Cliffs, NJ: Prentice-Hall.

Bandura, A. (1977a). Self-efficacy: Toward a unifying theory of behavioral change. *Psychological Review, 84,* 191-215.

Bandura, A. (1977b). *Social learning theory.* Englewood Cliffs, NJ: Prentice-Hall.

Bandura, A., and Huston, A. C. (1961). Identification as a process of incidental learning. *Journal of Abnormal and Social Psychology, 63,* 311-318.

Bandura, A., Reese, L., and Adams, N. E. (1982). Microanalysis of action and fear arousal as a function of differential levels of perceived self-efficacy. *Journal of Personality and Social Psychology, 43,* 5-21.

Bandura, A., Ross, D., and Ross, S. (1961). Transmission of aggression through imitation of aggressive models. *Journal of Abnormal and Social Psychology, 63,* 575-582.

Bandura, A., Ross, D., and Ross, S. (1963). Imitation of film-mediated aggression models. *Journal of Abnormal and Social Psychology, 66,* 3-11.

Barber, T. X., and Silver, M. J. (1968). Fact, fiction, and the experimenter bias effect. *Psychological Bulletin Monograph Supplement, 70,* 1-29.

Barefoot, J. C., Hoople, M., and McClay, D. (1972). Avoidance of an act which would violate personal space. *Psychonomic Science, 28,* 205-206.

Bargh, J. A. (1982). Attention and automaticity in the processing of self-relevant information. *Journal of Personality and Social Psychology, 43,* 425-436.

Barker, R., Dembo, T., and Lewin, K. (1941). Studies in topological and vector psychology: II. Frustration and regression. *University of Iowa Studies in Child Welfare, 18, 1.*

Barlow, J. D. (1969). Pupillary size as an index of preference in political candidates. *Perceptual and Motor Skills, 28,* 587-590.

Barnard, W. A., and Bell, P. A. (1982). An unobrusive apparatus for measuring interpersonal distance. *Journal of Genetic Psychology, 107,* 85-90.

Barnes, R. D., Ickes, W., and Kidd, R. F. (1979). Effects of the perceived intentionality and stability of another's dependency on helping behavior. *Personality and Social Psychology Bulletin, 5,* 367-372.

Baron, R. A. (1970). Magnitude of model's apparent pain and ability to aid the model as determinants of observer reaction time. *Psychonomic Science, 21,* 196-197.

Baron, R. A. (1972). Aggression as a function of ambient temperature and prior anger arousal. *Journal of Personality and Social Psychology, 21,* 183-189.

Baron, R. A. (1974). The aggression-inhibiting influence of heightened sexual arousal. *Journal of Personality and Social Psychology, 30,* 318-322.

Baron, R. A. (1977). *Human aggression.* New York: Plenum.

Baron, R. A. (1978). The aggression-inhibiting effect of sexual humor. *Journal of Personality and Social Psychology, 36,* 189-197.

Baron, R. A. (1983). The control of human aggression: An optimistic perspective. *Journal of Social and Clinical Psychology, 1,* 97-119.

Baron, R. A., and Bell, P. A. (1975). Aggression and heat: Mediating effects of prior provocation and exposure to an aggressive model. *Journal of Personality and Social Psychology, 31,* 825-832.

Baron, R. A., and Eggleston, R. J. (1972). Performance on the "aggression machine": Motivation to help or harm. *Psychonomic Science, 26,* 321-322.

Baron, R. A., and Ransberger, V. M. (1978). Ambient temperature and the occurrence of collective violence: The "long, hot summer" revisited. *Journal of Personality and Social Psychology, 36,* 351-360.

Baron, R. S., Sanders, G. S., and Baron, P. H. (1975). *Social comparison reconceptualized: Implications for choice shifts, averaging effects and social facilitation.* Unpublished manuscript, University of Iowa, Ames.

Bart, P. B. (1975, June). Rape doesn't end with a kiss. *Viva,* pp. 39-41, 100-101.

Bartlett, F. C. (1932). *Remembering.* Cambridge, England: Cambridge University Press.

Barton, J., Chassin, L., Presson, C., and Sherman, S. (1983). Social image factors as motivators of smoking initiation in early and middle adolescence. *Child Development, 53,* 1499-1511.

Bartos, O. J. (1966). Concession-making in experimental negotiations. *General Systems 10* (SSRI Preprint No. 6), 145-156.

Bartos, O. J. (1970). Determinants and consequences of toughness. In P. Swingle (Ed.), *The structure of conflict.* New York: Academic Press.

Basow, S. A. (1980). *Sex-role stereotypes: Traditions and alternatives.* Monterey, CA: Brooks/Cole.

Bass, B. M. (1949). An analysis of the leaderless group discussion. *Journal of Applied Psychology, 33,* 527-533.

Bass, B. M. (1963). Amount of participation, coalescence, and profitability of decision-making discussions. *Journal of Abnormal and Social Psychology, 67,* 92-94.

Batson, C. D., Cochran, P. J., Biederman, M. F., Blosser, J. L., Ryan, M. J., and Vogt, B. (1978). Failure to help when in a hurry: Callousness of conflict? *Personality and Social Pscyhology Bulletin, 4,* 97-101.

Batson, C. D., Coke, J. S., Janoski, M. L., and Hanson, M. (1978). Buying kindness: Effect of an extrinsic incentive for helping on perceived altruism. *Personality and Social Psychology Bulletin, 4,* 86-91.

Batson, C. D., Duncan, B., Ackerman, P., Buckley, T., and Birch, K. (1981). Is empathic emotion a source of altruistic motivation? *Journal of Personality and Social Psychology, 40,* 290-302.

Batson, C. D., Harris, A. C., McCaul, K. D., Davis, M., and Schmidt, T. (1979). Compassion or compliance: Alternative dispositional attributions for one's helping behavior. *Social Psychology Quarterly, 42,* 405-409.

Baum, A., and Valins, S. (Eds.). (1977). *The social psychology of crowding: Studies of the effects of residential group size.* Hillsdale, NJ: Erlbaum.

Baum, A., and Valins, S. (1979). Architectural mediation of residential density and control: Crowding and the regulation of social contact. In L. Berkowitz (Ed.), *Advances in experimental social psychology* (Vol. 12). New York: Academic Press.

Baumann, D. J., Cialdini, R. B., and Kendrick, D. T. (1981). Altruism as hedonism: Helping and self-gratification as equivalent responses. *Journal of Personality and Social Psychology, 40,* 1039-1046.

Baumeister, R. F. (1982). A self-presentational view of social phenomena. *Psychological Bulletin, 91,* 3-26.

Baumeister, R. F., Cooper, J., and Skib, B. A. (1979). Inferior performance as a selective response to expectancy: Taking a dive to make a point. *Journal of Personality and Social Psychology, 37,* 424-432.

Baumeister, R. F., and Darley, J. M. (1982). Reducing the biasing effect of perpetrator attractiveness in jury simulation. *Personality and Social Psychology Bulletin, 8,* 286-292.

Baumeister, R. F., and Jones, E. E. (1978). When self-presentation is constrained by the target's knowledge: Consistency and compensation. *Journal of Personality and Social Psychology, 36,* 608-618.

Baumeister, R. F., and Steinhilber, A. (in press). Paradoxical effects of supporting audiences on performance under pressure: The home field advantage in sports championships. *Journal of Personality and Social Psychology.*

Baumeister, R. F., and Tice, D. M. (1984). Role of self-presentation and choice in cognitive dissonance under forced compliance: Necessary or sufficient causes. *Journal of Personality and Social Psychology, 43,* 838-852.

Beach, F. (1976). Cross-species comparison and the human heritage. *Archives of Sexual Behavior, 5,* 469-485.

Beaman, A. L., Cole, C. M., Preston, M., Klentz, B., and Steblay, N. M. (1983). Fifteen years of foot-in-the-door research: A meta-analysis. *Personality and Social Psychology Bulletin, 9,* 181-196.

Beaman, A. L., Klentz, B., Diener, E., and Svanum, S. (1979). Objective self-awareness and transgression in children: A field study. *Journal of Personality and Social Psychology, 37,* 1835-1846.

Beck, A. (1970). Cognitive therapy: Nature and relation to behavior therapy. *Behavior Therapy, 1,* 184-200.

Beck, K. H., and Frankel, A. (1981). A conceptualization of threat communication and protective health behavior. *Social Psychology Quarterly, 44,* 204-217.

Beck, S. B., Ward-Hull, C. I., and McLear, P. M. (1976). Variables related to women's somatic preferences of the male and female body. *Journal of Personality and Social Psychology, 34,* 1200-1210.

Becker, F. O. (1973). Study of spatial markers. *Journal of Personality and Social Psychology, 26,* 439-455.

Becker, H. S. (1963). *Outsiders: Studies in the sociology of deviance.* New York: Free Press.

Becker, L. J., and Seligman, C. (1978). Reducing air-conditioning waste by signalling it is cool outside. *Personality and Social Psychology Bulletin, 4,* 412-415.

Becker, M., Dixit N., and Tedeschi, J. T. (1984). *Combining information about a source's credibility.* Unpublished manuscript, State University of New York, Albany.

Becker-Haven, J. F., and Lindskold, S. (1978). Deindividuation manipulations, self-consciousness, and bystander intervention. *Journal of Social Psychology, 105,* 113-121.

Beer, F. A. (1981). *Peace against war: The ecology of international violence.* San Francisco, CA: W. H. Freeman.

Bell, G., and French, R. (1950). Consistency of individual leadership position in small groups of varying membership. *Journal of Abnormal and Social Psychology, 45,* 764-767.

Bell, P. A. (1978). Affective state, attraction and affiliation: Misery loves happy company, too. *Personality and Social Psychology Bulletin, 4,* 616-619.

Bem, D. J (1967). Self-perception: An alternative interpretation of cognitive dissonance phenomena. *Psychological Review, 74,* 183-200.

Bem, D. J. (1972). Self-perception theory. In L. Berkowitz (Ed.), *Advances in experimental social psychology* (Vol. 6). New York: Academic Press.

Bem, D. J., and McConnell, H. K. (1970). Testing the self-perception explanation of dissonance phenomena: On the salience of premanipulation attitudes. *Journal of Personality and Social Psychology, 14,* 23-31.

Bem, D J., Wallach, M. A., and Kogan, N. (1965). Group decision making under risk of aversive consequences. *Journal of Personality and Social Psychology, 1,* 453-460.

Bem, S. L. (1974). The measurement of psychological androgyny. *Journal of Counseling and Clinical Psychology, 42,* 155-162.

Bem, S. L. (1975). Sex role adaptability: One consequences of psychological androgyny. *Journal of Personality and Social Psychology, 31,* 634-643.

Bem, S. L. (1979). Theory and measurement of androgyny: A reply to the Pedhazur-Tetenbaum and Locksley-Colton critiques. *Journal of Personality and Social Psychology, 37,* 1047-1054.

Bem, S. L., Martyna, W., and Watson, C. (1976). Sex-typing and androgyny: Further explorations of the expressive domain. *Journal of Personality and Social Psychology, 34,* 1016-1023.

Bennis, W. G., Berkowitz, W., Affinito, M., and Malone, M. (1958). Authority, power, and the ability to influence. *Human Relations, 11,* 143-155.

Benton, D. (1981). The extrapolation from animals to man: The example of testosterone and aggression. In P. Brain and R. Benton (Eds.), *Aggression: A multidisciplinary view.* New York: Elsenier North-Holland.

Berg, B. (1978). Helping behavior on the gridiron: It helps if you're winning. *Psychological Report, 42,* 531-534.

Berg, J. H. (1984). Development of friendship among roommates. *Journal of Personality and Social Psychology, 46,* 346-356.

Berger, P. L., and Luckmann, T. (1966). *The social construction of reality: A treatise on the sociology of knowledge.* Garden City, NY: Doubleday.

Berglas, S., and Jones, E. E. (1978). Drug choice as a self-handicapping strategy in response to non-contingent feedback. *Journal of Personality and Social Psychology, 36,* 405-417.

Berkowitz, H., and Zigler, E. (1965). Effects of preliminary positive and negative interactions and delay conditions on children's responsiveness to social reinforcement. *Journal of Personality and Social Psychology, 2,* 500-505.

Berkowitz, L. (1962). *Aggression: A social psychological analysis.* New York: McGraw-Hill.

Berkowitz, L. (1969). The frustration-aggression hypothesis revisited. In L. Berkowitz (Ed.), *Roots of aggression: A reexamination of the frustration-aggression hypothesis.* New York: Atherton.

Berkowitz, L. (1983). Aversively stimulated aggression: Some parallels and differences in research with animals and humans. *American Psychologist, 38,* 1135-1144.

Berkowitz, L., Cochran, S. T., and Embree, M. C. (1981). Physical pain and the goal of aversively stimulated aggression. *Journal of Personality and Social Psychology, 40,* 687-700.

Berkowitz, L., and Connor, W. H. (1966). Success, failure, and social responsibility. *Journal of Personality and Social Psychology, 4,* 664-669.

Berkowitz, L., and Daniels, L. R. (1963). Responsibility and dependency. *Journal of Abnormal and Social Psychology, 66,* 429-436.

Berkowitz, L., and Geen, R. G. (1966). Film violence and the cue properties of available targets. *Journal of Personality and Social Psychology, 3,* 525-530.

Berkowitz, L., and Green, J. A. (1962). The stimulus qualities of the scapegoat. *Journal of Abnormal and Social Psychology, 64,* 293-301.

Berkowitz, L., and LePage, A. (1967). Weapons as aggression-eliciting stimuli. *Journal of Personality and Social Psychology, 7,* 202-207.

Berkowitz, L., and Lundy, R. M. (1957). Personality characteristics related to susceptibility to influence by peers or authority figures. *Journal of Personality, 25,* 306-316.

Berkun, M. M., Bialek, H. M., Kern, R. P., and Yagi, K. (1962). Experimental studies of psychological stress in man. *Psychological Monographs, 76* (15, Whole No. 534).

Berman, J. S., and Kenny, D. A. (1976). Correlational bias in observer ratings. *Journal of Personality and Social Psychology, 34,* 263-273.

Bernikow, L. (1982, August 15). Alone: Yearning for companionship in America. *New York Times Sunday Magazine,* pp. 24-32.

Berscheid, E., Brothern, T., and Graziano, W. (1976). Gain/loss theory and the "law of infidelity": Mr. Doting vs. the admiring stranger. *Journal of Personality and Social Psychology, 33,* 709-718.

Berscheid, E., Dion, K., Walster, E., and Walster, G. (1971). Physical attractiveness and dating choice: A test of the matching hypothesis. *Journal of Experimental Social Psychology, 7,* 173-189.

Berscheid, E., and Walster, E. (1967). When does a harm-doer compensate a victim? *Journal of Personality and Social Psychology, 6,* 435-441.

Berscheid, E., and Walster, E. H. (1971). Adrenaline makes the heart grow fonder. *Psychology Today, 5,* 46-50.

Berscheid, E., and Walster, E. (1974). Physical attractiveness. In L. Berkowitz (Ed.), *Advances in experimental social psychology* (Vol. 7). New York: Academic Press.

Berscheid, E., and Walster, E. H. (1978). *Interpersonal attraction* (2nd ed.). Reading, MA: Addison-Wesley.

Bettleheim, B. (1958). Individual and mass behavior in extreme situations. In T. M. Newcomb and E. L. Hartley (Eds.). *Readings in social psychology* (3rd ed.). New York: Henry Holt.

Bickman L. (1971). The effect of social status on the honesty of others. *Journal of Social Psychology, 85,* 87-92.

Biri, J., Orcutt, B. A., and Leaman, R. (1963). Anchoring effects in sequential clinical judgments. *Journal of Abnormal and Social Psychology, 67,* 616-623.

Biggers, T., and Pryor, B. (1982). Attitude change: A function of emotion-eliciting qualities of environment. *Personality and Social Psychology Bulletin, 8,* 94-99.

Blake, R. R., and Mouton, J. S. (1961). Reactions to intergroup competition under win-lose conditions. *Management Science, 7,* 420-435.

Blalock, H. H., Jr. (1971). *Causal models in the social sciences.* Chicago: Aldine-Atherton.

Blane, H. T. (1968). *The personality of the alcoholic: Guises of dependency.* New York: Harper and Row.

Blau, P. M. (1964). *Exchange and power in social life.* New York: John Wiley.

Blood, R. O., Jr., and Woolfe, D. M. (1960). *Husbands and wives: The dynamics of married living.* New York: Free Press.

Blumenthal, M., Kahn, R. L., Andrews, F. M., and Head, K. B. (1972). *Justifying violence: Attitudes of American men.* Ann Arbor, MI: Institute for Social Research.

Bogart, F., Geis, F., Levy, M., and Zimbardo, P. (1970). No dissonance for Machiavellians. In R. Christie and F. Geis (Eds.), *Studies in Machiavellianism.* New York: Academic Press.

Boice, R., Hanley, C. P., Shaughnessy, P. and Gansler, D. (1982). Eyewitness accuracy: A general observational skill? *Bulletin of the Psychonomic Society, 20,* 193-195.

Bond, C. F. (1981). Dissonance and the pill: An interpersonal simulation. *Personality and Social Psychology Bulletin, 7,* 398-403.

Bond, C. F., Jr. (1982). Social facilitation: A self-presentational view. *Journal of Personality and Social Psychology, 42,* 1042-1050.

Bond, C. F., Jr., and Titus, L. J. (1983). Social facilitation: A meta-analysis of 241 studies. *Psychological Bulletin, 94,* 265-292.

Bond, M. H., Leung, K., and Wan, K. C. (1982). The social impact of self-effacing attributions: The Chinese case. *Journal of Social Psychology, 118,* 157-166.

Bons, P. M., and Fiedler, F. E. (1976). Changes in organizational leadership and the behavior of the relationship- and task-motivated leaders. *Administrative Science Quarterly, 21,* 433-472.

Bootzin, R. R., Herman, C. P., and Nicassio, P. (1976). The power of suggestion: Another examination of attribution and insomnia. *Journal of Personality and Social Psychology, 34,* 673-679.

Bond, M. H., Chin, C. K., and Wan, K. C. (1984). When modesty fails: The social impact of group-effacing attributions following success or failure. *European Journal of Social Psychology, 14,* 335-338.

Borgida, E., and Howard-Pitney, B. (1983). Personal involvement and the robustness of perceptual salience effects. *Journal of Personality and Social Psychology, 45,* 560-570.

Borgida, E., Locksley, A., and Brekke, N. (1981). Social stereotypes and social judgment. In N. Cantor and J. F. Kihlstrom (Eds.), *Personality, cognition, and social interaction.* Hillsdale, NJ: Erlbaum.

Borgida, E., and Nisbett, R. E. (1977). The differential impact of abstract vs concrete information on decisions. *Journal of Applied Social Psychology, 7,* 258-271.

Boski, P. (1983). A study of person perception in Nigeria: Ethnicity and self versus other attributions for achievement-related outcomes. *Journal of Cross-Cultural Psychology, 14,* 85-108.

Bossard, J. H. S. (1932). Residential propinquity as a factor in mate selection. *American Journal of Sociology, 38,* 219-224.

Bower, G. H. (1981). Mood and memory. *American Psychologist, 36,* 126-148.

Bradley, G. W. (1978). Self-serving biases in the attribution process: A reexamination of the fact or fiction question. *Journal of Personality and Social Psychology, 36,* 56-71.

Braginsky, B. M., Braginsky, D. D., and Ring, K. (1969). *Methods of madness: The mental hospital as a last resort.* New York: Holt, Rinehart, and Winston.

Braginsky, D. D. (1970). Machiavellianism and manipulative interpersonal behavior of children. *Journal of Experimental Social Psychology, 6,* 77-99.

Bramel, D. (1962). A dissonance theory approach to defensive projection. *Journal of Abnormal and Social Psychology, 64,* 121-129.

Bramel, D. (1969). Interpersonal attraction, hostility, and perception. In J. Mills (Ed.), *Experimental social psychology.* New York: Macmillan.

Brandt, A. (1980, October). Self-confrontations. *Psychology Today,* pp. 78-101.

Brehm, J. W. (1966). *A theory of psychological reactance.* New York: Academic Press.

Brehm, J. W., and Mann, M. (1975). Effects of importance of freedom and attraction to group members on influence produced by group pressure. *Journal of Personality and Social Psychology, 31,* 816-824.

Brehm, J. W., Stires, L. K., Sensenig, J., and Shaban, J. (1966). The attractiveness of an eliminated choice. *Journal of Experimental Social Psychology, 2,* 301-313.

Brehm, S. S. and Weinraub, M. (1977). Physical barriers and psychological reactance: Two-year-olds' responses to threats to freedom. *Journal of Personality and Social Psychology, 34,* 830-836.

Brewer, M. B. (1979). The role of ethnocentrism in intergroup conflict. In W. G. Austin and S. Worchel (Eds.), *The social psychology of intergroup relations.* Monterey, CA: Brooks/Cole.

Briggs, S. R., Cheek, J. M., and Buss, A. H. (1980). An analysis of the self-monitoring scale. *Journal of Personality and Social Psychology, 38,* 679-686.

Brigham, J. C., and Richardson, C. B. (1970). Race, sex and helping in the marketplace. *Journal of Applied Social Psychology, 9,* 314-322.

Brock, T. C., and Becker, L. A. (1965). Ineffectiveness of overheard counter-propaganda. *Journal of Personality and Social Psychology, 2,* 654-660.

Brock, T. C., and Becker, L. A. (1966). "Debriefing" and susceptibility to subsequent experimental manipulations. *Journal of Experimental Social Psychology, 2,* 314-323.

Brockner, J., Rubin, J. Z., and Lang, E. (1981). Face-saving and entrapment. *Journal of Experimental Social Psychology, 17,* 68-79.

Bronfenbrenner, U. (1961). The mirror image in Soviet-American relations: A social psychological report. *Journal of Social Issues, 7,* 45-56.

Broverman, I. K., Broverman, D. M., Clarkson, F. E., Rosenkrantz, P., and Vogel, S. R. (1970). Sex-role stereotypes and clinical judgments of mental health. *Journal of Counseling and Clinical Psychology, 34,* 1-7.

Broverman, I., Vogel, S. R., Broverman, D. M., Clarkson, F. E., and Rosenkrantz, P. S. (1972). Sex-role stereotypes: A current appraisal. *Journal of Social Issues, 28,* 59-78.

Brown v. Board of Education of Topeka, Kansas, 347 U.S. 483 (1954).

Brown, B. R. (1968). The effects of need to maintain face in interpersonal bargaining. *Journal of Experimental Social Psychology, 4,* 107-122.

Brown, C. (1981). Shared space invasion and race. *Personality and Social Psychology Bulletin, 7,* 103-108.

Brown, P., and Elliott, R. (1965). Control of aggression in a nursery school class. *Journal of Experimental Child Psychology, 2,* 103-107.

Brown, R. (1965). *Social psychology.* New York: Free Press.

Brown, R. C., Jr., and Tedeschi, J. T. (1976). Determinants of perceived aggression. *Journal of Social Psychology, 100,* 77-87.

Brownmiller, S. (1975). *Against our will: Men, women, and rape.* New York: Simon and Schuster.

Bruner, J. S., Shapiro, D., and Tagiuri, R. (1958). The meaning of traits in isolation and combination. In R. Tagiuri and L. Petrullo (Eds.), *Personal perception and interpersonal behavior.* Stanford, CA: Stanford University Press.

Bruner, J. S., and Tagiuri, R. (1954). The perception of people. In G. Lindzey (Ed.), *Handbook of social psychology* (Vol. 2). Reading, MA: Addison-Wesley.

Bryan, J. H., Redfield, J., and Mader, S. (1971). Words and deeds about altruism and the subsequent reinforcement power of the model. *Child Development, 42,* 1501-1508.

Bryan, J. H., and Schwartz, J. (1971). Effects of film material upon children's behavior. *Psychological Bulletin, 75,* 50-59.

Bryan, J. H., and Test, M. (1967). Models and helping: Naturalistic studies in aiding behavior. *Journal of Personality and Social Psychology, 6,* 400-407.

Bryan, J. H., and Walbek, N. H. (1970). The impact of words and deeds concerning altruism upon children. *Child Development, 41,* 747-757.

Bryant, J., and Zillman, D. (1979). Effect of intensification of annoyance through unrelated residual excitation on substantially delayed hostile behavior. *Journal of Experimental Social Psychology, 15,* 470-480.

Bryden, M. P. (1979). Evidence of sex-related differences in cerebral organization. In M. A. Witting and A. C. Peterson (Eds.), *Sex-related differences in cognitive functioning: Developmental issues.* New York: Academic Press.

Buckhort, R. (1979). Psychology of the eyewitness. In A. Pines and C. Mashlach (Eds.), *Experiencing social psychology.* New York: Alfred A. Knopf.

Burger, J. M., and Petty, R. E. (1981). The low-ball compliance technique: Task or person commitment? *Journal of Personality and Social Psychology, 40,* 492-500.

Burger, J. M., Oakman, J. A., and Bullard, N. G. (1983). Desire for control and the perception of crowding. *Personality and Social Psychology Bulletin, 9,* 475-479.

Burns, E. (1972). *Theatricality: A study of convention in the theater and in social life.* New York: Harper and Row.

Burnstein, E., and Vinokur, A. (1975). What a person thinks upon learning that he has chosen differently from others: Nice evidence for the persuasive-arguments explanation of choice shifts. *Journal of Experimental Social Psychology, 11,* 412-426.

Burt, M. R. (1980). Cultural myths and supports for rape. *Journal of Personality and Social Psychology, 38,* 217-230.

Burt, M. R., and Albin, R. S. (1981). Rape myths, rape definitions, and probability of conviction. *Journal of Applied Social Psychology, 11,* 212-230.

Buss, A. H. (1961). *The psychology of aggression.* New York: John Wiley.

Buss, A. H. (1966). Instrumentality of aggression, feedback, and frustration as determinants of physical aggression. *Journal of Personality and Social Psychology, 3,* 153-162.

Buss, A. R. (1978). Causes and reasons in attribution theory: A conceptual critique. *Journal of Personality and Social Psychology, 36,* 1311-1321.

Byrd, R. E. (1938). *Alone.* New York: Putnam.

Byrne, D. (1961). The influence of propinquity and opportunities for interaction on classroom relationships. *Human Relations, 14,* 63-69.

Byrne, D. (1971). *The attraction paradigm.* New York: Academic Press.

Byrne, D., and Blaylock, B. (1963). Similarity and assumed similarity between husbands and wives. *Journal of Abnormal and Social Psychology, 67,* 626-630.

Byrne, D., and Buehler, J. A. (1955). A note on the influence of propinquity upon acquaintanceships. *Journal of Abnormal and Social Psychology, 51,* 147-148.

Byrne, D., Ervin, C., and Lamberth, J. (1970). Continuity between the experimental study of attraction and real-life computer dating. *Journal of Personality and Social Psychology, 16,* 157-165.

Bryne, D., and Nelson, D. (1965). Attraction as a linear function of proportion of positive reinforcements. *Journal of Personality and Social Psychology, 1,* 659-663.

Cacioppo J. T., Harkins, S. G., and Petty, R. E. (1981). The nature of attitudes and cognitive responses and their relationship to behavior. In R. E. Petty, T. M. Ostrom, and T. C. Brock (Eds.), *Cognitive responses to persuasion.* Hillsdale, NJ: Erlbaum.

Cacioppo, J. T., and Petty, R. E. (1979). Effects of message repetition and position on cognitive responses, recall and persuasion. *Journal of Personality and Social Psychology, 37,* 97-109.

Cacioppo, J. T., and Petty, R. E. (1982). The need for cognition. *Journal of Personality and Social Psychology, 42,* 116-131.

Cacioppo, J. T., and Sandman, C. A. (1981). Psychophysiological functioning, cognitive responding and attitudes. In R. E. Petty, T. M. Ostrom, and T. C. Brock (Eds.), *Cognitive responses to persuasion.* Hillsdale, NJ: Erlbaum.

Cairns, R. B. (1979). *Social development: The origins and plasticity of interchanges.* San Francisco: W. H. Freeman.

Calder, B. J., Insko, C. A., and Yandell, G. (1974). The relation of cognitive and memorial processes to persuasion in a simulated jury trial. *Journal of Applied Social Psychology, 4,* 62-93.

Campbell, D. T., and Stanley, J. C. (1963). Experimental and quasi-experimental designs for research on teaching. In N. L. Gage (Ed.), *Handbook of research on teaching.* Chicago: Rand McNally.

Campbell, J. (1980). Complementarity and attraction: A reconceptualization in terms of dyadic behavior. *Representative Research in Social Psychology, 11,* 74-95.

Cansler, D. C., and Stiles, W. B. (1981). Relative status and interpersonal presumptuousness. *Journal of Experimental Social Psychology, 17,* 459-471.

Cantor, N., and Mischel, W. (1979). Prototypes in person perception. In L. Berkowitz (Ed.), *Advances in experimental social psychology* (Vol. 12). New York: Academic Press.

Carlsmith, J. M., and Anderson, C. A. (1979). Ambient temperature and the occurrence of collective violence: A new analysis. *Journal of Personality and Social Psychology, 37,* 337-344.

Carnegie, D. (1940). *How to win friends and influence people.* New York: Pocket Books.

Carol, J. S., and Wiener, R. L. (1982). Cognitive social psychology in court and beyond. In A. H. Hastorf and A. M. Isen (Eds.), *Cognitive social psychology.* New York: Elsevier North-Holland.

Carter, L., Haythorn, W. W., Shriver, B., and Lanzetta, J. T. (1951). The behavior of leaders and other group members. *Journal of Abnormal and Social Psychology, 46,* 589-595.

Carter, L. F. (1954). Recording and evaluating the performance of individuals as members of small groups. *Personnel Psychology, 7,* 477-484.

Carver, C. S. (1980). Perceived coercion, resistance to persuasion, and the Type A behavior pattern. *Journal of Research in Personality, 14,* 467-481.

Carver, C. S., Coleman, A. E., and Glass, D. C. (1976). The coronary-prone behavior pattern and the supression of fatique on a treadmill test. *Journal of Personality and Social Psychology, 33,* 460-466.

Carver, C. S., DeGregorio, E., and Gillis, R. (1981). Challenge and Type A behavior among intercollegiate football players. *Journal of Sport Psychology, 3,* 140-148.

Carver, C. S., and Glass, D. C. (1978). Coronary-prone behavior and interpersonal aggression. *Journal of Personality and Social Psychology, 36,* 361-366.

Carver, C. S., and Humphries, C. (1982). Social psychology of the Type A coronary-prone behavior pattern. In G. S. Sanders and J. Suls (Eds.), *Social psychology of health and illness.* Hillsdale, NJ: Erlbaum.

Cash, T. F., and Derlega, V. J. (1978). The matching hypothesis: Physical attractiveness among same-sexed friends. *Personality and Social Psychology Bulletin, 4,* 240-243.

Cash, T. F., Kehr, J. A., Polyson, J., and Freeman, V. (1977). Role of physical attractiveness in peer attribution of psychological disturbance. *Journal of Counseling and Clinical Psychology, 45,* 987-993.

Cassirer, E. (1944). *An essay on man.* New Haven: Yale University Press.

Catt, V., and Benson, P. L. (1977). Effect of verbal modeling on contributions to charity. *Journal of Applied Psychology, 62,* 81-85.

Chaiken, S., and Eagly, A. H. (1976). Communication modality as a determinant of message persuasiveness and message comprehensibility. *Journal of Personality and Social Psychology, 34,* 605-614.

Chambliss, W. J. (1966). The deterrent influence of punishment. *Crime and Delinquency, 12,* 70-75.

Chandler, T. A., Shama, D. D., Wolf, F. M., and Planchard, S. K. (1981). Misattributional causality: A five cross-national samples study. *Journal of Cross-Cultural Psychology, 12,* 207-221.

Chapanis, N., and Chapanis, A. (1964). Cognitive dissonance: Five years later. *Psychological Bulletin, 61,* 1-22.

Chapman, J. R., and Gates, M. (1978). *The victimization of women.* Beverly Hills, CA: Sage Publications.

Chasdi, E. H., and Lawrence, M. S. (1955). Some antecedents of aggression and effects of frustration in doll play. In D. McClelland (Ed.), *Studies in motivation.* New York: Appleton-Century-Crofts.

Chertkoff, J. M., and Esser, J. (1976). A review of experiments in explicit bargaining. *Journal of Experimental Social Psychology, 12,* 464-487.

Christie, R., and Geis, F. L. (1968). Some consequences of taking Machiavelli seriously. In E. F. Borgatta and W. W. Lambert (Eds.), *Handbook of personality theory and research.* Chicago: Rand McNally.

Christie, R., and Geis, F. L. (Eds.). (1970). *Studies in Machiavellianism.* New York: Academic Press.

Cialdini, R. B., Borden, R. J., Thorne, A., Walker, M. R., Freeman, S., and Sloan, L. R. (1976). Basking in reflected glory: Three (football) field studies. *Journal of Personality and Social Psychology, 34,* 366-374.

Cialdini, R. B., Cacioppo, J. T., Bassett, R., and Miller, J. A. (1978). Low-ball procedure for producing compliance: Commitment then cost. *Journal of Personality and Social Psychology, 36,* 463-476.

Cialdini, R. B., Levy, A., Herman, P., and Evenback, S. (1973). Attitudinal politics: The strategy of moderation. *Journal of Personality and Social Psychology, 25,* 100-108.

Cialdini, R. B., Levy, A., Herman, P., Kozlowski, L., and Petty, R. E. (1976). Elastic shifts of opinion: Determinants of direction and durability. *Journal of Personality and Social Psychology, 34,* 663-672.

Cialdini, R., and Mirels, H. (1976). Sense of personal control and attributions about yielding and resisting persuasion targets. *Journal of Personality and Social Psychology, 33,* 395-402.

Cialdini, R. B., Petty, R. E., and Cacioppo, J. T. (1981). Attitude and attitude change. In M. R. Rosenzweig and L. W. Porter (Eds.), *Annual Review of Psychology* (Vol. 32). Palo Alto, CA: Annual Reviews.

Cialdini, R. B., and Richardson, K. D. (1980). Two indirect tactics of image management: Basking and blasting. *Journal of Personality and Social Psychology, 39,* 406-415.

Cialdini, R. B., and Schroeder, D. A. (1976). Increasing compliance by legitimizing paltry contributions: When even a penny helps. *Journal of Personality and Social Psychology, 34,* 599-604.

Cialdini, R. B., Vincent, J. E., Lewis, S. K., Catalan, J., Wheeler, D., and Danby, B. L. (1975). Reciprocal concessions procedure for inducing compliance: The door-in-the-face technique. *Journal of Personality and Social Psychology, 31,* 206-215.

Cimbalo, R. S., Faling, V., and Mousaw, P. (1976). The course of love: A cross-sectional design. *Psychological Report, 38,* 1292-1294.

Clark, A. C. (1952). An examination of the operation of residual propinquity as a factor in mate selection. *American Sociological Review, 27,* 17-22.

Clark, R. D., and Word, L. E. (1972). Why don't bystanders help? Because of ambiguity? *Journal of Personality and Social Psychology, 24,* 392-400.

Cleaver, E. (1968). *Soul on ice.* New York: McGraw-Hill.

Clifford, M. M., and Walster, E. (1973). The effect of physical attractiveness on teacher expectation. *Sociology of Education, 46,* 248-258.

Clore, G. L., and Byrne, D. (1974). A reinforcement-affect model of attraction. In T. Huston (Ed.), *Foundations of interpersonal attraction.* New York: Academic Press.

Coch, L., and French, J. R. P., Jr. (1948). Overcoming resistance to change. *Human Relations, 1,* 512-532.

Cockburn, A. (1983). *The threat: Inside the Soviet military machine.* New York: Random House.

Cohen, A. R. (1955). Social norms, arbitrariness of frustration, and status of the agent of frustration in the frustration-aggression hypothesis. *Journal of Abnormal and Social Psychology, 51,* 222-226.

Cohen, A. R. (1959). Some implications of self-esteem for social influence. In C. I. Hovland and I. L. Janis (Eds.), *Personality and persuasibility.* New Haven: Yale University Press.

Cohen, F. (1980). Personality, stress and the development of physical illness. In. G. C. Stone, F. Cohen, and H. E. Adler (Eds.), *Health psychology.* San Francisco: Jossey-Bass.

Cohen, R. (1972). Altruism: Human cultural, or what? *Journal of Social Issues, 28,* 39-57.

Cohen, S., Krantz, D. S., Evans, G. W., and Stokels, D. (1981). Cardiovascular and behavioral effects of community noise. *American Scientist, 69,* 528-535.

Cohen, S., and Weinstein, H. (1981). Nonauditory effects of noise on behavior and health. *Journal of Social Issues, 37,* 36-70.

Coke, J. S., Batson, C. D., and McDavis, K. (1978). Empathic mediation of helping: A two-stage model. *Journal of Personality and Social Psychology, 36,* 752-766.

Coleman, D. (1984, March 6). Excuses: New theory defines their role in life. *New York Times,* pp. C1-C8.

Coleman, J. F., Blake, R. R., and Mouton, J. S. (1958). Task difficulty and conformity pressures. *Journal of Abnormal and Social Psychology, 57,* 120-122.

Collins, B. E., and Hoyt, M. G. (1972). Personal responsibility and consequences: An integration and extension of the "forced compliance" literature. *Journal of Experimental Social Psychology, 8,* 558-593.

Collins, J. J. (1981). *Drinking and crime: Perspectives on the relationships between alcohol consumption and criminal behavior.* New York: Guilford Press.

Cooley, C. H. (1909). *Social organization.* New York: Scribner.

Coombs, R. H., and Kenkel, W. F. (1966). Sex differences in dating aspirations and satisfaction with computer-selected partners. *Journal of Marriage and the Family, 28,* 62-66.

Cooper, E., and Dinerman, H. (1951). Analysis of the film "Don't be a sucker": A study of communication. *Public Opinion Quarterly, 15,* 243-264.

Cooper, J. (1980). Reducing fears and increasing assertiveness: The role of dissonance reduction. *Journal of Experimental Social Psychology, 16,* 199-212.

Coopersmith, S. (1967). *The antecedents of self-esteem.* San Francisco: Freeman.

Corry, J. (1983, November 20). "The Day After": TV as rallying force. *New York Times,* p. B2.

Coser, L. A. (1956). *The functions of social conflict.* Glencoe, IL: Free Press.

Coser, L. A. (1967). *Continuities in the study of social conflict.* New York: Free Press.

Cotton, J. L. (1981). A review of research on Schachter's theory of emotion and the misattribution of arousal. *European Journal of Social Psychology, 11,* 365-397.

Cottrell, N. B. (1972). Social facilitation. In C. G. McClintock (Ed.), *Experimental social psychology.* New York: Holt, Rinehart and Winston.

Cowan, C., Thompson, W., and Ellsworth, P. C. (1984). The effects of death qualification on juror's predisposition to convict and on the quality of deliberation. *Law and Human Behavior, 8,* 53-80.

Cowan, P. A., and Walters, R. H. (1963). Studies of reinforcement of aggression: Part I: Effects of scheduling. *Child Development, 34,* 543-551.

Cowen, E., Landes, K., and Schaet, D. E. (1959). The effects of mild frustration on the expression of prejudiced attitudes. *Journal of Abnormal and Social Psychology, 58,* 33-38.

Cox, D. F., and Bauer, R. A. (1964). Self-confidence and persuasibility in women. *Public Opinion Quarterly, 28,* 453-466.

Cozby, P. C. (1972). Self-disclosure, reciprocity and liking. *Sociometry, 35,* 151-160.

Cozby, P. C. (1973). Self-disclosure: A literature review. *Psychological Bulletin, 79,* 73-91.

Craig, J. R., and Metze, L. (1979). *Methods of psychological research.* Philadelphia: W. B. Saunders.

Croner, M. D., and Willis, R. H. (1961). Perceived differences in task competence and asymmetry of dyadic influence. *Journal of Abnormal and Social Psychology, 62,* 705-708.

Crosbie, P. V. (1972). Social exchange and power compliance: A test of Homan's proposition. *Sociometry, 35,* 203-222.

Cross, J. F., and Cross, J. (1971). Age, sex, race, and the perception of facial beauty. *Developmental Psychology, 5,* 433-439.

Crowne, D. P., and Marlow, D. (1964). *The approval motive: Studies in evaluative dependence.* New York: John Wiley.

Cullen, D. M. (1968). Attitude measurement by cognitive sampling. *Dissertation Abstracts, 29,* 1597A.

Cullen, E. (1960). Experiments on the effects of social isolation on reproductive behavior in the three-spined stickleback. *Animal Behavior, 8,* 235.

Cunningham, M. R. (1979). Weather, mood and helping

behavior: Quasi experiments with the sunshine Samaritan. *Journal of Personality and Social Psychology, 37,* 1947-1956.

Darby, B. W., and Schlenker, B. R. (1982). Children's reactions to apologies. *Journal of Personality and Social Psychology, 43,* 742-753.

D'Arcy, E. (1963). *Human acts: An essay in their moral evaluation.* London: Oxford University Press.

Darley, J. M., and Batson, C. D. (1973). "From Jerusalem to Jericho": A study of situational and dispositional variables in helping behavior. *Journal of Personality and Social Psychology, 27,* 100-108.

Darley, J. M., and Gross, P. H. (1983). A hypothesis-confirming bias in labeling effects. *Journal of Personality and Social Psychology, 44,* 20-33.

Darley, J. M., Teger, A. I., and Lewis, L. D. (1973). Do groups always inhibit individuals' responses to potential emergencies. *Journal of Personality and Social Psychology, 26,* 395-399.

Davidson, A. R., and Jaccard, J. (1979). Variables that moderate the attitude-behavior relation: Results of a longitudinal survey. *Journal of Personality and Social Psychology, 37,* 1364-1376.

Davis, J. H. (1969). *Group performance.* Reading, MA: Addison-Wesley.

Davis, K. E., and Florquist, C. C. (1965). Perceived threat and dependence as determinants of the tactical usage of opinion conformity. *Journal of Experimental Social Psychology, 1,* 219-236.

Davis, G. E. (1978). Designing for residential density. In A. Baum and Y. M. Epstein (Eds.), *Human response to crowding.* Hillsdale, NJ: Erlbaum.

Dawes, R. (1980). Social dilemmas. *Annual Review of Psychology, 31,* 169-193.

Dawes, R. M., McTavish, J., and Shaklee, H. (1977). Behavior, communication and assumptions about other peoples' behavior in a commons dilemma situation. *Journal of Personality and Social Psychology, 35,* 1-11.

Dawkins, R. (1976). *The selfish game.* New York: Oxford University Press.

Dean, L. M., Pugh, W. M., and Gunderson, E. K. E. (1975). Spatial and perceptual components of crowding: Effects on health and satisfaction. *Environment and Behavior, 7,* 225-237.

Deaux, K. (1984). From individual differences to social categories: Analysis of a decade's research on gender. *American Psychologist, 39,* 105-116.

Deaux, K., and Emswiller, T. (1974). Explanation of successful performance in sex-linked tasks: What is skill for the male is luck for the female. *Journal of Personality and Social Psychology, 29,* 80-85.

Deaux, K., White, L., and Farris, E. (1975). Skill versus luck: Field and laboratory studies of male and female preferences. *Journal of Personality and Social Psychology, 32,* 629-636.

deCharms, R. (1968). *Personal causation: The internal effective determinants of behavior.* New York: Academic Press.

Deci, E. L., and Ryan, R. M. (1980). The empirical exploration of intrinsic motivational processes. In L. Berkowitz (Ed.), *Advances in experimental social psychology* (Vol. 13). New York: Academic Press.

DeJong, W. (1979). An examination of self-perception mediation of the foot-in-the-door effect. *Journal of Personality and Social Psychology, 37,* 2221-2239.

DeJong, W., Marber, S., and Shaver, R. (1980). Crime intervention: The role of a victim's behavior in reducing situational ambiguity. *Personality and Social Psychology Bulletin, 6,* 113-118.

de Lenero, D. C. (1969). *Hacia donde va la mujir mexicana.* [where does the Mexican woman go from here?] Mexico: Instituto Mexicano de Estudios Sociales, A.C.

Delgado, J. M. R. (1960). Emotional behavior in animals and humans. *Psychiatric Research Report, 12,* 259-271.

Dembrowski, T. M., MacDougall, J. H., Herd, J. A., and Shields, J. L. (1983). Perspectives on coronary-prone behavior. In D. Krantz, A. Baum, and J. E. Singer (Eds.), *Handbook of psychology and health* (Vol. 3). Hillsdale, NJ: Erlbaum.

DePaulo, B. M., Brown, P. L., Ishii, S. H., and Fisher, J. D. (1981). Recipient reactions to kindly and unkindly bestowed help. *Journal of Personality and Social Psychology, 41,* 478-487.

de Tocqueville, A. (1961). *Democracy in America.* New York: Shocken Books.

Deutsch, M. (1973). *The resolution of conflict.* New Haven: Yale University Press.

Deutsch, M. (1980). Fifty years on conflict. In L. Festinger (Ed.), *Retrospections on social psychology.* New York: Oxford University Press.

Deutsch, M., Canavan, D., and Rubin, J. (1971). The effects of size of conflict and sex of experimenter upon interpersonal bargaining. *Journal of Experimental Social Psychology, 7,* 258-267.

Deutsch, M., and Gerard, H. G. (1955). A study of normative and informational social influence on individual judgment. *Journal of Abnormal and Social Psychology, 51,* 629-636.

Deutsch, M., and Krauss, R. M. (1960). The effect of threat upon interpersonal bargaining. *Journal of Abnormal and Social Psychology, 61,* 181-189.

Dewey, J. (1922). *Human nature and conduct.* New York: Henry Holt.

Dickoff, H. (1961). *Reactions to evaluations by another*

person as a function of self-evaluations and the interaction context. Unpublished manuscript, Duke University, Durham, NC.

Diener, E., and Crandall, R. (1978). *Ethics in social and behavioral research.* Chicago: University of Chicago Press.

Diener, E., and Crandall, R. (1979). An evaluation of the Jamaican anticrime program. *Journal of Applied Social Psychology, 33,* 178-183.

Diener, E., Dineen, J., Endresen, K., Beaman, A. L., and Fraser, S. C. (1975). Effects of altered responsibility, cognitive set, and modeling on physical aggression and deindividuation. *Journal of Personality and Social Psychology, 31,* 328-337.

Dillehay, R. C. (1973). On the irrelevance of the classical negative evidence concerning the effect of attitudes on behavior. *American Psychologist, 28,* 887-891.

Dion, K., Berscheid, E., and Walster, E. (1972). What is beautiful is good. *Journal of Personality and Social Psychology, 24,* 285-290.

Dion, K. L., and Dion, K. K. (1973). Correlates of romantic love. *Journal of Counseling and Clinical Psychology, 41,* 51-56.

Dipboye, R. L. (1977). Alternative approaches to deindividuation. *Psychological Bulletin, 84,* 1057-1075.

Dobbs, J. M., Jr. (1972, August). *Sex, siting and reactions to crowding on sidewalks.* Paper presented at the meeting of the American Psychological Association, Honolulu.

Doise, W., Cespeli, G., Dann, H. D., Gouge, C., Larsen, K., and Ostell, A. (1972). An experimental investigation into the formation of intergroup representations. *European Journal of Social Psychology, 2,* 202-204.

Dollard, J., Doob, L. W., Miller, N. E., Mowrer, O. H., and Sears, R. R. (1939). *Frustration and aggression.* New Haven: Yale University Press.

Donnerstein, E., Donnerstein, M., and Evans, R. (1975). Erotic stimuli and aggression: Facilitation and inhibition. *Journal of Personality and Social Psychology, 32,* 237-244.

Donnerstein, E., and Wilson, D. W. (1976). The effects of noise and perceived control upon ongoing and subsequent aggressive behavior. *Journal of Personality and Social Psychology, 34,* 774-781.

Doob, A. N., and Gross, A. E. (1968). Status of frustrator as an inhibitor of horn-honking responses. *Journal of Social Psychology, 76,* 213-218.

Doob, A. N., and Wood, L. E. (1972). Catharsis and aggression: Effects of annoyance and retaliation on aggressive behavior. *Journal of Personality and Social Psychology, 22,* 156-162.

Dorn, D. S. (1968). Self-concept, alienation, and anxiety in a contraculture and subculture: A research report. *The Journal of Criminal Law, Criminology and Police Science, 59,* 531-535.

Dornbush, S. M., Hastorf, A. H., Richardson, S. A., Muzzy, R. E., and Vreeland, R. S. (1965). The perceiver and perceived: Their relative influence on categories of interpersonal perception. *Journal of Personality and Social Psychology, 1,* 434-440.

Dowling, J. H. (1970). Individual ownership and the sharing of game in hunting societies. *American Anthropologist, 70,* 502-507.

Downs, A. C. (1983). Letters to Santa Claus: Elementary school-age children's sex-typed toy preferences in a natural setting. *Sex Roles, 9,* 159-163.

Driscoll, R., Davis, K. E., and Lipetz, M. E. (1972). Parental interference and romantic love: The Romeo and Juliet effect. *Journal of Personality and Social Psychology, 24,* 1-10.

Duchacek, I. W. (1971). *Nations and men: An introduction to international politics* (2nd ed.). New York: Holt, Rinehart and Winston.

Dutton, D., and Aron, A. (1974). Some evidence for heightened sexual attraction under conditions of high anxiety. *Journal of Personality and Social Psychology, 30,* 510-517.

Duval, S., Duval, V. H., and Neely, R. (1979). Self-focus, felt responsibility, and helping behavior. *Journal of Personality and Social Psychology, 37,* 1769-1778.

Duval, S., and Wicklund, R. A. (1972). *A theory of objective self-awareness.* New York: Academic Press.

Dyck, R., and Rule, B. (1978). Effect on retaliation of causal attributions concerning attack. *Journal of Personality and Social Psychology, 36,* 521-529.

Eagly, A. H. (1974). Comprehensibility of persuasive arguments as a determinant of opinion change. *Journal of Personality and Social Psychology, 29,* 758-773.

Eagly, A. H. (1978). Sex differences in influenceability. *Psychological Bulletin, 85,* 86-116.

Eagly, A. H. (1981). Recipient characteristics as determinants of responses to persuasion. In R. E. Petty, T. M. Ostrom, and T. C. Brock (Eds.), *Cognitive responses to persuasion.* Hillsdale, NJ: Erlbaum.

Eagly, A. H. (1983). Gender and social influence: A social psychological analysis. *American Psychologist, 38,* 971-981.

Eagly, A. H., and Carli, L. I. (1981). Sex of researchers and sex-typed communications as determinants of sex differences in influenceability: A meta-analysis of social influence studies. *Psychological Bulletin, 90,* 1-20.

Eagly, A. H., and Himmelfarb, S. (1978). Attitudes and opinions. In M. R. Rosenzweig and L. W. Porter (Eds.), *Annual Review of Psychology* (Vol. 29). Palo Alto, CA: Annual Reviews.

Eagly, A. H., and Steffen, V. J. (1984). Gender stereotypes stem from the distribution of women and men into social roles. *Journal of Personality and Social Psychology, 46,* 735-754.

Eagly, A. H., and Telaak, K. (1972). Width of the latitude of acceptance as a determinant of attitude change. *Journal of Personality and Social Psychology, 23,* 388-397.

Eagly, A. H., and Warren, R. (1976). Intelligence, comprehension, and opinion change. *Journal of Personality, 44,* 226-242.

Eagly, A. H., and Wood, W. (1982). Inferred sex differences in status as a determinant of gender stereotypes about social influence. *Journal of Personality and Social Psychology, 43,* 915-928.

Eagly, A. H., Wood, W., and Chaiken, S. (1978). Causal inferences about communicators and their effect on opinion change. *Journal of Personality and Social Psychology, 36,* 424-435.

Eagly, A. H., Wood, W., and Fishbaugh, L. (1981). Sex differences in conformity. Surveillance by the group as a determinant of male nonconformity. *Journal of Personality and Social Psychology, 40,* 384-394.

Earle, W. B., Giuliano, T., and Archer, R. L. (1983). Lonely at the top: The effect of power on information flow in the dyad. *Personality and Social Psychology Bulletin, 9,* 629-637.

Ebbesen, E. G., and Bowers, R. J. (1974). Proportion of risky to conservative arguments in a group discussion and choice shifts. *Journal of Personality and Social Psychology, 29,* 316-327.

Edney, J. J. (1980). The commons problem: Alternative perspectives. *American Psychologist, 35,* 131-150.

Edwards, A. L., and Kenney, K. F. P. (1946). A comparison of the Thurstone and Likert techniques of attitude scale construction. *Journal of Applied Psychology, 30,* 72-83.

Edwards, A. L., and Klockars, A. J. (1981). Significant others and self-evaluation: Relationships between perceived and actual evaluation. *Personality and Social Psychology Bulletin, 7,* 244-251.

Eisenstadt, S. N. (1952). Processes of communication among new immigrants. *Public Opinion Quarterly, 16,* 42-58.

Ekman, P., and Friesen, W. V. (1975). *Unmasking the face.* Englewood Cliffs, NJ: Prentice-Hall.

Ekman, P., Friesen, W. V., and Ancoli, S. (1980). Facial signs of emotional experience. *Journal of Personality and Social Psychology, 39,* 1125-1134.

Elder, G. (1969). Appearance and education in marriage mobility. *American Sociological Review, 34,* 519-533.

Ellsworth, P. C., Carlsmith, J. M., and Henson, A. (1972). The stare as a stimulus to flight in human subjects: A series of field experiments. *Journal of Personality and Social Psychology, 21,* 302-311.

Ellul, J. (1965). *Propaganda: The formation of men's attitudes.* New York: Alfred Knopf.

Emerson, R. M. (1962). Power-dependence relations. *American Sociological Review, 27,* 31-41.

Enzle, M. E. (1980). Self-perception of motivation. In D. M. Wegner and R. R. Vallacher (Eds.), *The self in social psychology.* New York: Oxford University Press.

Epstein, S. (1965). Authoritarianism, displaced aggression and social status of the target. *Journal of Personality and Social Psychology, 2,* 585-589.

Epstein, S. (1973). The self-concept revisited: Or a theory of a theory. *American Psychologist, 28,* 404-416.

Epstein, Y. M., Suedfeld, P., and Silverstein, S. J. (1973). The experimental contract: Subjects' expectations of and reactions to some behaviors of experimenters. *American Psychologist, 28,* 212-221.

Epstein, Y. M., Woolfolk, R. L., and Lehrer, P. M. (1981). Physiological, cognitive and nonverbal responses to repeated exposure to crowding. *Journal of Applied Social Psychology, 11,* 1-13.

Eron, L. D. (1980). Prescription for reduction of aggression. *American Psychologist, 35,* 244-252.

Etzioni, A. (1970). The Kennedy experiment. In E. I. Megargee and J. E. Hokanson (Eds.), *The dynamics of aggression.* New York: Harper and Row.

Evans, R. I. (1980). Behavioral medicine: A new applied challenge to social psychologists. In L. Bickman (Ed.), *Applied social psychology annual* (Vol. 1). Beverly Hills, CA: Sage Publications.

Evans, R. I., Rozelle, R. M., Mittlemark, M. B., Hansen, W. B., Bane, A. L., and Havis, J. (1978). Determining the onset of smoking in children: Knowledge of immediate physiological effects and coping with peer pressure, media pressure and parent modeling. *Journal of Applied Social Psychology, 8,* 126-125.

Evans-Pritchard, E. E. (1937). *Witchcraft, oracles and magic among the Azande.* Oxford, England: Clarendon.

Exline, R. V. (1957). Group climate as a factor in the relevance and accuracy of social perception. *Journal of Abnormal and Social Psychology, 55,* 382-388.

Exline, R. V., and Fehr, B. J. (1978). Applications of semiosis to the study of visual interaction. In A. W. Siegman and S. Feldstein (Eds.), *Nonverbal behavior and communication.* Hillsdale, NJ: Erlbaum.

Exline, R. V., Thibaut, J., Hickey, C. B., and Gumbert, P. (1970). Visual interaction in relation to Machiavellianism and an unethical act. In R. Christie and F. Geis (Eds.), *Studies in Machiavellianism.* New York: Academic Press.

Fagot, B. I. (1974). Sex differences in toddlers' behavior and parental reactions. *Developmental Psychology, 10,* 554-558.

Fancher, R. E. (1979). *Pioneers of psychology.* New York: W. W. Norton.

Fanon, F. (1963). *The wretched of the earth.* New York: Grove Press.

Farina, A., Fischer, E. H., Sherman, S., Smith, W. T., Groh, T., and Mermin, P. (1977). Physical attractiveness and mental illness. *Journal of Abnormal Psychology, 86,* 510-517.

Faris, R., and Dunham, H. W. (1965). *Mental disorders in urban areas.* Chicago: Phoenix Books.

Fazio, R. H., and Zanna, M. P. (1978). Attitudinal qualities relating to the strength of the attitude-behavior relationship. *Journal of Experimental Social Psychology, 14,* 398-408.

Fazio, R. H., Zanna, M. P., and Cooper, J. (1977). Dissonance and self-perception: An integrative view of each theory's proper domain of application. *Journal of Experimental Social Psychology, 13,* 464-479.

Feldman, N. S., and Ruble, D. N. (1981). Social comparison strategies: Dimensions offered and options taken. *Personality and Social Psychology Bulletin, 7,* 11-16.

Feldman, S. D. (1971, August). The *presentation of shortness in everyday life—height and heightism in American society; Toward a sociology of stature.* Paper presented at the meeting of the American Sociological Association.

Feldstein, J. H., and Feldstein, S. (1982). Sex differences on televised toy commercials. *Sex Roles, 8,* 581-587.

Felson, R. B. (1978). Aggression as impression management. *Social Psychology Quarterly, 41,* 205-213.

Felson, R. B. (1980). Physical attractiveness, grades and teachers' attributions of ability. *Representative Research in Social Psychology, 11,* 64-71.

Felson, R. B. (1981a). Aggression and violence between siblings. *Social Psychology Quarterly, 46,* 271-285.

Felson, R. B. (1981b). An interactionist approach to aggression. In J. T. Tedeschi (Ed.), *Impression management theory and social psychological research.* New York: Academic Press.

Felson, R. B. (1981c). Self and reflected appraisal among football players: A test of the Meadian hypothesis. *Social Psychology Quarterly, 44,* 116-126.

Felson, R. B. (1982). Impression management and the escalation of aggression and violence. *Social Psychology Quarterly, 45,* 245-254.

Felson, R. B. (1983). Aggression and violence between siblings. *Social Psychology Quarterly, 46,* 271-285.

Fenigstein, A. (1979). Self-consciousness, self-attention, and social interaction. *Journal of Personality and Social Psychology, 37,* 75-86.

Fenigstein, A., Scheier, M. F., and Buss, A. H. (1975). Public and private self-consciousness: Assessment and theory. *Journal of Consulting and Clinical Psychology, 43,* 522-527.

Ferguson, C. K., and Kelley, H. H. (1964). Significant factors in overevaluation of own groups' product. *Journal of Abnormal and Social Psychology, 69,* 223-228.

Feshback, N. D., Dillman, A. S., and Jordan, T. S. (1979). Portrait of a female on television: Some possible effects on children. In C. B. Kopp (Ed.), *Becoming female: Perspectives on development.* New York: Plenum Press.

Feshbach, S. (1961). The stimulating versus cathartic effect of a vicarious aggressive activity. *Journal of Abnormal and Social Psychology, 63,* 381-385.

Feshbach, S., and Singer, R. (1971). *Television and aggression: An experimental field study.* San Francisco: Jossey-Bass.

Festinger, L. (1954). A theory of social comparison processes. *Human Relations, 7,* 117-140.

Festinger, L. (1957). *A theory of cognitive dissonance.* Evanston, IL: Row, Peterson.

Festinger, L., and Carlsmith, J. M. (1959). Cogitive consequences of forced compliance. *Journal of Abnormal and Social Psychology, 158,* 203-210.

Festinger, L., Pepitone, A., and Newcomb, T. (1952). Some consequences of deindividuation in a group. *Journal of Abnormal and Social Psychology, 47,* 382-389.

Festinger, L., Riecken, H. W., and Schachter, S. (1956). *When prophesy fails.* Minneapolis: University of Minnesota Press.

Festinger, L., Schachter, S., and Back, K. (1950). *Social pressures in informal groups: A study of human factors in housing.* New York: Harper and Row.

Fiedler, F. E. (1964). A contingency model of leadership effectiveness. In L. Berkowitz (Ed.), *Advances in experimental social psychology* (Vol. 1). New York: Academic Press.

Fiedler, F. E. (1978). The contingency model and the dynamics of the leadership process. In L. Berkowitz (Ed.), *Advances in experimental social psychology* (Vol. 11). New York: Academic Press.

Fillenbaum, S. (1966). Prior deception and subsequent experimental performance: The "faithful" subject. *Journal of Personality and Social Psychology, 4,* 532-535.

Finck, H. T. (1902). *Romantic love and personal beauty: Their development, causal relations, historic and national peculiarities.* London: Macmillan.

Findlay, S. (1981, June 6). Most sex-ed classes don't alter behavior. *USA Today,* p. 1D.

Findlay, S. (1984, August 28). "Day After": Impact lingers. *USA Today,* p. 1D.

Fischhoff, B. (1975). Hindsight/foresight: The effect of outcome knowledge on judgment under uncertainty. *Journal of Experimental Psychology: Human Perception and Performance, 1,* 288-299.

Fischhoff, B., Slovic, P., and Lichtenstein, S. (1977). Knowing with certainty: The appropriateness of extreme confidence. *Journal of Experimental Psychology: Human Perception and Performance, 3,* 552-564.

Fishbein, M., and Ajzen, I. (1972). Attitudes and opinions. *Annual Review of Psychology, 23,* 487-544.

Fishbein, M., and Ajzen, I. (1974). Attitudes towards objects as predictors of single and multiple behavioral criteria. *Psychological Review, 81,* 59-74.

Fishbein, M., and Ajzen, I. (1975). *Belief, attitude, intention and behavior: An introduction to theory and research.* Reading, MA: Addison-Wesley.

Fisher, J. D., DePaulo, B. M., and Nadler, A. (1981). Extending altruism beyond the altruistic act: The mixed effects of aid on the help recipient. In J. P. Rushton and R. M. Sorrentino (Eds.), *Altruism and helping behavior.* Hillsdale, NJ: Erlbaum.

Fisher, J. D., and Nadler, A. (1976). Effect of donor resources on recipient self-esteem and self-help. *Journal of Experimental Social Psychology, 12,* 139-150.

Fisher, R., and Ury, W. (1983). *Getting to yes: Negotiating agreement without giving in.* New York: Penguin Books.

Fisher, W. A., and Byrne, D. (1978). Sex differences in response to erotica: Love or lust. *Journal of Personality and Social Psychology, 36,* 117-125.

Fitzgerald, M. P. (1963). Self-disclosure and expressed self-esteem, social distance and areas of the self-revealed. *Journal of Psychology, 56,* 405-412.

Fitzgerald, R., and Ellsworth, P. C. (1984). Due process vs. crime control: Death qualification and jury attitudes. *Law and Human Behavior, 8,* 31-51.

Fitzpatrick, A. R., and Eagly, A. H. (1981). Anticipatory belief polarization as a function of the expertise of a discussion partner. *Personality and Social Psychology Bulletin, 7,* 636-642.

Fling, S., and Manosevitz, M. (1972). Sex typing in nursery school children's play interests. *Developmental Psychology, 7,* 146-152.

Foley, L. A., and Chamblin, M. (1982). The effect of race and personality on mock jurors. *Journal of Psychology, 112,* 47-51.

Folkes, V. S. (1982). Forming relationships and the matching hypothesis. *Personality and Social Psychology Bulletin, 82,* 631-636.

Forsyth, D. R., Riess, M., and Schlenker, B. R. (1977). Impression management concerns governing reactions to a faulty decision. *Representative Research in Social Psychology, 18,* 12-22.

Foss, R. D., and Dempsey, C. B. (1979). Blood donation and the foot-in-the-door technique: A limiting case. *Journal of Personality and Social Psychology, 37,* 580-590.

Francis, S. J. (1979). Sex differences in nonverbal behavior. *Sex Roles, 5,* 519-535.

Frank, F., and Anderson, L. R. (1971). Effects of task and group size upon group productivity and member satisfaction. *Sociometry, 34,* 135-149.

Freedman, J. L. (1969). Role playing: Psychology by consensus. *Journal of Personality and Social Psychology, 13,* 107-114.

Freedman, J. L., and Fraser, S. C. (1966). Compliance without pressure: The foot-in-the-door technique. *Journal of Personality and Social Psychology, 4,* 195-202.

Freedman, J. L., Heshka, S., and Levy, A. (1975). Population density and pathology: Is there a relationship? *Journal of Experimental Social Psychology, 11,* 539-552.

Freedman, J. L., Levy, A. S., Buchanan, R. W., and Price, J. (1972). Crowding and human aggressiveness. *Journal of Experimental Social Psychology, 8,* 528-548.

Freidenberg, E. Z. (1959). *The vanishing adolescent.* New York: Harcourt, Brace.

Freidrich, C. J. (1963). *Man and his government.* New York: McGraw-Hill.

French, J. R. P., Jr., and Raven, B. (1959). The bases of social power. In D. Cartwright (Ed.), *Studies in social power.* Ann Arbor: University of Michigan Press.

French, J. R. P., Jr., and Snyder, R. (1959). Leadership and interpersonal power. In D. Cartwright (Ed.), *Studies in social power.* Ann Arbor: University of Michigan Press.

Freud, S. (1938). *A general introduction to psychoanalysis.* New York: Garden City Publishing Co.

Fried, R., and Berkowitz, L. (1979). Music hath charms . . . and can influence helpfulness. *Journal of Applied Social Psychology, 9,* 199-208.

Friedman, H., and Rosenman, R. H. (1974). *Type A behavior and your heart.* New York: Alfred Knopf.

Frieze, I., and Ramsey, S. (1976). Nonverbal maintenance of traditional sex roles. *Journal of Social Issues, 32,* 133-141.

Frieze, I. H., Parsons, J. E., Johnson, P. B., Ruble, D. N., and Zellman, G. L. (1978). *Women and sex roles: A social psychological perspective.* New York: W. W. Norton.

Frodi, A. (1977). Sexual arousal, situational restrictiveness, and aggressive behavior. *Journal of Research in Personality, 11,* 48-58.

Frodi, A., Macaulay, J. and Thome, P. R. (1977). Are women always less aggressive than men. A review of the experimental literature. *Psychological Bulletin 84,* 634-660.

Froming, W. J., and Carver, C. S. (1981). Divergent influence of private and public self-consciousness in a compliance paradigm. *Journal of Research in Personality, 15,* 159-171.

Fromkin, H. L., Goldstein, J. H., and Brock, T. C. (1977). The role of "irrelevant" derogation in vicarious aggression catharsis: A field experiment. *Journal of Experimental Social Psychology, 13,* 239-252.

Gabrenya, W. K., and Arkin, R. M. (1980). Self-monitoring scale: Factor structure and correlates. *Personality and Social Psychology Bulletin, 6,* 12-22.

Gaes, G. G., Kalle, R. J., and Tedeschi, J. T. (1978). Impression management in the forced compliance situation: Two studies using the bogus pipeline. *Journal of Experimental Social Psychology, 14,* 493-510.

Gaes, G. G. and Tedeschi, J. T. (1978). An evaluation of self-esteem and impression management theories of anticipatory belief change. *Journal of Experimental Social Psychology, 14,* 579-582.

Gager, N., and Schurr, C. (1976). *Sexual assault: Confronting rape in America.* New York: Grosset and Dunlap.

Galizio, M., and Hendrick, C. (1972). Effect of musical accompaniment on attitude: The guitar as a prop for persuasion. *Journal of Applied Social Psychology, 2,* 350-359.

Gallup, G. G., Jr. (1977). Self-recognition in primates: A comparative approach to the bidirectional properties of consciousness. *American Psychologist, 32,* 329-338.

Gamson, W. A. (1968). *Power and discontent.* Homewood, IL: Dorsey Press.

Gardner, M. (1957). *Fads and fallacies in the name of science.* New York: Dover Publications.

Garfinkel, H. (1964). Studies of routine grounds of everyday activities. *Social Problems, 11,* 225-250.

Gastorf, J. W. (1980). Time urgency and the Type A behavior pattern. *Journal of Consulting and Clinical Psychology, 48,* 299.

Gatchel, R., and Baum, A. (1983). *An introduction to health psychology.* Reading, MA: Addison-Wesley.

Geen, R. G., and Berkowitz, L. (1967). Some conditions facilitating the occurrence of aggression after the observation of violence. *Journal of Personality, 35,* 666-676.

Geen, R. G. and Quanty, M. B. (1977). The catharsis of aggression: An evaluation of a hypothesis. In L. Berkowitz (Ed.), *Advances in experimental social psyckology* (Vol. 10). New York: Academic Press.

Geen, R. G., and Stonner, D. (1971). The effects of aggressiveness habit strength upon behavior in the presence of aggression-related stimuli. *Journal of Personality and Social Psychology, 17,* 149-153.

Geis, F., Christie, R., and Nelson, C. (1970). In search of the Machiavel. In R. Christie and F. Geis (Eds.), *Studies in Machiavellianism.* New York: Academic Press.

Geise, L. A. (1979). The female role in middle class women's magazines from 1955 to 1976: A content analysis of nonfiction selections. *Sex Roles, 5,* 51-62.

Gelfand, D. M. (1962). The infleunce of self-esteem on the rate of verbal conditioning and social matching behavior. *Journal of Abnormal and Social Psychology, 65,* 259-265.

Geller, D. M. (1978). Involvement in role-playing situations: A demonstration with studies on obedience. *Journal of Personality and Social Psychology, 36,* 219-235.

Gelles, R. J. (1979). *Family violence.* Beverly Hills, CA: Sage Publications.

Gemmill, G. R., and Heisler, W. J. (1972). Machiavellianism as a factor in managerial job strain, job satisfaction and upward mobility. *Academy of Management Journal, 15,* 51-62.

Gentry, W. D. (1970). Effects of frustration, attack, and prior aggressive training on overt aggression and vascular processes. *Journal of Personality and Social Psychology, 16,* 718-725.

Geraldy, P. (1939). L'Amour. In W. Geoffrey (Ed.), *The compleat lover.* New York: Harrison-Hilton Books.

Gerard, H. B. (1963). Emotional uncertainty and social comparison. *Journal of Abnormal and Social Psychology, 66,* 568-573.

Gerard, H. B., and Mathewson, G. C. (1966). The effects of severity of initiation on liking for a group: A replication. *Journal of Experimental Social Psychology, 12,* 278-287.

Gerard, H. B., and Rabbie, J. M. (1961). Fear and social comparison. *Journal of Abnormal and Social Psychology, 61,* 586-592.

Gergen, K. J., Ellsworth, P., Maslach, C., and Seipel, M. (1975). Obligation, donor resources, and reactions to aid in three nations. *Journal of Personality and Social Psychology, 31,* 390-400.

Gergen, K. J., and Gergen, M. M. (1981). *Social psychology.* New York: Harcourt Brace Jovanovich.

Gergen, K. J., and Taylor, M. G. (1969). Social expectancy and self- presentation in a status hierarchy. *Journal of Experimental Social Psychology, 5,* 79-92.

Gergen, K. J., and Wishnov, B. (1965). Others self-evaluation and interaction anticipation as determinants of self-presentation. *Journal of Personality and Social Psychology, 2,* 348-358.

Gerth, H., and Mill, C. W. (1953). *Character and social structure.* New York: Harcourt, Brace, & World.

Gibb, C. A. (1969). Leadership. In G. Lindzey and E. Aronson (Eds.), *The handbook of social psychology* (Vol. 4, 2nd ed.) Reading, MA: Addison-Wesley.

Gibb, J. R. (1951). The effects of group size and of threat upon certainty in a problem-solving situation. *American Psychologist, 6,* 324.

Gibbons, F. X. (1978). Sexual standards and reactions to pornography: Enhancing behavioral consistency through self-focused attention. *Journal of Personality and Social Psychology, 36,* 976-987.

Gibbons, F. X., and Wicklund, R. (1982). Self-focused attention and helping behavior. *Journal of Personality and Social Psychology, 43,* 462-474.

Gibbs, J. P. (1968). Crime, punishment, and deterrence. *Southwestern Social Science Quarterly, 48,* 515-530.

Gilbert, G. M. (1951). Stereotype persistence and change among college students. *Journal of Abnormal and Social Psychology, 46,* 245-254.

Gilchrist, J. C., Shaw, M. E., and Walker, L. C. (1954). Some effects of unequal distribution of information in a wheel group structure. *Journal of Abnormal and Social Psychology, 49,* 554-556.

Giles, H. (1977). *Language, ethnicity, and intergroup relations.* London: Academic Press.

Gillig, P. M., and Greenwald, A. G. (1974). It is time to lay the sleeper effect to rest? *Journal of Personality and Social Psychology, 29,* 132-139.

Gillin, J. C., and Ochberg, F. M. (1970). Firearms control and violence. In D. N. Daniels, M. F. Gilula, and F. M. Ochberg (Eds.), *Violence and the struggle for existence.* Boston: Little, Brown.

Gilovich, T. (1981). Seeing the past in the present: The effect of associations to familiar events on judgments and decisions. *Journal of Personality and Social Psychology, 40,* 797-808.

Gintner, G., and Lindskold, S. (1975). Rate of participation and expertise as factors influencing leader choice. *Journal of Personality and Social Psychology, 32,* 1085-1089.

Glass, D. C. (1977). *Behavior patterns, stress and coronary disease.* Hillsdale, NJ: Erlbaum.

Glass, D. C., and Carver, C. S. (1980). Environmental stress and the Type A response. In A. Baum and J. E. Singer (Eds.), *Advances in environmental psychology: Applications of personal control* (Vol. 2). Hillsdale, NJ: Erlbaum.

Glass, D. C., and Singer, J. E. (1972). *Urban stress: Experiments on noise and social stressors.* New York: Academic Press.

Goethals, G. R., and Darley, J. M. (1977). Social comparison theory: An attributional approach. In J. M. Suls and R. L. Miller (Eds.), *Social comparison processes: Theoretical and empirical perspectives.* Washington, DC: Hemisphere/Halstead.

Goffman, E. (1959). *The presentation of self in everyday life.* Garden City, NY: Doubleday.

Goffman, E. (1963). *Stigma.* Englewood Cliffs, NJ: Prentice-Hall.

Goffman, E. (1967). *Interaction ritual.* New York: Anchor.

Goffman, E. (1971). *Relations in public.* New York: Harper Colophon Books.

Goffman, E. (1974). *Frame analysis: An essay on the organization of experience.* New York: Harper and Row.

Goldberg, P. (1968). Are women prejudiced against women? *Trans-Action, 5,* 28-30.

Goldberg, P. A. (1974, August). Prejudice toward women: Some personality correlatives. Paper presented at the meeting of the American Psychological Association, Honolulu, HI.

Goldman, W., and Lewis, P. (1977). Beautiful is good: Evidence that the physically attractive are more socially skilled. *Journal of Experimental Social Psychology, 13,* 125-130.

Goldstein, I. L. (1971). The application blank: How honest are the responses? *Journal of Applied Psychology, 55,* 491-492.

Goldstein, M., and Davis, E. E. (1972). Race and belief: A further analysis of the social determinants of behavioral intentions. *Journal of Personality and Social Psychology, 22,* 346-355.

Goleman, D. (1984, March 6). Excuses: New theory defines their role in life. *New York Times,* pp. C1-C8.

Golembiewski, R. T. (1962). *The small group: An analysis of research concepts and operations.* Chicago: University of Chicago Press.

Gonzales, M. H., Davis, J. M., Loney, G. L., Lukens, C. K., and Junghans, C. M. (1983). Interactional approach to interpersonal attraction. *Journal of Personality and Social Psychology, 44,* 1192-1197.

Goodacre, D. M., III. (1951). The use of a sociometric test as a predictor of combat unit effectiveness. *Sociometry, 14,* 148-152.

Goodstadt, B., and Hjelle, L. A. (1973). Power to the powerless: Locus of control and the use of power. *Journal of Personality and Social Psychology, 27,* 190-196.

Goranson, R. E. (1970). Media violence and aggressive behavior: A review of experimental research. In L. Berkowitz (Ed.), *Advances in experimental social psychology* (Vol. 5). New York: Academic Press.

Goranson, R. E., and Berkowitz, L. (1966). Reciprocity and responsibility reactions to prior help. *Journal of Personality and Social Psychology, 3,* 227-231.

Gorer, G. (1968). Man has no "killer" instinct. In A. Montagu (Ed.) The new sociology. New York: Oxford University Press.

Gottlieb, J., and Carver, C. S. (1980). Anticipation of future interaction and the bystander effect. *Journal of Experimental Social Psychology, 16,* 253-260.

Gouaux, C. (1971). Induced affective states and interpersonal attraction. *Journal of Personality and Social Psychology, 20,* 37-43.

Gouldner, A. W. (1960). The norm of reciprocity: A preliminary statement. *American Sociological Review, 25,* 161-178.

Gove, W. R., Hughes, M., and Geerken, M. R. (1980). Playing dumb: A form of impression management with undesirable side effects. *Social Psychology Quarterly, 43,* 89-102.

Gravenkemper, A., and Paludi, M. A. (1983). Fear of success revisited: Introducing an ambiguous cue. *Sex Roles, 9,* 897-900.

Green, S., Nebeker, D., and Boni, A. (1976). Personality and situational effects on leader behavior. *Academy of Management Journal, 19,* 189-194.

Greenberg, J. (1979). Group vs. individual equity judgments: Is there a polarization effect? *Journal of Experimental Social Psychology, 15,* 504-512.

Greenberg, M. S., and Shapiro, S. F. (1971). Indebtedness: An adverse aspect of asking for and receiving help. *Sociometry, 34,* 290-301.

Greenwald, A. G. (1968). Cognitive learning, cognitive response to persuasion, and attitude change. In A. G. Greenwald, T. C. Brock, and T. M. Ostrom (Eds.), *Psychological foundations of attitudes.* New York: Academic Press.

Greenwald, A. G. (1980). The totalitarian ego: Fabrication and revision of personal history. *American Psychologist, 35,* 603-613.

Greenwell, J., and Dengerink, H. A. (1973). The role of perceived versus actual attack in human physical aggression. *Journal of Personality and Social Psychology, 26,* 66-71.

Greer, D. L. (1983). Spectator booing and the home advantage: A study of social influence in the basketball arena. *Social Psychology Quarterly, 46,* 252-261.

Griffitt, W. (1968). Attraction towards a stranger as a function of direct and associated reinforcement. *Psychonomic Science, 11,* 147-148.

Griffitt, W. (1970). Environmental effects on interpersonal affective behavior: Ambient effective temperature and attraction. *Journal of Personality and Social Psychology, 15,* 240-244.

Griffitt, W., and Veitch, R. (1971). Hot and crowded: Influence of population density and temperature on interpersonal affective behavior: Ambient effective temperature and attraction. *Journal of Personality and Social Psychology, 17,* 92-98.

Griffitt, W., and Veitch, R. (1974). Preacquaintance attitude similarity and attraction revisited: Ten days in a fall-out shelter. *Sociometry, 37,* 163-173.

Gross, A. E., and Fleming, I. (1982). Twenty years of deception in social psychology. *Personality and Social Psychology Bulletin, 8,* 402-408.

Gross, E. (1954). Primary functions of the small group. *American Journal of Sociology, 60,* 24-30.

Gruder, C. L., Cook, T. D., Hennigan, K. M., Flay, B. R., Alessi, C., and Halamaj, J. (1978). Empirical tests of the absolute sleeper effect predicted from the discounting cue hypothesis. *Journal of Personality and Social Psychology, 36,* 1061-1074.

Gruder, C. L., Romer, D., and Korth, B. (1978). Dependency and fault as determinants of helping. *Journal of Experimental Social Psychology, 14,* 227-235.

Gruner, C. R. (1965). An experimental study of satire as persuasion. *Speech Monographs, 32,* 149-153.

Grusec, J. E., and Skubiski, S. L. (1970). Model nurturance, demand characteristics of the modeling experiment, and altruism. *Journal of Personality and Social Psychology, 14,* 352-359.

Grush, J. E. (1980). The impact of candidate expenditures, regionality, and prior outcomes on the 1976 Democratic presidential primaries. *Journal of Personality and Social Psychology, 38,* 337-347.

Grush, J. E., McKeough, K. L., and Ahlering, R. F. (1978). Extrapolating laboratory exposure research to actual political elections. *Journal of Personality and Social Psychology, 36,* 257-270.

Guillen, M. A. (1983). Life as a lottery. *Psychology Today, 17,* 59-61.

Gullahorn, J. T. (1952). Distance and friendship as factors in the gross interaction matrix. *Sociometry, 15,* 123-134.

Haas, J., and Roberts, G. C. (1975). Effect of evaluative others upon learning and performance of a complex motor task. *Journal of Motor Behavior, 7,* 81-90.

Hall, E. (1973, November). A conversation with Charles Osgood. *Psychology Today,* pp. 54-72.

Hall, E. T. (1959). *The silent language.* New York: Doubleday.

Hall, E. T. (1966). *The hidden dimension.* New York: Doubleday.

Halpin, A. W. (1955). The leader behavior and leadership ideology of educational administrators and aircraft commanders. *Harvard Educational Review, 25,* 18-32.

Halpin, A. W. (1956). Evaluation through the study of the leader's behavior. *Educational Leadership, 14,* 172-176.

Halpin, A. W., and Winer, B. J. (1952). *The leadership behavior of the airplane commander.* Columbus: Ohio State University Research Foundation.

Hamachek, D. E. (1971). *Encounters with the self.* New York: Holt, Rinehart and Winston.

Hamilton, D. L. (1979). A cognitive-attributional analysis of stereotyping. In L. Berkowitz (Ed.), *Advances in experimental social psychology* (Vol. 12). New York: Academic Press.

Hansen, R. D., and Stonner, D. M. (1978). Attributes and attributions: Inferring stimulus properties, actors' dispositions, and causes. *Journal of Personality and Social Psychology, 36,* 657-667.

Hardin, G. (1968). The tragedy of the commons. *Science, 162,* 1243-1248.

Hardyck, J. A., and Braden, M. (1962). Prophecy fails again: A report of a failure to replicate. *Journal of Abnormal and Social Psychology, 65,* 136-141.

Hare, A. P. (1962). *Handbook of small group research.* Glencoe, NY: Free Press.

Harkins, S. G., and Petty, R. E. (1981). Effects of source magnification of cognitive effort on attitudes: An information processing view. *Journal of Personality and Social Psychology, 40,* 401-413.

Harnett, J. J., Bailey, K. G., and Gibson, F. W., Jr. (1970). Personal space as influenced by sex and type of movement. *Journal of Psychology, 76,* 139-144.

Harre, R., and Secord, P. F. (1973). *The explanation of social behavior.* Totowa, NJ: Littlefield, Adams.

Harrell, W. A., and Hatnagel, T. (1976). The impact of Machiavellianism and the trustfulness of the victim on laboratory theft. *Sociometry, 39,* 157-165.

Harris, M. B. (1974). Mediators between frustration and aggression in a field experiment. *Journal of Experimental Social Psychology, 10,* 561-571.

Harris, R. J., and Joyce, M. A. (1980). What's fair? It depends on how you phrase the question. *Journal of Personality and Social Psychology, 38,* 165-179.

Harrison, A. H. (1977). Mere exposure. In L. Berkowitz (Ed.), *Advances in experimental social psychology* (Vol. 10). New York: Academic Press.

Hartmann, D. P. (1969). Influence of symbolically modeled instrumental aggression and pain cues on aggressive behavior. *Journal of Personality and Social Psychology, 11,* 280-288.

Harvey, J. H., and Weary, G. (1981). *Perspectives on attributional processes.* Dubuque, IA: Wm. C. Brown.

Harvey, M. D., and Enzle, M. E. (1978). Effects of retaliatory latency and provocation level on judged blameworthiness for retaliatory aggression. *Personality and Social Psychology Bulletin, 4,* 579-582.

Hass, R. G. (1981). Presentational strategies and the social expression of attitudes: Impression management within limits. In J. T. Tedeschi (Ed.), *Impression management theory and social psychological research.* New York: Academic Press.

Hass, R. G., and Mann, R. W. (1976). Anticipatory belief change: Persuasion or impression management. *Journal of Personality and Social Psychology, 34,* 105-111.

Hastie, R. (1981). Memory for information that is congruent or incongruent with a conceptual schema. In E. T. Higgins, C. P. Herman, and M. P. Zanna (Eds.), *Social cognition: The Ontario Symposium on Personality and Social Psychology.* Hillsdale, NJ: Erlbaum.

Hastorf, A. H., and Cantril, H. (1954). They saw a game. *Journal of Abnormal and Social Psychology, 49,* 129-134.

Hastorf, A. H., Schneider, D. J., and Polefka, J. (1970). *Person perception.* Reading, MA: Addison-Wesley.

Hayduk, L. A. (1983). Personal space: Where we now stand. *Psychological Bulletin, 94,* 293-335.

Heelas, P., and Lock, A. (Eds.). (1981). *Indigenous psychologies: The anthropology of the self.* London: Academic Press.

Heider, F. (1946). Attitudes and cognitive organization. *Journal of Psychology, 21,* 107-112.

Heider, F. (1958). *The psychology of interpersonal relations.* New York: John Wiley.

Heilman, M. E. (1974). Threats and promises: Reputational consequences and transfer of credibility. *Journal of Experimental Social Psychology, 10,* 310-324.

Heiman, J. (1975). The physiology of erotica: Women's sexual arousal. *Psychology Today, 8,* 90-94.

Helm, B., Bonoma, T. V., and Tedeschi, J. T. (1972). Reciprocity for harm done. *Journal of Social Psychology, 87,* 89-98.

Helmreich, R. L., Spence, J. T., and Gibson, R. H. (1982). Sex-role attitudes: 1972-1980. *Personality and Social Psychology Bulletin, 8,* 656-663.

Hemphill, J. K. (1961). Why people attempt to lead. In L. Petrullo and B. M. Bass (Eds.), *Leadership and interpersonal behavior.* New York: Holt, Rinehart and Winston.

Hemphill, J. K., and Sechrest, L. (1952). A comparison of three criteria of air crew effectiveness in combat over Korea. *American Psychologist 7,* 391.

Hemsley, G. D., and Doob, A. M. (1978). The effect of

looking behavior on perceptions of a communicator's credibility. *Journal of Applied Social Psychology, 8,* 136-144.

Henchy, T., and Glass, D. C. (1968). Evaluation apprehension and the social facilitation of dominant and subordinate responses. *Journal of Personality and Social Psychology, 10,* 446-454.

Henderson, J. B., Hall, S. M., and Lipton, H. L. (1979). Changing self-destructive behaviors. In G. C. Stone, F. Cohen, and N. E. Adler (Eds.), *Health psychology.* San Francisco: Jossey-Bass.

Hendrick, C. (1977). Social psychology as an experimental science. In C. Hendrick (Ed.), *Perspectives on social psychology.* Hillsdale, NJ: Erlbaum.

Henley, N. M. (1973). Status and sex: Some touching observations. *Bulletin of the Psychonomic Society, 2,* 91-93.

Henley, N. M. (1977). *Body politics: Power, sex and nonverbal communication.* Englewood Cliffs, NJ: Prentice-Hall.

Henry, A. F., and Short, J. F., Jr. (1954). *Suicide and homicide: Some economic, sociological and psychological aspects of aggression.* Glencoe, IL: Free Press.

Hepburn, C., and Locksley, A. (1983). Subjective awareness of stereotyping: Do we know when our judgments are prejudiced? *Social Psychology Quarterly, 46,* 311-318.

Hersh, S. M. (1970). *My Lai 4: A report on the massacre and its aftermath.* New York: Vintage.

Heslin, R., and Boss, D. (1980). Nonverbal intimacy in airport arrival and departure. *Personality and Social Psychology Bulletin, 6,* 248-252.

Hess, E. H. (1965). Attitude and pupil size. *Scientific American, 212,* 46-54.

Hewitt, J. P., and Stokes, R. (1975). Disclaimers. *American Sociological Review, 40,* 1-11.

Hicks, D. J. (1965). Imitation and retention of film-mediated aggressive peer and adult models. *Journal of Personality and Social Psychology, 2,* 97-100.

Higbee, K. L. (1969). Fifteen years of fear arousal: Research on threat appeals, 1953-1968. *Psychological Bulletin, 72,* 426-444.

Higbee, K. L., Lott, W. J., and Graves, J. P. (1976). Experimentation and college students in social-personality research. *Personality and Social Psychology Bulletin, 2,* 239-241.

Higbee, K. L., Millard, R. J., and Folkman, J. R. (1982). Social psychology research during the 1970s: Predominance of experimentation and college students. *Personality and Social Psychology Bulletin, 8,* 180-183.

Higbee, K. L., and Wells, M. G. (1972). Some research trends in social psychology during the 1960s. *American Psychologist, 27,* 963-966.

Higgins, E. T., King, G. A., and Mavin, G. H. (1982). Individual construct accessibility and subjective impressions and recall. *Journal of Personality and Social Psychology, 43,* 35-47.

Higgins, E. T., Rhodes, W. S., and Jones, C. R. (1977). Category accessibility and impression formation. *Journal of Experimental Social Psychology, 13,* 141-154.

Hilgard, E. R., and Bower, G. H. (1975). *Theories of learning* (4th ed.). Englewood Cliffs, NJ: Prentice-Hall.

Hill, C. T., Rubin, Z., and Peplau, L. A. (1976). Breakups before marriage: The end of 103 affairs. *Journal of Social Issues, 32,* 147-168.

Hinkle, S., Corcoran, C. J., and Grene, A. E. (1980). Self-attributions of having exerted influence: The effects of target admission or denial of influence. *Personality and Social Psychology Bulletin, 6,* 447-453.

Hinkle, S., and Schopler, J. (1979). Ethnocentrism in the evaluation of group products. In W. G. Austin and S. Worchel (Eds.), *The social psychology of intergroup relations.* Monterey, CA: Brooks/Cole.

Hiroto, D. S., and Seligman, M. E. P. (1975). Generality of learned helplessness in man. *Journal of Personality and Social Psychology, 31,* 311-327.

Hirschfield, N. (1983, June 26). The shame of New Bedford. *New York Sunday News Magazine,* pp. 4-16.

Hobbes, T. (1909). *Leviathan.* Oxford, England: Clarendon. (Reprint of 1st ed. 1651)

Hoffman, L. W. (1977). Fear of success in 1965 and 1974: A follow-up study. *Journal of Counseling and Clinical Psychology, 45,* 310-321.

Hoffman, M. L. (1981). Is altruism part of human nature? *Journal of Personality and Social Psychology, 40,* 121-137.

Hofling, C. K., Brotzman, E., Dalrymple, B., Graves, N., and Pierce, C. M. (1966). An experimental study in nurse-physician relationships. *Journal of Nervous and Mental Disorders, 143,* 141-159.

Hofstadter, R. (1963). *Anti-intellectualism in American life.* New York: Alfred Knopf.

Hokanson, J. E. (1970). Psychophysical evaluation of the catharsis hypothesis. In. E. I. Megargee and J. E. Hokanson (Eds.), *The dynamics of aggression.* New York: Harper and Row.

Hokanson, J. E., and Burgess, M. (1962). The effects of three types of aggression on vascular processes. *Journal of Abnormal and Social Psychology, 64,* 446-449.

Hokanson, J. E., and Edelman, R. (1966). Effects of three social responses on vascular processes. *Journal of Personality and Social Psychology, 3,* 442-447.

Hokanson, J. E., and Shetler, S. (1961). The effect of overt aggression on physiological arousal. *Journal of Abnormal and Social Psychology, 63,* 446-448.

Hollander, E. P. (1958). Conformity, status, and idiosyncrasy credit. *Psychological Review, 65,* 117-127.

Hollander, E. P. (1960). Competence and conformity in the acceptance of infleunce. *Journal of Abnormal and Social Psychology, 61,* 365-369.

Hollander, E. P. (1964). *Leaders, groups and influence.* New York: Oxford University Press.

Hollander, E. P., and Julian, J. W. (1970). Studies in leader legitimacy, influence, and innovation. In L. Berkowitz (Ed.), *Advances in experimental social psychology* (Vol. 5). New York: Academic Press.

Holmes, D. S., and Bennett, D. H. (1974). Experiments to answer the questions raised by the use of deception in psychological research. *Journal of Personality and Social Psychology, 29,* 358-367.

Homans, G. C. (1961). *Social behavior: Its elementary forms.* New York: Harcourt, Brace and World.

Homans, G. C. (1974). *Social behavior: Its elementary forms* (2nd ed.). New York: Harcourt, Brace and World.

Horai, J., and Tedeschi, J. T. (1969). The effects of threat credibility and magnitude of punishment upon compliance. *Journal of Personality and Social Psychology, 12,* 164-169.

Hornberger, R. H. (1959, August). *The differential reduction of aggressive responses as a function of interpolated activities.* Paper presented at the 67th annual convention of the American Psychological Association, Cincinnati, OH.

Horner, M. (1968). *Sex differences in achievement motivation and perfomance in competitive and noncompetitive situations.* Unpublished Ph.D. thesis, University of Michigan, Ann Arbor.

Hosch, H. M., and Cooper, D. S. (1982). Victimization as a determinant of eyewitness accuracy. *Journal of Applied Psychology, 67,* 649-652.

House, J. S. (1977). The three faces of social psychology. *Sociometry, 40,* 161-171.

Hovland, C. I. (1958). The role of primacy and recency in persuasive communication. In E. E. Maccoby, T. M. Newcomb, and E. L. Hartley (Eds.), *Readings in social psychology* (3rd ed.). New York: Henry Holt.

Hovland, C. I., Campbell, E. H., and Brock, T. C. (1957). The effects of "commitment" on opinion change following communication. In C. I. Hovland (Ed.), *Order of presentation in persuasion.* New Haven: Yale University Press.

Hovland, C. I., Harvey, D. J., and Sherif, M. (1957). Assimilation and contrast effects in reactions to communication and attitude change. *Journal of Abnormal and Social Psychology, 55,* 244-252.

Hovland, C. I., and Janis, I. L. (1959). *Personality and persuasibility.* New Haven: Yale University Press.

Hovland, C. I., Janis, I. L., and Kelley, H. H. (1953). *Communication and persuasion.* New Haven: Yale University Press.

Hovland, C. I., Lumsdaine, A. A., and Sheffield, F. D. (1949). *Experiments on mass communication.* Princeton: Princeton University Press.

Hovland, C. I., and Mandell, W. (1952). An experimental comparison of conclusion-drawing by the communicator and by the audience. *Journal of Abnormal and Social Psychology, 47,* 581-588.

Howard, J., and Rothbart, M. (1980). Social categorization and memory for in-group and out-group behavior. *Journal of Personality and Social Psychology, 38,* 301-308.

Howard, J. W., and Dawes, R. M. (1976). Linear prediction of marital happiness. *Personality and Social Psychology Bulletin, 2,* 478-480.

Howell, L. T., and Becker, S. W. (1962). Seating arrangement and leadership emergence. *Journal of Abnormal and Social Psychology, 64,* 148-150.

Hoyenga, K. B., and Hoyenga, K. T. (1979). *The question of sex differences: Psychological, cultural and biological issues.* Boston: Little, Brown.

Hoyt, M. F., Henley, M. D., and Collins, B. E. (1972). Studies in forced compliance: The confluence of choice and consequences on attitude change. *Journal of Personality and Social Psychology, 23,* 205-210.

Hull, J. G., and West, S. G. (1982). The discounting principle in attribution. *Personality and Social Psychology Bulletin, 8,* 208-213.

Humphreys, L. (1970). *Tearoom trade: Impersonal sex in public places.* Chicago: Aldine-Atherton.

Humphreys, L. (1978). *Tearoom trade.* Chicago: University of Chicago Press.

Hunt, M. (1974). *Sexual behavior in the 1970s.* Chicago: Playboy Press.

Hunt, M. (1982, September 12). Research through deception. *New York Times Sunday Magazine* pp. 66, 138, 140-143.

Hurwitz, J. I., Zander, A. F., and Hymovitch, B. (1968). Some effects of power on the relations among group members. In D. Cartwright and A. F. Zander (Eds.), *Group dynamics* (3rd ed.). New York: Harper and Row.

Husband, R. W. (1931). Analysis of methods in human maze learning. *Journal of Genetic Psychology, 39,* 258-277.

Huston, T. (Ed.). (1974). *Foundations of interpersonal attraction.* New York: Academic Press.

Huston, T., and Cate, R. (1979). Social exchange in intimate relationships. In M. Cook, and G. Wilson (Eds.), *Love and attraction.* Oxford, England: Pergamon Press.

Huston, T. L. (1973). Ambiguity of acceptance, social desirability and dating choice. *Journal of Experimental Social Psychology, 9,* 32-42.

Huston, T. L., Ruggerio, M., Conner, R., and Geis, G. (1981). Bystander intervention into crime: A study based on naturally occurring episodes. *Social Psychology Quarterly, 44,* 14-23.

Hyde, J. S. (1981). How large are cognitive gender differences? A meta analysis using ω2 and *d. American Psychologist, 36,* 892-901.

Hyde, J. S., and Rosenberg, B. G. (1980). *Half the human experience: The psychology of women.* Lexington, MA: D. C. Heath.

Ickes, W. J., and Barnes, R. D. (1977). The role of sex and self-monitoring in unstructured dyadic interactions. *Journal of Personality and Social Psychology, 35,* 315-330.

Indik, B. P. (1965). Organization size and member participation: Some empirical tests of alternatives. *Human Relations, 18,* 339-350.

Ingham, A., Levinger, G., Graves, J., and Peckham, V. (1974). The Ringelmann effect: Studies of group size and group performance. *Journal of Personality and Social Psychology, 10,* 371-384.

Insko, C. A. (1964). Primacy versus recency in persuasion as a function of the timing of arguments and measures. *Journal of Abnormal and Social Psychology, 69,* 381-391.

Insko, C. A. (1965). Verbal reinforcement of attitude. *Journal of Personality and Social Psychology, 2,* 621-623.

Instone, D., Major, B. R., and Bunker, B. B. (1983). Gender, self-confidence, and social influence strategies: An organizational simulation. *Journal of Personality and Social Psychology, 44,* 322-333.

Isen, A. M., Clark, M., and Schwartz, M. F. (1976). Duration of the effect of good mood on helping: "Footprints in the sands of time." *Journal of Personality and Social Psychology, 34,* 385-393.

Isen, A. M., and Levin, P. F. (1972). Effect of feeling good on helping: Cookies and kindness. *Journal of Personality and Social Psychology, 21,* 384-388.

Isen, A. M., Shalker, T. E., Clark, M., and Karp, L. (1978). Affect, accessibility of material in memory, and behavior: A cognitive loop? *Journal of Personality and Social Psychology, 36,* 1-12.

Isen, A. M., and Simmonds, S. (1978). The effect of feeling good on a helping task that is incompatible with good mood. *Social Psychology, 41,* 346-349.

Izard, C. E. (1977). *Human emotions.* New York: Plenum.

Jackson, J. M., and Latane, B. (1981). Strength and number of solicitors and the urge toward altruism. *Personality and Social Psychology Bulletin, 7,* 415-422.

Jackson, J. M., and Padgett, V. R. (1982). With a little help from my friend: Social loafing and the Lennon-McCartney songs. *Personality and Social Psychology Bulletin, 8,* 672-677.

Jackson, L. A. (1983). The influence of sex, physical attractiveness, sex role and occupational sex-linkage on perceptions of occupational suitability. *Journal of Applied Social Psychology, 13,* 31-44.

Jacoby, J., and Hoyer, W. D. (1982). Viewer miscomprehension of televised communication. *Journal of Marketing, 46,* 12-26.

Jaeger, M. E., Anthony, S., and Rosnow, R. L. (1980). Who hears what from whom and with what effect: A study of rumor. *Personality and Social Psychology Bulletin, 6,* 473-478.

Jaffe, Y., Malamuth, N., Feingold, J., and Feshbach, S. (1974). Sexual arousal and behavioral aggression. *Journal of Personality and Social Psychology, 30,* 759-764.

Jaffe, Y., and Yinon, Y. (1979). Retaliatory aggression in individuals and groups. *European Journal of Social Psychology, 9,* 177-186.

James, G., and Lott, A. (1964). Reward frequncy and the formation of positive attitudes toward group members. *Journal of Social Psychology, 62,* 111-115.

James, W. (1890). *Principles of psychology.* New York: Henry Holt.

James, W. (1950). *The principles of psychology.* New York: Dover Publications.

James, W. H., Woodruff, A. B., and Werner, W. (1965). Effects of internal and external control upon changes in smoking behavior. *Journal of Consulting Psychology, 29,* 184-186.

Janis, I. L. (1972). *Victims of groupthink.* Boston: Houghton Mifflin.

Janis, I. L., and Feshbach, S. (1953). Effects of fear-arousing communications. *Journal of Abnormal and Social Psychology, 48,* 78-92.

Janis, I. L., and Field, P. B. (1959). Sex differences and personality factors related to persuasibility. In C. I. Hovland and I. L. Janis (Eds.), *Personality and persuasibility.* New Haven: Yale University Press.

Janis, I. L., and Hoffman, D. (1971). Facilitating effects of daily contact between partners who make decisions to cut down on smoking. *Journal of Personality and Social Psychology, 17,* 25-35.

Janis, I. L., Kaye, D., and Kirschner, P. (1965). Facilitating effects of "eating while reading" on responsiveness to persuasive communications. *Journal of Personality and Social Psychology, 1,* 181-186.

Janis, I. L., and Rodin, J. (1979). Attribution, control, and decision making: Social psychology and health care. In G. C. Stone, F. Cohen, and N. E. Adler (Eds.), *Health psychology: A handbook.* San Francisco: Jossey-Bass.

Janis, I. L., and Terwillinger, R. F. (1962). An experimental study of psychological resistances to fear-arousing communications. *Journal of Abnormal and Social Psychology, 65,* 403-410.

Jegard, S., and Walters, R. (1960). A study of some determinants of aggression in young children. *Child Development, 31,* 739-747.

Jellison, J. M. (1981). Reconsidering the attitude concept: A behavioristic self-presentation formulation. In J. T. Tedeschi (Ed.), *Impression management theory and social psychological research.* New York: Academic Press.

Jellison, J. M., and Arkin, R. M. (1977). Social comparison of abilities: A self-presentational interpretation of decision making in groups. In J. M. Suls and R. L. Miller (Eds.), *Social comparison processes: Theoretical and empirical perspectives.* Washington, DC: Hemisphere.

Jellison, J. M., and Gentry, R. A. (1978). Self-presentation interpretation of the seeking of social approval. *Personality and Social Psychology Bulletin, 4,* 227-230.

Johnson, H. H., and Izzett, R. R. (1969). Relationship between authoritarianism and attitude change as a function of source credibility and type of communication. *Journal of Personality and Social Psychology, 13,* 317-321.

Johnson, M. K., Bransford, J. D., and Solomon, S. (1973). Memory for tacit implications of sentences. *Journal of Experimental Psychology, 98,* 203-205.

Johnson, P. (1974, May). *Social power and sex role stereotypes.* Paper presented at the meeting of the Western Psychological Association, San Francisco.

Johnson, R. N. (1972). *Aggression in man and animals.* Philadelphia: W. B. Saunders.

Johnson, T. J., Feigenbaum, R., and Weiby, M. (1964). Some determinants and consequences of the teacher's perception of causation. *Journal of Educational Psychology, 55,* 237-246.

Jones, C., and Aronson, E. (1973). Attribution of fault to a rape victim as a function of respectability of the victim. *Journal of Personality and Social Psychology, 26,* 413-419.

Jones, E. E. (1964). *Ingratiation: A social psychological analysis.* New York: Appleton-Century-Crofts.

Jones, E. E., and Berglas, S. (1978). Control of attributions about the self through self-handicapping strategies: The appeal of alcohol and the role of underachievement. *Personality and Social Psychology Bulletin, 4,* 200-206.

Jones, E. E., and Davis, K. E. (1965). From acts to dispositions: The attribution process in person perception. In L. Berkowitz (Ed.), *Advances in experimental social psychology* (Vol. 2). New York: Academic Press.

Jones, E. E., Davis, K. E., and Gergen, K. J. (1967). Role playing variations and their informational value for person perception. *Journal of Abnormal and Social Psychology, 63,* 302-310.

Jones, E. E., and deCharms, R. (1957). Changes in social perception as a function of the personal relevance of behavior. *Sociometry, 20,* 75-85.

Jones, E. E., Farina, A., Hastorf, A. H., Markus, H., Miller, D. T., and Scott, R. A. (1984). *Social stigma: The psychology of marked relationships.* New York: W. H. Freeman.

Jones, E. E., and Gerard, H. B. (1967). *Foundations of social psychology.* New York: John Wiley.

Jones, E. E., Gergen, K. J., and Davis, K. E. (1962). Some determinants of reacting to being approved or disapproved. *Psychological Monographs, 76* (2, Whole No. 521).

Jones, E. E., Gergen, K. J., Gumport, P., and Thibaut, J. W. (1965). Some conditions affecting the use of ingratiation to influence performance evaluation. *Journal of Personality and Social Psychology, 1,* 613-625.

Jones, E. E., Gergen, K. J., and Jones, R. G. (1964). Tactics of ingratiation among leaders and subordinates in a status hierarchy. *Psychological Monographs, 77* (3, Whole No. 566).

Jones, E. E., Jones, R. G., and Gergen, K. J. (1963). Some conditions affecting the evaluation of a conformist. *Journal of Personality, 31,* 270-288.

Jones, E. E., and Nisbett, R. E. (1972). The actor and the observer: Divergent perceptions of the causes of behavior. In E. E. Jones, D. E. Kanouse, H. H. Kelley, R. E. Nisbett, S. Valins, and B. Weiner (Eds.), *Attribution: Perceiving the causes of behavior.* Morristown, NJ: General Learning Press.

Jones, E. E., and Pittman, T. S. (1982). Toward a general theory of strategic self-presentation. In J. Suls (Ed.), *Psychological perspectives on the self* (Vol. 1). Hillsdale, NJ: Erlbaum.

Jones, E. E., and Sigall, H. (1971). The bogus pipeline: A new paradigm for measuring affect and attitudes. *Psychological Bulletin, 76,* 349-364.

Jones, E. E., Wood, G. C., and Quattrone, G. A. (1981). Perceived variability of personal characteristics of in-groups and out-groups: The role of knowledge and evaluation. *Personality and Social Psychology Bulletin, 7,* 523-528.

Jones, E. E., and Wortman, C. (1973). *Ingratiation: An attributional approach.* Morristown, NJ: General Learning Press.

Jones, J. W., and Bogat, G. A. (1978). Air pollution and human aggression. *Psychological Reports, 43,* 721-722.

Jones, K. E., Epstein, J., and O'Neal, E. C. (1981). *Experience with firearms mitigates the weapons effect.*

Unpublished manuscript, Tulane University, New Orleans.

Jones, R. (1984). The third wave. In A. Pines and C. Maslach (Eds.), *Experiencing social psychology: Readings and projects* (2nd ed.). New York: Alfred Knopf.

Jones, R. O., Linder, D., Kiesler, C., Zanna, M., and Brehm, J. (1968). Internal states or external stimuli: Observers' attitude judgments and the dissonance theory vs. self-persuasion controversy. *Journal of Experimental Social Psychology, 4,* 247-269.

Jones, S. C. (1974). The psychology of interpersonal attraction. In C. Nemeth (Ed.), *Social psychology: Classic and contemporary integrations.* Chicago: Rand McNally.

Jones, S. C., and Schneider, D. J. (1968). Certainty of self-appraisal and reactions to evaluations from others. *Sociometry, 31,* 395-403.

Jones, W. H., Chernovetz, M. E., and Hansson, R. O. (1978). The enigma of androgyny: Differential implications for males and females. *Journal of Counseling and Clinical Psychology, 46,* 298-313.

Jones, W. H., Freeman, J. F., and Goswick, R. A. (1981). The persistence of loneliness: Self and other determinants. *Journal of Personality, 49,* 27-48.

Jones, W. H., Sansone, C., and Helm, B. (1983). Loneliness and interpersonal judgments. *Personality and Social Psychology Bulletin, 9,* 437-441.

Joseph, J. M., Gaes, G. G., Tedeschi, J. T., and Cunningham, M. R. (1979). Impression management effects in the forced compliance situation. *Journal of Social Psychology, 107,* 89-98.

Joseph, J. M., Kane, T. R., Nacci, P. L., and Tedeschi, J. T. (1977). Perceived aggression: A re-evaluation of the Bandura modeling paradigm. *Journal of Social Psychology, 103,* 277-289.

Jung, J. (1982). *The experimenter's challenge.* New York: Macmillan.

Kaats, G. R., and Davis, K. E. (1970). The dynamics of sexual behavior of college students. *Journal of Marriage and the Family, 32,* 390-399.

Kahn, R., and Katz, D. (1953). Leadership practices in relation to productivity and morale. In D. Cartwright and A. Zander (Eds.), *Group dynamics: Research and theory.* Evanston, IL: Row, Peterson.

Kahneman, D., and Tversky, A. (1973). On the psychology of prediction. *Psychological Review, 80,* 237-251.

Kahneman, D., and Tversky, A. (1979). Intuitive prediction: Biases and corrective procedures. *Management Science, 12,* 313-327.

Kalven, H., Jr., and Zeisel, H. (1966). *The American jury.* Chicago: University of Chicago Press.

Kane, T., Joseph, J. M., and Tedeschi, J. T. (1976). Person perception and the Berkowitz paradigm for the study of aggression. *Journal of Personality and Social Psychology, 33,* 663-673.

Kanin, E. J., Davidson, K. D., and Scheck, S. R. (1970). A research note on male-female differentials in the experience of heterosexual love. *Journal of Sex Research, 6,* 64-72.

Kaplan, M. F. (1977). Judgments by juries. In M. F. Kaplan and S. Schwartz (Eds.), *Judgment and decision processes in applied settings.* New York: Academic Press.

Kaplan, M. F., and Miller, C. E. (1977). Judgments and group discussion: Effect of presentation and memory factors on polarization. *Sociometry, 40,* 337-343.

Kardes, F., Kimble, C., DaPolito, F., and Biers, D. (1982, August). *Reluctant communication: A self-presentational analysis.* Paper presented at the meeting of the American Psychological Association.

Karlin, R. A., and Epstein, Y. M. (1979). Acute crowding: A reliable method for inducing stress in humans. *Research Communications in Psychology, Psychiatry and Behavior, 4,* 357-370.

Karlin, R. A., Rosen, L. S., and Epstein, Y. M. (1979). Three into two doesn't go: A follow-up on the effects of overcrowded dormitory rooms. *Personality and Social Psychology Bulletin, 5,* 391-395.

Karlins, M., Coffman, T. L., and Walters G. (1969). On the fading of social stereotypes: Studies in three generations of college students. *Journal of Personality and Social Psychology, 13,* 1-16.

Kassarjian, H. H., and Cohen, J. B. (1965). Cognitive dissonance and consumer behavior. *California Management Review, 8,* 55-64.

Kassin, S. (1979). Consensus information, prediction, and causal attribution: A review of the literature and issues. *Journal of Personality and Social Psychology, 37,* 1966-1981.

Katz, D. (1960). The functional approach to the study of attitudes. *Public Opinion Quarterly, 24,* 163-204.

Katz, D., and Braly, K. W. (1933). Racial prejudice and racial stereotypes. *Journal of Abnormal and Social Psychology, 30,* 175-193.

Katz, E., and Lazarsfeld, P. F. (1955). *Personal influence.* Glencoe, IL: Free Press.

Kazdin, A. E., and Bryan, J. H. (1971). Competence and volunteering. *Journal of Experimental Social Psychology, 7,* 87-97.

Kazee, T. (1981). Television exposure and attitude change: The impact of political interest. *Public Opinion Quarterly, 45,* 507-518.

Keene, M. (1976). *The Psychic Mafia.* New York: Dell.

Kelley, H. H. (1950). The warm-cold variable in first impressions of persons. *Journal of Personality, 18,* 431-439.

Kelley, H. H. (1967). Attribution theory in social psychology. In D. Levine (Ed.), *Nebraska Symposium on Motivation.* Lincoln: University of Nebraska Press.

Kelley, H. H. (1973). The processes of causal attribution. *American Psychologist, 28,* 107-128.

Kelley, H. H., and Stahelski, A. J. (1970). Social interaction bases for cooperators' and competitors' beliefs about others. *Journal of Personality and Social Psychology, 16,* 66-91.

Kelley, H. H., and Thibaut, J. W. (1978). *Interpersonal relationships: A theory of interdependence.* New York: John Wiley.

Kellog, R., and Baron, R. S. (1975). Attribution theory, insomnia, and the reverse placebo effect: A reversal of Storms and Nisbett's findings. *Journal of Personality and Social Psychology, 32,* 231-236.

Kelly, G. A. (1955). *The psychology of personal constructs.* New York: W. W. Norton.

Kelman, H. C. (1950). Effects of success and failure on "suggestibility" in the autokinetic situation. *Journal of Abnormal and Social Psychology, 45,* 267-285.

Kelman, H. C. (1958). Compliance, identification, and internalization: Three processes of attiude change. *Journal of Conflict Resolution, 2,* 51-60.

Kelman, H. C. (1967). Human use of human subjects: The problem of deception in social psychological experiments. *Psychological Bulletin, 67,* 1-11.

Kelman, H. C., and Hovland, C. I. (1953). Reinstatement of the communicator in delayed measurement of opinion change. *Journal of Abnormal and Social Psychology, 48,* 327-335.

Kelman, H. C., and Lawrence, L. H. (1972, June). Violent man: American response to the trial of Lt. William L. Calley. *Psychology Today,* pp. 14-45, 78-81.

Kennan, G. F. (1947). The sources of Soviet conduct. *Foreign Affairs, 25,* 568-582.

Kenrick, D. T., Cialdini, R. B., and Linder, D. E. (1979). Misattribution under fear-arousing circumstances: Four failures to replicate. *Personality and Social Psychology Bulletin, 5,* 329-335.

Kenrick, D. T., and Guitierres, S. E. (1980). Contrast effects and judgments of physical attractiveness: When beauty becomes a social problem. *Journal of Personality and Social Psychology, 38,* 131-140.

Kerckoff, A. C., and Davis, K. E. (1962). Value consensus and need complementarity in mate selection. *American Sociological Review, 27,* 295-305.

Kerr, N. L. (1983). Motivation losses in small groups: A social dilemma analysis. *Journal of Personality and Social Psychology, 45,* 829-838.

Key, M. R. (1975). The role of male and female in children's books: Dispelling all doubt. In R. K. Unger and F. L. Denmark (Eds.), *Woman: Dependent or independent variable?* New York: Psychological Dimension.

Kiesler, C. A., Collins, B. E., and Miller, N. (1969). *Attitude change.* New York: John Wiley.

Kiesler, C. A., and Kiesler, S. B. (1969). *Conformity.* Reading, MA: Addison-Wesley.

Kiloh, L. G., Gye, R. S., Rosenworth, R. G, Bell, D. S., and White, R. T. (1974). Stereotactic amygdaloidotomy for aggressive behaviors. *Journal of Neurology, Neurosurgery and Psychiatry, 37,* 437-444.

Kimmel, A. J. (Ed.). (1981). *Ethics of human subjects research.* San Francisco: Jossey-Bass.

Kinsey, A. C., Pomeroy, W. B., and Martin, C. E. (1948). *Sexual behavior in the human male.* Philadelphia: W. B. Saunders.

Kinsey, A. C., Pomery, W. B., Martin, C. E., and Gebhard, P. H. (1953). *Sexual behavior in the human female.* Philadelphia: W. B. Saunders.

Kipnis, D. (1957). Interaction between members of bomber crews as a determinant of sociometric choice. *Human Relations, 10,* 263-270.

Kipnis, D. (1974). The powerholder. In J. T. Tedeschi (Ed.), *Perspectives on social power.* Chicago: Aldine-Atherton.

Kipnis, D., and Consentino, J. (1969). Use of leadership powers in industry. *Journal of Applied Psychology, 53,* 460-466.

Kipnis, D., and Misner, R. P. (1972). *Police actions and disorderly conduct.* Unpublished manuscript, Temple University, Philadelphia.

Kite, W. R. (1964). *Attributions of causality as a function of the use of reward and punishment.* Unpublished manuscript, Stanford University, Stanford, CA.

Klein, K., and Creech, B. (1982). Race, rape and bias. Distortion of prior odds and meaning changes. *Basic and Applied Social Psychology, 3,* 21-33.

Knapp, M. L. (1978). *Nonverbal communication in human interaction* (2nd ed.). New York: Holt, Rinehart & Winston.

Knapp, R. H. (1944). A psychology of rumor. *Public Opinion Quarterly, 8,* 22-37.

Knowles, E. S. (1983). Social physics and the effects of others: Test of the effects of audience size and distance on social judgments and behavior. *Journal of Personality and Social Psychology, 5,* 1263-1279.

Knox, R. E., and Inkster, J. A. (1968). Postdecision dissonance at posttime. *Journal of Personality and Social Psychology, 18,* 319-323.

Knox, R. E., & Safford, R. K. (1976). Group caution at the race track. *Journal of Experimental Social Psychology, 21,* 317-324.

Kogan, N., & Wallach, M. A. (1967). Risk taking as a function of the situation, the person, and the group. In *New directions in psychology* (Vol. 3). New York: Holt, Rinehart & Winston.

Kolditz, T. A., and Arkin, R. M. (1982). An impression management interpretation of the self-handicapping strategy. *Journal of Personality and Social Psychology, 43,* 492-502.

Komorita, S. S., and Chertkoff, J. M. (1973). A bargaining theory of coalition formation. *Psychological Review, 80,* 149-162.

Konecni, V. J. (1975). The mediation of aggressive behavior: Arousal level versus anger and cognitive labeling. *Journal of Personality and Social Psychology, 32,* 706-712.

Konecni, V. J., and Doob, A. N. (1972). Catharsis through displacement of aggression. *Journal of Personality and Social Psychology, 23,* 379-387.

Konecni, V. J., and Ebbesen, E. G. (1976). Disinhibition versus the cathartic effect: Artifact and substance. *Journal of Personality and Social Psychology, 34,* 352-365.

Koocher, G. P. (1977). Bathroom behavior and human dignity. *Journal of Personality and Social Psychology, 35,* 120-121.

Kopera, A. A., Maier, R. A., and Johnson, J. E. (1971, August). Perception of physical attractiveness: The influence of group interaction and group coaction on ratings of the attractiveness of photographs of women. Paper presented at the meeting of the American Psychological Association, Washington, DC.

Korda, M. (1975). *Power.* New York: Random House.

Kramer, B. M., Kalick, S. M., and Milburn, M. A. (1983). Attitudes toward nuclear weapons and nuclear war: 1945-1982. *Journal of Social Issues, 39,* 7-24.

Krantz, D., Baum, A., and Singer, J. E. (Eds.). (1983). *Handbook of psychology and health* (Vol. 3). Hillsdale, NJ: Erlbaum.

Krauss, R. M. (1966). Structural and attitudinal factors in interpersonal bargaining. *Journal of Experimental Social Psychology, 2,* 42-55.

Krauss, R. M., Geller, V., and Olson, C. (1976, August). Modalities and cues in perceiving deception. Paper presented at the meeting of the American Psychological Association, Washington, DC.

Kraut, R. E., and Price, J. D. (1976). Machiavellianism in parents and their children. *Journal of Personality and Social Psychology, 33,* 782-786.

Krebs, D. L. (1970). Altruism: An examination of the concept and a review of the literature. *Psychological Bulletin, 73,* 258-302.

Krech, D., Crutchfield, R. S., and Ballachey, E. L. (1962). *Individual in society: A textbook of social psychology.* New York: McGraw-Hill.

Kruglanski, A. W., and Freund, T. (1983). The freezing and unfreezing of lay-inferences: Effects on impressional primacy, ethnic stereotyping, and numerical anchoring. *Journal of Experimental Social Psychology, 19,* 448-468.

Kuhlman, C. E., Miller, M. J., and Gungor, E. (1973). Interpersonal conflict reduction: The effects of language and meaning. In L. Rappoport and D. A. Summers (Eds.), *Human judgment and social interaction.* New York: Holt, Rinehart and Winston.

Kuhlman, D. M., and Marshello, A. (1975). Individual differences in game motivation as moderators of preprogrammed strategy effects in prisoner's dilemma. *Journal of Personality and Social Psychology, 32,* 922-931.

Kuhn, A. (1963). *The study of society: A unified approach.* Homewood, IL: Richard D. Irwin.

Kuhn, M. H., and McPartland, T. S. (1954). An empirical investigation of self-attitudes. *American Sociological Review, 19,* 68-76.

Kuhn, T. (1962). *The structure of scientific revolutions.* Chicago: University of Chicago Press.

Kuiper, N. A., and Rogers, T. B. (1979). Encoding of personal information: Self-other differences. *Journal of Personality and Social Psychology, 37,* 2014-2024.

LaFrance, M., and Mayo, C. (1978). *Moving bodies: Nonverbal communication in social relationships.* Monterey, CA: Brooks/Cole.

Lagerspetz, K. (1981). Combining aggressive studies in infra-humans and man. In P. Brain and D. Benton (Eds.), *Multidisciplinary approaches to aggressive research.* New York: Elsevier North-Holland.

Laird, J. D. (1974). Self-attribution of emotion: The effects of expressive behavior on the quality of emotional experience. *Journal of Personality and Social Psychology, 29,* 475-486.

Laird, J. D., Wagener, J. J., Halal, M., and Szegda, M. (1982). Remembering what you feel: Effects of emotion on memory. *Journal of Personality and Social Psychology, 42,* 646-657.

Lalljee, M. (1981). Attribution theory and the analysis of explanations. In C. Ataki (Ed.), *The psychology of ordinary explanations of social behaviour.* London: Academic Press.

Langer, E., and Rodin, J. (1976). The effects of choice and enhanced person responsibility for the aged: A field experiment in an institutional setting. *Journal of Personality and Social Psychology, 34,* 191-198.

Langer, E. J., & Abelson, R. P. (1974). A patient by any other name . . . : Clinician group difference in labeling bias. *Journal of Consulting and Clinical Psychology, 42,* 4-9.

Langer, E. J., Blank, A., and Chanowitz, B. (1978). The mindlessness of ostensibly thoughtful action. *Journal of Personality and Social Psychology, 36,* 635-642.

Langer, E. J., and Roth, J. (1975). Heads I win, tails it's chance: The illusion of control as a function of the sequence of outcomes in a purely chance task. *Journal of Personality and Social Psychology, 32,* 951-955.

Lanzetta, J. T., Cartwright-Smith, J., and Kleck, R. E. (1976). Effects of nonverbal dissimulation in emotional experience and autonomic arousal. *Journal of Personality and Social Psychology, 33,* 354-370.

LaPiere, R. T. (1934). Attitudes versus actions. *Social Forces, 13,* 230-237.

Lasswell, H. D. (1966). Conflict and leadership: The process of decision and the nature of authority. In A. S. de Reuck and J. Knight (Eds.), *Ciba Foundation Symposium: Conflict in Society.* Boston: Little, Brown.

Latane, B., and Bidwell, L. D. (1977). Sex and affiliation in college cafeterias. *Personality and Social Psychology Bulletin, 3,* 571-574.

Latane, B., and Darley, J. M. (1968). Group inhibition of bystander intervention in emergencies. *Journal of Personality and Social Psychology, 10,* 215-221.

Latane, B., and Darley, J. M. (1970). *The unresponsive bystander: Why doesn't he help.* New York: Appleton-Century-Crofts.

Latane, B., and Nida, S. (1981). Ten years of research on group size and helping. *Psychological Bulletin, 89,* 308-324.

Latane, B., and Rodin, J. (1969). A lady in distress: Inhibiting effects of friends and strangers on bystander intervention. *Journal of Experimental Social Psychology, 5,* 189-202.

Lauer, R. H., and Handel, W. H. (1977). *Social psychology: The theory and application of symbolic interactionism.* Boston: Houghton-Mifflin.

Laufer, W. S., Johnson, J. A., and Hogan, R. (1981). Ego control and criminal behavior. *Journal of Personality and Social Psychology, 41,* 179-184.

Lazarus, R. S., Speisman, J., Mordkoff, A., and Davison, L. (1962). A laboratory study of psychological stress produced by a motion picture film. *Psychological Monographs, 76,* 34, Whole No. 553.

Leavitt, H. J. (1951). Some effects of certain communication patterns on group performance. *Journal of Abnormal and Social Psychology, 46,* 38-50.

Lefcourt, H. M. (1972). Recent developments in the study of locus of control. In B. A. Maher (Ed.), *Progress in experimental personality research* (Vol. 6). New York: Academic Press.

Lefkowitz, M., Blake, R. R., and Mouton, J. S. (1955). Status factors in pedestrian violation of traffic signals. *Journal of Abnormal and Social Psychology, 51,* 704-706.

Lerner, M. J., and Mathews, G. (1967). Reactions to suffering of others under conditions of indirect responsibility. *Journal of Personality and Social Psychology, 5,* 319-325.

Leung, K., and Bond, M. H. (1981). *How Chinese and Americans reward task-related contributions: A preliminary study.* Unpublished manuscript, Chinese University of Hong Kong.

Leventhal, H. (1980). Toward a comprehensive theory of emotion. In L. Berkowitz (Ed.), *Advances in experimental social psychology* (Vol. 13). New York: Academic Press.

Leventhal, H., Watts, J. C., and Pagano, F. (1967). Effects of fear and instructions on how to cope with danger. *Journal of Personality and Social Psychology, 6,* 313-321.

Levinger, G., and Breedlove, J. (1966). Interpersonal attraction and agreement: A study of marriage partners. *Journal of Personality and Social Psychology, 3,* 367-372.

Levinger, G., and Schneider, D. J. (1969). Test of the "risk is a value" hypothesis. *Journal of Personality and Social Psychology, 11,* 165-169.

Levinger, G., and Moles, D. C. (Eds.) (1979). *Close relationships.* New York: Basic Books.

Levinger, G., and Snoek, J. D. (1972). *Attraction in relationships: A new look at interpersonal attraction.* New York: General Learning Corporation.

Levi-Strauss, C. (1967). *Structural anthropology.* Garden City, NY: Anchor Books.

Lewin, K. (1935). Some social psychological differences between the United States and Germany. *Character and Personality, 4,* 265-293.

Lewin, K. (1946). *Resolving social conflicts.* New York: Harper & Row.

Lewin, K. (1948). *Resolving social conflicts: Selected papers on group dynamics (1935-1946).* New York: Harper & Row.

Lewin, K. (1951). *Field theory in social science.* New York: Harper & Row.

Lewin, K., Lippitt, R., and White, R. K. (1939). Patterns of aggressive behavior in experimentally created "social climates." *Journal of Social Psychology, 10,* 271-299.

Lewinsohn, P. M., Mischel, W., Chapline, W., and Barton, R. (1980). Social competence and depression: The role of illusory self-perceptions. *Journal of Abnormal Psychology, 89,* 203-212.

Lewis, M. (1972). Parents and children: Sex-role development. *School Review, 80,* 229-240.

Lewis, M., and Brooks, J. (1978). Self-knowledge and emotional development. In M. Lewis and L. Rosenblum (Eds.), *The development of affect.* New York: Plenum.

Lewittes, D. J., and Simmons, W. I. (1975). Impression management of a sexually motivated behavior. *Journal of Social Psychology, 96,* 39-44.

Lichtenstein, E. (1982). The smoking problem: A behavioral perspective. *Journal of Consulting and Clinical Psychology, 50,* 804-819.

Lieberman, S. (1956). The effect of changes in roles on the attitude of role occupants. *Human Relations, 9,* 385-402.

Liebert, R. M., Smith, W. P., Keiffer, M., and Hill, J. H. (1968). The effects of information and magnitude of initial offer on interpersonal negotiation. *Journal of Experimental Social Psychology, 4,* 431-444.

Liebert, R. M., Sprafkin, J. N., and Davidson, E. S. (Eds.). (1982). *The early window: Effects of television on children and youth.* New York: Pergamon Press.

Linder, D., and Worchel, W. (1970). Opinion change as a result of effortly drawing a counterattitudinal conclusion. *Journal of Experimental Social Psychology, 6,* 432-448.

Lindskold, S. (1981). Trust development, the GRIT proposal, and the effects of conciliatory acts on conflict and cooperation. *Psychological Bulletin, 85,* 772-793.

Lindskold, S., and Bennett, R. (1973). Attributing trust and conciliatory intent from coercive power capability. *Journal of Personality and Social Psychology, 28,* 180-186.

Lindskold, S., and Finch, M. (1981). Styles of announcing conciliation. *Journal of Conflict Resolution, 25,* 145-155.

Lindskold, S., Forte, R. A., Haake, C. S., and Schmidt, E. K. (1977). The effects of directness of face-to-face requests and sex of solicitor on street corner donations. *Journal of Social Psychology, 101,* 45-51.

Lindskold, S., McElwain, D. C., and Wayner, M. (1977). Cooperation and the use of coercion by groups and individuals. *Journal of Conflict Resolution, 21,* 531-550.

Lindskold, S., and Propst, L. R. (1981). Deindividuation, self-awareness, and impression management. In J. T. Tedeschi (Ed.), *Impression management theory and social psychological research.* New York: Academic Press.

Lindskold, S., Walters, P. S., and Koutsourais, H. (1983). Cooperators, competitors, and response to GRIT. *Journal of Conflict Resolution, 27,* 521-532.

Linville, P. W., and Jones, E. E. (1980). Polarized appraisals of out-group members. *Journal of Personality and Social Psychology, 38,* 689-703.

Lippa, R. (1976). Expressive control and the leakage of dispositional introversion-extraversion during role-played teaching. *Journal of Personality, 44,* 541-559.

Lippa, R. (1978). The effects of expressive control on expressive consistency and on the relation between expression behavior and personality. *Journal of Personality, 46,* 438-461.

Lippman, W. (1922). *Public opinion.* New York: Harcourt, Brace.

Lips, H. (1981). *Women, men and the psychology of power.* Englewood Cliffs, NJ: Prentice-Hall.

Liska, A. E. (1977). The dissipation of sociological social psychology. *American Sociologist, 12,* 2-8.

Liska, A. E. (1984). A critical examination of the causal structure of the Fishbein/Ajzen model. *Social Psychology Quarterly, 47,* 61-74.

Locksley, A., Ortiz, V., and Hepburn, C. (1980). Social categorization and discriminatory behavior: Extinguishing the minimal intergroup discrimination effect. *Journal of Personality and Social Psychology, 39,* 773-783.

Loftus, E. F. (1974a). *Memory.* Reading, MA: Addison-Wesley.

Loftus, E. F. (1974b, December). The incredible eyewitness. *Psychology Today,* pp. 117-119.

Loftus, E. F. (1975). Leading questions and eyewitness report. *Cognitive Psychology, 7,* 560-572.

Loftus, E. F. (1979). *Eyewitness testimony.* Cambridge: Harvard University Press.

Loftus, E. F. (1980). *Memory.* Reading, MA: Addison-Wesley.

Loftus, E. F. (1984, February). Essential but unreliable. *Psychology Today,* pp. 22-26.

Loftus, E. F. (1983). Whose shadow is crooked? *American Psychologist, 38,* 576-577.

Loftus, E. F. (1984, February). Eyewitnesses: essential but unreliable. *Psychology Today,* pp. 22-26.

Loftus, E. F., and Palmer, J. C. (1974). Reconstruction of automobile destruction: An example of the interaction between language and memory. *Journal of Verbal Learning and Verbal Behavior, 13,* 585-589.

London, P. (1970). The rescuers: Motivational hypotheses about Christians who saved Jews from the Nazis. In J. Macaulay and L. Berkowitz (Eds.), *Altruism and helping behavior.* New York: Academic Press.

Loo, C. (1972). The effects of spatial density on the social behavior of children. *Journal of Applied Social Psychology, 4,* 372-381.

Loo, C. M. (1979). A factor analytic approach to the study of spatial density effects of preschoolers. *Journal of Population, 2,* 47-68.

Lord, C. G. (1980). Schemas and images as memory aids:

Two modes of processing social information. *Journal of Personality and Social Psychology, 38,* 257-269.

Lott, A. J., Aponte, J. F., Lott, B. E., and McGinley, W. H. (1969). The effect of delayed reward on the development of positive attitudes toward persons. *Journal of Experimental Social Psychology, 5,* 101-113.

Lott, A. J., and Lott, B. E. (1961). Group cohesiveness, communication level, and conformity. *Journal of Abnormal and Social Psychology, 62,* 408-412.

Lott, A. J., and Lott, B. E. (1972). The power of liking. In L. Berkowitz (Ed.), *Advances in experimental social psychology* (Vol. 6). New York: Academic Press.

Lott, A. J., and Lott, B. E. (1974). The role of reward in the formation of positive interpersonal attitudes. In T. L. Huston (Ed.), *Foundations of interpersonal attraction.* New York: Academic Press.

Luchins, A. S. (1945). Social influence on perception of complex drawings. *Journal of Social Psychology, 21,* 257-273.

Luchins, A. S. (1957). Primacy-recency in impression formation. In C. Hovland (Ed.), *The order of presentation in persuasion.* New Haven: Yale University Press.

Lucke, J. F., and Batson, C. D. (1980). Response suppression to a distressed conspecific: Are laboratory rats altruistic? *Journal of Experimental Social Psychology, 16,* 214-227.

Lull, P. E. (1940). The effectiveness of humor in persuasive speeches. *Speech Monographs, 7,* 26-40.

Lumsdaine, A. A., and Janis, I. L. (1953). Resistance to "counterpropaganda" produced by one-sided and two-sided "propaganda" presentations. *Public Opinion Quarterly, 17,* 311-318.

Lussier, R., Perlman, D., and Breen, L. (1977). Causal attribution, attitude similarity, and the punishment of drug offenders. *British Journal of Addictions, 72,* 357-364.

Macaulay, J. (1970). A skill for charity. In J. Macaulay and L. Berkowitz (Eds.), *Altruism and helping behavior: Social psychological studies of some antecedents and consequences.* New York: Academic Press.

Maccoby, E. E., and Jacklin, C. N. (1974). *The psychology of sex differences.* Stanford, CA: Stanford University Press.

Maccoby, N. (1980). Promoting positive health behaviors in adults. In L. A. Bond and J. C. Rosen (Eds.), *Competence and coping during adulthood.* University Press of New England.

MacDonald, J. M. (1971). *Rape offenders and their victim.* Springfield, IL: Charles C. Thomas.

Machiavelli, N. (1966). *The prince and selected discourses* (D. Donne, Trans.). New York: Bantam Books. (Original work published 1513)

Mahoney, E. R. (1983). *Human sexuality.* New York: McGraw-Hill.

Maisonneuve, J., Palmade, G., and Fourment, C. (1952). Selective choices and propinquity. *Sociometry, 15,* 135-140.

Maki, J. E., and McClintock, C. G. (1983). The accuracy of social value prediction: Actor and observer influences. *Journal of Personality and Social Psychology, 45,* 829-838.

Malamuth, N., Haber, S., and Feshbach, S. (1980). Testing hypotheses regarding rape: Exposure to sexual violence, sex differences, and the "normality" of rape. *Journal of Research in Personality, 14,* 121-137.

Malinowski, B. (1929). *The sexual life of savages in northwestern Menanesia.* New York: Harcourt, Brace and World.

Malkis, F. S., Kalle, R. J., and Tedeschi, J. T. (1982). Attitudinal politics in the forced compliance situation. *Journal of Social Psychology, 117,* 79-91.

Mallick, S. K., and McCandless, B. F. (1966). A study of catharsis of aggression. *Journal of Personality and Social Psychology, 4,* 591-596.

Mann, L. (1981). The baiting crowd in episodes of threatened suicide. *Journal of Personality and Social Psychology, 41,* 703-709.

Mann, L., Newton, J. W., and Innes, J. M. (1982). A test between deindividuation and emergent norm theories of crowd aggression. *Journal of Personality and Social Psychology, 42,* 260-272.

Markovsky, B., and Berger, S. M. (1983). Crowd noise and mimicry. *Personality and Social Psychology Bulletin, 9,* 90-96.

Markus, H. (1977). Self-schemata and the processing of information about the self. *Journal of Personality and Social Psychology, 35,* 63-78.

Markus, H. (1978). The effect of mere presence on social facilitation: An unobtrusive test. *Journal of Experimental Social Psychology, 14,* 389-397.

Markus, H. (1980). The self in thought and memory. In D. M. Wegner and R. R. Vallacher (Eds.), *The self in social psychology.* New York: Oxford University Press.

Markus, H., Crane, M., Bernstein, S., and Siladi, M. (1982). Self-schemas and gender. *Journal of Personality and Social Psychology, 42,* 38-50.

Markus, H., and Sentis, K. (1982). The self in social information processing. In J. Suls (Ed.), *Psychological perspectives on the self* (Vol. 1). Hillsdale, NJ: Erlbaum.

Marlatt, G. A., Kosturn, C. F., and Lang, A. R. (1975). Provocation to anger and opportunity for retaliation as determinants of alcohol consumption in social drinkers. *Journal of Abnormal Psychology, 84,* 652-659.

Marquis, D. G., Guetzkow, H., & Heyns, R. W. (1951). A social psychological study of the decision-making conference. In H. Guetzkow (Ed.), *Groups, leadership and men.* Pittsburgh: Carnegie Press.

Marrow, A. J. (1969). *The practical theorist.* New York: Basic Books.

Marshall, G. (1976). *Affective consequences of "inadequately explained" physiological arousal.* Unpublished Ph.D. thesis, Stanford University, Stanford, CA.

Marshall, G., and Zimbardo, P. G. (1979). Affective consequences of inadequately explained physiological arousal. *Journal of Personality and Social Psychology, 37,* 970-988.

Maslach, C. (1979). Negative emotional biasing of unexplained arousal. *Journal of Personality and Social Psychology, 37,* 953-969.

Masling, J. (1966). Role-related behavior of the subject and psychologist and its effects upon psychological data. In D. Levine (Ed.), *Nebraska Symposium on Motivation.* Lincoln: University of Nebraska Press.

Mason, K. O., Czajka, J. L., and Arber, S. (1976). Change in U.S. womens' sex-role attitudes, 1964-1974. *American Sociological Review, 41,* 573-596.

Masters, W. H., and Johnson, V. E. (1966). *Human sexual response.* Boston, Little, Brown.

Masters, W. H., and Johnson, V. E. (1970). *Human sexual inadequacy.* Boston: Little, Brown.

Mathes, E. W., and Kahn, A. (1975). Diffusion of responsibility and extreme behavior. *Journal of Personality and Social Psychology, 31,* 881-886.

Matthews, K. A., and Carra, J. (1982). Suppression of menstrual distress symptoms: A study of Type A behavior. *Personality and Social Psychology Bulletin, 8,* 146-151.

Matthews, K. A., and Siegel, J. M. (1983). Type A behaviors by children, social comparison, and standards for self-evaluation. *Developmental Psychology, 19,* 135-140.

Matthews, K. A., Helmreich, R. L., Beane, W. E., and Lucker, G. W. (1980). Pattern A, achievement striving, and scientific merit: Does Pattern A help or hinder? *Journal of Personality and Social Psychology, 39,* 962-967.

Matthews, K. E., Jr., and Canon, L. K. (1975). Environmental noise level as a determinant of helping behavior. *Journal of Personality and Social Psychology, 32,* 571-577.

Matthews, R. W., Paulus, P. B., and Baron, R. A. (1979). Physical aggression after being crowded. *Journal of Nonverbal Behavior, 4,* 5-17.

Maurer, D. (1976). *Whiz mob.* New Haven: College and University Press.

Mausner, B. (1954). The effect of prior reinforcement on the interaction of observer pairs. *Journal of Abnormal and Social Psychology, 49,* 65-68.

Mauss, M. (1967). *The gift.* (I. Cunnison, Trans.). New York: W. W. Norton.

Mazis, M. B. (1975). Antipollution measures and psychological reactance theory: A field experiment. *Journal of Personality and Social Psychology, 31,* 654-660.

McArthur, L. A. (1972). The how and what of why: Some determinants and consequences of causal attribution. *Journal of Personality and Social Psychology, 22,* 171-193.

McCain, G., Cox, V. C., and Paulus. P. B. (1976). The relationship between illness complaints and degree of crowding in a prison environment. *Environment and Behavior, 8,* 283-290.

McCauley, C., Stitt, C. L., and Segal, M. (1980). Stereotyping: From prejudice to prediction. *Psychological Bulletin, 87,* 195-208.

McCauley, C., Stitt, C. F., Woods, K., and Lipton, D. (1973). Group shift to caution at the racetrack. *Journal of Experimental Social Psychology, 9,* 80-86.

McClelland, D. C., Kalin, R., Wanner, H. E., and Davis, W. (1972). *Alcohol and human motivation.* New York: Free Press.

McCorkle, L. W., and Korn, R. R. (1954). Resocialization within walls. *Annals of the American Academy of Political and Social Science, 293,* 88-98.

McDougall, W. (1908). *Introduction to social psychology.* London: Methuen.

McGhee, P. E., and Teevan, R. C. (1967). Conformity behavior and need for affiliation. *Journal of Social Psychology, 72,* 117-121.

McGinley, H., LeFevre, R., and McGinley, P. (1975). The influence of a communicator's body position on opinion change in others. *Journal of Personality and Social Psychology, 31,* 686-690.

McGuire, W. J. (1964). Inducing resistance to persuasion: Some contemporary approaches. In L. Berkowitz (Ed.), *Advances in experimental social psychology* (Vol. 1). New York: Academic Press.

McGuire, W. J. (1968). Personality and susceptibility to social influence. In E. F. Borgatta and W. W. Lambert (Eds.), *Handbook of personality theory and research.* Chicago: Rand McNally.

McGuire, W. J. (1969). The nature of attitudes and attitude change. In G. Lindzey and E. Aronson (Eds.), *Handbook of social psychology* (Vol. 3, 2nd ed.). Reading, MA: Addison-Wesley.

McGuire, W. J., and McGuire, C. V. (1982). Significant others in self-space: Sex differences and developmental trends in the social self. In J. Suls (Ed.), *Psychological perspectives on the self* (Vol. 1). Hillsdale, NJ: Erlbaum.

McGuire, W. J., McGuire, C. V., Child, P., and Fijioka, T. (1978). Salience of ethnicity in the spontaneous self-concept as a function of one's ethnic distinctiveness in the social environment. *Journal of Personality and Social Psychology, 36,* 511-520.

McGuire, W. J., and Millman, S. (1965). Anticipatory belief lowering following forewarning of a persuasive attack. *Journal of Personality and Social Psychology, 62,* 327-337.

McGuire, W. J., and Padawer-Singer, A. (1976). Trait salience in the spontaneous self-concept. *Journal of Personality and Social Psychology, 33,* 743-754.

McGuire, W. J., and Papageorgis, D. (1961). The relative efficacy of various types of prior belief-defense in producing immunity against persuasion. *Journal of Abnormal and Social Psychology, 62,* 327-337.

McGuire, W. J., and Papageorgis, D. (1962). Effectiveness of forewarning in developing resistance to persuasion. *Public Opinion Quarterly, 26,* 24-34.

McKenna, R. H. (1976). Good Samaritanism in rural and urban settings: A nonreactive comparison of helping behavior of clergy and control subjects. *Representative Research in Social Psychology, 7,* 58-65.

McNemar, Q. (1946). Opinion-attitude methodology. *Psychological Bulletin, 43,* 289-374.

Mead, M. (1935). *Sex and temperament in three primative societies.* New York: William Morrow.

Meade, R. D. (1967). An experimental study of leadership in India. *Journal of Social Psychology, 72,* 35-43.

Megargee, E. I. (1970). Undercontrolled and over-controlled personality types in extreme antisocial aggression. In E. I. Megargee and J. E. Hokanson (Eds.), *The dynamics of aggression.* New York: Harper & Row.

Mehrabian, A. (1981). *Silent messages: Implicit communication of emotions and attitudes* (2nd ed.). Belmont, CA: Wadsworth.

Meichenbaum, D. (1977). *Cognitive-behavior modification: An integrative approach.* New York: Plenum.

Melges, F. T., and Harris, R. F. (1970). Anger and attack: A cybernetic model of violence. In D. N. Daniels, M. F. Gilula, and F. M. Ochberg (Eds.), Boston: Little, Brown.

Messick, D. M., and McClelland, C. L. (1983). Social traps and temporal traps. *Personality and Social psychology Bulletin, 9,* 105-110.

Meyer, J. P., and Mulherin, A. (1980). From attribution to helping: An analysis of the mediating effects of affect and expectancy. *Journal of Personality and Social Psychology, 39,* 201-210.

Meyer, J. P., and Pepper, S. (1977). Need compatibility and marital adjustment in young married couples. *Journal of Personality and Social Psychology, 35,* 331-342.

Meyer, T. P. (1972). The effects of sexually arousing and violent films on aggressive behavior. *Journal of Sex Research, 8,* 324-333.

Staff. (1978, March 1). 'Ask and ye shall get'—It's rule in richest nation. *Miami Herald,* pp. 1G, 3G.

Michaels, J. W., Blommel, J. M., Brocato, R. M., Linkous, R. A., and Rowe, J. S. (1982). Social facilitation and inhibition in a natural setting. *Replications in Social Psychology, 2,* 21-24.

Michener, H. A., and Burt, M. R. (1974). Legitimacy as a base of social influence. In J. T. Tedeschi (Eds.), *Perspectives on social power.* Chicago: Aldine-Atherton.

Middlemist, D., Knowles, E. S., and Matter, C. F. (1976). Personal space invasion in the lavatory: Suggestive evidence for arousal. *Journal of Personality and Social Psychology, 33,* 541-546.

Middlemist, R. D., Knowles, E. S., and Matter, C. F. (1977). What to do and what to report: A reply to Koocher. *Journal of Personality and Social Psychology, 35,* 122-124.

Milgram S. (1963). Behavioral study of obedience. *Journal of Abnormal and Social Psychology, 67,* 371-378.

Milgram, S. (1965). Some conditions of obedience and disobedience to authority. *Human Relations, 18,* 57-76.

Milgram, S. (1970). The experience of living in cities: A psychological analysis. *Science, 167,* 1461-1468.

Milgram, S. (1974). *Obedience to authority.* New York: Harper & Row.

Milgram, S., Bickman, L., and Berkowitz, L. (1969). Note on the drawing power of crowds of different size. *Journal of Personality and Social Psychology, 13,* 79-82.

Miller, A. G. (1972). Role-playing: An alternative to deception? A review of the evidence. *American Psychologist, 27,* 623-636.

Miller, C. T. (1982). The role of performance-related similarity in social comparison of abilities: A test of the related attributes hypothesis. *Journal of Experimental Social Psychology, 18,* 513-523.

Miller, D. T., Norman, S. A., and Wright, E. (1978). Distortion in person perception as a consequence of the need for effective control. *Journal of Personality and Social Psychology, 36,* 598-607.

Miller, G. A. (1956). The magical number seven, plus or minus two: Some limits on our capacity for processing information. *Psychological Review, 63,* 81-97.

Miller, G. R., and Hewgill, M. A. (1966). Some recent research on fear-arousing message appeals. *Speech Monographs, 33,* 377-391.

Miller, H. L., and Rivenbark, W. H. (1970). Sexual differences in physical attractiveness as a determinant of heterosexual liking. *Psychological Reports,77,* 701-702.

Miller, L. C., and Cox, C. L. (1982). For appearance sake: Public self-consciousness and makeup use. *Personality and Social Psychology Bulletin, 8,* 748-751.

Miller, N., and Butler, D. (1969). Social power and communication in small groups. *Behavioral Science, 14,* 11-18.

Miller, N., and Campbell, D. T. (1959). Recency and primacy in persuasion as a function of the timing of speeches and measurement. *Journal of Abnormal and Social Psychology, 59,* 1-9.

Miller, N., Maruyama, G., Beaber, R. J., and Valone, K. (1976). Speed of speech and persuasion. *Journal of Personality and Social Psychology, 34,* 615-625.

Miller, R. L., Brickman, P., and Bolen, D. (1975). Attribution versus persuasion as a means for modifying behavior. *Journal of Personality and Social Psychology, 31,* 430-441.

Miller, R. L., and Suls, J. (1977). Helping, self-attribution, and size of an initial request. *Journal of Social Psychology, 103,* 203-208.

Mischel, W., Ebbesen, E., and Zeiss, A. R. (1976). Determinants of selective memory about the self. *Journal of Consulting and Clinical Psychology, 44,* 92-103.

Mitford, J. (1973). Kind and unusual punishment: The prison business. New York: Alfred Knopf.

Mittelmark, M. B., and Evans, R. I. (1978, August). Communicating imminent health consequences: Smoking control strategy for children. Paper presented at the meeting of the American Psychological Association, Toronto, Canada.

Mixon, D. (1972). Instead of deception. *Journal of the Theory of Social Behaviour, 2,* 145-177.

Modigliani, A. (1971). Embarrassment, face-work and eye-contact. Testing a theory of embarrassment. *Journal of Personality and Social Psychology, 17,* 15-24.

Moede, W. (1927). Die Richtlinien der Leistungs-Psychologie. [the accurate function of the psychology of performance] *Industrielle Psychotechnik, 4,* 193-207.

Molm, L. D. (1981). The conversion of power imbalance to power use. *Social Psychology Quarterly, 44,* 151-163.

Monahan, J., and Loftus, E. (1982). The psychology of law. *Annual Review of Psychology, 33,* 441-475.

Money, J., and Ehrhardt, A. A. (1972). *Man and woman, boy and girl.* Baltimore: Johns Hopkins University Press.

Money, J., and Tucker, P. (1975). *Sexual signatures: On being a man or a woman.* Boston: Little, Brown.

Montagu, A. (1968). *Man and aggression.* New York: Oxford University Press.

Montemayer, R., and Eisen, M. (1977). The development of self-conceptions from childhood to adolescence. *Developmental Psychology, 13,* 314-319.

Monteverde, F., Paschke, R., and Tedeschi, J. T. (1974). The effectiveness of honesty and deceit as influence tactics. *Sociometry, 37,* 583-591.

Moore, J. C. (1964). *A further test of interactionist hypotheses of self-conception* (Tech. Rep. No. 6). Stanford, CA: Stanford University Laboratory for Social Research.

Moray, N. (1959). Attention in dichotic listening: Affective cues and the influence of instructions. *Quarterly Journal of Experimental Psychology, 11,* 56-60.

Morgenthau, H. (1969). *Politics among nations* (5th ed.). New York: Alfred Knopf.

Moriarty, T. (1975). Crime, commitment, and the unresponsive bystander: Two field experiments. *Journal of Personality and Social Psychology, 31,* 370-376.

Morse, S. J., Gergen, K. J., Peele, S., and van Ryneveld, J. (1977). Reactions to receiving expected and unexpected help from a person who violates or does not violate a norm. *Journal of Experimental Social Psychology, 13,* 397-402.

Morris, E. (1979). *The rise of Theodore Roosevelt.* New York: Coward, McCann & Geoghegan.

Moscovici, A., and Faucheux, C. (1972). Social influence, conformity bias, and the study of active minorities. In L. Berkowitz (Ed.), *Advances in experimental social psychology* (Vol. 6). New York: Academic Press.

Moscovici, S. (1976). *Social influence and social change.* New York: Academic Press.

Moscovici, S. (1980). Toward a theory of conversion behavior. In L. Berkowitz (Ed.), *Advances in experimental social psychology* (Vol. 13). New York: Academic Press.

Moyer, K. E. (1976). *The psychobiology of aggression.* New York: Harper & Row.

Muir, D., and Weinstein, E. (1962). The social debt: An investigation of lower-class and middle-class norms of social obligation. *American Sociological Review, 27,* 532-539.

Mulder, M., and Stemerding, A. (1963). Threat, attraction to group and need for strong leaderhip: A laboratory experiment in a natural setting. *Human Relations, 16,* 317-334.

Munsterberg, H. (1908). *On the witness stand.* New York: Clark, Boardman.

Myers, D. G., and Kaplan, M. F. (1976). Group-induced polarization in simulated juries. *Personality and Social Psychology Bulletin, 3,* 63-66.

Myers, D. G., and Ridle, J. (1979, August). Can we all be better than average? *Psychology Today,* pp. 89-98.

Mynatt, C., and Sherman, S. J. (1975). Responsibility attribution in groups and individuals: A direct test of the diffusion of responsibility hypothesis. *Journal of Personality and Social Psychology, 32,* 1111-1118.

Nadler, A., Fisher, J. D., and Ben-Itzhak, S. (1983). With a little help from my friend: Effect of single or multiple act aid as a function of donor and task characteristics. *Journal of Personality and Social Psychology, 44,* 310-321.

Nadler, A., Shapira, R., and Ben-Itzhak, S. (1982). Good looks may help: Effects of helper's physical attractiveness and sex of helper on males' and females' help-seeking behavior. *Journal of Personality and Social Psychology, 42,* 90-99.

Napoleon, T., Chassin, L., and Young, R. D. (1980). A replication and extension of "Physical attractiveness and mental illness." *Journal of Abnormal Psychology, 89,* 250-253.

Nelson, B. (1983, June 20). Aggression: Still a stronger trait for males. *New York Times,* p. 6.

Nemeth, C. (1970). Effects of free versus constrained behavior on attraction between people. *Journal of Personality and Social Psychology, 15,* 302-313.

Nemeth, C., and Wachtler, J. (1983). Creative problem solving as a result of majority vs. minority influence. *European Journal of Social Psychology, 13,* 45-55.

Staff. (1981, September 13). Untitled article on subscriptions to cable television service. *New York Times,* pp. 127-129.

Newcomb, T. M. (1961). *The acquaintance process.* New York: Holt, Rinehart & Winston.

Staff. (1978, December 4). The cult of death. *Newsweek* pp. 38-53.

Staff. (1983, December 5). After "The Day After." *Newsweek,* p. 62.

Staff. (1983, June 13). Sally Ride: Ready for liftoff. *Newsweek,* pp. 36-51.

Newtson, D. A. (1973). Attribution and the unit of perception of ongoing behavior. *Journal of Personality and Social Psychology, 28,* 28-38.

Newtson, D. A., and Engquist, G. (1976). The perceptual organization of ongoing behavior. *Journal of Experimental Social Psychology, 12,* 847-862.

Nicholls, J. G. (1975). Causal attribution and other achievement-related cognitions: Effect of task outcomes, attainment, value and sex. *Journal of Personaity and Social Psychology, 31,* 379-389.

Nickerson, D. and Newhall, S. M. (1943). A psychological color solid. *Journal of the Optical Society of America, 33,* 419-422.

Nisbett, R., and Ross, L. (1980). *Human inference: Strategies and shortcomings of social judgment.* Englewood Cliffs, NJ: Prentice-Hall.

Nisbett, R. E., Caputo, C., Legant, P., and Marecek, J. (1973). Behavior as seen by the actor and as seen by the observer. *Journal of Personality and Social Psychology, 27,* 154-164.

Nisbett, R. E., and Wilson, T. D. (1977). Telling more than we can know: Verbal reports on mental processes. *Psychological Review, 84,* 231-259.

Nizer, L. (1961). *My life in court.* New York: Pyramid.

Nkpa, N. K. U. (1975). Rumor mongering in war time. *Journal of Social Psychology, 96,* 27-35.

Norman, R. (1976). When what is said is important: A comparison of expert and attractive sources. *Journal of Experimental Social Psychology, 12,* 294-300.

O'Dell, J. W. (1968). Group size and emotionl interaction. *Journal of Personality and Social Psychology, 8,* 75-78.

O'Grady, K. E. (1982). Sex, physical attractiveness and perceived risk for mental illness. *Journal of Personality and Social Psychology, 43,* 1064-1071.

Ohbuchi, I. (1982). On the cognitive integration mediating reactions to attack patterns. *Social Psychology Quarterly, 45,* 213-218.

Oppenheim, A. N. (1966). *Questionnaire design and attitude measurement.* New York: Basic Books.

O'Quin, K., and Aronoff, J. (1981). Humor as a technique of social influence. *Social Psychology Quarterly, 44,* 349-357.

Orne, M. T. (1962). On the social psychology of the psychological experiment: With particular reference to demand characteristics and their implications. *American Psychologist, 17,* 776-783.

Orne, M. T. (1969). Demand characteristics and the concept of quasi controls. In R. Rosenthal and R. L. Rosnow (Eds.), *Artifacts in behavioral research.* New York: Academic Press.

Orne, M. T., and Evans, F. J. (1965). Social control in the psychological experiment: Antisocial behavior and hypnosis. *Journal of Personality and Social Psychology, 1,* 189-200.

Osgood, C. E. (1959). Suggestions for winning the real war with communism. *Journal of Conflict Resolution, 3,* 295-325.

Osgood, C. E. (1962). *An alternative to war or surrender.* Urbana: University of Illinois Press.

Osgood, C. E. (1974). Exploration of semantic space: A personal diary. In T. S. Krawiec (Ed.), *The psychologists* (Vol. 2). New York: Oxford University Press.

Osgood, C. E., Suci, G. J., and Tannenbaum, P. H. (1957). *The measurement of meaning.* Urbana: University of Illinois Press.

Oskamp, S. (1971). Effects of programmed strategies on cooperation in the prisoner's dilemma and other mixed-motive games. *Journal of Conflict Resolution, 15,* 225-229.

Oskamp, S. (1984). *Applied social psychology.* Englewood Cliffs, NJ: Prentice-Hall.

Packard, V. O. (1966). *The status seekers: An exploration of class behavior in America and the hidden barriers that affect you, your community, your future.* New York: D. McKay.

Padget, V. R., and Jorgenson, D. O. (1982). Superstition and economic threat: Germany, 1918-1940. *Personality and Social Psychology Bulletin, 8,* 736-741.

Page, A. L., and Hood, T. (1981). Attitude change among teachers in U.S. Department of Energy educational workshops. *Journal of Social Psychology, 115,* 183-188.

Page, M. M., and Scheidt, R. J. (1971). The elusive weapons effect: Demand awareness, evaluation apprehension and slightly sophisticated subjects. *Journal of Personality and Social Psychology, 20,* 304-318.

Palmer, E. L., and Dorr, A. (1980). *Children and the faces of television: Teaching violence, selling.* New York: Academic Press.

Paludi, M. A., and Bauer, W. D. (1983). Goldberg revisited: What's in an author's name? *Sex Roles, 9,* 387-390.

Pancer, S. M., McMullen, L. M., Kabatoff, R. A., Johnson, K. G., and Pond, C. A. (1979). Conflict and avoidance in the helping situation. *Journal of Personality and Social Psychology, 37,* 1406-1411.

Park, B., and Rothbart, M. (1982). Perception of out-group homogeneity and levels of social categorization: Memory for the subordinate attributes of in-group and out-group members. *Journal of Personality and Social Psychology, 42,* 1051-1068.

Parke, R. D., Berkowitz, L., Leyens, J. P., West, S. G., and Sebastian, R. J. (1977). Some effects of violent and non-violent movies on the behavior of juvenile delinquents. In L. Berkowitz (Ed.), *Advances in experimental social psychology* (Vol. 10). New York: Academic Press.

Parker, S. D., Brewer, M. B., and Spencer, J. R. (1980). Perceived control and attributions to fate. *Personality and Social Psychology Bulletin, 6,* 454-459.

Parkes, K. R. (1983). Smoking as a moderator of the relationship between affective state and absence from work. *Journal of Applied Psychology, 68,* 698-708.

Parsons, T. (1963). On the concept of influence. *Public Opinion Quarterly, 27,* 37-62.

Pastore, N. (1952). The role of arbitrariness in the frustration-aggression hypothesis. *Journal of Abnormal and Social Psychology, 47,* 728-731.

Patterson, G. R., Littman, R. A., and Bricker, W. (1967). Assertive behavior in children: A step toward a theory of aggression. *Monographs of the Society for Research in Child Development, 32,* (5, Whole No. 113).

Patterson, M. L., Mullens, S., and Romano, J. (1971). Compensatory reactions to spatial intrusion. *Sociometry, 34,* 114-121.

Paulhus, D. (1982). Individual differences, self-presentation and cognitive dissonance: Their concurrent operation in forced compliance. *Journal of Personality and Social Psychology, 43,* 838-852.

Pearce, P. L. (1980). Strangers, travelers, and Greyhound terminals: A study of small-scale helping behaviors. *Journal of Personality and Social Psychology, 38,* 935-940.

Peirce, C. S. (1951). The fixation of belief. In M. H. Fiscn (Ed.), *Classic American philosophers.* New York: Appleton-Century-Crofts (Original work published 1877 in Popular Science Monthly).

Pendleton, M., and Batson, C. D. (1979). Self-presentation and the door-in-the-face technique for inducing compliance. *Personality and Social Psychology Bulletin, 5,* 77-81.

Pennebacker, J. W., Dyer, M. A., Caulkins, R. S., Litowitz, D. L., Ackerman, P. L., Anderson, D. B., and McGraw, K. M. (1979). Don't the girls get prettier at closing time: A country and western application to psychology. *Personality and Social Psychology Bulletin, 5,* 122-125.

Pennebacker, J. W., and Sanders, D. Y. (1976). American graffitti: Effects of authority and reactance arousal. *Personality and Social Psychology Bulletin, 2,* 264-267.

Peplau, L. A., and Perlman, L. A. (Eds.). (1982). *Loneliness: A sourcebook of current theory, research and therapy.* New York: John Wiley.

Perlman, D., and Cozby, P. C. (Eds.). (1983). *Social psychology.* New York: Holt, Rinehart & Winston.

Pessin, J. (1933). The comparative effects of social and mechanical stimulation on memorizing. *American Journal of Psychology, 45,* 263-270.

Peterson, P. D., and Koulack, D. (1969). Attitude change as a function of latitudes of acceptance and rejection. *Journal of Personality and Social Psychology, 11,* 309-311.

Petty, R. E., and Cacioppo, J. T. (1979). Issue involvement can increase and decrease persuasion by enhancing message-relevant cognitive responses. *Journal of Personality and Social Psychology, 37,* 1915-1926.

Petty, R. E., and Cacioppo, J. T. (1981). *Attitudes and persuasion: Classic and contemporary approaches.* Dubuque, IA: Wm. C. Brown.

Petty, R. E., Cacioppo, J. T., and Heesacker, M. (1981). The use of rhetorical questions in persuasion: A cognitive response analysis. *Journal of Personality and Social Psychology, 40,* 432-440.

Petty, R. E., Ostrom, T. M., and Brock, T. C. (1981). Historical foundations of the cognitive approach to attitudes and persuasion. In R. E. Petty, T. M. Ostrom, and T. C. Brock (Eds.), *Cognitive responses to persuasion.* Hillsdale, NJ: Erlbaum.

Piaget, J. (1966). *The moral judgment of the child.* New York: Free Press. (Original work published 1932)

Piehl, J. (1977). Integration of information in the "Courts": Inlfuence of physical attractiveness on amount of punishment for a traffic offender. *Psychological Reports, 41,* 551-556.

Pihl, R. O., Zeichner, A., Niaura, R., Nagy, K., and Zacchia, C. (1981). Attribution and alcohol-mediated aggression. *Journal of Abnormal Psychology, 90,* 468-475.

Piliavin, I. M., Rodin, J., and Piliavin, J. A. (1969). Good Samaritanism: An underground phenomenon? *Journal of Personality and Social Psychology, 13,* 289-299.

Piliavin, J. A., Callero, P. L., and Evans, D. E. (1982). Addiction to altruism? Opponent-process theory and habitual blood donation. *Journal of Personality and Social Psychology, 43,* 1200-1213.

Piliavin, J. A., and Piliavin, I. M. (1972). Effects of blood on reactions to a victim. *Journal of Personality and Social Psychology, 23,* 353-361.

Pittman, T. S., Pallak, M. S., Riggs, J. M., and Gotay, C. C. (1981). Increasing blood donor pledge fulfillment. *Personality and Social Psychology Bulletin, 7,* 195-200.

Platt, J. (1973). Social traps. *American Psychologist, 28,* 641-651.

Platt, J. R. (1964). Strong inference. *Science, 146,* 347-353.

Pliner, P., Hart, H., Kohl, J., and Saari, D. (1974). Compliance without pressure: Some further data on the foot-in-the-door technique. *Journal of Experimental Social Psychology, 10,* 17-22.

Plutchik, R., and Ax, A. F. (1967). A critique of "determinants of emotional state" by Schachter and Singer (1962). *Psychophysiology, 4,* 79-82.

Pocs, O., and Godow, A. G. (1977). Can students view parents as sexual beings. *The Family Coordinator, 26,* 31-36.

Post, E. (1960). *Etiquette: The blue book of social usage.* New York: Funk & Wagnalls.

Powell, F. A., and Miller, G. R. (1967). Social approval and disapproval cues in anxiety-arousing communications. *Speech Monographs, 34,* 152-159.

Premack, D. (1971). Language in chimpanzees? *Science, 172,* 808-822.

Price, K. H., and Garland, H. (1981). Influence mode and competence: Compliance with leader suggestions. *Personality and Social Psychology Bulletin, 7,* 117-122.

Price, R. A., and Vandenberg, S. G. (1979). Matching for physical attractiveness in married couples. *Personality and Social Psychology Bulletin, 5,* 398-400.

Pruitt, D. G. (1968). Reciprocity and credit building in a laboratory dyad. *Journal of Personality and Social Psychology, 8,* 143-147.

Pruitt, D. G., and Drews, J. L. (1969). The effects of time pressure, time elapsed and the opponent's concession rate on behavior in negotiation. *Journal of Experimental Social Psychology, 5,* 43-60.

Pruitt, D. G., and Gahagan, J. P. (1974). Campus crisis. In J. T. Tedeschi (Ed.), *Perspectives on social power.* Chicago: Aldine-Atherton.

Pugh, M. D. (1983). Contributory fault and rape convictions: Loglinear models for blaming the victim. *Social Psychology Quarterly, 46,* 233-242.

Quattrone, G. A., and Jones, E. E. (1978). Selective self-disclosure with and without correspondent performance. *Journal of Experimental Social Psychology, 14,* 511-526.

Quattrone, G. A., and Jones, E. E. (1980). The perception of variability within in-groups and out-groups: Implications for the law of small numbers. *Journal of Personality and Social Psychology, 38,* 141-152.

Quigley-Fernandez, B., and Tedeschi, J. T. (1978). The bogus pipeline as lie detector: Two validity studies. *Journal of Personality and Social Psychology, 36,* 247-256.

Rabbie, J. (1963). Differential preference for companionship under stress. *Journal of Abnormal and Social Psychology, 67,* 643-648.

Ramirez, J., Bryant, J., and Zillman, D. (1982). Effects of erotica on retaliatory behavior as a function of level of prior provocation. *Journal of Personality and Social Psychology, 43,* 971-978.

Rand, C. S., and Hall, J. (1983). Sex differences in the accuracy of self-perceived attractiveness. *Social Psychology Quarterly, 46,* 359-363.

Rankin, R. E., and Campbell, D. T. (1955). Galvanic skins response to Negro and white experimenters. *Journal of Abnormal and Social Psychology, 51,* 30-33.

Rasmussen, C., and Zander, A. (1954). Group membership and self-evaluation. *Human Relations, 7,* 239-251.

Read, S. J. (1983). Once is enough: Causal reasoning from a single instance. *Journal of Personality and Social Psychology, 45,* 323-334.

Regan, D. T., and Fazio, R. H. (1977). On the consistency between attitudes and behavior: Look at the method of attitude formation. *Journal of Experimental Social Psychology, 13,* 28-45.

Regan, D. T., Williams, M., and Sparling, S. (1972). Voluntary expiation of guilt: A field experiment. *Journal of Personality and Social Psychology, 24,* 42-45.

Regan, J. W. (1976). Liking for evaluators: Consistency and

self-esteem theories. *Journal of Experimental Social Psychology, 12,* 156-169.

Reich, C. A. (1970). *The greening of America.* New York: Random House.

Reisenzein, R. (1983). The Schachter theory of emotion: Two decades later. *Psychological Bulletin, 94,* 239-264.

Reiss, I. L. (1960). *Premarital sexual standards in America.* New York: Free Press.

Rettig, S. (1956). An exploratory study of altruism. *Dissertation Abstracts, 16,* 2229-2230.

Reynolds, P. D. (1982). *Ethics and social science research.* Englewood Cliffs, NJ: Prentice-Hall.

Rholes, W. S., Bailey, S., and McMillan, L. (1982). Experiences that motivate moral development: The role of cognitive dissonance. *Journal of Experimental Social Psychology, 18,* 524-536.

Richardson, D., and Campbell, J. L. (1982). Alcohol and rape: The effect of alcohol on attributions of blame for rape. *Personality and Social Psychology Bulletin, 8,* 468-476.

Richardson, D. C., Bernstein, S., and Taylor, S. P. (1979). The effects of situational contingencies on female retaliative behavior. *Journal of Personality and Social Psychology, 37,* 2044-2048.

Rickel, A. U., and Anderson, L. R. (1981). Name ambiguity and androgyny. *Sex Roles, 7,* 1057-1066.

Riess, M., and Rosenfeld, P. (1980). Seating preferences as nonverbal communication: A self-presentational analysis. *Journal of Applied Communications Research, 8,* 22-30.

Riess, M., Rosenfeld, P., Melburg, V., and Tedeschi, J. T. (1981). Self-serving attributions: Biased private perceptions and distorted public descriptions. *Journal of Personality and Social Psychology, 41,* 224-231.

Riess, M., and Salzer, S. (1981, August). *Individuals avoid invading the space of males but not females.* Paper presented at the meeting of the American Psychological Association, Los Angeles, CA.

Riess, M., and Taylor, J. (in press). Ego-involvement and attributions for success and failure in a field setting. *Personality and Social Psychology Bulletin.*

Riordan, C. A., Marlin, N. A., and Kellogg, R. T. (1983). The effectiveness of accounts following transgressions. *Social Psychology Quarterly, 46,* 213-219.

Riordan, C. A., and Tedeschi, J. T. (1983). Attraction in aversive environments: Some evidence for classical conditioning and negative reinforcement. *Journal of Personality and Social Psychology, 44,* 683-692.

Rittle, R. H., and Bernard, N. (1977). Enhancement of response rate by the mere physical presence of the experimenter. *Personality and Social Psychology Bulletin, 3,* 127-130.

Robinson, C. L., Lockard, J. S., and Adams, R. M. (1979). Who looks at a baby in public? *Ethology and Sociobiology, 1,* 87-91.

Rochon, J. (1977). *An evaluation of the seat belt education campaign.* Ottawa, Canada: Department of Transport.

Rodin, J., and Baum, A. (1978). Crowding and helplessness: Potential consequences of density and loss of control. In A. Baum and Y. M. Epstein (Eds.), *Human response to crowding.* Hillsdale, NJ: Erlbaum.

Rodin, J., Bohm, L. C., and Wack, J. T. (1982). Control, coping and aging: Models for research and intervention. In L. Bickman (Ed.), *Applied social psychology annual* (Vol. 3). Beverly Hills, CA: Sage Publications.

Rodin, J., and Langer, E. (1977). Long-term effect of a control-relevant intervention. *Journal of Personality and Social Psychology, 35,* 897-902.

Rodin, J., Solomon, S., and Metcalf, J. (1978). Role of control in mediating perceptions of density. *Journal of Personality and Social Psychology, 36,* 988-999.

Roethlisberger, F. J., and Dickson, W. J. (1939). *Management and the worker.* Cambridge: Harvard University Press.

Rogers, M., Miller, N., Mayer, F. S., and Duval, S. (1982). Personal responsibility and salience of the request for help: Determinants of the relation between negative affect and helping behavior. *Journal of Personality and Social Psychology, 43,* 956-970.

Rogers, R. W., and Thistlethwaite, D. L. (1970). Effects of fear arousal and reassurance on attitude change. *Journal of Personality and Social Psychology, 15,* 227-233.

Rogers, T. B., Kuiper, N. A., and Kirker, W. S. (1977). Self-reference and the encoding of personal information. *Journal of Personality and Social Psychology, 35,* 677-688.

Rohrbaugh, J. B. (1979). *Woman: Psychology's puzzle.* New York: Basic Books.

Rokeach, M. P., Smith, P. W., and Evans, R. E. (1960). Two kinds of prejudice or one? In M. Rokeach (Ed.), *The open and closed mind.* New York: Basic Books.

Rosen, S., and Tesser, A. (1970). On reluctance to communicate undesirable information: The MUM effect. *Sociometry, 33,* 253-263.

Rosenberg, M. (1979). *Conceiving the self.* New York: Basic Books.

Rosenberg, M. (1982). Psychological selectivity in self-esteem formation. In M. Rosenberg and H. B. Kaplan (Eds.), *Social psychology of the self-concept.* Arlington Heights, IL: Harlan Davidson.

Rosenberg, M. J. (1965). When dissonance fails: On eliminating evaluation apprehension from attitude measurement. *Journal of Personality and Social Psychology, 1,* 28–42.

Rosenberg, M. J. (1969). The conditions and consequences of evaluation apprehension. In R. Rosenthal and R. W. Rosnow (Eds.), *Artifacts in behavioral research.* New York: Academic Press.

Rosenfeld, H. M. (1965). Effect of approval-seeking induction on interpersonal proximity. *Psychological Reports, 17,* 120–122.

Rosenfeld, P. and Hessel, M. B. (1982). *The effects of status on avoidance of personal space invasions at a water fountain.* Unpublished manuscript, Pennsylvania State University/Behrend, Erie.

Rosenfeld, P., Giacalone, R. A., and Tedeschi, J. T. (1983). Cognitive dissonance vs. impression management. *Journal of Social Psychology, 120,* 203–211.

Rosenfeld, P., Giacalone, R., Tedeschi, J. T., and Bond, M. (1983) The cross-cultural efficacy of entitlements in American and Hong Kong Chinese students. In J. B. Deregowski, S. Dziuraurec, and R. C. Annis (Eds.), *Explications in cross-cultural psychology.* Lisse: Swets and Zeitlinger.

Rosenhan, D. L. (1973). On being sane in insane places. *Science, 179,* 250–258.

Rosenhan, D. L., Salovey, P., and Hargis, K. (1981). The joys of helping: Focus of attention mediates the impact of positive affect on altruism. *Journal of Personality and Social Psychology, 40,* 899-905.

Rosenhan, D. L., Underwood, B., and Moore, B. S. (1974). Affect moderates self-gratification and altruism. *Journal of Personality and Social Psychology, 30,* 546–552.

Rosenkrantz, P., Vogel, S. R., Bee, H., Broverman, I. K., and Broverman, D. M. (1968). Sex-role stereotypes and self-concepts in college students. *Journal of Counseling and Clinical Psychology, 32,* 287–295.

Rosenman, R. H., Brand, R. J., Jenkins, C. D., Friedman, M., Straus, R., and Wurm, M. (1975). Coronary heart disease in the Western Collaborative Group Study: Final follow-up experience of 8½ years. *Journal of the American Medical Association, 233,* 872–877.

Rosenthal, R. (1969). Interpersonal expectations: Effects of experimenter's hypothesis. In R. Rosenthal and R. L. Rosnow (Eds.), *Artifacts in behavioral research.* New York: Academic Press.

Rosenthal, R. (1976). *Experimenter effects in behavioral research.* New York: Irvington.

Rosenthal, R., and Fode, K. L. (1963). The effect of experimenter bias on the performance of the albino rat. *Behavioral Science, 8,* 183–189.

Rosenthal, R., and Jacobson, L. (1968). *Pygmalion in the classroom: Teacher expectation and pupil intellectual development.* New York: Holt, Rinehart & Winston.

Rosenzweig, S. (1933). The experimental situation as a psychological problem. *Psychological Review, 40,* 337–354.

Rosnow, R. L. (1980). Psychology of rumor reconsidered. *Psychological Bulletin, 87,* 578–591.

Rosnow, R. L. (1981). *Paradigms in transition: The methodology of social inquiry.* New York: Oxford University Press.

Rosnow, R. L., and Fine, G. A. (1976). *Rumor and gossip: The social psychology of hearsay.* New York: Elsevier North-Holland.

Ross, A. S. (1971). Effect of increased responsibility on bystander intervention: The presence of children. *Journal of Personality and Social Psychology, 19,* 306–310.

Ross, E. A. (1908). *Social psychology.* New York: Macmillan.

Ross, L. (1977). The intuitive psychologist and his shortcomings: Distortions in the attribution process. In L. Berkowitz (Ed.), *Advances in experimental social psychology* (Vol. 10). New York: Academic Press.

Ross, L. Amabile, T. M., and Steinmetz, J. L. (1977). Social roles, social control, and biases in social-perception processes. *Journal of Personality and Social Psychology, 35,* 485–494.

Ross, L., Bierbruer, G., and Polly, S. (1974). Attribution of educational outcomes by professional and nonprofessional instructors. *Journal of Personality and Social Psychology, 29,* 609–618.

Ross, L., Greene, D., and House P. (1977). The "false consensus effect": An egocentric bias in social perception and attribution processes. *Developmental Psychology, 13,* 279-301.

Ross, M., and Sicoly, F. (1979). Egocentric biases in availability and attribution. *Journal of Personality and Social Psychology, 37,* 322-336.

Rothbart, M. K., and Maccoby, E. E. (1966). Parents' different reactions to sons and daughters. *Journal of Personality and Social Psychology, 4,* 337-343.

Rotter, J. B. (1954). *Social learning and clinical psychology.* Englewood Cliffs, NJ: Prentice-Hall.

Rotter, J. B. (1966). Generalized expectancies for internal versus external control of reinforcement. *Psychological Monographs, 80,* (1, Whole No. 609), 1–28.

Rotter, J. B. (1967). Beliefs, social attitudes, and behavior: A social learning analysis. In R. Jessor and S. Feshbach (Eds.), *Cognition, personality, and clinical psychology.* San Francisco, CA: Jossey-Bass.

Rotter, J. B. (1978). A new scale for the measurement of interpersonal trust. *Journal of Personality, 35,* 651-655.

Rotton, J., Barry, T., Frey, J., and Soler, E. (1978). Air pollution and interpersonal attraction. *Journal of Applied Social Psychology, 8,* 57-71.

Rubenstein, C., and Shaver, P. (1979). Loneliness in two northeastern cities. In J. Hartog and J. Audy (Eds.), *The anatomy of loneliness.* New York: International University Press.

Rubenstein, C., Shaver, P., and Peplau, L. A. (1982). Loneliness. In D. Krebs (Ed.), *Readings in social psychology* (2nd ed.). New York: Harper & Row.

Rubin, J. Z. (1981, March). Psychological traps. *Psychology Today,* pp. 52-63.

Rubin, J. Z., Provenzano, F. J., and Luria, Z.(1974). The eye of the beholder: Parents' views on sex of newborns. *American Journal of Orthopsychiatry, 44,* 512-519.

Rubin, Z. (1970). Measurement of romantic love. *Journal of Personality and Social Psychology, 16,* 265-273.

Rubin, Z. (1974). From liking to loving: Patterns of attraction in dating relationships. In T. L. Huston (Ed.), *Foundations of interpersonal attraction.* New York: Academic Press.

Ruble, D. N., and Higgins, E. T. (1976). Effects of group sex composition on self-presentation and sex-typing. *Journal of Social Issues, 32,* 125-132.

Ruble, T. L. (1983). Sex stereotypes: Issues of change in the 1970s. *Sex Roles, 9,* 397-402.

Runyan, D. L. (1974). The group risky-shift effect as a function of emotional bonds, actual consequences, and extent of responsibility. *Journal of Personality and Social Psychology, 29,* 670-676.

Runyan, W. M. (1981). Why did Van Gogh cut off his ear? The problem of alternative explanations in psychobiography. *Journal of Personality and Social Psychology, 40,* 1070-1077.

Rushton, J. P. and Campbell, A. C. (1977). Modeling, vicarious reinforcement and extraversion on blood donating in adults: Immediate and long-term effects. *European Journal of Social Psychology, 7,* 297-306.

Saegert, S. (1978). High-density environments: Their personal and social consequences. In A. Baum and Y. M. Epstein (Eds.), *Human response to crowding.* Hillsdale, NJ: Erlbaum.

Saegert, S. C., Swap, W. C., and Zajonc, R. B. (1973). Exposure, context, and interpersonal attraction. *Journal of Personality and Social Psychology, 25,* 234-242.

Safilios-Rothschild, C. A. (1969). The study of family power structure: A review of 1960-1969. *Journal of Marriage and the Family, 32,* 539-552.

Saks, M. J. (1976, January). Some scientists can't rig juries. *Psychology Today,* pp. 48-50, 55-57.

Sales, S. M. (1973). Threat as a factor in authoritarianism: An analysis of archival data. *Journal of Personality and Social Psychology, 28,* 44-57.

Sampson, E. E. (1977). Psychology and the American ideal. *Journal of Personality and Social Psychology, 35,* 767-782.

Sampson, E. E., and Insko, C. A. (1964). Cognitive consistency and performance in the autokinetic situation. *Journal of Abnormal and Social Psychology, 68,* 184-192.

Sanders, G. S. (1978). An integration of shifts toward risk and caution in gambling situations. *Journal of Experimental Social Psychology, 14,* 409-416.

Sanders, G. S., Baron, R. S., and Moore, D. L. (1978). Distraction and social comparison as mediators of social facilitation effects. *Journal of Experimental Social Psychology, 14,* 219-303.

Sarnoff, I., and Zimbardo, P. (1961). Anxiety, fear and social affiliation. *Journal of Abnormal and Social Psychology, 62,* 356-363.

Saulnier, K., and Perlman, D. (1981). The actor-observer bias is alive and well in prison: A sequel to Wells. *Personality and Social Psychology Bulletin, 7,* 559-564.

Sbordone, R. J., Gorelick, D. A., and Elliot, M. L. (1981). An ethological analysis of drug-induced pathological aggression. In P. Brain and R. Benton (Eds.), *Aggression: A multidisciplinary view.* New York: Elsenier North-Holland.

Schachter, S. (1951). Deviation, rejection, and communication. *Journal of Abnormal and Social Psychology, 46,* 190-207.

Schachter, S. (1959). *The psychology of affiliation.* Stanford, CA: Stanford University Press.

Schachter, S. (1964). The interaction of cognitive and physiological determinants of emotional state. In L. Berkowitz (Ed.), *Advances in experimental social psychology* (Vol. 1). New York: Academic Press.

Schachter, S. (1977). Nicotine regulation in heavy and light smokers. *Journal of Experimental Psychology, 106,* 5-12.

Schachter, S., and Burdick, H. (1955). A field experiment on rumor transmission and distortion. *Journal of Abnormal and Social Psychology, 50,* 363-372.

Schachter, S., Ellertson, N., McBride, D., and Gregory, D. (1951). An experimental study of cohesiveness and productivity. *Human Relations, 4,* 229-238.

Schachter, S., and Singer, J. (1962). Cognitive, social and physiological determinants of emotional state. *Psychological Review, 69,* 379-399.

Schaffer, K. F. (1981). *Sex roles and human behavior.* Cambridge, MA: Winthrop Publishers.

Schaps, E. (1972). Cost, dependency, and helping. *Journal of Personality and Social Psychology, 21,* 74-78.

Scheff, T. J. (1966). *Being mentally ill.* Chicago, IL: Aldine-Atherton.

Scheier, M. F. (1980). Effects of public and private self-consciousness on the public expression of personal beliefs. *Journal of Personality and Social Psychology, 39,* 514-521.

Scheier, M. F., and Carver, C. S. (1977). Self-focused attention and the experience of emotion: Attraction, repulsion, elation, and depression. *Journal of Personality and Social Psychology, 35,* 625-636.

Scheier, M. F., and Carver, C. S. (1983). Self-directed attention and the comparison of self with standards. *Journal of Experimental Social Psychology, 19,* 205-222.

Scheier, M. F., Carver, C. S., and Gibbons, F. X. (1979). Self-directed attention, awareness of bodily states, and suggestibility. *Journal of Personality and Social psychology, 37,* 1576-1988.

Schell, J. (1982). *The fate of the earth.* New York: Alfred Knopf.

Schelling, T. C. (1966). *Arms and influence.* New Haven: Yale University Press.

Scherer, K. R., Abeles, R. P., and Fischer, C. S. (1975). *Human aggression and conflict.* Englewood Cliffs, NJ: Prentice-Hall.

Schlenker, B. R. (1980). *Impression management: The self-concept, social identity, and interpersonal relations.* Monterey, CA: Brooks/Cole.

Schlenker, B. R., Bonoma, T. V., Tedeschi, J. T., and Pivnick, W. P. (1970). Compliance to threats as a function of the wording of the threat and the exploitativeness of the threatener. *Sociometry, 33,* 394-408.

Schlenker, B. R., and Darby, B. W. (1981). The use of apologies in social predicaments. *Social Psychology Quarterly, 44,* 271-278.

Schlenker, B. R., Helm, B., and Tedeschi, J. T. (1973). The effects of personality and situational variables on behavioral trust. *Journal of Personality and Social Psychology, 25,* 419-427.

Schlenker, B. R., and Leary, M. R. (1982). Social anxiety and self-presentation: A conceptualization and model. *Psychological Bulletin, 92,* 641-669.

Schlenker, B. R., and Miller, R. S. (1977a). Egocentrism in groups: Self-serving biases or logical information processing? *Journal of Personality and Social Psychology, 35,* 755-764.

Schlenker, B. R., and Miller, R. S. (1977b). Group cohesiveness as a determinant of egocentric perceptions in cooperative groups. *Human Relations, 30,* 1039-1055.

Schlenker, B. R., Nacci, P., Helm, B., and Tedeschi, J. T. (1976). Reactions to coercive and reward power: The effects of switching influence modes on target compliance. *Sociometry, 39,* 316-323.

Schlenker, B. R., and Tedeschi, J. T. (1972). Interpersonal attraction and the exercise of reward and coercive power. *Human Relations, 25,* 427-439.

Schlelsinger, A. M., Jr. (1965). *A thousand days.* Boston: Houghton Mifflin.

Schmid, C. (1969). Urban crime areas: Part I. *American Sociological Review, 25,* 527-542.

Schmidt, D. E., and Keating, J. P. (1979). Human crowding and personal control: An integration of the research. *Psychological Bulletin, 86,* 680-700.

Schmidt, G., and Sigusch, V. (1970). Sex differences in responses to psychological stimulation by films and slides. *Journal of Sex Research, 6,* 268-283.

Schmutte, G. T., and Taylor, S. P. (1980). Psychical aggression as a function of alcohol and pain feedback. *Journal of Social Psychology, 110,* 235-244.

Schneider, D. J. (1969). Tactical self-presentation after success and failure. *Journal of Personality and Social Psychology, 13,* 262-268.

Schneider, D. J., Hastorf, A. H., and Ellsworth, P. C. (1979). *Person perception* (2nd ed.). Reading, MA: Addison-Wesley.

Schopler, J., and Bateson, N. (1965). The power of dependence. *Journal of Personality and Social Psychology, 2,* 247-254.

Schopler, J., and Thompson, V. D. (1968). Role of attribution processes in mediating amount of reciprocity for a favor. *Journal of Personality and Social Psychology, 10,* 243-250.

Schulman, J., Shaver, P., Colman, R., Emrick, B., and Christie, R. (1973). Recipe for a jury. *Psychology Today, 6,* 37-44, 77-84.

Schultz, R. (1976). Effects of control and predictability on the physical and psychological well-being of the institutionalized aged. *Journal of Personality and Social Psychology, 33,* 563-573.

Schwab, J. Nadeau, S. E., and Warheit, G. J. (1979). Crowding and mental health. *Pavlovian Journal of Biological Science, 14,* 226-233.

Schwartz, B., and Barsky, S. (1977). The home advantage. *Social Forces, 55,* 641-666.

Schwartz, B., Tesser, A., and Powell, E. (1982). Dominance cues in nonverbal behavior. *Social Psychology Quarterly, 45,* 114-120.

Schwartz, G., Kane, T., Joseph, J. M., and Tedeschi, J. T. (1978). The effects of remorse on reactions to a harm-doer. *British Journal of Social and Clinical Psychology, 17,* 293-297.

Schwartz, S. H. (1970). Elicitation of moral obligation and self-sacrificing behavior. *Journal of Personality and Social Psychology, 15,* 283-293.

Schwartz, S. H. (1977). Normative influences on altruism. In L. Berkowitz (Ed.), *Advances in experimental social psychology* (Vol. 10). New York: Academic Press.

Schwartz, S. H., and Clausen, G. T. (1970). Responsibility, norms, and helping in an emergency. *Journal of Personality and Social Psychology, 16,* 299-310.

Schwartz, S. H., and Gottlieb, A. (1980). Bystander anonymity and reactions to emergencies. *Journal of Personality and Social Psychology, 39,* 418-430.

Schwarzwald, J., Bizman, A., and Raz, M. (1983). The foot-in-the-door paradigm: Effects of second request size on donation probabiity and donor generosity. *Personality and Social Psychology Bulletin, 9,* 443-450.

Scott, M. R., and Lyman, S. M. (1968). Accounts. *American Sociological Review, 33,* 46-62.

Seeman, M. (1967). Powerlessness and knowledge: A comparative study of alienation and learning. *Sociometry, 30,* 105-123.

Segal, M. W. (1974). Alphabet and attraction: An unobtrusive measure of the effect of propinquity in a field setting. *Journal of Personality and Social Psychology, 30,* 654-657.

Seligman, M. E. P. (1975). *Helplessness: On depression, development, and death.* San Francisco, CA: W. H. Freeman.

Shaw, D. L., and McCombs, M. (1977). *The emergence of American political issues: The agenda-setting function of the press.* St. Paul, MN: West.

Shaw, M. E. (1964). Communication networks. In L. Berkowitz (Ed.), *Advances in experimental social psychology* (Vol. 1). New York: Academic Press.

Shaw, M. E. (1981). *Group dynamics: The psychology of small group behavior* (3rd ed.). New York: McGraw-Hill.

Shaw, M. E., and Shaw, L. M. (1962). Some effects of sociometric grouping upon learning in a second grade classroom. *Journal of Social Psychology, 57,* 453-458.

Sheard, M. H., and Flynn, J. P. (1967). Facilitation of attack behavior by stimulation of the midbrain of cats. *Brain Research, 4,* 324-333.

Sheposh, J. P., Deming, M., and Young, L. E. (1981, May). *The radiating effects of status and attractiveness of a male upon evaluation of the female partner.* Paper presented at the annual meeting of the Western Psychological Association, Seattle.

Sherif, C. W. and Sherif, M. (1967). *Attitude, ego-involvement, and change.* New York: John Wiley.

Sherif, C. W., Sherif, M., and Nebergall, R. E. (1965). *Attitude and attitude change: The social judgment-involvement approach.* Philadelphia: W. B. Saunders.

Sherif, M. (1936). *The psychology of social norms.* New York: Harper & Row.

Sherif, M., Harvey, O. J., White, B. J., Hood, W. R., and Sherif, C. W. (1961). *Intergroup conflict and cooperation: The robber's cave experiment.* Norman: University of Oklahoma Books Exchange.

Sherif, M., and Sherif, C. W. (1956). *Groups in harmony and tension.* New York: Harper & Row.

Sherman, M. A., and Hass, A. (1984). Man to man, woman to woman. *Psychology Today, 18,* 72-73.

Sherman, S. J. (1980). On the self-erasing nature of errors of prediction. *Journal of Personality and Social Psychology, 39,* 211-221.

Sherman, S. J., Presson, C. C., Chassin, L., Corty, E., and Olshavsky, R. (1983). The false consensus effect in estimates of smoking prevalence. *Personality and Social Psychology Bulletin, 9,* 197-207.

Shibutani, T. (1966). *Improvised news: A sociological study of rumor.* Indianapolis: Bobbs-Merrill.

Shoredone, R. J., Gorelick, D. A., and Elliot, M. L. (1981). An ethological analysis of drug-induced pathological aggression. In P. Brain and D. Benton (Eds.), *Multidisciplinary approaches to aggression research.* New York: Elsevier North-Holland.

Shotland, R. L., and Goodstein, L. (1983). Just because she doesn't want to doesn't mean it's rape: An experimentally based causal model of the perception of rape in a dating situation. *Social Psychology Quarterly, 46,* 220-232.

Shotland, R. L., and Straw, M. K. (1976). Bystander response to an assault: When a man attacks a woman. *Journal of Personality and Social Psychology, 34,* 990-999.

Shrauger, J. S., and Schoeneman, T. J. (1979). Symbolic interactionist view of self-concept: Through the looking glass darkly. *Psychological Bulletin, 86,* 549-573.

Shubik, M. (1971). The dollar auction game. *Journal of Conflict Resolution, 15,* 109-111.

Sieber, J. E. (Ed.). (1982). *The ethics of social research* (Vol. 1). New York: Springer-Verlag.

Sigall, H., Aronson, E., and Van Hoose, T. (1970). The cooperative subject: Myth or reality? *Journal of Experimental Social Psychology, 6,* 1-10.

Sigall, H., and Landy, F. (1973). Radiating beauty: The effects of having an attractive partner on person perception. *Journal of Personality and Social Psychology, 28,* 218-224.

Sigall, H., and Ostrove, N. (1975). Beautiful but dangerous: Effects of offender attractiveness and nature of crime on juridic judgment. *Journal of Personality and Social Psychology, 31,* 410-414.

Sigall, H., and Page, R. (1971). Current stereotypes: A little fading, a little faking. *Journal of Personality and Social Psychology, 18,* 247-255.

Silberman, C. E. (1978). *Criminal violence, criminal justice.* New York: Random House.

Silver, L. B., Dublin, C. C., and Lourie, R. S. (1969). Does violence breed violence? *American Journal of Psychiatry, 126,* 404-407.

Silverman, I. (1964). Differential effects of ego threat upon persuasibility for high and low self-esteem subjects. *Journal of Abnormal and Social Psychology, 69,* 567-572.

Simon, J. (1983, August 5). Review of Woody Allen's *Zelig. National Review,* p. 950.

Singer, J. L. (1971). The influence of violence portrayed in television or motion pictures upon overt aggressive behavior. In J. L. Singer (Ed.), *The control of aggression and violence: Cognitive and physiological factors.* New York: Academic Press.

Sivacek, J., and Crano, W. D. (1982). Vested interest as a moderator of attitude-behavior consistency. *Journal of Personality and Social Psychology, 43,* 210-221.

Skinner, B. F. (1974). *About behaviorism.* New York: Alfred Knopf.

Skrypnek, B. J., and Snyder, M. (1982). On the self-perpetuating nature of stereotypes about women and men. *Journal of Experimental Social Psychology, 18,* 277-291.

Slater, P. E. (1958). Contrasting correlates of group size. *Sociometry, 21,* 129-139.

Smetana, J. G., and Adler, N. E. (1980). Fishbein's value X expectancy model: An examinantion of some assumptions. *Personality and Social Psychology Bulletin, 6,* 89-96.

Smith, G. F., and Dorfman, D. D. (1975). The effect of stimulus uncertainty on the relationship between frequency of exposure and liking. *Journal of Personality and Social Psychology, 31,* 150-155.

Smith, H. (1977). *The Russians.* New York: Ballantine Books.

Smith, M. J. (1982). *Persuasion and human action.* Belmont, CA: Wadsworth.

Smith, R. (1962). Restraints on American foreign policy. *Daedalus, 91,* 705-716.

Smith, T. W., Snyder, C. R., and Handelman, M. M. (1982). On the self-serving function of an academic wooden leg: Test anxiety as a self-handicapping strategy. *Journal of Personality and Social Psychology, 42,* 314-321.

Smith, T. W., Snyder, C. R., and Perkins, S. C. (1983). The self-serving function of hypochondriacal complaints: Physical symptoms as self-handicapping strategies. *Journal of Personality and Social Psychology, 44,* 787-797.

Smith, W. P., and Leginski, W. A. (1970). Magnitude and precision of punitive power in bargaining strategy. *Journal of Experimental Social Psychology, 6,* 57-76.

Snyder, C. R., Stucky, R. J., and Higgins, R. L. (1983). *Excuses: Masquerades in search of grace.* New York: John Wiley.

Snyder, M. (1974). Self-monitoring of expressive behavior. *Journal of Personality and Social Psychology, 30,* 526-537.

Snyder, M. (1979). Self-monitoring processes. In L. Berkowitz (Ed.), *Advances in experimental social psychology* (Vol. 12). New York: Academic Press.

Snyder, M., and Ebbesen, E. B. (1972). Dissonance awareness: A test of dissonance theory versus self-perception theory. *Journal of Experimental Social Psychology, 8,* 502-517.

Snyder, M., and Swann, W. B., Jr. (1976). When actions reflect attitudes: The politics of impression management. *Journal of Personality and Social Psychology, 34,* 1034-1042.

Snyder, M., and Swann, W. B., Jr. (1978). Hypothesis testing processes in social interaction. *Journal of Personality and Social Psychology, 36,* 1202-1212.

Solomon, H., Solomon, L. Z., Arnone, M. M., Maur, B. J., Reda, R. M., and Roth, E. O. (1981). Anonymity and helping. *Journal of Social Psychology, 113,* 37-43.

Solomon, M. R., and Schopler, J. (1982). Self-consciousness and clothing. *Personality and Social Psychology Bulletin, 8,* 508-514.

Solomon, R. (1980). The opponent-process theory of acquired motivation: The costs of pleasure and the benefits of pain. *American Psychologist, 35,* 691-712.

Solomon, R. C. (1981). *Love: Emotion, myth and metaphor.* Garden City, NY: Doubleday.

Sommer, R. (1969). *Personal space.* Englewood Cliffs, NJ: Prentice-Hall.

Sommer, O. (1976). *The end of imprisonment.* New York: Oxford University Press.

Sorensen, T. C. (1966). *Kennedy.* New York: Bantam Books.

Spector, P. E., Cohen, S. L., and Penner, L. A. (1976). The effects of real vs. hypothetical risk on group choice-shifts. *Personality and Social Psychology Bulletin, 2,* 290-293.

Speroff, B., and Kerr, W. (1952). Steel mill "hot strip" accidents and interpersonal desirability values. *Journal of Clinical Psychology, 8,* 89-91.

Spradley, J. (1970). *You owe yourself a drunk.* Boston: Little, Brown.

Stagner, R., and Congdon, C. S. (1955). Another failure to

demonstrate displacement of aggression. *Journal of Abnormal and Social Psychology, 51,* 695-696.

Stang, D. J. (1972). Conformity, ability and self-esteem. *Representative Research in Social Psychology, 3,* 97-103.

Stark, R. (1975). *Social problems.* New York: Random House.

Steele, C. M., Sothwick, L. L., and Critchlow, B. (1981). Dissonance and alcohol: Drinking your troubles away. *Journal of Personality and Social Psychology, 41,* 831-846.

Steiner, I. D. (1972). *Group process and productivity.* New York: Academic Press.

Stephens, W. N. (1963). *The family in cross-cultural perspectives.* New York: Holt, Rinehart & Winston.

Stephenson, B., and Wicklund, R. A. (1983). Self-directed attention and taking the other's perspective. *Journal of Experimental Social Psychology, 19,* 58-77.

Sternglaz, S. H., and Serbin, L. H. (1974). Sex role stereotyping in children's television programs. *Developmental Psychology, 10,* 710-715.

Stewart, R. H. (1965). Effect of continuous responding on the order effect in personality impression formation. *Journal of Personality and Social Psychology, 1,* 161-165.

Stokols, D. (1972). On the distinction between density and crowding: Some implication for future research. *Psychological Review, 79,* 275-278.

Stolz, H. R., and Stolz, L. M. (1951). *Somatic development of adolescent boys.* New York: MacMillan.

Stoner, J. A. F. (1961). *A comparison of individual and group decisions involving risk.* Unpublished master's thesis, Sloan School of Management, MIT, Cambridge.

Storms, M., and Nisbett, R. E. (1970). Insomnia and the attribution process. *Journal of Personality and Social Psychology, 16,* 319-328.

Storms, M. D. (1973). Videotape and the attribution process: Reversing actors' and observers' points of view. *Journal of Personality and Social Psychology, 27,* 165-175.

Stotland, E. (1969). Exploratory investigations of empathy. In L. Berkowitz (Ed.), *Advances in experimental social psychology* (Vol. 4). New York: Academic Press.

Straus, M. A., Gelles, R. J., and Steinmetz, S. K. (1980). *Behind closed doors: Violence in the American family.* Garden City, NY: Anchor Press.

Strawson, P. F. (1959). *Individuals.* New York: Metheun.

Stricker, G. (1967). A pre-experimental inquiry concerning cognitive determinants of emotional state. *Journal of General Psychology, 76,* 73-79.

Strobe, W. (1980). Self-esteem and attribution: Individual differences in the causal explanation of success and failure. In D. Gorlitz (Ed.), *Perspectives on attribution research and theory.* Cambridge, MA: Ballinger.

Strodbeck, F. L., and Hook, L. H. (1961). The social dimensions of a twelve-man jury table. *Sociometry, 24,* 297-315.

Strong, B., and Reynolds, R. (1982). *Understanding our sexuality.* St. Paul, MN: West.

Strong, S. R. (1982). Emerging integration of clinical and social psychology: A clinician's perspective. In G. Weary and H. L. Mirels (Eds.), *Integrations of clinical and social psychology.* New York: Oxford University Press.

Strube, M. J. (1982). Time urgency and Type A behavior: A methodological note. *Personality and Social Psychology Bulletin, 3,* 563-565.

Strube, M. J., and Garcia, J. E. (1981). A meta-analytic investigation of Fieldler's contingency model of leadership effectiveness. *Psychological Bulletin, 90,* 307-321.

Suinn, R. H. (1982). Intervention with Type A behaviors. *Journal of Consulting and Clinical Psychology, 50,* 933-949.

Sullivan, H. S. (1953). *The interpersonal theory of psychiatry.* New York: W. W. Norton.

Suls, J., Gastorf, J. W., and Lawhorn, J. (1978). Social comparison choices for evaluating a sex- and age-related ability. *Personality and Social Psychology Bulletin, 4,* 102-105.

Suls, J. M., and Miller, R. C. (Eds.) (1977). *Social comparison processes: Theoretical and empirical perspectives.* Washington, DC: Halsted-Wiley.

Summers, G. F., and Hammonds, A. D. (1966). Effect of racial characteristics of investigator on self-enumerated responses to a Negro prejudice scale. *Social Forces, 44,* 515-518.

Sundstrom, E., and Altman, I. (1976). Personal space and interpersonal relations: Research review and theoretical model. *Human Ecology, 4,* 47-67.

Sussman, S., Mueser, K., Grau, B. W., & Yarnold, P. (1983). Stability of females' facial attractiveness during childhood. *Journal of Personality and Social Psychology, 44,* 1231-1233.

Svalastoga, K. (1962). Rape and social structure. *Pacific Sociological Review, 5,* 48-53.

Swann, W. B., Jr. (1984). Self-verification: Bringing social reality into harmony with the self. In J. Suls and A. G. Greenwald (Eds.), *Psychological perspectives on the self* (Vol. 2). Hillsdale, NJ: Erlbaum.

Swann, W. B., Jr., and Hill, C. A. (1982). When our identities are mistaken: Reaffirming self-conceptions through social interaction. *Journal of Personality and Social Psychology, 43,* 59-66.

Sweeney, P., and Moreland, R. L. (1980, August). *Self-sche-*

mas of gender and the perseverance of beliefs about the self. Paper presented at the annual convention of the American Psychological Association, Montreal.

Tajfel, H. (1978). *Differentiation between social groups: Studies in the social psychology of intergroup relations.* New York: Academic Press.

Tajfel, H., Billig, M. G., Bundy, R. F., and Flament, C. (1971). Social categorization and intergroup behavior. *European Journal of Social Psychology, 1,* 149-177.

Tajfel, H., and Turner, J. (1979). An integrative theory of intergroup conflict. In W. G. Austin and S. Worchel (Eds.), *The social psychology of intergroup relations.* Monterey, CA: Brooks/Cole.

Tanford, S., and Penrod, S. (1984). Social influence model: A formal integration of research on majority and minority influence processes. *Psychological Bulletin, 95,* 189-225.

Tannenbaum, P. H., and Zillman, D. (1975). Emotional arousal in the facilitation of aggression through communication. In L. Berkowitz (Ed.), *Advances in experimental social psychology* (Vol. 8). New York: Academic Press.

Tapp, J. L. (1976). Psychology and the law: An overture. *Annual Review of Psychology, 27,* 359-404.

Tavris, C., and Offir, C. (1977). *The longest war: Sex differences in perspective.* New York: Harcourt Brace Jovanovich.

Tavris, C., and Wade, C. (1984). *The longest war: Sex differences in perspective* (2nd ed.). San Diego: Harcourt Brace Jovanovich.

Taylor, D. (1966). The monster. In N. E. Hoopes and R. Peck (Eds.), *Edge of awareness: Twenty-five contemporary essays.* New York: Dell.

Taylor, M. C., and Hall, J. A. (1982). Psychological androgyny: Theories, methods and conclusions. *Psychological Bulletin, 92,* 347-366.

Taylor, R. L., and Weiss, A. E. (1970). American presidential assassination. In D. H. Daniels, M. F. Gilula, and F. M. Ochberg (Eds.), *Violence and the struggle for existence.* Boston: Little, Brown.

Taylor, S. E., and Fiske, S. T. (1978). Salience, attention, and attribution: Top of the head phenomena. In L. Berkowitz (Ed.), *Advances in experimental social psychology* (Vol. 11). New York: Academic Press.

Taylor, S. E., Fiske, S. T., Etcoff, N. L., and Ruderman, A. J. (1978). Categorical and contextual bases of person memory and stereotyping. *Journal of Personality and Social Psychology, 36,* 778-793.

Taylor, S. P. (1967). Aggressive behavior and physiological arousal as a function of provocation and the tendency to inhibit aggression. *Journal of Personality, 35,* 297-310.

Taylor, S. P., Gammon, C. B., and Capasso, D. R. (1976). Aggression as a function of alcohol and threat. *Journal of Personality and Social Psychology, 34,* 938-941.

Taylor, S. P., Shuntich, R. J., and Greenberg, A. (1979). The effects of repeated aggressive encounter on subsequent aggressive behavior. *Journal of Social Psychology, 97,* 199-208.

Taylor, S. P., Vardaris, R. M., Rawitch, A. B., Gammon, C. B., Cranston, J. W., and Lubetkin, A. I. (1976). The effects of alcohol and delta-9-tetra hydrocannabinal on human physical aggression. *Aggressive Behavior, 2,* 153-161.

Tedeschi, J. T., Gaes, G. G., and Rivera, A. M. (1977). Aggression and the use of coercive power. *Journal of Social Issues, 33,* 101-125.

Tedeschi, J. T., Horai, J., Lindskold, S., and Faley, T. E. (1970). The effects of opportunity costs and target compliance on the behavior of a threatening source. *Journal of Experimental Social Psychology, 6,* 205-213.

Tedeschi, J. T., Melburg, V., and Rosenfeld, P. (1981). Is the concept of aggression useful? In P. Brain and D. Benton (Eds.), *Multidisciplinary approaches to aggression research.* New York: Elsevier North-Holland.

Tedeschi, J. T., and Riess, M. (1981). Identities, the phenomenal self, and laboratory research. In J. T. Tedeschi (Ed.), *Impression management theory and social psychological research.* New York: Academic Press.

Tedeschi, J. T., and Riess, M. (1981). Predicaments and verbal tactics of impression management. In C. Antaki (Ed.), *Ordinary language explanations of social behavior.* London: Academic Press.

Tedeschi, J. T., and Riordan, C. A. (1981). Impression management and prosocial behavior following transgression. In J. T. Tedeschi (Ed.), *Impression management theory and social psychological research.* New York: Academic Press.

Tedeschi, J. T., and Rosenfeld, P. (1981). Impression management and the forced compliance situation. In J. T. Tedeschi (Ed.), *Impression management theory and social psychological research.* New York: Academic Press.

Tedeschi, J. T., Schlenker, B. R., and Bonoma, T. V. (1971). Cognitive dissonance: Private ratiocination or public spectacle? *American Psychologist, 26,* 685-695.

Tedeschi, J. T., Schlenker, B. R., and Bonoma, T. V. (1973). *Conflict, power and games: The experimental study of interpersonal relations.* Chicago: Aldine-Atherton.

Tedeschi, J. T., Schlenker, B. R., and Bonoma, T. V. (1975). Compliance to threats as a function of source attractiveness and esteem. *Sociometry, 38,* 81-98.

Tedeschi, J. T., Schlenker, B. R., and Lindskold, S. (1970).

The exercise of power and influence: The source of influence. In J. T. Tedeschi (Ed.), *The social influence processes.* Chicago: Aldine-Atherton.

Tedeschi, J. T., Smith, R. B., III, and Brown, R. C., Jr. (1974). A reinterpretation of research on aggression. *Psychological Bulletin, 81,* 540-563.

Teger, A. I. (1980). *Too much invested to quit.* New York: Pergamon Press.

Tesser, A., and Brodie, M. (1971). A note on the evaluation of a computer date. *Psychonomic Science, 23,* 300.

Tesser, A., and Campbell, J. (1980). Self-definition: The impact of the relative performance and similarity of others. *Social Psychology Quarterly, 43,* 341-347.

Tesser, A., Gatewood, R., and Driver, M. (1968). Some determinants of gratitude. *Journal of Personality and Social Psychology, 9,* 233-236.

Tesser, A., and Rosen, S. (1975). The reluctance to transmit bad news. In L. Berkowitz (Ed.), *Advances in experimental social psychology* (Vol. 8). New York: Academic Press.

Tetlock, P., and Manstead, T. (in press). Impression management versus intrapsychic explanations in social psychology. *Psychological Review.*

Tetlock, P. E. (1980). Explaining teacher explanations of pupil performance: A self-presentational interpretation. *Social Psychology Quarterly, 43,* 283-290.

Thibaut, J. W., and Kelley, H. H. (1959). *The social psychology of groups.* New York: John Wiley.

Thomas, C. C., Batson, C. D., and Coke, J. S. (1981). Do good Samaritans discourage helpfulness: Self-perceived altruism after exposure to highly helpful others. *Journal of Personality and Social Psychology, 40,* 194-200.

Thomas, E. H., Webb, S., and Tweedie, J. (1961). Effects of familiarity with a controversial issue on acceptance of successive persuasive communications. *Journal of Abnormal and Social Psychology, 63,* 656-659.

Thomas, G., and Batson, C. D. (1981). Effect of helping under normative pressure on self-perceived altruism. *Social Psychology Quarterly, 44,* 127-131.

Thomas, W. I. (1937). *Primative behavior: An introduction to the social sciences.* New York: McGraw-Hill.

Thomas, W. I., and Znaniecki, F. (1918). *The Polish peasant in Europe and America.* New York: Alfred Knopf.

Thompson, W. C., Cowan, C. L., and Rosenhan, D. L. (1980). Focus of attention mediates the impact of negative affect on altruism. *Journal of Personality and Social Psychology, 38,* 291-300.

Thorndike, E. L. (1920). A constant error in psychological ratings. *Journal of Applied Psychology, 4,* 25-29.

Tinbergen, N. (1955). The curious behavior of the stickleback. In Scientific American (Ed.), *Twentieth Century Bestiary.* New York: Simon & Schuster.

Tobey, E. L., and Tunnell, G. (1981). Predicting our impressions on others: Effects of public self-consciousness and acting, a self-monitoring subscale. *Personality and Social Psychology Bulletin, 7,* 661-669.

Toch, H. H. (1969). *Violent men: An inquiry into the psychology of violence.* Chicago: Aldine-Atherton.

Torrance, E. P. (1954). Some consequences of power differences on decision making in permanent and temporary three-man groups. *Research Studies, State College of Washington, 22,* 130-140.

Tourangeau, R., and Ellsworth, P. C. (1978). *The role of facial response in the experience of emotion.* Unpublished manuscript, Yale University, New Haven, CT.

Tresemer, D. W. (1974). Fear of success: Popular but unproven. *Psychology Today, 7,* 82-85.

Triandis, H. C., and Fishbein, M. (1963). Cognitive interaction in person perception. *Journal of Abnormal and Social Psychology, 67,* 446-453.

Triplett, N. (1897). The dynamogenic factors in pacemaking and competition. *American Journal of Psychology, 9,* 507-533.

Trope, Y., and Bassok, M. (1982). Confirmatory and diagnosing strategies in social information gathering. *Journal of Personality and Social Psychology, 43,* 22-34.

Troutman, C., Michael, R., and Shanteau, J. (1976). Do consumers evaluate products by adding or averaging attribute information? *Journal of Consumer Research, 3,* 101-106.

Tuchman, B. W. (1978). *A distant mirror.* New York: Alfred Knopf.

Turner, J. C. (1981). The experimental social psychology of intergroup behavior. In J. C. Turner & H. Giles (Eds.), *Intergroup behavior.* Chicago: University of Chicago Press.

Turner, R. G. (1977). Self-consciousness and anticipatory belief change. *Personality and Social Psychology Bulletin, 3,* 438-441.

Tyler, T. R., and McGraw, K. M. (1983). The threat of nuclear war: Risk interpretation and behavioral response. *Journal of Social Issues, 39,* 25-40.

Uhleman, T., and Walker, N. D. (1980). "He takes some of my time, I take some of his": An analysis of sentencing patterns in jury cases. *Law and Society Review, 14,* 323-342.

Underwood, B., Berenson, J. F., Berenson, R. J., Cheng, K. K., Wilson, D., Kulik, J., Moore, B. S., and Wenzel, G. (1977). Attention, negative affect and altruism: An ecological validation. *Personality and Social Psychology Bulletin, 3,* 51-53.

Unger, R. K. (1979). *Female and male.* New York: Harper & Row.

Unger, R. L., Hilderbrand, M., and Maden, T. (1982). Physical attractiveness and assumptions about social deviance: Some sex-by-sex comparisons. *Personality and Social Psychology Bulletin, 8,* 293-301.

Ursin, H. (1981). Neuroanatomical basis of aggression. In P. Brain and R. Benton (Eds.), *Aggression: A multidisciplinary view.* New York: Elsenier North-Holland.

Staff. (1983, November 22). "Day After" not changing many minds. *USA Today,* p. 1.

Staff. (1984, August 7). Heart attacks cut in half. *USA Today,* p. 1A.

Valeriani, R. (1979). *Travels with Henry.* Boston: Houghton Mifflin.

Valins, S., and Baum, A. (1973). Residential group size, social interaction and crowding. *Environment and Behavior, 5,* 421-439.

Valins, S., and Nisbett, R. E. (1972). Attribution processes in the development and treatment of emotional disorders. In E. E. Jones, D. E. Kanouse, and H. H. Kelley (Eds.), *Attribution: Perceiving the causes of behavior.* Morristown, NJ: General Learning Press.

Van Zelst, R. H. (1952a). Sociometrically selected work teams increase production. *Personnel Psychology, 5,* 175-186.

Van Zelst, R. H. (1952b). Validation of a sociometric regrouping procedure. *Journal of Abnormal and Social Psychology, 47,* 299-301.

Veitch, R., DeWood, R., and Bosko, K. (1977). Radio news broadcasts: Their effects on interpersonal helping. *Sociometry, 40,* 383-386.

Veitch, R., and Griffitt, W. (1976). Good news, bad news: Affective and interpersonal effects. *Journal of Applied Social Psychology, 6,* 69-75.

Vinokur, A., and Burnstein, E. (1974). Effects of partially shared persuasive arguments on group-induced shifts: A group problem-solving approach. *Journal of Personality and Social Psychology, 29,* 305-315.

Vinokur, A., and Burnstein, E. (1978). Depolarization of attitudes in groups. *Journal of Personality and Social Psychology, 36,* 872-885.

Vinokur, A., and Selzer, M. L. (1975). Desirable versus undesirable life events: Their relationship to stress and mental distress. *Journal of Personality and Social Psychology, 32,* 329-337.

von Baeyer, C. L., Sherk, D. L., and Zanna, M. P. (1981). Impression management in the job interview: When the female applicant meets the male (chauvinist) interviewer. *Personality and Social Psychology Bulletin, 7,* 45-51.

Wagner, R. V. (1975). Complementary needs, role expectations, interpersonal attraction and the stability of work relationships. *Journal of Personality and Social Psychology, 32,* 116-124.

Wallace, J., and Sadalla, E. (1966). Behavioral consequences of transgression: I. The effect of social recognition. *Journal of Experimental Research in Personality, 1,* 187-194.

Wallace, S. (1968). Routes to Skid Row. In E. Rubington and M. Weinberg (Eds.), *Deviance: The interactionist perspective.* New York: Macmillan.

Wallston, B. S., and O'Leary, V. E. (1981). Sex makes a difference: Differential perceptions of women and men. In L. Wheeler (Ed.), *Review of personality and social psychology* (Vol. 2). Beverly Hills, CA: Sage Publications.

Walster, E., Aronson, V., Abrahams, D., and Rottman, L. (1966). Importance of physical attractiveness in dating behavior. *Journal of Personality and Social Psychology, 4,* 508-516.

Walster, E., and Festinger, L. (1962). The effectiveness of "overheard" persuasive communications. *Journal of Abnormal and Social Psychology, 65,* 395-402.

Walster, E., and Walster, G. (1978). *A new look at love.* Reading, MA: Addison-Wesley.

Walster, E., Walster, G. W., and Berscheid, E. (1978). *Equity: Theory and research.* Boston, MA: Allyn & Bacon.

Walters, R. H., and Brown, M. (1963). Studies of reinforcement of aggression: III. Transfer of responses to an interpersonal situation. *Child Development, 34,* 536-571.

Wan, K. C., and Bond, M. H. (1982). Chinese attributions for success and failure under public and anonymous conditions of rating. *Acta Psychologica Taiwanica, 24,* 23-31.

Watson, C. G., and Daly, W. K., Zimmerman, A., and Anderson, D. (1979). Effects of patient attitude and staff indulgence on improvement in schizophrenics: A test of impression management theory. *Journal of Abnormal Psychology, 88,* 338-340.

Watson, D. (1982). The actor and the observer: How are their perceptions of causality divergent? *Psychological Bulletin, 92,* 682-700.

Webb, E. J., Campbell, D. T., Schwartz, R. D., Sechrest, L., and Grove, J. B. (1981). *Nonreactive measures in the social sciences* (2nd ed.). Boston: Houghton Mifflin.

Weber, S. J., and Cook, T. D. (1972). Subject effects in laboratory research: An examination of subject roles, demand characteristics, and valid inference. *Psychological Bulletin, 77,* 273-295.

Wegner, D. M., and Vallacher, R. R. (1977). *Implicit psychology: An introduction to social cognition.* New York: Oxford University Press.

Wegner, D. M., Wenzlaff, R., Kerker, R. M., and Beattie, A. E. (1981). Incrimination through innuendo: Can media questions become public answers? *Journal of Personality and Social Psychology, 40,* 822-832.

Weick, K. E. (1984). Small wins: Redefining the scale of social problems. *American Psychologist, 39,* 40-49.

Weigel, R. H., and Newman, L. S. (1976). Increasing attitude-behavior correspondence by broadening the scope of the behavioral measure. *Journal of Personality and Social Psychology, 33,* 793-802.

Weiss, R. (1973). *Loneliness: The experiences of emotional and social isolation.* Cambridge: MIT Press.

Weiss, W. (1957). Opinion congruence with a negative source of one issue as a factor influencing agreement on another issue. *Journal of Abnormal and Social Psychology, 54,* 180-186.

Weiss, W. (1969). Effects of the mass media of communication. In G. Lindzey and E. Aronson (Eds.), *Handbook of social psychology* (Vol. 5, 2nd ed.). Reading, MA: Addison-Wesley.

Weitzman, L. J., Eifler, D., Hokada, E., and Ross, C. (1972). Sex-role socialization in picure books for preschool children. *American Journal of Sociology, 77,* 1125-1150.

Wells, G. L., and Harvey, J. H. (1977). Do people use consensus information in making causal attributions? *Journal of Personality and Social Psychology, 35,* 279-293.

Wells, G. L., and Petty, R. E. (1980). The effects of overt head-movements on persuasion: Compatibility and incompatibility of responses. *Journal of Basic and Applied Social Psychology, 1,* 219-230.

Wells, G. L., and Ronis, D. L. (1982). Discounting and augmentation: Is there something special about the number of causes? *Personality and Social Psychology Bulletin, 8,* 566-572.

West, S. G., and Brown, T. J. (1975). Physical attractiveness, the severity of the emergency and helping: A field experiment and interpersonal simulation. *Journal of Experimental Social Psychology, 11,* 531-538.

West, S. G., Gunn, S. P., and Chernicky, P. (1975). Ubiquitous Watergate: An attributional analysis. *Journal of Personality and Social Psychology, 32,* 55-65.

West, S. G., and Wicklund, R. A. (1980) *A primer of social psychological theories.* Monterey, CA: Brooks/Cole.

Wheeler, L. (1966). Toward a theory of behavioral contagion. *Psychological Review, 73,* 179-192.

Wheeler, L., Koestner, R., and Driver, R. E. (1982). Related attributes in the choice of comparison others: It's there, but it isn't all there is. *Journal of Experimental Social Psychology, 18,* 489-500.

Wheeler, L., Reis, H., and Neziek, J. (1983). Loneliness, social interaction and sex roles. *Journal of Personality and Social Psychology, 45,* 943-953.

White, C. B. (1982). Sexual interest, attitudes, knowledge and sexual history in relation to sexual behavior in the institutionalized aged. *Archives of Sexual Behavior, 11,* 11-21.

White, G. (1980). Inducing jealousy: A power perspective. *Personality and Social Psychology Bulletin, 6,* 222-227.

White, J. W., and Gruber, K. J. (1982). Instigative aggression as a function of past experience and target characteristics. *Journal of Personality and Social Psychology, 42,* 1069-1075.

White, L. A. (1979). Erotica and aggression: The influence of sexual arousal, positive affect, and negative affect on aggressive behavior. *Journal of Personality and Social Psychology, 37,* 591-601.

White, R. K. (1965). Images in the context of international conflict: Soviet perceptions of the U.S. and the U.S.S.R. In H. C. Kelman (Ed.), *International behavior: A social psychological analysis.* New York: Holt, Rinehart & Winston.

Whorf, B. L. (1956). *Language, thought, and reality.* Cambridge: MIT Press.

Wicker, A. W. (1969). Attitudes versus actions: The relationship of verbal and overt behavioral responses to attitude objects. *Journal of Social Issues, 25,* 41-78.

Wicklund, R. A. (1975). Objective self-awareness. In L. Berkowitz (Ed.), *Advances in experimental social psychology* (Vol. 8). New York: Academic Press.

Wicklund, R. A., and Brehm, J. W. (1968). Attitude change as a function of felt competence and threat to attitudinal freedom. *Journal of Experimental Social Psychology, 4,* 64-75.

Wicklund, R. A., and Brehm, J. W. (1976). *Perspectives on cognitive dissonance.* Hillsdale, NJ: Erlbaum.

Wilder, D. A. (1978). Reduction of intergroup discrimination through individuation of the out-group. *Journal of Personality and Social Psychology, 36,* 1361-1374.

Wilke, H., and Lanzetta, J. T. (1970). The obligation to help: The effects of amount of prior help on subsequent helping behavior. *Journal of Experimental Social Psychology, 6,* 488-493.

Will, J. A., Self, P. A., and Datan, N. (1976). Maternal behavior and perceived sex of infant. *American Journal of Orthopsychiatry, 49,* 135-139.

Willerman, B., and Swanson, L. (1953). Group prestige in voluntary organizations: A study of college sororities. *Human Relations, 6,* 57-77.

Williams, J. G., and Solano, C. H. (1983). The social reality of feeling lonely: Friendship and reciprocation. *Personality and Social Psychology Bulletin, 9,* 237-242.

Williams, K., Harkins, S., and Latane, B. (1981). Identifiability as a deterrent to social loafing: Two cheering experiments. *Journal of Personality and Social Psychology, 40,* 303-311.

Williams, K. B., and Williams, K. D. (1983). Social inhibition and asking for help: The effects of number, strength, and immediacy of potential help givers. *Journal of Personality and Social Psychology, 44,* 67-77.

Williams, K. D. (1981, May). *The effects of group cohesion on social loafing.* Paper presented at the annual meeting of the Midwest Psychological Association, Detroit.

Wilson, D. W. (1981). Is helping a laughing matter? *Psychology, 18,* 6-9.

Wilson, D. W., and Donnerstein, E. (1977). Guilty or not guilty: A look at the simulated jury paradigm. *Journal of Applied Social Psychology, 7,* 175-190.

Wilson, D. W., and Schafer, R. B. (1978). Is social psychology interdisciplinary? *Personality and Social Psychology Bulletin, 4,* 548-552.

Wilson, E. O. (1978). *On human nature.* Cambridge: Harvard University Press.

Wilson, L., and Rogers, R. W. (1975). The fire this time: Effects of race of target, insult and potential retaliation in black aggression. *Journal of Personality and Social Psychology, 32,* 857-864.

Wilson, L. R., and Nakajo, H. (1966). Preference for photographs as a function of frequency of presentation. *Psychonomic Science, 3,* 577-578.

Wilson, W., and Miller, H. (1968). Repetition, order of presentation, and timing of arguments and measures as determinants of opinion change. *Journal of Personality and Social Psychology, 9,* 184-188.

Winch, R. F. (1958). *Mate selection: A study of complementary needs.* New York: Harper & Row.

Wingfield, A. (1979). *Human learning and memory: An introduction.* New York: Harper & Row.

Winick, C., and Holt, H. (1961). Seating position as nonverbal communication in group analysis. *Psychiatry, 24,* 171-182.

Winkler, J., and Taylor, S. E. (1979). Preference, expectations and attributional bias: Two field studies. *Journal of Applied Psychology, 9,* 183-197.

Wolfe, R., Lennox, R., and Hudiburg, R. (1983). Self-monitoring and sex as moderator variables in the statistical explanation of self-reported marijuana and alcohol use. *Journal of Personality and Social Psychology, 44,* 1069-1074.

Wolfgang, M. E., and Ferracuti, F. (1967). *The subculture of violence.* London: Tavistock.

Womack, W. M., and Wagner, N. N. (1967). Negro interviewers and white patients. *Archives of General Psychiatry, 16,* 685-692.

Wood, R. E., and Mitchell, T. E. (1981). Manager behavior in a social context: The impact of impression management on attributions and disciplinary actions. *Organizational Behavior and Human Performance, 28,* 356-378.

Worchel, S., Lind, E., and Kaufman, K. (1975). Evaluations of group products as a function of expectations of group longevity, outcome of competition and publicity of evaluations. *Journal of Personality and Social Psychology, 31,* 1089-1097.

Worchel, S., and Teddlie, C. (1976). The experience of crowding: A two-factor theory. *Journal of Personality and Social Psychology, 34,* 30-40.

Newspaper Enterprises Associates. (1982). *World Almanac.* New York: Author.

Wortman, C. B., and Brehm, J. W. (1975). Responses to uncontrollable outcomes: An integration of reactance theory and the learned helplessness model. In L. Berkowitz (Ed.), *Advances in experimental social psychology* (Vol. 8). New York: Academic Press.

Wrong, D. H. (1961). The oversocialized conception of man in modern sociology. *American Sociological Review, 26,* 183-193.

Yakimovitch, D., and Saltz, E. (1971). Helping behavior: The cry for help. *Pychonomic Science, 23,* 427-428.

Yarkin, K. L., Town, J. P., and Wallston, B. S. (1982). Blacks and women must try harder. *Personality and Social Psychology Bulletin, 8,* 21-24.

Yinon, Y., and Bizman, A. (1980). Noise, success, and failure as determinants of helping behavior. *Personality and Social Psychology Bulletin, 6,* 125-130.

Zajonc, R. (1965). Social facilitation. *Science, 149,* 269-274.

Zajonc, R. B. (1968a). Attitudinal effects of mere exposures. *Journal of Personality and Social Psychology Monograph Supplement, 9,* 1-27.

Zajonc, R. B. (1968b). Cognitive theories in social psychology. In G. Lindzey and E. Aronson (Eds.), *Handbook of social psychology* (Vol. 1, 2nd ed.). Reading, MA: Addison-Wesley.

Zander, A., and Havelin, A. (1960). Social comparison and interpersonal attraction. *Human Relations, 13,* 21-32.

Zanna, M., Goethals, G. R., and Hill, J. (1975). Evaluating a sex-rated ability: Social comparison with similar others and standard setters. *Journal of Experimental Social Psychology, 11,* 86-93.

Zanna, M. P., Kiesler, C. A., and Pilkonis, P. A. (1970). Positive and negative attitudinal affect established by classical conditioning. *Journal of Personality and Social Psychology, 14,* 321-328.

Zeiss, A. M. (1982). Expectations for the effects of aging on sexuality in parents and average married couples. *The Journal of Sex Research, 18,* 47-57.

Ziller, R. C., and Lewis, D. (1981). Orientations: Self, social, and environmental percepts through auto-photography. *Personality and Social Psychology Bulletin, 7,* 338-341.

Zillman, D. (1971). Excitation transfer in communication-mediated aggressive behavior. *Journal of Experimental Social Psychology, 7,* 419-434.

Zillman, D., and Bryant, J. (1974). Effect of residual excitation on the emotional response to provocation and delayed aggressive behavior. *Journal of Personality and Social Psychology, 30,* 782-791.

Zillman, D., Johnson, R. C., and Day, K. D. (1974). Attribution of apparent arousal and proficiency of recovery from sympathetic activation affecting motivation transfer to aggressive behavior. *Journal of Experimental Social Psychology, 10,* 503-515.

Zillman, D., and Sapolsky, B. S. (1977). What mediates the effect of mild erotica on annoyance and hostile behavior in males? *Journal of Personality and Social Psychology, 35,* 587-596.

Zimbardo, P. G. (1970). The human choice: Individuation, reason, and order versus deindividuation, impulse, and chaos. In W. J. Arnold and D. Levine (Eds.), *Nebraska Symposium on Motivation* (Vol. 17). Lincoln: University of Nebraska Press.

Zimbardo, P. G., and Anderson, S. (1981). Induced hearing deficit generates experimental paranoia. *Science, 212,* 1529-1531.

Zimbardo, P. G., Ebbesen, E. B., and Maslach, C. (1977). *Influencing attitudes and changing behavior.* Reading, MA: Addison-Wesley.

Zimbardo, P. G., and Formica, R. (1963). Emotional comparison and self-esteem as determinants of affiliation. *Journal of Personality, 31,* 141-162.

Zimbardo, P. G., Haney, C., and Banks, W. C. (1973, April 8). A Pirandellian prison. *New York Times Sunday Magazine,* pp. 38-60.

Zimmerman, D. H., and West, C. (1975). Sex roles, interruptions and silence in language. In B. Thorne and N. Henley (Eds.), *Language and sex: Difference and dominance.* Rowley, MA: Newbury House.

Zipf, S. G. (1960). Resistance and conformity under reward and punishment. *Journal of Abnormal and Social Psychology, 61,* 102-109.

Zuckerman, M. (1978). Use of consensus information in prediction of behavior. *Journal of Experimental Social Psychology, 14,* 163-171.

Zuckerman, M. (1979). Attribution of success and failure revisited, or: The motivational bias is alive and well in attribution theory. *Journal of Personality, 47,* 245-287.

Zuckerman, M., Lazzaro, M. M., and Waldgeir, D. (1979). Undermining effects of the foot-in-the-door technique with extrinsic rewards. *Journal of Applied Social Psychology, 9,* 292-296.

Zuckerman, M., and Wheeler, L. (1975). To dispell fantasies about the fantasy-based measure of fear of success. *Psychological Bulletin, 82,* 932-946.

Subject Index

Name Index